NEWHOUSE

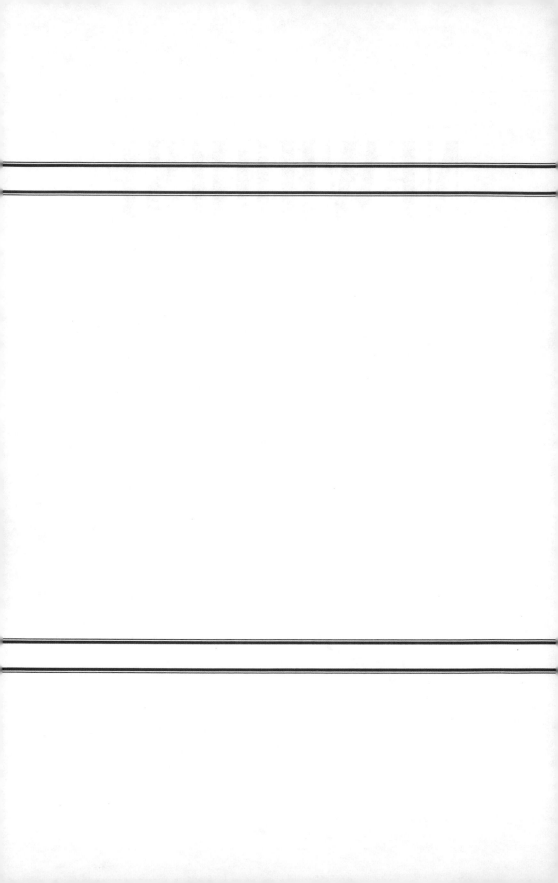

NEWHOUSE

All the Glitter, Power, and Glory

of America's Richest Media Empire

and the Secretive Man Behind It

Thomas Maier

St. Martin's Press   New York

LIBRARY OF CONGRESS CATALOGING-IN-PUBLICATION DATA

Maier, Thomas
    Newhouse / Thomas Maier.
      p.   cm.
    "A Thomas Dunne book."
    ISBN 0-312-11481-8 (hardcover)
    1. Newhouse, Samuel I.   2. Publishers and publishing—United States—Biography.   3. Newspaper publishing—United States—History—20th century. 4. American newspapers—History—20th century.   I. Title.
    Z473.N47M35   1994
    070.5'092—dc20
    [B]   94-19816
                                                CIP

First Edition: October 1994

10 9 8 7 6 5 4 3 2 1

For my parents

Contents

Acknowledgments

The reporting that resulted in the writing of this book began in November 1990 as an assignment from the editors of *Newsday*'s Sunday magazine. They asked for a feature about the management changes at Random House. Most Random House company executives were quite responsive to interview requests for the *Newsday* piece and their names appear on page 391 as sources interviewed as a result of that process. At the time, this author had only a passing familiarity with Si Newhouse. But the mere mention of Newhouse's name sparked a curious response and a desire to know more about him. (Months later in preparing this book, several of these same Random House executives declined requests for further interviews when they were informed that the focus had been broadened into a book about Newhouse and his media empire).

For the record, Si Newhouse never responded to a written request for an interview. Eventually, this author called Newhouse's longtime assistant, who said Mr. Newhouse had received my letter but wouldn't be cooperating. His brother, Donald, whose brief comments are included in the text, and other family members had much the same reaction. Even more curious was the reaction of some journalists who were approached for interviews. "Is this an *authorized* biography?" was a constantly posed question, a true curiosity when one thinks about its implications. In its truest sense, this book was never intended to be an authorized biography—at least not by its implied definition. Instead, it relied on the tools of the craft—examining hundreds of pages of court testimony and documents, conducting more than 250 interviews, and reading numerous books, newspapers, and periodicals, including Newhouse's own—to examine the history of Advance Publications and its impact on America's media and cultural life.

There are many people to be thanked, none more so than my wife, Joyce, whose love, patience, and encouragement never diminished. She and our three sons, Andrew, Taylor, and Reade, endured many hours wondering when Daddy would emerge from his basement office. Both my agent, Faith Hamlin, and my editors at St. Martin's Press, Thomas Dunne and David Sobel, were wonderfully supportive and courageous in their determination to see this work published. I am also grateful to the financial grant provided by the Fund for Investigative Journalism, Inc., whose board of distinguished journalists lent a significant helping hand to the completion of this project. There are several librarians who helped immeasurably; my particular thanks to Charles Young of the Queensboro Public Library, Betty Macholz and Joanne Kelleher of the Commack, New York, Public Library, and the staff of the Cleveland State University Press Collection.

Several of my friends and colleagues at *Newsday* shared their insights from the start, especially Noel Rubinton and Brian Donovan. Anthony Marro, Kenneth C. Crowe, Mary Ann Skinner, Ridgely Ochs, Richard Galant, and my longtime mentor, Robert W. Greene, who founded *Newsday*'s investigative team, bear special mention. Richard Laudor added his unique insights as both a lawyer and a journalist of the first order. Raymond A. Schroth, S.J. brought many keen insights from a lifetime of teaching students that journalism is a public trust. One other friend, who carefully read this manuscript in its earliest form, was perhaps the most helpful, but his name cannot be mentioned here for reasons that are his own. Let it be said no writer ever had a better team of supporters.

T.M.

New York City

May 1994

"A publisher is known by the company he keeps."
ALFRED A. KNOPF

NEWHOUSE

Off with Their Heads . . .

A nd now, Liz Smith with the latest . . ."

The image of New York's doyenne of gossip flashed on the television screen, a smiling face of celebrity dish and Hollywood delights on the chatty WNBC-TV news program called "Live at Five." This hardly seemed the place for a public beheading. Yet all that was missing on this lazy summer afternoon in June 1988 was scaffolding and a black hood.

In one fell swoop, Liz Smith told her audience that Grace Mirabella was being fired from *Vogue,* the world's best-known fashion magazine, and would be replaced by Anna Wintour. After thirty-six years at *Vogue,* nearly half as the magazine's editor in chief, Mirabella was gone. And now everyone in the world seemed to know about Grace Mirabella's firing—except her.

Soon the telephone was ringing at Mirabella's home. Her husband picked it up.

"Listen, have you heard Liz Smith?" a friend on the other end asked in a tone of grave finality. "Turn on the TV."

Mirabella's husband, Dr. William Cahan, a well-respected surgeon, dutifully recorded the information. Before Mirabella arrived home from work, he called her with the bad news. At first, she didn't believe it. She was just about to leave the office. Surely, she would have been told before departing. The whole notion of learning about one's firing from a TV show seemed tacky, unworthy of a *Vogue* editor—too *unstylish.*

Undoubtedly, though, the departure signs were there. Those little intimations of mortality an editor in the Condé Nast magazine kingdom receives before the Scythe of Death appears. Mirabella had witnessed the same treatment accorded to Diana Vreeland, the mercurial high priestess of haute couture, whom she had abruptly replaced in 1971 as *Vogue's* editor. There were the same none-too-subtle, contrary remarks that Alexander Liberman, Condé Nast's suave, commanding editorial director, would leave scattered throughout conversations with her, usually concerning an upcoming issue or layout. Or one of those condescending ways

Alex would begin, letting you know just how deep the trouble you were in. "Dear friend . . ." Liberman would intone, with his icy continental manner, finely chiseled face, and penetrating stare.

As the éminence grise of Condé Nast magazines, a brilliant and turbulent force of nature for more than forty years, Liberman was the prophet of perpetual change, a man who could sense the oncoming tides of upheaval and always manage to survive. With fear and awe, he was called "The Silver Fox," though never to his face. Liberman had been Mirabella's mentor, a source of support when she transformed *Vogue* into a magazine more appealing to working women—a move that proved to be a tremendous success.

Now, this one last time, Mirabella called upon him, hoping he would tell her the truth. Their conversation was brief.

"I'm afraid it's true," Liberman told her. "Talk to Si."

He was right. Only one person could say with utmost certainty whether Mirabella had been fired—S. I. Newhouse, Jr., the billionaire owner of the Condé Nast magazine empire and the most powerful American publisher of his generation.

As ruler of the largest privately held fortune in the United States, Newhouse owns and controls such magazines as *Vanity Fair* and *The New Yorker,* the Random House publishing company, and dozens of daily newspapers, as well as cable television franchises and other media properties. Some Newhouse publications rank among the most celebrated in the world; others boast virtual monopolies of the daily press in several American cities. Together, the Newhouse family's wealth is greater than that of Queen Elizabeth II or the House of Saud.

Despite his extraordinary influence, Si, as he is called by friends and enemies alike, remains barely known to the American public and often misunderstood even by those who claim to know him. A seemingly shy, diminutive man who finds personal conversations awkward, Newhouse developed a certain self-assuredness only after he passed the age of fifty, possessing an intuitive sense for the way his publications should operate. As the oldest son of newspaper magnate S. I. Newhouse, Sr., he had been given *Vogue* and four other Condé Nast women's magazines to run in the early 1960s—a sideline business in his father's eyes but one that would become the centerpiece of Si's media empire by the 1990s.

To preserve this multibillion-dollar enterprise, Si Newhouse's moves were often stunning, even brutal. His actions were sometimes portrayed as part of some overall philosophy, vital to the company's success. "Change is change—it doesn't happen slowly," Newhouse once stated, giving a rare public explanation. "The concept of complete satisfaction is like the concept of truth. You can move toward it, but you never entirely get there." This epistemology of change—even the momentary sacrifice of stability that the swift chop of an errant editor's head would bring—seemed necessary to keep his company's revenues flowing. Indeed, the Newhouse verve for an occasional bloodletting had a familiar eighteenth-century ring: *Quand il y avait la guillotine, il y avait du pain!* For Si Newhouse, change was essential, the secret ingredient to his family's perpetual success.

Grace Mirabella understood all of this, though she still refused to believe her firing would ever happen in this way.

At her home that evening, Mirabella decided to call Newhouse and inquire about the TV news report.

Is it true? she asked.

"I'm afraid it is," replied Newhouse, with hardly a word of apology or explanation.

The next afternoon, Newhouse attempted to repair some of the damage by offering a sizable severance package and labeling Mirabella's departure as a "resignation." Still, there was no denying this bloody mess. Mirabella was livid at the public spectacle of becoming the latest *sans tête,* another in a long line of editorial decapitations for which Si Newhouse would become notorious.

"The way it was handled was graceless—without making a pun," Newhouse later admitted. "The P.R. of it got all bitched up. So fine. But it wasn't a spur of the moment decision."

Despite his protestations, Newhouse's sudden off-with-their-heads ways were recorded by the press with a certain morbid fascination, the body counts piling up like a prolonged St. Valentine Day's Massacre. With each firing, the public import seemed magnified, often played out prominently on the front pages of America's most-respected newspapers. No one was safe, no matter how firmly affixed to a publication's masthead. Newhouse's management style resembled "a revolving door," as *Time* magazine described it in 1990, featuring a photographic lineup of severed Newhouse editors.

The head shots of the beheaded looked like a Who's Who of New York's literary world:

William Shawn, the legendary *New Yorker* editor, who was praised by Newhouse as one of the great influences on his life shortly before Shawn was canned.

Anthea Disney, the editor of Condé Nast's *Self* magazine, who learned of her firing during her vacation, when Newhouse unexpectedly stopped by her home with the grim news.

Robert Bernstein, the chairman of Random House, Inc.'s book-publishing group, who was forced to "resign" and endure a seemingly orchestrated media campaign by Newhouse's organization that portrayed Bernstein, a guiding force behind the company's phenonmenal growth, as inattentive to the bottom line.

André Schiffrin, the publisher of Pantheon Books, who was pushed out in a way that provoked dozens of writers and editors to protest publicly outside the doors of Random House.

Other lesser-known editors fell victim to the Newhouse chopping block in a variety of ignominious ways. Louis Oliver Gropp, the editor of *House & Garden,* found out he was being axed when he called in for messages while standing at a public telephone at a California airport. Even those who replaced the beheaded were not spared the blade. Robert Gottlieb replaced Shawn as *The New Yorker*'s editor and believed himself to be a close Newhouse friend. But while Gottlieb was on a trip to Japan, Newhouse announced *Vanity Fair*'s Tina Brown as his successor. A cartoon character in Gottlieb's final issue of *The New Yorker* in September 1992 seemed to capture the gallows humor gripping the entire staff. In it, a boss with a manic smile looked about an empty room. "*Ahhh,* the smell of freshly mowed employees," he chirps.

Perhaps the cruelest departure was inflicted upon Margaret Case, a longtime society editor at *Vogue.* Case had been associated with the magazine since 1926, the halcyon days of Condé Nast himself, the man who established *Vogue* as the bible of the fashion industry and who employed an office full of young women whose surnames appeared in the *Social Register.* A very dignified woman, Case had a well-developed sense of who belonged and who didn't in *Vogue*'s rarefied strata, as though she could sniff out a person's breeding. For more than forty years, Case went to work every day at *Vogue,* until she arrived one morning in 1971 to find movers in her office. No one in the Newhouse organization bothered to tell her that she had been fired. "They decided to get rid of her," as Diana Vreeland later wrote in her memoir. "She didn't get the hint."

The moving men explained they were here to take her desk away.

"But it's my desk," Case said. "It's got all my things in it."

No matter. The moving men poured her belongings—years of papers, photographs, and letters—into cardboard boxes, which were later dumped at her apartment.

Margaret Case, almost eighty years old, was devastated. She went home and stayed there, until one morning when her body was found in the courtyard of her apartment building. The next morning's obituary page said Miss Case "fell or jumped" from the bedroom window of her Park Avenue apartment. One of her neighbors, Mrs. Vreeland, had no doubts about the cause.

"She threw herself out a window because she was eighty, she was out of work, she had no money—and she'd been dismissed in the most terrible way," Vreeland later wrote. "She'd gone out the window, sixteen floors. She was as neat as a pin. She was in a raincoat fastened to here, a little handkerchief, all the buttons to the very bottom, and a pair of slacks. I mean she had thought everything out!"

Whatever the reason, Margaret Case managed to exit her window with more dignity than when she had left through Si Newhouse's door.

By the 1990s, tales of rapid departures and bloody ruptures cast a certain phantasmagoria about Si Newhouse and his media-hyped reign of terror.

Si, the Omnipotent! "The Lord High Executioner," as one business magazine called him. Another likened him to Howard Hughes. S. I. Newhouse, Jr.—the mysterious, cryptic head of the largest media fortune in American history.

The speculation about his family's wealth underscores how little is known about him. Eight billion dollars, $10 billion, even $13 billion, as *Fortune* estimated in late 1993, are the figures bandied about when trying to establish his worth. "There aren't many absolute rulers around these days, on thrones or in executive suites, but S. I. ("Si") Newhouse Jr. comes close," *Time* magazine observed in 1992 after his controversial switch of *New Yorker* editors.

Inside the Condé Nast building in midtown Manhattan where Si Newhouse makes his headquarters, whispers of intrigue and betrayal fill the halls and are compounded by the byzantine secret methods of Newhouse himself. He is famous for arriving at his office in the dark every morning, sometime before 5:00 A.M. Some top editors who report directly to him are said to receive their pay in separate checks, from different subsidiaries inside the Newhouse company, so that no one but Si knows the true amount. For more than two generations, the Newhouses' international media conglomerate has been run like a neighborhood grocery store, with dozens of family members personally overseeing every detail. As if their fortune could be found somewhere under a mattress, the family has avoided any large-scale borrowing to finance new acquisitions, often preferring to pay fully in cash. During lunch at The Four Seasons or on long plane flights with his executives, Si doesn't tolerate inquiries about other parts of his kingdom. Like his father, Si Newhouse disdains corporate meetings and eschews most small talk. Family questions just lie there untouched.

Despite all the media hype and public speculation, however, no outsider really seems to know much about Si Newhouse. He remains, in many ways, an enigma.

Repeatedly, the story of Newhouse and his family fortune has been enmeshed in myths and embellished half truths. The few who have tried to examine the Newhouses closely were either stonewalled or threatened with lawsuits. For a man who has reaped a fortune from free speech, Si Newhouse paradoxically demands a wall of silence about himself and his activities. His money does the talking instead. Top executives fired by Newhouse often are given generous severance packages and paid to remain quiet. Several of his highest-paid writers act as if courtiers at his court, offering whatever advice he may require. At extravagant affairs, they will call him a man of great intellect, a benefactor of Venetian graces, or other accolades. And in hushed asides to the workaday press, these famous writers will assure doubters that their claims about this taciturn billionaire are indeed so. For in the upper reaches of America's media hierarchy, Si Newhouse's name is spoken with the same fear and reverence that another generation reserved for Citizen Hearst. With few remaining independent voices—and an oligarchy of media power held by a handful of conglomerates like Newhouse's—it is hard not to come under his sway.

As a result, many of the most pivotal aspects of Si Newhouse's public life and his stewardship of a public trust remain unexamined or ignored. Nor has much been written about him personally—even when *Fortune* named the Newhouses as one of the wealthiest families in the United States or when *Newsweek* ranked him and two of his top editors, Tina Brown and Knopf's Sonny Mehta, among the top one hundred members of America's "cultural elite." Most Americans know little about Si Newhouse—the most influential American media baron of our time—other than the fact that he is very rich and sometimes goes to fancy parties. To be sure, any other high-profile billionaire like Newhouse would likely have been treated to smothering attention in the media. Indeed, any other American potentate with Newhouse's history would have almost surely landed inside the pages of *Vanity Fair* with his own Annie Leibovitz portrait, or in *Vogue, The New Yorker, GQ, Details,* or in Newhouse's Sunday supplement, *Parade,* found in dozens of daily newspapers, including his own.

There are many well-known "secrets" about Si Newhouse that are told at Manhattan media parties but never examined in the press. One example is his lifelong friendship with Roy Cohn—the unrepentant avatar of McCarthyism and legal confidant of Mafia dons. His extensive financial, social, and legal ties to Newhouse and his family have remained glossed over for years as Cohn managed to plant, fix, and incite stories about the powerful and well-connected in their publications. For those aware of these details, Si Newhouse's unquestioning devotion to Roy Cohn remains a troubling paradox, providing much insight into Newhouse's personal life and how he views his public responsibilities.

The full extent of the Newhouse family's ethical lapses in handling so important a public institution as a major American daily newspaper, however, remains virtually unknown even among today's media cognoscenti. There are repeated examples of the Newhouse papers' union busting, political malleability, and their willingness to allow advertisers to influence improperly their editorial judgment. Nevertheless, one of the most persistent myths surrounding the Newhouse empire is a much-vaunted reputation as hands-off owners who pay attention only to the financial bottom line. During the lifetime of Si's father, S. I. Newhouse, Sr., this facade of "local autonomy" was repeated over and over in news stories, some of which were planted by his press agent. They served the elder Newhouse well as he dangled huge sums of cash before poor little rich heirs in such cities as Newark and Portland, trying to convince them to hock a family heirloom—their dear dead daddy's newspaper—to a virtual stranger with deep pockets.

Unlike the populist publications of Joseph Pulitzer or William Randolph

Hearst, which sprang forth as the political voices of their owners, the Newhouse empire began as a fix-it shop of editorially neutered money losers that were magically turned around into profit-making concerns. As press critic A. J. Liebling described him, Sam Newhouse was a "journalistic chiffonier," a scavenger of third-rate newspapers who possessed "no political ideas, just economic convictions." Without a single exception, Sam Newhouse's purchase meant nothing in the way of better journalism. In his own way, though, Sam Newhouse was a harbinger of change who would define much of today's newspaper industry.

By keeping his eye fixed on the bottom line rather than the editorial page, Sam Newhouse gathered a collection of newspapers that became the prototype for the modern newspaper chain. After slashing away the fat (such as more reporters, in-depth news pages, or faraway bureaus), these chronically mediocre newspapers became cash cow subsidiaries, generating money for more newspaper properties to be attached to the Newhouse conglomerate. His profit margins were estimated as large as 25 percent of every million dollars collected, allowing him to finance bids that were repeatedly heralded as the highest ever paid for a newspaper at the time. In this equation, however, public service for the only newspaper in town usually meant providing better movie tables, more of the next day's weather, and a humdrum recitation of local events.

Journalists—who look warily at politicians and preachers but are fond of romantic illusions about their own craft—were convinced that the Newhouse promises of local autonomy would mean a free hand for themselves, the editorial hired hands. Of course, this freedom came with a short leash, for Newhouse's newsrooms were given as little money as necessary to perform their tasks. Nevertheless, the myth of local autonomy with a benign hands-off owner was rolled out, in city after city, before old man Newhouse was finally laid to rest. Even a year after his death in 1979, when his middle-aged sons, Si and Donald, bought Random House, the family's image as hands-off owners was revisited prominently on the front page of *The New York Times,* a prediction that proved so erroneous as to be laughable in hindsight.

By the late 1980s, Si Newhouse had sufficiently disabused the literary world of any illusions regarding his intent. He ruled with a velvet fist. But oh, what a splendid fist it could be. Like their billionaire owner, a collector of modern art and contemporary opinion, Si Newhouse's hip slick magazines celebrated the acquisitiveness of the eighties—a gilded time when America pulsed to the rhythms of junk-bond kings, Ronald Reagan, and Madonna. Like its owner, Newhouse's empire epitomized the ethos of the age. And his approach to publications—what Alex Liberman once called "the Newhouse concept"—set a pervasive tone for many of America's top media companies.

With a gambler's flair, Si Newhouse spent as much as $75 million in order to breathe new life into *Vanity Fair*—a defunct magazine left for dead during the Depression—and turned this forgotten corpse into the most-talked-about publication of this generation. Its young and talented editor, Tina Brown, seemed to capture the trappings and every nuance of the decade's greed, avarice, and power: Madonna in the buff, Claus von Bülow in black leather, the Reagans dancing at the White House. All these were part of the cavalcade of eighties icons embraced or vilified, sometimes simultaneously, in its glossy pages. No matter how real or contrived, the singular impact of *Vanity Fair*—and its unique view of just how the 1980s looked and felt to the nation—was immeasurable, with media from august newspapers to TV's "Lifestyles of the Rich and Famous" seeming to emulate its style.

Similarly, Newhouse's bold moves at Random House or in purchasing *The New Yorker* were conducted with the guile of a Wall Street raider and, in some quarters, greeted with the same emotions as a hostile takeover. His decision to revamp Random House's traditions and his willingness to spend millions in attempts to dominate the market for "big books" had a profound impact on American publishing. But his decision to buy *The New Yorker* clearly put the two polar aesthetics of Si Newhouse's universe on a collision course: the Condé Nast world, where marketing and advertising demands permeated the editorial pages of its fashion magazines, and *The New Yorker*'s "Chinese Wall" culture, where no editorial decision would ever be made except for the purest literary reasons. Newhouse's ouster of Shawn and his numerous shake-ups at *The New Yorker* sent the magazine into convulsions, especially when Tina Brown arrived as its new editor. Whether she has ruined or saved *The New Yorker,* perhaps the finest magazine America has ever known, is still very much debated. Indisputably, though, the magazine has learned to live within the Newhouse concept, with its standards of integrity diminished.

More than that of any other American media figure in our time, Si Newhouse's fortune, which he shares with his younger brother, Donald, has remained shrouded in secrecy. Their billions are taken for granted as part of an inherited birthright. Yet what is so remarkable about these Newhouses is the immense distance they have journeyed in the span of only three generations—from a ramshackle apartment on New York's Lower East Side to their children's uptown Park Avenue duplexes and well-mannered country estates. To attain such an empire, they relied on remarkable business acumen, which at times bordered on genius. Since Si Newhouse's birth in 1927, when his father began a little privately owned company on the outer borough of Staten Island, Advance Publications has grown to become an American powerhouse dominant in the media industry. His Condé Nast empire is now international, with versions of magazines like *Vogue* appearing in Britain, France, Italy, and Australia and his book imprints read around the world. Beyond print, his family's cable-television franchises reach more than 1 million American homes, including some cities where he also owns the local newspaper. His family's newspaper collection includes a powerful Washington-based news syndicate, the largest Sunday rotogravure magazine in the land, and several daily newspapers with virtual monopolies in their region. Si and his brother have become major investors in the newest forms of global media, part of a much-touted "superhighway of information" expected to redefine the way we live. In the broadest sense, the Newhouses, like other great family dynasties, have secured a place in the American pantheon of wealth and power, as much as the Rockefellers, Fords, du Ponts, and even the Kennedys.

For all of the Machiavellian power and corporate influence attributed to him, Si Newhouse remains a refractive personality, like some mirrored ball found swirling above the dance floor, reflecting many different insights with no certainty of what is inside. Most of his personal life—far from his often-repeated image as a self-assured tyrant—has been spent in a confusing struggle for a clear identity, a true sense of self. He has been difficult to understand even for some members of his own family. "How he is within the family, I can't say," said his son Wynn, who remained distant from his father for part of his young adulthood. "I'm knowing him better all the time. He's a complex person." Si Newhouse's propensity for secrecy and control seems boundless—the stuff of legend every bit as potent as the paternalistic Horatio Alger–like myth carved out for his own father. Indeed, understanding the relationship between father and son in the Newhouse family, from one generation to the next, appears crucial to deciphering the character and motivations of Si Newhouse.

To those few in whom he confided, Si depicted his early life as a struggle to distinguish himself from his famous father, a hard-driving spirit who kept dominating his oldest son until well into adulthood. After the shame and uncertainty of dropping out of Syracuse University—which received millions from his father and later dedicated a journalism school bearing his name—Si Newhouse floundered in various parts of his father's newspaper company. He was a sullen, awkward lad who resembled the comic figure of Jerry Lewis, an object of coworkers' ridicule. He endured a failed early marriage, a difficult relationship with his children, and a lingering doubt about his ability to be entrusted with the Newhouse family fortune.

At times, these expectations and pressures became overwhelming. Suicide became a threat, sometimes an obsession. As a high school teenager and later as a college student, Si Newhouse spoke to a friend of his loneliness, his sense of alienation, and the continuous thoughts of ending his pain. The fear of failing his exacting father, a constant standard-bearer, seemed a source of unspoken torment destined to shape Newhouse's life as much as any other force. This uncertainty about himself would linger for many years.

Si Newhouse did not fully achieve his own sense of public identity until late in life, after his father became infirm and eventually died at the age of eighty-four. Over time, Si would give up the more frivolous aspects of his bachelorhood and settle into a long marriage with an attractive, fashionable woman, Victoria de Ramel, the ex-wife of a French count, who would share his interest in the arts. He would also take his place in the Newhouse company as chairman, the greater among equals with his brother, Donald, a solid, steady type who once seemed destined to inherit his father's leadership mantle. Finally free of his father's long shadow, Si Newhouse fashioned the Newhouse empire in his own image, adding billions to its coffers and a great luster to the family name. In doing so, Newhouse became very much his father's son.

Whatever the root cause, S. I. Newhouse, Jr., has become legendary for perpetual and often tumultuous change and his constant need to rediscover an identity and recreate himself. It is a lasting irony that Si Newhouse, who once felt so desperate and dominated himself, is now portrayed to the world by some as an intolerant beast, a source of torment, an imperial boss who would just as soon fire and hire as compromise or concede.

Publicly, the Newhouse name is no longer likened to that of a ragpicker or a comic buffoon. Over the past decade, his father's traditional approach of grinding out each possible penny from the family's chain of undistinguished daily newspapers has been transmogrified by Si into a much more sophisticated, jaded aesthetic. Unlike his father's vision, reflected in his grimy collection of drab dailies, Si's view of what a publication should look like emanates from his colorful experiences at Condé Nast, working with Alexander Liberman, who would forever have a profound influence on Newhouse's career.

After failing to find a place within his father's newspaper empire, Si Newhouse found himself comfortable in the world of Condé Nast, which was supervised by Liberman and favored by Newhouse's mother, Mitzi, who shared her son's taste for art, fashion, and the finer accoutrements of wealth. In his private memoir to his adult children, the elder Newhouse hardly mentioned Condé Nast at all. Yet within this realm of haute couture that was barely a footnote to his father's story, Si Newhouse found a haven, a place where his own sensibilities developed. Over time, Liberman became Si's close confidant, championing the many changes Si brought to Condé Nast and sometimes acting like a paternal figure to him.

Alex Liberman's influence extended to the American media, as well. A mystical, dashing Russian émigré and lifelong sculptor and painter, Liberman taught Newhouse about the power of images, the language of art, and how to translate that into commerce. "The now-bad word *advertising,* in its true sense of communicating, displaying meaning, comes to mind," Liberman once wrote about Irving Penn, whose photographs helped give *Vogue* its distinctive look. "In our epoch, there is no patience for Rembrandt's modulated chiaroscuro. We need the black-and-white lighting of Guernica." Wrapping the merchandise in such elegant terms, a Liberman trademark, became part of the Newhouse mystique. In this Condé Nast aesthetic, the separate realms of editorial and advertising matter often blended into one thin veneer, rather than an impenetrable wall, between paid advertising and editorial content.

With this approach, Newhouse publications have fundamentally changed the role and responsibilities of today's American media and what readers can expect from it. Madison Avenue marketing gimmicks—with names like "outserts" and "advertorials"—have often been introduced in Condé Nast publications before being offered and accepted by the rest of the magazine world. These glossy advertising devices for high-priced goods, such as Calvin Klein clothing or Revlon perfumes, look almost identical to the editorial text and photos found elsewhere within the magazine, often because they are prepared by the same people. The results can be insidiously pleasing and appalling. In the late 1980s, *Vanity Fair* featured separate laudatory cover stories about designers Klein and Ralph Lauren, posing as they might in one of their ads—life imitating advertising.

Even *The New Yorker,* which once prided itself for editorial autonomy before Newhouse acquired it, was no longer immune to these commercial compromises. In the first issue under Tina Brown's leadership, the semi-nude pictures in a Calvin Klein underwear ad seemed to announce her arrival more than the table of contents on the opposite page. In her first year, the addition to its pages of Gianni Versace, an advertising-rich designer from Italy, was heralded as much as any new writer Brown brought on board. After all, the British-born editor didn't need a can of spray paint to understand the writing on these New York walls: Commerce rules!

In Si Newhouse's world, creating a new magazine like *Self* or *Vanity Fair* is decided primarily through the business side—a matter of market research and demographics rather than editorial voice. In this equation, marketing a story or an ad seems indistinguishable. Likewise, books are sold as "units" by top editors with more flair for finance than literature. And his newspapers, which provide great revenue streams like moats surrounding Newhouse's publishing fortress, are sought in monopoly markets, where competition has been artfully eliminated and profits maximized. In more fashionable terms than his father ever imagined, Si Newhouse has reaffirmed the view that publications exist to sell products. That he has done so with more panache than anyone in America's media world is indisputable.

By the early 1990s, with a nationwide recession and an ever-widening gap between rich and poor, Newhouse's critics saw a more sinister motive in this redefinition of the media. To many, the Condé Nast stylization of celebrity and gossip over the previous decade became a permanent part of the American cultural diet, displacing whatever sense of social responsibility these editors and their billionaire owners may once have felt toward their audience. Call it trickle-down media, the modern equivalent of "Let them eat cake."

In Newhouse's publications, this hybrid of highbrow and lowbrow tastes applied as much to the once-vaunted Alfred A. Knopf imprint as to the covers of *Glamour* and *Mademoiselle* found in grocery store checkout shelves. Foreign dictators, wealthy tycoons, and a veritable parade of Hollywood stars were treated ever so lightly by Si Newhouse's editors, as friends to be toasted and never examined closely. Many of these prize editors were influenced more by Fleet Street and England's rigidly class-conscious society than by the traditional schools of American journalism, whose practitioners, they pointed out, blather on incessantly about ethics. At times, the Newhouse headquarters at 350 Madison Avenue seemed like a boarding school for transplanted Brits, who recognized only one journalistic crime: being boring. They would waste no time postulating about media's responsibilities or about information as a means of social ascendancy. Only in their most grandiose moments did these Brits wax poetic, as with Tina Brown's farewell to *Vanity Fair,* proclaiming her discovery of the "postmodern" publication on this strange new continent.

The sharp difference between pretense and reality in the Newhouse kingdom—and the lack of culpability for what Americans read—is sometimes galling, even to friends on the social circuit. "Last month, Ivana Trump, perhaps the single greatest creation of the idiot culture, a tabloid artifact if ever there was one, appeared on the cover of Vanity Fair," complained Watergate journalist Carl Bernstein shortly before Tina Brown departed for *The New Yorker* in 1992. "On the cover, that is, of Condé Nast's flagship magazine, the same Condé Nast/Newhouse/Random House whose executives will yield to nobody in their solemnity about their profession, who will tell you long into the night how seriously in touch with American culture they are, how serious they are about the truth."

What remains unanswered, though, are the many broader truths and public issues inherent in one man's control of a dominant conglomerate in a democratic society—questions that deal with the very essence of what Americans read and learn about their world, the accountability of the press in a time of growing public distrust, and the narrowing boundaries between news and commercial boosterism. Just who is running America's media? Can they be trusted with so great a power to influence public opinion? What exactly can Americans expect from the media companies that reap fortunes from their patronage? Can a city's only major daily newspaper with an all-but-government-sanctioned monopoly still be considered the private domain of just one individual? There is no more apropos place to begin this inquiry than with Si Newhouse and his assemblage of newspapers, magazines, books, television and radio stations, and cable franchises.

During his lifetime, Sam Newhouse had the dubious distinction of generating angry and sometimes violent confrontations with his own reporters, who picketed over working conditions at his newspapers. But in this generation, his son has provoked even more disturbing confrontations, which go well beyond a matter of money. In separate incidents during the past decade, writers and editors at Random House, *The New Yorker*, and Newhouse's newspaper in Cleveland have protested publicly, not about wages and benefits but over what they perceived as matters of conscience, principle, and good journalism. In all of these dramas, Si Newhouse was the central character, condemned as a symbol of corrupt greed or defended mightily by those in his employ. Rarely has Si Newhouse offered any public explanation for his actions or reasons. Yet the underlying issues in these disputes—far beyond the ego clashes of well-known writers and publishers—belie some of the fundamental tensions of this new age of commercialism in American media, with its concentration of power and its widening breach between the public interest and the interests of a very few. In the coming century, these questions about the integrity of America's information and media ownership are likely to be as fundamental to society as the purity of the water we drink or the air we breathe.

From this vantage, Si Newhouse's silence seems to derive more from the arrogance of his power than from a foible of his personality. Accountability is the last thing he wants, except to his relatives, who look to him to ensure that this great family enterprise continues running. As in any self-respecting dynasty, keeping the fortune intact for future generations of Newhouse children remains paramount. In this regard, Si Newhouse has been an unqualified success, a son who has built upon the mighty fortress his father left him rather than presiding over its demise.

Anyone who questions how Si Newhouse has done this—or who poses a possible threat to this multibillion-dollar media empire—will receive only a silent quizzical gaze. Or perhaps the same curious response Newhouse gave when he refused a *Fortune* magazine interview for a 1987 profile about his company, which has made countless millions from selling his brand of journalism to readers. His answer was as elliptical as the man himself: "My brother and I feel this goes against all our principles."

CHAPTER ONE

Man of the House

Pink roses blanketed the dark wood coffin as his family and closest friends sat in the front pews near his remains. Almost unbelievably, after eighty-four years of tireless thought and motion, Sam Newhouse was at rest.

There was an overwhelming sense of finality on this August day in 1979 as the body of S. I. Newhouse, Sr.—a five-foot-two-inch giant of journalism—lay in repose. Inside the cavernous Temple Emanu-El, a house of worship along Manhattan's Fifth Avenue, the elaborate funeral services befit the solemn grandeur required for such an individual. "We are here to mourn a great and enduring man who lived his life in such a manner that it will be written large on twentieth-century America," Rabbi Ronald Sobel told those assembled.

All the signs of greatness were on display. Powerful politicians, such as United States senator Jacob Javits and the governor of New York, Hugh Carey, were among more than six hundred mourners who filled the synagogue. That morning, newspapers across the country carried Newhouse's obituary—some on the front page—including his thirty-one papers, which featured a carefully constructed version of Newhouse's life written by one of his top editors. More than a half century earlier, the Newhouse media empire was started with the purchase of a failing newspaper on Staten Island. By the time of his death, Newhouse had added seven magazines, six television stations, five radio stations, and several cable-television franchises, employing fifteen thousand people in eleven states. Sam Newhouse was the most familar kind of American success story: the single-minded struggle of an enterprising young man who rises from a life of poverty to achieve untold wealth and power. Somehow, it seemed fitting that one of Newhouse's acquisitions would include Street & Smith, the pulp publisher of Horatio Alger stories.

On this day, those who spoke at the funeral services were careful to make sure the myths surrounding Sam Newhouse remained unchallenged and intact. One eulogist was publisher Ashton Phelps, the man who most bayou residents thought was the owner of their daily newspaper, the *New*

Orleans Times-Picayune. Phelps, a proud, aristocratic man whose white-shoe family long ago had sold out to the Yankee Newhouses, paid his tribute to the real boss of his publication and his reputation as a hands-off owner. "I have never known him or any other member of his family to attempt to dictate editorial policy," Phelps assured. "S. I. began the tradition of editorial autonomy. He was a great defender of the First Amendment and a great believer in the challenge of responsible editors. My friend referred to his group of newspapers as a family, and that is how we felt—as a family."

Another who spoke was Dr. William Tolley, the chancellor emeritus of Syracuse University, who had welcomed Newhouse as a great benefactor, accepting millions for a journalism school in Newhouse's name. Tolley had seen Newhouse's two sons, Si and Donald, grow from their teenage years to middle age and was privy to some of the family's hopes and worries. Tolley was sure to touch the familiar chords of Newhouse's life and declare them the acts of a genius. No other comment would do.

"How else can you explain the phenomenal drive of a man who began with nothing and built an editorial empire?" Tolley asked.

Si Newhouse, seated in the front row with his grieving family, didn't speak at his father's funeral. At fifty-two years of age, Si was well aware of the myths surrounding the name of Newhouse and the awesome challenges facing a son who follows in his father's business. It would be a hard act to follow. For years, Si Newhouse had trained for the day when he and his younger brother, Donald, would take over as stewards of the family business. No one was certain of what would happen with the Newhouse empire. For all of the lionizing myths at his father's funeral, what remained conspicuously unresolved was who would carry on and whether they were up to the task.

Sam Newhouse had been slow to address these questions himself. Those who knew him well seemed to think he trusted the judgment of his younger son, Donald, more than of Si. Only age forced Sam Newhouse to concede his powers over the family franchise. By the mid-1970s, when Sam was past eighty, he began cutting back on his frantic travel to his various "properties"—the term he used for his newspapers and magazines. He would even joke about his imminent retirement.

"I've eased up," he told an interviewer in 1976. "My sons have assumed more responsibility. I'm more or less being shoved into the background."

But the elder Newhouse, who disdained using a desk and preferred to carry his important papers in a battered brown briefcase, continued to spend four days a week inspecting his publications on a tightly managed schedule. Even close family friends realized that Si and Donald were still being treated as sons, not as heirs apparent. "S. I. has to make a conscious effort to allow his sons to make decisions," said one family friend at the time.

After years of vigorous activity, Sam Newhouse suffered a slight stroke in 1977, shortly after his purchase of the Booth newspaper chain, the largest newspaper sale of its time. Initially, he appeared unaffected, though soon his mental health began to deteriorate rapidly. His near-encyclopedic mind, which had once mastered so many complex media deals, was crippled by an advancing senility that rendered him childlike. He begged for candy or to "go outside and play." His family kept him from public view, and those rare visitors allowed into the family's home were shocked at his condition. With crayons or chalk, Sam would spell out words.

"C-A-T," he would say, mouthing each letter. "See? C-A-T. Cat!"

In July 1979, Sam Newhouse suffered a more severe stroke and died a few weeks later. After the funeral, his body was carried aboard the Staten Island ferry and laid to rest in a cemetery not far from where he had bought his first newspaper. The future of his empire now was very much in the hands of Sam Newhouse's sons.

During the time when their father became increasingly incapacitated, Si and Donald had assumed much more responsibility for running the Newhouse operations. At first, it seemed that the sons wanted to reap their rewards from the family fortune immediately rather than follow the advice of their father, who once declared, "The only thing to do with money earned in newspapers [is] leave it in newspapers." After years of modest salary increases under his father's watchful eye, Si boosted his salary from $239,500 to $407,859 in 1979. Rather than reinvest profits back into the business, Si and his brother also decided to pay themselves a $1.5 million dividend from the family's broadcasting company. For all of the changes Si would bring about, however, he still remained faithful to many of his father's most closely held rules.

In rare public interviews, Si talked about the family's devotion to local autonomy among its publications. Privately, he appeared determined to live up to his father's expectations and his drive to "build something of significance to leave to my children and family." Si shared his father's penchant for secrecy and carefully avoided, as his father had, any public spectacles or similarities to such grandiose American newspaper barons as Hearst or Pulitzer. Like his father, he seemed to sense the inherent dangers of too much publicity, the corrosive effect it can have on maintaining a financial empire and avoiding government scrutiny.

Two months after his father's death, Si caught himself while making an inadvertent but inevitable comparison to another famous American newspaper legend. The slip occurred inside his office while he was uncharacteristically engaged in small talk with a reporter from a business publication. They were waiting for his brother, Donald, who was caught in traffic and was running late for the interview. Relaxed and in shirtsleeves, Si steered the conversation to the subject of movies. Ever the cinema buff, he began recalling some haunting lines from the classic *Citizen Kane*—the part where Bernstein speaks:

. . . One day, back in 1896, I was crossing over to Jersey on a ferry and as we pulled out there was another ferry pulling in—and on it there was a girl waiting to get off. A white dress she had on—and she was carrying a white parasol—and I only saw her for one second and she didn't see me at all—but I'll bet a month hasn't gone by since that I haven't thought of that girl. . . .

Suddenly, Si pulled himself from his reverie, as if struck by the irony of the passage.

After a long pause, Si Newhouse, the new ruler of America's largest publishing fortune, addressed the reporter. "You know," he said, "you're not going to find any Citizen Kane here."

It was on the ferry, crossing the wide expanse of the Hudson River back and forth each day from Jersey, where Sam Newhouse embarked on his career as a newspaperman. Though he would later remember this time with a vague fondness, his journey was hardly idyllic.

In the spring of 1908, Newhouse's immigrant parents heard of a school in Manhattan where he could be trained in bookkeeping and typing—the skills necessary for a small thirteen-year-old boy to land a job and help his family survive. On the ferry ride back and forth to school, Newhouse helped another boy carry bundles of newspapers, saving the nickel he earned for the fare. Money was crucial to the impoverished Newhouse family. To earn a few extra pennies, Newhouse's mother, Rose, worked as a peddler. With unspeakable embarrassment, young Sammy watched his mother "put a huge pack on her back and peddle dry goods from house to house." For a few years, his ne'er-do-well father managed to eke out a small living by running a suspender factory in Jersey City, until it failed in 1905. This was but one of many disappointments for his father, whose life could only be described in Job-like terms. He was a man of many miseries.

Meier Neuhaus, Sam's father's name before arriving in the United States, was born in a small village near Vitebsk in czarist Russia. He was the son of a rabbi and trained to become a Talmudic scholar. In the old country, Meier's father had married four times and buried all of his wives before deciding to join his son on the trip to America. In steerage during the crossing, his father became ill, died, and was buried at sea. When he arrived, Meier settled in New York City's Lower East Side ghettos of the 1890s, unable to speak English and without a trade. Eventually, he adopted a new spelling to his name: Meyer Newhouse. In 1894, he met and married Rose Fatt, then an eighteen-year-old farm girl who had emigrated from Austria. The following year, the couple bore a son, Solomon—who later used the name Samuel—the first of eight children.

In a year or two, they managed to relocate across the Hudson to an area near Bayonne, New Jersey, moving six different times in a decade as the number of children increased. But the most desperate turn for the family involved Meyer Newhouse's health. For years, he had been plagued by asthma, and his condition worsened when Sam turned thirteen years old. Under his doctor's order, Meyer left his wife and children for a more arid climate, living first in upstate New York, then in Texas, and later in Arizona. He would return only during the summer months, when the climate would allow. This decision placed a tremendous burden on the family and forced Sam, at a time when most youngsters are starting high school, to become the man of the house.

"I had to become head of the family because Poppa was a sick man," Newhouse would recall seventy years later in his privately published memoir. "My mother and father, my sisters and brothers and I simply lived with that fact. That was the way it was, the way it had to be. I was the oldest. It was my job to take over. And I did it."

This relentless determination helped him win a job from a local lawyer, Hyman Lazarus, who laughed when he was first introduced to the pint-sized lad. Accompanied by his desperate father, Sam Newhouse gained full-time employment at two dollars a week after offering to work for nothing for the first month. Lazarus became so impressed with the industrious young man that he eventually asked him to oversee a small failing daily newspaper he owned called the *Bayonne Times*.

"Sammy, go down and take care of the paper until we get rid of it," said Lazarus, a politically connected attorney who also served as a police magistrate and liked to be called by the honorific *Judge*.

Newhouse, who was planning to study to become a lawyer, seized the opportunity and quickly saved the drowning publication. The turnabout didn't come from inspired editorial content but, rather, from copying the successful advertising pitches of other big-city papers. He convinced Bayonne's downtown merchants to advertise through a variety of discounts, special placements, and other hard-sell incentives. Some of his techniques, as he later admitted, "couldn't be used today because they might be considered illegal preferential discounts." As the paper turned flush with new revenues, Sam asked for, and received, a percentage of the profits from a grateful Judge Lazarus and allowed his siblings and other family members to get various odd jobs connected with the paper. In 1922, with his own money and loans from his family and Judge Lazarus, Sam Newhouse bought a controlling interest in another troubled newspaper, the *Staten Island Advance*. This was the first newspaper that Sam, still in his twenties, would own outright; it would form the centerpiece of his company, Advance Publications.

Within the Newhouse family, all eyes turned to Sam, the undeterred dynamo who pulled them out of poverty almost by sheer will. At home, Sam was more father than son, sitting at the head of the table and given his own room in a house still cramped with kids. His mother was forever grateful. Still, Sam couldn't hide his sense of frustration at his father's failings, as witnessed in his memoir, written years later. Indeed, the differences between father and son—a tension that would emerge again with another successive generation—was never more evident in the Newhouse family than between Meyer and his oldest son, Sam.

Meyer Newhouse chose his own separate path in life, unashamedly. Despite his father's example as a rabbi and his own religious schooling, Meyer showed little interest in the religious life (Sam would later describe his father as an agnostic). Yet it was some of Meyer's more down-to-earth decisions that appalled his ambitious, energetic son. When the suspenders business failed—"after Pop's partner walked out one Sunday morning with all the assets," as he later recalled it—the family moved back to Bayonne from Jersey City and mistakenly allowed young Sammy to repeat the first grade in a new school. The blunder seemed inexcusable. "I lost a year in school because my parents didn't know that I could start where I had left off in the previous school," he recalled. "They never mentioned it and so I spent a second year in the first grade."

But Meyer's personal failings also included a lack of business acumen, much to his oldest's son chagrin. "When Pop came home in the summers he tried to help, but he just wasn't a businessman," Newhouse recalled. "If a customer wanted a hundred dollars worth of merchandise, Poppa simply gave it to him. No questions about credit." This was hardly the hard-edged business approach of Sam, who sent out threatening lawyer's letters to errant creditors for those who advertised in his paper.

Sam became the dominant figure. In conversations, he sometimes referred to his brother Norman, several years younger, as "son." He paid for a new house for the family and college costs for Norman and his younger sisters. He even doled out punishment to his siblings. When nine-year-old Norman referred to their absent father as "the old man," Sam slapped him across the face in front of a roomful of people. Such a sign of disrespect for their father could not be tolerated among the children. Yet, when his business interests thrived in the 1920s, Sam provided a helpful, though somewhat condescending, gesture to his father. "I was able to set up Poppa in Connecticut with four newsstands—two in Hartford, one in Bristol, and one in New Britain," Sam recalled. "He struggled with these for about three years, but nothing much came of that venture."

If there was any father figure in young Sam's life, it was Judge Lazarus, who had provided many insights and opportunities. In November 1924, Judge Lazarus, a vigorous man in his early fifties, died suddenly. "I was quite shaken by his death," recalled Newhouse. "I mourned so deeply that my father told [my sister] Naomi he hoped that when he died I would mourn for him as I did the judge." But there was never any such deep affinity between father and son.

For a young man who yearned to become an ideal capitalist, Sam Newhouse found it difficult to reconcile himself with his father's political views as a socialist. Meyer's two brothers and one of his four sisters—a free-wheeling woman who bore two children out of wedlock—were even more committed to socialism than he was. (The leftist political orientation of his family members was ironic, particularly given the Red-baiting campaign in the mid-1950s by Newhouse's largest newspaper, the *Newark Star Ledger,* which printed reckless allegations provided by Senator McCarthy's committee.)

Underscoring his overall detachment, Sam Newhouse kept a careful distance from his father's political philosophy. "My father and his socialistic brothers and sister looked outward, away from themselves towards some kind of collective salvation and state control to meet their needs," Sam would later say. "I have always looked inward, toward individual responsibility and the potentials of the free marketplace." For the official family history, Sam diplomatically said he picked up good traits from both his parents. But clearly, Sam favored his mother's silent, determined pragmatism and held his father's hapless life in contempt. "My father was a reflective man, happier with words and ideas than with action," recalled Sam. "My mother, an unschooled farm girl, was the opposite. Impatient with too much talk, she was practical, energetic and clear of mind, concentrating always on the way to survive."

In his recollections, Sam Newhouse shared one particular encounter between his father and himself—a deathbed scene. "We were so sure of our goals and so intent on pursuing them that we never thought of questioning them. If any one of us ever wondered why, it was my father—even as he lay dying." Meyer Newhouse's life was slowly ebbing away inside a hospital room at the time his son came to visit. For months in 1945, Sam Newhouse had jockeyed to gain control of the *Jersey Journal,* another daily newspaper in northern New Jersey, and brought the news of the sale with him to his father's bedside.

"Pop, I've just bought the *Jersey Journal,*" the young dynamo announced.

His seventy-five-year-old father, undoubtedly preoccupied by other matters, seemed unimpressed.

"Sammy, why do you need that?" he asked.

Sam was dumbfounded; even years later he seemed at a loss to explain the encounter. "What could I say to him?" he later commented. "That he should ask and that I should find it so hard to answer was typical of each of us. I'm not sure yet that I can find the words."

Reflection was never Sam Newhouse's strength, and his memoir barely addresses some of the glaring discrepancies in his life's story. Why Meyer Newhouse never took his wife and children with him—leaving them abandoned except for an occasional visit—remains one of the family's central mysteries. If there was a "Rosebud" to Sam Newhouse's life, a driving force behind his relentless pursuits as a media tycoon, its source seems to reside somewhere in his relationship with his father. When Meyer

Newhouse left, he took whatever remained of Sam's childhood with him. Sam's only answer to these family travails caused by his father seemed a stiff-lipped resoluteness, a solace found in perpetual work. "Perhaps it was my way, without being aware of it, of realizing his dream." This was the only explanation he could offer decades later.

In this sense, Sam Newhouse was truly American, a man of action, shedding the more introspective European traits of his father, who never adapted to this new world. By being tougher and smarter, by sticking together as a family and never quite allowing anyone full access to the inner sanctum, young Newhouse and his siblings amassed a great fortune, a testament to their resolve. "We never had time for self-pity or tears," Sam said later. "Our energies had to be concentrated for what had to be done and our intelligence concentrated on how to do it. That's why Pop's absence, for example, left no aftertaste of bitterness. His sickness was just another problem, and I took over leadership of the family long before I was out of my teens as the natural, logical solution to that problem."

With that same tenacity, Sam Newhouse set out to find his fortune.

The ship was barely within sight of New York harbor when angry union workers began chanting the name Newhouse through a megaphone. The sounds of the rancorous demonstration filled the air, and a small plane flew overhead with the message BACK THE GUILD painted on its side.

Waiting at the pier, Si Newhouse, almost seven years old, stood beside the family's nurse, who held his younger brother, Donald, by the hand as the happy occasion of their parents' arrival home from a long trip to Europe turned sour. Though too young to comprehend fully what was going on, the two boys witnessed one of the first public demonstrations of their father's power and the kind of antipathy that the name Newhouse could stir.

On this August afternoon in 1934, Sam Newhouse was returning to New York after several weeks in Europe with his wife, Mitzi. They had married ten years earlier, but business at his newly acquired newspaper, the *Staten Island Advance,* had prevented him from taking a honeymoon. "I told her that, along with my devotion to her, she would also have to accept my commitment to my work," Sam later said. The embarrassment of this day's public demonstration against her husband certainly tested that devotion. As the European cruiser *Aquitania* neared the shore, a small boat containing Newspaper Guild leader Heywood Broun approached. After stepping on board the ocean liner, Broun and the Guild leaders told Newhouse they were angered by his firing of an editorial writer who had tried to organize the *Advance*'s editorial staff. While he was away, the union had already set up pickets throughout the small island borough to protest Newhouse's action. Unless he reinstated the editorial writer, Broun warned, there would be more trouble.

When the cruise ship finally docked, Sam Newhouse and his mortified wife hurried into taxicabs with their two sons. They were surrounded by shouting union supporters carrying signs. When they arrived home, there were other Guild workers waiting, and through the night, a sound truck blared and a huge spotlight aimed its beam against the Newhouse windows. "They set up pickets and loudspeakers around the house, upsetting the kids and Mitzi," he later complained. Yet, Newhouse remained undeterred. "I will not be intimidated by picketing, hippodromizing or ballyhooing," the young publisher said the next day in a formal statement.

Sam Newhouse's hard-line position prevailed. The Guild's picketing against the *Advance*—which by then had secured a near monopoly on Staten Island thanks to Newhouse's circulation maneuvers—barely made a dent, and it actually caused a slight surge in readership due to the sudden publicity. After the purchase of the *Staten Island Advance,* Sam Newhouse revamped its business operations and, rather than improving its tepid editorial quality, funneled the profits into the purchase of other newspapers. He bought the *Long Island Press* in 1932 and during the next two decades bought seven more papers in Newark, Syracuse, Jersey City, Long Island City, and Harrisburg, Pennsylvania. Eventually, he controlled more of the circulation surrounding New York City than *The New York Times.*

Often these newspapers were in failing health, but Newhouse seemed able to revive most by using the formula he had first learned at the *Bayonne Times*—cutting costs, maximizing advertising, and focusing on local news. "If he has not debased the quality of U.S. journalism, he has not notably improved it either," *Time* magazine would later conclude. "Most of his papers are editorially as good, bad or indifferent as when he bought them." For Sam Newhouse, newspapers were properties from which great fortunes, rather than great truths, could be obtained. "Sam never pretended to be a public benefactor," said Phil Hochstein, Newhouse's longtime editorial adviser. "He doesn't claim to be with the people. He's a capitalist."

By weaving through the narrow constraints of the Internal Revenue Service's tax codes, Newhouse expanded his empire by reinvesting his retained earnings—the excess profits from his company kept in bank accounts—to buy new properties or make necessary capital improvements at his existing newspapers, such as updated printing presses. During the 1960s, Newhouse bought nine other daily newspapers for a total $128 million, several of them at record prices, like the *Cleveland Plain Dealer* and the *New Orleans Times-Picayune.* Only rarely did he have to borrow. According to Richard Meeker, author of a biography on Sam Newhouse, he even "cleaned out" the account of the Samuel I. Newhouse Foundation—his private charity set up years earlier as a legal tax dodge—so he could buy the *Birmingham News* in 1955 with a minimum of outside borrowing.

More often than not, the Newhouses seized the opportunity to purchase other family-owned newspapers, usually right after the death of a founding owner, when Sam could entice the surviving heirs with a ripe money offer and straight-faced promises never to interfere in the newsroom. Around this approach, the Newhouses even fashioned a philosophy of local autonomy. It would become the model for other newspaper groups such as Gannett and Thomson. (Sam Newhouse disliked the term *chain* publisher, preferring the more sanguine *group*.) "Mr. Samuel I. Newhouse, the archetype, specializes in disgruntling heritors, or profiting from their disgruntlement," observed press critic A. J. Liebling in 1961. "A family feud is grist for his mill, but if he can't get a paper that way he will talk beautifully of the satisfactions of cash, rapidly quoting sections of the capital-gains law as he accepts his hat. If the owner shows him the door, he exhibits no resentment." By seizing on the misfortunes of other families and their independently owned newspapers, the Newhouses enriched their own empire while determining not to repeat that pattern themselves.

Sam Newhouse and his family generally disdained talking to reporters, though he was not above a little mythmaking in the press to help ease his way with an important deal. Before buying the Booth newspaper chain in Michigan—one of the largest newspaper deals of the century, which included the Sunday supplement *Parade*—the Newhouses, father and his two sons, agreed to sit for a rare interview in 1976 with *Business Week*. The magazine later printed a flattering profile that stressed the Newhouse family's hands-off approach. "With the *Business Week* piece, he had to be convinced to do it," recalled Ray Josephs, the longtime Newhouse publicist. "When he first decided to use PR, it was to help buy newspapers. Many of the newspapers he bought were family-owned, and they had a sense of being proprietors of important civic enterprises. They were concerned with who was going to buy their newspaper."

Some of the newspaper deals were consummated with handshake deals; others seemed possible only through outright deception. For example, the widow who sold the *Harrisburg Patriot and Evening News* in the late 1940s to a Newhouse business associate had no idea who was secretly financing the sale. If she knew of Newhouse's involvement, she would never have sold the family heirloom to Newhouse, as biographer Meeker wrote, for her departed husband despised the idea of newspaper chains.

With some rejections, however, more than money or editorial stance came into play. When he moved to buy the *Oregon Journal,* its managing editor at the time referred to him in print as Samuel Isidor Newhouse, a clear-cut error with a thinly veiled tone of anti-Semitism. (His middle initial didn't stand for anything.) He also encountered examples of religious discrimination at other newspapers. "Other deals at other times and in other places fell through for other reasons, but none of them bothered me as much as those that failed because of my being a Jew," Sam Newhouse said in his memoir. "I have always been reluctant to talk about this or even to acknowledge that I have run into it. Sometimes, I would like to think I only imagined the prejudice, but I knew only too well that it was there."

Those who had genuine cause for concern with Newhouse were newspaper union leaders, who were well aware of his history of labor strife. At the *Long Island Press* in the 1930s, Newhouse set up a special spy network to find, harass, and sometimes fire those who thought of unionizing his newsroom. For this, the spies received bonuses and better hours and assignments. Sam Newhouse developed notoriety as a union-busting newspaper owner. After one political fracas, New York City's then mayor Fiorello La Guardia accused Newhouse of asking him to dispatch police officers against striking *Press* employees. "When [Newhouse] came to my office, he went on his knees and asked for police to beat up his reporters," La Guardia said three years after a bloody 1937 confrontation in which five union members had to be hospitalized, including one with a fractured skull. "He said to me, 'Let us use a stick on these fellows. How can anybody make money by paying the wages they want?' " Although Newhouse denied the mayor's remarks, the Guild strike at the *Press* had resulted in violence and would remain a source of bitterness until the paper closed thirty years later.

The Newhouse history of labor trouble stretched across the continent. In 1959, two of Newhouse's biggest newspapers suffered through prolonged strikes, although the company eventually prevailed, stronger than ever. At the *St. Louis Globe-Democrat,* the Guild members walked out over Newhouse's failture to agree to an adequate pension fund. Newhouse outfoxed the striking workers when he decided to sell the paper's production plant to the rival *St. Louis Post-Dispatch* in return for several million dollars in cash and a promise of cheap printing rates. Perhaps the most acrimonious labor confrontation with Newhouse, however, involved the *Portland Oregonian* that same year.

Long considered one of the best newspapers in the West, the *Portland Oregonian* was purchased by Newhouse in 1950 for an unprecedented price of $5.8 million, a sale that drew national attention to the burgeoning newspaper collector. Newhouse, who had carefully studied the *Oregonian*'s worth and estimated it to be much higher than the asking price, was delighted. He called it "the best buy I've ever made in my life." In 1957, the *Oregonian* won a Pulitzer Prize for investigative reporting. "For a Newhouse paper to get a Pulitzer Prize, that's something," he exclaimed. Yet Newhouse could scarcely claim credit. He acknowledged he knew nothing about the stories, which would cost thousands of dollars in expenses and legal fees. "They had courage," Newhouse said of the intrepid reporters. "I didn't even know they were doing it."

Newhouse's benevolent approach to the *Oregonian* soon changed. Although the paper's profitability had increased, few signs of the new prosperity could be found among employees. A bitter strike erupted as

Newhouse imported nearly five dozen strikebreakers from Oklahoma, some with rifles and shotguns, and trained his nonunion supervisors to run the newspaper in the event of a walkout. When the strike occurred, Newhouse managed to keep publishing the *Oregonian,* but at a terrible cost. Violent attacks on homes and delivery trucks continued for months. One of the most seriously injured victims was Don Newhouse, Sam's first cousin, who oversaw the *Oregonian*'s production side. One night, nearly a year after the strike began, a shotgun blast came through the basement window of Don Newhouse's home. "He was seriously wounded, and the attack—as we would find out—shortened his life," Sam would say later. "But we refused to yield, even to this extreme provocation."

The *Oregonian* strike dragged on through 1961, when Newhouse bought the competing *Oregon Journal* and consolidated both papers' operations. Those who crossed the picket line or replaced the striking employees were given permanent positions after the strike was settled. Officially, the bloody Portland strike was not resolved until five years after it had started.

Newhouse's strong anti-labor moves in Portland prompted an outcry from Senator Wayne Morse of Oregon. "The American people need to be warned before it is too late about the threat which is arising as a result of the monopolistic practices of the Newhouse interests," Morse said in a stinging 1960 speech on the Senate floor. After the sale of the *New Orleans Times-Picayune,* the House Judiciary Committee chairman announced an investigation into newspaper monopolies. Yet none of these governmental or judicial reviews ever came to anything, mostly because of the sophisticated financial techniques employed by Newhouse to ensure his empire would stay intact. His actions—which often skirted on the precipice of antitrust violations and reduced major cities to a single daily newspaper—were rarely scrutinized by other media. This was especially so in five cities—St. Louis, Portland, Birmingham, Syracuse, and Harrisburg, Pennsylvania—where Newhouse owned not only the daily newspaper but also a television and radio station or a cable-television franchise, as well.

Part of the reason why Newhouse escaped much scrutiny is because he deliberately avoided the bombast and political advocacy of old-time big-city newspaper barons such as William Randolph Hearst. "Going way back, when my father and his brothers were putting together their business, there was considerable public concern about the imposition of an individual owner's editorial judgment on the country as a whole," Si Newhouse testified years later when asked about his father's policy of local autonomy. Rather than a roaring yellow journalist competing in the cities, Sam Newhouse served as the prototype of a new age: bottom-line media corporations that prefer to own newspaper groups in exclusive markets. As Liebling remarked in his 1961 *New Yorker* article, "The men of the new order do not meddle with the locals as long as they come up with the tithe. They are, for the public, faceless and their coups are often inside jobs. Hearst tried to take cities by storm, but the new men prefer a rendezvous at the back gate."

Quietly, the elder Newhouse demonstrated his determined will, a remarkable fingertip feel for a newspaper's worth and a community's advertising potential. His mastery of modern-day media techniques was often well ahead of his time. In the mid-1930s, for example, Newhouse used a marketing survey to find out readers' interests in his New Jesey circulation area—a reliance on marketing that directly affected its brand of journalism and that today pervades the entire newspaper industry. He pioneered improved circulation methods—such as a reliance on home delivery rather than impulse sales at newsstands on the street—and steered his newspapers' focus toward the expanding suburbs, where he had the market all to himself. After buying into a newspaper, he quickly turned around its financial performance or, without sympathy or remorse, closed down a loser. "I'm not interested in buying funerals," he declared more than once, taking a pass, for example, on the purchase of the now-defunct *New York Herald Tribune*.

In this lifelong quest to build an empire, Sam Newhouse's brothers, in-laws, and especially his two sons would become central players. A chronic insomniac, Sam called his brothers sometimes late into the night with arcane questions and specific details that filled his restless mind. "After all, if I can't sleep, why should you?" he would tell his brothers. "I don't like to waste my time sleeping." With unwavering regularity, he and other senior family members would fly across the country to visit their newspapers, perfecting the ability to spot problems and then confer as a group in an attempt to find answers. Because they were a family, they could be brutally honest in their appraisals. "I remember years ago, when I was real young, going to my grandfather's house and seeing my father and uncle and grandfather having some argument, shouting at one another," recalled Wynn, Si's second-oldest son. "It was just the sort of Woody Allen stereotype of a Jewish family, where we all got together and one expressed his viewpoint more loudly than the next."

Though Sam was undoubtedly the ruler, the rest of the family took important jobs throughout the company. His brother Ted served as business manager to a number of papers, while Norman, the only Newhouse brother who ever worked full-time in the newsroom, was everything from a waterfront reporter and political writer to executive editor. "You know, I don't think any of us has any vanity," Norman once told a reporter. "And when you're free of vanity, you're free of a lot of other problems." Another brother, Louis, was mechanical superintendent; his sisters, Naomi and Estelle, worked in circulation and marketing. At various times, Sam Newhouse employed sixty-four cousins, nephews, in-laws, and other relatives in his family-owned company.

For all of the modern, sophisticated techniques of his company, there was still an old-fashioned paternalistic nature to Sam Newhouse. After all, he and his siblings had been through so much together. Whatever would be achieved or lost, as he defined it, would be a drama performed together. "We are a family," he explained in his memoir. "The ties that matter are the ties to each other. We build as a family and we shall continue to build as a family as long as we can."

Ultimately, Sam Newhouse knew he couldn't trust anyone to run the Advance company other than his namesake, S. I. Newhouse, Jr., and his younger son, Donald, both of whom had traveled with him since they were teenagers. They were aware of all the family secrets. The elder Newhouse had seen too many other family-owned newspapers collapse under the weight of dissension or uncertainty among the survivors. He would place great emphasis on the training of his sons to run his far-flung media colossus someday. This was a mixed blessing for Si Newhouse. During his childhood, Si and his brother were not abandoned by their father, as Sam had experienced with his absentee father. Rather, "the boys" were dominated by their father's boundless energy and genius well into their adult lives. They did not feel the satisfaction of building an empire or establishing their own name; instead, they were charged with the burdensome responsibility of maintaining a fortune, lest they suffer the ignominy of losing it. There was no room for failure, no opportunity for the family blood to weaken.

"I'm very hardboiled about the boys," the ever-confident media giant proclaimed in a profile story about himself that was featured on the cover of *Time* magazine. "I've built this thing up and I'm not going to let it go to pieces. The boys have been trained differently from myself. The older son, Si, is very interested in politics and public affairs, and he may eventually have more to say about policy than I have."

Eventually, his father's judgment about Si Newhouse's place in the family business would seem quite accurate. But just how difficult this legacy would be for Si Newhouse—as a young man then struggling with his own identity—would not be known except to his closest friend.

CHAPTER TWO

In His Father's Shadow

Allard Lowenstein didn't say where he was going. He was on a mission of mercy, an act of compassion for someone in need. Hurriedly, he slipped out of the family's house in Westchester without his parents knowing and journeyed to Manhattan to be with his troubled friend, Si Newhouse.

Over the telephone, Si had talked about killing himself, doing something to end the pain he felt inside. This wasn't his first crisis. Newhouse's thoughts of suicide would persist through high school and, as his letters to Lowenstein would show, linger until at least his early years in college. There was a profound sense of unhappiness and desperation about Si. At times, the burden of his father's all-encompassing expectations seemed crushing. Allard was one of the few friends he could trust to listen.

Usually, it wasn't until the following morning when Allard's younger sister found out where her brother had been the night before. As a secret shared among siblings, Lowenstein told her about Si's troubles.

"Si was very close to my brother," Lowenstein's sister, Dorothy Di-Cintio, recalled years later. "There were actual times when Al ran over in the middle of the night. . . . I think he was very worried. He would dash off to shore him up, and he was very concerned that there was a real danger that he might take his life or go off the deep end in one way or the other. My feeling is that Al felt very sorry for him, particularly in relation to his father."

In the early 1940s, the two boys became friends at the Horace Mann School, then a bucolic, all-male private high school in the northernmost section of the Bronx, near where the New York City borough meets the Westchester County suburbs. By his junior year, Allard Lowenstein, in the same class of 1945 as Si Newhouse, had already distinguished himself as a leader. At such a competitive school, it was important to stand out. Lowenstein was a bright, popular, and outspoken teenager. He showed more than a few glimpses of the political savvy he would someday use as a civil rights activist and New York congressman before he was murdered in 1980.

Lowenstein had a penchant for befriending "lost puppies," as his sister called them. "My brother was the kind of guy who spent his life helping people who needed help, and that would include somebody who needed emotional help. He liked to help the downtrodden, which is what Si was. Not in a sense of money, but Si was a very unhappy young man. On several occasions, Al ran to his rescue when Si was deeply in trouble with himself."

From his letters and interviews with other classmates, it is clear Si Newhouse, then a painfully shy sixteen-year-old, looked up to Allard Lowenstein, almost as he might to an older brother, as someone who cared and possessed the kind of self-confidence Si so often lacked as a teenager. Allard gently dissuaded Newhouse from acting upon his suicidal impulses.

Si's private pressures during his years at Horace Mann were part of a pattern of dark, brooding emotions and uncertainty about himself that would continue well into adulthood—sometimes to the bewilderment or ridicule of his peers and often as a source of dismay to his demanding father. His thoughts of suicide were only the most dramatic of many emotional upheavals surrounding Si Newhouse's early life—a painful road to maturity that included dropping out of college, an unhappy marriage with three children, a broken engagement to another woman, and a pro-longed period as a devil-may-care, middle-aged bachelor. Some wondered whether Si Newhouse would ever assume his rightful place at the head of his father's company. Most thought Donald would prevail. "I remember that Donald was more like his father than Si was," recalls William Tolley, a former Syacuse University chancellor, who came as close as anyone to being a true confidant to Sam Newhouse. "Si took a little longer to grow up. He had a little wild period, but not too wild. But Donald had his head on straight all the time."

For those who knew Si Newhouse only as a quiet, unprepossessing high school student with curly black hair and a slender build, the troubles surrounding him were a mystery. That this confused, socially inept young man would someday metamorphose into one of the world's most powerful media moguls would become an even greater surprise. Young Si barely made an impression. "I don't think I spoke more than ten words with him the whole time I was in school," recalls one classmate, Paul Haberman. "I don't know anybody that he was particularly friendly with."

Another classmate, John Halderstein, who was the class president, re-calls little about Si Newhouse other than his most familiar characteristic—being known as Allard Lowenstein's friend. "When you mention Si, I immediately think of Allard," Halderstein recalled five decades later. "He was kind of quiet, shy. I knew him then, but we weren't particularly good friends. I think Si needed a good friend. I just had that feeling."

None of his classmates—other than Allard Lowenstein—knew just how much Si Newhouse was in need of a friend.

For all of his obsession with bulding an empire, Sam Newhouse realized, at least late in life, that he had often neglected his family. The constant travel, the many hours spent at his various newspapers, and even the solitude he demanded while reviewing financial papers in his study at home kept him away from the concerns of daily life. His sons were almost nuisances for this newspaperman on the rise. "I did not have much time to spend with them and to do the things conventional fathers conventionally did with their sons," he admitted in his memoir.

To the extent Sam Newhouse shared poignant moments with his children, they seemed part of their training to inherit one of America's largest private fortunes. On Sunday mornings, rather than play baseball or go fishing, the elder Newhouse took his sons with him to the office—a practice that began when Si was five years old. Although his own father had mostly abandoned the family due to his asthma, Sam Newhouse felt no compulsion to be a traditional father with his sons. There was no room for frivolity or a sense of ease. "It just would not have been like me to be out there in the backyard swatting a baseball or wading through a stream, casting for trout," Sam later explained. "What's more, I didn't have the time."

Most of the burden for keeping Sam Newhouse's family together rested with his petite wife, Mitzi Epstein Newhouse, who tried to make up for her husband's constant absences by lavishing time and affection on her sons. "I think she may have been bothered by the fact that I was always so terribly involved with the paper," Sam admitted years later. Si was particularly close to his mother, and he appeared to physically resemble her side of the family more than the Newhouses. For years, Mitzi's immigrant mother lived with them following the death of her father, a garment manufacturer, and she helped in rearing the two boys.

The Newhouses moved to Staten Island, the mostly rural and least-populated borough of New York City, where Sam had already purchased the local newspaper soon after they were married in 1924. Everything within the family seemed to revolve around Sam's quest to build a newspaper empire. As part of an advertising promotion, the couple's first house was bought and furnished by Newhouse's Staten Island paper, the *Advance*. Eventually, Sam and his bride moved into a home he constructed on a few plots of land situated along Ward Hill, with a panoramic view of New York bay. Shortly after they moved into the new home, their first child—Samuel I. Newhouse, Jr.—was born on November 8, 1927. After a difficult labor, Si was delivered by cesarean section, the same way in which his younger brother, Donald Edward, would be born less than two years later. Mitzi had planned on having four children, but her physicians advised it would be too dangerous to have any more.

A woman with taste for the finer things, Mitzi Newhouse appeared to smooth Sam Newhouse's rough edges. When they met, she was a student at the Parsons School of Design and, though somewhat flighty in conversation, exuded both vitality and a certain charm. After an eight-month courtship, Sam presented an expensive diamond ring to her and they were married. Not incidentally, Mitzi, at just five feet tall, was slightly shorter than Sam Newhouse—height being something he was constantly aware of all his life in relation to others.

As a lifelong social climber, Mitzi loved the nightlife and warm glow of affluence found in Manhattan. There were frequent opening nights at the opera and Broadway plays, followed by dinner at Sardi's. As her husband's income grew, she treated herself to annual trips abroad to view the latest Paris fashions by such famous designers as Dior and Givenchy. Eventually, Mitzi uged her husband to move from the provincial environs of Staten Island to a large fourteen-room duplex on Park Avenue, on the Upper East Side of Manhattan, which she furnished with French-style antiques. The Newhouse home was very much in the image of Louis XIV: floors of parquet de Versailles covered with handmade French rugs, period furniture with bone white paneled walls glazed in pale sea blue to match the ceiling. "Mrs. Newhouse prefers soft color schemes to set off her blonde good looks and to form a pleasing background for feminine guests," gushed a 1957 *Herald Tribune* feature, with Mitzi pictured sitting by her opulent dining room table like a queen.

Unlike those minions who worked for him, Sam saw money as no object when it came to Mitzi. "I always talked to Sam before we went into any depth on money," decorator John Gerald once said. "He was never tight-fisted with anything Mitzi wanted."

When she got bored, Mitzi brought in a new decorator and revamped the look of the family's living quarters.

"It's a mess. You know what I want. Fix it," Mitzi would order.

In his father's world, however, there were no such indulgences for young Si Newhouse. After initially ignoring his sons until they could accompany him to work, Sam Newhouse embarked on what seemed like a junior-executive training program for his future heirs. He arranged with his public-relations man, Ray Josephs, to send the boys by train to Washington, D.C., so they could be taken on a special tour of the Capitol and meet important, powerful men of the kind they were destined to be. Summers were spent inside the offices of their father's newspapers, learning each aspect of the business. He demanded both boys "go through periods of rigorous training that developed their aptitudes." During the summer of 1943, for example, Si worked at his father's paper, the *Long Island Press,* as a cub reporter. One week, he covered the police beat, calling the morgue to inquire about curious deaths and watching the speeders and drunk drivers passing through traffic court. He spent another week in the state supreme courthouse, watching the trials of those accused of murder and other violent felonies. And as part of a week-long apprenticeship at City Hall, young Si met Mayor Fiorello La Guardia.

Work was an essential part of the family discipline. Although, in reality, his children's fate would be secured by trust accounts already in place for them, Sam Newhouse presented himself as a stern taskmaster, one with exacting and unforgiving standards. "They will have jobs," Sam once told the *New York Times* about his sons' future claim to his empire. "If they don't do their jobs well, they will be out of luck."

Sam Newhouse determined that Si and Donald would be educated in select private schools to prepare them for the rigors of a competitive world. Horace Mann seemed the perfect place. Each class had about one hundred students, many were the second- and third-generation sons of immigrant families, mostly Jewish like the Newhouses. There was a firm emphasis on achievement and several of the students of Si's era would become well known as successful adults, such as *Times* columnist Anthony Lewis, former Manhattan congressman William Green, James Schlesinger, who served in the cabinet under two presidents, and lawyer Roy Cohn.

Some say the atmosphere at Horace Mann resembled the movie *Goodbye, Mr. Chips,* as close to the spirit of a British boarding school as one could expect to find in the Bronx. "At the time, it was a very elitist school, very small—I think ninety percent of the graduates went to Ivy League schools," recalled classmate Charles Slotnik. "There were some real old-line teachers with fifteen or twenty years experience—not so much from Horace Mann but from England and other areas. It was a very intense academic regimen—very few written exams; everything was oral examination. You'd have to stand up and recite. We never took Regents [state-mandated written tests]. They thought we were above that."

In such a competitive atmosphere, the shy and awkward young Newhouse struggled to distinguish himself. "Good things come in small packages and diminutive Si was Staten Island's present to Horace Mann back in 1940," his class yearbook stated. The yearbook mentions that Si made his "clear imprints" at the school as president of the Speakers' Club and as one of the two managing editors of the school's newspaper, with Allard as its editor in chief. He won the Speakers' Club presidency by one vote. As a member of this club, Si helped to found the school's Wendell Willkie Award, willing to champion the memory of that failed Republican presidential candidate. At the newspaper, Si authored several articles and columns, including an elaborately detailed feature about attending the Metropolitan Opera and a bylined series about the inner workings of Horace Mann, entitled "How the School Runs." At year's end, the paper's staff held a small party at Newhouse's home. But he was hardly popular among his peers. "You never heard him laugh," remembered Robert Carniero, the newspaper's other managing editor. "He gave the impression of someone who wasn't happy, wasn't content with himself."

With the rest of the nation consumed by World War II, young Newhouse commented in his letters to Lowenstein about the world outside his home and school. When Allard suggested that the defeat of Winston Churchill was a "good omen," Newhouse wrote back strongly about his admiration for the British leader ("one of the greatest figures who ever lived") and warned that Churchill's political demise, so soon after Franklin D. Roosevelt's death, would "put the control of the world almost squarely in the lap of Stalin."

Privately, Si also voiced concern about labor leader Sidney Hillman's activity within the Democratic party and worried that the party would be controlled by "extreme leftists, Communists and socialists controlled by labor." Whatever personal disagreements between them, Si seemed in unison with his father's views on the issue of labor. Almost as if he were the voice of Sam Newhouse, Si expressed sheer disgust at the "disgraceful" 1945 newspaper strike in New York. He characterized it this way: "Imagine 3,000 fugitives from a chain gang, keeping 17,000,000 people from reading newspapers. They all should have been thrown in jail."

Despite his tough talk on politics, Si remained demurely on the sidelines and seemed to relish his role as a behind-the-scenes adviser to his friend Allard Lowenstein—the budding student politician. In the summer before his senior year at Horace Mann, Si exchanged several letters with him about Lowenstein's plans to run for class office. His main competitor was John Halderstein, who eventually won the race for class president, though Allard managed to become vice president of the student body's general organization. During that summer, in anticipation of the upcoming student vote when school resumed, Newhouse suggested strategy to his friend, methodically counting the votes of fellow classmates and identifying who they could count on. At times, Si Newhouse sounded like a Tammany Hall politician, barking commands at his candidate. "When anyone says you know anything at all about politics, I'll laugh in his face," Si chided Lowenstein. The handwritten missives were remarkably blunt and Machiavellian, commenting critically on numerous students. He advised Lowenstein not to push those who had already committed themselves to his candidacy, warning that: "We don't want to oversell our product."

From their correspondences, it is clear young Newhouse's political heroes were distinctly men capable of shrewd and daring maneuvers, while the fools were naïve idealists. Mindful of his friend's heroes, he admonished Lowenstein, the young idealist, not to become another Henry Wallace, the liberal presidential candidate.

For all of their plotting, however, the student election didn't turn out quite as Si and Allard had hoped. Another candidate—a student named Joseph Bernstein, a younger relative of the composer Leonard Bernstein—siphoned votes from Lowenstein's tally, causing the vote to result in a dead heat between John Halderstein and Lowenstein. Decades later, Halderstein recalled the election with a laugh. "It turned out that the school election was a tie, between Lowenstein and myself," said Halderstein. "So I got Joseph Bernstein to drop out, and I got his supporters, and that's how I won."

With less dramatic goals, Si Newhouse managed to fulfill his wish to become president of the Speakers' Club, though he expressed concerns that it might become filled with too many liberals. The job was undoubtedly a minor triumph for Si, who seemed to dislike small talk and was terrified of public speaking himself but who obviously had visions of someday being actively engaged in the arena of opinions and ideas. "The only thing I remember Al saying about Newhouse was, at one point, he mentioned that he was the wealthiest boy in our class," remembers Paul Haberman. "Obviously, most of the kids were well-to-do, given that it was a private school. Newhouse certainly didn't give any indication that he was that rich when he was in high school. Actually, he kept to himself and was unassuming."

Toward the end of his senior year, however, Si Newhouse's intentions of following other classmates to an Ivy League school evaporated. In his school yearbook, next to a picture of a chubby-cheeked Si Newhouse, is written: "Cornell can look forwad to Si's arrival at Ithaca." Si never arrived, however, acknowledging in a letter to Lowenstein that he had been rejected by Cornell. A few days after his rejection, Si received a telephone call from a Cornell fraternity man, unwittingly offering to let him use the frat house while he searched for a room. Appalled, young Si verbally abused the friendly caller, all but spitting in his face through the receiver.

The rejection from Cornell didn't seem to faze his father. Sam Newhouse was intent that both his sons would attend Syracuse University, a large private university in the same upstate New York town where the Newhouse family owned both the morning and afternoon newspapers as well as television and radio stations. Indeed, Sam Newhouse, who never had had the chance to attend college full-time, embraced Syracuse with his usual vigor, determined to become a big man on campus himself. He was elected as an honorary member of a Jewish fraternity on campus and was courted by William Tolley, then the university chancellor, as a potential benefactor with deep pockets. On many Saturday afternoons, Sam Newhouse sat with the university chancellor in his private box at the university stadium, rooting for the school's football team. Tolley and Sam Newhouse became close friends, but there was never a hint that Syracuse might not have been his son's first choice.

"He changed his mind about Cornell; I don't know why," Tolley said years later about Si Newhouse, calling him a "brilliant" student. "He could've gotten into Cornell, all right. He just changed his mind. Sam told me that both of them would come to Syracuse, so I imagine he influenced both boys. He told me before they came, 'I want both my boys to be at Syracuse, and they will be.' And I did not meet the boys until they came to Syracuse."

His son's rejection by Cornell wasn't the only fact Sam Newhouse kept from his new confidant, the university chancellor. Tolley says he first met

Sam Newhouse in 1945 "before he bought the *Syracuse Post-Standard*." But Newhouse did indeed own the newspaper at that time—a fact he kept secret for several years because of the anti-Semitic overtones he had once encountered before buying the paper. Tolley's relationship with Sam Newhouse included keeping an eye on his sons while they were away at school. Over the next several decades, Tolley's friendship with the newspaper baron flourished, with Sam Newhouse donating millions of dollars to the university.

Si Newhouse's stay at Syracuse was far less satisfying, sometimes erupting in verbal fights when his parents arrived for a visit. On their way up to Canada for a vacation, Sam and Mitzi inspected their son's room and his mother nearly fainted, comparing it with an East Side tenement, the kind where his father had grown up as a boy. Though Si was away from home, he still hadn't evaded the pull of his father's emotional orbit. Shortly after arriving for his freshman year Si described a visit by his parents which degenerated into "the same sort of scrapping between us, and lecturing on their part, which always occurs."

On campus, Si Newhouse found himself lost among a huge mass of students, including eighteen hundred in the freshman class. After years at an all-boys high school, having few dates, Si Newhouse was enchanted by the "coeds" he discovered. He described a model he met as "the most beautiful child I've ever laid eyes upon. . . ."

Still, Si Newhouse, the millionaire's son, found plenty to complain about at his new school. While keeping a brave front, he mentioned that his dormitory room was like a monk's sparse living quarters. The student daily looked more like toilet paper than a real newspaper, he complained. In a letter, he said the newspaper was poorly managed "almost entirely by 'women' " and sorely in need of good ideas. Around Syracuse, he said, the general atmosphere was boring and lacking any interest in politics. In his private correspondence to Lowenstein, Newhouse depicted one new Syracuse acquaintance as combining the "femininity and bitchiness" of a mutual friend from Horace Mann.

While Si struggled at Syracuse, Allard Lowenstein went to the University of North Carolina and gradually fell out of touch with his friend from Horace Mann. After a disastrous term at Syracuse, Si Newhouse was moved to reach out to his old friend and tell him of his problems. For not showing the right attitude, he was blackballed from his college fraternity— an ouster, Si admitted, bound to make his father furious. At the *Daily Orange,* the Syracuse student newspaper, he wrote a scathing unsigned editorial calling for a strong show of force in containing the expansion by the Soviet Union and stopping Stalin before a war erupted. After he was identified as the author of the anonymous editorial, Newhouse said, he was vilified by teachers in classes, including a political science professor who attempted to get the entire issue of the newspaper suppressed. "I have turned very rightist in spite of myself," he told his liberal friend.

At Syracuse, Si was away for the first time from the pressing influence of his father and began the very messy emotional business of growing up, finding his own identity. With an almost reckless abandon that winter and spring semester, Si enjoyed himself as never before—a more wonderful time, he would say, than any in his whole life—getting drunk and seeming to anger and alienate many in his path. This uncertain self-discovery was often crude and sophomoric, yet Si Newhouse finally was allowed to be himself. These happy times didn't last long. There seemed an underlying self-destructiveness to these actions, the mark of a student destined to drop out of school. When not ecstatic over his defiant moments, the emotional pendulum seemed to swing in the other direction, and then there were his black moods to contend with.

Suicide remained an option for Si. After recounting some of his hell-raising experiences in a letter, he confided to his old friend Allard: "But at the same time, I have never had so many low periods (remember my old talk of suicide, well, I was thinking of it again.)" The talk of suicide, however, stayed a secret between the two high school friends. There were other matters that also remained unsaid.

Allard Lowenstein, who felt sympathy toward Newhouse as perhaps no one else did in high school, was troubled by his own identity. Lowenstein's diaries and private papers later showed he had doubts about his sexuality, a constant source of tension between his image as a heterosexual young man and his own homosexual impulses. "The urge I get when I see certain boys is getting out-of-control," Lowenstein wrote in his diary in 1943, while he was still a student at Horace Mann. "God, God, what will I do?" During high school, Lowenstein apparently sublimated his homosexual urges, a pattern that would continue for the rest of his adult life. "I can only see one solution," as Lowenstein confided to his diary, "very good friendships." But Lowenstein never revealed these inner doubts to any of his Horace Mann friends at that time, according to his biographer, William H. Chafe.

Most of Si's own anxieties seemed to emanate from a fear of failure—the risk of not living up to the expectations set by his father, the great and powerful S. I. Newhouse, Sr. This dread would cast a pall over Si Newhouse's emotions for years. "I think Mr. Newhouse was tough and I think he was very tough, very hard on Si, rightly or wrongly," said Lowenstein's sister, Dorothy. "I don't know what he could have done wrong. But what I think was the problem was that Si didn't come up to his father's expectations—whether his father's expectations were extremely high or whether his father didn't realize that he wasn't the kind of person he wanted him to be. I think what he wanted was somebody who was imposing, capable, and bright—an outstanding figure—and Si certainly wasn't that."

By his sophomore year of college, Allard Lowenstein had gradually distanced himself from Si Newhouse, who struggled to find new friends on the Syracuse campus, a particularly difficult feat after he was thrown out of his fraternity. "Even then, there was something different about him," recalled Donald Brooks, who attended Syracuse at the time and later became a well-known New York designer. "My room was adjacent to his in our off-campus living quarters, and I remember that when everyone else was playing Benny Goodman or Glenn Miller, the music you heard from Si's room was Mahler or Sibelius."

Undoubtedly, Si was a bright young man, yet he seemed too immature or restless to stay at Syracuse. He was unable to maintain the needed grade-point average in the college's journalism department and was forced to drop it as a major. By his junior year, Newhouse was confused and unfocused on his future goals and dropped out of Syracuse University altogether, never to return again as a student. For Sam Newhouse, his oldest son's decision to become a college dropout—to leave the school he had picked for him—left him greatly saddened. The idea of going away to college as a full-time student must have seemed a luxury to Sam Newhouse. Because of his family's dire financial problems, Sam had been compelled to leave school after the eighth grade, forcing him to take the state's Regents exam to qualify as a high school graduate. Then he sandwiched night classes at the New Jersey College of Law for four years in between his daytime work resuscitating the *Bayonne Times*—until he gained a law degree in 1916. Now, thirty years later, his eldest son, who had been given virtually every chance and opportunity, had thrown it all away.

Once filled with enthusiasm for the college scene, Sam Newhouse couldn't hide his disappointment. "He loved it and enjoyed his relationship with the university—it was a brand-new world for him," Chancellor Tolley recalled about Sam Newhouse's initial response to the Syracuse campus. The elder Newhouse and the university chancellor became fast friends. "He loved football and he came to all the home games," recalled Tolley. "He sat in my box and he enjoyed every minute of it. He knew football. He learned a lot about both fooball and basketball. He wasn't a talker, though. He was a quiet man, and I think I spoke with him about as much as anybody." After Si's decision to drop out, however, Sam was never quite as enthusiastic for Syracuse, even though Donald also entered Syracuse at the time. Tolley conferred with Sam, hoping they could somehow convince Si to stay in school. But Sam Newhouse declined the offer.

"Look, I'm not going to fight it," the elder Newhouse told Tolley during one conversation. "If they want to drop out, let them drop out."

Sam Newhouse continued to support the school as a benefactor, but not as the proud father of an alumnus. After the decision to drop out was made, "He wasn't the same," Tolley recalled. "He was disappointed. We all were. I thought it was a mistake, but I didn't try to influence him. Both boys dropped out and went back to work."

Years later, Donald, who also quit school roughly at the same point during his college career at Syracuse, put the best possible face on their departure. "We got restless," Donald said. "The lure of working took us away from college." Somehow, Donald's decision to drop out didn't seem to have the same sting as Si's failure at Syracuse. Donald Newhouse, who greatly resembled his father in looks and demeanor, had worked on the business side of the student newspaper and trained under his Uncle Ted at the family's newspaper, the *Long Island Press*. Donald's decision to leave college made him appear to be a young man in a hurry, someone with purpose and direction. At Syracuse, Donald had met a beautiful coed, Susan Marley, the daughter of a local junk dealer turned self-made millionaire. Donald and Suzie, as she was affectionately called, would eventually marry and have several children. Success and happiness, even without a college degree from Syracuse, seemed assured for Donald.

Si Newhouse was a different story. At Syracuse, he also met a young woman to whom he would later get married—yet there remained a level of personal unhappiness and self-doubt that would linger for years, afflicting nearly everyone in his life. There was no sure path that Si Newhouse seemed intent on following when he dropped out. He left Syracuse only after a long streak of self-indulgence and lingering thoughts of committing suicide. While his younger brother made it clear that he was marching off the college campus to stake his claim in the Newhouse empire, Si's course seemed aimless. There would remain many more years of heartache and family difficulties before Si Newhouse seemed to find his niche inside his father's kingdom.

Jane Franke was a friendly, bright, and sensitive young woman who graduated from Syracuse University with a degree in fine arts. While they were Syracuse undergraduates in the late 1940s, she met Si Newhouse and fell in love. One family friend would describe her as a "nice Jewish girl from the Bronx." Actually, her family lived in Westchester County, near the Connecticut border, where her father, Chester Frankenstein, was president of Port Chester Auto Parts. Though hardly a multimillionaire newspaper owner, Frankenstein earned enough so that Jane could attend the private Cherry Lawn School in Darien, Connecticut, about twenty minutes from their home, and then Syracuse. Eventually, Jane decided to change her name legally to Franke, a shortened and undoubtedly more socially acceptable version of her family's surname.

With her short brunette hair, a wide smile, and deep dark eyes, Jane Franke was attracted to the slightly older Si Newhouse, a brooding, melancholy young man of considerable intelligence. After they met at Syracuse, Jane and Si managed to remain a steady couple even after Si dropped out of college, worked at the *Long Island Press*, and entered the Air Force for a two-year hitch. The Newhouse family—particularly Si's mother, Mitzi—liked the fiancée her son had selected. The wedding was welcomed as a sign that Si might be willing to settle down after a tumultuous college experience.

One month after she graduated from Syracuse's College of Fine Arts in February 1951, Jane walked down the aisle, escorted by her father, at an evening marriage ceremony held in the Jade Room of the Waldorf-Astoria Hotel. At the time, Si Newhouse, who had enlisted the previous August, was stationed at Sampson Air Force Base in upstate Geneva, New York. Donald Newhouse served as Si's best man, while Jane's sister was her bridesmaid.

The marriage didn't prove to be a happy one, however. After he was discharged in 1952 as an airman second class, Si was sent to Portland, Oregon, to work at one of his father's radio stations; he later returned to New York to work again at the *Long Island Press*. Si had yet to find a comfortable spot within the family business. At home, things were even worse. Within five years, Si and Jane's marriage had produced three children, Samuel, Wynn, and Pamela, but their life together remained a struggle, at least emotionally. "I think they simply grew apart," recalls Ray Josephs, the Newhouse company's PR man. "I remember visiting them early on at Park Avenue, where they had a big apartment. But it was on the other side of Ninety-sixth Street. It wasn't very attractive. I thought it was rather second-rate." After Pamela was born, Si and Jane separated and eventually divorced. Unhappy and increasingly distant, Si Newhouse hadn't been ready for the demands that family life would place upon him, at least with the young coed he had met at Syracuse.

"We were really too young," recalled Jane many years later, after she was remarried to a textile executive. "We kept changing and eventually we both learned what we wanted. He respected intellect. And it might be fair to say he is cool and distant. He's never relaxed. And you'd have to go back to his childhood to understand that." Si seemed too consumed by his complex relationship with his father and the need to find his own identity.

Despite the difficulties with Jane, Si tried to remain a good father, showing an interest in the lives of their three children, even if he was no longer living in their home. But the divorce seemed to shock Si's parents, who were deeply troubled by their son's failed marriage. "That was a bad time, especially for Mitzi," Ernie Doepke, a close confidant of Sam Newhouse, would later say. "She thought divorces were not part of the Newhouse family. For a couple of years, when we went to their home, Si wasn't there. She wouldn't have him. She practically disowned him."

His father's treatment was even worse. Sam Newhouse, domineering and supremely self-assured, often seemed intent on humiliating his oldest son. The story most often repeated involved eleven dollars' worth of shaving cream. Sam Newhouse spotted the expense on a financial report shortly after he purchased the *New Orleans Times-Picayune* in 1962. He grilled his son on the need for charging eleven dollars for shaving cream to the family-owned business. Somehow, the incident seemed to underline the strong doubts Sam Newhouse harbored about his eldest son, then a thirty-five-year-old college dropout estranged from his wife and children. This surely wasn't the manner in which Sam Newhouse was accustomed to ruling his life. As Richard Meeker, the elder Newhouse's biographer, concluded about their relationship, "His father must have wondered if he would ever overcome the sense of disappointment he sometimes felt about his first child."

At his father's newspapers, Si Newhouse was viewed as something of a buffoon. One of his coworkers at the *Long Island Press* remembered Si sitting around the office, rarely writing anything, and reading the *Daily Worker* until the end of the day, when he would offer to give this man a ride back to Manhattan in his Cadillac. At his father's Washington-based news service, Jules Witcover, who later became a nationally syndicated columnist, recalled how Si Newhouse seemed perfectly suited as the bumbling son of the wealthy owner. "He was known in the bureau as Jerry Lewis," Witcover told Meeker. "He looked like Jerry Lewis. He acted like Jerry Lewis. They'd line him up with press credentials for these big foreign trips, and he would come in with about four cameras hanging all over him. The kid was just ludicrous."

After his divorce, Si's personal life became increasingly solitary and self-indulgent. Even his hobbies, such as collecting fine art and watching old movies, were essentially individual preoccupations. He dated a number of women, including Geraldine Stutz, who eventually became president and part owner of Henri Bendel's, and Nadine Bertin, who worked within the Condé Nast company. He steadily dated another young woman, Rachel Crespin, whom he eventually proposed to. In late October 1962, the couple's engagement announcement was placed in the society pages of *The New York Times*. Crespin, who was also divorced at the time, was a fashion editor of "Junior Bazaar," a section within *Harper's Bazaar*—the main competitor to Condé Nast's fashion powerhouse, *Vogue*. Their engagement ended abruptly; Si never married Crespin.

"I was engaged to Si for a month," Crespin recalled years later. "It was not significant. We met; it was at a party. It was a very short relationship. There were a lot of people who were closer to him than I was. I think everybody whom I could even remotely think of who was a friend of his from that period isn't alive anymore." Crespin declined to discuss why the engagement was broken. "I have a tremendous fondness for him," she said. "He's a nice man."

Rather than allay his parents' concerns, Si appeared determined to maintain his cavalier lifestyle. As if to underline the point, the usually media-shy Newhouse consented to an interview with *The New York Times* for a floridly detailed feature story on bachelors living in Manhattan. In this article, the thirty-eight-year-old publisher's son recounted how he had watched a movie with "a marvelous bachelor apartment" and decided to move into a similar East Side duplex apartment with two terraces.

"It's very much me at the moment," Si told the *Times,* which pictured him relaxing with his abstract paintings, jackal fur rug (made from fifty skins imported from Greece), and wearing black espadrilles on his feet. As he sat with his legs crossed, Si was pictured waiting for his Filipino houseboy, Pedro, to finish pouring him a cup from an elegant white teapot. Raving about his houseboy, whose cooking range extended from spaghetti to duck, Si described him as "one of the great luxuries of the world."

Surely, such an indulgent lifestyle could not be expected to gain the approval of his Spartan and demanding father. Publicly, though, Sam Newhouse would never let on about any disappointment. He seemed to have a higher mission in mind for his sons—pushing them to find their place in the family business and ensure its survival. Whatever the setbacks, Sam Newhouse was committed to the notion of family and its lasting ties of loyalty. "The boys learned the business early and well," Sam Newhouse said near the end of his life. "This has been true for my grandsons and the other youngsters coming up with them. All of them have been born into a world of means I could only dream of as a child, yet all have been born into an awareness that their comforts carry obligations to the family, to the organization, to the community."

Almost seventy years old by the mid-1960s, S. I. Newhouse, Sr., had become a newspaper legend. He was celebrated in weekly newsmagazines and enjoyed the honor of having the journalism school at Syracuse University named for him. At the dedication ceremony in 1964, President Johnson appeared personally to make a speech and pose with Sam Newhouse and his family for an official photograph. In this picture, Donald and Susan gathered with their children next to the President and Lady Bird Johnson, while Si stood alone, behind his parents. The image suggests a strange and unsettling dichotomy about the relationship between father and son. Here was his father, smiling broadly as he received a much-publicized honor at the same school from which Si had dropped out so ignominiously. Although he was well into his thirties, Si Newhouse still moved in his father's shadow, experiencing a bittersweet mix of awe and fear. Even Si's children understood the emotional tumult he endured as a son who had to bend to his father's will.

"Nobody really knew him," Pamela Newhouse, Si's daughter, told an interviewer in 1980 about her famous grandfather. "You probably heard that he was mild and unassuming, but he had an iron will. He got people to do what he wanted. There's the paradox. Maybe he didn't whip my father [Si Newhouse] into joining him, but when you are brought up in a certain way and given certain opportunities, it makes it difficult to reject them. My father was given a great deal. Perhaps he was spoiled. So when it came time to decide what he would do as an adult, it is possible he needed a certain way of life."

Si's decision to find a different way of life would indeed take him beyond his father's world of grimy newspapers situated in out-of-the-way places, far from the social circles of New York. His son's reputation would be forged on the island of Manhattan, with its sophisticated brew of trendy magazines and highbrow literature, contemporary art and fashion, and all of the trappings of immeasurable wealth. After years of failing to find a place in his father's newspaper kingdom, Si discovered the one place in the family business in which Sam Newhouse showed little interest: the world of Condé Nast magazines.

CHAPTER THREE

A Grand Acquisition–Condé Nast

As the story goes, Sam Newhouse was leaving his Park Avenue town house for a walk one morning in 1959 when he asked his wife, Mitzi, what she would like for their upcoming thirty-fifth wedding anniversary.

"She asked for a fashion magazine," said Newhouse, who by this time in his life had learned how to tell a good yarn. "So I went out and got her *Vogue!*"

Anyone acquainted with Sam Newhouse's career knew this often repeated tale had been embroidered, if not outright fabricated, for he was hardly inclined to do anything on a whim. True, Mitzi Newhouse was pleased by the cachet that owning a magazine like *Vogue* would bring. But the $5 million purchase of *Vogue*—the perennial fashion bible and a virtual pictorial tribute to the social calendars of America's elite—and the assortment of other Condé Nast fashion magazines was only a small part of Newhouse's effort to diversify his burgeoning media empire. After learning of its availability, Newhouse was willing to pay almost any price to acquire a controlling interest in this stable of advertising-rich publications.

As Si Newhouse later recalled, his father was told at first by the broker handling the deal that the asking price for the Condé Nast magazines was $500,000.

"It seems like a good deal," the elder Newhouse replied, authorizing the sale.

Later, the broker was forced to call back with the bad news that he had misunderstood the price, which was actually ten times greater.

Sam Newhouse barely blinked. "It still sounds good."

The offer also sounded good to Iva Sergei Voidato Patcévitch, the elegant silver-haired president and publisher of Condé Nast Publications, Inc., which still carried the name of its legendary former owner, who had died nearly two decades earlier. Patcévitch, known as "Mr. Pat," was willing to sell his exclusive option on 470,000 shares for control of the company to Newhouse. In less than three weeks, Newhouse added another fifty thousand shares from other sources (for a total 52 percent ownership of the company) and convinced Patcévitch to stay and continue overseeing the company. Patcévitch told the staff of the sale to the Newhouses, informing them that the Newhouses were only acting as "private investors," with assurances there would be "no change whatsoever in the policies, management or operations of Condé Nast Publications."

For years, the magazine company made famous by Condé Nast had carried on merrily, insulated and somewhat oblivious to their slipping finances. Since 1909, when it was purchased by Nast, *Vogue* had been single-minded in its mission as an arbiter of style and taste among the rich. Along with his longtime editor Edna Woolman Chase, the dapper Gatsby-like Nast, once a poor boy from St. Louis, projected a vision in *Vogue* of Paris fashions and New York high life. Rather than aim his magazines at a wide audience, Nast positioned *Vogue* as a publication for the elite and sold it to advertisers with discriminating appeal. "Class, not mass," he insisted. The magazine featured some fine writing and photography, but its essential purpose was never in doubt: to sell merchandise. His intent was to "bait the editorial pages," as Nast described it, "in such a way as to lift out of all the millions of Americans just the 100,000 cultivated people who can buy these quality goods."

From a small society periodical, *Vogue* evolved into a powerhouse fashion magazine that became the centerpiece of Nast's collection of publications, which included *Vanity Fair* and *House & Garden*. In 1929, Nast lost control of the company following the stock market crash and his finances never fully recovered. *Vanity Fair,* which was perhaps the best magazine of its era in the 1920s, ceased publication in 1936 as times changed. Three years before he died, Nast managed to found *Glamour* magazine in 1939, which became one of the most popular young women's magazines in the United States and at times the company's biggest moneymaker. Even though Nast's ownership stock was eventually transferred into the hands of British publishers, *Vogue* never seemed to lose Nast's sense of social flair or entitlement. With *Vogue* showing the way, the Condé Nast magazines would have an impact on the rest of the country, based on his self-professed theory that "taste percolates downward."

Vogue was constant in its effete approach, chronicling the accoutrements of the beautiful people of the 1960s just as Condé Nast had celebrated New York's café society in the 1920s. "It becomes increasingly apparent after a short visit at *Vogue* that most of the staff acts, dresses, and talks as if it had walked right out of its own magazine pages," writer Gay Talese observed in a 1961 *Esquire* magazine feature entitled "Vogueland." "Whatever else may be said for it, *Vogue* does offer a kind of balmy escape for those thousands of female Walter Mittys who, under the hair dryer each week, can flip through the gossamer pages and perchance dream that *they* are the Countess Crespi lolling on the Niarchos' three-masted schooner, *they* are at Monaco being sketched by Rene Bouche, *they* are flying their own Beechcraft toward some exotic spot far, far from Oshkosh . . . far, far from the Bronx.''

Patcévitch, as chief editorial executive and publisher, managed the company for the next two decades, until the British owners, the Berry family, offered him an option to buy their controlling stock. Unable to afford the company himself, Patcévitch shopped his option around unsuccessfully (Henry Luce's Time Inc., rejected the asking price) until the Newhouses entered the picture. At the time, the Condé Nast publications included *Vogue,* with its circulation of 415,000 readers, *Glamour, Bride's, House & Garden*, and the *Vogue Pattern Book*, as well as a Connecticut printing plant used by other publications, including *The New Yorker*. Behind this chic veneer, however, the Condé Nast magazines were losing money. Before its sale in 1959 to the Newhouses, the then publicly traded company reported a net loss of $225,000 on sales of $20 million for 1958, and a similar deficit of $132,000 on $19 million in sales the year before that. Sam Newhouse acted swiftly to stem the red ink. Shortly after he acquired Condé Nast, Newhouse also bought out the Street & Smith publishing house, which produced a number of slick magazines and once published pulp potboilers with such folk heroes as Buffalo Bill and the works of Horatio Alger, Jr. After paying $4 million to acquire Street & Smith, Newhouse shut down one of its magazines, *Charm*, and melded it into *Glamour*, which essentially appealed to the same young readership. He did the same with the magazine *Living for Young Homemakers*, whose readers were combined with those of *House & Garden*. By buying out the competition, Newhouse's ad salesmen were able to sell *Glamour* as the first women's magazine with a circulation of more than a million. Another Street & Smith title, *Mademoiselle*, became a prominent player in Newhouse's group of glossy magazines. Although Patcévitch stayed in place during this transition, he reported to Sam Newhouse every Monday or Tuesday over lunch. Before the first year of Newhouse's ownership was complete, the Condé Nast finances had been turned around, with reported net profits of $1.6 million.

The transformation was much more than financial, however. The man once described as a ragpicker among newspaper owners, whose mother had toted clothing on her back to sell to other immigrants in New Jersey, was now the wealthy owner of the world's best-known fashion magazine. Sam Newhouse still looked to his monopoly newspapers as the financial engine for his empire, churning out profits in much greater amounts than could ever be realized from monthly magazines. But he realized the buoyant effect that owning *Vogue* had on his social-climbing wife. "I thought Mitzi would get a thrill out of it," he said when asked about the purchase.

Sam Newhouse and his wife became members of the Condé Nast board of directors, with Mitzi flying once a year to Europe to make the rounds of the fashion houses and to be treated royally as the new owner of *Vogue*. She threw lavish parties for her friends, who included a number of top

Condé Nast editors and advertisers. She even took credit for making sure *Vogue* employed models in her petite dress size. In its pages, the magazine celebrated Mitzi as a pillar of New York society, with little mention to readers that her husband owned *Vogue*. In one 1964 feature, entitled "People Are Talking About . . ."—a familiar place of honor in the magazine—Mitzi Newhouse was reverently profiled and described as "pastel, fragile, with the look of Belleek porcelain."

The most profound change resulting from the purchase of Condé Nast, however, occurred with Si Newhouse, who had wandered from job to job within the family enterprise, never quite finding his place in his father's kingdom. Before then, he had spent a number of years at the *Newark Star-Ledger*, the provincial newspaper whose dull, bulky appearance must have seemed even more so compared to the luster of trendsetting *Vogue*. As with all of the Newhouse properties, there was a family member assigned to watch over Condé Nast. At first, Sam Newhouse kept an eye on the company, but soon that responsibility fell to Si, whose interest in the world of Condé Nast expanded rapidly. Away from the day-to-day oversight of his father's newspaper empire, Si seemed to relish the challenge. Although the purchase was publicized as a gift for Mitzi, as one *Fortune* writer later observed, "It also turned out to be a present for Si, who moved in to learn the business and found the world of slick magazines entirely to his taste."

Shortly after the acquisition, Si began working at *Glamour* in a number of positions where he could learn all the aspects of the magazine business. By the mid-1960s, he had established himself in the magazine world of Condé Nast and was appointed as the publisher of the American edition of *Vogue*, one of the positions once held by Patcévitch. Some who had worked with the family for many years recognized how quickly Si Newhouse responded. "He loved it much more—right from the start—than the newspapers," recalls Ray Josephs, the family's longtime publicist. "That was his niche, and Sam was never interested in the magazines. Sam was raised in the newspaper world."

To guide him through the hodgepodge of magazine publishing, Si relied heavily on Richard A. Shortway, an energetic advertising manager at *Glamour* who would work daily with Newhouse for the next five years. Shortway was a handsome man with a deep voice, rugged appearance, and personal charm reminiscent of the actor William Holden. Within the business, Dick Shortway was considered a great salesman—an outside guy—who was able to entertain clients at luncheons or dinners and convince them to advertise with Condé Nast. Not everyone had it in his gut to be a pitchman, certainly not the ever-shy Newhouse. "Si never went outside; he was always an inside guy," recalled Peter Diamandis, a *Glamour* salesman at the time, who later became a top Newhouse publisher and then formed his own multimillion dollar magazine company. "But with Dick, he went out and talked to retailers, cosmetic-company executives. Dick was a little bit of a mentor for him. He was a terrific sales-man—a very tough, no-nonsense outside guy who would take rejection well. I think he taught Si something about taking rejection, if you can work your way through it."

Dick Shortway, like his new boss at the time, was in his mid-thirties and had recently seen his marriage fall apart. The similarities, though, ended there. He still remembers the day he first walked into Si Newhouse's office.

"Have you got a minute?" Shortway asked.

Newhouse looked up from his desk and smiled meekly. "Yes, I'm . . . *honored,*" said the boss's son.

From all appearances, Shortway, with a bit of the salesman's swagger, possessed the unswerving self-confidence young Newhouse lacked. At *Glamour,* Si was a socially inept executive who remained guarded in con-versation. At times, he could be both sad and self-deprecating about his inner mood swings. Upon returning to work after a few days on vacation, Si showed up at an advertising sales meeting sporting a deep tan and a new suit.

"I was in the room when someone said, 'Boy, you look great, Si,' " Diamandis recalled.

Si just looked without expression.

"That's on the *outside,*" he replied.

Given his own piece of the family empire to run, Si Newhouse became enthusiastic about the newly purchased magazines as he learned about the business from Shortway. After he arrived at *Glamour,* Newhouse relocated next to Shortway's office, where they would talk endlessly about strategy and how best to sell the magazine. Si was a quick study and soon was suggesting new ideas for special issues or features, asking Shortway whether he thought they could sell enough advertising for them. At least once a week, Shortway would join Si for informal dinners, where the conversation usually remained focused on business. "I'd go to Si's house and it would be just he and I—or I might bring one of our senior adver-tising people along—and we would discuss things," said Shortway. "His houseboy would come to the door and say, 'Hello, Mr. Shortway, would you like a scotch and soda?' Si would come up in blue jeans, no shoes, no socks, and a sweatshirt. And Pedro, his houseboy, would serve us dinner."

Through their work together, Shortway and Si became friendly and would occasionally double-date. When Sam and Mitzi hosted an engage-ment party, marking Si's intention to marry Rachel Crespin in the early 1960s, Dick was one of the guests who attended, though he was surprisesd weeks later when "all of a sudden, the whole thing was off." Si trusted him enough so that he occasionally asked Shortway to escort his mother, Mitzi, to social functions. "Si didn't go to those things; he avoided them," Shortway recalled. "Si would ask me, 'Do you mind taking my mother?' "

At family parties, Shortway would sometimes encounter Sam New-house. Invariably, Sam would pull Shortway aside and ask him privately, "How's business?" Although Shortway was in the old man's employ, his loyalties were clearly to Si. He fobbed off the elder Newhouse's inquiry with a quick answer: "Good," or "Promising."

Somehow, these unexplicit responses satisfied Sam Newhouse. "Okay, good, keep working," he replied, then walked off to rejoin the party.

Shortway's ascent through the company was part of his close working relationship with Si. In 1962, Shortway moved from *Glamour* to *Vogue* as its advertising director. At that point, Si was overseeing *Vogue*'s operations as well as the rest of the Condé Nast magazines. Shortway suggested Si take the title of publisher, but Si objected. "Newhouses don't take titles," he told him. But by 1964, Si Newhouse was formally named *Vogue*'s publisher and Shortway was made his associate publisher two years later. Much of the reason for that promotion was that Si didn't like to go out to meet people. "Si was never an outside person, didn't really want to be on the outside," recalled Shortway. "I said, 'You have to have someone on the outside with some degree of power,' and so he made me associate publisher and let me be the outside guy and he was the inside guy. He made every decision, though, I assure you."

For old family hands like Ray Josephs, the difference in Si Newhouse's demeanor and approach was quite evident. Very early one morning, Josephs recalled, he met with the boss's son at his Condé Nast office and was struck by the change. The young man who had once seemed lost in the family business now seemed quite focused and assured.

Hours before his employees would arrive, Si was busy at work in his stark white office, with a few paintings hanging from the walls and an assortment of magazines stacked up in a corner. "He was at the desk with a calculator, toting things up on his own, figuring out percentages, what this paper was doing and what that magazine was doing," recalls Josephs. "Not with a bevy of assistants around, but by himself, scribbling things down. He used this system of early starts, doing it himself and getting a feel for all the publications by the calculations that he himself does. He had a desire to find those areas where he could make constant improvement."

One of those areas of improvement for Si Newhouse, aside from any business interests, was his own self-esteem. For all of its inherent commercial appeal, Condé Nast also provided entrée to some of the most select social circles in Manhattan and the glamorous world of art and fashion. To help lead him through this realm was someone who was already in the company and who would become both a close friend and teacher to young Si Newhouse, an ever-engaging and sophisticated man known by some as "the Silver Fox." He would become the dominant voice of Condé Nast for the next quarter century.

Alexander Liberman stood at the glass layout tables, peering endlessly at each tiny photograph with a cubelike magnifying glass or the naked eye, like some meticulous miner panning for gold. Somewhere in these celluloid strips was the next cover, the one with just the right look: a photo with *charm,* as he might say.

A stern-looking man with a hawklike nose, a neatly trimmed salt-and-pepper mustache, and a shock of flowing white hair pushed back against his head, Liberman, at nearly eighty, still managed to strike a commanding pose, making the rounds of the different Condé Nast magazines in 1990, trying to stay in touch. During office hours, he usually wore a nondescript dark suit, with a blue shirt and navy tie or some other ensemble of bland tones and hues. He preferred black Reeboks to leather shoes, allowing him to make only the slightest sound as he entered a room. It wasn't necessary for the longtime editorial director of Condé Nast to make a statement with his clothes.

As he reviewed the possible cover photos or scanned the layouts of his art directors, Liberman dispensed his comments with imperial detachment, often using endearing phrases like "friend" and "my dear" to veil or soften his otherwise-blunt comments. It could be a grueling process even for seasoned professionals. Véronique Vienne remembers this ordeal vividly. In her short tenure as art director for *Self* magazine, Vienne quickly learned the linguistic nuances and corporate doublespeak of Condé Nast. In many ways, this atmosphere reflected the quirky personalities of Si Newhouse and his mentor and confidant, Alex Liberman. She recalls one particular layout that Liberman admonished for being too "nice."

"Un peu plus de brutalité, s'il vous plaît, ma chère amie," Liberman murmured. Literally translated, he was urging her to use "a little more brutality, if you please, my dear friend." But in the language of Condé Nast, as she well understood, it meant not to be too provincial, too predictable in her layouts. The master's cutting comments were stylish but direct as any knife.

"Like most victims of abuse, Condé Nast employees worship their abuser—and Liberman is their hero," Vienne later observed. "At *Self* magazine we were no exception. When Mr. Liberman, as we called him, came into the room, there was a heightened sense of purpose, a childlike excitement, and a delicious urgency."

Liberman's taste for violence extended to both the artistic realm and in-house politics. For a time, the screaming tabloid covers of the *New York Post,* splashed with bloody scenes and tales of human misery, were posted on the walls of the *Vogue* layout room as a sort of inspiration to Liberman. To be *journalistic* was the supreme compliment, the visual ideal. The torn black-and-white pieces of paper under the bold headlines, the certain way of cropping photos, the emphasis on movement and being of the moment—all were Liberman trademarks, as distinctive as a Rauschenberg. "I want to look journalistic, darling," he would implore his corps of designers and art directors. In office politics as well, Liberman was an acknowledged master. For fifty years, he managed to survive numerous owners and legendary editors. However, it was not until the Newhouses assumed control of the company that Liberman rose as the preeminent creative force at Condé Nast, the one whose aesthetic would forever influence Si Newhouse and so much of the American media.

Soon after the family's acquisition of Condé Nast Publications in 1959, Sam Newhouse went to his oldest son and, as Si later recalled, "asked me to go in and learn what made it work." The person who showed him was Alexander Semeonovitch Liberman, then a debonair forty-seven-year-old artist who had edited well-known magazines on both sides of the Atlantic. On the *Vogue* masthead, Liberman was listed as art director, below the names of Patcévitch and editor Jessica Daves, though few art directors wielded anywhere near as much influence as Liberman did. Young Newhouse realized that Liberman—a veritable charm-school teacher of old-world culture, modern art, and personal comportment—was the one to go to to "learn what made it work." As Si Newhouse made his way to the top of the company, Liberman's power increased as well, eventually resulting in his appointment in 1962 as editorial director for all of the Condé Nast magazines, including *Vogue*. In the view of Si Newhouse, watching Liberman was like observing a maestro before an orchestra or a great painter with a palette. Each photo and graphic "is all explored and re-examined in the same way Alex explores and re-examines his art," as Newhouse once described it. "Alex has never settled on one solution."

Everything about Liberman was expressed in superlatives, spoken with the knowing, inflated air that had for so long been part of the Condé Nast style. With his breathy, slightly haughty voice, in a manner that suggested the actor John Houseman, Liberman paid special attention to the cover shots and inside photos, the layout and graphic design—those signature characteristics that gave the magazines their look. But he also kept an eye on what was being written, remaining very hands-on in overseeing each magazine's editorial content. Like his cryptic mannerisms inside the halls and elevators at Condé Nast's offices, Liberman's impact on the rest of the magazine industry over time was both subtle and yet remarkably pervasive. A cultural czar who combined both highbrow art and mass-market appeal, Liberman could speak of Picasso's way of painting inside his studio or of watching Marie Osmond on TV—and he would search for ways to combine both sensibilities in the Condé Nast magazines.

Alex Liberman was a wondrously complex figure—the kind that a young American like Si Newhouse could have encountered only in reading some Russian novel depicting an epic-like life filled with extravagant characters and dramas of great pain and emotion. Liberman's personal odyssey stretched from the last days of czarist Russia, through the struggle in occupied France during World War II, to the jet-setting days of modern art and women's fashions in postwar America. His remarkable experiences forged a distinctively resolute but multifaceted identity, reflecting a life played out in many different worlds. At times, he was a classical idealist who nevertheless was adaptable and attuned to the changing times; a polyglot who spoke purely of art's highest purposes and yet remained conversant in the ways of commerce. "He is a Dostoevskian personality," observed Barbara Rose, a Liberman friend and biographer, "a larger-than-life gambler, adventurer, and mystic haunted by a double who acts as conscience and often requires him to act unpredictably."

Liberman's oldest memories are of upheaval, terror, and abandonment set against the backdrop of the Russian Revolution, with his father's difficult act of walking a political tightrope in a nation swept up in chaos and blood. Semeon Liberman was a Russian economist and lumber specialist working for the czar's family. His wife, Henriette Pascar, a beautiful self-absorbed actress, gave birth to their son, Alexander, in September 1912. He was the couple's only child. The Libermans lived in St. Petersburg during the Russian Revolution of 1917 and later moved to Moscow when his father managed to become an adviser to Lenin. "I don't know if anyone realizes what it meant to be a child brought up in the Revolution," Alex Liberman recalled years later. "You become prepared for any disruption— upheaval is natural."

Semeon Liberman survived because he knew how to cultivate the favor of powerful men. Although his expertise in finance and his long-held socialist beliefs helped him to gain a position in the Soviet government, the elder Liberman refused to become a Bolshevik. "Comrade Lenin, Bolsheviks, like singers, are born, not made," he reportedly told the revolutionary leader. Equally headstrong was his wife, Henriette, who established the first state children's theater in 1919. At the urging of the government, the theater became a workplace for Constructivists, though the authorities were less than pleased by Henriette's fondness for Kipling, Robert Louis Stevenson, and Mark Twain. "Her favorite plays, which she read to me, were dramatizations of 'Tom Sawyer' and 'Treasure Island,' " Alex Liberman recalled for a profile in *The New Yorker* in 1960, shortly after Newhouse's purchase of Condé Nast. "Maybe that is why I'm so happy in America, where I've lived for twenty years."

His mother's idealization of Americans and her wish for him to become an artist were reinforced in Alexander Liberman's psyche from the youngest age. In her memoirs, Henriette tells of young Alexander's gift for mimicry and his artistic flair, which made him capable of transforming pieces of paper into a costume. As biographer Barbara Rose described Liberman's mother, "She taught her son that through imagination, tawdry reality could be made beautiful and marvelous." By age six, however, Liberman, a sometimes sick and precocious youth, often felt neglected by his parents. His childhood memories included scenes of alcoholism he witnessed at home, where his once-bourgeois parents were forced to share a multifamily dwelling with other Communists. "I still remember (being then about six) coming home or looking down from upstairs and seeing my mother and father dead drunk with their friends, lying sprawled on the floor," Liberman once said. "To this day, when I open a door, I expect to see a figure lying on the floor."

The cruelest moments were suffered after he left Russia, to join his father in England, where he was setting up a trade mission for the Soviet government. Liberman was placed by his father in a boarding school, St. Piran's in Maidenhead, the first Jewish student to enroll, where he was continually abused and beaten by other students. "Those English beatings! They teach you to smile when it hurts," Liberman recalled. "That is the purpose of the operation. It has great merit—if you survive. When you smile, the punishment stops. It teaches you to accept life's blows with a smile. . . . Two years of sadistic refinement, but in retrospect I'm grateful for them."

After the death of Lenin, Semeon Liberman realized he could not return to the Soviet Union and so he arranged his wife's transport to Paris, where the family relocated in 1926. As white Russian émigrés adapting to a foreign land, the couple decided to enroll their son in an exclusive school, where he honed his artistic skills. Alexander, by then a teenager, attended André Lhote's school, considered the avant-garde place for aspiring young painters. Lhote's teaching methods were heavy-handed and met with firm resistance from the petulant young Russian, who felt more inclined to challenge than to copy his teacher. When Liberman presented a painting—a study in Pointillism rather than Lhote's favored Cubism—it was returned with angry comments and a whole section of the work wiped out. "The eye must have rest!" he angrily scribbled on Liberman's painting. The confrontation caused Alex to leave the school.

During the Depression, Liberman helped support his family by taking numerous odd jobs as a designer of windows and posters. He landed a position as a graphic artist at the weekly illustrated magazine *Vu,* which became the prototype for the American magazine *Life.* Despite their hardships, Liberman's parents made their mark on Parisian café society, especially his mother, Henriette, a bohemian free spirit who took on a series of influential lovers. At age forty-five, Henriette decided to resume her career as a dancer. She enlisted Bronislava Nijinska, the sister of Nijinsky, to be her choreographer, for Chagall to prepare the costumes and sets, and for Alexandre Iacovleff, the Russian émigré painter and Henriette's lover, to make the posters along with her son. His mother's affair with Iacovleff, as Liberman would later say, "was a love that gave me everything—Tatiana and my career."

Tatiana Iacovleva was the fifteen-year-old niece of the painter, who was smuggled out of Russia when her uncle learned she was starving in the streets. Tatiana took up residence in Paris with her uncle at about the same time as Alexandre Iacovleff's affair with Henriette took flight. It became Tatiana's task to occupy Alexander Liberman, a few years younger, while his mother visited with the painter. "Iacovleff would tell Tatiana, 'Get rid of that brat' and she'd take me to the beach or a museum to keep me out of the way," Liberman recalled. Although they were playmates, there was no romance between Liberman and Tatiana Iacovleva until more than a decade later. By that point, Liberman's marriage to a German skier had failed and Tatiana's marriage to Bertrand du Plessix, a French diplomat who fathered their daughter, Francine, was near collapse.

After a chance encounter in the south of France, Alex and Tatiana, the two Russian émigrés so much a part of each other's world, became lovers, their lives increasingly entangled in the greater drama of the German invasion. When Bertrand du Plessix, a French Resistance hero, was shot down in Gibraltar, Liberman arranged for the escape of Tatiana and her young daughter, Francine, to Portugal and later New York in January 1941. The following year, Liberman and Tatiana were married.

Once in Manhattan, Liberman's life was again assisted by another of his mother's lovers, Lucien Vogel, the founder of *Vu*. Before the war, Alex had worked for Vogel and rose quickly from an art assistant to one of *Vu*'s top editors. Vogel had gotten his job as art director at *Glamour* magazine from his friend Condé Nast after fleeing Paris during the Nazi invasion. Vogel was well aware of Liberman's talents and ability to speak in a proper English tongue. He arranged a job for Liberman as a lowly assistant working for Mehemed Fehmy Agha—the "Great God of art directors," as Liberman called him. Agha had helped create *Vanity Fair* with editor Frank Crowninshield and now oversaw *Vogue*'s look. At fifty dollars a week, Liberman was assigned to sit at the last desk in a row of seven. On a Friday, he was summoned by the fabled "Dr. Agha." This would be his first taste of bloody intrigue in the world of Condé Nast.

"I'm terribly sorry, but you're not good enough for *Vogue*," Agha said as he summarily fired Liberman.

At the same time, however, Vogel and his close friend Iva Patcévitch had arranged for Liberman to meet Condé Nast the following Monday, unaware of what had happened on Friday. Devastated by Agha's firing, Liberman nevertheless was determined to keep his appointment with Nast. During their meeting, Liberman brought along one of the few possessions he had taken with him from Europe—his gold medal, which he had won for magazine design at the 1937 Exposition Internationale in Paris. He spoke of his experiences in Paris, which included working for the famous 1930s poster artist Cassandre before he began his brilliant career at *Vu*.

Duly impressed, Nast declared, "A man like you must be on *Vogue*!" Then Condé Nast called Agha into his office. Agha, who spotted Liberman sitting there with the owner, never mentioned anything about the firing.

"I want Liberman on *Vogue*," Nast instructed his art director, who quietly kept his anger to himself.

Within his first week at Condé Nast, Liberman managed to survive one of many attempts at his ouster. When Nast died suddenly the following year, Agha again pressured the company's management—Patcévitch, by then the company's president, and *Vogue*'s editor, Edna Woolman Chase—with an ultimatum. Either get rid of Liberman, Agha warned, or he would leave.

By then, however, Liberman's remarkable talents as a graphic designer capable of updating *Vogue*'s image had made him an invaluable commodity. Crowninshield, for one, was a fan of the young Russian designer; he had been ever since Liberman designed a *Vogue* cover with a girl holding a balloon and used the balloon as an *O* in the magazine's name. In the months before he died, Nast's assessments had been even blunter. No longer following the rigidly formal procedure of picking a cover, Nast would turn to his new wunderkind and ask his opinion.

"Mr. Liberman, would you come here and tell us which of these you like?" Nast would say, then hand Liberman's choice to Agha and tell him to run it.

In forcing a showdown with the higher-ups, Agha ensured his own demise. "There were great promenades and whisperings in the corridors, but in the end, they chose me," Liberman recalled. "I was cheaper, probably."

By the time Si Newhouse arrived, eager to learn how things worked, Liberman was the long-established art director for all of Condé Nast magazines, as well as a weekend painter and sculptor who introduced readers to the works of modern artists, which sometimes served as backdrops for the fashion photos of such talents as Cecil Beaton, Irving Penn, Horst P. Horst, and later Richard Avedon. The same year Condé Nast magazines were acquired by the Newhouses, Liberman enjoyed some of his greatest acclaim for a collection of photographs and interviews he had taken over the past twelve years with the great painters and sculptors of the School of Paris. Portraits of living artists such as Picasso, Matisse, Chagall, and Balthus, along with the empty studios of some dead greats like Cézanne and Renoir, were reverently captured by Liberman, who had spent his two-month vacations taking the photographs himself. The collection was shown at the Museum of Modern Art and later published as a book: *The Artist in His Studio*.

This remarkable effort seemed to underscore Liberman's own desire to become an accomplished artist, a longtime wish sublimated by war and the need to support his family. "I think most of these artists were, as the French say, *monstres sacrés*," Liberman observed. "They all had the overpowering drive, the sort of self-centered selfishness that, perhaps, profound art demands." The following year, Liberman enjoyed a one-man showing of his paintings at the Betty Parsons Gallery. One of those prominent collectors of Liberman's paintings would be his new benefactor, Si Newhouse. "I'm grateful for my job at Condé Nast and for the inspiration that it gives me," he told *The New Yorker* in November 1960. "I believe that money should be used to facilitate a creative life and to eliminate fatigue."

Young Newhouse, like one of those debutante daughters of wealthy blue-blooded families employed for years in great numbers at *Vogue,* was escorted by Liberman through the byzantine world of high society and haute couture and instructed on the intricacies. The reserved and socially awkward millionaire's son was taken to the most fashionable restaurants, trendsetting parties, and cultural salons and imbued with an aesthetic that extended from Manhattan's art world to a shared vision of what the Newhouse publications should be. In doing so, Liberman forged a personal friendship with Si that has lasted for more than thirty years. As much as Si's father had given him money and opportunity, it was Liberman who helped Si Newhouse find his own identity.

"Alex has been a surrogate father to Si," said Peter Diamandis, who eventually worked for Condé Nast in a number of positions, including publisher of two of its magazines. He explained further: "I don't think he spent much time with his father. Liberman found a very shy, somewhat under-exposed guy named Si Junior and took him under his wing. He took him to parties, took him to functions. He exposed him to a different world. Nobody had ever spent a lot of time with Si or showed any great interest in him. So Si's attitude about Alex was not only that he was a talented human being but that he was somebody who took an interest in *me,* somebody who spent time with *me.* It was a much stronger bonding than just somebody who admires someone else's intellect."

In selecting Liberman to become the editorial director for Condé Nast in 1962, the Newhouses made a considerable departure from Sam Newhouse's traditional hands-off approach to running a newspaper. For years under the old system, Sam's longtime trusted adviser, Phil Hochstein, had served as the editorial adviser, but each publication's editors were allowed to make most decisions on their own. "We have never had an editorial director, because a director implies someone who tells others what to do," the elder Newhouse wrote in his memoir.

At Condé Nast, the traditional Newhouse approach would be altered. Liberman would become the *monstre sacré,* the singular dominant voice heard above all others. He decided the image of *Vogue* as some illustrated tribute to the wealthy Park Avenue ladies listed in the *Social Register* must change. To survive in postwar America, where many wives worked, including his own (Tatiana became the leading hat designer at Saks Fifth Avenue), *Vogue* had to become more sophisticated and contemporary. To accomplish this feat in a company so bound by genteel traditions, Liberman took a very hands-on approach. He attempted to break the mind-set of those who did not dare to be great. "Alex's greatest characteristic is that he will never leave well enough alone," Si Newhouse observed later. "He is always probing and pushing."

This change in mood was hastened by the reality that *Vogue* was slipping in its circulation battle with the Hearst-owned magazine *Harper's Bazaar,* which at that time was enjoying perhaps the best run in its history. In a bold stroke in 1962, the decision was made to lure Diana Vreeland, who had been fashion editor of *Harper's Bazaar* for more than two decades, with an offer to become the new editor of *Vogue*. Jessica Daves, the cautious and level-headed editor of *Vogue* who had replaced the legendary Edna Woolman Chase, seemed unable to enliven its pages, at least to Liberman's satisfaction. With fistfuls of Newhouse's money, Liberman and Patcévitch courted Vreeland and agreed to let her bring her own unique vision of women's fashions to *Vogue*.

The timing for Vreeland couldn't have been better. The Sixties, with its roaring and revolutionary upheavals in American pop culture and in women's lives, was captured in imaginative and daring ways inside Vreeland's *Vogue*. The Pill, The Rolling Stones, Andy Warhol, flower children, Truman Capote, Jacqueline Kennedy—all of the beautiful people seemed part of the ensemble gracing Vreeland's pages. "She was the first editor to say to me, 'You know, this is entertainment,' " Liberman recalled. "In many ways, she acted as a brilliant theatrical producer. She visualized *Vogue* as theater . . . she was the most talented editor of her period because she was able to stamp an era in the reader's mind."

Gone were the carefully contrived "white glove" pictorials of photographers like Beaton, whose romantic still-life artifices of ideal beauty were once the magazine's hallmark. At center stage now were Irving Penn, who was hired in 1943 and brought about many of the photographic breakthroughs that Liberman wanted, and Richard Avedon, perhaps the most innovative photographer of all, who was lured from *Harper's Bazaar* in 1965 and became a fixture at *Vogue*. Avedon's pictures, like his twirling multiple-exposed portrait of waiflike Penelope Tree, expressed the youthful individualism and freedom of that decade. Irving Penn's portfolio seemed to stretch from one *Vogue* era to another, dating back to the highly stylized tableaux featuring such beautiful models as his wife, Lisa Fonssagrives, of the late 1940s and early 1950s. With Vreeland at the helm, however, Penn's most artistic innovations burst forth in everything from Dali-like surrealistic studies of fashion models and celebrities to faraway trips capturing vividly realistic photos of tribesmen in the wild. Vreeland delighted in the experimentation. "Fashion must be the intoxicating release from the banality of the world," she declared, one of many bons mots that flowed like champagne from her creative mind. "Never fear being vulgar—just boring, middle class or dull."

At the time, Vreeland's selection underlined *Vogue*'s commitment first and foremost as a fashion magazine, with its determination to remain ahead of the curve in a world of radically changing tastes and mores. With her extravagant flair and exquisite taste, Vreeland emblazoned her flamboyant personality on the pages of *Vogue,* as if the magazine and its editor had taken on the same character. From her plush, regal red office, with scented Rigaud candles burning, she would write morning memos: *"Today, let's think pig white! Wouldn't it be wonderful to have stockings that were pig white! The color of baby pigs, not quite white and not quite pink!"*

With more curiosity and energy than anyone on the staff, Vreeland, then nearly seventy years old, moved effortlessly through the social circles of Manhattan and along the fashion runways of Paris. She seemed perfect for Liberman, just what he was searching for, the kind of editor the Newhouses needed to rejuvenate the magazine. Vreeland also knew how to play to the new owners of Condé Nast, and she became a fixture at Mitzi Newhouse's parties. "Diana seduced Mitzi Newhouse," said one Condé Nast editor, remembering Vreeland's behavior at a fashion show before she was hired away from *Harper's Bazaar.* "Afterwards, she rushed over to Mitzi, practically threw herself at her, and showered her with compliments."

For Vreeland, *Vogue* was an art form filled with what she called "pizzazz." Those who tried to capture her vision of film were challenged as never before. "I always felt we were selling dreams, not clothes," as Irving Penn described it. After her arrival at *Vogue, Harper's Bazaar* began a slow fade as a major competitor to *Vogue,* an eclipse that would last for more than two decades. During much of the 1960s, Diana Vreeland reigned supreme. "She's an original," said her friend Jacqueline Kennedy Onassis, who didn't mind lighting this oracle's Lucky Strike cigarettes and years later would edit a book based on Vreeland's reminiscences. "You don't get many, and when you do you should tip your hat to them."

Others were not so generous. Stanley Kauffmann, in a review of *The World in Vogue,* an elaborate anthology of the magazine published in 1964, commented on the Anglophile obsessions at Condé Nast. To Kauffmann, the world of *Vogue* was peopled with affected British accents and a pseudo-English longing for some form of American royalty. "Man does not live by cake alone, and only spiritual White Russians pine for the days when," Kauffmann said. For all of its faults, however, Kauffmann acknowledged the magazine satisfied the need for frivolity, regardless of social strata. *"Vogue* glitters for us all," he wrote, "and one wants glitter as well as gold."

During most of her tenure, Vreeland enjoyed the support of her benefactor, Alexander Liberman, who seemed to share her flair for the dramatic and her inclination for the provocative and truly extraordinary. For much of his tenure, Liberman had wanted to bring a sense of art to the pages of *Vogue,* most notably by paying for the work of some of the world's best photographers. He provided an almost-philosophical framework for *Vogue*'s message to its readers, encapsulated in a 1961 cover essay, "Beauty in Our Time." This essay, accompanied by Irving Penn photographs (and reprinted ten years later as "*Vogue*'s Point of View"), underlined the fundamentally contradictory message of women's fashion magazines. To some extent, Liberman was celebrating the independent-minded modern woman who had "destroyed the erotic straitjacket" of men's concept of beauty. But this was hardly a feminist manifesto, for within Liberman's own mind, women still remained "natural" seduc-tresses. As Liberman defined her, this modern woman "reveals the tra-ditional charms of her sex, but they are proudly shown as the attributes of her femininity, not coyly as teasers to man's appetites."

Liberman's essay also hinted at the double-edged sword for those who live and die by the dictates of fashion. "Man has until recently played the role of Paris in the judgment and contemplation of the opposite sex—always from a man's point of view," Liberman complained. "Now woman does not have to mimic an ideal established by male taste. She has gained enough assurance and power to risk pleasing, but above all, to dare displeasing and still be admired." At Condé Nast, however, this was not true, because male taste still dominated. Only two men—Alex-ander Liberman and, increasingly throughout the decade, Si Newhouse—would control this collection of magazines read by millions of American women. And when Diana Vreeland dared to displease, she was shown the door.

The end for Vreeland began in the early 1970s as a recession hit the nation, which was still mired in the Vietnam War and no longer felt in the mood to party. Vreeland's invitation to *Vogue* was a bit of a dare for readers, as well. As presented in the pages of *Vogue,* the crazy furs and wigs, the plastic dress and see-through blouses were garb that even the most fashion-conscious wouldn't be caught dead wearing on the boulevard. Perhaps the biggest crisis, the Waterloo of the runway, took place over the introduction of the midiskirt. When the Paris designers deigned that this dullard skirt—caught rather unappealing in the middle of the calf—was the new look, millions of American women revolted. No longer were they going to listen to the pronouncements from Paris and slavishly follow them, nor were they going to read those glossy magazines echoing the dictates of high fashion, with *Vogue* as the number-one culprit on their list. "*Vogue* has always been like the Imperial Russian court," one insider told *Newsweek* at the time, "and Mrs. Vreeland's period of favor was over."

Despite all of Vreeland's artistry and extravagant style, *Vogue*'s cir-culation plummeted and its advertisers fled, with a 38 percent drop in ad pages in the first three months of 1971. Many of the important advertisers—designers and upscale department stores with racks of unsold midi-skirts trumpeted in *Vogue*—were incensed at Vreeland's stewardship. There was also a generation gap. Iconoclastic young women of the baby boom generation seemed turned off by *Vogue* and its elitist Establishment air of excessive leisure. Many were now in the workforce, professional women with greater concerns in life than appearing like Marisa Berenson, Cher, or Veruschka. Suddenly, Vreeland, the marvelous eccentric who didn't get to work until after noon, didn't seem fun anymore, certainly not to the likes of Si Newhouse.

Newhouse's displeasure over *Vogue*'s finances was expressed to Liberman, who quietly distanced himself from the Vreeland mess. The rumors of a rift between Vreeland and her editorial director raged for months, until she was abruptly demoted to consulting editor in May 1971. Vreeland insisted on hearing the words from Si himself. "We just sat there for what seemed to me like ten minutes, each waiting for the other to say something," Newhouse later recalled. "Finally, I said that it wasn't working out, and that we were going to ask her to retire. She just watched me deal with her, perhaps in amusement, perhaps in shock. She was very cool. That night I had a very bad dream about it, a wild nightmare."

Friends of Vreeland never forgave Alex Liberman for not defending her. In departing, at least in the version Vreeland later recounted to her friends, she left this epigram for Liberman: "Alex, we've all known many White Russians, and we've known a few Red Russians. But, Alex, you're the only Yellow Russian I've ever known."

In her place, Liberman appointed Vreeland's longtime assistant, Grace Mirabella, a golden-haired forty-year-old aide-de-camp whom everyone at Condé Nast, including Vreeland, said they adored. Mirabella later recounted the selection process: "I suppose Alex looked around and thought, 'Who is likely to think the way I do?' And there I was. We rarely disagree on anything."

But the vision of *Vogue* was no longer the exclusive domain of Alex Liberman, as he would begin to realize. This new view was radically different from Vreeland's "take it or leave it" approach and it forced Liberman, ever the survivor, to adapt himself to what could be expected with the new thinking at Condé Nast magazines. For during the attention-grabbing editorship of Diana Vreeland, Si Newhouse had quietly accomplished what his father had asked him to do: to find out how the magazines work. From his editorial training with Liberman and inexorably through his own experiences with Dick Shortway on the business side of the magazines, Si developed his own ideas of what a magazine is all about—*"The Newhouse concept,"* as Liberman called it. This concept involved Si Newhouse's much more sophisticated approach to upscale publications, a far cry from his father's austere, no-frills method to newspapering in mass markets. Now, well into his mid-forties, Si Newhouse was prepared to exert his influence in a way that had once seemed beyond him. He would continue to allow Liberman, his friend and mentor, great leeway and scope in shaping the look and feel of his magazines. To the artists and editors, Liberman still reigned supreme. From this point on, however, there was no doubt who held the strings at Condé Nast, that artful contrivance to the fashion world. Finally, Si Newhouse had found a home.

CHAPTER FOUR

The Newhouse Concept

Andy Warhol became aware of the Newhouse concept in the early 1970s when his friend Diana Vreeland was catapulted out of her editor's chair and *Vogue* no longer seemed quite the cultural barometer it had once been. "*Vogue* decided it wanted to go middle-class," he told the press.

Warhol remained curious, though, about the Newhouses, who at one point were interested in buying the artist's *Interview* magazine, his free-wheeling digest of Manhattan's downtown scene, Eurotrash, and monthly pick of the glitz. Warhol and his crew edited *Interview* not as a serious editorial venture but, rather, by the seat of their pants. Maybe he didn't want to sell his magazine, but that didn't mean Warhol couldn't do business with the Newhouses. A masterful appraiser of potential buyers for his work, Warhol was quite aware that Si Newhouse was very wealthy and emerging as a major player in the art market.

Shortly after Sam Newhouse's death in 1979, Warhol received a call from the Newhouses, who were looking to immortalize the image of their recently departed patriarch. For Warhol, it would be a chance to learn how Si Newhouse operated his magazines.

At their request, Warhol met with Si and Mitzi at his Union Square offices. The Newhouses said they wanted Warhol to paint a portrait of Sam Newhouse, something in Warhol's distinctive style—with the strokes and splashes of brilliant color over cameralike images, just as he had painted famous portraits of Marilyn, Elvis, James Dean, and other pop icons. By then, Warhol had painted several portraits of rich people in this style and had even bartered them for ads in his magazine. The portrait commissions paid Warhol handsomely and he was pleased with the outcome, though he considered it more a moneymaking venture than pure art.

"They brought pictures of the husband who just died, but they weren't right so they're going to send down some more for a portrait," Warhol recorded for his diaries. The idea of a Warhol rendition of himself probably never occurred to Sam Newhouse. Somehow, though, this posthumous portrait seemed a strange metaphor for the changes about to happen, when Si Newhouse would remake his father's business in his own image, with the kind of fame only a Warhol could appreciate.

During the visit with Si and his mother, Warhol managed to turn to the subject of magazines. As with most of Warhol's creations, art may have seemed the driving force for *Interview,* but commerce was his constant concern. A month before the Newhouse visit, Warhol bemoaned the lack of advertising in one issue featuring Liza Minnelli on the cover, especially compared with the special September issue of Newhouse's *Vogue.* "I was disappointed because it didn't seem that thick," Warhol wrote. "Only forty pages of ads, the issue was only eighty-eight pages. And *Vogue* this month is so fat it looks like the telephone book."

Through their conversation, Warhol would learn the secret of the Newhouse concept. Foremost on Warhol's mind was Condé Nast's newly created magazine, *Self,* which was one of the publishing industry's notable success stories at that time. "I asked the son about *Self* magazine—he said they survey everything by computer every month," Warhol wrote. "That's how they know what's happening."

Although marketing surveys were pioneered by the Newhouse papers back in the 1930s, the advent of the computer allowed Si Newhouse to conduct a monthly or weekly vox populi to see how his magazines were performing. Rather than pressing the flesh like the politician publisher Hearst or using some intuitive feel for the zeitgeist like Warhol, this bloodless but calculatingly acurate approach seemed ideal for a shy, secretive billionaire's son. In effect, Si Newhouse could run a magazine empire and stay in touch with readers without ever having to meet any of them.

Beginning in the 1970s, the company employed the Mark Clements research firm to conduct market surveys to serve as the eyes and ears of the Newhouse publications. The Clements firm was renowned for its comprehensive surveys, attempting to gauge reactions of readers through elaborate tests that asked for opinions rating different features and story subjects, graphics and design, just about anything involved with selling the magazine. Using these tools, the Newhouse organization marketed their magazines as any other consumer item—like toothpaste, perfume, or dog food is researched and tested—in a way that greatly influenced the rest of the print media. "I think they are at the forefront of understanding the value of research," explained Mark Clements, who worked closely with Liberman and Newhouse for more than two decades. "As a result, many of the other companies have become aware of the importance of understanding editorial research—what I call *product research,* because their magazine is a product. The consumer looks at their magazine as a product; the only difference is that the editor has to come up with a new product that has certain consistencies from issue to issue. That's the important thing with a magazine."

This reliance on marketing and surveys, while increasingly common at nearly every large media company, took on almost-religious proportions within the Newhouse organization. The most ardent believer was Si Newhouse. "Si was very much into research and it's been very helpful to the success of the magazines of the company," said Dick Shortway, the publisher of *Vogue* for much of the 1970s and 1980s. "Mark [Clements] was his key research guy in terms of trying to figure out what the readers liked and didn't like about all of the magazines."

Ascending to the role of chairman of Condé Nast Publications in 1975, Si became a devotee of market surveys and scrutinized the circulation reports to see how readers reacted to each magazine's cover (a crucial factor for newsstand sales) and how they liked each feature inside. "Mark would come in and say, 'Okay, on this page, we have a sixty-eight percent 'interested' or a forty-eight percent 'most interested' or a thirty percent 'read,' " recalled Shortway. "And we'd determine then the kind of editorial that was appealing to the reader. Si was very intrigued by all this. He's that kind of person, to be involved in research and all the things about readership of the magazine."

Armed with this information, the editors working for Si Newhouse were expected to adhere to the computer results in making their decisions. Not everyone agreed with this approach. One Condé Nast editor who came from a major newspaper was surprised to see "how seriously" research was taken by editors. With the aid of market research to guide him, Newhouse decided to start the health and fitness magazine called *Self* in 1979, to revive *Vanity Fair* in 1983, and to revamp *House & Garden* into a more upscale *HG* in the late 1980s—all by taking advantage of the market trends Newhouse's computer scanners detected on the horizon. (Surveys discovered all sorts of remarkable facts about readers, such as the *Glamour* market test in 1992, which found that 18 percent of the magazine's male audience is gay or bisexual, with one-fifth of this group being cross-dressers looking for beauty and fashion tips.)

"That's the first time I ever worked at a publication where you sat around a table with a man who whips through these reports and every editor has to sit there and go through the postmortem," recalled one editor. Another said the decision-making was too dominated by research. "They used Mark Clements on all of the magazines, but I found it useless," complained one former top editor at Condé Nast. "I'm a believer in research, but I didn't find what Clements told me was helpful. I never learned anything from it. It just seemed that it told you the obvious."

Diana Vreeland particularly objected to the Newhouse concept and its reliance on marketing rather than artistic considerations or editorial judgment. "If you broaden your public so that you have to keep each and every reader in mind, then perhaps you lessen the impact of everything," she said in an interview several years after leaving *Vogue*. "The real question is whether you're trying to anticipate what the reader wants, or whether you have a dream of your own that you want to do something about."

After *Vogue*'s near financial collapse under Vreeland in the early 1970s, Newhouse was convinced he could no longer afford dreamers. And he became even more convinced about market research. The entire staff of *Vogue* was reorganized to seek a broader, younger audience, and Grace Mirabella was instructed by Liberman and Newhouse to pay much more attention to research, circulation, advertising, and all those other boring bottom-line concerns to which Mrs. Vreeland had paid little heed. "Under the great Diana Vreeland, *Vogue* almost went out of business—a lot of people don't know that," said Clements. "In the early 1970s, they retired Diana Vreeland because *Vogue* was going downhill. She was not aware that she was editing the book—a lot of people felt—for her own small clique, so to speak, and not the total market. Then they brought in Grace Mirabella and, between Mirabella and Alex Liberman, they brought that book up and up and up. A lot of people are under the impression that Diana Vreeland was the great editor of *Vogue*. It's not true. She did a lot of great things, but that was not one of them."

Mirabella would never be so harsh on her former mentor. After Vreeland returned from a four-month vaction, she was allowed to keep an office in the Condé Nast building on a different floor from her old one and given the title of contributing editor. Even Margaret Case's suicide—theorized by Vreeland and many others to have resulted from the cruel manner in which the former society editor had been booted out of Condé Nast—was handled in a faux cheery manner that never even hinted at the circumstances surrounding her death. ("She understood only the best—recognized it, demanded it, gave it," read the full-page tribute in *Vogue*.)

Still, Mirabella's editorship would set a different tone, much more than a matter of repainting her new office from Vreeland's regal red to her favorite color, a creamy beige. Mirabella's concerns seemed much more complicated than her mentor's. "Diana Vreeland was interested in fantasy," Mirabella explained years later. "You were never reporting, you were never talking about women in real life. It was make-believe, the wilder shores of love. I was a great fan of hers, and I followed her around like a bird dog. But when I took over that wasn't wanted anymore." Mirabella was in California on a photographic shoot for an upcoming issue when she learned of her selection as the new editor of *Vogue*. She believed Liberman had picked her, but she was never sure and never found out. "It's that kind of place," she later observed. "They are in the communications business, but they don't know how to communicate."

Working closely with Liberman, much more so than Vreeland had during her final years, Grace Mirabella made sure *Vogue* responded to the demands of Newhouse's market surveys as well as to the changes within the women's movement and the fashion industry itself. The magazine added more features about health and fitness, personal finance, and the arts. Working women and their daily concerns became a central focus, with less emphasis on the extremes of Paris designers. "Fashion can't stand alone," Mirabella declared. "It needs an environment. It makes the clothes more valid actually."

As a college-educated woman who grew up in the suburbs of New Jersey and had worked her way up from staff "shop hound" to Vreeland's top assistant, the young and vibrant Mirabella seemed to personify the new, more Middle American look that *Vogue* was seeking. No longer was *Vogue* out to shock a puritanical nation; rather, it sought to celebrate the more accessible, wholesome look of such models as Lauren Hutton and Lisa Taylor and the more conservative but popular designs of Geoffrey Beene, Giorgio Armani, and Halston. As Si Newhouse assured readers of *The New York Times* in 1971 after the Vreeland bloodbath, "Highly volatile-looking models have been cycled out."

Over the next decade, a remarkable turnaround transpired at *Vogue* as its readership began to climb from 428,000 when Vreeland was fired to more than a million by the early 1980s. Mirabella, with considerable justification, became a star. "I think at the midpoint of the '70s there was a very decisive change in the way we all lived and in people's attitudes toward fashion, culture and health. It was a change from the headiness of the '60s and the whole exoticism from Britain—the lifestyle Diana Vreeland caught perfectly," Si Newhouse said years later. "I'm not a social historian but there was a settling down and a seriousness that Grace, who came in at the beginning of it, really caught. The magazine flourished, became deeper and more enriching."

Vogue also became friendlier to its advertisers as the magazine's mission seemed to change from "selling dreams" to selling merchandise again. Under Vreeland, *Vogue*'s traditional symbiotic relationship with the fashion industry was strained and she declined to do some of the obligatory editorial layouts for important advertisers—all part of the reasons leading to her demise. But Mirabella restored *Vogue*'s willingness to accommodate its biggest advertisers. The "must list" remained a standard policy at *Vogue*, listing those advertisers who must be written about, based not necessarily upon journalistic merit but upon advertising dollars. This list comprised Seventh Avenue designers and top-flight department stores whose clothing was to be featured in *Vogue*'s editorial pages, presented as "reporting" that was objective. When asked about the must list by one interviewer in 1979, Mirabella dismissed any thought of impropriety. "There's always been a tradition of it," she replied. It was not a formal written rule, but something understood. As Dick Shortway, by then *Vogue*'s publisher, acknowledged to *Advertising Age* in 1972, "The cold hard fact is that those who advertise get coverage."

Where Mirabella did take a strong stand was in her attempts to ban photographs in *Vogue* of women smoking cigarettes, even though Condé

Nast continued to accept advertising from tobacco companies. Mirabella, married to a physician, understood the threat of cancer and related illnesses for millions of women who smoke. At this same time, Si himself was trying and eventually did quit his several-packs-a-day cigarette habit. Nevertheless, the health of the bottom line usually prevailed in these in-house debates. Dick Shortway recalled his skirmishes with Mirabella over cigarettes: "Grace was so antismoking—with a lot of tobacco industry advertising—she would want to do articles that were antismoking. And I would go to Alex and say, 'You're going to kill a hundred pages of advertising for me.' And he would step in and say, 'Gracie, darling, do you really think we have to?' At one point, she wanted to do—in every issue—an article that was antismoking and I said, 'Please, enough! Once a year, twice a year, okay. But let's not go crazy.' I'd go to Alex and he'd say, 'Gracie, I don't think that would be terribly appropriate. After all, Dick is getting a lot of advertising from those people.' " On occasion, when the crusade against smoking or another editorial idea became too costly, Shortway would approach Si directly for a solution. But inevitably, Newhouse replied, "Talk to Alex; see what he thinks."

The business-side people at Condé Nast, like the circulation director, always got a final look at the editorial product to make sure it would sell. The covers of Si's magazines were never the sole domain of his editors and journalists. "He has to approve each cover," Alex Liberman once said, after acknowledging that each new issue's front was shown to the company's circulation chief for his approval. "Newsstand sales are terribly important for us these days and [the circulation official] knows which covers sell magazines."

At Condé Nast, these compromises seemed to present no burdensome moral qualms or ethical dilemmas. While other journalists might be vilified for such actions, the Newhouse method was to blur the distinction between editorial and advertising, the difference between what was used to inform and what was used to sell. In the final analysis, everything existed to push the product. Although his domain was the world of women's fashion magazines, Si Newhouse was still a very practical bottom-line publisher like his father.

Over time, Sam Newhouse recognized this transformation in his eldest son and eventually turned over complete rein of the Condé Nast magazine company to him. Si Newhouse had demonstrated his ability to run things to his father's satisfaction, and he even began offering his creative ideas. One of his most successful innovations as publisher was to showcase New York designers in *Vogue*'s special September issue, which debuted in the early 1970s and emerged as a hugh moneymaker for the company. The September issues—often containing eight hundred glossy pages and weighing three pounds— were so large that the U.S. Postal Service had to issue special warnings to its district managers. With an eye toward lowering costs, Si also decided to pare down *Vogue*'s oversized pages to the more standard magazine format, and he trimmed its publication schedule from twice monthly to once a month.

Yet, Si was far from hesitant to invest money needed to expand the reach of the company. When research showed there was a niche in the travel market, Newhouse bought *Signature* magazine from Diner's Club, killed it, and sold its subscribers on the newly revamped *Condé Nast Traveler,* a slick upscale monthly that became notable for sometimes running critical articles about the travel industry—one of the rare Newhouse publications ever to bite the hand that fed it. The *Traveler*'s attempts at truth telling were aimed at the informed, affluent readers it was pursuing, in line with Si Newhouse's overall concept of magazines for the elite. At *House & Garden,* after a market research firm studied its demographics as part of a $5 million overhaul of the magazine in the early 1980s, Newhouse nearly tripled the cover price and pulled it off such downscale venues as grocery store shelves. In the trickle-down media of Condé Nast, truth and style were for those who could pay for it.

"Our magazines represent a certain tone and audience," Newhouse explained. "It was that initial direction of Condé Nast. He invented the form of the specialized magazine. He didn't want a large audience. He wanted one in which everyone counted."

Marketing could completely redefine a Newhouse magazine's editorial voice. For instance, the numbers showed the appeal of *Gentlemen*'s *Quarterly,* which the Newhouse organization bought in 1979, had to be widened among heterosexual men if it wanted to improve its profit margins. "*GQ* was too gay," as Tina Brown bluntly put it. There was more than a little irony in this decision. For decades, gays had worked at Condé Nast under conditions considered much more tolerant than at other media companies. "My business—as far as the men in it go—is a gay business," said Anna Wintour in a 1992 story entitled "Vanity Fairies" for *The Advocate,* a gay and lesbian newsmagazine. In the early 1980s, however, the decision was made at *GQ* to tone down the homoerotic images of such photographers as Bruce Weber and to appeal more to a heterosexual audience. Such celebrities as Billy Crystal, Sting, and Patrick Swayze were featured prominently and photo displays of male models almost always included women.

"They sell better," *GQ* editor Art Cooper explained, "and we have the figures to prove it."

As Si Newhouse's magazine empire expanded, so did the demands placed on Alexander Liberman, whose realm was extended far beyond the pages of *Vogue.* In effect, Liberman was the supra-editor of all Condé Nast publications, supervising their overall direction and sometimes even engrossing himself in the day-to-day details. The changes for Alex were subtle and, as he noted, filled with a certain ambivalence.

For a time in the early 1960s, Liberman served as the helpful mentor, instructing Si Newhouse on the rudiments of fashion magazines. In many ways, what Si considered quality journalism was learned with Liberman at these magazines—a view that would extend itself to book publishing and more serious publications like *The New Yorker* in coming years. But their relationship shifted almost diametrically by the late 1970s as Liberman found himself being increasingly defined by the wealth and fame of Si Newhouse's publishing success.

"Up to a certain point I was known as an artist, but as Si Newhouse bought magazines and the company became an empire, I find I'm suddenly known more as a magazine executive," he observed. No longer was Condé Nast the slow-paced haven Liberman had once enjoyed, where he could go swimming at lunchtime and afford the luxury of concentrating on his painting and sculpture during weekends. In a sense, the Newhouse concept had transformed Alexander Liberman, just as Liberman's views about the look of American magazines had so infused Si Newhouse's aesthetic.

By his own definition, Alex Liberman was an artist. Condé Nast was a pleasant distraction that provided an elegant lifestyle. Whether he was perceived as a serious artist, though, was of paramount concern to Liberman. As an artist, he was another Paris-influenced exotic, not unlike Diana Vreeland, in his taste for the avant-garde, creating works that were daring, provocative, and sometimes inexplicable. If he was not working as an artist, Liberman theorized, he developed ulcers, suffering a succession of attacks until two-thirds of his stomach was removed in 1960. "I still basically thought I was a painter, and yearned for some kind of safe job that would allow me to continue painting," he explained years later. "I progressed in my career at *Vogue* and . . . things became a little easier. I had a history of bleeding ulcers; I needed to be surrounded by a certain atmosphere of warmth, which I felt through the years at Condé Nast. It gave me reassurance and courage, for in art there is no 'success.' "

By the time Newhouse arrived at Condé Nast, Liberman's canvases were filled with circles, precisely drawn from compasses or even poker chips in a hard-edged geometrical form that Liberman called "Circlism." Part of the fascination for circles comes from Liberman's longtime devotion to the Russian mysticism of Georgei Gurdjieff and Peter Ouspensky and other cosmological writings having to do with the occult. In the Gurdjieff way of thinking, the use of circles represents the higher levels of consciousness, the essence of the Russian desire for spirituality. Circlism would be Liberman's challenge to the modern-day Cubism of Picasso, whom he had met and greatly admired. Afterward, Liberman's paintings became more freely abstractionist, influenced by Jackson Pollock and others, with his precision-oriented technique giving way to elemental thrusts of paint applied to the canvas with a squeegee. In the early 1960s, he turned to sculpture, creating metallic forms in the barn of the Connecticut farm owned by Tatiana's daughter, Francine du Plessix Gray. To critics, though, Liberman's work seemed an adaptation of styles rather than one compelling vision. His artistic assault, to the extent Liberman's art challenged his contemporaries at all, remained largely misunderstood.

One of Alex's great patrons was Si Newhouse, whose taste for modern art was clearly influenced and enhanced by Liberman. In the 1960s, Si bought several of Liberman's works for his personal collection, particularly some of the paintings composed during Liberman's search for a certain *terribilita,* with his emphasis on sharp, domineering black-and-white abstractions. "If you know the collection, you know it is serious, austere," Liberman once assured a journalist, who was curious about Si's tastes in art. "It is the most severe art anybody could collect. The paintings of his friend Barnett Newman or Jasper Johns aren't frivolous. They aren't entertaining."

Despite the success of *The Artist in His Studio,* Liberman's photographic collection of Picasso and other great artists, his own artwork didn't sell very well. "This is a revival that should have closed out of town," wrote well-known art reviewer Hilton Kramer about a Liberman show in 1978. Even his wife, Tatiana, upon viewing one giant sculpture in the backyard, exclaimed, "Oh, it's so frightening," and asked her husband to at least paint his welded stuctures in lipstick red rather than funereal black. Perhaps the most embarrassing criticism was made in 1971 by then President Richard Nixon, who ordered that one of Liberman's sculptures be removed from the view of his Executive Office window.

The nearly thirty-foot-high sculpture titled *Adam,* a configuration of huge red-painted cylinders that resembled a smokestack, was parked on the lawn of the nearby Corcoran Gallery of Art, which was featuring a retrospective of Liberman's work. To mark its opening, a gala ball was held for sixteen hundred guests, with tables decorated in circles of orange and white. Those who were invited to the gallery included Sam and Mitzi Newhouse. And one of the featured works, *Six Hundred Thirty-Nine,* was a 1959 experiment with random patterns, dozens of black polka-dots scattered about a white background, which was borrowed from Si's personal collection.

Nixon's disdain for Liberman's sculpture, however, prompted top officials of the National Endowment for the Arts and the National Park Service to ship it to a wooded site along the Potomac River. Misleadingly, government officials promoted the move as the first step in bringing important art works to the national parks, an idea they convinced Liberman to support. Shortly afterward, Nixon was floating down the Potomac in the presidential yacht, the *Sequoia,* when he spotted a red monstrosity along the tree-lined shores.

"What in hell is that?" Nixon asked his advisers.

"It's *Adam,*" a top aide, Leonard Garment, reportedly replied. "We all think he looks very well in his new setting."

Nixon seemed placated, if not pleased. "Well, it's better there than where it was before," said the President.

When Liberman was told the full story, recounted in a book by a government official who knew of the ruse, he proclaimed it a "great honor" that his art had aroused such a violent reaction from the President. "The worst thing is indifference," Liberman said. "Great political figures have never been connoisseurs of art, and Nixon is no exception."

Those who questioned Liberman's art invariably mentioned his status as editorial director of Condé Nast. Some suggested that he enjoyed greater attention than his work deserved because of his role within the Newhouse media empire. "I have always been plagued by suspicions that in some indefinable way I am not serious," he bemoaned to his friend Robert Hughes, *Time* magazine's art critic. "And that's because I have a job."

Whatever his response to criticism, however, the fear of being "not serious" about his art seemed to unnerve Liberman. The great sacrifice he knew other artists had paid, both emotionally and financially, was too exacting a toll for him. Perhaps his mother had wanted him to become a great artist, but there were bills to pay once he and Tatiana landed in the United States, including the care of Liberman's mother. His studio would not be found in some forgotten foothills but, rather, featured on the "Home Design" page of the Sunday *New York Times* rotogravure. "Poverty is not conducive to good art," he said in an interview about the time of his seventieth birthday, "and I have always believed in living life to the hilt."

This disquieting ambivalence about his life as an artist and his need to make a living seemed to affect Liberman's work at Condé Nast. For more than twenty years, he had tried to bring an appreciation for contemporary art to the mass of *Vogue* readers. These affluent subscribers were hardly the proletarian masses of Marxist doctrine, yet Liberman, true to his self-image as an idealist, felt the same messianic fervor for introducing great artists to these people as his mother once had at her theater in Russia. At *Vogue,* Liberman solicited the illustrations of such unconventional artists as Marcel Duchamp and Salvador Dali, and he instructed photographers to take their pictures of models in beautiful clothes against the backdrop of modern art found in Manhattan galleries. He encouraged photographers such as Irving Penn, Cecil Beaton, and Horst P. Horst to seek the "wonderful possibilities of creative experimentation" by giving them their own studios and paying for their expensive productions. As Liberman presented it, the exquisitely executed photograph, a picture of beauty captured in time, could somehow suggest a higher consciousness, a glimpse at the eternal verities.

But by the mid-1970s, with the ignominious departure of Vreeland and the rise of the Newhouse concept, Liberman adopted a more detached view of what was possible with magazines. He was still willing to give assignments to Penn and play to the inventive styling of Richard Avedon and the provocatively erotic photos of Helmut Newton, whose *Vogue* portrait of a nude Charlotte Rampling before a gilded mirror seemed to vibrate with all the raw sexuality of that narcissistic decade. Yet Liberman no longer viewed photography as art, not even when taken by his favorites. "There was once a possibility that one's work could be an artistic fulfillment, but *Vogue* has changed," said Irving Penn by the late 1970s. "It has a different public. Nowadays, my best work doesn't get into the magazine." Avedon was even more critical. After Vreeland's ouster, he commented years later, "It was the beginning of fashion at its lowest common denominator, the pandering to mass appeal that ends with Madonna on the cover of *Vogue*."

Liberman's intent no longer seemed a personal quest to unleash a vision of beauty strong enough to shake the Calvinist roots of American culture, as it once had in the 1940s and 1950s. "For all his cosmopolitan background, Liberman in his late thirties and early forties was still, at root, an extremely idealistic Russian, and he believed—rather too much, perhaps, for the taste of the eighties—in the image of the senior artist as monk, seer, starets, and prophet, the last Holy Man in a secular age," his friend Robert Hughes observed. Suddenly, it was as if Alexander Liberman, after nearly three decades of working on *Vogue*, had discovered it was just a fashion magazine after all. As he later told writer Marie Winn, he had decided by the mid-1970s that he had been "kidding myself and the public. I know I'll get shot for this, but I don't consider photography an art." After *Vogue*'s near financial demise under Vreeland, Liberman adopted a new outlook, declawing the effete attitude of *Vogue,* which seemed to cry out, Take it or leave it, I'm a beautiful thing!

Under the rule of Si Newhouse, the true purpose of *Vogue* was unmistakably commercial. "It's a business after all," Liberman said in 1991, expressing his new mercantile view. Art for Alex Liberman would find its place on the weekend, out at the Connecticut farm, welding massive sculptures amid the sparks. Workdays were for making sure that all of the Condé Nast magazines were running according to the Newhouse concept—an amalgram of reader surveys, circulation figures, and advertising revenues leading to financial success. Si Newhouse would tolerate nothing less.

Fashion was about change, Liberman theorized, as he himself changed. Though growing older, he could still provide hip streetwise window dressing for his magazines. By the 1980s, the slashingly violent look of the paparazzi, rather than the mannered theatrical productions of yesterday, became the visual ideal. "Liberman found the trick of walking a middle ground—making high art more accessible and making the low tabloid end more chic," observed Derek Ungless, then creative director for one of Newhouse's new magazines, *Details*.

As Liberman described it, this new reality was about *speed* and *journalism*—a certain kind of communication that expressed itself in darting headlines, quicky moving graphics, and the rapid eye movements of a generation of readers accustomed to video sound bites. "I'm not interested in the fashion magazine as masterpiece," Liberman explained. "We are not making magazines to be preciously saved. I like the discardable quality of life."

For the first time in his life, Si Newhouse exuded confidence—a quiet, relaxed kind of steadiness that seemed to say he had mastered the job. Indeed, Si Newhouse was synonymous with the name Condé Nast by the early 1980s.

The family's vast media holdings were supervised by Si's in-house editors, lawyers, and advisers in the same buildings on Madison Avenue. Donald Newhouse worked out of the *Newark Star-Ledger* offices in nearby New Jersey and dutifully conferred on the financial results of the newspapers and broadcast properties with his older brother. Few, if any, company officials knew about the inner workings of the whole Newhouse empire. "The only crossover is between my brother and me," Si explained. But most of the action seemed to occur inside the Condé Nast building, where Si could be found in the thick of it.

Although nearly sixty, Si appeared younger than his years. His thinning hair, which had once been allowed to grow in a modified Afro-like style, was now coiffed in a razor-cut style, a "power cut" that almost made him look like Caesar. At work, he often favored casual clothing, frequently wearing khaki pants, polo shirts, and loose-fitting sweaters with the sleeves rolled up, which allowed him to unfasten his collar and project a sense of ease. Throughout his office, there were a number of cartoons on display, including the one behind his desk that had a swirl of agonized-looking characters encircling two words—*pills* and *ouch!* Unlike his round-faced father, who constantly had to watch his weight, Si stayed thin and usually left his fourteenth-floor Condé Nast offices by late afternoon, finding time to relax and exercise at a nearby club.

Si could still be very ill at ease in social situations, often muttering replies in abstruse phrases and rarely being forthcoming. Unlike some who suffer an awkward adolescence but become more pleasing in appearance as they mature, Si was still essentially a man whose droll, gapped-tooth smile, wide proboscis, and short stature made more than one of his detractors refer uncharitably to him as "the Frog Prince." Another attribute that seemed unchanged since adolescence (when at the Horace Mann School, he remarked disparagingly about his other classmates' mental agility in his letters to Lowenstein) was Si's capacity, when provoked, for rather pointed condescension. One longtime colleague recalled a social encounter in which a man who was barely an acquaintance attempted to ingratiate himself with Si Newhouse by talking at length about kosher delis.

"So, Si, what do you think is the best Jewish restaurant in New York?"

the man reportedly asked, finally coming up for air after reeling off name after name where good pastrami could be found.

"Grenouille," Newhouse replied, as tart as vinegar.

A tale about Newhouse's imperial manner was repeated by some guests who had attended an elaborate dinner at Si's East Side residence. After his invitees gushed with praise about the culinary presentation, Si let his displeasure be known. He had decided to send his cook back to culinary school, he announced. The guests were aghast and asked why. "It's not that the food isn't good," replied the demanding billionaire. "It's the *presentation* that needs work."

Something did seem to change from the time of Si's youth, however. The fear of displeasing his father had slowly dissipated, if not completely passed from memory. Well before Sam's death in 1979, Si demonstrated the mental toughness needed to assume his father's place in the family business. Surprisingly, Condé Nast expanded even further than anticipated in the 1980s, with a swashbuckling aggressivemess that became part of Si Newhouse's public persona. In one *Wall Street Journal* profile of him, a top rival at the Hearst Corporation, John Mack Carter, noted that the Newhouse company became "much more competitive" after Si took charge. "He's become daring in launching magazines," said the rival executive.

The success of *Self* magazine and his other publications during the booming economy of the mid-1980s buoyed Newhouse's faith in his own judgment. "We have changed from a small family-owned company to a major force in the industry," one Condé Nast executive told *The New York Times* by 1992. "When Si's father died, Si started to really take control of the operation. For the last five or six years, he has really hit his style. He is now a confident, mature executive who really knows the business." He had learned how the publishing industry works from two acknowledged geniuses of the craft—Alexander Liberman and his own father. And now, Si had developed his own reputation for brilliance. Along with it, he also developed a certain intolerance for those he considered incompetent, ineffectual, or simply dated.

Firing became an indelicate but often engrossing art form at Condé Nast, especially when handled by the boss. Si Newhouse's propensity for change—and his ever-widening notoriety for brutal endings with his editorial staffers—created a fearsome aura around the son who many thought would never make it. "I don't know if I was ever patient," Newhouse commented in a *Times* story headlined HEADS HAVE A HISTORY OF ROLLING AT NEWHOUSE. "Somebody else has to comment on that. I'm not sure I'm any different as an executive. I think I've just been me."

His signature style was everywhere. When the time came for *House & Garden*'s editor, Louis Oliver Gropp, to depart in 1987, Newhouse was still suffering from one of his most notable debacles in personnel management. Only few months earlier, his sudden dismissal of William Shawn, the longtime editor of *The New Yorker,* had caused an uproar among the staff and a great deal of negative attention about the way in which Newhouse dismissed one of America's most respected literary figures. Gropp's firing received little attention but was equally abrupt.

For much of the 1980s, Gropp was the editor of *House & Garden* as the home-furnishings magazine experienced a number of renovations to its image. Unlike *Vogue* or some other Condé Nast magazines, *House & Garden* was not the leader among those devoted to, as the industry called it, "the upper-class shelter magazines." In the early 1980s, with Gropp as editor, Newhouse invested heavily in a revamped *House & Garden,* appealing to a more upscale audience, hoping to siphon away more advertising dollars from dominant rival *Architectural Digest.* By 1987, Newhouse and Liberman had concluded that another overhaul was needed, especially after the worrisome surge of another rival, *Metropolitan Home,* which was increasingly read by many free-spending baby boomers. Once the decision was made to pull the plug on Gropp, however, there remained only one problem: where to find him.

Louis Gropp was on vacation in California when his fate was sealed back in New York. Rumors about his impending departure were already circulating throughout the Condé Nast building and had reached the press. When Gropp finally called back at the office for his messages, he learned that Si Newhouse—whom he had seen maybe once a month or so for the past twenty years at Condé Nast—wanted to talk to him. The cross-country conversation that later followed was anything but smooth. "I'm sure Si wished that I had been in town, but I wasn't," recalled Gropp, a pleasant, soft-spoken man. "I don't think he wanted me to read it somewhere—not that I was reading *W* on my vacation in Southern California. So he called me and said he had decided to make the change and that we'd get together as soon as I got back."

At times, Gropp almost felt sorry for Newhouse, who seemed tortured in relating the bad news. "It was not an easy thing for him to do," said Gropp, who eventually became the new editor at a rival magazine, *House Beautiful.* "It wasn't like we had a fight or that he didn't like me. It was difficult for him to do that, and difficult for me to hear that. But that's how life is. He didn't tell why he was doing it. He just said he had decided to name Anna Wintour editor."

Wintour's arrival was actually more electrifying news for the wags at Condé Nast than the departure of Gropp. Since 1983, when Wintour was hired away from *New York* magazine and appointed to the newly created position of creative director at *Vogue,* she had seemed to lead a charmed existence. Her fashion work at *New York* magazine—notably her use of some of the city's artists to paint backdrops for models wearing the latest clothes—caught the eye of Liberman, who had relied on a similar concept decades earlier. Ever the mystic, Liberman said he felt "an absolute certitude that I needed this presence." After talking with his mentor, Si Newhouse was determined to clear the way for this new force. As Newhouse later explained, "Alex's mind is quite subtle and complex. I won't dare to say what was in his mind. Everything I heard was 'Here is a great talent.'"

With these overtones of mystical fate and greatness, many thought Wintour—who was given the amorphous task of overseeing *Vogue*'s look—was being groomed to take over someday from Grace Mirabella. Certainly, Wintour, then an attractive, strikingly thin woman in her mid-thirties with a fondness for wearing Chanel and pitch-black sunglasses inside the office, seemed to embody the stylish essence of *Vogue*. And as the daughter of a well-known London journalist, she seemed to have the requisite British accent.

If Liberman was charmed by the new young editor, Si Newhouse was even more so. Two decades her senior, Si seemed enraptured by her youthful presence and took special care to ensure that she was happy and often praised. Some insiders at Condé Nast were upset by her special status and wrongly suggested that Wintour, though recently married, was having an affair with Newhouse—something both vehemently denied. The rumors of infidelity persisted nevertheless. "Dirt-diggers have suggested that it's not only Si Newhouse's ear that Anna Wintour commands," the industry magazine *Adweek* later observed. "The nature of their relationship is debated the way comic-book aficionados argued over Superman and Lois Lane—did they or didn't they?" Others say Wintour's rapid rise was due to her affinity for what Liberman and Newhouse wanted with their magazines. "She's cold and she's tough," said one former colleague. "But she knows about image and she looks good. She's also intelligent— no one can blow on about the future of *Vogue* better than she can. Si Newhouse likes that."

At *Vogue*, however, Wintour's presence seemed to unnerve Mirabella and her top associates, leaving Wintour unhappy and feeling left out of the creative process of the magazine. "Perhaps I was silly," Liberman later explained. "In my innocence, I thought she could collaborate with Grace and enrich the magazine."

Eventually, Wintour decided to return home, at least temporarily. In 1986, Bernard Leser, an Australian-born publisher of Condé Nast's London subsidiary who shared Si's zest for work and magazine acquisitions, heard of her uhappiness and offered her the post of editor of British *Vogue*. Leser launched a relentless campaign to bring Wintour back to England, initially against the wishes of both Newhouse and Liberman. "I think it was Bernie's persuasive powers," Wintour later explained. "He made them both [Newhouse and Liberman] decide it was for the good of the company."

As the financial-side guru, Leser assured Wintour that she could have an unfettered rein with the editorial side of British *Vogue,* a magazine that was very much like the Italian and French versions of *Vogue,* which still seemed to hold some of the panache and quest for beauty left from Diana Vreeland's days. In Leser's estimation, there was a considerable difference among the various international editions of the same magazine. "The Anglo-Saxon *Vogues*—American, Australian, German—are more active in moving merchandise, and are characterized by featuring products and services that are within the reach of people with good incomes," Leser explained.

Wintour's arrival in London hardly evoked cheers. Acting like some visiting field marshal, she insisted that the London staff arrive earlier, work harder, and accede to her judgments on photos. She turned the magazine upside down, adding certain features on gardening and essays from Paris and New York. She relished the upheaval. "I'm the Condé Nast hit man," she reported told a friend. "I love coming in and changing magazines." The critical reaction was harsh, however, and British *Vogue* lost some advertising and key editors during Wintour's first year, although things later rebounded. Among her British press critics, she was nicknamed "Nuclear Wintour" and "Wintour of Our Discontent" for her chilly manner. Her personal life became more difficult, as well. She was pregnant with her second child and spent weekends commuting at company expense on the Concorde from London to New York to be with her husband, chief of child psychiatry at Columbia-Presbyterian Medical Center in Manhattan. "I was having a hard time personally," she told an interviewer afterward. "It wasn't a secret."

When word spread to Si Newhouse that another media company was talking with Wintour, he acted swiftly. With uncommon concern, Si personally flew to London to keep her in the fold, and, without informing the current occupant, offered her the editor's seat at *House & Garden* in New York. "I suggested she come back and take it over," Newhouse said later.

Wintour's stewardship at *House & Garden* proved to be remarkably similar to her experience at British *Vogue,* however. In short measure, she reshaped the magazine, stressing a bigger format with *Vogue*-like headlines, and changed the name to *HG.* The photo essays were broadened to include not only interior shots but pictures of those celebrities who lived in these chosen mansions and villas. Some critics again lambasted Wintour's moves and ridiculed her use of celebrities, calling it "Vanity Chair," parodying another famous Condé Nast magazine. But Si was enchanted by Wintour and her idea of a magazine devoted to style. "People either loved or hated what I did there," she later admitted. Advertisers were cool to the newly Wintourized *HG,* with some of the more traditional advertisers fleeing. After only five months Wintour would leave abruptly again for another Condé Nast magazine in crisis, while *HG* would return to its old format, with a new editor who proved more reassuring to both its affluent readers and advertisers.

This time, Anna Wintour was headed to an even greater stage, forever earning her the praises of Si Newhouse. This time, she was going to reclaim *Vogue* as her own.

The source of distress leading to Wintour's selection as the new editor of *Vogue*—the unsurpassed jewel of the Condé Nast magazine empire—came mainly from outside the company, from a newly introduced American version of the innovative French magazine *Elle*.

For years, Newhouse and Liberman were content as *Vogue* dominated the fashion-magazine market. Under the steady, tasteful hand of Grace Mirabella, *Vogue* had tripled its audience and enjoyed a similar increase in revenues in the mid-1980s. *Vogue*'s number of advertising pages rose to about 3,200 annually—more than any other monthly magazine in the United States. The affluence of the 1980s renewed the interest in women's fashion and in beauty and health, and *Vogue* seemed the fortunate recipient of this trend.

But in 1985, *Elle* entered the fray with a splash. A lively, hip monthly magazine with vibrantly colorful photographs, *Elle* was started as a joint project by the French media compay Hachette and media mogul Rupert Murdoch. Within several months, *Elle*'s circulation rose rapidly to more than 800,000, still far from *Vogue*'s commanding circulation of 1.2 million but exceeding that of longtime rival *Harper's Bazaar*. Though he never let on publicly, the red-hot circulation reports about *Elle* virtually set off fire alarms inside Si Newhouse's office. Research studies—the real bible in Newhouse's magazine empire—showed that *Elle*'s audience was both younger and more affluent than the average *Vogue* reader. Suddenly, *Vogue*'s vaunted perch in the world of haute couture seemed quite vulnerable. "The fact that it was as successful as it was," Newhouse later explained, "was a sign that we should be looking at. It seemed a change at the top was necessary."

However, the ineptly handled firing of Grace Mirabella—particularly the oft-repeated story of how she learned about it via Liz Smith's TV report—reinforced Newhouse's public image as a boorish billionaire without the slightest hint of loyalty to someone who had served him so well. His words only hinted at personal remorse. "There are certain decisions I have to make," he told the *Times* a year later. "I don't think there is any ideal way of handling this very sensitive area. I think it's quite true that the Grace Mirabella thing was handled awkwardly and could have been handled better. I try my best."

Certainly, Si Newhouse had enough time to prepare. Liberman later conceded he had talked privately with Si for months about the ouster of Grace Mirabella and her replacement with Wintour. "These rumors and discussions had been going on a long, long time," Liberman said, although he had never breathed a word of it to Mirabella. "There were discussions about it before Anna left for British *Vogue*. It was certainly nothing new."

Dick Shortway recalls his discussion with Wintour when he found out she had agreed to leave British *Vogue* for *House & Garden*. What are you doing? Are you crazy? he asked when she broke the news to him. "But she just smiled," Shortway said years later in an interview. "She always wanted to be the editor of American *Vogue* and I think Si had that in mind. But at that point, he wasn't going to do anything about it. I think he wanted her back first and maybe planned the whole move with Grace from the inception of bringing Anna back."

The shock waves caused by *Elle*'s rapid success prompted Newhouse to consider changes in *Vogue*'s graphics and layout and to embrace a more youthful approach. Despite several hints from Liberman, Mirabella seemed unable or unwilling to make *Vogue* more like the new upstart. "I had a slightly different view of the way the world is going from [Newhouse and Liberman]," Mirabella said months after her firing. "My favorite subject is women, and their favorite subject, which is glitz, do not go together."

Wintour's brusque handling of Mirabella's staff earned her few admirers. She held a virtual inquisition of *Vogue* editors in her *HG* ofices before she arrived in order to decide who would stay and who would be cast adrift. Determined to change the magazine's look, she paid a reported $480,000 to buy out the remaining two years on the contract of Richard Avedon—who had taken nearly all of *Vogue*'s cover shots since the mid-1960s. To some, *Vogue* without Avedon was unfathomable.

Nevertheless, Si Newhouse backed his new editor. "I couldn't face the replacement of Grace," Liberman later told Dodie Kazanjian and Calvin Tomkins in their 1993 biography of him. "Newhouse wanted the change. I didn't push for Anna Wintour. She was a demand of Si's." Indeed, Newhouse's fondness for his new editor again stirred the rumor mill about the nature of their relationship as she once more ascended to a better title. On her first day as *Vogue*'s new editor, Wintour addressed the whisperings head-on. That morning, Liz Smith had devoted space in her column to the rumors, with a bemused denial from Newhouse. ("I am very much in love with my wife and my wife's dog," Si quipped.) Before the assembled writers, photographers, and editors, Wintour made an impassioned speech about women who rise quickly to the top and how they are falsely accused of trading on their sexuality. Anyone who believed that she was having an affair with Si Newhouse, Wintour declared, "is still living in the era when a woman could only make it to the top by pleasing a man. This is the 1980s. You don't have to do that anymore."

For all of the anguish, Wintour's selection proved to be a hit with both young readers and advertisers. Setting the pace quickly, her first issue featured a very un-*Vogue*-like cover. Forgoing the cool, meticulous studio close-ups of perfect beauties, this November 1988 issue debuted with an outdoors shot of a model with windswept blond hair. She was wearing inexpensive jeans and a ten-thousand-dollar dark Christian Lacroix top stitched with a cross of jewels across her chest. Most noticeably, her tummy peeked through in a winsome, sexy way. "I'm not an advocate of the plastic, every-piece-of-hair-in-place look," explained Wintour, who continued to experiment, even presenting Madonna out of character for one *Vogue* cover as a fresh-faced girl-next-door type. Admirers suggested Wintour was the true successor to Diana Vreeland. The bold selection of Wintour stunted *Elle*'s further advance and only seemed to bolster Si Newhouse's view that he had done the right thing in repositioning *Vogue* for the 1990s. "I think the magazine is superb," Newhouse declared in his most effusive Liberman-like cadences. "The look is fresh, it's full of surprise, and I think the feature content is up to date, relevant and upbeat. There's a brightness, a sharpness, I hadn't seen before."

Still, after more than a generation of change and a radical redefinition of women's place in society, nearly all of the crucial decisions about Condé Nast's magazines with their millions of female readers remained very much in the hands of Alexander Liberman and Si Newhouse. They would decide what women want—just as they had during the waning days of the Eisenhower administration. "Certainly, Alex—and Alex's relationship with Si—is the focal point of Condé Nast," recalled a former associate editor at *Vogue* who enjoyed her stay for two decades but harbored no illusions. "What you have is a company that gets the overwhelming majority of their revenues from women and they're creating products for women. The overwhelming majority of the staff who create these magazines are women. And still, you have the couple of people who have the ultimate power in the company are male. . . . A lot of the Condé Nast way of operating is the male-female dynamic: how Alex relates to women, how Si relates to women."

Approaching the age of eighty, Liberman was particularly hesitant to show any signs that he might be losing his creative powers as a cultural czar. In uneasy conversations, editors and art directors sometimes felt it was necessary to assure Liberman that he still reigned supreme, that he was still in touch. To fail to do so, not to pay homage, was to risk a serious breach in one's future. Some women at Condé Nast liked to fawn over the attentions of Liberman, who for years strutted about as the grand peacock in a world of beauty and femininity. "Alex has a way to guide, to inspire, to make you think harder," Edith Locke said in 1979, only months before she was canned as editor of *Mademoiselle*. "And he's an extremely handsome man. It makes you feel good to know that he notices what you're wearing and how you look."

Even the subtlest challenges to Liberman's authority were quickly detected on his radar screen. Rochelle Udell, an editor who grew up in the Bronx and worked for Condé Nast magazines in the late 1970s, returned in 1988 to become the second in command under Alex. With her quick wit and candid manner, Udell ingratiated herself quickly with Newhouse. "Si clearly enjoys working with her," observed Steve Florio, one of his top publishers. "They'll be talking about something and she'll say, 'Now, Si, this is how it is.' Then he'll get this sly grin on his face and begin to laugh, and you can see that they understand each other." Shortly after she arrived, a cover story in 1988 in the business publication *Manhattan Inc.* touted Udell as the company's new editorial power, picturing her sitting atop a pile of Condé Nast magazines. The story gave the clear impression Udell was the emerging power. "Liberman is about grandeur," the magazine story quoted one insider as saying. "Udell is about energy. It marks the beginning of a new era."

Neither Liberman nor Newhouse was amused. The Udell cover story created a complicated dilemma at 350 Madison Avenue when it also mentioned the possibility that Amy Levin might be replaced as editor at *Mademoiselle,* another of Condé Nast's magazines. Levin's husband, Art Cooper—who was also the editor of the highly successful men's magazine *GQ*—expressed his displeasure and concern over the article. Newhouse felt compelled to write a letter to Clay Felker, the editor of *Manhattan Inc.*, reaffirming his "tremendous conviction in and commitment to [Levin's] talents as an editor." (Levin was eventually removed in 1992.)

For Udell, the *Manhattan Inc.* story proved to be a disaster. It upset Liberman, caused Si Newhouse some public embarrassment, and wound up derailing Udell's future as the heir apparent. Alex Liberman was not ready to say good-bye just yet. "Si said 'Alex, you need someone to help you in this great mission of yours, you're not getting any younger,' and my understanding is that he chose Rochelle because he knew her and trusted her," said one former Condé Nast editor who worked closely with Udell at the time. "The moment she got there, he [Liberman] started undermining her because he couldn't stand any threat, even one chosen by himself. I can tell you, he did everything he could to undermine Rochelle."

In an interview at the time, Liberman hinted at his annoyance regarding the rumors. As always, he underlined his determination to press on. "I'm being retired every other day in the newspapers," he said. "All sorts of fascinating names are being suggested to replace me. But for the time being I enjoy it here very much."

Anthea Disney was another strong-willed woman at Condé Nast who didn't always pay attention to the intrigue and protocol in the White Russian's court. A raven-haired British woman with a resemblance to the actress Marlo Thomas, Disney grew up as a reporter working for several Fleet Street papers and was eventually sent to New York as a star correspondent and bureau chief. She was later hired as an editor for the *New York Daily News* and *Us* magazine in the mid-1980s before she became the new editor of Condé Nast's *Self* magazine in 1988.

Despite its remarkable initial success, Newhouse was unhappy with the direction of *Self.* With the right editor, he hoped it might take off as a mass-circulation magazine. Disney's predecessor, Val Weaver, lasted only a short time before Si came knocking at her door. "Would you mind if we made a change in editors in chief?" Newhouse asked Weaver before lowering the boom.

Disney quickly took charge of the magazine. With her tabloid sense, she put several young celebrities on the cover, along with bold headlines that asked young, health-conscious readers: BREAST OBSESSED: IS THE BODY BIZ THROWING WOMEN A CURVE? She seemed in synch with Liberman's desire for a faster-paced magazine. "American journalists ramble on and you have to read 3,000 dully laid-out words before you say, *Oh!* this is what it's about," Disney said. "At *Self,* you should have the sense that you've read the whole article from reading the headline, the subhead, the outquotes and captions. It's then up to you whether you want to read it or not, but at least you'll feel entertained."

With this formula, both advertising and circulation at *Self* began to revive and Disney felt confident she was headed on the right path. The rejuvenation of *Self* was noticed by the media and soon there were stories in the press about this bright new British star at Condé Nast. Shortly afterward, Disney received a telephone call from Si.

"I really wish you'd work with Alex . . ." Newhouse told her.

"Why would I want to work with Alex?" she asked, still not getting it.

"Well, you know, Alex is feeling left out," Si replied, somewhat sheepishly, to his new star editor.

Her biggest crime, as Disney later learned, was that the media accounts of her success at *Self* never mentioned Liberman or that she never referred to his part in the magazine's redesign. In fact, he played a very minimal role in the new look of *Self.* But, as her friends and confidants explained to her, deference to Alex was crucial to surviving at the top at Condé Nast.

"Anthy, just go to Alex and say you want him involved, you care about his feelings," advised one top person in the company.

"Bullshit!" Disney replied, preferring to take her own chances and, if necessary, accept the consequences.

For Si Newhouse, though, there was no other relationship quite like his friendship with Alex Liberman. Like a grown child who is mindful of an aging parent, Si was protective and sometimes defensive of the man who had taught him so much. It seemed impossible he would even consider removing Liberman, as he had so many other top people at Condé Nast. The protectiveness toward Liberman was especially acute as his beloved wife, Tatiana, withered away in frail health and was cared for by a private nurse. Alexander Liberman simply meant too much to the history of the company—and, even more so, to Si's own personal history—ever to see him depart unwillingly.

For a time, Disney held her admittedly sharp tongue during conversations with Liberman, even as she fumed at the ridiculousness of a man nearly eighty telling her what young women, those between the target ages of twenty-eight and thirty-two, really wanted. As he tried to exert more control, Disney finally lost her composure.

"Alex, what exactly would you know about a woman of thirty years old?" demanded the forty-four-year-old *Self* editor. "How would you know what her hopes, fears, and desires are? You have no contact with anybody like this!"

Liberman appeared befuddled but determined to reply. He muttered, "But Tatiana's nurse . . . I talk with her a great deal."

"And she earns fifteen thousand dollars a year and gets shouted at," Disney shot back. "I mean, that's not our readership, you know."

Shortly afterward, there was another confrontation over the selection of a new cover for the next issue of *Self,* this time with Si Newhouse in attendance. In this conversation, Liberman announced with great satisfaction that they should run a cover photograph he preferred rather than the one proposed by Disney.

"On what evidence?" Disney asked.

Liberman explained that he had taken the two proposed covers of *Self* home that evening. It was Tatiana's nurse who had told him which one she liked.

"That's the most absurd thing I ever heard in my life," Disney declared. She then showed the research for *Self,* the market studies showing who the readers were and what the magazine's overall demographic target should be.

Liberman seemed to roll his eyes. "Oh . . . research," he moaned in exasperated horror. "I can't . . . I can't. I'm sorry, I *can't* believe in research. I mean research, *really*. Who cares about research?"

"Well, why'd you pay to have it done, then, if you don't believe it?" Disney replied. She looked over at Si Newhouse, seated with his feet not touching the ground. But he remained silent, as though gripped in terror at the thought of interrupting Alex during one of his creative moments.

By August 1989, little more than a year after she had arrived, Disney was asked to leave—not in so many words, but the message, as delivered personally by Si Newhouse, was clear enough. On his way from Liberman's Connecticut family home, Si decided to stop at Disney's nearby house to speak with her and perhaps mitigate the blow. Much to her surprise, Anthea Disney found herself being fired on her own doorstep.

At first, Newhouse rambled on, saying how sorry he was and mentioning his respect for Disney's talents as an editor. He sounded like a man whose hand was being forced.

"Let's face it, Si," Disney interrupted him, knowing full well that her fate had already been decided regardless of what she might say. "This is *your* company. It's got your name on it. If you think I'm such a brilliant journalist, then what's the problem? You have admitted the numbers are fine and the advertisers like it. What problem do we have here?"

Newhouse didn't reply, obviously pained by the untidy task he was obligated to perform.

"Look, it's obviously me or Alex—and clearly it's not going to be Alex," Disney continued. "I understand that. We don't have to have that discussion."

Si just nodded and looked miserable as he thanked her and soon departed.

Disney's replacement at *Self,* the company's third-largest-selling magazine, was a woman more accustomed to pleasing men. Alexandra Penney, who was appointed in September 1989, had been a magazine writer for *Glamour* and *Vogue* and author of the best-selling book *How to Make Love to a Man.* Penney had never edited a magazine before when she was recruited for *Self* by Newhouse.

Unlike her predecessor, though, Penney knew how to play to the top men at Condé Nast. In a 1990 *Times* article about the latest makeover at *Self,* she made sure Alexander Liberman, who was quoted prominently, was given credit for the magazine's redesign. Penney's words of praise about her boss gushed forth later in the same story. "Oh, it's divine," she said, holding up a layout designed by Liberman for the magazine. "Oh, you're a doll." Cupping her hand over the phone, she told the visiting reporter in an aside, "He's heaven." Penney also found ways to please Newhouse. Even though she didn't have a dog at the time, Penney reportedly held a birthday party for Si's dog at her apartment one evening in March 1992, along with seven other pooches owned by friends. The dogs sipped Evian while the owners enjoyed caviar.

The influence of Alexander Liberman continued unabated throughout the early 1990s, despite his public attempts to minimize his impact. ("What power? You mean because I choose pink instead of blue?") Ever the grateful pupil and steadfast friend, Si Newhouse often paid tribute to Liberman's contributions. "He has had an enormous influence on Condé Nast," said Newhouse. "And by extension, I think Condé Nast has had an important impact on the magazine world."

But the vision that truly prevailed and was much more emblematic of America's media in the 1990s was the Newhouse concept—the hybrid of advertising imagery and editorial content. As much as Sam Newhouse had pioneered modern-day newspaper-chain ownership aimed at capturing mass audiences in near-monopoly settings, Si Newhouse and his stable of slick, demographically select magazines became harbingers of the class-driven changes in America's media in the 1990s—no longer for everyone, as Si Newhouse freely admitted, but, rather, for a desirable few.

The impact of Newhouse's pervasive concept was underlined when *Vogue* magazine celebrated its hundredth anniversary in 1992. Kennedy Fraser, who wrote about fashion for *The New Yorker* during the 1970s and early 1980s, examined the state of fashion photography in writing a preface to the Random House book marking the event, *On the Edge: Images from One Hundred Years of Vogue.* Although some aspects of fashion magazines hadn't changed since she had followed fashion in her column, Fraser later observed that "the biggest difference between then and now is that the division between commercial and editorial work has almost vanished."

Some who critiqued *Vogue* learned to accept it on its own terms as something other than purely editorial matter. In reviewing the collection of *Vogue* photographs shown at the New York Public Library as part of the birthday celebration, *New York Times* critic Charles Hagen noted the "strongly self-congratulatory air to this exhibit" and judged the work on its own terms as "the alluring blend of fantasy and commerce that fashion, and *Vogue,* represents." The overall impression of *Vogue*'s pages contained an undeniable message—both about its content and, by association, the editorial vision of Newhouse, who by then had owned the magazine for nearly one-third of its existence. As Hagen wrote, "For all the craft and style that goes into them, fashion photographs are in the end a form of advertising; their main purpose is to sell clothes."

Photographers, in particular, represented this new hybrid, an aesthetic where the traditional church-and-state type of separation of editorial fact and advertising promotion melded into one. For example, Patrick Demarchelier or Herb Ritts, whose photographic work appeared in *Vogue* or other Newhouse magazines, derived much of their income from work performed for such Condé Nast advertisers as Estée Lauder, Yves Saint Laurent, Ralph Lauren, or Lancôme. Often their photos in advertisements and those accompanying stories seemed almost indistinguishable. For their pivotal roles in setting the tone for an entire "book," top magazine photographers were paid handsomely. When Demarchelier decided to leave Newhouse's company for rival Hearst's *Harper's Bazaar,* the bidding for another star photographer, Steven Meisel, became intense. Rumors abounded that Meisel, whose popularity peaked as Madonna's favorite lensman, would soon land at the newly revived *Harper's Bazaar,* run by Liz Tilberis, who had been hired away from Newhouse's British *Vogue.* Si kept Meisel by giving him a new $2 million contract and turning him into one of the highest-paid photographers in the fashion world. Condé Nast officials reportedly convinced Meisel to remain by pointing out that he might lose some of his lucrative advertising accounts if he strayed to Hearst.

The most perfect marriage of Newhouse editorial product and advertisement, however, debuted later in the anniversary year. For this union, the folks at Condé Nast even invented a new name, "outsert." It was a typically audacious word for what was clearly the oldest trick in the business. Accompanying the October 1992 issue of *Vogue* was a virtual twin—another charming glossy advertising supplement with two of *Vogue*'s favorite models on its cover: Cindy Crawford and Claudia Schiffer. This second publication had an uncanny resemblance to *Vogue,* sharing the same typeface and the same fashion layouts. It looked and felt like a Newhouse magazine, but Si's marketing people insisted on calling it an outsert, as though some new test-tube creature from their media laboratory. Despite its uncanny similarity to *Vogue,* the big bold title on this sixty-eight-page publication was imprinted with the trademark name Revlon. Inside, the stories were written with the help of *Vogue*'s editorial staff and made to appear just like its reportage.

"It isn't an accident. We want it to look like *Vogue,*" said Dick Tarlow, whose advertising firm is owned by Revlon. Of course, the pictures were by *Vogue*'s longtime photographers—including the cover shot by Bruce Weber, whose own clients included such Newhouse advertising favorites as Gianni Versace, Ralph Lauren, Banana Republic, and Calvin Klein. Weber was an old hand at this new hybrid, having produced a similar 116-page outsert for *Vanity Fair* in 1991. The willingness of *Vogue*'s editors to open the floodgates—virtually to recreate an advertising supplement in its own image—simply delighted the cosmetics giant. "*Vogue* has a lot of credibility with consumers," declared Michael Hammond, Revlon's North American president. "What we're offering is not just from us, but from *Vogue.*"

The outcry over these outserts came from press critics and those in academia, who said they shamelessly interfered with the autonomy of *Vogue*'s editorial content. "It apes *Vogue* so precisely," observed *Wall Street Journal* writer Joanne Lipman, "that it leaves itself open to charges of breaching the Chinese Wall separating advertising and editorial." At Condé Nast, however, these ethical standards no longer applied. They seemed as dated as yesterday's fashions. The Newhouse concept had fully taken root. To the extent that any metaphoric Chinese wall still existed, it was now made of Swiss cheese. "We're lending our fashion and beauty expertise," pooh-poohed *Vogue*'s publisher, Anne Sutherland Fuchs, when asked about any ethical conflicts. "It's a wonderful marriage."

Certainly, neither Si Newhouse nor his editorial director was much concerned with the disturbing trend to confuse ads with editorial content. "There's a joke that when an issue is fat with advertising, it's a well-edited issue," Liberman observed. "Fat issues sell more copies. And advertising has become so good that it's harder and harder to tell it from the editorial."

The reminders that Newhouse's influence stretched beyond fashion magazines and into the realm of serious journalism were evident as well at the celebration for *Vogue*'s hundredth anniversary. On this occasion, the New York Public Library was filled with frivolity, flowers, and the sounds of a Latin band as Si Newhouse hosted a special party, with his editorial director, Alexander Liberman, by his side. For a time, Liberman stood in a small circle with Newhouse, his patron and admirer, smiling wanly as the swells of New York's literary and fashion worlds swirled about them. Amidst this crème de la crème, in the quintessential Condé Nast style, the superlatives were flowing that night.

"This is the first party of the Nineties!" proclaimed Paloma Picasso.

"Tonight bridges the best of the Seventies with what's coming with the Nineties," seconded Karl Lagerfeld.

For all the hyperbole, the night was indeed a remarkable triumph for the two men from Condé Nast. As all the world could see, Si Newhouse was one of New York's most powerful literary lions, a man whose sensibilities emanated from fashion magazines but whose reach and influence on the rest of America's media was still very much expanding. This once-failing enterprise, Condé Nast, was now the heart and soul of Newhouse's internationally renowned company, his gift and lasting legacy from his father. Si Newhouse's extraordinary wealth—exhibited in this library hall with a smattering of famous writers, designers, photographers, and editors in his employ—was unmatched by anyone in New York during the second half of the twentieth century. As he stood in this public library, a magnificent tribute to America's egalitarian philosophy regarding the printed word, Si Newhouse toasted his prize magazine designed for the affluent and select few. No longer the painfully shy young man struggling in his father's wake, Newhouse was now a giant in the industry himself, embodying the remarkable transformation of American media into the hands of a few billionaires and their vanishing sense of noblesse oblige.

For Alexander Liberman, this party seemed to mark another turning point, a celebration of his remarkable capacity for change. In a lifetime filled with exquisite beauty and unspeakable horrors, Liberman's style and grace had survived intact. In 1991, he endured the death of his beloved wife, Tatiana, and suffered from failing health considered so grave that some friends worried aloud what would become of him. Even the disappointment of never becoming a great artist, as he once hoped, seemed to have faded.

For a time following Tatiana's death, Liberman moved from his East Side town house to a $1 million apartment at United Nations Plaza, directly below the palatial apartment where Si and his second wife, Victoria, lived. The close proximity of his residence to Alex Liberman's only seemed to underline their special paternal bond, the lasting loyalty Si Newhouse felt to those who taught him how things really work. Few others would ever be so close. On the occasion of Liberman's eightieth birthday, Si sent him a personal note summarizing their thirty years together. ". . . What wonderful times we've shared! And how you've shaped and changed me!" Si wrote. "Associate, friend, brother, father . . . there have been elements of all these in our relationship with none of the tensions there might have been . . ."

By the time of *Vogue*'s hundredth anniversary in 1992, Liberman's health had improved markedly and life was blooming about him again.

After a short absence, he returned to the hallways and composing rooms of Condé Nast, peering at the covers and layouts of the company's magazines before they appeared in print. "When I walk down the corridors at *Vogue,* especially in the summer, with all those ravishing young creatures in their summer nothings, I feel like Matisse with his odalisques," Liberman confided to Wintour upon his return. Alex consulted with Si on the latest personnel changes in the Condé Nast empire and carried on fervently, as though he intended to remain there forever. He found time as well to prepare an opulently produced photographic memoir of his departed friend Marlene Dietrich, which was published by Newhouse's publishing arm, Random House. And mostly, Liberman discovered a new love—Tatiana's nurse and companion. Melinda Pechángco, the fifty-year-old Philippine-born nurse whose opinions he valued and whose care he had come to depend on, would become Liberman's bride, a death-defying feat for most men at age eighty.

Somehow, both love and Alexander Liberman seemed vital and new and . . . *in touch again.* As the master once exclaimed about his fabled magazines, "Youth is everyone's dream."

My Friend Roy

Power was invigorating to Roy Cohn, a magical tonic that made his sleepy-looking eyes move faster around a room, and his sometimes-prickly personality turn witty and effervescent.

In the early years of the Reagan administration, there was no better place for Cohn to exercise his unique talents as a political fixer—a schmoozer supreme—than by holding his own private pre-inaugural gala. From this font of presidential favor, Cohn lavished praise and attention upon those U.S. senators, state governors, and top White House aides who attended along with his friends and clients. Even for those who may never have seen the six personally autographed photographs of President Reagan prominently displayed back in his office, the message was clear: Roy Cohn had clout.

On this special night in 1985, shortly after Ronald Reagan's reelection, Cohn worked the room like a master. The guest list included his best friend, someone who had known him for many years. And so, when the moment came to greet Secretary of State George P. Schultz, Cohn did all the talking, as he always did when he was with his best friend.

"You know Si Newhouse, of Newhouse Newspapers," Cohn said, solicitous and ever so engaging.

Cohn's gentle reminder hardly seemed necessary. After all, Newhouse's *Vanity Fair* magazine would later feverishly extol Cohn's preball reception at the Dolly Madison ballroom of the Madison Hotel during the long inauguration weekend in Washington, D.C. POWER PARTY was the headline above the story written by *Vanity Fair* featurist Bob Colacello, an ace at this sort of thing. In the magazine's photo essay, CIA director William Casey is seen talking with "die-hard deb" Cornelia Guest. Ambassadors, U.S. senators, governors, and other media tycoons like Rupert Murdoch were all on Cohn's guest list celebrating Ronald Reagan's victory.

But Cohn's introduction and all of Newhouse's money and influence failed to register a note of familiarity with Shultz. The secretary of state gave a blank look when he was asked whether he knew Si Newhouse.

"No," Shultz replied.

There were no further recorded accounts of this meeting to determine whether Cohn showed his amazement to the secretary of state or whether Newhouse displayed expression of any sort. Perhaps their presence together at a White House function given by Cohn, nearly forty years after he and Newhouse had met at Horace Mann in the Bronx, was enough satisfaction. Once again, as so many times before, Roy had introduced another interesting person to his best friend, Si.

On nights like this, Roy seemed able to forget all the turmoil he had created, the secret deals and the character assassination. He was the life of the party. There was something exciting about being with Roy, something edgy and paradoxical but also searing, vital, and alive. Indeed, just standing in front of the secretary of state, being introduced to Shultz, was one of those moments with Roy Cohn that was both wonderful and a bit absurd. All of his life, Cohn had been a registered Democrat, yet he felt most at home with conservative Republicans like Reagan and, during an earlier, more confrontational time, Senator Joseph McCarthy. This pattern of contradictions and subterfuge, of trading in favors big and small, continued endlessly throughout Cohn's life. To his closest friends, Si Newhouse among them, this transparent buoyancy was part of his charm; to his many detractors, it was just one of many character flaws that made Roy Cohn so dangerous.

Over the next year and a half, Cohn would be unceremoniously disbarred from the practice of law in New York for a number of offenses, including stealing money from a client. Cohn provided help and advice not only to the President and senators but, as court documents would show, to Mafia dons and an assortment of crooked New York politicians. And despite a lifetime of publicly ridiculing homosexuals and denying his sexual preferences to his circle of married friends, the slow but inevitable march of the AIDS virus, contracted somewhere along a prolific line of chance encounters with young men, was already spreading throughout Cohn's body and would finally claim him in April 1986.

From beginning to end, one of the few constants in Roy Cohn's life was Si Newhouse's friendship. After he was forced from government following the disastrous 1954 Army-McCarthy hearings, Cohn began his career in private life by working for a distribution company run by a family friend of Si's and originally financed by Si's father, Sam. One of the last telephone calls Roy took before he died in his hospital bed was from Si.

Over a lifetime that included few friends and true intimates, no one came closer to Si Newhouse, his family, and the inner workings of their business empire than Roy Cohn. Newhouse's long-term friendship with Cohn remains one of the most complex relationships of his life, both personally and professionally. This union reached back to their days as young boys from well-to-do Jewish families who gravitated together as like-minded friends. It developed during the days when Roy was retained as an in-house counsel by Newhouse's father and his business associates and matured during those difficult times when Si Newhouse was newly divorced and estranged from part of his family. Their friendship would last through the 1980s, by which time they had both achieved prominence and power and, dressed in tuxedos, could look out at the world and simply grin.

Their relationship, which was based on shared experiences and similar views about the world, provides one of the most revealing glimpses into Newhouse's character, how his family empire works, and what he deems to be important. More than anyone outside the direct kinship of blood, Cohn seemed to hold the keys to Si Newhouse's world.

He used the Newhouse name, money, or endorsement to gain the bargaining chips that he could later trade for clients or for himself. He could punish his political enemies with "exposés" in Newhouse newspapers or get the news items planted or fixed for those whose favor he needed. Nosy reporters who began to look under the rocks of Cohn's business deals were told to back off. Cohn's guile and political insight were used by the Newhouses like some *consigliere* who knew how to solve the most intractable problems and seemed wise to the ways of the world.

As a man who courted power all his life, gauging its ups and downs and acting accordingly, Cohn could only marvel at those who didn't know Si Newhouse, at the relative anonymity of a man near the top of the list of America's wealthiest men and owner of the country's most powerful publishing company. After Secretary Shultz's dumbfounded expression, indicating he was unsure whether he should know Newhouse, Cohn could only express amazement. As he told a reporter: "It's a phenomenon of American life that nobody knows who Si Newhouse is."

Roy and Si, usually in that order. Ever since their days together at Horace Mann, Roy Cohn always seemed a few steps ahead of Si Newhouse. Where Si was shy and nervous, Cohn was quick-witted, outspoken, and funny, sometimes brilliantly so. While Roy was fiercely directed, Si was more demure and uncertain of himself. In many respects, though, Si Newhouse and Roy Cohn were very much alike, creating a bond of loyalty that would last for years. They knew many of the same schoolmates, such as Allard Lowenstein, and often shared the same views about what they wanted from life.

"I spent five years at Horace Mann, and they rank with the best years of my life," Cohn recalled in his autobiography. "I made good friendships there—not many, I wasn't gregarious, I wasn't a mingler—but quality friendships, two of which have stood the test of time: Si Newhouse and Gene Pope. Both happened to be heirs to empires, and both more than filled their father's shoes."

In those days, Cohn claimed he was more liberal than most of his classmates, including Anthony Lewis, who was Cohn's close friend and later became a reporter and columnist for *The New York Times.* (Cohn and Lewis would eventually have a falling out, exacerbated by their diverging political philosophies.) But Si and Roy remained friends, both preferring to take a backstage role in the intrigue of high school politics. The school's yearbook described Cohn in a way that would become familiar: "Roy's chief interest is politics; and he made good use of this bent at Horace Mann, becoming H.M.'s 'man behind the scenes.' "

Like Newhouse, Cohn shared the burden of having a successful father who was determined to see him succeed. Both boys also enjoyed particularly close relationships with mothers who favored and protected them. In Roy's case, his father, Albert Cohn, was a state appellate court judge with strong connections to the Bronx Democratic party, a political link that Roy would maintain throughout his life. "My parents were forever trying to provide me with a 'normal' childhood, and never succeeding," Cohn later observed. His mother, Dora Marcus Cohn, was a strong-willed, plain-looking woman who doted on her only child to the point where many family and friends wondered whether she was doing more harm than good. As Dora's influence on her son grew, Al Cohn's presence seemed to fade so much that he was rarely around at home, even on weekends. When Roy was eight, his family moved at Dora's urging from their apartment near the Bronx courthouse and Yankee Stadium to Manhattan's Park Avenue, not far from the Newhouse residence. At his parents' get-togethers, young Roy would join the adults and carry on precocious conversations beyond the grasp of most people his age. By the time he went to Horace Mann, Roy was a fastidiously dressed adolescent who was often called a mama's boy. His devotion to Dora would last well into middle age, with Roy always choosing to live with his mother until she died in the 1960s.

Roy Cohn possessed a restless ambition, which was evident by his junior year, when he made an important decision. "I had gotten all there was for me to get out of Horace Mann," he later recalled. "I was antsy to get my life moving quicker towards the real world." With the approval of the school's headmaster, Cohn was allowed to take several summer courses taught by private tutors and to skip his senior year. At age seventeen, Cohn entered Columbia College and was twenty years old when he had graduated from Columbia Law School. "Even my worst enemies have said, 'Well, we have to admit, he's a brilliant little bastard.' "

Si Newhouse didn't seem to burn with the same ambition as Cohn. Roy's tenacious approach and his rapid advance through school likely made a difficult period in Si Newhouse's life even tougher by comparison. In those dark moments when Si considered suicide because of the tensions he felt, it is unclear how much comfort or support Roy provided as a friend. At times, Roy could embody the very essence of loyalty. Unlike

Allard Lowenstein, however, Roy could also be insensitive, a tough opportunist rarely in touch with other people's feelings. Some thought Cohn was simply a bad influence. "Roy was a crumb from the word go," recalled Dorothy DiCintio, Allard Lowenstein's sister. "Roy was a dastardly kind of guy from the time he was a young man. Al wouldn't shun him, but they weren't friends. When Si achieved something on his own, Roy latched onto him. Roy Cohn, to me, was the bottom of the barrel. Always was."

But what mattered most was that Sam Newhouse—the most dominant figure in Si's life—was impressed with Roy. Sam felt Roy was a good influence on his shy and sometimes unfocused son. He spoke up for himself in a way that seemed practical and clear-thinking to the elder Newhouse. Roy's sense of drive and political acumen was a source of both awe and admiration.

At age twenty-one, Cohn began his law career as an assistant U.S. attorney in the Southern District of New York, where he quickly moved on from prosecuting small-time violations of federal currency and drug laws to much larger prosecutions. Eventually, with the help of friendly newsmen to whom he fed a constant stream of tips and inside information, Cohn became best known as an organized crime prosecutor who busted the "biggest," "most sensational," and "worldwide" rackets. He became prominent enough to take on the most talked-about boogeyman of his time: America's fear of communism and its perceived threat to internal security. As a Red-hunting prosecutor, Cohn's prominent role in the New York trial of eleven Communist leaders and his involvement in the conviction of Ethel and Julius Rosenberg opened his way for the even greater opportunity of working for Senator Joseph McCarthy.

In January 1953, when Cohn was twenty-five years old, he was chosen to become chief counsel for the U.S. Senate's permanent investigations subcommittee, the chief staging ground for what would be known as the McCarthy era—a dark passage in American history, when scores of people were subpoenaed to testify and grilled about their political beliefs. Many innocent people lost their jobs or had their reputations ruined through the course of these hearings. Cohn was the chief protagonist for McCarthy, often whispering damaging questions in McCarthy's ear so that the senator could pose them to witnesses suspected of being subversives. McCarthy admired Cohn's nearly photographic memory and his aggressive, relentless demeanor. "Roy is one of the most brilliant young men I have ever met," McCarthy said later.

Cohn joined the Republican from Wisconsin at the height of his influence and power. But Cohn stayed for less than two years, leaving after the 1954 Army-McCarthy hearings, which led to McCarthy's censure by the Senate. McCarthy "was in many ways the most gifted demagogue ever bred on these shores," writer Richard Rovere later commented. "No bolder seditionist ever moved among us—nor any politician with a surer, swifter access to the dark places of the American mind." In these pursuits, Roy was the perfect aide-de-camp, an ambitious, intense former prosecutor willing to fight without regard to ethical constraints.

During this time, Cohn developed a running correspondence and fast friendship with then FBI director J. Edgar Hoover, a rabid anti-Communist who frequently gave advice to McCarthy's subcommittee, along with confidential information taken from FBI files. "It is very doubtful whether Senator Joseph McCarthy would have survived in his reckless smearing campaign without the ammunition provided by Hoover," former FBI agent W. W. Turner later observed. "FBI agents put in long hours poring over Bureau security files and abstracting them for Roy Cohn." Cohn would forever deny that he was privy to confidential FBI reports. But Cohn and McCarthy had plenty of access to the press.

One of the most virulently pro-McCarthy newspapers was the *Newark Star-Ledger,* then the largest newspaper in the Newhouse chain. Even when many newspapers began to question McCarthy's approach, the *Star-Ledger* remained staunchly in his camp. Praising McCarthy's 1952 re-election victory, a *Star-Ledger* editorial castigated his critics and firmly pronounced that "[We] do not believe 'McCarthyism' to be an important issue." The Newhouse paper refused to run columnist Drew Pearson's charges against McCarthy, and it gave exaggerated importance with banner headlines to news involving McCarthy, no matter how contrived. "Most reprehensible of all was the paper's practice of allowing itself to be used as a conduit for charges McCarthy himself wouldn't dare make in public," wrote Richard Meeker, whose biography of Sam Newhouse quotes a *Star-Ledger* reporter as saying "we'd get documents all the time from McCarthy."

The most scurrilous attack by the *Newark Star-Ledger* involved Clifford Case, the U.S. senator from New Jersey. Early in his 1954 campaign for the Senate, Case had criticized McCarthy's Red-baiting tactics and promised to try to push the Wisconsin senator out of his chairmanship of the permanent investigations subcommittee. On a tip from McCarthy's office, the Newhouse paper aggressively investigated and eventually published a story about Case's sister, who was a mental patient living in upstate New York and a former member of the Communist party. The *Star-Ledger*'s smear was intended to paint the moderate Republican Case as a Communist, or at least sympathetic to Communists.

There was more than a little irony to these charges coming from a newspaper owned by the Newhouses, whose relatives dallied with socialism upon arriving in the United States. Nor was there any evidence that Si Newhouse was troubled by his friend's reckless actions or his alliance with McCarthy. Typically, Roy Cohn was never tied directly to the Clifford Case exposé. But there were those, including the New Jersey senator himself, who saw Cohn's fingerprints all over it. "The story was true," Case later told author David M. Oshinsky in 1979. "I don't know how they found out about it and I never asked McCarthy if he was directly involved. Let's just say it came from his people." But Oshinsky said Case left no doubt during his interview that the source was Roy Cohn.

Si Newhouse remained a friend throughout the period of Cohn's most intense political entanglements, which included an enduring battle with another rich man's son. To get his job with McCarthy, Cohn was chosen over Robert F. Kennedy, whose multimillionaire father, former ambassador Joseph P. Kennedy, was a friend and political supporter of McCarthy's anti-Communist crusade. On the same day Cohn's appointment was announced, Kennedy was selected as assistant to the subcommittee's general counsel, Francis Flanagan. This mortal slight to young Kennedy's ego—and Cohn's questionable tactics with regard to the McCarthy committee—prompted the permanent wrath of Bobby Kennedy, which would last until his assassination years later.

After several verbal exchanges, Kennedy's simmering feud with Cohn, the chief counsel and main rival for McCarthy's attention, developed into an angry physical confrontation in June 1954. In the Senate corridor, Cohn and Kennedy exchanged a few punches, with little damage, before Senator Karl E. Mundt, a Republican from South Dakota and a member of the subcommittee, broke up the fight between its two top lawyers. For the rest of his life, Kennedy remained a staunch enemy of Roy Cohn. "Being anti-Communist does not automatically excuse a lack of integrity in every other facet of life," Kennedy said of Cohn in January 1955.

Years later, the feud was still very much alive when Si Newhouse and Cohn were dining in a restaurant in New York called Orsini's and Bobby Kennedy walked in. The year was 1967, one year before Kennedy was assassinated during his run for the presidency.

"I came into dinner with S. I. Newhouse, my best friend, and two young ladies," Cohn said. "We were seated. A few minutes later, in came Bobby Kennedy with Margot Fonteyn, and they were seated at a table directly next to ours. All of a sudden the conversation stopped at our table, and no conversation ever started at their table."

Newhouse looked at Cohn for his reaction. "Well, this is going to be ridiculous," Cohn said, "and at these prices we don't have to spend the evening in silence."

Roy stood up and walked over to Kennedy's table. "Bobby, look, you're here, I'm there," Cohn said, gesturing to the table where Si Newhouse was sitting. "I'm going to ruin your evening and you're going to ruin my evening just by looking at each other."

Despite their many past disagreements, Kennedy concurred. "You're absolutely right, you were here first, I'll move," said Kennedy, who was then New York's junior U.S. senator.

"He got the headwaiter and had his table changed to another part of the restaurant," Cohn later recalled. "That's the last time I ever saw Bobby Kennedy."

After the notorious McCarthy hearings, Roy Cohn was a young man fading fast from the limelight. With his resignation in the summer of 1954, Cohn had decided to jump before he was pushed off the committee by other senators tired of his reckless actions. "It has been a bitter lesson to come to Washington and see a reputation, gained at some effort, torn to shreds because I was associated with Senator McCarthy, who has become a symbol of hatred for all who fear the exposure of Communism," he later said. To gain a foothold in the private sector, Roy Cohn, then an ego-bruised twenty-seven-year-old, turned to the world of Si Newhouse, his family, and their circle of friends for help. And this helping hand came in the person of the Newhouses' longtime friend Henry Garfinkle.

During their lifetimes, both Cohn and Henry Garfinkle would share the distinction of becoming close friends of the Newhouses, and both had been loaned money by Sam Newhouse in times of difficulty. During the 1950s, Cohn's involvement with Garfinkle's company would set the controversial tone for his future business dealings. In turn, the Newhouses' reliance on friends like Cohn and Garfinkle underlined some of the more complex business relationships that helped their media empire to expand and flourish.

Henry Garfinkle's early history resembled Sam Newhouse's own background. In the 1920s, when he was about thirteen years old, Garfinkle began selling newspapers on street corners and at the ferry pier in Staten Island. To help support his family, he dropped out of school by age fifteen. Somehow, Henry Garfinkle's small enterprise along the ferry port overlooking New York harbor caught the attention of Sam Newhouse, the owner of the *Staten Island Advance,* the borough's main daily newspaper. Newhouse understood how important distribution was to his fledgling newspaper and he encouraged Garfinkle by providing him with a three-thousand-dollar interest-free loan to buy his first newsstand at the ferry terminal, where commuters traveled into Manhattan. Like Sam Newhouse, Garfinkle was born on the Lower East Side of New York and was the eldest son of eight children of a Russian immigrant family. They were both diminutive men, not much more than five feet tall, who were dynamos in their own ways. "Henry has two personalities," a former associate would tell *The Wall Street Journal* in a front-page profile about Garfinkle. "His business personality is gracious and charming and improves with the importance of his guest. His real personality is ruthless."

Garfinkle's immense drive and ambition soon enabled him to buy newsstands at Newark Airport, the Port Authority, and at other transportation hubs. Eventually, he became a multimillionaire owner of newspaper and magazine distribution systems in New York and much of the Northeast.

Garfinkle stayed forever grateful and loyal to Sam Newhouse, who had given him his first big break in business. "Let's face it, we were best friends," Garfinkle explained. "Anything I could have done to help the man, I'd do."

A few months after leaving the McCarthy subcommittee, Cohn became the general counsel in 1955 for the Union News Company—the original firm that Garfinkle had bought in Staten Island with Newhouse's loans. By the time Roy joined the company, Union News had become one of the leading newsstand and restaurant operations in the nation. Whether Roy Cohn convinced Si Newhouse or his father to clear the way for getting a job with Garfinkle remains unclear. Cohn likely came to Garfinkle's attention through the Newhouses, Garfinkle's son Myron said, though he was not sure whether Sam Newhouse had asked Garfinkle directly to hire Si's best friend. "My best guess is that my father hired him independently. But they had overlapping circles of social and business associates, I'm sure, and he may have met Cohn through them."

Less than a year after leaving McCarthy, Cohn used his hardball legal tactics to help Garfinkle take over the American News Company, acquired through an elaborate stockholder's lawsuit. Cohn later claimed to have engineered Garfinkle's successful coup. At the publicly held company's annual meeting in March 1955, Garfinkle headed a dissident group that eventually forced the management to resign. This bold move allowed Garfinkle to gain control of the ninety-one-year-old company, which called itself the world's oldest magazine wholesaler. Garfinkle revamped the ailing company, renamed it Ancorp National Services, Inc., and gained a near stranglehold on the distribution of newspapers and magazines in the Northeast.

The Newhouses benefited from Garfinkle's help. Being on friendly terms with the top distributor was vital to any newspaper and particularly to a company entering the U.S. magazine industry, which greatly depends on sales from newsstands to boost circulation and justify higher premiums from advertisers. Henry Garfinkle was well aware of his nexus of power and he used his control to wring every cent possible out of publishers. Even the mightiest media powers had to pay tribute. According to federal regulators, Garfinkle's firm would seek payments to ensure their papers and magazines got good display and promotion on his newsstands. In 1971, the Federal Trade Commission filed a civil lawsuit against Ancorp, seeking $585,000 in penalties for the scheme. From late 1965 to early 1969, FTC investigators alleged, Garfinkle's company would demand and get improper payments to the tune of $2,500 a month from *The New York Times* and $500 a week from the *New York Daily News*. The federal agency sought the high penalties, partly because Garfinkle's firm had violated an earlier FTC order in 1964 barring any such payments.

Behind Garfinkle's newsstands, there was another force: the persistent criminal element involved with New York's newspaper and magazine distribution industry. In the 1960s, organized-crime figures with alleged ties to the Bonnano crime family were involved with Garfinkle, according to a *Wall Street Journal* investigation. A *Times* obituary of Garfinkle observed: "He repeatedly denied charges that he hired underworld figures during circulation wars that were waged on his newsstands."

Unlike most other owners of media companies, however, the Newhouses actually got preferential treatment from Garfinkle. Part of the reason was simply personal, the fact that Henry Garfinkle and Sam Newhouse had remained friends for decades. They vacationed together and their families would come to know one another well. But in a more tangible way, Newhouse reaped the rewards of being Garfinkle's first benefactor when he bought the Condé Nast group of women's magazines in 1959. Such magazines as *Vogue, Glamour,* and *House & Garden* were helped immeasurably by this association with the company run by Garfinkle and his legal counsel, Roy Cohn. With their friends controlling almost 50 percent of America's newsstands at one point, the Newhouses' $5 million investment in the money-losing Condé Nast magazine company quickly paid dividends. "Let's be honest with each other," Garfinkle later said. "If you put one newspaper or magazine at the front of the stand, you know what happens."

Those who were close to Roy Cohn say the business relationship added another dimension to his friendship with Si Newhouse, giving him much greater access to the Newhouse empire. "S. I. Newhouse, Sr., was a friend and—they used the word *benefactor*—of Henry Garfinkle," said Neil Walsh, a lifelong buddy of Cohn. "And I believe that's how Roy got friendly with Sam, and through that, he got even more friendly with Si."

Riding horses through the wooded meadows was fun for the kids and another way in which Si, Roy, and their inner circle of friends were drawn closer together. On these weekend afternoons during the early 1960s, Newhouse accompanied his children—Sam, Pamela, and Wynn—and joined Cohn's friend Bill Fugazy and his children for relaxation. Usually, the gang would get together at riding clubs in Westchester County, north of New York City, or in nearby Connecticut. "Every Saturday or Sunday, we'd go riding together with the kids," recalled Fugazy, who had been introduced to Si Newhouse a few years earlier by Cohn.

Newhouse, then a wiry, thin man in his mid-thirties, was small and not very coordinated. But he was always game for a challenge. "Teaching Si how to ride horses was fun," Fugazy remembered years later with a smile. "We'd be going against each other for fun. If Si fell, if he'd get knocked off the horse, he'd get right back up again."

Fugazy was a tough-minded executive whose family had amassed a fortune by running one of the nation's top limousine firms. Like Roy Cohn, Fugazy seemed to know everyone in New York with special access—from choice box seats with the owners of the New York Yankees to the inner sanctum of the city's Roman Catholic cardinal, Francis J. Spellman. Si Newhouse was able to relax with these friends, a group of ambitious, self-assured young men. This band of friends—Roy, Fugazy, Si, and a group of others—were, to use a phrase from the early 1960s, their own Rat Pack. After suffering through a difficult divorce, Newhouse could unwind as he vacationed or spent time on the town with them. They would help him forget whatever family or business tensions existed.

Horseplay of all sorts was encouraged. On one weekend, Si and Roy conspired to surprise Fugazy. Somehow, while Fugazy was occupied elsewhere on the grounds of their club, the two friends managed to hoist a live goat into Fugazy's parked automobile. There, in the backseat, the wretched beast was found, to Fugazy's horror and his friends' delight. "Roy and Si bought a goat for my birthday and put it into my car," Fugazy would later recall. "I remember that weekend very well."

Roy and his friends seemed the kind of men his father would approve of, the kind Sam Newhouse might even be pleased to call friends. "Sam and Mitzi had a lot of respect for Roy and they felt that he was a good influence on Si," recalled Fugazy. "Parents think that their children are unprepared for the world's problems and they were that way with Si and Donald—more so with Si."

During those same years, Peter Diamandis remembers being invited by Si to join him and some of his pals, who included Fugazy, William Zeckendorf, Jr., son of the wealthy builder, and Roy, for lunch at the King Cole Room at the St. Regis Hotel. When lunch was over, there was a group of limousines waiting outside for them. "That's who his friends were, the sons of the very wealthy in New York," said Diamandis, who was then working for Si at Condé Nast. "Roy Cohn at that time was probably the most famous of the group—on his own hook."

The Newhouses were unshakable in their loyalty to Roy Cohn, despite his ignominious tenure with McCarthy and the succession of three remarkably dramatic trials during a ten-year period beginning in 1963. During this time, Cohn was indicted for obstruction of justice and perjury involving an alleged $5 million stock-swindle scheme. His first trial in 1964 resulted in a mistrial; the second trial wound up in a dismissal of the charges against Cohn. In 1971, Cohn was again acquitted on charges of bribery, conspiracy, and filing false documents with the Securities and Exchange Commission. At these trials, the testimony revealed some of Cohn's friends and business associates included such underworld figures as Moe Dalitz, who built the Desert Inn gambling casino in Las Vegas; a man described by authorities as an "underboss" to Mafia chieftain Vito Genovese; and Meyer Lansky, the Miami gangster. Despite an intense federal investigation, Cohn walked away from his ordeal of three trials, saying with some justification that the government's investigation was a personal "vendetta" by Robert Kennedy after he became U.S. attorney general.

Throughout these trials, Si remained a steadfast friend; he often went to court and dined with Cohn while the jury deliberated his fate. Sam Newhouse also offered his support. "There were periods of big trouble and I was lucky to have good friends who bailed me out with loans and outright gifts," Cohn later said in his autobiography. "The best of all was Samuel I. Newhouse, the founder of the publishing empire and the father of my best friend, Si. I remember going to see him, nervous as a cat, and he asked me what the trouble was."

According to Cohn, he told the elder Newhouse, "I'm broke."

"Tell me how much you need," Sam Newhouse said with a smile, as Cohn recalled it. "C'mon, Roy, give me a number."

Cohn said he told the publisher that he needed $250,000, and Newhouse, without missing a beat, wrote out a check for that amount. (In another account of the same meeting, Cohn said he asked Sam Newhouse for "at least $300,000 or $400,000" and received a check for half a million dollars.)

Overwhelmed by the generosity of a man known for his parsimonious approach to publishing, Cohn told the senior Newhouse that he was uncertain whether he could ever pay back the loan.

"You don't ever have to pay me back," Newhouse replied. "You've already paid me with friendship."

Friends and business associates say Cohn paid his debt to the Newhouses in myriad ways, both professionally and personally. During the 1960s, Cohn served as a Newhouse legal adviser on a number of matters. "I remember flying out together to St. Louis on business with Roy, Sam, Si—Roy was working for them at the time," recalled Fugazy. "Roy was helpful in a lot of their union problems. Roy was well connected and he knew a lot of union people."

Dick Shortway remembered Cohn's unexpected role in a discussion of an attractive offer from the rival Hearst organization for Shortway to become publisher of *Harper's Bazaar* in the late 1960s. Shortway told Si about the offer. Newhouse asked Shortway, then one of his top executives at *Vogue*, to wait until they could discuss it over lunch that same day. When they reconvened at the lunch table, Roy Cohn was there to join them, having been invited by Si. "He (Cohn) and Si convinced me it would be a bad move for me, so I turned them down," Shortway said. "Si thought Cohn could be an influence on me not to take the job." Soon afterward, Shortway was made *Vogue*'s publisher and Si assumed the broader title of publishing director for Condé Nast. The lasting memory for Shortway, though, was Si's great confidence in Roy's negotiating ability.

Cohn played another role for the Newhouses—as a big brother, an acceptable peer for Si, who seemed unsure of himself and inclined to repeat his mistakes with women. Friends from those days say the senior Newhouse paid Roy to keep an eye on his son—"sort of like a retainer to keep Si out of trouble," as one described it. Another Cohn friend, former New Jersey congressman Neil Gallagher, recalled Roy's frantic attempts to stop Si from marrying a woman deemed not worthy. "Jesus! Do anything to stop this! The father—" Cohn ranted. Sam's generous gift to Roy was, as others suggest, simply a way that a wealthy man tries to control his children by, in effect, paying his children's friends to monitor their behavior. "Si was divorced then and I would think that Sam had Roy keep an eye on him," said Neil Walsh, Cohn's friend. "Si had married very young and he really hadn't been around the bright spots. I could see how the father could have been nervous about Si hitting the bright lights and some of the hot spots."

In the wintertime, Si, Roy, and other pals escaped New York's frozen concrete for a few days in the sun, usually somewhere in the Caribbean, where they rented a house. "There were constant comings and goings of people," Walsh recalled. One of the most memorable trips was an earlier winter vacation in Havana, before Cuba was taken over by Castro. Cohn had made friends with some top officials in Batista's government after handling a troublesome matter involving an American company's interests in Havana. Typically, Roy worked a little of his legal magic, and the grateful Cubans treated Roy like visiting royalty. "Whenever Roy would go to Havana and get off the plane, there would be four members of the secret police waiting," said Walsh. "The cars, everything. They'd stay around the clock with him and his party."

For Si Newhouse's circle of friends, Havana meant relaxing on the beach by day and going to see the sights at night. While in Cuba, Walsh remembers meeting Sam and Mitzi Newhouse, who sometimes stayed at the same hotel as Roy, Si, and their friends. One rainy morning, Walsh spotted the couple by the hotel entrance, looking for a taxi during a tropical downpour. "I remember them coming out, and there were no cabs there, and Sam senior goes running down the street to get a cab so that Mitzi wouldn't get wet," he recalled. "I remember saying to myself, If I had his money, I'd have three or four guys running for cabs. I wouldn't get my ass soaking wet. But that was Sam Newhouse."

With his gang of friends, Si Newhouse felt relaxed enough to show a rarely visible side of his personality. "He always seemed to me a very quiet fellow with a good sense of humor," recalled Neil Gallagher, then a Democratic congressman from New Jersey who was one of Roy's pals at the time. "He was bright enough so that when somebody said something, he'd have a little quip, or top Roy when Roy was making a joke on somebody. Si could top him when he was in the mood to tell it. There was a lot of give-and-take in those days. We were all a lot younger and we were always joking about things."

As part of his macho image, Roy Cohn posed as a swinging single, not sure whether he wanted to get married. His buddies never doubted or asked. It seemed unthinkable that their friend—tough-talking lawyer Roy Cohn—was gay. Besides, there were the short items in the press that linked Cohn romantically to two women. Carol Horn, a Seventh Avenue designer, was said to have been Cohn's fiancée, though the relationship never went anywhere. Horn was one of the devoted friends in 1969 who, along with Si Newhouse, accompanied Cohn at some of his trials. ("I remember Si as being a very private person," said Horn in 1992. "He was personable, but he seemed to like doing things his own way. And I think he's the same way today.")

Si Newhouse was on the golf course with Roy when Cohn had a revelation about another important woman in his life: Barbara Walters. Cohn was first introduced to the future television personality by Walters's father, who then owned the famous Latin Quarter nightclubs in New York and Miami. He eventually asked Walters for a date and, according to Roy, enjoyed his time with Barbara until she mentioned that she was engaged. After that encounter, they didn't speak for three years, until one day when Walters called and left an obscure message with Cohn's telephone operator. At first, Cohn didn't know what to make of the garbled message. "Two days later, I'm playing golf with Si Newhouse, and on the tenth tee, it got to me," Cohn later recalled. "I said, 'God, I wonder if that was Barbara Walters?' So I ran off and called her." For years afterward, Cohn would share a long-lasting friendship with Walters. In the mid-1980s, for instance, Walters voiced support for him in the midst of a legal proceeding that resulted in Cohn's disbarment.

Even as he lay dying, Cohn carried on his duplicity. During one of his final interviews, he was asked about the great love of his life.

"Barbara Walters," he quickly answered. "Oh, boy, did we ever discuss getting married. . . .We discussed it before her marriage, after her marriage, during her marriage. . . . You know how those things are."

But whether Barbara Walters ever shared anything more than friendship with Cohn is a matter of speculation, since she has never spoken publicly about her relationship with him. Cohn's relationship with Walters, however, seemed to add to his macho image among his heterosexual friends. Like Si Newhouse's aborted engagement with Rachel Crespin in the 1960s, it was thought that Cohn simply appeared to have had second thoughts about getting hitched. As Morley Safer of "60 Minutes" would later say in a Cohn profile that briefly mentioned Walters, "He's just not the marrying kind."

Roy did become an important part of Newhouse's family life, acting like an uncle to Si's kids, enabling them to divine and translate the often-hidden moods and intentions of their father. In a family atmosphere where conformity was often an unspoken rule, Roy served as a refreshing anti-dote, very much the freewheeling individualist. "He was a great friend, as good as anyone can have," Si's son Wynn later said.

Wynn Newhouse, though he was only a youngster at the time, remembers the "extraordinary house in Acapulco" that his father, Roy, and their friends shared for years during holiday vacations. "My father would go down south with a girlfriend for these trips they had before he got remarried, and Roy's big comment was 'There goes the ex-future Mrs. Newhouse.' He came up with brilliant wisecracks, but they were never wicked, just always amusing," Wynn said. "He left, I'm sure, a string of small bills here and there that weren't paid, but in the big things in life Roy was a great guy. Very complex, much more complex than most people understand."

Cohn, whose legal specialties included messy divorce cases, found himself offering family advice to the Newhouses. Years later, Caroline Newhouse, who was Si's daughter-in-law, gushed about Cohn's unique insight into the family. Privately, Roy explained to her the mysteries of Si's family history and "made it possible for me to communicate with my father-in-law, whom few people can communicate with. My father-in-law is an extremely shy and protective man. . . . Roy gave us our engagement party. He and my brother gave us our wedding speeches at our wedding. My father-in-law was unable to do that. He has since learned to give a speech, but it was a very difficult thing for him."

Whether feeding rumors to reporters, negotiating with the Newhouse employees, or giving friendly insight to Si's children, Roy Cohn spoke with authority, assured in his claim that he was Si Newhouse's best friend. He knew Si's strengths and weaknesses and he never confused them. "Si is very shy," Cohn would explain. "He's terrorized by public appearances. When he has to give a five-minute speech, he rehearses four to eight weeks. If I have a party, he calls and his opening line is, 'Do I have to come?' "

As protector and confidant, Cohn ingratiated himself with the Newhouse family as perhaps no other outsider. To those curious about the ever-secretive Si Newhouse and his multibillion-dollar empire, Cohn was more than willing to be quoted, providing his own angle and "spin" to reporters, like a seasoned public-relations agent. By the 1980s, it was clear that Roy Cohn spoke for Si Newhouse.

Roy Cohn, the political fixer, was keenly aware of, and sometimes acknowledged, the more subtle forms of permanent power in American life. And there were few more powerful forces than the media—with its pervasive reach among the public and its ability to generate billions of dollars in revenues. Cohn was well aware of his best friend's place in that pantheon of power. He even repeated the Newhouse notion of local autonomy.

"If they wanted, the Newhouses could push a couple of buttons and become the most powerful publishing force in the United States," Roy Cohn told *The Wall Street Journal* in 1982. "But that would collide with their concept of local autonomy."

Because of his personal reticence, most people assumed Si shared his father's philosophy of local autonomy. Some flattering journalists erroneously concluded this philosophy meant Newhouse was solely interested in the bottom line and that reporters and editors were free to do their jobs without interference from above. To hear the Newhouses tell it, they were the epitome of the modern American newspaper publishers—conscientiously turning a profit and keeping their news pages sacrosanct. "I am interested in publishing successful newspapers, not in king-making," Sam Newhouse instructed his children. "I have no desire to curry favor with men just because they are famous or powerful. By avoiding such involvement and by not associating with any of their causes or organizations, I preserve my independence and the integrity of my newspapers. Readers know immediately when a newspaper becomes someone's mouthpiece, and that's bad business."

But Roy Cohn had every intention of using the Newhouse news pages to help his friends and to punish his political enemies. Although he might acknowledge such esoteric notions as local autonomy, Cohn's view of the press was much more pragmatic. His bare-knuckled opportunistic approach was something he had learned from his mentor, Senator Joseph McCarthy. Knowing the top people—what buttons to push—was paramount to Cohn. He spent his life seeking favor with publishers, owners, and top editors who commanded some of the nation's most influential media outlets. In the 1950s, these trusted confidants included columnist Walter Winchell; by the late 1970s and early 1980s, Cohn's influence spread from the gossip columns of Rupert Murdoch's *New York Post* to the front page of *The New York Times*. Reflecting on Roy's career as a power broker, former *Times* legal reporter Sidney Zion, who edited and rewrote Cohn's autobiography, acknowledges that Cohn was one of his best sources, and Cohn provided information to other journalists in a similar fashion. This symbiotic relationship between Cohn and the media was mutually beneficial. Aside from ideology or friendship, Roy Cohn's access to the nation's top politicians often depended on the perception he could influence the media for them. "Roy's power was that he had a lot of friends in the media, and it was Si Newhouse who was his best friend," Zion said.

One Republican insider who worked with Cohn to help influence the Newhouse editorial stance marveled at Cohn's ability to manipulate the press, which he pushed and shaped to his own liking like putty. "The Newhouses are people who are fundamentally interested in the bottom line," concluded this politician. "Their newspapers, when they buy them, are notoriously pro-Establishment. They are always for the 'ins'—whether the 'ins' be Democrats or Republicans. They love to kowtow to the Establishment. And they are very slow to cover any news that threatens the Establishment in any way. Essentially, the Newhouses' bottom line is, 'Is the newspaper making any money?' That's all they care about. Roy had the ability to shake them of that, which they did only under great duress."

An early example of Cohn's clout with the Newhouse organization happened in the early 1960s when the Kennedy administration wanted a favor and Cohn willingly obliged. This deal involved one of Kennedy's most important supporters in Congress, Hale Boggs, the House majority whip, whose Louisiana home district was based in New Orleans. Because he supported Kennedy's civil rights and other liberal programs, Boggs was sharply criticized in the usually conservative editorial pages of the local daily newspaper, *The New Orleans Times-Picayune*. President Kennedy realized how important Boggs's support was in gathering other southern Democrats to his cause, and he worried how the *Times-Picayune*'s criticism might hurt Boggs politically.

During one White House meeting where the Boggs dilemma was discussed, Kennedy confidant Neil Gallagher—the New Jersey congressman and, more importantly, a friend and business associate of Roy Cohn—offered a possible solution. Gallagher pointed out to President Kennedy that the New Orleans paper had recently been purchased by Sam Newhouse and, he added, Roy Cohn was very close with the Newhouses. Gallagher offered to talk with Cohn about intervening with the Newhouses on Boggs's behalf.

In the Kennedy administration, the idea of enlisting Roy Cohn's help toward anything was anathema, especially to Bobby Kennedy. During the 1960 Democratic convention, Cohn had tried his best to help Lyndon Johnson, rather than JFK, get the presidential nomination. At the same time Gallagher's offer was being discussed, Bobby Kennedy and a team of Justice Department lawyers and FBI agents were conducting an investigation that would result in Cohn's criminal indictment. Gallagher was well aware of the active Cohn investigation. He was feeling pressure from Roy and their circle of friends to get the Kennedy administration to drop their probe into Cohn's business activities. This was a chance for a backroom deal that would help everyone, if Newhouse was willing.

Bobby Kennedy vehemently objected to asking for Cohn's help, but cooler heads in the administration prevailed. "Go ahead and talk to him," the President said, sending Gallagher to work out an arrangement with Cohn.

"I didn't know what Roy's position was officially within the Newhouse organization but I knew he was quite influential with Mr. Newhouse," Gallagher said. He called Cohn and spelled out the deal. Roy seemed excited at the prospect of getting the Justice Department off his back. "Roy called me back and said the next time I was in New York why didn't we have dinner. And I did and came to New York that weekend, and that's when he told me that the Newhouses would support Boggs down there."

Gallagher recalled that during the dinner, Cohn indicated that he had personally spoken with Si Newhouse about the Boggs endorsement. "Roy said Newhouse could be helpful and he had not been entirely interested in what the editorial position was locally, since he left it to the local editors, but that he had respect for Boggs and felt that they could support Boggs and his position on civil rights." Cohn said Boggs should read the *Times-Picayune*'s editorial page and if he didn't like the new viewpoint, the Newhouses would find another editorial approach suitable to him.

Gallagher quickly contacted the White House, with firm assurances from Cohn that Newhouse had agreed to one part of the deal. He hoped the other part involving Cohn's legal problems would soon follow. "I went back and told Kennedy's chief political aide, Kenneth O'Donnell, that news, and he said, 'What does he want?' " said Gallagher.

As the go-between on this deal, Gallagher was amused by O'Donnell's question, because he had been wondering the same thing.

"To tell you the truth, he didn't say what he wanted," Gallagher recalled telling the President's aide. "Cohn didn't ask any quid pro quo on it. But if you're asking me, he's certainly interested in calling the war off between Bobby and himself."

The Newhouse editorials soon reflected a new appreciation toward Congressman Boggs's efforts in the House, and Boggs himself certainly understood the value of staying on Roy Cohn's good side. Cohn later claimed he spoke with Boggs personally about asking the President to drop the Justice Department probe against him. But Bobby Kennedy's effort to get Cohn prevailed.

"I got a call from Hale Boggs," Cohn recounted in his autobiography. "Boggs was a friend of mine and a friend of the President." Boggs told him that the President couldn't stop his brother or then U.S. Attorney Robert Morgenthau, who was assigned to the case, from proceeding with an indictment. "I said, 'Hale, you know, I'm not in a position to be making grandiose statements, but if the President of the United States can't control his brother, he's in pretty bad shape,' " Cohn wrote.

For those involved in the Hale Boggs episode, what was striking was Cohn's tremendous clout within the Newhouse organization, the kind of media connection that ambitious politicians dream of. But Gallagher said he wasn't surprised by the Newhouses' willingness to bend, if not break, their professed policy of local autonomy at Cohn's request. "Old man Newhouse was a legend where I came from, from being the clerk for old Judge Lazarus," said Gallagher, whose New Jersey district was dominated by another Newhouse newspaper, the *Newark Star-Ledger*. "Certainly, the trust that old man Newhouse had in Roy reflected that he was a contemporary of Si's and gave him good advice."

Zion shared the same view about Roy's ability to trade off his friendship with Si Newhouse. "Roy used the Newhouse connection in a myriad of ways to enhance his power and influence," according to Zion. "There are Newhouse papers all over the country, and Newhouse television stations and national Newhouse magazines and Sunday supplements. It's not exactly one congressman one paper, but it's not too far from it. So if you were a senator or a congressman or party leader or anybody in politics Roy Cohn wanted to reach, you risked something if you didn't take his call."

After surviving his three trials, Cohn returned to form as a full-fledged power broker in New York City and national politics. By the early 1980s, his political influence at city hall had expanded enough so that he could reportedly help Si Newhouse's oldest son, Sam, gain a much-coveted berth along the East River for his yacht. Early corruption allegations during the administration of Mayor Edward I. Koch involved Staten Island. However, Newhouse's newspaper in the city, the *Staten Island Advance,* rarely pursued any such signs of corruption with aggression, even when right under its nose.

Several of the allegations involved companies with connections to Roy Cohn. Dan Janison was a young reporter at the *Advance,* the seventy-thousand-circulation daily newspaper for which the entire Newhouse media empire is named. He remembers his experience when he tried to write about the companies and their ties to Cohn.

Late one day in 1981, Janison learned about a government investigation and filed a last-minute story, which was bannered on the newspaper's front page. He was pleased the *Advance,* with its staff of mostly underpaid young reporters like himself, had gotten a break on a story so vital to its readers before the other, much larger dailies in New York City. "The story came in late and went into the paper fast and I'm pretty sure they were hungry for a follow-up story," Janison recalled. "It was top of the front page. It led the paper."

The following morning, however, Janison learned he wouldn't be doing any more stories about the allegations—or anything involving Roy Cohn.

When he arrived at work, the *Advance*'s longtime editor walked over to Janison's desk. With a pipe in his mouth, Les Trauptman sat down with the twenty-four-year-old reporter and in a quiet, almost fatherly way killed Janison's investigation.

"I realize that this guy Cohn is a sleazy character, and I'm not knocking your story today," the Newhouse editor said. "But in our continuing coverage, we can't use the name of that lawyer."

"You realize that causes a big problem," Janison said, embarking on an explanation of Cohn's role in the scandal.

Trauptman quickly cut him off. "Trust me, we have to do this," said the editor.

Upset and frustrated, Janison dropped the story on his editor's order, though his every instinct rebelled against such a move. A few months later, a front-page *Wall Street Journal* profile about Si Newhouse's empire made Janison realize just how close Roy Cohn was to his newspaper's company. "Cohn acted as the spokesman for the Newhouse organization in that story," Janison said. "I think they routed the calls to him. So I had some inkling of what I was up against."

When it came to signing up big-name talent, Roy Cohn had remarkably good fortune as a literary impresario for the Newhouse organization.

With Cohn's help, Norman Mailer was convinced to become a contributor to Newhouse's *Parade* magazine and later to sign a lucrative book contract with Random House. Regardless of their obvious differences on political matters, Mailer, the liberal, and Cohn, the conservative, were similar in their bombast and feistiness, their capacity for self-promotion and sniffing out a good deal. Surely, Si Newhouse's largesse was a good deal for both of them.

Mailer's entrée into the world of Condé Nast began sometime in 1980, shortly after Si Newhouse acquired Random House. At that time, Si expressed a desire to sign up Mailer, hoping to add that lustrous name to his publishing house's stable of well-known authors and to have him as a potential contributor to his Condé Nast magazines. Cohn relayed this version of Si's intentions to Peter Manso, a writer who then was close with Mailer and would later write a biography about him. Si Newhouse wanted Mailer to write a magazine piece about his views on capital punishment, Cohn told Manso. This idea was timely because Mailer had just won the Pulitzer Prize for his book, *The Executioner's Song,* the novelistic and highly acclaimed account of Gary Gilmore's execution by firing squad. Cohn, feeling his way as he talked up Newhouse's offer, believed that Mailer would like a quick-pay day. "He'll pay cash," Cohn told Manso about the Newhouse offer. "We'll give him seven thousand dollars for the piece."

The idea for the essay on capital punishment was said to have come from Walter Anderson, who had recently been promoted to editor of *Parade*. Anderson later told Manso in his Mailer biography that Si Newhouse became very excited when he mentioned the proposal one day over lunch. In his interview with Manso, Anderson said he wasn't sure whether Si Newhouse had any grand scheme to acquire Mailer's services for his book company, as well. "I consider Norman the quality writer of our time, and Si shares that opinion absolutely," said Anderson. "He's extremely high on Norman, but he's high on William Styron, too, who's also at Random House, and I'm certainly not aware that he had an acquisition plan to get Norman. He wouldn't discuss that with me anyway."

To get the deal done, Newhouse relied on the unique skills of his long-time friend, whose great talent was making things happen. During his talks with Cohn, Manso made it plain that he was not Mailer's agent, but he told Cohn that he was sure the seven-thousand-dollar offer was much too low. "I think you might tell your friend Si to multiply by a factor of ten," Manso replied. Later, Roy Cohn called Mailer himself and they agreed to set up a luncheon with Si Newhouse. Usually, such a power lunch would be held at Si's favorite restaurant, The Four Seasons, or some other midtown eatery. Mailer, undoubtedly aware of Cohn's unsavory reputation in liberal circles, insisted instead that the three men have lunch in an obscure Italian restaurant in Greenwich Village. Eventually, Mailer agreed to write the piece on capital punishment for *Parade*.

When the magazine later commissioned Mailer to travel to Russia and file a report based on his impressions, Cohn couldn't stomach Mailer's sympathies for the Soviet system and expressed his outrage at the story to friends like Manso and Anderson. "These Commies'll drop a bomb on his house and he'll still be praising them," Cohn complained. Only after complaining to Si Newhouse did Cohn simmer down and drop his threat to write a reply to the *Parade* article. But Cohn recognized Mailer was one of the finest writers of his generation—"a genius," as Roy would call him. Despite their differences, the two men became friendly, with Cohn often debating Mailer about the issues of the day. Mailer's regard for Roy Cohn, once the vilified right-hand man of Senator McCarthy, warmed considerably after they met and he signed a lucrative writing deal with Newhouse.

"I think Norman was always a little embarrassed about his association with Roy—he didn't want to be too public with it," said Peter Fraser, Cohn's companion during the early 1980s when Roy's personal life became an open secret. Cohn became involved in other business matters with Mailer. He rented a small cottage for himself and Peter Fraser in Provincetown, Massachusetts. The house was owned by Mailer and was next to a larger house where Mailer's family stayed during the summer. On some summer evenings, Cohn and Mailer would hold court at a large dinner shared by family and friends. "Norman, being who he is, liked people and so respected Roy's differences," said Fraser. "I think Mailer enjoyed his conversation with Roy because they were so diametrically opposed. It was always a fun dinner."

Peter Manso was one of Mailer's friends who wasn't thrilled with his new alliance with Cohn and expressed some concerns. But Mailer brushed him off and replied, "It's about time I had a patron."

Indeed, he had found a patron—Si Newhouse. Newhouse's overtures to Norman Mailer, made through Roy Cohn, would pay him sizable fees and commissions throughout the decade of the 1980s and well into the 1990s, with some of the most lucrative deals ever seen by an American novelist. In 1983, Mailer left his longtime publisher, Little, Brown, and signed a four-book contract with Random House for more than $4 million over the next nine years. His first book for Random, *Tough Guys Don't Dance,* was excerpted in Newhouse's newly unveiled *Vanity Fair* magazine. (By the early 1990s, Mailer was listed on the *Vanity Fair* masthead as writer-at-large under the name of editor Tina Brown.) None of the New-house editors, however, were aware of Si's guiding hand or the help of Roy Cohn in securing Norman Mailer's services. "Upon reading the man-uscript it was my idea, purely my idea, to buy it for *Vanity Fair,*" insisted Leo Lerman, then *Vanity Fair*'s editor, in describing how he decided to run excerpts of *Tough Guys* after talking with Mailer's Random House editor, Jason Epstein. For his part, Mailer seemed to have found some comfort in the size and stability of Newhouse's fortune. "I sensed that what Norman really wanted was to clear the decks and have nothing to worry about financially for the rest of his life," Jason Epstein later said.

The highly publicized coup of signing Norman Mailer provided the sort of big-name literary quality Si Newhouse was seeking in the early 1980s as he established his own imprimatur on the family business. Unlike his father, Si Newhouse was willing to pay for the best talent, if necessary. At Condé Nast, he had learned that expensive photographers and top-line editors were important to the reputation, as well as financial success, of his properties. Mailer's marquee value would lend an air of sophisiti-cation to the Newhouse name, one that had been associated for so long with the pedestrian and mediocre. In return, the literary lion was feted by the Newhouse organization in the best places money could afford.

"I have to thank you all, and it goes against the grain," Mailer said at a Newhouse-sponsored celebration at New York's "21" for the 1991 pub-lication of *Harlot's Ghost,* a huge and critically acclaimed novel about the CIA. "As you get older, you have to change all those curmudgeonly ways. I am now in immediate spiritual danger of saying I love you all, but since I am a psychopath at bottom, this is only true for tonight." Mailer had enough presence of mind at that night's affair to thank his billionaire patron and the Random House editor who had helped follow through on the deal fashioned by Roy Cohn, by then dead for five years but still not forgotten. "Si Newhouse, who brings back Venetian graces, and my editor, Jason Epstein, the last mandarin," Mailer said, his bushy mane of white hair making him look every bit the part of a literary lion.

In the 1980s, Cohn was particularly brazen about using his friend's publications for his own ends. To press his right-wing political views, Roy gave *Parade*'s 21 million Sunday readers across the country a piece of his mind about the Internal Revenue Service. The diatribe was as bizarre and amusing as it was journalistically reckless for Newhouse to publish it.

Cohn was hardly in the position to be lecturing Newhouse's readers, since at this very time, he was allowing his Manhattan law office to be used as a meeting place for Mafia clients. Yet, while he was under active investigation for disbarment, Roy Cohn was pictured on the April 3, 1983 cover of *Parade,* posing with a big smile and holding his briefcase. Surrounding him was a group of average-looking Americans, as if they were direct from central casting, pictured laughing, waving their hands, and seeming in awe of the man before them.

YOU CAN BEAT THE IRS, by Roy Cohn. This cover story seemed full of the Reaganesque rah-rah of the early 1980s, a fantasy starring Roy Cohn in the Jimmy Stewart role, as the honest and truthful everyman lawyer, the populist avenger against the dreaded bureaucracy of big government. Though a little box in italic print below the story did accurately describe Cohn as "one of this country's most controversial and successful lawyers," very little else in the *Parade* story bears any semblance to reality. While Si Newhouse and his editors may have been unaware of the full extent of Roy's legal problems, the story itself seemed patently misleading.

In his version, Cohn was a just an average Joe who was persecuted for a $4 million back tax bill even though he "never once failed to file and pay substantial taxes." The story was filled with Cohn's sense of defiance and sarcasm. "At this point, we pause for the roll of honor—a brief tribute to the series of agents who have given the best years of their lives to the IRS's bungling of my case," he taunted midway through the *Parade* piece.

The truth of the matter, as court documents later showed, was that Cohn had been involved for years in an elaborate tax scheme in which he used his law firm to pay for nearly all of his personal expenses—which some say reached $1 million annually, including yachts, Rolls-Royces, vacations abroad—and to set up shell companies to hold the title to his Sixty-eighth Street town house and a Connecticut home worth an estimated $600,000 at the time. In 1986, the U.S. attorney's office in Manhattan would file a $7 million civil lawsuit against Cohn, seeking payment and an end to his alleged tax dodge. Only once in the *Parade* article did Cohn, the wounded taxpayer, suggest that his travail might be more like a cat-and-mouse game.

Even more reckless was Cohn's advice to *Parade* readers concerning their own tax problems. In a guide of how-to tips, Cohn counseled, "Keep one step ahead of them: If there is a problem, change bank accounts so they can't grab your funds by knowing from your records where you bank. If they get canceled checks and information from your bank, they will be in a position to know much more about your life than is acceptable. . . ." Of course, for many *Parade* readers—the vast majority of whom are working-class people who will never earn $1 million in their lifetimes, let alone spend it like Cohn—this questionable advice would be nearly impossible to follow. Certainly, the average American was not inclined to set up a maze of checking accounts to avoid detection by the government. Following Cohn's instructions, one would invariably need to retain a lawyer at considerable cost and face the likely prospect of an IRS audit, which would probably require an accountant to sort out.

Cohn's law partners, including longtime friend Tom Bolan, recognized the harmful consequences of the *Parade* article, which seemed to provoke the IRS into filing the federal lawsuit against Cohn and his law firm. In the final analysis, Cohn's story was more of a thumb in the eye of the IRS—an act of revenge rather than a public service. "Provocative is a euphemistic way of putting it," Bolan recalled. "We could have all done without it." Cohn's firm ultimately settled with the IRS without admitting any wrongdoing.

The fact that Cohn, Si's best friend, could use the cover of the nation's premier Sunday magazine for his own misleading portrayal of his personal tax problems underscored how much access Cohn had to the Newhouse empire, how he could use its news pages to fight his own private battles. Whether Newhouse agreed with his diatribe against the Internal Revenue Service is not certain. It is worth mentioning that at the same time Cohn's story appeared, Si and Donald Newhouse, as the executors of their father's estate, had been hit with one of the largest combined tax and penalties claims ever levied by the IRS, amounting to $942 million. Perhaps they were the only audience Roy Cohn needed.

The most remarkable public-relations coup Cohn engineered on the cover of Newhouse's *Parade* magazine, however, didn't involve himself. Rather, this cover story featured one of his most important political allies— the President of the United States, Ronald Reagan.

As the 1984 campaign season approached, Cohn had lunch with Ed Rollins, a top political aide to the President. Rollins was worried about poll results that showed Reagan's age, as well as lingering doubts that the President might not have recovered fully from the 1981 assassination attempt, posed one of the few obstacles to his otherwise-certain reelection. Cohn adopted these concerns as his own and soon had a perfect public-relations solution.

"I thought about it, and I said it seemed to me that a well-placed magazine article showing the President's physical prowess would be the best answer," Cohn told Sidney Zion, who recounted the anecdote in Cohn's autobiography. "The obvious magazine was *Parade*." According to Cohn's account, the magazine's editor, Walter Anderson, "engineered an article on the President's outdoor activities with a cover piece showing him diving into a swimming pool, his massive chest and strong body, and then leading into shots of him chopping wood at the California ranch. The article served its purpose. It was widely received and acclaimed."

The Cohn-planted story and the carefully staged photographs of the President attracted great attention in the media, more than adequately fulfilling its political purpose. As *Time* magazine commented, "With its Charles Atlas photos of a fit, firm Reagan, the *Parade* piece had a clear political payoff: if a President pumps iron, his age seems moot."

Documents made public years later at the Reagan Presidential Library show Cohn was quick to trade on the *Parade* cover story by asking for another favor from the President several months later. In his August 1984 letter to a Reagan aide, Cohn described himself as "Special Counsel" to the Newhouse Publications and boasted that he had "arranged the now famous picture and story of the President working out."

Cohn would get upset later when David Gergen, upon leaving the White House as communications director, seemed to take credit for the *Parade* cover with the President. But the GOP cognoscenti knew who had really fixed the deal. "That was absolutely Roy; that was Roy's handiwork—the cover of Ronald Reagan lifting weights," said Roger Stone, the GOP political strategist who got to know Cohn while serving as Northeast campaign manager for Reagan's 1980 presidential campaign. "Roy told me about the idea several weeks before it happened."

When the *Parade* cover story appeared, the White House was overjoyed. Cohn had worked his magic in the effort to restore Reagan's image as a rugged outdoorsman, much younger and healthier than his age suggested. With the help of Newhouse's magazine, the President had put the assassin's bullet behind him, at least in the mind of the American public. Especially pleased with the outcome was First Lady Nancy Reagan, who had a fondness for Cohn and his behind-the-scenes approach. "I remember Mike Deaver and Nancy Reagan thanked him profusely for it," recalled Stone. "She knew that Roy could get things done, and she respected and used people who could get things done."

At Roy's lavish birthday parties, Si preferred to stand in the background with a group of Cohn's older friends—a conclave of politicians, gangsters, judges, artists, writers, and old chums. In the late 1970s and early 1980s, these parties inevitably took place at Studio 54, with its pulsing disco beat and glittering dance floor, undoubtedly the most celebrated and notorious nightclub of the era.

The Dionysian aspect of Studio 54 was its main attraction, a raucous adult playpen where the gossip columns chronicled the goings-on of those single-name celebrities: Liza, Halston, Bianca, Andy, and other splendors of the night. Cohn was the lawyer for Studio 54 owners, Ian Schraeger and Steve Rubell, and he was rumored to have an interest in the club. When he threw a party, expenses were picked up by the nightspot. Cohn loved being treated as a VIP in a place where customers waited on long lines outside for the chance to come in and be seen. "I gave him a party at Studio 54," Rubell said at the time, recalling a scene where the exuberant wife of the Canadian prime minister provided unexpected entertainment at a Cohn affair. "He invited one hundred and fifty people. Three to four thousand showed up. Margaret Trudeau showed up. Everyone! I had a big cake made of Roy with a halo around his head. This big cake was on a stand. Then Margaret Trudeau went and sat on it."

Newhouse always made an effort to come to these birthday bashes and be there for his friend. "I think Si was at quite a few birthday parties for Roy," recalled Tom Bolan, Cohn's friend and law partner. In 1979, for example, Si Newhouse was one of the two hundred or more guests at Roy's fifty-second birthday gala, which included developer Donald Trump and *New York Times* columnist William Safire. As they rolled out a giant cake in the shape of Roy Cohn's face, Si remained happily in the background, off to the side. As Cohn would later tell *People* magazine for a profile of Si Newhouse, "At my annual birthday party, it is my favor to him never to call upon him to make a speech."

Studio 54 was a romping ground for Roy Cohn, where he could live in excess. Amid its lights and shadows, Roy could be himself. In the downstairs rooms of Studio 54's basement, where the most orgiastic encounters happened, Roy found his safest haven, arranging for sex with a variety of young men. "We went over to Studio 54," Andy Warhol would observe in his diary in the late 1970s. "Stevie [Rubell] introduced me to Roy Cohn who was with four beautiful boys. . . ."

During this time, Cohn's dual existence seemed to confuse his old friends who used to vacation together in the 1960s. "In those days, Roy was totally in the closet," Neil Walsh remembers. "There was absolutely zero, no idea of it, until his mother died. Fugazy and I can both tell you that we were both there when Roy was fucking broads. There's no question about that. Then, when his mother died, he started showing up with what we used to say were his 'bodyguards.' That was a polite term. I mean, Roy, up until the day he died—he went on '60 Minutes' and he was dying of AIDS—and he still said he wasn't gay."

Cohn's homosexuality didn't seem to disturb Si Newhouse as it did some of Roy's other longtime friends, Peter Fraser recalled. He and Cohn would go on vacations with the Newhouses to Acapulco or spend time at Si's palatial and very private mansion in Palm Beach, Florida, with the long, beautiful courtyard. "I have no idea when he knew" about Cohn's sexuality, Fraser said. "Obviously, I was made welcome in their home and never treated with anything but respect. But I doubt it was ever a subject of discussion between the two of them."

Even if they never talked about it, Newhouse likely knew Roy's secret, perhaps since their days as school chums, and chose to keep his friend's confidence for many years. If he learned later as an adult about Cohn's homosexuality, it never seemed to alter his affection for his best friend. They were friends because they had grown up together and were too loyal ever to part. "When they were together, they were very similar—they were the same height, slight build, and just their energy seemed very similar," recalled Fraser. "To me, they could have been brothers."

The controversy surrounding Cohn resurfaced in the press during the early 1990s, when the Broadway hit *Angels in America* won the Pulitzer Prize. The play portrayed Cohn as the ultimate self-denying, self-hating gay man in a heterosexual world. Even before the play, the revelation of

Cohn's homosexuality had made it difficult for some of his heterosexual friends. But not Si. "Speaking of friends, his best buddy was Si Newhouse, the all-powerful chairman of Condé Nast," wrote the columnist Taki in a defense of Cohn. "I have followed Mr. Newhouse's career rather closely. . . . It seems that Si Newhouse nowadays gets not a small amount of boot-licking. What I don't understand is this: Why the fear? Si is heterosexual and remained friends with Roy until the end. This is to Mr. Newhouse's credit. What is not admirable is the brown-nosing where the Condé Nast supremo is concerned. This is so because Mr. Newhouse can provide well-paid employment, even if it's writing about rich people's houses."

Roy Cohn never feared Si, or at least never showed it. That pugnacious, fiercely independent quality endeared him to Newhouse. An artist like Alexander Liberman could provide one view of the world and its fine accoutrements; a pragmatist like Cohn offered quite another perspective. As Nicholas von Hoffman, Cohn's biographer, suggests: "My hunch is that, in some ways, Si is a retiring man who, because of his father's wealth and the way he grew up, has an almost-intimidated feeling about the world out there. Roy, whom he came to know very early in life, was one of those strong people who could take care of things for him. I think there was this true connection of affection and this feeling that Roy understood all these mysterious things out there, how the strange world works. Of course, he could render real services. But in a way, he was almost a talisman—the rabbit's foot in the pocket. He had Roy and that made the world a little bit safer."

When the good times were over for Cohn, Si Newhouse remained a steadfast friend, one of several who served as references on Cohn's behalf in his ill-fated attempt to be listed in the Martindale-Hubbell legal directory. (Not enough lawyers could be found to approve conscientiously of Cohn's legal tactics.) The media attention surrounding Cohn's legal misdeeds became intensive in 1986 as he lay dying of AIDS. After a long review of his actions as an attorney, the Appellate Division of the New York State Supreme Court pulled Cohn's law license, despite the pleas of his powerful friends. The court agreed with a disciplinary panel's recommendation that Cohn be disbarred. "One need not be a lawyer to recognize the impropriety of such conduct," the five-judge panel concluded after reviewing the record against Cohn. "For an attorney practicing nearly 40 years in this state, such misconduct is inexcusable."

Nevertheless, Si continued to lend his name and reputation to help Cohn in any way he could. For many, his unwavering fidelity was an enigma. Fred Hughes, the longtime business partner of Andy Warhol and a friend of Newhouse, recalled a private dinner in the late 1980s when someone, with a pained expression, asked Si how he could be associated with such a man. "This was a long conversation, with some very powerful people, and he gave this lengthy, sincere avowal of his friendship," remembered

Hughes, who admires Si for his loyalty. "It was a very open thing for him to say in front of these people and he was as tactful as he could be."

Undoubtedly, Cohn had been driven by a certain self-hate, which seemed to manifest itself in his relentless attacks on Communists, gays, and even fellow Jews. How many of these views were shared by Newhouse is uncertain, even for those who witnessed many conversations between the two. In 1985, Cohn would describe Newhouse as "one of the most apolitical people I know," though in the same breath, he added that his best friend was "a conservative with a high tolerance for ultraliberals." Newhouse claimed he and Cohn were far apart ideologically. But Si and Roy did seem to share a similar view about human nature—a common link that over time brought them closer together. Newhouse never felt comfortable enough with himself to express his views as forcefully as Roy. "Si was kind of noncommittal, let's put it that way," recalled Tom Bolan. "He would tend to listen more and not volunteer his opinions. He was just interested in getting your opinion."

As death neared, Cohn's suntanned face appeared drawn, his bulging eyes and cranium even more prominent. His thin bantamlike frame had become frail, almost brittle, from the disease. At a New Year's party in 1986, he made an appearance through sheer determination. When Cohn was hospitalized and dying, Si Newhouse visited or telephoned virtually every day. If Roy thought they would be coming for a visit, Si and his wife, Victoria, made every effort to be there. After his death, the press repeated Roy's claim that he suffered from liver cancer, although later reporting accurately that he had died of AIDS.

On his deathbed, Cohn made a change in his will so that he could leave one last gift for his best friend. It was a large marble sculpture of a man's head created by a French modernist; it had been left in Cohn's East Side town house. "Of course, it'll probably end up going to the IRS, but Roy really wanted to try to do something special for Si, who was one of his dearest friends and has one of the best contemporary art collections," said another of Cohn's friends to the press.

For nearly four decades, Roy Cohn had provided friendship and advice to Si, who was always loyal to him—no matter how much Cohn exploited the Newhouses for his own purposes or how much the family relied on Cohn to fix their own problems. The full extent of how Roy Cohn compromised the Newhouse media empire would not be publicly detailed until after his death in 1986, when a federal trial revealed how Cohn had assisted his Mafia friends in fixing a story in a Newhouse newspaper to help elect Jackie Presser as Teamster president. In the end, the legacy of Roy Cohn would prove to be a disgraceful one, a testament to how greed and criminality pervade so much of America's life.

Yet the laughter, fun times, and lasting friendship seemed worth whatever price for Si Newhouse, a lonely, insecure boy when he first met Cohn. Roy had lived the kind of exciting public life that Si, as the custodian to one of America's greatest media fortunes, could only watch from the sidelines and perhaps enjoy vicariously. There would be those who would wonder why they were friends at all and what they had ever shared in common. It no longer mattered, though. Roy was gone, and all that was left was the marble sculpture and Si's gratitude.

"I don't know the price," Newhouse said when apprised of the bequest, "but anything Roy had will be meaningful to me."

CHAPTER SIX

Stop the Presses

At the *Cleveland Plain Dealer,* Si Newhouse was just a name. Reporters and editors vaguely recognized him as the owner of their newspaper, the son of the man who had founded the Newhouse newspapers chain. For most journalists in Cleveland, Si Newhouse was largely a mystery figure ensconced in some faraway Manhattan tower. Only occasionally did a few hired hands in Cleveland manage to catch a glimpse of their billionaire owner.

"I saw him once or twice—he was not a regular there," recalls Bill Woestendiek, who served as editorial-page editor and later executive editor of the *Plain Dealer* in the late 1980s. "I never had a meeting with him, except to say hello."

Walt Bogdanich was another journalist at the *Plain Dealer* who had never met Si Newhouse. There didn't seem a need for Bogdanich to know much about the newspaper's absentee owner or who his friends were. He had been lured from the city's other competing daily newspaper, the *Cleveland Press,* and arrived at the *Plain Dealer* in November 1979. In a relatively short time, Bogdanich quickly established himself as one of the best investigative reporters on the *Plain Dealer*'s staff, with numerous tough stories to his credit. A tall, studious young man with curly dark brown hair, deep-set eyes, and a full beard, Bogdanich inspired trust among his editors and fellow reporters. He was both talented and level-headed. He was no one's fool.

Although he had been born in Chicago and raised in nearby Gary, Indiana, Bogdanich was enticed by Cleveland's political roguishness and blatant corruption when he was a journalism student, studying in the Kiplinger program for public-affairs reporting at Ohio State University. As a student, Bogdanich searched through reams of documents and court records to study the relationship among the Teamsters union, organized crime, and the Cleveland Establishment. From the campus in Columbus, Ohio, he would drive up to Cleveland to read through records for hours, day after day. He began to see patterns of how things worked in Cleveland

and this understanding helped him land a job with the *Cleveland Press,* where he worked for two and a half years.

"That's what brought me to Cleveland—the Teamsters and organized crime and corruption," recalls Bogdanich. "It was such a thoroughly corrupt city that it was just fun." When the *Plain Dealer* made an offer, Bogdanich considered the ailing financial condition of the *Press* and decided it was a good time to jump. He became the first hire the *Plain Dealer* had made directly from the *Press* in recent memory.

Everything was going well for Bogdanich until the subject turned to Jackie Presser, the man being pushed by Mafia leaders in both Cleveland and New York for the presidency of the nation's largest union. From the moment he was given that assignment in mid-1981 and for the next several months, Bogdanich would become involved in a story of remarkable intrigue—one far greater than what would ever appear in the *Plain Dealer*. It would underline some of the darkest aspects of Si Newhouse's friendship with Roy Cohn and would expose Cohn's corrosive influence on the Newhouse newspapers. Cohn's role as a go-between with the mob and Newhouse officials would threaten to ruin Bogdanich's reputation as a reporter and forever change his life. And when the full story was eventually revealed years later in federal court, even Bogdanich was stunned at how Newhouse and his top editors had allowed the Mafia virtually to dictate a front-page story in their paper to please Jackie Presser.

Yet the truth about Jackie Presser was just one of several behind-the-scenes dramas at the *Cleveland Plain Dealer* during the 1980s that were never fully told to its readers. The Presser incident can be examined only against the larger backdrop of Si Newhouse's attempt to secure a virtual monopoly on daily newspapering in Cleveland—a prize undoubtedly worth millions of dollars in added revenues for the Newhouse media empire. The series of ethical compromises and other legally questionable actions in Cleveland would prompt a federal criminal antitrust investigation into the deal crafted by Si Newhouse. Overall, this air of manipulation and editorial compromise surrounding the *Plain Dealer* compelled some of its most talented journalists to leave and opened the door for advertisers to influence unduly news judgments through the early 1990s.

What happened in Cleveland, however, would have consequences far beyond the shattering of Newhouse's image as a benign out-of-town owner with a professed hands-off editorial policy. It permanently set in place the way in which Cleveland's citizenry obtains vitally important newspaper information about their region, the twelfth-largest in the United States. More importantly, what happened at the *Plain Dealer* was a perverse and powerful warning to Americans concerned about the integrity of their news media and how it can be improperly tainted and professionally compromised. In an era in which many of America's major cities are increasingly serviced by only one daily newspaper—acting in each city like private utilities with almost complete control on the printed word—the lessons were indeed profound. The actions in Cleveland would forever mark Si Newhouse and his company as unworthy stewards of a public trust, a flawed vessel for so important a task as the free flow of information in a democratic society. And with so much at stake, it raises the question of what an informed public would do about it if only they knew the full extent of the story.

The *Cleveland Plain Dealer* was one of the newspapers on Si Newhouse's "paper route," a jocular reference inside the company to the way in which the Newhouses divided their newspaper chain. Each family member, including Si, was responsible for overseeing a portion of it. Si was accustomed to flying to these newspapers for a day or two to be briefed by the family's handpicked executives and would then relay his findings to the Newhouse's main offices in New York. Thursday was usually the day Si flew to Cleveland, a pattern repeated for years, even after he became the top executive at Condé Nast. Peter Diamandis, a former Condé Nast publisher, said Sam Newhouse "extracted a deal from Si that the only way Si could work at Condé Nast was if he went to Cleveland every Wednesday night and worked on the *Plain Dealer* on Thursday." After flying back to La Guardia, Si was in his Condé Nast office by Friday morning. "He was never there on Thursdays and this went on for years," said Diamandis, "even after Sam's death."

When Sam Newhouse died in 1979, Si continued to share the responsibility for the Cleveland property, along with his uncle, Norman, who was a more frequent visitor. Except for these behind-the-scenes updates by the Newhouses, everything at the *Plain Dealer* made it appear that publisher Thomas Vail was still in charge.

Vail took command of the *Plain Dealer* in 1963 when it was reorganized following a bitter 129-day strike. His tenure began with great promise. As a thirty-six-year-old newspaper executive, Vail was determined to infuse more life into the sleepy *Plain Dealer* by recruiting a team of Young Turks with a taste for investigative journalism. Vail's roots were deep. He was the great-grandson of Liberty E. Holden, a gold-mine millionaire who bought the *Plain Dealer* in 1885 and transformed it from a struggling weekly into one of the Midwest's most influential daily newspapers. After Holden's death in 1912, the paper was bequeathed to his five children and their heirs. But in 1967, the holding company that controlled the paper, the Forest City Publishing Company—by then owned among several family members and trusts that were unhappy about their fragmented earnings— decided to accept Sam Newhouse's unprecedented buyout offer. The sale of the *Plain Dealer* for $50 million was heralded in a front-page *New York Times* story as "the highest price ever paid for a single newspaper in the history of American journalism."

As with other Newhouse dailies, the *Cleveland Plain Dealer* appeared to remain under local management—with Vail still at the top of the masthead—even though the paper's purse strings were held firmly in New York. "Complete control of The Plain Dealer, its business, personnel, and editorial policies have been left in my hands," Vail said in an interview after the paper was sold.

In those rare moments when he commented publicly for the company, Si Newhouse seemed a preacher of his father's local autonomy doctrine. "We are essentially a nonbureaucratic, decentralized, highly autonomous organization, with each unit acting very much on its own initiative but with personal or indirect contact with various members of the family," Si Newhouse told *Business Week* in the mid-1970s in his own monochromatic version of the family's formula for success. "We don't tie down different elements in our organization to formulas or limit their thinking to ground rules coming out of a center."

In the early 1980s, Si Newhouse's Manhattan world of glossy magazines, haute couture, and power lunches seemed light years away from the gritty work, lunch-pail lunches and everyday concerns of the readers of the *Cleveland Plain Dealer,* the largest daily newspaper in the state of Ohio. At the time, Cleveland was in the throes of a deep recession and its local government seemed gripped by the forces of racial division, rampant corruption, and the pervasive influence of organized crime in many facets of urban life.

Unlike many American cities, however, Cleveland still had two daily newspapers, which in 1981 were locked in a costly war for readers and advertisers. For a short time, the vigorous competition between the *Plain Dealer* and the financially ailing *Cleveland Press* seemed good news for Cleveland's reading public and for its need to understand what was going on in that complex industrial city. The competition was also good news for young reporters like Bogdanich, who was eager to pursue investigative stories for the *Plain Dealer*. In early 1981, when the *Plain Dealer* began hearing corruption rumors about Jackie Presser—then the regional head of the Teamsters union and a potential future president of the national organization—the newspaper's executive editor, Dave Hopcraft, decided to pair Bogdanich with another reporter, Mairy Jayn Woge, to investigate and determine the truth.

Any major story about the Teamsters and organized crime, especially one involving Jackie Presser, seemed like a natural for Bogdanich. From his earlier reporting, though, he knew that dealing with Presser would be difficult. This smooth and media-savvy Teamsters official had retained two public-relations people to try to deflect nosy reporters such as Bogdanich. Jackie Presser, like his father, who also had been a powerful Teamsters official, was very much a part of the power structure in Cleveland. Bogdanich, who came from a working-class background, was appalled by the excess and sheer greed of the Teamster leader. The rank-and-file members of the union made a mere pittance compared to Presser's income. So when Hopcraft told Bogdanich about the assignment, he readily accepted, eager to expose Presser's methods. What Bogdanich didn't know at that time, however, was that the management of the *Plain Dealer* was already involved in secret discussions with Presser.

For months, Presser, his lawyers, and his public-relations experts had been complaining privately to Hopcraft about the journalistic practices of Mairy Jayn Woge. They considered her unfair and biased, and they were determined to get her off the Presser story. An energetic woman in her fifties, Woge nevertheless was very well wired into the Teamsters' labyrinthine machinery. She had cultivated several excellent sources who knew about Presser and his inside deals. Sometimes she appeared to know more than the FBI. "She had connections everywhere," recalled Bogdanich, who would help verify Mairy Jayn's reporting and provide the writing skill and scope that these high-profile stories would demand.

But neither reporter was aware that Hopcraft had been privately talking with Presser and his surrogates for months. When he offered the assignment to Bogdanich, it was in large measure because Hopcraft shared Presser's concerns about Woge. If Woge was somehow too close to government investigators or to dissident Teamster members anxious to push Presser out of the union, then Hopcraft figured it was prudent to have another reporter involved in the story. "Jackie had said all these things to me over the years, how there was some connection between [Mairy Jayn] and some of the people who [were Presser's enemies]," Hopcraft told James Neff, the former *Cleveland Plain Dealer* reporter who first detailed the paper's capitulation to Presser in his 1989 biography about the Teamsters leader. "They clearly saw her as someone being used by the government and the gangster element of the Teamsters to weaken Jackie and solidify whatever control they did or didn't have on the union. I think she is the kind of person who could be used. I believed it. That's why I got Walt involved in it. Because nobody's going to use Walt." (Hopcraft, now a public-relations man in Cleveland, declined to be interviewed, except to confirm Neff's account of the story. "Jim Neff had it right in his book," he said.)

Once the two reporters were put on the trail together, it didn't take long to confirm rumors that Jackie Presser had been an informant for the FBI, serving as a mole inside the Teamster organization as he rose in the national ranks. The story was remarkably sensitive. Even with FBI agents whom Bogdanich knew and trusted, he noticed an uneasiness. They acted very peculiar whenever the subject of Presser came up. The two reporters interviewed several people in law enforcement and every conversation was taped so there would be no misunderstanding about what was said. Sometimes, Bogdanich would listen to Mairy Jayn's interviews and then go confirm them with his own FBI sources. After a time, Bogdanich became convinced Presser was an informer. Quickly, they developed a two-part series that appeared in their paper in late August 1981.

The first story detailed how Presser received $300,000 in kickbacks from a Las Vegas public-relations firm hired by the Teamsters to upgrade the union's image. The story was based on a sworn deposition by a partner in the P.R. firm and backed up by other interviews and documents. On the face of it, the first-day kickback story seemed the most important, prompting the Justice Department to conduct a criminal probe. The next day, Presser's denials of the kickback charges were duly noted in a sidebar story accompanying the second part of the *Plain Dealer*'s series.

But that second part of the series would prove to be a story much more troublesome to both Presser and the two reporters who wrote it. CHARGES DIDN'T STOP PRESSER AS A U.S. INFORMER read the front-page headline above that story by Bogdanich and Woge. Based on federal sources and court records, the article showed how Jackie Presser and his late father, William E. Presser, were informants for the Internal Revenue Service starting in 1971 and that Jackie Presser also had been an informant for the FBI during the latter half of the 1970s. The well-documented stories were picked up by newspapers across the nation and seemed to please the *Plain Dealer*'s upper management.

"Good job," publisher Vail told Bogdanich when he spotted him in the newsroom after the stories appeared.

The exposé, particularly the story documenting Jackie Presser's role as a government informant, caused a strong undercurrent of concern in both federal law enforcement and within the upper echelon of the Mafia. These stories, like some huge gong, at first stunned those within its reach and continued reverberating for what seemed a very long time. Over several months, they would set in motion a series of events that would directly include several top Mafia leaders, Roy Cohn, and the Newhouses themselves. And the product of this strange alliance would be another front-page *Plain Dealer* story—appearing more than a year after the original stories outlining Presser's corruption—that repudiated the essential truth of Bogdanich and Woge's stories.

For years, there were rumors within Mafia circles, a repeated suspicion that Jackie Presser was an informant and could not be trusted. This view was certainly shared by Mafia leaders in Chicago, who objected to the idea of Presser someday becoming the national president of the Teamsters union. For the mob, the Teamsters, with their multimillion-dollar pension and welfare fund, was a virtual cornucopia of corruption, a treasure chest of loans and financial schemes for all sorts of questionable ventures. It was too important to be left in the hands of a snitch, someone who could not be trusted.

But it seemed inevitable that the Teamsters would fall eventually into Presser's hands. In 1981, Frank Fitzsimmons, then president of the Teamsters, died after a long bout with cancer. He was replaced by Roy L. Williams, who was being secretly promoted and controlled by the Chicago mob. The other possible contender for the job had been Jackie Presser.

Those who were backing Presser included both Maishe Rockman, who had long-standing ties to the Cleveland Mafia and had known Jackie for most of his life, and an even more powerful mob figure, Anthony "Fat Tony" Salerno, the cigar-chomping chief of New York's Genovese crime family. These two mobsters wanted Jackie Presser simply because they could control him.

Presser's fortunes improved when Roy Williams faced the unfortunate calamity of a federal indictment shortly into his tenure as president of the Teamsters. Williams was charged with other top union officials in a conspiracy to offer bribes to a U.S. senator. By the spring of 1982, the common wisdom among Mafia leaders was that Williams would soon be headed for prison and they should look to promote a successor. Once again, the door to the Teamsters presidency was opened to Presser.

This time, Presser made every effort to add to his considerable political clout, including his success in getting the Teamsters support for Ronald Reagan in 1980. In return, Reagan later appointed Presser to his presidential transition team. One of the few remaining obstacles to Presser's ascendancy was the festering suspicion that he was a government stool pigeon. To quell these doubts, Maishe Rockman traveled to Chicago to personally assure Joey Aiuppa, the top Mafia boss there, that he had known Presser for years and was sure that he wasn't a government snitch. Presser could be trusted and controlled just like Roy Williams, Rockman promised. After a few days, Chicago indicated it would go along, but only reluctantly. Somehow, in any way possible, it seemed the *Plain Dealer*'s series documenting Presser's actions as an FBI informer had to be denied.

The mob's dilemma was discussed at a secret meeting in New York, where Presser's two godfathers, Maishe Rockman and Fat Tony Salerno, tried to figure out a way to refute the newspaper's stories.

When he wasn't at his Manhattan apartment, his one-hundred-acre estate in upstate New York, or at his penthouse apartment in Miami, Salerno was at his East Harlem social club, overseeing the mob's massive loan-sharking and gambling operations and helping to control the Teamsters union. Government bugs were secretly recording the conversation inside the social club, where investigators would later find a Teamsters membership directory among Salerno's possessions.

"You know anybody connected with the *Plain Dealer*?" Rockman asked Salerno at a meeting taped inside a restaurant near Salerno's Palma Boys Social Club on 116th Street in East Harlem.

"No, I don't," said Salerno, the nearly seventy-year-old New York mob boss. "But wait a minute, I'll try and find out."

As federal court testimony would later show, Salerno instructed one of his top aides to call Roy Cohn. For years, Cohn had served as a special counselor to the Mafia don, instructing Salerno on the legal niceties that might disrupt his gravy train of illegal acts. Cohn even allowed Salerno to use his Manhattan town house—which also served as home to Cohn's law offices—as a safe haven, free from government wiretaps, where Salerno could conduct meetings with other mobsters. Cohn performed similar legal services for Salerno as he had for Carmine Galante, another Mafia don who was fond of cigars and was found with the remnants of one still between his teeth when he was shot dead a few years earlier in the garden of a Brooklyn restaurant.

After speaking with Cohn on the telephone, Salerno was quite pleased. Once again, Roy Cohn had proved he could do the trick. Salerno told his visiting mafiosi from Cleveland—Rockman and his underboss, Angelo Lonardo—about their remarkable stroke of good luck. Not only was Roy Cohn serving as Salerno's lawyer but he was also a lawyer for the owners of the *Cleveland Plain Dealer*. The remarkable stroke of luck was delightful news, as if divine providence was shining on the Palma Boys Social Club.

"Tony . . . asked Roy Cohn if he knew who owned the Plain Dealer or was connected with the Plain Dealer," Lonardo would later testify as a government witness in the 1987 commission trial. "He [Cohn] says, 'Well I represent him.' And Tony Salerno told him, told Roy Cohn, that he would talk to him about it."

Salerno didn't want to mention the Presser matter over the telephone, fearing—with more than ample justification—that his conversations were being recorded by the government. The New York Mafia boss set up a meeting with Cohn, Maishe Rockman, and himself—which was recorded by government surveillance cameras. Inside Cohn's office, the Cleveland mobster talked about the trouble that the *Plain Dealer*'s articles had caused for Jackie Presser. Rockman said he wanted a front-page retraction, claiming that Presser wasn't a government informer.

This request was a tall order even for Roy Cohn, who had been able to influence the content of Newhouse publications in the past. Whether something was true was rarely of consequence to Cohn, the master manipulator. But this wasn't some political endorsement or some puff-piece feature initiated at Roy's request. In effect, the mob was demanding that a major American newspaper deny something perfectly true and that Cohn employ his influence with Newhouse to undermine the credibility of his own newspaper.

As the meeting with Salerno and Rockman ended, Cohn assured them that "he would speak to his client about a retraction," as Lonardo later told the FBI. (Lonardo, who was sentenced to life for directing mob murders and drug trafficking in Cleveland, later became an important federal witness in the government's commission trial in New York against Salerno and other mob figures.)

Once set in motion by Roy Cohn, the negotiations on the retraction were largely handled by three people—Charles Sabin, the Newhouse lawyer who worked out of the Condé Nast building in New York; John Climaco, the attorney for Presser; and Dave Hopcraft, who realized it would be his job to put a story to Jackie Presser's liking in the Cleveland paper.

But Si Newhouse was the crucial link in the mob's attempt to get a front-page retraction about Presser, based on what Dave Hopcraft told author Jim Neff. "Here's how the play went—from Climaco to Roy Cohn to Si Newhouse to Charley Sabin and Norman Newhouse," recalled Hopcraft. Si reportedly "wasn't very amendable right away" but eventually he was convinced to go along.

The carrier pigeon was Norman Newhouse, Si's amiable bow-tied uncle, who told Hopcraft that he must run a front-page story about Presser. Norman was good at taking orders. In 1967, after years of living in the New York City area, Norman moved to New Orleans, where his family "paper route" expanded to include constant flights to the *Plain Dealer* and overseeing the *New Orleans Times-Picayune* and other smaller Newhouse papers in the South. At that time, Sam Newhouse decided at a family meeting that one of them had to move to watch their properties in that region. "They looked at me, and I said, 'I'm ready.' And so we came down the following Wednesday," Norman later recalled.

To make sure the deed was done, Newhouse's lawyer flew out to Cleveland and, over dinner with Vail and Hopcraft, repeated Presser's denials about the $300,000 in kickbacks and about being a government informer. Pressed by his newspaper bosses and Si Newhouse's own attorney, Hopcraft said he would run a face-saving story about Presser if the government would say that it had dropped its investigation of the kickback scheme. This would be in keeping with *Plain Dealer* practice to cover acquittals with as much prominence as the original charge. In an extraordinary act, Hopcraft later called and convinced David Margolis, then head of the Justice Department's organized-crime section, to write a letter in July 1982 to Presser's attorney saying that their investigation had ended. In effect, the stories by Walt Bogdanich and Mairy Jayn Woge were being torpedoed by their own editor. The actual reason why the government dropped its probe of the kickbacks was that the seven-year statute of limitations on such a crime had expired. But that seemed of little consequence to Hopcraft, who was pressured to make sure a story refuting the Presser exposé appeared in the *Plain Dealer*.

In a sense, the story about Jackie Presser would come full circle on a Thursday in early October 1982, degenerating from a genuine journalistic triumph into what would become a corrupting tragedy leaving many embittered. On that day, Hopcraft called Bogdanich and they discussed the possibility of running an update about the government's investigation into Jackie Presser's alleged kickback scheme.

"I hear the investigation has run its course, and they are not going to indict him," Hopcraft told his reporter. He didn't let on how he knew this fact.

"Yeah, I'm sort of hearing the same thing," Bogdanich said.

"Well, maybe we ought to write a story about it."

Bogdanich agreed, adding that "my information is that the reason they are not going to do it is that they couldn't find anything within the statute of limitations." At the time, Bogdanich felt it was fair to write an update about the federal probe, since they had written so much negatively about Presser. "No big deal, that's the fair thing to do," Bogdanich told his editor.

So Bogdanich went back to his desk and wrote the story, putting in the reason why the case hadn't gone anywhere. At one point, Bogdanich showed his editor a rough draft and Hopcraft thanked him for it. From there, things became quite strange.

Hopcraft took much longer than would be usual with such a story. Eventually, Bogdanich wandered over to the editor's desk to inquire about it. Hopcraft seemed worried and anxious.

"The Newhouses are interested in this. . . . New York is interested in this," Hopcraft told him. "We need to put something more in here."

"Like what?"

Bogdanich was told to take one more try at the story and he again handed it in. Hopcraft later added more detail and some rambling quotes from Presser's lawyer, Climaco, and deleted some of the reasons that Bogdanich had cited as to why the government probe had been dropped. When Bogdanich finally got to see the new Hopcraft-revised story, he was outraged. As he would later tell friends, "It was a totally different story— and it was an apology."

As Bogdanich eventually learned, the FBI was also anxious not to have Presser publicly identified as an informer. He was a good source involved in several ongoing criminal investigations, including one probe that eventually resulted in the conviction of his longtime mentor, Maishe Rockman. Just as there was no honor among mobsters, there also appeared to be little among the journalistic regime at the *Plain Dealer*.

The following day, Bogdanich made a valiant appeal to his editors to stick by the original exposé. "This is a totally bogus story from top to bottom," he argued with them.

Hopcraft and other senior editors assured Bogdanich that he should trust their judgment. "We're working on it," one editor told him. "Just be quiet."

By then, it was Friday afternoon, and Bogdanich realized that people would be going home soon. If the *Plain Dealer* editors were to run such a story, there would be little time for any objection by Bogdanich and his fellow staffers. At that moment, he felt an awful sense of dread, as if he was about to become the fall guy in some melodramatic plot he still didn't understand fully. Once more, he approached Hopcraft's desk.

"Why are you doing this? You know this isn't true. I'll show you the tapes, and the documents," Bogdanich pleaded.

"I know you have it, Walt," Hopcraft replied, not completely unsympathetic. "But I'm not interested in seeing them."

Nor was anyone else in the *Plain Dealer* management. Bogdanich realized their dilemma, for these same editors who had supported him a year ago were now being told by the owners in New York that they would have to rework the original story. Up until then, Bogdanich had thought of Hopcraft and other editors as honorable journalists who would eventually make sure the right thing was done. But now, he realized that his trust had been betrayed and his own reputation was about to be ruined. He decided to tell an influential member of the newsroom about what was going on with the Presser story, and the word of the cover-up spread like wildfire. Reporters gathered in small groups inside the newsroom, which effectively stopped functioning that afternoon. The word was that a crooked deal was afoot.

When the rumors reached the editors' desks, they became upset with Bogdanich. One came over to his desk, visibly angry. "I told you not to say anything public," the editor told him.

"Hey, look, at this point, everyone's on their own . . . obviously," Bogdanich replied. "I have to do what's right. You're going to publish this crooked story and the truth has to be known."

On Saturday morning, before the deadline for the *Plain Dealer*'s massive Sunday edition, Bogdanich came back to the newsroom to meet with Hopcraft and some of the lower-echelon editors, arguing about the story and what it was going to say. Only one of the editors seemed to side with Bogdanich's view, though Hopcraft was beginning to waver. Clearly, the question for these Newhouse editors was whether they were going to refuse to go along and maybe be fired or forced to resign or to do what was ordered of them. The answer still hadn't been determined when Bogdanich left the newsroom to go home that Saturday afternoon.

The article was to appear the next day, which happened to be the date of Walt's birthday, October 10. As was their custom, Walt and his wife planned to go out to celebrate, and they were joined by reporter James Neff and his wife at a French restaurant. Throughout the evening, as Bogdanich later told friends, he kept telephoning the newsroom to find out whether the story was going to run. Eventually, he learned, the story— without Bogdanich's byline—appeared in the newspaper's first edition.

The front-page article was at best misleading, and in some places, an outright falsehood regarding Presser's status as an FBI informant. The letter from Margolis—the one Hopcraft had urged him to write—was cited prominently in the story, saying "please be advised that the Department of Justice considers this matter closed." The story put much of the blame for the Presser exposé on a convict named Harry Haler, who was hired by a company doing public relations for the Teamsters. Haler claimed in a civil lawsuit that he had kicked back part of his salary to Presser. The two reporters, Bogdanich and Woge, had independently verified the kickback accusations, as well as their other story, which declared that Presser was a government informant. In the new upside-down version of the truth, however, the *Plain Dealer* quoted Presser's lawyer,

Climaco: "The IRS as well as the Justice Department have advised me that Jackie and William Presser have never acted as informants."

Presser was delighted by the *Plain Dealer* story, which was all but a formal correction and written apology. He waved the phony story in triumph when he later met the FBI agents who had used him as an informant. True to form, Jackie Presser still managed to complain that the *Plain Dealer* story was not "above the fold" (the top half of the newspaper's front page), where the original exposé had appeared. At a press conference where TV reporters and the city's other media pounced on what appeared to be the *Plain Dealer*'s mea culpa, Presser gloated. He boasted to the assembled journalists how Hopcraft had agreed with his complaints concerning reporter Mairy Jayn Woge. "He [Hopcraft] says, 'I concur with you and I'm going to put another reporter on with her because I question the credibility of Mairy Jayn,' " the crooked union leader declared.

Hopcraft's betrayal of his staff was underlined in Presser's own words and in the deliberately misleading story that he changed and edited and put into the newspaper for all to read and believe. He even quoted himself in the article. "Reporters and editors who prepared the story adhered to the highest of journalistic standards in preparing the articles in question," Hopcraft said about the original story, before pulling the rug out from his own reporters.

The issue was not dead with the *Plain Dealer* staff, however. In reaction to what the Newhouse-controlled management had done—and as a way of trying to "balance" the TV coverage about the Presser press conference—about fifty *Plain Dealer* reporters, editors, and other staff members marched with picket signs and chanted in protest outside the front offices of their own newspaper. The staff's moral disgust and outrage could barely be contained. Parodying the paper's advertising slogan—"When the News Breaks, We Put It Together," one protest sign proclaimed, WHEN THE NEWS BREAKS, WE APOLOGIZE. The Newspaper Guild in Cleveland, which had a long history of promoting solid journalistic standards as well as union issues of wages and benefits, supported the picketing. Another sign, again playing off the *Plain Dealer*'s marketing boast as the state's biggest newspaper, put it as Lincoln Steffens might have: OHIO'S LARGEST SHAME.

The staff later demanded to meet with Hopcraft so he could explain his actions concerning the Presser story. Hopcraft eventually agreed to sit down with a small delegation of reporters. At the *Plain Dealer*, editorial integrity and true local autonomy were something the hired hands would have to insist upon. In a newsroom memo, Hopcraft said reporters should not "bite the hand that feeds them" and that "disloyal" acts like speaking against the *Plain Dealer* could lead to dismissal. In its account of the *Plain Dealer*'s civil war over the story, *Cleveland Magazine* observed that Presser "was the clear winner." The magazine noted that publisher Thomas Vail's attention during the Presser fiasco was focused on another matter—why he hadn't been invited to a White House dinner by President Reagan.

A few theorized that the Newhouses caved in because of Presser's threat of a libel lawsuit and the sizable cost of defending the stories through a protracted legal battle. For all of his bluster, Presser was unlikely to bring such a legal action, one that would force him to reveal many of his secrets and one that he stood little chance of winning legally. In the 1980s, however, the countless stories of multimillion-dollar libel awards against newspapers seemed to chill a number of bottom line–oriented news organizations like the Newhouse newspaper chain. Another explanation shared by more reporters was that the Newhouses were fearful of upsetting the unions controlled by Presser that delivered the *Plain Dealer* at doorsteps every day. This seemed to make the most sense to reporters who wondered why their newspapers had acted so disgracefully. Even though they heard Roy Cohn was somehow involved, Bogdanich and the paper's reporters didn't realize the retraction story—when fully traced to its point of origin—was concocted at the request of two Mafia bosses.

Jackie Presser knew it, though. When the *Plain Dealer*'s retraction appeared, Presser managed to make sure that the clipping was sent to Fat Tony Salerno, whose favorite lawyer, Roy Cohn, a consigliere without portfolio, had made it all happen. Like some successful public-relations agent who had hit pay dirt, the New York Mafia don sent copies of the story he helped to plant in Newhouse's paper to his fellow mafiosi in Chicago, sure they still doubted Presser's claims that he was not an informant. When Bogdanich and Woge's stories first appeared and were picked up nationally, Salerno was heard complaining on government surveillance tapes: "Did you read in the papers that Jack Presser is a stool pigeon for the government? These fucking Chicago guys are going to knock my brains in." But after putting Roy Cohn on the job to get a retraction from the Newhouses' Cleveland paper, Salerno expressed his satisfaction with the results and could be heard saying, "So I sent the fucking paper to Chicago."

Thus, with help from the Newhouses as well as both the mob and federal law-enforcement authorities, the path was cleared for Jackie Presser to become the next national Teamsters president. In April 1983, Roy Williams was convicted in the attempted bribery case involving Senator Howard Cannon—a criminal charge that Presser, as a secret government informant, had helped the FBI to secure a few years earlier. Williams was forced to step down. Soon afterward, Presser took power, opening the doors to the mob bosses who wanted to control the union.

In 1986, Presser was eventually indicted on racketeering and embezzlement charges that he pocketed $700,000 for nonexistent "ghost" employees in his local Cleveland office. That same year, the President's organized crime commission said in a lengthy report that Presser would not have become Teamsters president without the help of New York Mafia leader Anthony Salerno, a man who once was heard to say, "without me, there wouldn't be no mob." While he was awaiting trial, Presser was paid more than $800,000 in annual salary from the Teamsters, but he died from brain cancer before the case could go before a jury.

However, it was another mob-related trial that would reveal publicly how Cohn and Salerno had induced the Newhouse-owned *Plain Dealer* to run the phony story about Jackie Presser.

During the late 1980s, federal authorities in New York conducted a series of trials against the top bosses of several New York Mafia crime families, highly publicized investigations that became known as the "commission trials." After reviewing almost four hundred tapes taken from Salerno's headquarters and boxes of other surveillance evidence, prosecutors were able to convict Salerno and other top bosses of forming a "commission" to oversee the mob's racketeering. The abundant proof of the Mafia's grip on the nation's largest union echoed the conclusions reached nearly thirty years earlier by Robert Kennedy, Cohn's old nemesis. After three years as chief counsel to the McClellan committee in the late 1950s, Kennedy called the Teamsters "the most powerful institution in the country, aside from the United States government itself."

In the federal government's second commission trial in 1988—which this time dealt with corruption inside the Teamsters union—federal authorities made public the private conversations inside Salerno's mob headquarters. On these government-recorded tapes, the Mafia leader can be heard conspiring to fix the Presser story with the help of Roy Cohn. In preparing for this second trial against Salerno, Assistant U.S. Attorney Mark Hellerer became well acquainted with the nexus of power among the Teamsters, organized crime, crooked politicians, and greedy businessmen. Hellerer said the mob chieftains who backed Jackie Presser felt a front-page retraction in the *Plain Dealer* was essential to removing the bull's eye from their man's chest. As a rumored government informer, Presser was almost certain to wind up dead. "It was of great concern to the organized-crime people who had influence in the Teamsters union," said Hellerer. "The proof at trial showed that Presser was felt to be Cleveland's boy, and they were pushing him to get the top spot. And they got Salerno of the Genovese family to back him. They were concerned that this story about Presser being an FBI informant might be true, and they took steps to squelch the story. Otherwise, it would have allowed any family—in Chicago or wherever else—to rise to the top spot and have a lot of influence with the Teamsters."

After watching how Mafia leaders and crooked lawyers like Roy Cohn operated during the 1980s, prosecutor Hellerer said he learned that even fundamental institutions like an American daily newspaper are not immune from the reach of the mob. Nor did the federal prosecutor express any surprise that a billionaire newspaper owner like Si Newhouse would fail to stop such a purposeful charade. "I don't think it's wild at all,"

Hellerer said after recalling how the Presser story was fixed. "I think it's how Roy Cohn did business, and I think it's how newspapers do business. The news is a very malleable thing and certain people have a lot of influence on how it is reported, and it's a great rare day when a full and truthful story comes out in the media. And I would say this is a particularly good example of it. That's my jaded view of how things happened. It's my understanding that the reporters there at the *Plain Dealer* were upset . . . and with good reason."

Despite the *Plain Dealer*'s cover-up, federal authorities, through a series of stunning courtroom maneuvers in the late 1980s, finally began to remove permanently elements of organized crime from the top ranks of the Teamsters. At the same time of the phony Presser story, however, there was emerging another criminal investigation by U.S. Justice Department officials that was directly aimed at the *Plain Dealer* and would prove to be equally murky.

This was a complex antitrust investigation that senior Justice Department officials in Washington, D.C., failed to pursue vigorously and, according to the two local federal prosecutors involved in it, mishandled. It was a dispute with millions of dollars at stake for the Newhouse empire, one that such *Plain Dealer* reporters as Walt Bogdanich had little or no idea about at the time. Yet this drama served as the financial backdrop needed to understand the pressures inside the *Plain Dealer* newsroom as Bogdanich and Woge pursued allegations against Presser, the Teamster leader whose members each day drove the trucks that delivered their newspaper. The government's botched investigation into Newhouse's attempt to secure an all-but-total monopoly on daily newspapering in Cleveland would have profound and long-lasting consequences for the city and would lead directly to the death of the *Plain Dealer*'s only competition, the *Cleveland Press*.

And unlike the scheme to kill the Presser exposé, this was a deal with Si Newhouse's signature on it.

In the early 1980s, Joseph E. Cole suddenly appeared as a savior, as if descending from some journalism heaven, to keep Cleveland from becoming a one-newspaper town. To hear him speak, Cole—the overweight, balding sixty-five-year-old manufacturer of keys who had recently bought the nearly comatose *Cleveland Press*—was the man who could save the city from the brink. Or, at the very least, Cole spoke as though he could. Certainly no one had any idea that Cole would strike a secret deal with Si Newhouse to kill his own newspaper.

Quite the contrary, Cole went out of his way to make it appear he would never concede to Newhouse's mammoth morning daily. In May 1981, as the keynote speaker before three hundred business executives at the annual Cleveland Business Show and Management Conference, Cole invoked images of his political hero, John F. Kennedy, and talked of a future that called for "new vision and new dangers, new frontiers and permanent crisis, suffering and achievement."

At times, Cole's inspirational message seemed almost Zen-like, as if Kahlil Gibran had come to Cleveland. "He is powerless, however exalted his station, if he believes that he can impose his will," he intoned, as if quoting from the Book of Cole. "He is all powerful, no matter how lowly, if he knows himself to be responsible." Before he wandered too far, Cole translated his lofty thoughts into the very real newspaper battle he had on his hands with the *Plain Dealer*. "Meaning no offense to my esteemed competitor on Superior Avenue, I bought The Press to remove the thorny temptations that might confront him if his were the only voice, his the only rostrum, his the only philosophy in town," Cole warned. "A publisher's potential for mischief is no less than that of anyone else if the conditions are right. Give a publisher—or anyone else for that matter—a monopoly and you run a very real risk of seeing a square deal converted into a rigged deal . . . a plain deal into a raw deal. Simply said, I don't like monopolies."

Hollywood couldn't have directed a better scene for Cole. His speech was a call to arms for freedom of expression, spirited discussion, and a full and varied account of daily life by two vigorous newspapers with the city's best interests in mind. Cole took his banner and made it his own. "I was not ready to stand by and idly lament while one of our great institutions perished," he proclaimed. "Cleveland is too great a city to suffer the humiliation of being a one-newspaper town."

Seven months earlier, Cole had stepped forward to buy the ailing *Cleveland Press*, proclaiming his love for his city and the concept of a two-newspaper town. After 102 years, the Scripps Howard newspaper chain had decided to shed the money-losing afternoon paper, which had reportedly lost as much as $5 million a year when Joseph Cole emerged as its only suitor. When he heard the paper was for sale, Cole called the owners of the Scripps company and worked out a deal in which he bought the *Press* and assumed its liabilities for an estimated $1 million. Yes, this was a risk, he told the business crowd, but one well worth taking.

"I bought it, too, in the full knowledge of a publisher's potential to make an enduring contribution—both materially and spiritually—to the common good," Cole assured them, with apparent conviction. "The prospects for civic good far outweighed the potential of personal economic risk."

Compared to past transactions involving Joseph Cole, the deal for the *Cleveland Press* was fairly straightforward. A complicated series of buyouts had allowed Cole to put together the Cole National Corporation, a Cleveland-based company worth millions of dollars. This fortune was built largely on the money scratched together from small key-duplicating machines placed in hardware shops and Sears department stores across the land. Ever the enterprising entrepreneur, Cole was always looking for the next big deal or other ways to make money. When he owned a small part of the Cleveland Indians major-league team, for example, he reportedly discussed his intensions of taking a tax write-off by depreciating baseball players.

In the late 1950s, Cole met John F. Kennedy and soon switched his Republican registration to Democrat, contributing heavily to Kennedy's presidential campaign. He later became a prominent supporter of Hubert Humphrey in 1968, hoping to be appointed to the Court of St. James if Humphrey was elected president. Again in the 1972 campaign, Cole floated a $250,000 loan to the former vice president and later became finance chairman of the Democratic National Committee. His political ambitions were viewed as part of Cole's desire to be recognized, to be accorded some degree of prestige. Owning a newspaper—the lone underdog voice in his hometown—seemed another way to satisfy that desire.

"I'll tell you this—the *Cleveland Press* is going to be run on the highest ethical and moral basis that exists," Cole told a magazine writer when he purchased the paper. "It is clear to me and to those associated with me that in order to make this venture a success, this newspaper, above all, has to be a journal of integrity. . . . I know how important it is for me not to involve my personal interests in the running of the newspaper."

But what the audience at the May 1981 business show didn't know—the fact that Cole never mentioned in his inspired speech about newspaper competition—was that privately he had already approached his rival, Si Newhouse, with a plan to merge the operations of the two papers. Indeed, as Si would later testify, Cole approached him with a plan almost as soon as he bought the *Cleveland Press*.

While they were both in Florida in December 1980, Cole telephoned Newhouse, shortly after his purchase of the *Cleveland Press*, to discuss the possibility of a joint venture. Si Newhouse agreed to go over to Cole's Palm Beach estate, not far from the Newhouse family's own property in the same Florida enclave for the wealthy.

As the two men spoke, far from the cold environs of Cleveland, Cole confided why he had purchased the newspaper. He also expressed his surprise at the poor condition of the paper once he took over.

"Look, I'm an amateur at this thing and I don't really know much about the newspaper business," Si Newhouse later recalled Cole telling him. "But I have got some people there who are handling things for me and they tell me that some newspapers in competitive markets get together and they do some collaboration. I don't know exactly what it's called, but don't you think we ought to be talking about something like that in Cleveland?"

Newhouse was unmoved. Cole pressed him further.

"I am sure you have just as much a problem as we do and wouldn't it be in our mutual interests?" Cole asked.

Newhouse later would say Cole's initial offer was too vague and didn't specify exactly what type of "collaboration" he had in mind. After all, Si Newhouse's morning newspaper was well ahead of the *Press,* and his strategy seemed to be to wait for its inevitable collapse.

But within the next two years, Si Newhouse would change his mind and pay more than $22.5 million to buy an all-but-worthless subscription list and a newly formed bulk-mail advertising circular from Cole, in return for Cole's promise to shut down the *Cleveland Press*, the only competing daily newspaper in town. The secret two-page agreement between Si Newhouse and Cole would cover Cole's losses from the *Press* and even allow him to make a tidy profit for himself. And it would finally provide Si Newhouse and his family-owned empire with the prize they had long sought—a virtual monopoly in Cleveland worth millions of dollars in added revenues.

When Si Newhouse's secret business deal to eliminate his only competitor was revealed by another out-of-town newspaper, the *Akron Beacon-Journal,* the federal government launched a criminal antitrust investigation. If indicted and found guilty, both Si Newhouse and Cole could face three-year jail terms and $100,000 fines. Moreover, Newhouse faced the possibility of some seriously damaging publicity at about the same time he was polishing his image in New York by reviving *Vanity Fair* and buying *The New Yorker.* DID SI NEWHOUSE CONSPIRE TO KILL THE CLEVELAND PRESS? asked one *Business Week* headline in a 1985 story.

But no one would ever find out for sure. The federal probe into the death of the *Cleveland Press* would later end without citing Si Newhouse for any wrongdoing. In one crucial move, senior Justice Department officials decided to remove the two federal prosecutors who had recommended that a grand jury pursue criminal charges against Si Newhouse, Joseph Cole, and others involved in the closing of the *Cleveland Press*. Instead, Si Newhouse, a central focus of the federal criminal antitrust investigation, was granted immunity for his grand jury testimony, essentially ensuring that he would walk away unscathed.

This decision seemed directly at odds with the findings of a federal district judge, who, in another related lawsuit involving the printers who had lost their jobs at the *Cleveland Press*, found ample evidence of an alleged antitrust conspiracy. "The record is replete with facts from which the jury could conclude that Plain Dealer, Press Publishing and Cole conspired together in restraint of trade . . . ," wrote U.S. District Court Judge Ann Aldrich. The judge's written opinion was a veritable road map for the federal prosecutors, but they chose not to follow.

The full story of why the Justice Department didn't pursue antitrust charges in the demise of the *Cleveland Press* remains unclear. The two federal prosecutors who originally handled the investigation, Assistant U.S. Attorneys Russell Twist and Marilyn Bobula, have both claimed that their attempts to bring the full case before a grand jury were stymied by higher officials. The end of the *Cleveland Press* can be understood only by tracing events and decisions that have come to light since its presses closed, its editorial voice was silenced, and more than eight hundred people lost their jobs.

As Joseph Cole told Si Newhouse that day at his Palm Beach estate, both Cleveland newspapers were hurting financially in the early 1980s. When Cole bought the competing paper, Newhouse's *Plain Dealer* had lost 21,000 readers from its circulation record of 410,646 only eight years earlier; Sunday circulation had fallen even more during the 1970s, by nearly ninety thousand readers. The *Press*'s circulation problems mirrored the deeper problems of its rivals. Among the citizens of Cleveland, both newspapers were considered losers. At the time, a random survey of newspaper readers later published by *Cleveland Magazine* underlined how poorly the people of the city thought its two newspapers were doing. "Comments from the respondents were brutally critical of both newspapers—ranging from a belief that the papers deliberately cover up and distort the news, to a feeling that their writers and editors are simply incompetent," the magazine found. "The message is clear enough: Readers of both newspapers are desperate for thoughtful, comprehensive, well-written, well-edited and well-packaged news and features. And it is clear they feel they are cheated by both newspapers now."

For most of the 1970s, the Newhouse strategy was to hang on, firm in the belief that Cleveland could support only one daily newspaper, until the competition finally collapsed. With the Cleveland economy in a recession in 1980, however, the dominant *Plain Dealer* still managed to lose 3.1 million lines of advertising that year, a sizable chunk of its overall revenues. When the Scripps company finally unloaded the *Press* on the media neophyte Joseph Cole, the Newhouse strategy slowly changed.

After Newhouse's initial rebuff on any collaboration, Cole attempted to revive the *Press* through a number of well-publicized improvements, such as increasing the size of the paper's type. By April 1981, Cole announced a flashy tabloid Sunday edition that gobbled up more *Plain Dealer* readers and advertisers. In early 1982, the *Press* launched a new magazine called *Go,* aimed at teenagers, and unveiled plans for a revamped business section. Cole and his top management seemed upbeat, pointing to signs they were making headway against the *Plain Dealer*.

In the meantime, the *Plain Dealer* seemed headed for difficulty. While Cole had already made his peace with the Teamsters when he bought the newspaper, the *Plain Dealer* faced the uncertainty of a new labor contract with the Teamsters in 1982. This negotiation came at the same time that Jackie Presser was pushing the *Plain Dealer* for a retraction of the Bogdanich-Woge exposé. Presser was a familiar figure to newspaper managers in Cleveland. Back in 1980, he had told the FBI that the *Plain*

Dealer's assistant to the publisher, Alex Machaskee, had asked him to help shut down the *Press* by creating "problems" with its Teamsters local, according to Neff, who noted Machaskee's denial. In a rare moment of principle, Presser told the FBI that he had refused the offer from the Newhouse management to help them kill their competition because he strongly believed Cleveland should be a two-newspaper town.

David Hopcraft would later tell Neff he wasn't aware of any threat by Presser to launch a strike if the retraction story didn't run. But clearly, the *Plain Dealer* was well aware of how a Teamsters strike could damage its fortunes. "You have to remember the timing," Hopcraft later explained. "There's no way in God's green earth the *Cleveland Press* could survive as a newspaper unless you can get the Guild or the Teamsters to close down the *Plain Dealer* for six months."

As the *Press*'s publisher, Cole decided to up the ante by announcing the end of the long-standing publishers' agreement in Cleveland. In the past, if a union struck one newspaper, the publisher of the competing paper would close down for the duration. Cole now said he wouldn't shut down and plans were made to deliver the *Press* in the morning if there was a strike. "Obviously, the Press is hoping that its new look will catch on in time," wrote local columnist Fred McGunagle as 1982 approached. "That time could be this summer when labor contracts come up at the Plain Dealer. A strike would cost the Plain Dealer circulation and advertising losses it might never recover. A settlement on the union's terms would cost it millions of dollars. That could make the Plain Dealer start thinking again about a joint operating agreement, in which two papers merge all but their editorial departments."

But a joint-operating agreement would not be necessary. In mid-1982, Si Newhouse made two important decisions that, coincidence or not, would greatly affect the *Plain Dealer*'s future. The first permitted Cohn to place a retraction-like story on the *Plain Dealer*'s front page that would please Jackie Presser. The other was to meet once again with Joseph Cole about a plan that would pay Cole handsomely to close the *Cleveland Press* and forever cede a stranglehold on the Cleveland market to the Newhouse company.

As Si Newhouse would later testify, the plans to kill the *Cleveland Press* began with a telephone call from Cole. The *Press* publisher said he wanted to meet with Si Newhouse at the Condé Nast building in New York. Cole said he also wanted to bring his lawyer. When asked later in court whether he considered that call unusual, Newhouse replied, "I didn't think about it. The man wanted a meeting. So I agreed to that."

For the past several months, Cole had kept a brave but misleading public front as the savior of a resurgent *Press*. But privately, a group of auditors who reviewed the paper's books concluded its revenues would never exceed its debts and recommended that Cole get out as soon as possible.

Some of the executives pointed to the progress they had made in a short time, however. "I just felt that if we had kept going we could have made it," said Robert W. Hatton, Jr., the paper's advertising chief. But Cole was ready to quit if Newhouse made the right offer.

During their meeting in New York, Joseph Cole mentioned the sale of several items like trucks and printing presses, which Newhouse would later say held no value to him. The value of the land beneath the *Cleveland Press* building was never discussed, Newhouse would say. But Si Newhouse did mention something that he considered of value to him.

"I said that I could use his subscription list and I would be interested in it and I asked what he thought it was, what he would want for it," Newhouse recalled. "He kind of hemmed and hawed."

Cole said he wanted $20 million for the subscription list—an unheard-of figure for a list of names that could be culled largely from the local telephone books. Newhouse protested that the price was too high but still offered $14.5 million for it. "He breathed a sigh—he said, 'Yes,' " as Newhouse recalled the conversation. "I don't know how I would characterize it, but I had a feeling that this man lost a bundle of money and he was very, very upset at the situation he found himself in, and that's where I thought he was."

Newhouse would later testify that he didn't ask Cole how he had arrived at such a figure or what he'd paid for the *Cleveland Press*—reportedly only $1 million. In a sense, this didn't matter. For the true price of the agreement was the elimination of competition and clear sailing financially for the *Plain Dealer*—a price well worth $20 million. During the 1980s, with the *Press* gone, the *Plain Dealer* was free to collect tens of millions in additional advertising revenues, what some in the industry call a license to print cash.

During this meeting, Cole also indicated he wanted an agreement on a newly formed company called Del-Com, which delivered advertising supplements in the mail to those people who didn't subscribe to the *Press*. Newhouse said he was interested but didn't have time to commit himself because of his plan to leave on vacation. "I am going off for three weeks on a trip I take every year and I will turn this over to the lawyers, yours and mine, and leave it with them," Si said, now that the important business was decided. "Let them figure out what there is here and try and reach some kind of an understanding, if everyone agrees it's something we want to get involved with."

Eventually, Newhouse's underlings arrived at a price of another $8 million for the Cole-owned advertising-supplement company. In total, Newhouse agreed by May 1982 to pay $22.5 million to Cole for what was, in essence, his acquiescence in closing the *Cleveland Press*. A two-page agreement was signed by Si Newhouse and Joseph Cole on June 10, 1982.

Gentlemen:

We intend to cease publication of the Cleveland Press and to terminate its active operations after its June 17, 1982 edition. This letter confirms our understandings and, when executed by you, it shall constitue a binding agreement between you (sometimes referred to as the "Plain Dealer") and the undersigned (sometimes referred to as the "Press").

A week later, the Cleveland Press died, after 103 years of publication. At the time of its demise, the *Press* was still the twenty-first-largest American daily newspaper. To an unwitting media and public, the paper appeared to be simply a victim of poor economic conditions and a society relying increasingly on television rather than print for its news. There was no suggestion of the behind-the-scenes deal that had actually killed the paper.

One of the first outsiders to question the *Cleveland Press* closing was John R. Malone, a Chicago media broker who called Cole the day the paper folded and made an offer to buy it. Five days later, a Cole associate rejected Malone's $7.4 million offer for the *Press* and its equipment and refused to discuss it further. Malone found the answer surprising, given Cole's stated desires to see Cleveland remain a two-newspaper city. He later found out Cole had sold the subscription list to the *Plain Dealer*, but that fact didn't bother Malone. He still wanted to buy and revive the *Press* before it was too late, before rigor mortis set in with its faithful readers and advertisers. In July, a Malone representative toured the paper's shutdown offices, and found that computers were in boxes and wires were pulled out of the ceiling. It would take months to restore the newsroom, Malone's scout told him, even if Cole was willing to sell the *Press*. "It occurred to us that the plant was made inoperative so that there could be no continuing operations there," Malone later said.

Observing what happened with the *Press,* federal antitrust prosecutors in the U.S. attorney's office in Cleveland informed their Justice Department bosses that Cole might have been paid by Si Newhouse to close down the newspaper. The prosecutors warned that these actions "raise the specter of a possible violation" of two sections of the Sherman Anti-Trust Act, which prohibits restraint of trade and creation of monopolies. They asked for permission to subpoena documents and to take sworn statements from Cole and other *Press* executives. But in September 1982, Joseph Widmar, a Justice Department director of operations in the antitrust division, shot back a curt reply: "You are authorized to take no further action into the above matter." There was no explanation why.

The case was far from over, however. The *Press*'s printers, who had signed a labor contract with lifetime job guarantees approved by the Scripps company, sued over the shutdown, which they claim resulted from an antitrust conspiracy between Si Newhouse and Joseph Cole. In that case, Si Newhouse gave a sworn deposition detailing his meetings with Cole and other aspects concerning the sale of the subscription list. Although the judge who reviewed the printers' claim dismissed it on technical grounds, she clearly raised a red flag of possible illegality involved in the deal. The opinion by U.S. District Court Judge Ann Aldrich was based on reviewing the record that included Si Newhouse's testimony. Still, there was no change of heart by Justice Department officials.

A newspaper exposé about the deal, however, finally tipped the government's hand. When the *Akron Beacon Journal,* a newspaper located about fifty miles south of Cleveland, published a highly detailed story in January 1984 about the demise of the *Cleveland Press*, it outlined Si Newhouse's multimillion-dollar offer to Cole and raised many questions surrounding the deal. This exposé about the nation's most powerful publisher and his privately owned newspaper company was both brave and unique. In American journalism, even the biggest newspapers rarely throw rocks at another publisher.

In their story, reporters Dan Cook and Peter Phipps, who had once worked at the *Press,* underlined how the subscription list Si Newhouse purchased for $14.5 million was essentially worthless. They interviewed newspaper executives from the *Washington Post, Philadelphia Inquirer,* and the recently defunct *Buffalo Courier Express,* who said subscription lists were never traded when newspapers in those cities closed. Their story dovetailed with similar sworn statements made in the printers' lawsuit, including one by Charles Griner, the *Press*'s circulation director in 1982, saying the subscription list was valueless. The printers' lawyer was even more blunt. "The subscription list was just a ruse, a charade, to cover the payoff to Cole to take a dive," said attorney Robert Phillips. "Who would pay fourteen million dollars for a phone book?"

Newspaper-industry executives also expressed doubts about the deal. "If the *Cleveland Press* was going out of business, the list was worthless to Newhouse," said James B. Shaffer, who had been an assistant to the publisher at the *Buffalo Courier Express.* "If the *Cleveland Press* wasn't going out of business, Newhouse would have been glad to pay $14.5 million to kill the competition." Indeed, the *Press*'s closure proved to be a bonanza for Newhouse's paper, enabling the *Plain Dealer* to raise its advertising rates by 28 percent in less than two years and increase its circulation by more than 80,000 to an all-time high level.

Two weeks later, embarrassed Justice Department officials—whose interoffice memo stopping the initial antitrust probe was also highlighted in the *Beacon-Journal*'s story—announced they were authorizing a criminal investigation into Si Newhouse's $22.5 million payment to Joseph Cole.

The two local antitrust prosecutors assigned to the case were Charles Russell Twist and Marilyn Bobula. But things soon went awry. After a short review of the case, these two prosecutors realized how difficult their investigation would be to pursue. Ultimately, their decision to challenge the Justice Department's handling of the wrongdoing in the *Cleveland Press* case would forever impact on their careers within the Justice Department.

As he pursued the case, Russell Twist became alarmed by what he considered the special consideration granted to Si Newhouse. One memo from his superiors particularly appalled him. It suggested that the Justice Department invite the lawyers for Cole and Newhouse "to make a presentation of the facts, as they perceive them, before proceeding to call a grand jury." To be sure, inviting defense lawyers to the table was not unprecedented. But this memo, in Twist's view, suggested that a less-than-vigorous approach would be taken.

Most importantly, Twist was shocked to find that the Justice Department had already decided to grant immunity to Si Newhouse and Joseph Cole—even before the full evidence was presented to a federal grand jury. A March 1985 memo from J. Paul McGrath, then an assistant attorney general in the Justice Department's antitrust division, summarized this two-sided view. It was the government's belief that something illegal probably had happened but there also appeared to be a determination to keep Si Newhouse from being held personally responsible for it. McGrath wrote: "We opened the investigation because of strong suspicion that this transaction involved a Section 1 conspiracy along these lines: the parties [Newhouse and Cole and their associates] realized that an acquisition of the Press by Newhouse would have violated the antitrust laws and thus they devised a sham transaction." McGrath said the deal involved Newhouse's purchase of the *Press* subscription list and advertising supplement "at extraordinarily inflated amounts." McGrath said there was also a "side-deal" in which Cole agreed to get rid of his printing presses and other equipment so that "Newhouse would not thereafter be faced with competition in Cleveland. This made the large purchase price attractive, because Newhouse would then be in a monopoly position and thus would be able to charge more for advertising."

But despite this evidence, McGrath's memo also shows how a decision was made within the Justice Department to keep Si Newhouse from ever having to face criminal indictment in the case. McGrath said that Newhouse and Cole were granted immunity for their testimony. "We did, of course, all agree last year that, if a criminal case was authorized, it would be authorized against corporate, and not individual, defendants," McGrath said in one Justice Department memo. (In a 1993 interview, McGrath, by then in private practice, declined to comment on specifics. But he said his decision making was based on the facts of the case.)

When Twist and Bobula became aware of this predetermination to in-
sulate Newhouse and Cole, they were outraged. Simply put, this meant
Si Newhouse would get away unscathed before prosecutors had a chance
to make a case against him. They came to believe that senior Justice
Department officials did not want to pursue the case aggressively.

"What I do know is that there has been a course of conduct in this
investigation to derail it and impede it," Twist later testified. "The intent
is not to get all the evidence, to minimize the evidence that you have, and
to immunize the targets. And there is so much of that, that it is inescapable
that it was improper."

Twist and Bobula eventually decided to write a joint memo expressing
their concerns. One of those whom they criticized was their own boss,
John Weedon, chief of the Cleveland antitrust office. When the matter
didn't seem to go anywhere, Twist confided his disagreement to a law
clerk for the judge presiding over the case. Soon, top Justice Department
officials found out about his comments and they pulled both Twist and
Bobula off the *Cleveland Press* case. Twist was fired a year later for in-
subordination and unprofessional conduct and Bobula was transferred.

For a time, Twist was determined to air his grievances about the way
in which the Newhouse case was handled. At a closed-door hearing in
1986 about his conduct, Twist criticized Douglas Ginsburg—who at the
time of the *Cleveland Press* investigation was the assistant attorney general
for antitrust—for not pursuing Twist's concerns about his superiors' handling of the Newhouse case. "He doesn't want this investigated too thoroughly and doesn't want it brought forward, which some people
characterize as a cover-up," Twist testified at his own disciplinary hearing.
For his part, Ginsburg would later swear Twist was fired because of his
poor judgment and recalcitrancy, and he denied that Twist's comments to
the judge's law clerk had had anything to do with the firing. In 1987, a
federal judge supported the Justice Department's dismissal of Twist. That
same year, Ginsburg would be nominated to the Supreme Court by President Reagan (a nomination eventually derailed because of Ginsburg's
admission that he had previously used marijuana).

Privately, those who were familiar with the case portrayed Twist as a
man who was too often strident and conspiratorial. Twist, who had once
worked as a lawyer with the American Bar Association's ethics section,
insisted it was his duty under the legal code of conduct to bring to light
any evidence of a cover-up in the *Cleveland Press* case. But Bobula, who
remained a federal prosecutor, said several years later that she still agreed
with Twist's concern about the actions of Si Newhouse and Joseph Cole
in the *Cleveland Press* deal. "Everything that Russell said in the lawsuit
was correct in my opinion, there was nothing wrong," said Bobula. "He
was the best lawyer I ever worked with. He was not treated well."

For all the accusations swirling around him, however, Si Newhouse was treated very well. Although he did endure a nearly week-long stay in Cleveland to appear before a federal grand jury in May 1985, he did so with a promise of immunity. The *Plain Dealer* wrote virtually nothing about the grand jury probe into Newhouse's deal, though reporters were assigned to monitor it. Local television reporters largely ignored the story. In effect, virtually no one in Cleveland knew about the investigation into this secret deal. The few reporters who showed up at the courthouse for the billionaire's testimony found Newhouse and his lawyers unwilling to answer any questions about their actions in the case.

As he passed one group of reporters in a hallway, company lawyer Richard Urowsky walked by briskly with his client, Si Newhouse. "Lovely day, isn't it?" Urowsky said sardonically, turning his head to Newhouse and away from the reporters as they quickly marched past.

Bobula remembers talking with Newhouse during a break in his testimony before the grand jury. "He was an interesting person," recalled the prosecutor. "At one point, we went to the snack bar and he had no change and I bought him a coffee. Here's this man with all the billions of dollars, and I bought him a cup of coffee. He was an extremely polite gentleman."

With Twist and Bobula pulled off the case, the *Cleveland Press* investigation withered for months, then finally died. In June 1987, almost exactly five years from the date that the *Cleveland Press* had shut down, the Justice Department announced the grand jury deliberations had concluded with no charges filed. Mark Sheehan, the department spokesman, said Justice Department officials had not found enough evidence to continue the investigation. A five-year statute of limitations was about to expire, Sheehan said. He declined comment on Twist's accusations except to say that the department's Office of Professional Responsibility had found them without merit.

With the theoretical but never very real threat of prosecution behind them, the two wealthy newspaper barons of Cleveland were free to pursue their own ventures.

Joseph Cole, even without a newspaper, fared well. He tore down the building where the *Cleveland Press* had been and went ahead with his plans to build an office complex on the site.

Newhouse also got what he wanted: complete control of the daily newspaper market in the Cleveland region. Such a lock on the Cleveland market during the 1980s and well into the mid-1990s created a virtual wellspring of cash, one of several monopoly-like newspaper franchises that Newhouse and his family enjoyed across the nation. In January 1984, more than a year after the *Press* was killed, the *Plain Dealer* took out a full-page notice in *Advertising Age,* the main industry magazine catering to advertisers and advertising agencies, to tout its good fortune.

"Attention All Print Buyers," the newspaper proclaimed. "The Plain

Dealer now delivers 66.7% of a Plum terrific market!" The advertisement said the paper's 497,386 daily circulation was "the highest in our history." In this promotional ad, there was no mention that this boost in circulation came about as the result of the *Cleveland Press*'s closing or that Si Newhouse had paid $22.5 million to eliminate, in effect, the possibility that it might somehow be revived.

The only hint of what had happened, though clearly unintentional, appeared at the bottom of the ad:

"The PLAIN DEALER—One Great Buy For The Cleveland Market."

Newspapers are translucent creatures, where even the deepest rumblings of the soul usually make their way to the surface. In the case of the *Cleveland Plain Dealer*, Si Newhouse's abuse of a public trust, his tolerance and sometimes deliberate participation in ethically vacuous deals, and the many untold stories both unknown to the public and yet of concern to the commonweal would cast a pall over the integrity of his newspaper. Like some dark lingering cloud, this journalistic affliction continued throughout the 1980s and early 1990s. The suspicious deal to kill the *Press* and the staff's outcry over the phony Jackie Presser story seemed to have an immutable effect on the pages of the newspaper.

"The problem of the Plain Dealer's inadequacies has become more than a problem of a newspaper," local media critic Roldo Bartimole wrote soon after the *Cleveland Press* collapsed in 1982. "In the past few weeks particularly, it's become a problem for the community. When the Press died in June, it left the Plain Dealer—fat and arrogant—the only kid on the block in a city with all the terminal illnesses of a big, old northern American city."

Many of the bright young reporters at the *Cleveland Plain Dealer* seemed to stay for only a short time and then leave. As Bartimole observed, "Upper echelon editors may be too gun-shy about hiring reporters who get too aggressive. The PD has had its problems with such reporters in the past and has gotten bad national publicity from acts by its own reporters." Now that it had a lock on the Cleveland market, the paper's management seemed to prefer reporters who didn't want to examine important political or economic controversies closely. They wanted reporters who simply didn't want to rock the boat. "It troubles me," one reporter told Bartimole. "They don't want to do anything but puff pieces." Another *Plain Dealer* reporter observed, "They hired nice people but they don't have drive. There's no enthusiasm. There's no anger. No drive. They don't get excited about their work."

After the *Press* collapsed, the *Plain Dealer* decided it would not hire any of the *Press*'s former staff writers and editors, something that dominant newspapers in other cities, like the *Philadelphia Inquirer,* felt an obligation to do after the deaths of their main competitors. In promotional ads, the *Plain Dealer* said it was now offering "The Best of the Press," which actually meant adding a few syndicated columnists, comics, and features. There was no expansion of the paper's local coverage with additional reporters. Newhouse's coup poured tens of millions more into the coffers of his empire headquartered in New York—with a pretax profit level estimated by some experts to be as high as 20 percent or more during the heyday of the 1980s—but brought very little tangible benefit for readers in Cleveland, many of whom now relied on the *Plain Dealer* as the only source of printed news.

For all of the newspaper's failings, however, Thomas Vail, the publisher on the masthead, remained the target of public scorn rather than the newspaper's owner. "Unfortunately, the history of Vail's reign has already been written. It's called failure," concluded Bartimole. "The newspaper—which could be the most powerful in the state, a crucial political state—doesn't have the impact it should or could." It is unlikely that Vail could ever have brought about the quality of news coverage under Newhouse that he once talked of as a young publisher in the early 1960s. Vail's long-held dream of winning a Pulitzer Prize for the paper seemed to have faded during the Newhouse ownership. Even attempts to improve the newspaper became suspect. In a 1982 column, Bartimole noted that Vail "recently went outside the *Plain Dealer* to bring in an editor of the editorial page, one who was connected with a Pulitzer Prize winning newspaper. . . . Vail may think he can buy a Pulitzer."

What happened to that new editor at the *Cleveland Plain Dealer* would come to illustrate just how deep the ethical and journalistic morass remained at the Newhouse paper.

Bill Woestendiek began with high hopes when he arrived at the *Plain Dealer* in 1982. During his long career, Woestendiek, a graduate of the Columbia University School of Journalism and a former Nieman fellow at Harvard, had worked as a top editor in the 1960s at *Newsday* on Long Island and later served as executive editor of the *Arizona Star* when it won a Pulitzer Prize. Woestendiek joined the *Plain Dealer* as editorial-page editor and became its executive editor about a year later. "It wasn't that bad when I first came there," he recalled. "We made a lot of changes and we made a lot of progress. We really made the editorial page a lot livelier, which is one of the things the P-D didn't have. We did a lot more aggressive investigative reporting. There were a lot of good things. I didn't consider it a hot seat when I went there. I saw it as another paper I could help improve."

With a large news section and an abundant amount of new advertising flowing in after the death of the *Press,* Woestendiek felt there was a great opportunity for the *Cleveland Plain Dealer* to become, as Vail had once expressed, the best newspaper between New York and Chicago. As executive editor directly in charge of the paper's news coverage, however,

Woestendiek was surprised to find that there was no sense of obligation to improve or at least increase the paper's coverage after the loss of the *Press*. "Having one newspaper is bad enough—it's always a tragedy when a city loses one of its newspapers," Woestendiek said. "Usually when a second newspaper folds, the editorial side is very upset. You know, it's a fraternity and it's a sad occasion. But I doubt that the business office or the advertising department or the Newhouses were very upset by it because it really gave them a stranglehold on the market."

Efforts to launch more in-depth stories that poked and prodded the Cleveland establishment were frowned upon by Woestendiek's bosses, he said, especially Alex Machaskee, the assistant to the publisher and one of Newhouse's top managers. "The *Plain Dealer* management did not like, and probably still does not like, anybody who rocks any boat or raises any questions about the way they want things done—no questions about that," said the paper's former top editor.

During his watch, the *Plain Dealer* virtually ignored the stories about the Justice Department's investigation into Newhouse's alleged attempts to gain a monopoly. But Woestendiek did harbor his own doubts about the deal that killed the *Press*. "I was, happily, not there when it happened. It was one of the things that I was pleased that I was not involved in," said Woestendiek. "But I have my suspicions. I think they paid an enormous amount of money for a subscription list that wasn't needed, in my opinion. And, I think, in a lot of people's opinions. It took a long time—that antitrust case—and I know there was a lot of money spent by the Newhouses in fighting it."

Whatever his ethical misgivings about the past, the clear dividing line for Woestendiek concerned the repeated attempts by Newhouse business executives to allow advertisers, such as large department stores in Cleveland, to influence the news and how it appeared in the *Plain Dealer*. Far from a neophyte, Woestendiek knew every newspaper, even the largest, can have sacred cows that are handled gingerly, if at all, in the news pages. But at the *Plain Dealer*, he said the breakdown of the "Chinese wall"— that traditional separation between advertising and the news pages considered essential by most modern-day journalists—made his position intolerable.

By 1987, "the complaints of advertisers were really taken very seriously by the publisher and the general manager, Alex Machaskee, in particular," said Woestendiek. "There was the inauguration of special puff sections on automobiles and real estate. The auto dealers and realtors were very upset that they did not get enough good coverage. Even to the point where the then Sunday magazine editor and I were asked to meet with the advertising director for [a local department store], because the company didn't like the covers of the Sunday magazine. He gave suggestions on how it could be improved. And the company objected frequently to the stories on page three, which they considered their page and which I considered theirs for three-fourths of the page but not the news section. It was that kind of thing."

In private meetings, Woestendiek objected to what he considered an improper encroachment on the news, but he was waved off by the top Newhouse management. Eventually, after enough protestation about journalistic morality, the *Plain Dealer*'s executive editor was shown the door. He never got to speak to Si Newhouse about it. "I was asked to leave," said Woestendiek. "I had never been very bashful about accepting my position and in taking a stand on what is proper and what is improper. A lot of the very good people who were there are now elsewhere, like the editorial-page editor, assistant editorial page editor, the city editor—a whole bunch of people. They were all good people and they all felt very strongly about the direction the paper was taking."

Those who questioned the way Si Newhouse ran his newspaper in Cleveland didn't last long but did manage to flourish elsewhere. Woestendiek later became director of the University of Southern California's School of Journalism. Walt Bogdanich survived the body blow to his reputation caused by the phony Presser story and eventually joined *The Wall Street Journal,* where he won a Pulitzer Prize. James Neff was supposed to return to the *Plain Dealer* after he finished his leave of absence to write the Jackie Presser biography, but his detailed account of the *Plain Dealer*'s handling of the Presser stories all but sealed his fate. And J. Paul McGrath—the Justice Department antitrust official who had questioned the deal but was part of the decision to grant immunity to Newhouse and Cole—soon afterward went into private practice, where, four years later, he was retained by the Newhouses as an expert witness in another complicated legal matter.

At the *Plain Dealer,* there was the sense that the newspaper had sold out, compromising its standards of truth and fairness. This pattern seemed to extend from one generation of management to the next at the paper—with Newhouse's ownership as the common link. Efforts to bury the truth about the Jackie Presser story lasted for years. In 1989, when Neff's book about Presser was published, the *Plain Dealer* commissioned a freelance review by Howard Bray, the director of the Knight Center for Specialized Journalism at the University of Maryland. In his review, Bray paid particular attention to the Newhouse intervention on behalf of Presser and said the book "reveals how the paper's credibility fell victim to the influence of Teamster-Mob powers" with a front-page "editorial surrender" repudiating its own exposé. But Bray's review never appeared in the *Plain Dealer*. Accompanying a *Washington Journalism Review* story about Neff's book, Vail offered one of his few public comments about the Presser affair. "At no time did we apologize," Vail said. "No 'retraction' was ever printed. We just published a news story [to the effect that] the government, in a sense, had signed off on the investigation of Presser, and we had an obligation to print that." By then, however, the weight of evidence contained in government tapes and court documents detailing the interplay of Roy Cohn, the Newhouses, and the mob made Vail's protestations seem hollow. When he left the *Plain Dealer,* Vail signed an agreement never again to discuss publicly what went on at the newspaper.

For his part, Si Newhouse would survive the Cleveland fiasco by typically refusing to talk about it. In his silence, there were nevertheless some revelations into his character and his business methods. Perhaps the most significant was how much power was wielded by Si Newhouse, once viewed by outsiders as the black sheep in his family. In the few published profiles about the Newhouses, writers would give the impression that Si's brother, Donald, was the dominant voice in running the family's $5 billion newspaper empire and that Si confined himself mainly to magazine and book publishing. On a day-to-day basis, this may appear so. But the signature on the *Cleveland Press* deal belied what most insiders already understood: In matters that count, Si Newhouse calls the shots in the family business, in the same way his father once did.

Newhouse's silence also underlined a more troubling problem within the American media, the fundamental questions involving accountability and public trust. No matter how much criticism there was about the *Plain Dealer*, there was never any reason for Si Newhouse to have to explain himself. In 1989, when the top-rated national television show "60 Minutes" reprised the Jackie Presser stories and the cover-up at the *Plain Dealer*, Si Newhouse still refused to comment. He didn't have to. Nor did he ever explain his part in the shutdown of the *Cleveland Press*. To hold the key to what millions of Americans read every day in Ohio's largest city, Si Newhouse needed only one credential: ownership of the *Plain Dealer*'s printing presses.

This domineering grip on the dissemination of news was a far cry from earlier in the century when cities had several competing newspapers. "It is for this buying public that newspapers are edited and published, for without that support the newspapers cannot live," Walter Lippmann wrote in 1922. "A newspaper can flout an advertiser, it can attack a powerful banking or traction interest, but if it alienates the buying public, it loses the one indispensable asset of its existence." With the collapse of competition and a certain lock on the market, newspapers like Newhouse's *Cleveland Plain Dealer* could afford a "take it or leave it" approach to serving the public.

The profound distrust of Americans toward the media in the 1990s, the nagging suspicion that local newspapers act too often as gatekeepers withholding vital information from the public, found its exemplar in Si Newhouse, the man whose newspaper in Cleveland housed the secrets of the mob, its crooked unions, and its own self-serving advertisers. The public's skepticism about the tainted news they consumed, as readership surveys would repeatedly show, grew out of the belief that newspapers had become mere house organs for the wealthy, that the interests of the powerful held far greater sway than those of mere readers. When it involved embarrassing matters to billionaires (or at least those with glossy printing presses and lucrative assignments to offer at the most elite publications in New York), the press often seemed perplexed or feigned disinterest. That was certainly the case in the media's examination of Si Newhouse's role in Cleveland. And the press would be largely complacent again when Newhouse faced an even greater legal challenge from the government, one that was aimed at the very heart of the family fortune.

The Artful (Tax) Dodger

One summer before Sam's death, the family gathered together for a day of celebration rather than work. In the air was an expansive mood created by open lawns, a gentle breeze, and the sounds of young people. There was little hint of the dramatic changes that would soon take place within the Newhouse family, though a single gesture would be remembered for years to come as proof of just how important he had been to their lives.

On this day, Sam's younger brother Ted smiled appreciatively as the family arrived at his summer estate, hidden behind the privets and granite walls of upstate Connecticut. He was unaccustomed to being the center of attention. For this occasion, nearly every Newhouse family member, in-law, and loved one had come—a sizable group to honor Ted and his wife, Caroline, on their twentieth wedding anniversary.

Before long, the family and their guests were called to the luncheon table, where an elaborate meal was waiting. As the family watched, Ted rose to give the first toast. Most of the family gazed expectantly at Caroline. But a sense of family history and gratitude filled Ted for the moment, compelling him to recognize the one person who had made it all happen for them.

"To Sam," said Ted, raising his glass and beaming proudly at his oldest brother, Samuel Newhouse, Sr.

There was no better tribute for a man, then in his eighties, who had spent his life carefully arranging each deal and structuring the family's finances so that they would never again face the hardships he and his generation had known. Ted Newhouse felt indebted to his oldest brother for bringing about the luxurious life their whole family now enjoyed. Somehow, it seemed fitting that Ted should recognize Sam on this day, above even his wife.

Of all the Newhouses, Sam had perhaps the deepest sense of family. The life Sam Newhouse had constructed for his family was truly magnificent. In moments like this, his accomplishments were recognized by some of the older Newhouses, such as soft-spoken Ted, who remembered the poverty and the anti-Semitism they once had felt. The younger Newhouses had little such experience. They had grown up in Park Avenue duplexes, attended the best private schools, and had guaranteed jobs waiting for them in the family business.

In particular, Si appeared to lack this fundamental understanding of his family's struggle to achieve. For the longest time, he seemed to suffer from the frivolousness so often found among the sons of successful, driven men. Not only did Si lack his father's sense of gravitas; he appeared intent on frittering away whatever talents he possessed and embarrassing his father. Si's messy divorce from his first wife, Jane, which separated him from his children for a time and deeply disappointed his parents, only underlined the question of succession, of whether theirs would be a family dynasty or just another newspaper chain with fractious heirs.

Some of these questions were answered when Si met Victoria de Ramel, a sophisticated dark-haired woman whom he married in April 1973. Their marriage would bring much needed stability to Si's life and an end to his cavalier image. Although there remained some distance from his children, this second marriage formed a steady foundation for the empire Si Newhouse would soon inherit.

Victoria de Ramel was a much different woman from Jane Franke. When she married her forty-six-year-old husband, Victoria was a mature woman with a sophisticated taste in art and culture that complemented Si's array of interests. Victoria worked as a senior editor for the George Braziller book publishing company in Manhattan and moved within many of the same social circles as Si Newhouse and his Condé Nast editors. Unlike her husband, she had distinguished herself in college, graduating magna cum laude from Bryn Mawr. She was the daughter of New York investment broker John C. Benedict, who had sent her to the private Brearley School. She later married a Frenchman, Count Régis de Ramel, a union that ultimately ended in divorce. Her abiding interest in architecture prompted her to join the board of the Municipal Arts Society, New York City's architectural watchdog group, whose members also included Jacqueline Kennedy Onassis, and to write a book herself about one of her favorite architects.

Increasingly, Si and Victoria Newhouse made the social rounds and were received at some of the best parties in New York. They lived in a modern-looking white concrete town house on East Seventieth Street, just off Lexington Avenue, which was filled with Si's expensive collection of abstract art. Si purchased some of the best works of contemporary artists such as Jasper Johns, Barnett Newman, Mark Rothko, Roy Lichtenstein, and Willem de Kooning. "It's like a gallery; there's no place to put the ashes," a visitor complained. (Si's taste in abstract art was so eclectic that a burglar once misjudged the worth of his valuables, preferring to heist the silver flatware and some lithographs instead of the more costly art left hanging on his walls.) Si became an important patron and later a board member of the Museum of Modern Art. And Victoria, an ever-smiling, ever-knowledgeable companion, was often by his side at those functions and fund-raisers. Victoria would never enjoy the same closeness with Mitzi Newhouse as Jane Franke once had, partly because she would never give her any grandchildren. But Victoria seemed dedicated to her husband and their life together, a stabilizing force for Si as he prepared to assume more responsibility.

For much of the 1970s, however, even though Si was well into middle age and had proved himself with the turnaround of Condé Nast magazines, even though he had remarried and become an important part of the family's inner circle, he still did not seem quite whole. He was still only a son.

That perception would change when Sam Newhouse died on August 29, 1979 at the age of eighty-four, leaving the largest American media enterprise of its kind still in private hands. This legacy included thirty daily newspapers, including monopolylike franchises in Newark, Cleveland, New Orleans, Portland, and Syracuse, as well as the *Parade* Sunday supplement. The family's Condé Nast stable of glossy magazines as well as the television stations and cable-television franchises proved to be a gold mine. No American publishing tycoon, not even Pulitzer or Hearst, had left his heirs an empire as large, financially diverse, and profitable as Sam Newhouse's Advance Publications, Incorporated.

Sam's death was a turning point for the entire family, none more so than for his eldest son. Though emotionally difficult, his father's passing seemed to liberate Si, who was now free to place his own imprimatur on the family business and to build it beyond anything his father could have anticipated. Si's comments sometimes conveyed this sense of obligation, of the emotional debt he felt to the family enterprise. But he would be much more than a mere custodian of his father's memory.

In the 1980s, publishing jewels of a kind his father had once dreamed of owning—like *The New Yorker* or Random House, bringing class and prestige as well as a steady stream of revenues—became attainable. As the multimillion-dollar acquisitions of once-priceless media properties accelerated during the decade, Si showed his willingness to spend money. "Si Newhouse has shaken up the company his father left behind, snapping up old magazines, starting new ones, refashioning those he already owns, hiring and firing at a sometimes dizzying pace, and installing one British editor after another," said one magazine profile. By the late 1980s, Si and his brother, Donald, were worth billions more than much better-known tycoons. Together, they possessed the largest private fortune in the United States.

And yet in a sense, his father's death did set the stage for what was to come. Si's ability to finance the Random House purchase or to continue pouring millions into *Vanity Fair* would likely have been difficult, if not impossible, without Sam Newhouse's final achievement—an artfully constructed tax scheme that allowed the Newhouse empire to frustrate the United States government's claim for nearly $1 billion in back taxes and penalties. Aided immeasurably by the government's poor handling of the case, it was an elaborate plan, a perfectly executed gamble, that would save and solidify the Newhouse family fortune for generations to come.

Sam Newhouse's lasting legacy, ensuring an uninterrupted cash flow for his beloved Advance Publications, would not be finalized until more than a decade after his death. The protracted legal battle over the Newhouse estate—which threatened to break apart their far-flung communications franchise and saddle them with huge tax bills—would prove to be the family's greatest challenge. As never before, the surviving Newhouses, including Si, would be compelled to testify publicly about their finances, in far greater detail than they had ever previously allowed. For example, Donald Newhouse would be required to tell in court papers how he had managed to get by one year on a salary of $397,839, plus dividends totaling more than $650,000—an amount he termed as "nominal"—for running the family's chain of television and cable stations. And Si Newhouse, in an odd and revealing way, would testify how his family's method of making business decisions was almost too ephemeral for words, like explaining love.

Despite whatever possible discomfort the Newhouses felt, however, the Internal Revenue Service and its army of federal lawyers, auditors, and expert tax witnesses would bear the greatest embarrassment. "This case represents a monumental defeat for the Service," said noted tax lawyer Richard Covey after the dust had settled and the full consequences were realized.

The elaborate tax plan would not only bring about the government's courtroom defeat—one of the biggest in the history of the U.S. tax code— but also ensure that the Newhouse family fortune would be kept intact for another generation. And it was achieved by the Newhouses carefully setting a plan to outfox their opponent and then patiently waiting for their moment to arrive. Indeed, that moment did not come until 1989, in the gray marble confines of the United States Tax Court in Washington, a place where America's wealthiest corporations and individuals often drag out their cases until their tax debts are whittled to a fraction. Faced with a $1 billion bill for back taxes, the Newhouses managed to get away with paying only a fraction of the amount the government originally required.

One of the most remarkable aspects of this stunning tax victory turned on Si Newhouse's ability to deny and mitigate what virtually everyone believed to be true: that Sam Newhouse was the principal owner of the family business and that, regardless of whatever discussion took place among the Newhouses, he always called the final shots. Certainly, most of the media thought this to be true, especially those journalists in his employ. Sam Newhouse's tightfistedness about wages and his closely held reins on the newspaper chain were legendary. Shortly after pulling off "the biggest newspaper deal in U.S. journalistic history," Sam Newhouse was featured on the cover of *Time* magazine in 1962, which underlined his extraordinary ability to appraise and acquire newspapers. "Among the country's newspaper giants, Sam Newhouse seems to know best how to make daily newspapering pay," the magazine concluded. To suggest Newhouse was not wholly in control of his empire seemed like questioning whether Henry Ford really ran his car company or whether the Pope ruled the Catholic Church. The very idea seemed preposterous.

Nevertheless, Si and Donald Newhouse, as executors of their father's estate and its imperiled fortune, made just such an argument. Under oath, Si and his brother swore that their father had not really been in charge and that every business decision was made by the family as a group—testimony that, of course, conformed to their attorneys' tax theories. Financial experts could only shake their heads and marvel at its sheer ingenuity.

As the economist Paul Samuelson later observed: "The scheme's beauty, of course, is that the Newhouses can apparently have it both ways. For estate purposes the value of the company is artificially lowered. But should the family ever want to sell, it can easily recover the company's full market value by offering all the firm's securities as a package."

These troubling questions posed by the Newhouse tax case were of little concern outside the courtroom, however. With scant attention paid by the news media, the outcome of the tax trial barely made a ripple among the public. Far more effective than a censor's order, this form of silence was a lasting lesson in the true power of the press. It was as if an unwritten rule or a gentleman's agreement applied: The finances of great publishers were not grist for the pulp mills they owned, not to be showcased and displayed in exacting detail like the affairs of Leona Helmsley, Imelda Marcos, Michael Milken, or other more vulgar titans of commerce.

"The U.S. Tax Court is only a short cab ride from the Washington bureau of Newhouse Newspapers, but the dedicated news hounds employed there somehow have managed to miss the compelling tale just concluded," Richard Pollak later observed in *The Nation*. "This demonstrates puzzling news judgment, for the several million readers of the chain's twenty-six newspapers doubtless would find instructive an exploration of the government's accusation that the Newhouse family has dodged more than $1 billion in taxes."

The Newhouses' stunning tax gambit—ensuring that they would not have to sell any valued properties to pay their taxes—was a masterful business maneuver by Sam Newhouse, the seeds of which were planted and carefully cultivated decades earlier. But the final stroke to ensure victory in U.S. Tax Court needed the full participation of Si and Donald and their lawyers. More than anything, the Newhouses' billion-dollar tax case sealed their fates together—from father to son, one generation to the next—as nothing they had ever shared before.

Over the years, the original charter for Advance Publications, Inc.—the Newhouse family's holding company that formed the centerpiece of its communications empire—was layered with so many amendments and revisions that it was rendered almost unintelligible. And that's just the way Sam wanted it.

In the codicils and fine print, there was no way of conveying Sam Newhouse's sense of family, the intricacies of blood and personal loyalties. Yet these documents reflected the changes in the family, its growing newspaper chain, and its own embrace of secrecy regarding its operations. These legal papers traced the history of the business as it emerged from a small family enterprise into one of America's most powerful media conglomerates. In many ways, these arcane papers look like a cryptographer's nightmare. But to understand the IRS's billion-dollar claim on the Newhouse finances—and how it was successfully defeated—it was necessary to follow these carefully drawn documents like some intricate road map to understand their implications.

In the early 1920s, the incorporation papers for the privately held Newhouse company were filed, and then changed repeatedly throughout the following decades. Sam Newhouse, a young man who exuded great seriousness, had already shown his ability to turn around successfully a faltering newspaper, the sleepy Bayonne rag owned by his friend and mentor Judge Hyman Lazarus. In 1922, he convinced Lazarus to form a partnership with him to buy the *Staten Island Advance*. Two years later, Newhouse bought out Judge Lazarus and filed the incorporation papers for the Staten Island Advance Company, the predecessor of Advance Publications, Inc.

The paper's brand of intensely local news coverage and the willingness to cater to its provincial audience and advertisers soon made the enterprise profitable. Despite the hard times of the Depression, Newhouse was willing to plow his profits back into expansion, and he began buying up other newspapers by the early 1930s, starting with the nearby *Long Island Press*. In 1936, Newhouse made the first significant change in the company's charter, which created three types of common stock. All of the voting rights, however, were concentrated in the class A common stock, which he owned himself. From the clear delineation in the company's stock, there did not seem to be any question of who was in control.

As the family's newspaper chain grew, Newhouse employed numerous relatives, entrusting his two brothers, Norman and Ted, to help manage the business with him. The charter was repeatedly amended over the coming decades—in 1938, in 1949, in 1952, and again in 1956—eventually to include Norman and Ted among the company's preferred stockholders. Their shares of preferred stock would prove to be worth a fortune, but the voting rights and common stock still remained with Sam Newhouse.

Ownership was so intricate and so little discussed that Si was surprised as an adult to read in a *Time* magazine article about two kinds of stock in the family company. It was not until after Sam Newhouse's death in 1979, however, that anyone outside the family and its employ tried to figure its worth.

Six months after his father's death, Si and the other fiduciaries of the Newhouse estate filed tax papers with the IRS, valuing the gross adjusted worth of Sam Newhouse's stake in Advance at approximately $181.9 million. Based on that figure, they filed a return listing the net tax bill as just shy of $48.7 million. Their father's business affairs were all carefully explained in attached documents sworn to by Si and Donald.

Under the law, the Newhouse tax filing was kept confidential and would not become public until Si and Donald decided to appeal their bill from the IRS through the U.S. Tax Court. But to many media experts at the time, the Newhouses' two prosperous daily newspapers in Newark and Cleveland alone were probably worth more than $181 million—without counting some two dozen Newhouse newspapers, the magazines, and the broadcast outlets. The Newhouses' lowball estimate to the IRS was based on a theory that ownership of their empire was shared among the family. After carefully examining their account of the family finances, the government concluded it was all a big lie.

But typical of its performance throughout this case, the IRS didn't arrive at its own estimated tax bill for another three years, not until 1983, when the government said it had finished a lengthy review of Newhouse family fiscal statements. At the time of Sam's death, the agency claimed the Newhouse estate was worth $1.2 billion. Therefore, the IRS determined, the two brothers' tax payment was deficient by $609 million.

The government took a further step, as well. The Newhouses' tax return was deliberately intended to deceive, the IRS charged, and they filed a 50 percent penalty for civil fraud, amounting to another $304 million. By the time the tax dispute came to trial, the projected total, including interest, was expected to exceed $1 billion—the largest tax assessment ever filed by the U.S. government in a family estate case.

Ironically, as the case developed, there were signs that the government had also seriously underestimated the true worth of the Newhouse fortune. One of the government's expert witnesses—James Kobak of James B. Kobak & Co., a magazine consultant who had appeared in more than thirty-five cases as an expert witness in media appraisals—issued a report before the trial, concluding that the true value of the Newhouse empire was nearly double what the IRS had estimated. According to Kobak, the fair market value of the Advance company's common stock—all of which was owned by Sam Newhouse at the time of his death—was not $1.2 billion, as the IRS originally figured, but actually $2.1 billion. Kobak's report meant that the IRS should have doubled not only the true value of the Newhouse estate but also demand a higher bill for back taxes. What the Newhouses owed should have been $1.2 billion, not $609 million, as the agency had earlier estimated.

Kobak's new estimate made the Newhouses' attempt to settle a tax bill of only $48 million seem even more outrageous. After all, most Americans in that stratospheric tax bracket would pay, at the time of death, about one-third of their estate's value to Uncle Sam. If Kobak's assessment was correct, the comparison was striking: The Newhouses' estimate of their estate-tax liability was only 2 percent of the actual worth of the Newhouse empire. In the meantime, the Newhouse empire, unencumbered by its huge tax bill, had mushroomed to an estimated worth of nearly $10 billion by the time of the trial in 1989.

"I thought the government's approach was correct," Kobak said later about his reason for testifying as an IRS expert. "We know who owned that company—that was a matter of fact. I thought the government was right. That was a trick that [Sam Newhouse] pulled."

But the trick worked. In fact, the government's attempts to use Kobak's report to reassess the Newhouse empire and double its tax liability was later thrown out by Judge B. John Williams, Jr., because, he said, it had been received too late. The Newhouse attorney complained that they would be too unprepared for such a report so close to trial. Judge Williams agreed with such reasoning. It was a pretrial decision that would set the tone for the deliberations to come.

Robert Shilliday moved slowly and with great purpose as he explained what he described as the size and scope of the huge tax gamble being perpetrated by the Newhouses. His opening statement for the government in a nearly empty courtroom in January 1989 was filled with a sense of outrage at the deception he felt had occurred. When Si Newhouse and his brother filed the tax return on their father's estate nearly ten years earlier, they were, in effect, cashing in on the strategy that Sam Newhouse had planned for decades, with its multiple changes to the family company's charter. This strategy was meant, Shilliday argued, to keep the Newhouse estate from paying its fair share of taxes.

"The genesis of the plan was confusion," Shilliday insisted. "The plan was murky. It was dark. It was without form. In a word, it was vagueness. This plan was built on a magician's card trick, a sleight of hand."

Shilliday, no stranger to melodrama in the court, contended the changes made in 1956—by then about the fifth or sixth major change to the Advance company's charter—held the key to this deception. "It was to be a trick, an illusion," he told the court. "This illusion began a great gamble and put the estate of Newhouse on a collision course with the Internal Revenue Service."

As a result of the changes made in 1956, the preferred shareholders of

Advance Publications—who numbered only Si and Donald, their mother, Mitzi, and their uncles Norman and Ted—were given the right to vote on a voluntary liquidation. At the tax trial, the Newhouse attorneys never offered a reason for the 1956 changes in the charter and suggested that whatever Sam Newhouse's intent was for the peculiar capital structure of the company, it would remain a mystery, buried forever with him.

But to Shilliday, these modifications were no mystery; the patriarch's intent was quite clear. As he portrayed it, Sam Newhouse was a "businessman's businessman" who was determined to see that his company remain in his family's hands long after he had died. The elder Newhouse was, according to the government's attorney, "All business all the time in every sense of the word, but at the same time . . . a family man with strong ties to the past."

Like some overgrown artichoke, with layer upon layer, the changes made to the Newhouse company in 1956 were built on previous amendments to Advance's charter, including one in 1949 that set a low fixed price for the preferred stockholders if they chose to liquidate and sell their interests in the company—so low, in fact, that the Newhouse family members were essentially locked in for as long as Sam continued to run the company. The compelling reason for this complex stock configuration seemed clear enough. Sam Newhouse had learned from the bitter struggles for money and control that ripped apart the families of other newspaper tycoons like Hearst and Pulitzer. He was determined to prevent these internecine wars after his death.

There was plenty of room for deception and misinterpretations in the Newhouse financial documents. Although on paper the 1956 changes granted the family's preferred shareholders the right to voluntary liquidation at any point, they would not, in reality, ever do so during Sam Newhouse's lifetime. When he died, however, whoever laid claim to the common stock and its voting rights would still need the approval of the preferred stockholders—the Newhouse family—to gain full control of Advance. In terms of estimating the true value of Newhouse stock, this arrangement was a Catch-22. After all, what was Sam's stock worth to a potential buyer if the other Newhouses, who retained the right to prevent a liquidation, didn't want to sell theirs? This arrangement left things wide open come tax time. It also seemed to be Sam Newhouse's way of assuring that the family business did not shatter after one generation under the weight of a crushing tax payment on his estate.

Crucial to the future tax case, the 1956 amendments posed a legally murky question of fiduciary rights and class voting rights under the law. To Shilliday and the IRS, the changes in 1956 were an artifice designed to make it appear—at least for estate tax purposes—that the preferred shareholders were equal owners of the company, on the same plane as the common stockholder, Sam Newhouse. This amendment enabled Si Newhouse and his brother, as the executors, to claim that the value of Sam's estate's holdings was much less than the total value of the company. However, the IRS auditors concluded the family's byzantine charter changes were all a ruse, essentially made up to avoid taxes.

"The plan was to make the common shares and the preferred shares equal but without doing anything to make it so," Shilliday insisted in his opening statement. All of the power and money of the Advance company was ruled by Sam Newhouse, he said, with a dominating grip on the company's common stock and voting rights throughout his lifetime. Yet after Sam's death, the government was being asked to believe his company was somehow jointly run through a group decision-making process, with little differences in stock ownership. This scenario didn't wash with Shilliday as he reviewed the case and studied the documents. "At some point, whether it was 1956 or some other date, one would conclude Mr. Newhouse started out controlling the company and then wound up not controlling the company," Shilliday would say years later in an interview, underlining the essential paradox of the Newhouse company charter.

But it was Shilliday's job to disprove the Newhouse tax theories. Despite his visceral and emotional appeals, the government seemed unprepared for a tax case so complex and for the sharply honed arguments of the Newhouse estate attorneys. The byzantine structure of the Newhouse finances "was very unusual; it was one of a kind," he recalled. "Up to that date, I'd not seen a corporate organization anywhere similar to that."

Indeed, Shilliday wound up litigating the case only because of a quirk in the IRS's own rules. Under the government's procedures, because Sam Newhouse died at his winter estate in Florida, it would be the IRS southern division that would handle the case—even though Sam Newhouse spent nearly every moment of his adult life as a New York resident. The estate tax return was filed with the Jacksonville, Florida, office of the Internal Revenue Service, and it was assigned by late 1983 to Shilliday, then an Atlanta-based special trial attorney.

Shilliday had spent most of his career with the IRS after graduating at the top of his class from Florida State University Law School in 1970. For a decade, he had worked in a variety of legal posts, overseeing technical questions on tax audits and reviews, and developing a taste for trying cases in court. Since 1980, he had been one of only a handful of special IRS attorneys who handled the cases in U.S. Tax Court, a rarefied level of review usually involving large estates or multimillion-dollar corporate tax debts that focused on minute interpretations of the tax code. There were no run-of-the-mill cases for collection, refund litigation, or criminal tax cases involved in this line of work. Shilliday, who was forty-six when the trial began in late 1988, had full authority. The Newhouse case was his to win or lose, without the usually bureaucratic tendency to look over one's shoulder or to be second-guessed.

At first, Shilliday was not convinced that it would be necessary to go to trial with the Newhouse case. From 1983 and for the next two years, he met periodically with the tax lawyers hired by the Newhouse family, hoping for a settlement. In his own way, Shilliday signaled his willingness to accommodate with a style that Newhouse attorneys later agreed was gentlemanly and professional. He listened intently as the Newhouse lawyers from the Washington firm of Dow Lohnes Long, which specialized in media-related tax cases, argued that there was no merit in the IRS's fraud penalty. The Newhouses had hired an independent third-party analyst to come up with their estimate of the estate's worth, and they argued that there were no legal precedents for the IRS levying a fine based solely on a different valuation.

Shilliday came around to their point of view. He wasn't part of the penalty decision, but inherited it with the case. As a sign of good faith, Shilliday agreed with the Newhouse attorneys and consented to a December 1986 court stipulation to dismiss the $304 million claim for penalties and interest.

This was the last time the government would relent. As the talks continued, Shilliday became determined not to concede any further.

For both sides, the remaining issue revolved around the worth of Sam Newhouse's common stock on the open market and whether or not the tax bill would reflect its true value. The Newhouse lawyers argued that the question of voting rights with the common stock was like "playing with the trains"—an essentially meaningless endeavor because the preferred shareholders held the keys to the company. Sam Newhouse's common stock was more or less the same as his family members' preferred shares, they contended. He had to share dividends proportionally with the preferred shareholders and couldn't liquidate the company without their consent. No one in their right mind would buy the Newhouse common stock without the prior approval of the preferred shareholders, and thus it was worth far less than the IRS had estimated.

Shilliday wasn't buying that argument. Over the next several months, he became more convinced of the inequity in the Newhouse tax payment as both sides hired experts to bolster their positions, trying to convince the other side to settle. To say that Sam Newhouse's common stock didn't reflect his overall control of the company just seemed absurd. It defied the fundamental reality of the Newhouse empire. "The term control implies the entire voting control the common [stock] has. It implies control over mergers. It implies control over the destiny of the company, acquisitions, and the entire life stream of a corporation," as Shilliday explained in his opening statement in court.

To decide who was in charge, the judge would only have to review Sam Newhouse's words before he died. In his memoir to his children, the elder Newhouse described his role as a decision maker. "The head of the family—the position I have held ever since I was 13—carries the most weight in reaching any final decision," Sam Newhouse wrote. "But this is done just as it was done around the kitchen table with Momma in those early years, with a good deal of give and take by everyone." In another section of the book, Newhouse elaborated: "Although I have generally held the ultimate responsibilities for our major decisions, there have always been thorough discussions among all of us."

If the Newhouses were willing to throw the dice and go to trial, Shilliday was confident of the gamble. To help win the case, Si Newhouse and his brother would get on the stand and convince the judge that their father—the man who built the family fortune—had not been fully in charge.

"Please state your name for the record."

"Samuel I. Newhouse, Jr."

"Sir, would you tell the court whether you are now employed?"

"I am."

"What is your present employment?"

"I'm chairman of Advance Publications, chairman of Condé Nast Publications and I may have a number of other titles."

On this dreary January day in 1989, Si Newhouse, a slight and almost-unassuming man, sat in the dark recesses of the witness chair, raised his hand, and swore to tell the truth. Despite his deadpan understatement, in the nearly ten years since his father's death, Si Newhouse had become the richest and most powerful media baron in America.

"What is your relationship, sir, with Mr. S. I. Newhouse whose estate is a party in this action?"

"I was Mr. Newhouse's eldest son," he replied, "and I'm an executor of his estate."

At this hearing in Washington, D.C., Si Newhouse's testimony was much more than a defense of his father's empire building, more than just a how-to course in collecting multimillion-dollar media properties and avoiding taxes. Newhouse's words were testament to his drive and how his family's empire had grown dramatically. In this chamber, he would be required to testify in truthful detail about the family business—a forbidden topic outside of the Newhouse household. Concerned about secrecy, the family's attorney would ask the court to seal the record, to keep the sworn testimony of the press lord and the myriad revealing documents about the Newhouse finances from the inquiring minds of the Fourth Estate and their other competitors. But this request for a gag order on the proceedings was denied by Judge Williams, in deference to the First Amendment—the same constitutional provision that the Newhouses had invoked so often in running their presses.

To ensure the family's future and stave off possible further inquiries by the IRS into their finances, it was necessary for Si Newhouse's performance on the witness stand to conform neatly with the tax theories postulated by his high-powered legal team. He was ready to be led by his attorneys. At first, Newhouse spoke of his education and career, a portrait of the media tycoon as a young man. To the unfamiliar, his version seemed quaint and almost believable. Only occasionally did the added detail or telling phrase belie his true existence as the heir to one of America's great fortunes.

Newhouse told the court that he began working for the family business in 1948 as a twenty-one-year-old obituary writer for the old *Long Island Press*—a now-defunct broadsheet that at the time found its largest audience among the rows of two-story flats in working-class neighborhoods of Queens. Si described himself as a "cub reporter," dutifully absorbing the lessons of the craft. Matter-of-factly, he mentioned in his testimony that he happened to work for his Uncle Norman, the editor-in-chief of the *Press* and that he, as a mere cub, somehow managed to get invited three times a week to the 9:00 A.M. meetings where Uncle Norman, Uncle Ted, and his father decided the fate of the company.

On the stand, Si Newhouse fancied himself a young man of boundless drive and unremitting purpose, a portrait very much at odds with those who remembered him from the 1940s and 1950s. Both he and Donald could not be held by the constraints of academe, as Si portrayed it to the court. "Each went to college for three years and we were too impatient to wait around and get a degree," Si testified about his reasons for leaving Syracuse University. Later on the stand, Donald would be more frank. Asked about his major in college, he replied, "Having a good time."

Soon, Si's personal history was dispensed with so that the Newhouse attorneys could lay the foundation for the estate's tax defense. Much of their case was handled by a lawyer named Albert Turkus, a Harvard Law graduate who had once worked for Ralph Nader's Tax Reform Research Group. It was imperative for Turkus's consensus theory that Si Newhouse testify that decision-making in the Newhouse family business was done as a group and that Sam was only one among equals. On the stand, the back-and-forth, the seemingly well-rehearsed exchange between Newhouse and his media attorney, went with barely a hitch.

"Was there ever a time, Mr. Newhouse, when your father S.I. dictated a decision to the rest of the group?" Turkus asked.

For a moment, the direct approach seemed to take Newhouse aback.

"No, there was—I never remember him dictating a business decision. It was totally outside of his nature. He—the business was founded on the kind of consensus management and consensus concept and any—it never would have occurred to him to dictate a decision."

Such a view surely would have surprised many who worked for years under Sam Newhouse. Still, his son's version of the family business continued under oath without interruption.

"Can you tell the Court, Mr. Newhouse, when you first became aware of the fact that you were a shareholder in Advance?"

"The first time I knew it was when I got a dividend check," Si replied.

"Did there ever come a time, Mr. Newhouse, when you became aware of the fact that there were any differences in the nature of the different shareholders' interest?"

"Yes."

"Would you describe that for the Court, please?"

"Well, I can't pin it down to a period, but after awhile, there started to be stories in *Time* and some of the other magazines and we started to get written up. People began to notice us and there were references in these articles to classes of stock and that's when I first became aware of— that it was—that there were differences in the stock."

As he went on, this sixty-one-year-old media scion, his coarse silver-gray hair bristling off his scalp, told his own coming-of-age story, Newhouse-style.

Newhouse explained he got his first check in the 1950s (when, according to his account, he slowly became aware of the stock differences in the company). By this time, he was nearly thirty years old, married with children, had already spent two years in the air force, and had attended countless family meetings where virtually all aspects of the family business were discussed. Yet, Si Newhouse testified, he had to learn who owned what in the family's multimillion-dollar business by reading it in a magazine.

Si Newhouse's claim of being oblivious and unconcerned with the differences in the Advance stock conformed nicely with his tax attorneys' arguments. If there was little meaning in the varying classes of stock in the Newhouse business, as the attorneys contended, then Sam Newhouse's complete control of the company's common stock could not be fully taxed. As dubious as this legal theory might seem to the government, it was a trial balloon that seemed to float in court.

"At the time of your father's death, Mr. Newhouse, on August 29 of 1979, what was your understanding of the nature of the ownership of Advance?"

"Well, S.I. was a great loss," said his son. "He had been a powerful factor in our operations and in the ownership. He did a great deal of work but instead of there being four—five of us, the new situation was that there were four of us who owned the company. It certainly made a difference but it was the facts and so instead of five—"

He was beginning to wander. Turkus quickly interrupted. "Sir, what was your understanding of the nature of each individual's share of the ownership as compared to each other?"

Newhouse stared blankly at his attorney. "I have to say that I did not think about each individual's number of shares or percent of ownership. To the extent that I was aware of it, it was something that was in the back of my mind and had absolutely nothing to do with what we were involved in, which was running a business."

Determinedly, the tax attorney drove home the point. "At that time, Mr. Newhouse, what if any significance did you attach to the fact that some of the shares of the company were common shares and some of the shares of the company were preferred shares?"

"I did not attach any significance to it," Newhouse replied.

Turkus posed the same question about voting rights.

"I did not attach any significance to it in terms of the ownership of the business and the operation of the business," Newhouse said again.

Revisiting his father's legacy, Si Newhouse contended that his father was not the dominant force that the entire publishing industry assumed he was for decades. In determining whether to plow money back into the business, or pay a dividend, or make almost any decision at all involving the family business, Sam Newhouse was not a lion but a lamb, his son asserted.

"He was not a dictator," Si Newhouse testified, "and he—in this and everything else, he became part of a group discussion."

For virtually every other question concerning the family's portfolio, Newhouse had a stock answer. Slouched in the witness chair, Newhouse took on a certain incongruous appearance, like a reluctant witness sticking to the rehearsed presentation of fact and leaving the rest in a shroud of haze.

"We didn't think about stock," Newhouse replied to one inquiry. "We never thought about the corporate legalities, the corporate aspects of it. We were involved together—the family business—so I can't tell you when I really thought about it all being equal. I've always felt we were equal. There was never any thought that there was an inequality about any of us in the family."

Only once or twice on the stand did Newhouse seem to share the commonly held view about the powerhouse media company built by his father—that old man Newhouse knew every circulation figure, every display advertiser, and seemingly every nubby pencil and paper clip in the newsroom. The obsessive drive for detail, this ant-like approach, was what made the Newhouse newspapers grow from a molehill to a mountainous communications empire without peer. Near the end of his testimony, Newhouse became as expansive as he would ever be on the witness stand, providing a short lecture on the secret of the family's good fortune.

"I think the reason for our success—what makes us unique as operators—is the very intense interest that we have in the small parts of the operation and the large parts of the operation," Newhouse conceded on the stand, perhaps his most revealing moment that day in court. "So, the last thing I would say about us is that we are passive."

In fact, *passive* may have been the right word to describe the IRS's attorneys in this case. The cross-examination by Shilliday and his associate counsel, Howard Levine, hardly seemed threatening to Newhouse's ever-faithful version of the facts. After all, would a publisher with such a professed strong interest in every operational detail remain so vastly unfamiliar with the basic underpinnings of the company's stock structure?

The question remained essentially unanswered, like a mystery clue that would hover throughout the court proceeding.

As his testimony continued, Si Newhouse waxed on almost nostalgically about the family enterprise and how as a young man he eschewed such workaday notions as compensation.

"We worked, I think, like demons from the time we were youngest—at a very young age. There was an example set for us by our uncles and our father and it never occurred to us to ask what we were getting paid. Whatever we were getting paid, we were paid. He was not a father who said if you work a little harder, I'll pay you more. Or, if you don't work—if you're not working hard enough I'm not going to pay you. That was not part of his life. We were so committed to this family enterprise that this question did not arise."

The matter of what Si was paid as a Newhouse executive arose later during the cross-examination. When his father was dying, Si acknowledged that he became quite concerned with what he was paid and that it accurately reflect his increased workload.

"Could you tell the Court what your net worth was on August 29, 1979," Levine asked. Immediately, Newhouse's attorney sprung into action before he could answer.

"Objection, Your Honor," Turkus retorted. Pushing his luck, Turkus then went on to argue that Newhouse was incapable of saying what he was worth. "To ask him to opine as to his net worth necessarily requires him offering expert testimony in areas that it's not clear he has any expertise in, and the relevance—"

This was too much to take, even for Judge Williams, who was already favorable to the Newhouse arguments. He couldn't accept this at face value.

"Well, I think people can probably opine on their net worth, just like they can opine on the value of an asset that they own," said the judge. "I don't think either one requires expert testimony."

The two sides argued until Williams decided to break for lunch. When the hearing resumed, Newhouse was again confronted with financial documents detailing his salary from Advance. These documents showed that when Sam fell ill, the rest of the family, including his son Si quickly paid themselves more to pick up the slack. In 1978, Si Newhouse's salary was $239,500. This jumped to $407,859 the next year, when his father died. So much for the demon-like work pace without concern for money.

"Okay, could you tell the Court why the huge increase in your salary?" Levine finally asked.

"Well, S.I. had become relatively inactive in the early part of '79 and of course totally inactive with a stroke and with—obviously with his death," Si Newhouse said. "You will notice that all the salaries went up and I believe that as a group we came to the conclusion that we were absorbing his work and that a salary increase based on an increase in our responsibility was in order."

If Si Newhouse's haziness on sticky details like stock ownership among the family members didn't exactly jibe with his lecture on the family's "very intense interest" in the company's operations, the government lawyers never seemed to notice. If Si's lack of concern for what he was paid early in his career—if this struck the attorneys as disingenuous—they never expressed it. Even when Newhouse, who earlier testified that he had learned about the stock differences from a story in *Time* magazine, later said he didn't know what his father's reputation as a newspaper appraiser was in the industry, the government attorneys didn't make much of a fuss.

"At the time of death," Levine began, "isn't it a fact that your father was known as one of the premier appraisers of media properties?"

"Objection, Your Honor," Turkus interjected. "Known by whom? I mean, does he mean was that his reputation in the general community or is he quoting from a particular source? I'm just not sure how the witness can be presumed to know—"

Judge Williams nodded in agreement. "Mr. Levine, I think you should be more specific. Is it a question of reputation or in the general community or known by other executives—"

"In the general community, Your Honor," Levine replied.

". . . in the media publishing industry or other segments of the world?" Judge Williams continued.

The government's inquisitor seemed confused. "Well, I suppose I would say all of the above," Levine said. "Was he generally known as that in the media business?" Levine looked at the witness stand.

Finally, it was Newhouse's turn to answer. After watching his father for his entire life and getting to know the family media business in detail, surely S. I. Newhouse, Jr., could cast some light on his father's reputation.

"I don't know," Newhouse said with a drone-like tone in his voice. "I think that we conducted our business and we did fairly well and we made mistakes in some things and we were right about others, and I just don't know what he was known as."

In a way, Newhouse's time under oath—when not withstanding the rigors of what passed for the government's cross-examination—actually provided the opportunity to expand further on the Newhouse's unique place in the history of America's media business. To Si, Advance Publications was a purely democratic entity, careful not to wield unduly any power or influence like other press barons. Si could advance his arguments in historical terms, with a keen insight to his father's concerns about remaining invisible while the Advance company grew at a galloping pace. Even in this account, though, there was still no doubt whose hands were on the reins of the family business.

"Going way back, when my father and his brothers were putting together their business, there was considerable public concern about the imposition of an individual owner's editorial judgment on the country as a whole," Newhouse recalled. "It reflected primarily old Mr. Hearst, but I think to a certain extent Pulitzer and even Scripps were involved in common editorial policy. My father developed the concept of local autonomy and I think perhaps gave it those words, because it was his policy and this is followed consistently throughout his life and was followed by all of us in our handling of the newspapers. It was our policy to leave editorial endorsements and editorial judgments to the local editor, local publisher, dependent on the situation. In fact, at times we got just as much criticism for leaving editorial judgments to the local people as Hearst got for superimposing his judgments. But that's another story.

"As to autonomy of decision-making beyond that, I believe I described at considerable length the procedure that we followed, and while the judgment of the local publisher was certainly an important factor in our thinking, we are in fact very tight close operators who know almost everything that's going on in each one of our newspapers and participate in-depth in the decision-making."

Shilliday, the government's lawyer, later explained he felt it was "very unusual" for Si, given his detailed knowledge of the operations of the company, to testify that he was unaware of the basic structure of the company for so long. Shilliday later recalled Si's "difficulty in answering questions on cross-examination." But the two government lawyers, Shilliday and Levine, never made a dent in Newhouse's testimony.

Unchallenged, Si Newhouse instead explained the Newhouses' intricate company charter in terms of continuing a family saga. The different amendments to the family business's charter were not designed to avoid paying millions in taxes, but simply, as Si put it, to continue the "great fun" of running the company for themselves and their children.

"We have had considerable experience in the destructiveness of divisiveness in families that led to their sale of newspapers," Newhouse told the court. "In fact, almost every newspaper—probably every newspaper we acquired—we acquired because of family problems and at a certain point, we became concerned enough about the potential of that divisiveness to lead to some form of fragmentation of the company in the future so that someone proposed to our attorneys and our attorneys came back to us with a plan for the stockholder's agreement that we felt would accomplish a number of purposes, the first and most important being to maintain a stability for the company in the future."

For the Newhouse fortune to escape unscathed, the patriarch's shares had to be minimized and taxed as little as possible. And so, the Newhouse charter was made to appear as amorphous, as impenetrable, and as difficult to fathom for income purposes as legally possible.

Whatever the IRS and its hordes of auditors and attorneys would make of it, Si Newhouse was now at one with the business that his father had placed in his hands. His performance on the stand likely would have made his tight-lipped father feel proud. No matter how much he was challenged by the government's questions—which was not much at all—Si remained a font of often confusing information. And he glossed it over in terms so vague that at times even he was at a loss for words.

"As I said in the beginning, to put a formula on it almost destroys the concept," Newhouse explained to the government's lawyer. "It is a delicate concept. It depends on the tight working relationship and the good will that prevails among all of us, a sense of common goal, a feeling that we're all involved in this thing together. . . . There's no lobbying, there's no sides to anything. There's discussion and I think that's about the best I can say about it. It's a subtle process that comes out of the Newhouse corporate culture and Newhouse family culture and it works. It's given us a wonderful result."

Si's near-mystical response served only to frustrate the government attorneys further; they searched for a juicy case study that they might catch him on. One such exchange happened near the end of cross-examination. Using the Newhouses' $150 million purchase of the Booth media empire in 1976, the government attorneys asked for a step-by-step description of the family's decision-making process in that specific sale. Perhaps in getting Si Newhouse to explain how the family obtained the group of Michigan dailies and also the Sunday supplement *Parade,* which was also owned by Booth, the government could show how Sam Newhouse really was the key player, as virtually everyone assumed.

"You were involved in that acquisition?" asked Levine, now appearing somewhat frustrated.

"I certainly was," Newhouse replied.

"All right," Levine said, then looked upon Newhouse to fill in the blanks.

Newhouse returned only a quizzical, nonplussed stare.

"Well," he said in a weary tone of utter boredom. "It's a little bit like trying to describe love. . . ."

The government's case was in a near shambles by the time one of its top witnesses, John Coffee, Jr., took the stand. Somehow—amazingly, in Coffee's view—the Newhouses seemed on the verge of winning, escaping from what once had been a $1 billion tax bill against them. After months of preparation and years of waiting, the Internal Revenue Service's case was falling apart, almost inexplicably to Coffee. He remained convinced that the Newhouses were trying to walk away with millions in unpaid taxes.

As a professor of corporate and securities law at Columbia University, Coffee had analyzed many complex internal stock transfers of closely held companies, often testifying as an expert witness at tax estate trials. In a sense, he was like a coroner, a forensic accountant, picking through the remains of a family-owned company to find its essential structure and determine its true value. To Coffee, though the machinations of stock transfers and different classes seemed complicated, the bottom line was fairly clear-cut: Sam Newhouse controlled the company.

"He may have loved his brothers, but he kept all the voting stock," Coffee later explained.

On the stand, Coffee testified that the estate should be taxed for the full value of the company, not on the paltry sum that the Newhouses had calculated. He gave a detailed analysis of the Newhouse media empire and on cross-examination he backed up his assertions with an impressive understanding of the company.

Somehow, though, it didn't seem enough. Coffee sensed that his testimony was having little impact with the court, and it was both baffling and frustrating to him. When appearing as a witness for a wealthy taxpayer challenging the government's assessment, Coffee was accustomed to being paid a handsome fee and being prepped in advance by attorneys well versed in the case. In this case, however, Coffee's fee was relatively modest and Shilliday seemed out of his league. Coffee's early entreatments to Shilliday to seek a possible settlement were rejected out of hand. The IRS had built much of its expert testimony on university professors like Coffee who were willing to take a much smaller fee for their services than some of the professional analysts working actively in the field. It was difficult for the government to find analysts willing to take on a powerful adversary like the Newhouse family, which could, of course, become a future client or employer. At least one analyst for a major Wall Street investment house declined the government's invitation to appear as a witness against the Newhouses.

What Coffee found most disconcerting, however, was the deeply antagonistic relationship that had developed between Shilliday and Judge B. John Williams, Jr., that had escalated dramatically during the course of the trial.

Theoretically, of course, legal decisions were supposed to turn on matters of fact and law, not personalities. But Judge Williams could barely contain his contempt for what he clearly considered Shilliday's lackluster performance. "They got into one of the strongest personality clashes that I've seen in such a matter," said Coffee months after the trial. "Usually, the government gets a great deal of deference from a judge, particularly in tax court."

Not so with Judge Williams. The judge himself had once been an IRS attorney and was familiar with the inner workings of the IRS. He had come to the bench after a time with one of Philadelphia's largest old-line firms and displayed a magisterial air that sometimes seemed condescending and tart. Despite his prior government service, Judge Williams made it clear that he had a distaste for the IRS lawyers, and for Shilliday in particular. Coffee would find the judge respectful to him personally, but he was appalled by Williams's treatment of Shilliday. "Williams made a number of statements during the trial, saying things like 'I have a billion-dollar case and they send me these attorneys,' " recalled Coffee. More than a half dozen times during the trial, Williams fretted aloud about the poor legal representation being made by the government's main attorney.

Surely, Shilliday could not be expected to know the entire background of every witness in the case. For instance, he was unaware that J. Paul McGrath—called as an expert witness for the Newhouses shortly after Si testified—had been part of the 1985 Justice Department's criminal anti-trust investigation of Newhouse and his former newspaper competitor in Cleveland. It was McGrath's memo that outlined why the government had decided to grant Si immunity from any prosecution in that matter. As an expert witness in the tax case, however, McGrath spoke in general terms about the government's antitrust concerns if the Newhouses chose to spin off some of their media properties and sell them to other large media companies.

Of course, McGrath's actions in the Cleveland antitrust probe had vir-tually nothing to do with the Newhouse tax case. Nor was there any testimony at the tax trial by McGrath detailing the Cleveland case. But when asked years later, Shilliday said he would have liked to have known this bit of information when McGrath took the stand and testified that he had no financial "relationship" with the Newhouses. (In a 1993 interview, McGrath said he was recruited by one of Newhouse's attorneys to be an expert witness on Justice Department antitrust reviews. McGrath said he charged his usual hourly rate. "I don't know why they asked me," he said.)

But Shilliday's awareness of another expert witness's background—this time called for the government—did provide perhaps the most dramatic confrontation between Judge Williams and himself. On February 15, 1989, a few days after Coffee appeared on the stand, the judge's impatience with Shilliday's case erupted. For all practical purposes, this was the day the IRS's six-year case against the Newhouse family started to unravel irreversibly.

By this point in the trial, Williams had already thrown out much of the government's case. He had refused to allow into evidence certain key parts of expert witnesses' testimony and disallowed the report from media con-sultant James Kobak, who contended that the true value of the Newhouse empire was worth nearly twice the earlier $1.2 billion estimate by the IRS. There was one last big-gun expert witness left for the government: media consultant John Morton, perhaps the best-known and most highly re-spected analyst in the newspaper business.

Pure and simple, Shilliday walked Morton through the case and his interpretation of Advance's corporate structure. Then, fatefully, Shilliday solicited his opinion of the differing expert witness reports offered by the two sides and asked who was correct.

Judge Williams, alarmed that Morton was being asked to make a legal judgment, spoke up.

"Business expertise doesn't give him [Morton] the ability to do that," the judge said in a condescending way. "Business expertise gives you the ability to decide what to do with the disagreement. It doesn't give you the ability to decide who's right and who's wrong. If you can't understand that, Mr. Shilliday, I don't think there's a lot about this case that you understand."

Shilliday couldn't keep still. "The issue in this case," he began, "is who is right or wrong from a legal point of view. . . ."

"Yes, that's right," Judge Williams quickly snapped. "And a business-person doesn't have the expertise to make that judgment, right?"

"That's correct, Your Honor."

"Thank you—but he made the judgment, didn't he?" Williams asked, determined to exact his pound of flesh from the erring litigator.

"Yes, he did, Your Honor," Shilliday said like a contrite schoolboy.

Williams pressed on, quizzing Shilliday about one of the assumptions that Morton used in his valuation of the Newhouse estate. Shilliday again conceded that his expert witness, Morton, was in error. The judge was visibly angered by this second erroneous assumption.

"He is wrong," the judge said, with Morton in the witness box next to him. "As a matter of law, he is wrong! So now he is wrong on two counts. I am going to strike his whole report. His entire report is stricken! He is wrong as a matter of law. He's incredible as an expert. As a business-person, that he would make a decision as to who's right and who's wrong among [ten] prominent and eminent legal experts . . . It is absolutely incredible to me that he could make that judgment as a businessperson."

Morton, an urbane man who at the time wrote a column on the media business for the *Washington Journalism Review* and was often quoted in *The New York Times* and other periodicals, appeared stunned.

"The only thing I can say is that it saves us this afternoon," Judge Williams said with an undeniable tone of contempt.

The judge then focused his attention on Shilliday.

"Your lack of understanding in this case is exceeded only by your lack of preparation," Williams said, full of scorn. "It's just unbelievable. Just unbelievable! This is the worst performance I have seen on the bench—and for you to bring the commissioner's case into here with this kind of testimony is absolutely beyond the bounds of reason."

Judge Williams paused and looked for a moment at the thunderstruck courtroom. "You have anything else you want to say?"

Shilliday shrugged. "No."

"Well, I think I am finished," the judge said. "You may sit down."

After that staggering blow, what had once been the government's $1 billion tax case against the Newhouses never seemed to recover. Despite whatever damage Judge Williams may have inflicted on the government's case, the fundamental fault arose from the tactics and legal decisions made by the IRS and its attorneys. One after another, the series of missteps and miscalculations by the government allowed the Newhouses' attorneys to gain a decided advantage in court.

The Newhouse presentation relied on Wall Street experts and publishing executives to give a realistic assessment of what Advance would fetch on the open market. Media baron Rupert Murdoch and Douglas McCorkindale, who was in charge of acquisitions for Gannett Co., Inc., America's largest newspaper chain, agreed to testify about the worth of the Newhouse stock if there was a possible outside purchase. Both Murdoch and McCorkindale said Sam Newhouse's one thousand voting shares of class A common were worth far less than the full value of the company, particularly if the potential buyer could not easily purchase the remaining preferred stock, with all of its liquidation rights and other attachments. "Just looking at it overall, we are not interested in getting into situations that get messy and get involved in litigation," said McCorkindale.

Rupert Murdoch took the stand in defense of the Newhouses for no fee. The Australian-born tycoon told the court that his relationship with Si Newhouse and his brother, Donald, was "cordial and a bit more of being social acquaintances" than strictly business.

But Murdoch did acknowledge that he and the Newhouses were competitors in several media markets. Only months before, Murdoch had bought the longtime book publisher Harper & Row and combined it with his British-owned publishing house to form the new firm called HarperCollins, a strong competitor to Newhouse's Random House. Murdoch also said he and the Newhouses were "pretty vigorous competitors" in the magazine business, often vying for the same readers. Most notable was Murdoch's fledgling women's magazine *Mirabella,* named for its founding editor, Grace Mirabella, whom Murdoch hired after Si Newhouse unceremoniously dumped her from the editorship of *Vogue.*

Despite this friendly competition, however, Murdoch testified that he wouldn't pay a nickel for the Newhouse common shares without some agreement with other family members.

"Would you please explain for The Court, Mr. Murdoch, why you would not have been interested in such a purchase?" he was asked.

In his most commanding voice, the Australian mogul replied, "We are not interested in buying minority stock in companies unless there is some strategic purpose, and one can see it as a stage to buying the whole of the company."

The testimony of Murdoch and the Gannett executive fit neatly into the broader theory proposed by the Newhouse legal team—that Sam Newhouse's voting stock was worth far less than what the IRS claimed and that the family had paid its fair share in taxes. As Murdoch's testimony underlined, there were many realistic doubts about who would be willing to purchase a family-run business with stock ownership as appealing as a thornbush.

During the trial, Shilliday and his government witnesses did little to overcome these doubts.

Joseph Baniewicz was the IRS expert in analyzing media businesses and determining what amount of taxes were owed to Uncle Sam. If Shilliday was the government's point man in the courtroom, it was Baniewicz who was the driving force, the bureaucrat behind the scenes, in the government's pursuit of the Newhouses for back taxes.

In 1983, Baniewicz pushed the IRS to reject the tax forms filed by Si Newhouse and his brother on their father's estate. After traveling during his IRS audit to the family's various newspapers and broadcast stations, Baniewicz became convinced that Sam's shares in the Newhouse empire were worth far more than the family had stated on its estate-tax forms. In its 1980 filing, Si Newhouse and his brother based their estate tax payment of $48 million on the claim that their father's total holdings amounted to only $178 million.

Baniewicz figured things much differently. He was convinced that Sam Newhouse's one thousand shares of Advance common stock controlled the company, and he made his calculations based on that premise. The IRS calculations were based on "the subtraction theory"—a phrase that would be repeated often throughout the tax trial. In short, it meant that the IRS estimated the full worth of the Advance company and then subtracted the cost of buying all of the stock that wasn't owned by Sam Newhouse at the time of his death. In this case, it meant the cost of disenfranchising the Advance company's 3,500 shares of preferred stock, which was owned by the rest of the Newhouse family.

As a result of this approach, Baniewicz estimated that the preferred stock was worth about $267 million. And, he further concluded, the one thousand shares of class A common stock with voting rights left by Sam Newhouse was worth no less than $1.2 billion—with a bill for estate taxes of $609 million owed to Uncle Sam. By this calculation, Baniewicz was also convinced that the Newhouses deliberately set out to mislead the IRS by seriously undervaluing the worth of Sam's shares. The estimated tax bills were so far apart that it had to be fraud, he concluded. In the halls of the IRS, Baniewicz's indignation prevailed, and on May 18, 1983, the IRS issued a notice of tax deficiency along with a $304 million fraud penalty.

"Baniewicz was the more zealous one," Coffee later said about the government's protagonists. "They believed from the outset that it was fraud. They never got into serious negotiations and they were just outclassed. They could have settled for a lot more, but the IRS analysts didn't want to back down. Shilliday, he was small-time and he was given a position to take in court, and he saluted like a good soldier. It was the IRS who made the decision. It was Baniewicz's theory."

The IRS tax theory contained a fatal flaw, however. And it was right in the fine print, in the government's regulations on how to value such an estate as Sam Newhouse's. The fair market value, it read, is determined by "the price at which the property would change hands between a willing buyer and a willing seller, neither being under any compulsion to buy or sell and both having reasonable knowledge of the relevant facts." The IRS emphasis was on determining the true value of the privately owned Newhouse empire, and did not satisfactorily address to the question of who would want to buy such an encumbered company and at what price. There was no indication that any real-world buyer would be willing to use a subtraction theory to arrive at a price tag or would be willing to negotiate a buyback or merger for the remaining Newhouse family shares.

It was a gaping hole in the government's case, and the Newhouse attorneys waited until the trial to drive a wedge through it.

When Baniewicz took the stand, he was cagily asked numerous questions as part of the voir dire, the initial procedure in court testimony to establish a witness's credibility as an expert. One of Newhouse's attorneys, Albert Turkus, asked him several questions about how the government estimated the value of Newhouse common stock. Turkus seized on what he perceived to be Baniewicz's weak spot, the government's Achilles heel—whether he examined the worth of this stock from the eyes of a willing buyer and a willing seller, as the law dictated. After listening to Baniewicz's explanation for a short time, Turkus appealed to Judge Williams.

"Mr. Baniewicz never sought advice from real-world buyers on how they would approach valuing the stock like this," Turkus argued. "Forget about how unique this stock is. He didn't even ask any questions about how they would approach valuing the stock in a closely held company where there were different classes of stock.

"He has never advised—he has never himself been involved in buying and selling a newspaper, buying and selling newspaper companies, magazine companies, stock in such companies. He's never advised buyers and sellers. . . . I'm not suggesting to this court on behalf of [the Newhouses] that there's anything wrong with Mr. Baniewicz having an opinion, or that there's anything wrong with the Service employing Mr. Baniewicz to provide valuations which may be the bases of notices of deficiency. . . . [But] the fact that he engages in that exercise does not make him . . . an expert in the things which the government is asking him to testify about here today."

With his key witness on the ropes, Shilliday scurried to his feet and defended Baniewicz to the judge. He pointed out that Baniewicz had performed IRS valuations for the past fifteen years and specialized in media companies.

Judge Williams demurred for the moment.

"Do you have any expert witness who's going to testify that buyers, any buyer of common stock, would pay a price determined by subtracting out from the value of the total enterprise the value of the preferred?" Judge Williams asked.

Shilliday nodded and said he would provide, with some caveats, such testimony from media consultants John Morton and James Kobak. With this assurance, Williams agreed to permit most of Baniewicz's report into evidence. It was a promise that Shilliday would be unable to keep.

By the time Morton and Kobak appeared in the case, things had already gone drastically awry for the government. In one instance, Turkus pointed out to the court that Shilliday had misidentified Richard Meeker—the author of a critical biography about Sam Newhouse published after his death—as a former friend or associate, according to a pretrial memorandum. Meeker was fifty years younger than Sam Newhouse, and Shilliday hoped to call him as an expert on Newhouse's iron grip on the family business. Because of this careless error, Judge Williams threatened to hold Shilliday in contempt, and the government soon dropped Meeker as a witness.

Shilliday made a more serious error in judgment by hoping to call another witness, William Worthington, Jr., a former Chemical Bank official who wrote a 1977 memo that seemed to foreshadow some of the IRS contentions about the Newhouse stock. In that memo, Worthington questioned Chemical's prevailing view that all classes of Newhouse were the same and said it could face a serious IRS challenge. "The common stockholders, currently only Mr. Newhouse, have complete control. Since the valuation of each class of stock is critical to the Newhouse family's estate plan, I recommend that the family seek the opinion of evaluation specialists."

When Worthington's memo was found in the files of Chemical Bank, the IRS felt it had discovered a smoking gun. To Shilliday, it indicated that there was doubt about the legality of the Newhouses' tax plan among their own bankers. It also seemed to undercut the family's claim that Sam Newhouse's shares were worth no more than the others.

Armed with this memo, Shilliday had hoped to show that Sam Newhouse had intended to trick the IRS out of millions in death taxes. His opening statement to Judge Williams, alluding to the Newhouses' alleged "trick" with its taxes, its financial "sleight-of-hand," seemed to be built on this evidence. But when Shilliday eventually called upon Worthington and tried to offer his memo as evidence, his efforts fell far short.

First of all, while Worthington expressed his doubts about the IRS interpretation, he didn't believe that the Newhouses were deliberately trying to deceive the IRS. More importantly, the Worthington memo failed to take into account the company's 1956 charter amendments, which gave the other Newhouses who owned preferred shares the option of blocking a potential sale. Worthington was unaware of those provisions and his memo was later discounted by his superiors at Chemical Bank, who were unlikely to disagree with the Newhouse tax strategy, anyway. When Shilliday tried to admit Worthington's memo into evidence, Turkus argued that it was ignorant of the 1956 charter changes and reflected only Worthington's individual view, not the opinion of the bank.

Judge Williams agreed and excused Worthington as a witness. The government's "smoking gun" never even made it to the stand.

Nor was the government ever able to back up its earlier testimony from its chief IRS analyst, Baniewicz, who contended that a prospective buyer of the Newhouse media empire would use the IRS subtraction theory to estimate the true value of the company's shares.

Magazine analyst James Kobak's report on the Newhouse empire had been dismissed by the court before he even took the stand. Kobak's assessment was that the Advance company was worth more than $2 billion when Sam Newhouse died—a figure twice the previous estimate by the IRS's own analyst, Baniewicz. Two months before the trial, the government unveiled their sudden increased estimate of the value of the Newhouse company, adapting to the updated figures provided by Kobak. But the tardiness of Kobak's report, on what the Newhouse lawyers portrayed as "the eve of trial" in the case, prompted Turkus to ask the judge to dismiss it, and Williams did.

Kobak's analysis on the stand only seemed to hasten the judge's dim view of the government's case. The magazine analyst had been retained in 1985, and the government later had to explain why it had taken him so long to produce his report. When called to testify, Kobak said he had been a consultant since 1971 and that each month he averaged about two valuations of media properties for tax and merger reasons. During Kobak's initial testimony, Shilliday led him through the basic tenets of the government's case and Kobak nodded and agreed. For a time, it still looked as if Kobak would prove to be one of the government's most effective witnesses, with a bloated estimate of the Newhouse fortune that made the government's assessment seem downright charitable.

However, the poor presentation of the government's case was never so devastatingly evident than with Kobak, particularly during cross-examination. At one point, under Turkus's questioning, Kobak admitted that he had made a $39 million mistake in his valuation of *Vogue,* the most prized of the Condé Nast magazines, and its related *Vogue Guides.* When asked about another discrepancy, Kobak offered a less-than-satisfying response: "My ladies may have picked that up from a clipping out of the newspaper or something and . . . wrote it wrong."

Judge Williams had endured enough; he decided to take matters into his own hands.

"I will entertain a motion to strike this report and his testimony from evidence," he said, interrupting Kobak's testimony.

With Kobak still in the witness stand, Turkus quickly took the judge's cue. "We so move, Your Honor," Turkus said.

"I will grant the motion."

Shilliday, still stunned by the sudden ouster of his expert witness, just looked at Judge Williams in disbelief.

"Is Mr. Morton going to be a little more credible than Mr. Kobak?" Judge Williams asked.

"Yes, Your Honor," Shilliday said without conviction.

Williams was unmistakably blunt. "For your client's sake, I hope so."

When John Morton was thrown off the stand, discredited as the government's last-gasp expert witness because of what the judge said were his erroneous assumptions on legal matters, the IRS case against the Newhouse estate was irretrievably lost.

It took nearly a year following the trial's completion for Judge Williams finally to issue his report. His findings were later considered well reasoned by legal scholars and contained none of the bombastic asides and personal affronts to Shilliday and the IRS witnesses that had marred the courtroom proceedings. Nevertheless, Judge Williams's findings in the tax case were a disaster for the government.

On February 28, 1990, the judge's one-hundred-page ruling was nothing short of total victory for Si Newhouse, his brother, Donald, and the generation of younger Newhouses, who, due to the form of complicated family trusts, stood as heirs to their grandfather's fortune. In short, Judge Williams agreed with the Newhouse lawyers. He ruled that the value of Advance Publications, the family's newspaper and magazine conglomerate, was worth about $1.5 billion at the time of Sam Newhouse's death but that his one thousand shares of common stock were worth only $176 million. As a result, the family owed $48 million in taxes, almost exactly as the Newhouses had claimed a decade earlier.

More than just one loss in a very expensive case, the Newhouse decision by Judge Williams became a troublesome precedent for the IRS in determining the value of wealthy private held companies. In the future, the IRS would have to prove with much greater specificity what a company might fetch on the open market from a willing buyer who might sharply lower the asking price if full control of the company wasn't clear.

According to Williams, the law was so unclear about the rights and duties regarding so many different classes of stock that any final determination on the value of the Newhouse fortune had to take into account the potential cost of expensive litigation to sort things out. Of course, any outside buyer would have to figure on "the likelihood of protracted and unpredictable litigation in negotiating a purchase price," Judge Williams declared. As a result of the logic in the judge's ruling, the worth of Sam Newhouse's stock plummeted and so did the estate taxes. In the end, Sam Newhouse's stock ownership was declared to be worth only about 10 percent of what the judge had agreed was the full value of Advance

Publications, the company that Newhouse built and controlled his entire adult life.

For some observers, the Newhouse decision was a galling excuse for every rich family business in the United States to come up with a new estate tax plan—making its capital structure so confusing, with multiple charter revisions and amendments, that no one could figure it out later without a costly legal battle. But the Newhouse side was obviously pleased by the outcome. "It's hard for anyone to say why the judge ruled the way he did," recalled Paul Scherer, the Newhouse family accountant who sat through most of the trial. "It was a landmark case in estate taxes. And in all the commentary I read, everyone has a different view and a different idea."

What was in Sam Newhouse's mind in formulating such a beehive business charter is forever lost to history, though he now holds an honored place in professional CPA journals as a mighty champion of interpreting the tax codes. In Coffee's opinion, sheer gall and utter obfuscation was the intent of Sam Newhouse, the kind of financial maneuver against the IRS that would have made Roy Cohn proud. "They were consciously thinking about this strategy all along," says Coffee. "There were about eleven changes in a twenty-year period, with all these arcane changes and wordings. There's no ordinary company that goes through these types of changes in their structure."

To save the family fortune, Sam Newhouse's secretive approach proved essential. Whatever threat the massive IRS investigation may once have posed, the Newhouse media kingdom, now worth more than $10 billion, was safe as its entered the 1990s. The tax strategy carried out by Sam Newhouse, his attorneys, and his bankers for decades had paid off handsomely for his sons. Unlike other family dynasties, which saw their power and fortune slip away in huge IRS payments and internal strife, that of the Newhouses had emerged unscathed and triumphant. Sam Newhouse's gift to his family was secure.

As this case moved glacially through the court, the ability to avoid any jarring tax payment on the patriarch's estate enabled the Newhouse company to grow exponentially. They were able to acquire such high-profile media properties as Random House and *The New Yorker,* as well as pay for a host of other developments. If the Newhouses had paid what the IRS said was their fair share of taxes, these purchases—which helped to redefine America's media industry during the past decade—would have been difficult, if not impossible. And it likely would have meant still further tax challenges by the IRS, endangering other parts of the family fortune.

Instead, the result was relatively painless. Aside from the high-priced attorneys and their witnesses, the tax fight had cost Si Newhouse very little in the way of lost prestige or embarrassing details. During this ordeal, Si was rarely challenged about his testimony—the hazy answers to specific questions and the overall claim under oath that his father really hadn't run the family company with an iron hand as so many had thought he had.

Si was spared such public embarrassment because the Newhouses' $1 billion tax case attracted little attention from Washington correspondents or the financial press corps. For some, their conspicuous absence at the Newhouse trial spoke volumes about the apparent willingness of the press to protect its own—or at least ignore their travails in open court. The nation's top newspapers seemed reluctant to explore the allegations of massive tax avoidance against the Newhouses, "members in good standing of the media conglomerate club whom fellow potentates might encounter any noon at the Four Seasons or later in black tie at Sotheby's," as *The Nation*'s Richard Pollak later commented. "Better to distract the vulgar plebes with circuses like the Steinberg and Myerson trials."

That is not to say that Si Newhouse wasn't grateful for the little help he did get from the media. For the day, he could even be pleasant with one of his chief rivals. "It is very nice of you to come," Si Newhouse said as fellow media baron Rupert Murdoch arrived in U.S Tax Court one morning to lend his voice to the Newhouses' tax arguments. Si shook Murdoch's hand vigorously, like that of a long-lost friend.

Murdoch, who had left his limousine and driver parked outside the courtroom, smiled and looked around. No matter how rich and powerful he had become, Murdoch still knew a meaty story when he encountered it and he had braced himself for the throng of reporters and photographers he expected upon his arrival. But the world's best-known media tycoon seemed surprised, almost disappointed, at the rows of empty seats in the courtroom.

"I was expecting more of a turnout," Murdoch said.

After testifying as the Newhouses had hoped—claiming that the purchase of Advance without all of the preferred shares would be "a very bad business proposition for anybody"—Murdoch put on his coat and began to leave.

As he neared the door, Murdoch smiled and nodded at Si Newhouse, who was looking at the list of witnesses with his son Wynn.

"See you in New York," Murdoch said, then dashed to his waiting limousine.

CHAPTER EIGHT

At Random

Dinner that evening was very special. When the sale was announced in February 1980, Si Newhouse invited those closest to him to a private celebration to mark his new acquisition. Random House was the prize, and now it was his. What his father had not been able to accomplish in a lifetime, Si Newhouse, along with his brother, Donald, had pulled off with one masterful stroke less than a year after Sam Newhouse's death.

Thirty people gathered at one of Si's favorite Japanese restaurants, inside the Ritz Hotel on the East Side of Manhattan, a place where Newhouse could be assured of privacy. One of the few outsiders invited to accompany him was Random House's longtime chairman, Robert L. Bernstein, a tall, shy man with a highly regarded reputation in the book-publishing business.

Many of the guests that night were friends of Mitzi Newhouse, still lively at seventy-six, who came dressed in a sequined gown as she might for a Broadway opening. She seemed pleased but said very little. Si, perhaps buoyed by the swift acquisition of America's premier book publisher, was a bit more talkative than usual. His comments, though, were little more than light patter.

At the head table, Roy Cohn carried most of the evening. He told several humorous anecdotes and seemed delighted by his friend's good fortune. Bernstein and his wife, Helen, were aware of Cohn's unsavory reputation, though his presence didn't engender any doubts about Newhouse's intentions with Random House. "I remember he was very charming that night," Bob Bernstein would later recall about Cohn. "I've been told that he could be that way."

There was an air of festivity surrounding the dinner, which in retrospect would make it seem like a coming-of-age party for Si Newhouse.

From this moment forward, the Newhouses' vast empire was Si's to own and manage with the acquiescent support of his brother. Random House was a bold statement of his intent. Never before had the Newhouses, despite all their money, been able to attract a media property quite like it. Owning one of the nation's top book publishers carried significant literary prestige as well as a steady stream of profits. In the newspaper world, prestige and quality were modifiers rarely attached to the Newhouse name. Even the elegantly produced *Vogue* magazine, the jewel of the Condé Nast assemblage, was dismissed in most New York literary circles as mere puffery. During his lifetime, Sam Newhouse hunted and sniffed for such prestigious properties as *The New Yorker, The Washington Post,* and *The New York Times,* but each time he was firmly rebuffed. Things would be different for his sons.

At the age of fifty-two, Si Newhouse was eager to make his own mark. The purchase of Random House less than a year after his father's death would certainly draw a great deal of media attention and push the name of Newhouse outside of its protective cocoon. Si Newhouse voiced concern about losing his near anonymity. Nevertheless, buying Random House was a firm and necessary signal that this second generation was intent on taking the family's once-pedestrian group of publications to a higher plane, one very much in the public eye.

Acquiring Random House was a personal triumph, as well. Whatever doubts that once lingered about Si's ability to run the family business had long since evaporated. In a style his father would have admired, the $70 million purchase of Random House from the RCA Corporation was executed swiftly and aggressively. Throughout the 1980s, Random House's total value grew exponentially, more than tenfold by the end of the decade. As his first major acquisition, Newhouse's purchase of Random House set a tone for the dramatic and often-convulsive actions within his family's company, a pattern of events that would leave an indelible imprint on the media industry at large.

Along with a handful of other book publishers owned by large multinational corporations, Newhouse's publishing house catapulted the business of selling books—once a rather modest cottage industry—into an unprecedented period of megabucks and blockbuster titles more akin to Hollywood than New York publishing academe. In luncheons at Manhattan's Four Seasons restaurant or over the telephone to his top executives, Si Newhouse articulated his formula for publishing success: Pay whatever price necessary for the big-name book. Inexorably, this new equation upset the equilibrium of the firm, redefining virtually everything about the publishing house. Editors would come and go in fast succession, and eventually the fundamental changes to Random House would bring about Robert Bernstein's departure. What happened to America's best-known book publisher would be debated in the media and within the publishing industry itself. By the 1990s, though, most agreed Random House was a far different company from the one Newhouse had purchased a decade earlier.

For his part, Robert Bernstein had little hint initially of the changes that would occur. After running Random House for nearly fifteen years,

Bernstein was simply looking for an owner he could trust. He hoped for the same kind of publishing marriage Bennett Cerf had arranged twenty years earlier with the house owned by Alfred A. Knopf, a union consummated through a simple handshake and their shared purpose in publishing the finest books possible. As he looked for a possible suitor for Random House in early 1980, Bernstein knew it wasn't going to be that easy.

Several weeks earlier, Bernstein—a courtly Harvard-trained executive whom Cerf had personally selected to lead Random House through the second half of the century—had learned his treasured publishing house was about to be put up for sale. Since 1966, the company had been owned by RCA, which paid Cerf handsomely for it. But RCA officials never really understood how to manage a publishing house, and they remained content to allow Bernstein a free hand in running it. Bernstein's relative autonomy was now threatened by RCA's decision to sell.

The prime mover in Random House's sale was RCA chairman Edgar H. Griffiths, a one-time credit analyst who rose in the company to become a successor to the legendary Gen. David Sarnoff, the broadcasting genius who built RCA and envisioned its NBC radio and television networks. To most, Griffiths was a humorless company man with razor-cut hair and an expressionless smile. He was criticized even by his board of directors for being too consumed by his job. Nevertheless, analysts liked him for improving RCA's bottom-line performance.

With one stroke in early 1980, Griffiths decided to spin off both Random House and Banquet Foods, two subsidiaries that no longer blended into his company's profit picture. For Random House's chairman, there was a certain gallows humor in sharing the same fate with a poultry company. "There seemed to be more of a problem to them with Banquet, because of what you do with ten thousand chickens every day," Bernstein recalled. The RCA officials assured him that Random House would be placed in responsible hands and that he would be informed before any final decision was made.

Shortly afterward, Bernstein received a telephone call from the Newhouse family. He learned one of the media brokers selected by RCA to find a buyer was putting together a proposed deal with the Newhouses. But both Newhouse brothers said they wanted to meet with Bernstein before any agreement was signed. Bernstein and the brothers agreed to lunch at the club inside the Pan Am building in Manhattan.

"I must say the Newhouses were terrific in the way they handled it," Bernstein recalled. "They told me that they wanted to buy it only if it was okay with the people at Random House and they asked me to check before they went ahead."

Bernstein did some checking of his own. In 1980, neither Si nor Donald Newhouse was well known, not even in Manhattan's tightly knit media community. It was presumed that the sons would follow the same path as their father, who, according to media folklore, had allowed the editorial side a free rein so long as his newspapers made money. This appeared similar to the arrangement Bernstein enjoyed with his RCA bosses. The Newhouse properties were also privately owned, another factor that appealed to Bernstein. Given the highs and lows of publishing, Bernstein felt Random House would be in better hands with a private owner like Newhouse than with a publicly held media company that was answerable to a board of directors and issued quarterly reports to its stockholders.

During their luncheon meeting, Bernstein tried to take a measure of both brothers and was favorably impressed. Despite the Newhouses' projected image of meticulously sharing family power, Bernstein sensed Si Newhouse held more sway than his younger sibling. "It was all Si who handled it," Bernstein recalled of the sale negotiations. "Si is much more aggressive than Donald." After that meeting, however, Bernstein remained in the dark about the proceedings until Griffith gave him an urgent call one day in early February 1980 and told him to come over to the RCA executive suite by 1:30 P.M. that afternoon. Bernstein assumed he would be asked his opinion about a possible bid. Instead, Griffiths offered a fait accompli.

"I just want to tell you before it goes out on the ticker at two o'clock that we're going to sell Random House," Griffiths said.

Bernstein, like a man never fully in control of his own fate, showed no surprise at the sudden announcement. He was grateful the buyer was Newhouse.

The next day, the purchase of Random House made headlines across the country and the familiar fiction about the Newhouses was once again repeated for a new generation. "According to publishing officials, Newhouse, because it makes a point of keeping its hands off its properties, will make a fitting parent at a time when many authors and editors are dismayed by the commercialization of the book business," the *Times* pronounced in its front-page story about the sale.

This hands-off view—which would later seem amusing to anyone familiar with Si Newhouse's very tactile ways—was repeated by a number of other knowledgeable publishing experts who had no idea of what was to come. Nor did Bernstein, who felt he had inherited a new owner with whom he could be comfortable. It wasn't until many months later that Robert Bernstein realized how wrong he had been.

For nearly a half century, Random House was Bennett Cerf's house. Actually, as his friends and colleagues learned with delight, it was more like his stage.

From the very outset in 1925, Cerf, then a young Columbia University graduate, and his best friend from college, Donald S. Klopfer, began publishing books with a certain flair and élan. Even their first titles— handsomely redesigned classics that were part of the Modern Library series, forming the cornerstone of what would later become Random House, Inc.—set the tone for a classy blend of highbrow literature and popular entertainment, which would become a Random House tradition.

Cerf, a short man with a ready smile, horn-rimmed glasses, and a remarkable ability to make friends, was the thinking man's P. T. Barnum, somehow able to ensnare the most interesting beasts under his tent. "Bennett runs Random House as a conservative branch of show business," Jason Epstein, one of its most talented editors, observed. "The company is vulgar to a degree. But what makes the difference with Bennett is how important he feels it is to have a Philip Roth and William Styron on the list. Some other publishers would know a thousand ways to get rich without having one author like that. Bennett Cerf doesn't."

Editors and writers alike enjoyed the editorial freedom allowed by Cerf and Klopfer, who published writers as diverse as William Faulkner, John O'Hara, Robert Penn Warren, Ayn Rand, James Michener, and Marcel Proust. Cerf nevertheless had a seasoned taste for best-sellers and healthy profits. He seemed to understand the public's tastes and reading habits and he presented a list of books that, as he described it, someone browsing through a bookstore might pick "at random." The Modern Library classics, which had sold more than 50 million copies by the time Cerf died in 1971, would prove to be a gold mine for the company, as would several other book deals Cerf engineered.

Cerf's bold decision to initiate a landmark lawsuit that challenged federal censorship and allowed James Joyce's *Ulysses* to be published in the United States brought the publishing firm its first true taste of fame. The highly publicized fight to publish Joyce's masterpiece made Random House a fearless champion of artistic expression, a publisher on the side of the literary angels. The so-called "dirty words" contained in the back of Joyce's novel were, as a federal judge later ruled, "a sincere and serious attempt to devise a new literary method for the observation and description of mankind." The courtroom drama over Joyce's novel, which was finally published in the United States in 1934, heightened the public's awareness of this Irish writer and the fledgling American publisher willing to fight its government's obscenity ban. At the time, Cerf's embrace of *Ulysses* could easily have backfired. Another well-known publisher of Joyce's work had already shied away from the novel because of possible repercussions. The timidity of larger, more established publishers in coming to the aid of what was already recognized as a great literary work made young Cerf's move seem even bolder and his legal victory that much sweeter.

With Random House's early success, a certain literary reputation and tradition developed. As a raconteur and habitué of the New York nightlife, Cerf signed up many of the writers and celebrities he met in his sojourns. For many Americans, Bennett Cerf was best known as a panelist on the long-running television show "What's My Line?" Yet his resounding achievement was to gather the creative talent needed to establish Random House as one of America's great book publishers.

After World War II, Cerf and company resided in the palatial old Villard house located on Madison Avenue, behind St. Patrick's Cathedral in midtown Manhattan, creating an intellectual atmosphere described with some hyperbole. When Jason Epstein arrived at Random House from another publisher in the mid-1950s, he expressed his happiness to the boss's wife. "When Jason Epstein came over, he said he was in 'Lotusland,' " recalled Phyllis Fraser Cerf, then also an editor at Random House. "It was one of the great places. He felt like he was in heaven."

Robert Bernstein shared the same sentiments about Random House, coming over from Simon & Schuster at about the same time as Epstein and rising quickly as a young star through the company's ranks. Both Epstein and Bernstein were reflective of Cerf's view that running a publishing house was much the same as managing a championship baseball team. He believed in developing such talented editors as Albert Erskine, Robert Loomis, Joe Fox, and later Robert Gottlieb, creating a vital enterprise that ensured Random House's continued success. Bernstein was brought in for his business expertise in selling popular books, while Epstein was hired for his acute literary taste and ability to find important works. As Cerf quipped succinctly, "Jason Epstein is my class editor and Robert Bernstein is my mass editor."

By 1965, Random House had grown into a mature company with many different publishing interests, including the distinguished imprints of Alfred A. Knopf and Pantheon purchased in the early 1960s. Cerf, who was sixty-seven years old at the time, decided he wanted to sell Random House and step down from the company's presidency. He chose Bernstein as his successor. "We had someone ready, the right man to step in," Cerf recalled in his memoir, praising Bernstein, who "had proved he had everything he needed to be responsible for our combined operations." That same year, Cerf held merger talks with Henry Luce's Time-Life company, which held several publishing advantages. Both sides were willing, but the Justice Department—in noticeable contrast to its decisions about media mergers later during the Reagan years—indicated it would block such a deal on antitrust grounds. RCA's chief, David Sarnoff, was willing to meet Cerf's asking price, however. A deal was struck as soon as Cerf and his wife, along with his friend Frank Sinatra and his soon-to-be wife, Mia Farrow, returned from a ten-day vacation—a trip that Cerf used as a "take it or leave it" ploy in his negotiations. The handsome contract stipulated that Cerf's staff would still run Random House and that RCA would not interfere with the publishing process.

Throughout his tenure as company president, Bernstein allowed his editors great leeway and initiative, keeping with the tradition of Cerf and Donald Klopfer. Yet Bernstein was fated to supervise Random House with someone always watching over his shoulder. Until he died in 1971, Cerf remained chairman and kept a mindful eye on the company. He admitted he sometimes caught himself second-guessing Bernstein, in whom he had great confidence, and felt it difficult to give up the reins of the business. During RCA's ownership, Bernstein found himself explaining the publishing house's business to a group of executives like Griffiths who had little interest in keeping it.

For Bernstein, having to talk with only one owner, Si Newhouse, seemed like an added bonus to the purchase of Random House in 1980, after years of RCA's disinterest and bureaucracy. "I had five or six bosses while at RCA," Bernstein told *The Wall Street Journal* two years later, praising Newhouse's singular syle. "Under RCA, we were a $40 million business in an $8 billion company, so we were not important to them," Bernstein explained. "At the monthly meetings, what they wanted to know was if the figures were above or below the previous month, and everything was done by committee." One particular bone of contention with RCA was satisfied in a matter of weeks under Newhouse. He quickly allowed Bernstein to acquire Fawcett Books, a mass-market publisher of paperbacks needed to complement Random House's long list of authors appearing in more expensive hardcover editions. Bernstein realized this new owner could size up a situation and make a swift decision.

While professing ignorance about some parts of the book industry, Si Newhouse readily became an avid pupil. In interviews after the sale, he invoked the familiar notion of local autonomy and of letting experts like Bernstein run their own show. In a way, Si Newhouse seemed a perfect owner: The shy, nondescript older son of a man grown wealthy beyond anyone's imagination, he seemed to indicate he was willing to sit back and only occasionally go through the books. To *Publishers Weekly,* the industry's major trade magazine, Newhouse portrayed himself as a mere "consultant" to Bernstein in running Random House. "I expect to see him from time to time and talk over any problems of interest," Newhouse said. "In my younger days, I was able to learn about the newspaper business and then the magazine business by working in them from the ground up. Unfortunately I can't do that now, but I can hope to get a feel for the opportunities and dynamics in the business." Newhouse indicated his main interests were in the "mundane aspects of publishing" such as production, distribution, marketing, and other financial matters. To any editor or writer wondering about Newhouse's intentions, this hardly seemed threatening.

Bernstein, a secure man with not much taste for corporate intrigue, welcomed Newhouse's curiosity and encouraged him to talk with many of his top editors. "I did not try to have his only vision of the business be mine," Bernstein recalled. The more Newhouse knew, Bernstein theorized, the more Random House would benefit within their billionaire owner's far-flung empire with all its competing interests. Editors were invited to tag along with Bernstein for his lunches at The Four Seasons with Si, where they were encouraged to speak about their part of the business. Occasionally, they would later receive handwritten notes from Newhouse, commenting favorably on a published work or suggesting an idea. The luncheons with Newhouse became notorious within the company for being ill-named, for editors rarely got the chance to consume anything more than repeated questions.

On Tuesday afternoons, week after week, Newhouse and Bernstein would meet at a circular banquette in the Grill Room of The Four Seasons, where they talked and went rapidly through a succession of company memos and reports. Newhouse scribbled his notes on yellow legal pads. "It was very quick," Bernstein said of the weekly luncheons. "You would discuss various parts of the business, what was happening. You'd discuss personnel; you'd discuss acquisitions of books—it'd be a general review of what was happening in the business in the past week. And on a week-to-week basis, a person is very informed on what is going on in the business."

With Newhouse's backing, Bernstein presided over a remarkable period of expansion for Random House, when revenues climbed from under $200 million at the time of the 1980 sale to nearly $900 million by the end of the decade. Far larger than when Bennett Cerf served as its president, Random House under Bernstein became the preeminent force in American trade-book publishing, entering headlong into the expensive bidding race for popular fiction, contemporary nonfiction, and other works by celebrity authors. To maximize earnings, Bernstein combined Fawcett with its existing Ballantine Books division to create one of the nation's top mass-market publishers, created Villard Books, and acquired the Times Books imprint from the New York Times Company. He also expanded Random House's distribution of smaller publishers like Reader's Digest Press and the AAA Road Atlas and starting putting its children's books and best-selling authors on audio and video tapes.

By the mid-1980s, Random House was enjoying a steady increase in revenues each year, with a profit level of about 15 percent—a remarkable achievement for the book industry, where the margins are usually much lower. In a few short years, Bernstein and his boss had transformed Random House—a company viewed as overpriced by analysts before its 1980 sale—into a moneymaking juggernaut that even Sam Newhouse would have been proud to own. "I think it represents one of the great buys of our time," Si Newhouse told the *Times* in 1985 in a rare moment of braggadocio.

Despite the company's remarkable financial success, Bernstein was never able to establish much of a relationship with Si Newhouse, whose personality seemed at odds with Bernstein's avuncular style. In their conversations, Si seemed to construct a maze of tightly fortified walls with only a few slight openings. Bernstein learned where he could venture in their talks as well as those certain areas considered off limits. All areas of Random House's finances were free for discussion, but the idea of any "synergy" with other Newhouse properties like *Vanity Fair* or other Condé Nast magazines was not to be discussed. What went on in other areas of the Newhouse empire was broached only if Si desired. The dividing lines were kept inviolate; inquiries were not appreciated.

Family, in particular, was a forbidden topic. Usually during long-distance flights together rather than the rigidly formatted Four Seasons luncheons, Bernstein tried to share stories about their families. The father of three sons, Bernstein was an admitted "son-worshiper" who talked proudly of their achievements and of his growing brood of grandchildren. Si Newhouse, the father of three children now in early phases of adulthood, was unwilling to partake in any such personal discussions, however. "I never met Si's children," Bernstein recalled. "He rarely talked about them. And if you started, he would stop, at least to me. . . . Si kept his family very much out of the discussions. One of the things about when you talk about your family is that you feel you have to give the other person equal time. But that never worked with Si. So I stopped talking about my family."

From time to time, however, the relationships within the Newhouse family nevertheless would make themselves known at Random House. When Si's daughter, Pamela, entertained thoughts of becoming a writer, it was Robert Gottlieb, publisher of the company's prestigious Alfred A. Knopf imprint (and later made editor of *The New Yorker*), who was dispatched to encourage her and offer advice. And during the weekly Four Seasons luncheon, Si was occasionally accompanied by Steven Newhouse, Donald's son. One of the third generation of Newhouses—Sam Newhouse's grandchildren and the heirs to much of his fortune—Steve Newhouse was generally viewed as the most likely to run the family business when his father and uncle were no longer able to. The preparation and grooming to run the Newhouse concern apparently required a certain monklike silence when in the presence of the elders tending to their affairs. As a young man, Si learned to sit quietly as his father and uncles discussed their newspapers. Now, while Si examined the events at Random House amid the bustle and lunchtime activity at The Four Seasons, Steve never voiced an opinion. His silence was unnerving to Bernstein. "Steve never said a word," he recalled. "You couldn't get an opinion out of him. Many times, he sort of just sat there without saying anything for the whole lunch. It was really sort of strange."

Part of the silence seemed to be enforced by Si, never explicitly in words but, rather, in gestures and silent pauses invoking the weight of a family code. "It was apparent that you were not to seek his opinion even though he was there," Bernstein says of the polite young man who did little but watch and listen. "My sons would have found it intolerable."

The unspoken differences between Si Newhouse and Bernstein also extended to their views about publishing and what role it should play in society. Far from a cultural brute, as some would portray him, Newhouse had developed a sophisticated aesthetic and taste, particularly about those subjects with which he felt familiar, like art, film, history, and architecture. Nevertheless, the purpose of the publishing business for the Newhouse family had been historically single-minded. "I do not like charity cases," Newhouse once adamantly stated. "I believe my operations should have the sense of security that comes from knowing their work leads to a profit. Businesses that lose money are insecure and do not take the chances they should to achieve quality."

Along with its financial rewards, Bernstein viewed publishing in more patrician tones, as a traditionalist who would sometimes publish a book because it deserved to be. He also refused some books he knew would make money simply because they would come at the expense of Random House's reputation. As his mentor, Bennett Cerf, once said in publishing a limited edition of the *Divine Comedy,* "Profit was not what we were looking for; it was the prestige." For Bernstein, who started out as a salesman on the business side, books had become a source of good for the commonweal as well as for the company's bottom line. Indeed, he believed quality and prestige were intrinsically linked to and essential for the success of the house. "A mountain range instead of a mountain," as he would describe his decentralized approach within Random House, Inc., with its more than a dozen imprints dealing with everything from fiction to biographies, cookbooks to children's books. "A book company is a service company for authors," he told his top editors. "It edits them, promotes them, and, in a way, it has to love them." One of his biggest admirers was Ted Geisel, whose Dr. Seuss books were a bedtime staple for children and a steady source of income for Random House for more than a generation. He once called Bernstein "our kaiser and pope."

As a natural extension of his view about publishing. Bernstein became personally committed to the ideals of free speech and human rights, helping to found such international groups as the Helsinki Watch, Human Rights Watch, and the Fund for Free Expression. Through his work as chairman of the Association of American Publishers in the early 1970s, Bernstein championed the international issue of protecting writers and journalists from government violence and abuse. He founded the independent Fund for Free Expession along with such members as Arthur Miller and E. L. Doctorow. He became deeply committed to human-rights issues after a visit to the Soviet Union in the mid-1970s, where he met dissident writers, some of whom had been imprisoned. In 1975, Bernstein and his wife traveled to Oslo when Yelena Bonner delivered the speech prepared by her husband, Andrei D. Sakharov, at the time he won the Nobel Peace Prize. His association with some of the world's leading dissidents, like Jacobo Timerman and Natan Sharansky, brought Random House both distinguished and sometimes best-selling books. Simply because he knew and trusted Bernstein, Sakharov allowed his memoirs to be smuggled out of the Soviet Union and printed by Knopf after a simple handshake agreement.

Bernstein, whose life and career were changing through this work, could be passionate about human rights. When a conversation lingered about what Knopf should pay for *Letters to Olga* by Vaclav Havel, the then-imprisoned Czech writer who would later become his nation's president, Bernstein became impatient.

"He's in jail," he directed. "Buy the book!"

The movement for human rights consumed much of Bernstein's heart and attention. "It's my life—it's all I do," he said in one interview. It was not uncommon for Bernstein to open a Random House sales conference with a comment about human rights. The executive conference room inside Random House's headquarters at 201 East Fiftieth Street—where the company relocated in 1969 when the Villard house became too crowded—was used for the weekly meetings of these human-rights groups. In 1985, Bernstein, then sixty-two years old, flew to Nicaragua with well-known attorney Orville Schell and Juan Menez, both top officials of the Americas Watch, to document for themselves the allegations that the Contras, the anti-Sandinista rebels, were terrorizing civilians. During the trip, the three men drove, without weapons, to the Honduras border to talk with local residents. Bernstein never sought or asked for Newhouse's approval before such a mission. But those familiar with Newhouse's thinking believe he couldn't have been pleased with the extracurricular activities of his company's chairman.

Essentially, Si Newhouse had always claimed that he was apolitical. To the extent his politics were discernible, Newhouse seemed to favor the status quo, whatever it was. Bernstein surmised that Newhouse privately endorsed the politics of conservatives like Ronald Reagan, at least from their few private moments together and Si's close friendship with Roy Cohn. Newhouse might be seen at an occasional political function or fundraiser, but he refrained from other obvious efforts to gain influence or favor with any administration. It was virtually unheard of for a Condé Nast editor to testify publicly before a congressional committee as Bernstein did and speak against an appointee selected by Reagan to become assistant secretary of state for Human Rights and Humanitarian Affairs. Consistently, Bernstein made a distinction between his role as human-rights advocate and chairman of Random House. But the Reagan administration officials criticized the Americas Watch as a politically biased group and questioned Bernstein's objectivity.

Seeking a sign of support, Bernstein encouraged Newhouse, whose family foundation gives only a small portion of their total wealth to charity, to make a major donation. After all, the Newhouse family had made billions of dollars essentially through the freedom to print and say whatever they wanted. Bernstein saw such a donation in primarily personal terms. He knew that Newhouse probably disagreed with several of his human-rights groups' findings, but he felt that the billionaire owner would bestow a gift as a way of backing his chairman, who had considerably lifted Random House's revenues. After one or two overtures were made, Newhouse finally bought a table at one of the human-rights fund-raising dinners. The major gift Bernstein had hoped for never materialized. He could not help but see Newhouse's lack of financial support, given Bernstein's up-front public commitment, as a subtle no-confidence vote for him personally.

In the following months, the differences between the two men became more pronounced, in large measure symbolizing what publishing once was and where it was now headed. The dramatic changes within Random House—and in American publishing in general during the boom years of the late 1980s—would soon make their shaky relationship untenable. In public, Bernstein remained supportive, though his comments seemed to acknowledge that the early common wisdom about Newhouse and his promise of complete autonomy were mistaken. "Si looks over your shoulder a lot," he told *The New York Times,* "but in a constructive way." Random House was no longer the publishing enterprise of Bennett Cerf and his successor, Bob Bernstein, but rather the prized property of Si Newhouse.

When Joni Evans's marriage to Simon & Schuster chairman Dick Snyder fell apart in 1987, the gossips treated their dissolution with the same mock horror as the breakup of Madonna and Sean Penn. When Evans was offered a top job at Random House and she accepted shortly afterward, the columns once again buzzed. When she was removed as publisher of Random House's signature imprint in late 1990, the news was headlined in *The New York Times.* "You've been fired on the front page of the *Times,*" a distraught friend gasped over the telephone.

Almost as much as best-selling authors, and sometimes more so, book editors in the late 1980s were suddenly celebs—touted, lionized, and castigated by the chroniclers of Manhattan's social scene. Even Evans was amazed at the lack of proportion people showed when discussing her fate. "The media has decided that editors and publishers are as glamorous as William Styron and Ed Doctorow, and it's really silly," she said in a 1991 interview. "It used to be Tina Brown and Anna Wintour and now it's spilled over into the book publishers."

To be a major player in Si Newhouse's empire was to invite attention. By the late 1980s, the whole aura of celebrity seemed to have rubbed off on Random House book editors like Evans, Sonny Mehta, and Erroll McDonald, once silent toilers in the literary vineyards who were now profiled in newspapers and magazines. Agents like Mort Janklow and Andrew Wylie were lauded in print and their record-setting million-dollar advances for blockbuster books not yet written were heralded like moon landings or foreign coups d'état. "The press is writing stories about the publishing business the way they used to write about Hollywood," said superagent Lynn Nesbit, herself an occasional column item. She later formed her own agency with Janklow.

This aura of celebrity was just the most visible change taking place during a decade in which publishing deals were auctioned, sold, and packaged like any Hollywood deal. Bigness—big books by big authors sold in big shopping malls by big media conglomerates became the driving force in American book publishing. Celebrity was just a part of the sophisticated mass marketing needed to promote and sell books. During Bernstein's tenure, Random House was more than willing to play along, at least to a point. "It was always Newhouse's theory to get the big books and pay a lot for them, as opposed to me, who wanted to know what was the previous sales record of an author," said Bernstein. "He always believed that a publishing house needs a big book to help carry things through and that whatever price you pay now will still be cheaper over the long run."

Newhouse appeared confident in his understanding of the book business by the mid-1980s and started offering a steady stream of ideas. His suggestions were usually treated as mandates. He became convinced Random House should compete head-on with any other publisher for the big-name book, regardless of Bernstein's reservations. In relying on such an approach, Bernstein realized his company's fortunes might become too dependent on high-risk ventures, with expensive books sometimes written by untested celebrity authors. Si's approach might also crowd out the available money for smaller, often more literary books that were a fundamental part of Random House's reputation as a quality publisher and that would provide a more prudent return on investment. But Newhouse was convinced he was right. His big-book theory changed Random House's character as well as transformed the world of publishing, accelerating its reliance on blockbusters. Because of Random House's deep pockets, small independent houses were sometimes forced to take the risks they might not have in order to compete. "We've overpaid," complained Roger Straus, head of the independent publishing house Farrar, Straus and Giroux in 1990. "But we're aware when we do it. And of how much we can afford to lose, because we can't put it under the rug the way they can at Newhouse's place."

Newhouse would push to sign big-name authors, leaving Bernstein and his management team to figure out the rest. His ideas could be quite good. From the earliest days of his ownership, for example, Si made known his wish that Norman Mailer become a Random House author. "He wanted Mailer and we put together a deal for Mailer," recalled Bernstein, who said he was unaware of the ways in which Roy Cohn had privately helped to midwife the deal. "Si was very instrumental in getting him and we then dealt directly with Scott Meredith [Mailer's longtime agent]."

Perhaps the most notable success, however, was Newhouse's personal effort to convince Donald Trump to write a book for Random House.

Trump's marquee value became evident to Si when "street sales"—issues bought at newsstands rather than through subscriptions—jumped for Newhouse's *GQ* magazine issue featuring "The Donald" on its cover. By early 1985, Newhouse was familiar with Trump from New York's social circles. They both shared the same attorney and close friend, Roy Cohn, who at various times had helped to broker sensitive deals for both men. At that time, Trump had not yet become the man of a thousand tabloid headlines. The young developer with a dashing appearance and a multi-million-dollar real estate portfolio seemed to capture the interest of readers, embodying the era's much-publicized ideal of the brash Yuppie on the make. Trump was the ideal billionaire. At lunch during a sales conference in Puerto Rico in December 1984, Newhouse made signing up Trump an immediate priority.

Soon afterward, Si personally called Trump, and that initial contact was followed by a series of follow-up meetings with Random House's then associate publisher Peter Osnos. During one conference with the developer, Osnos brought along, at Si's suggestion, a dummy book jacket with a picture of Trump standing splendidly in the atrium of his Trump Tower. TRUMP was emblazoned in large gold letters across a black background at the top of the jacket. Osnos wrapped the jacket around a thick Russian novel for further verisimilitude. Although what Si had in mind probably wasn't *War and Peace,* the sales pitch worked. "When I'm ready to do the book, I'd like to do it with Random House," Trump wrote to Newhouse soon afterward. Privately, he was flattered and slightly dumbfounded that Si Newhouse was interested enough to approach him personally. Trump told the press he would donate his royalties to charity and chose writer Tony Schwartz to be his Boswell. A year later, Trump's paean to himself, *The Art of the Deal,* became a huge best-seller for Random House. (Trump's sequel a few years later, *Surviving at the Top,* arrived in bookstores shortly after Trump's financial troubles became known, with very disappointing results.) The original book, however, secured Trump's place as a nationally recognized figure—a True Celeb in the bright firmament of American Hype.

For Newhouse, the Trump best-seller captured the spirit of what he was trying to do both at Random House and, even more so, at his Condé Nast magazines. "It's obvious that this book was like *Vanity Fair,* the preeminent example of a certain instinct that Si has for a kind of glamour and power and public presence," said one person who was involved in the first Trump book. "It's like Trump was a kind of shadow for him, in the sense that Si is so shy and so bumbling with words and so uncomfortable in social situations. I think his attraction to Trump was that he was so much his opposite. So out there, so aggressive, so full of himself." When the book party was held in the golden Trump Tower atrium, Si Newhouse greeted guests along with his new author.

Sometimes ideas sprang from Newhouse's own life or business interests.

At least twice, editors at Newhouse's publishing house were asked to consider autobiographies or memoirs by men who had been lawyers for the Newhouses: Clark Clifford and Roy Cohn. On the surface, both seemed like good ideas, though these books would later cause some considerable difficulty and embarrassment for Random House.

"Si is filled with ideas for books," said Osnos in an interview in 1990 as he was preparing Clifford's memoir, *Counsel to the President,* for publication. Osnos, a former top foreign editor at the *Washington Post,* had been recruited by Bernstein in the mid-1980s to help bolster Random House's lineup of nonfiction books. At one point in the late 1980s, Si Newhouse suggested a book about Clifford, once a top aide to Presidents Truman, Kennedy, and Johnson and a powerfully influential lawyer who once tried unsuccessfully to buy the *Washington Post* for the Newhouses. In an interview, Osnos would point to the Clifford memoir as an example of Si's good ideas. Before Clifford's memoir appeared in print, however, his august reputation was sullied by his participation in the international scandal involving the Bank of Commerce and Credit International (BCCI). He was later indicted on criminal charges by the Manhattan district attorney's office. There was no way that Osnos or Random House could have anticipated this crisis. Eventually, Clifford's law partner was acquitted of the charges by a jury, while Clifford was excused from standing trial because of his ill health. Nevertheless, the BCCI affair made Clifford's statesmanlike tome seem phony and discredited.

Roy Cohn's idea of producing a book about himself presented even more problems for Random House's editors. "We had to do it," recalled Bernstein. "I didn't see how we could not do it, given how close he was to Newhouse." Bernstein was never given any reasons why Newhouse wanted to buy the autobiography of his controversial best friend.

The assignment of producing the book fell to Jason Epstein and Howard Kaminsky, who had been installed as head of Random House's flagship imprint. For a time, there was a genuine hope within Random House that a revealing confession-like book by Cohn could become a best-seller. A writer and close pal of Cohn, former *New York Times* reporter Sidney Zion, was chosen to patch together Cohn's ramblings, both on paper and on tape, and assemble them into a cohesive book. Cohn lavished praise on friends like Si Newhouse, Ronald Reagan, and Barbara Walters and used the forum to criticize old enemies or those he simply didn't like, such as then Vice President George Bush and federal judge Irving Kaufman. Some familiar with Cohn's methods believe an unsubstantiated allegation against Kaufman was made simply as a payback for the final 1986 report of the President's organized crime commission, chaired by Kaufman, which contained a thinly veiled reference to lawyers who allow organized-crime figures to use their offices or provide other questionable assistance, as Cohn did with mob bosses Anthony Salerno and Carmine Galante.

After reading some of the rough drafts, Random House had a change of heart about a tell-all autobiography by the boss's best friend. Zion was nearly 80 percent finished with the Cohn manuscript when he received word from Random House that they were dropping the project. Zion said that only a week or so before, he had received a twenty-thousand-dollar check for his work on the Cohn book. Zion was angered by the sudden decision and later published the book elsewhere. Both the Zion-written autobiography and Nicholas von Hoffmann's biography, entitled *Citizen Cohn,* were reviewed together by Tom Wolfe on the front page of *The New York Times Book Review.* Yet one Random House executive told columnist Liz Smith that Zion's manuscript had problems. A *Washington Post* reviewer said the Zion book was "chattier and spottier" than von Hoffmann's effort.

Whatever the book's problems, Zion believes the potential trouble was evident from the very start. He remembered being surprised to find Jason Epstein at Roy Cohn's final party. "I said, 'Jason, fancy meeting you here,' " recalled Zion, a longime friend of Cohn who had gone to many parties with him and was familiar with Roy's friends. He felt Epstein was being solicitous of people with whom he usually wouldn't associate and was there simply for one reason. "Jason had to be there, because he wanted to be friends with Roy because he worked for Si Newhouse."

But finding out why his book had been killed became a mystery for Zion. By that time, Cohn had already died from AIDS and there was no one else to intervene on the book's behalf. "I think Si killed it," Zion later said. "Someone close to him later said to me that they thought it was best for everyone concerned."

Despite these occasional personal interventions, Newhouse allowed Bernstein and his staff to become more aggressive in the pursuit of big books and celebrity authors. His philosophical tug-of-war with Bernstein over large advances became apparent as Random House signed such popular fiction writers as Barbara Taylor Bradford and John Jakes to multimillion-dollar contracts, as well as such well-known political figures as former Speaker of the House Thomas P. "Tip" O'Neill, Jr., and First Lady Nancy Reagan. The $1 million advance paid for O'Neill's book was worth the price when it became a number-two nonfiction best-seller, but the huge $3 million payment to Nancy Reagan reportedly was never recouped. It was Si who pushed hard to sign the First Lady's book.

Bernstein's reluctance to up the ante in publishing upset some agents like Morton Janklow, who managed to get Si Newhouse's ear during this time. Janklow's financial interest was obvious: He wanted to get the most money possible for his clients through a large advance. What was more difficult to trace was how Janklow, a social acquaintance of Newhouse, managed to affect his thinking. As early as 1985, Janklow hinted publicly that he was unhappy with Bernstein. "It's a great publishing house, no question about that. They are easy to deal with on the personal level.

But there's still not a great deal of flexibility there." Janklow's carefully worded dart was aimed at Bernstein and the haughty kind of attitude Random House displayed in rejecting *Scruples* by Judith Krantz—an entertainingly salacious tale of little redeeming social value (despite the fact it spent thirty-six weeks on the best-seller list after Janklow sold it to another publisher for a measly fifty thousand dollars). Bernstein's lack of enthusiasm for large advances and the general disinterest of Random House editors in acquiring the widely popular pulp novelists—almost displaying an elitist disdain—stirred Janklow and others to point out privately to Si Newhouse what he was missing.

Within the industry, Jason Epstein, the brilliant and mercurial editorial director of "Little Random," as the flagship imprint is called in the company, was known to have declined some books that later became best-sellers, including *Mayor* by Edward I. Koch. Such works, it was reasoned, were not of the quality Random House traditionally published, and their authors not of the caliber Epstein was accustomed to editing, such as Gore Vidal, E. L. Doctorow, and Norman Mailer. When actress Shirley MacLaine offered *Out on a Limb,* her first opus on her extrasensory experiences, which later became an out-of-this world best-seller, Epstein firmly rejected it. "Did I know it was going to sell? Sure I did," Epstein said afterward, without a moment of self-doubt. "But I took one look at that book and saw that it was madness—*mishigoss* about coming from another planet. Being Cleopatra's best friend . . . the woman was obviously disturbed. That's millions of dollars of business we didn't do, but I've never had a moment of regret."

By the summer of 1984, Epstein was asked to stay at Random House as a top editor but relinquish his powers as publisher. In his place, Bernstein agreed with Newhouse to offer the position to Howard Kaminsky, the former chief of Warner Books, who had a flair for signing up commercial novelists and big-name books. A fast-paced and sometimes pungent conversationalist, Kaminsky rapidly developed a social relationship with Si Newhouse, which he liked to characterize as friendship. Kaminsky had a refreshing directness—what might be called street smarts in his native Brooklyn—that appealed to Newhouse. Kaminsky blended his aggressive tendencies ("a plunger," as Bernstein later described him) with humor in a way reminiscent of his older cousin, comedian Mel Brooks. He didn't seem as intellectually threatening or portentous as other Random House editors and his tastes in film and art were similar to Newhouse's.

Kaminsky was willing to take chances, the kind of calculated big-money gambles that Si wanted for his publishing company. He wasn't shy, either, about letting Newhouse know his thoughts about Random House's management. During their Four Seasons luncheons together, Bernstein noticed Newhouse's questions were becoming more detailed, as if he was being briefed about the company by others. "Si loved detail and got more and more involved as time went on," Bernstein said. "He was courted by Mort Janklow, and in the time of Howard Kaminsky, he got even more involved. Si liked the game of going higher and higher with the authors."

During his dozen years with Warner, Kaminsky turned that company around with such mass-market delights as *Never Say Diet* by TV jumping jack Richard Simmons and John Naisbitt's *Megatrends,* a pop survey of every social trend imaginable. With Si's blessings, Kaminsky was determined to "widen the net" of Random House's offerings and signed up a roster of celebrities like Carol Burnett and sure-hit novelists. Conservative columnist William F. Buckley, Jr., was signed up and Kaminsky won the rights to John Jakes's *California Gold* in an auction with Bantam Books and Simon & Schuster, Random House's two main rivals. The reported $4.3 million bid for both the hard and soft rights to Jakes's novel—before he had written a word—underlined the frenetic pace within the publishing industry. Simon & Schuster, once a struggling company, had revived in the early 1980s to become Random House's main competitor. A third major competitor, Bantam, stressed high-volume celebrity books in hardcover, like Kitty Kelley's biography of Frank Sinatra, which became a massive seller. Together, Random House and its two top rival publishing houses placed forty-nine books on the best-seller list in 1986 alone.

At Random, the old guard struggled to adapt while maintaining the quality that they believed had made Bennett Cerf's company a success. In the past, the firm, which published more than forty Pulitzer Prize–winning books and the writings of twenty-seven Nobel winners, was the place where quality and prestige ruled. Writers could depend on being nurtured in return for a certain loyalty to the house. Bernstein was fond of mentioning those well-known authors who had been with the company for two decades or more: William Styron, Robert Penn Warren, Ray Bradbury, John Hersey, and Truman Capote. To be sure, Bernstein was willing to pay a hefty advance to any writer with a proven track record. Mario Puzo once had a $6 million offer waved in front of him by Bernstein after the latter was alerted to Puzo's availability by the top editor at Knopf, Robert Gottlieb. Inexorably, such high-stakes gambles were transforming the publishing business and Random House itself. In the past, as one top agent told writer Joshua Hammer in 1987, the difference between Random House and Simon & Schuster was "the difference between Bendel's and Macy's. S&S was the crass, vulgar, we're-in-it-for-the-business publisher. Random House presented itself as 'We are the people of quality. You come to be with us, and we're not going to overspend for you.' Now Random House is becoming what S&S was five years ago. 'Give us the book, and we'll pay you top dollar.' "

As Si Newhouse once told another publishing executive, Kaminsky's role was to make sure Random House would spend big money as readily as any of its competitors. For Newhouse, Random House's sterling reputation of old could go only so far; money was the active agent of the day.

"To a certain extent, the lines are becoming blurred," acknowledged Kaminsky, who still appreciated the differences. "We're all making great expenditures for a few books that everybody wants."

As Random House changed under Si Newhouse's leadership, Bernstein realized how empty were the original promises of hands-off autonomy. Si was clearly calling the shots and Howard Kaminsky, as the most vigorous actor on Newhouse's behalf, became the personification of those changes. The tension between Kaminsky and Bernstein, two men with very different styles and tastes, was evident to those who attended editorial meetings with them.

Bernstein, whose soft-spoken manner often masked a strong sense of pride, seemed taken aback by Kaminsky's direct and sometimes-pointed comments. On more than one occasion, Kaminsky approved book deals with large advances without first asking Bernstein's approval. Bernstein assumed Kaminsky had sought Newhouse's approval directly, which further provoked his wrath. Implicity, Kaminsky's actions suggested Bernstein was almost irrelevant in the new order of things. Such bold moves by Kaminsky seemed predicated on his good personal connections with Si Newhouse—the kind of relationship that, ironically, Bernstein encouraged his top editors to develop with the owner.

What was most galling to Bernstein, however, was the persistent rumor that Kaminsky was Random House's heir apparent, the man selected by Newhouse to lead Random House into the future. Bernstein began to believe Kaminsky, who was not demure in speaking to the press, was the prime source of these rumors about him. He heard disparaging words that he was a "light hand on the tiller" or too obsessed with his human-rights causes to spend an adequate amount of time overseeing Random House. There were several editors who agreed with Kaminsky's criticisms or thought the company had grown too large for Bernstein and that it was best he retire. Though in his mid-sixties, Bernstein was not ready to leave. Nor did the think that Kaminsky, then forty-seven, was ready yet to succeed him, if ever.

By October 1987, Bernstein was determined to get rid of Kaminsky. It was an extraordinary step for him, because he preferred to ease people out of jobs rather than abruptly fire them. Confrontation was not his style. Ousting Kaminsky, however, seemed necessary to reestablish his grip on Random House's management. When Kaminsky returned from the Frankfurt Book Fair, the international book industry's annual showcase, he was asked to meet with Bernstein in the chairman's executive office and was then fired. Book editors within Little Random—many of whom had believed the gossip items about the social affairs attended by Kaminsky and Si Newhouse—were dumbfounded. Kaminsky gathered his staff to read a note announcing his departure. Some laughed, thinking it was a joke, until they realized from Kaminsky's choked voice that he was indeed leaving.

The departure was so abrupt, Bernstein had little time to consider who would be Kaminsky's replacement. Joni Evans was asked to run the Random House imprint, while other divisions like Times Books, Vintage Books, and Fodor would report to Bernstein temporarily until things could be worked out. Suddenly, the atmosphere was chaotic. This kind of public beheading might be inflicted by Si at Condé Nast, but it was not the management style for which Bernstein and Random House were known. In effect, the confrontations over Kaminsky had been prompted by the subtle competing pressures from Newhouse, who had installed a potential successor with whom Bernstein felt distinctly uncomfortable and philosophically at odds. Bernstein just couldn't picture Howard Kaminsky as Random House's chairman someday.

"In fairness to Si, I don't think he ever gave any indication that the 'heir apparent' thing was anyplace close on his agenda," Bernstein recalled. But Newhouse never showed any signs of wanting to halt Kaminsky's overtures to circumvent his boss. If anything, Si seemed to enjoy Kaminsky's company and favored the changes he wanted to bring to Random House.

Under the circumstances, there was little Newhouse could do but support Bernstein's decision. In all likelihood, Newhouse, no stranger to quick good-byes, was as surprised by the firing as Kaminsky. "Howard challenged Bob Bernstein and tried to usurp the role without being actually the president," recalled one editor who attended some of the tense meetings and conferences with the two men. "Everyone assumed that Bob went to Si and said, 'Him or me.' "

Newhouse's final break with Robert Bernstein began in 1989, apparently over the fallout from the purchase of the Crown Publishing Group, a major publisher that Newhouse had agreed to buy for under $200 million a year earlier. Si had long wanted to purchase Crown, known for its savvy marketing and distribution. In the mid-1980s, Crown was the nation's fifth-largest publisher of hardcover books. When the owners of Crown were finally ready to sell, they chose Random House, based partly on their long-standing admiration for Bernstein and his collegial style. As they reviewed the projected numbers, Bernstein and his staff recognized that Crown produced a huge stream of revenues, as much as $400 million in sales. But Crown's owners, Alan Mirken and eighty-six-year-old cofounder Nat Wartels, had yet to provide crucial information about their cost structure. Bernstein said he preferred to wait until all the numbers were considered, especially Crown's net income. During one of their Four Seasons luncheons, however, Newhouse countermanded his chairman and, in effect, ordered him to buy it. As Bernstein recalled, "Si was somebody who was a risk taker when he wanted something."

The suspicions about Crown's leaky finances were confirmed only after it became the property of Random House. By then, it was too late. Bernstein and his top aides realized that Crown was losing money, despite its huge flow of revenues. Two of the biggest moneymakers for Crown that looked so good from afar—its Outlet promotional books and particularly its direct-mail operation, the Publishers Central Bureau, with $170 million in revenues—were found, upon closer inspection, to suffer from overhead costs greater than their revenues. The difficult job of digesting Crown and fixing its problems fell to Bernstein at a time when the overall question of cost structure was being reevaluated in the publishing industry. After years of solid profits in the mid-1980s, the company was barely able to stay in the black by 1989. Suddenly, Random House's "mountain range" of imprints seemed unmanageable and Bernstein's golden touch became suspect.

During their weekly talks, Newhouse—by now fully conversant with the ways of the book-publishing industry—pressed Bernstein harder and harder for better financial results. It became apparent that Newhouse wanted someone different for Random House, finally to make over the publishing house in his own image. After months of resisting, Bernstein was suddenly vulnerable on the numbers and realized that Random House would no longer remain his company to run. In November 1989, after a lengthy period of private disagreements, it was announced that Bernstein would leave, with no successor named. Typical of their differences, Bernstein called his departure a "resignation," while Newhouse preferred to label it a retirement.

After a decade of highly publicized firings, Si Newhouse was already notorious for his bruising management style, prompting one editorial writer to wonder after Bernstein's abrupt dismissal if Newhouse might be "the George Steinbrenner of publishing." In his oblique way, Newhouse spoke only a few words. "We decided this was the right thing," Newhouse said, claiming he could not remember who first broached the subject of Bernstein's departure. "It's the way things worked out." To another writer, Newhouse denied Bernstein's firing followed any "pattern of traumatic decisions" like the abrupt departures at *The New Yorker, Vogue,* and other Condé Nast publications.

Keenly aware of his own reputation, Bernstein didn't indulge in recrimination, almost to the point of being misleading about his fundamental differences with Newhouse. "I thought this was the right time to do it," Bernstein said shortly after the announcement. "There was no serious disagreement between Si and myself." For more than a year, Bernstein remained silent about how Newhouse had transformed the Random House he had known. The company Bernstein was leaving on East Fiftieth Street was a huge international publishing conglomerate, not the "congenial, collegial, decent place to work," as Jason Epstein once said of the publisher he joined inside the old Villard houses.

In his chairman's office, before a group of sixty top editors, many longtime friends, and his wife, Helen, Robert Bernstein announced he was leaving the company he loved. "From the beginning I felt that Random

House was a special place where good writing and new ideas, particularly those fighting their way into existence from dark corners of the world would always be published just for themselves," Bernstein told one writer upon leaving, perhaps his most telling comment at the time. "In these days of hype and commercialism, I believe this is more important than ever."

One week afterward, Si Newhouse announced his selection of Alberto Vitale, the head of rival Bantam Doubleday Dell, to succeed Bernstein at Random House. Newhouse believed that Vitale, best known as a man of numbers rather than letters, could streamline Random House's varied and seemingly unwieldly operations and make the company even more competitive for the 1990s. Upon arrival, Vitale was gracious to his predecessor. "It is clear from the outpouring of affection and good wishes for Bob since he announced his retirement, that he is a legend in American publishing and, more important, a legend to his own people at Random House," Vitale said.

There was some relief within Random House that Newhouse had chosen a familiar publishing figure and not, as the gossip columns speculated, someone like baseball commissioner Peter Ueberroth or Si's thirty-two-year-old nephew, Steven. The good feelings would not last long. One of the first places Vitale looked to cut at Random House was one of Bernstein's own "dark corners" where good writing and new ideas were a tradition. And when he made his move, Vitale discovered how deep the feelings of resentment and concerns were at Si Newhouse's Random House.

CHAPTER NINE

Cleaning House

As Studs Terkel remembers, the idea seemed improbable, a bit crazy, and, as he thought some more, simply brilliant: Treat Chicago like some small village in a distant land and describe its life in vivid detail to American readers, including Chicagoans themselves.

Over the telephone André Schiffrin, the head of Pantheon Books, a division of Random House, suggested the idea to Terkel in the mid-1960s, when Terkel was known mainly as host of a radio talk show in the Chicago area. Use Jan Myrdal's book *Report from a Chinese Village* as a model to write about Chicago, Schiffrin suggested.

"You're crazy," Terkel protested. "How can you compare Chicago to a small village in China?"

Nevertheless, he followed his editor's advice and the result was *Division Street: America*—a critically acclaimed book capturing the voice of urban America as found on one street stretching across the heart of Chicago. The book established Terkel's reputation as an author and his unswerving loyalty to Schiffrin. "Everything I am as an author is because of André," said Terkel, who produced six books with Pantheon, including the 1985 Pulitzer Prize–winning *The Good War: An Oral History of World War II*.

Terkel's path was typical of many writers who came under Schiffrin's wing and eventually became part of the imprint's distinguished family tradition, which began with Schiffrin's father and was later carried on by his son. Pantheon was founded in 1942 by Kurt Wolff and his wife, Helen, and they were joined the following year by Jacques Schiffrin—all three well-known publishers who were forced to flee Nazi-occupied Europe. Jacques Schiffrin was the founder of the world-renowned *Bibliotheque de la Pleiade,* which published the complete works of great writers in carefully annotated volumes. A close friend of writer André Gide, Jacques was an integral part of Pantheon's success and its reputation for progressive thought.

When Bennett Cerf purchased Pantheon in 1961, he selected Schiffrin's son, André, to run the prestigious publisher, which already had a backlist of titles such as *Dr. Zhivago* by Boris Pasternak and *Born Free* by Joy Adamson. "We selected the ideal man to run it, André Schiffrin," Cerf wrote in his memoir. "André had important connections abroad and excellent judgment. Pantheon has been nursed by us to do fine books. We didn't expect them to produce best sellers, although every once in a while they have come across a big winner. They've done very well." Such well-known authors as Ariel Dorfman, Barbara Ehrenreich, George Kennan, and Noam Chomsky found a national outlet for books on sometimes-radical notions and provocative politics. "It had a special touch," said Chomsky, a professor at MIT, who had seven books published by Pantheon. "Sure, there are publishers taking chances on an offbeat book. But Pantheon did it regularly. Pantheon was different because Schiffrin made it different."

In the world of Random House, Pantheon was its own small village, a lonely outpost on the twenty-seventh floor of the building, where Schiffrin and his bright young editors kept to themselves. Even getting to the Pantheon offices required a separate elevator from the one traveled by other editors at Random House.

Some top executives within the company clearly resented Pantheon's freedom, both editorially and financially. How Si Newhouse felt about Pantheon was never really clear. But Schiffrin, whose wife was a friend of Victoria Newhouse, had socialized occasionally with the Newhouses and he never felt any reason to be alarmed.

When Robert Bernstein was forced out, however, Pantheon quickly became a target for Alberto Vitale, a bottom-line manager retained by Si Newhouse to cut costs. In 1989, the year that Bernstein left, Pantheon lost money. Most familiar with Random House's losses for that year say Pantheon's loss was particularly small compared with Crown's problems or books with huge advances that proved disappointing. Nevertheless, what upset Vitale was his impression that Schiffrin didn't seem bothered by the losses. "Pantheon wanted to publish the best books possible, even some that lost money, but that ethos changed when Vitale came in," recalled Schiffrin, a soft-spoken man who resembles a college English professor more than a corporate executive. "He felt it was a bad influence on the other imprints."

Two months after his arrival, Vitale told Schiffrin he must reduce Pantheon's list of new titles from about 120 books to 40 and shrink his staff by an equal proportion. Schiffrin refused and instead resigned. Recollections about this meeting remain hazy and conflicting. Schiffrin says Vitale told him that he wanted to change Pantheon's "mix of books" to include "right-wing books as well as left-wing." Vitale, who bristles at the thought, denied any such statement. "That's one hundred percent not true," he said. "The fact is I reacted to what I found. Pantheon was the most glaring problem, absolutely. Anyone could have a bad year, but to have one after another . . . it was not fair to the others."

Si Newhouse and his new chairman didn't seem to realize the furor they would unleash by letting Schiffrin go. Whatever clamor there may have been with Robert Bernstein's ouster was muted, mostly because the long-time chairman chose not to incite any outcry when asked to depart. Months afterward, Bernstein still felt it was bad form to complain about his own treatment. (Several editors speculated that Bernstein had agreed to remain silent for a period of time as part of his "golden parachute" severance package with Newhouse. Bernstein says he would never have signed such a gag agreement. Newhouse probably didn't ask for one, he later theorized, because of Bernstein's well-known position on human rights and free speech.)

As part of his severance package, however, Schiffrin agreed to refrain from making any public statements to the press for a year. In effect, Si Newhouse had bought his departing editor's silence. But Schiffrin's closely knit band of editors and their many prominent authors were determined not to let him go quietly into the night. Before they quit themselves, Schiffrin's top editors unleashed their own guerrilla war inside the company's headquarters. To publicize their side of the story, they faxed press releases and called friendly journalists. They painted a portrait of Alberto Vitale as a numbers-crunching philistine intent on trashing Pantheon and its literary tradition. Those who knew Vitale, a proud but amiable man genuinely excited by the new challenge of running Random House, were surprised at how he was cast as the villain. Though Vitale was primarily an administrator, he usually allowed considerable freedom to his editors.

Emotions were running high, however, and Vitale became a surrogate for the wrath many felt toward Si Newhouse and his overall treatment of Random House. To New York's literary world—which witnessed the departure of Robert Bernstein and then André Schiffrin in a matter of months—Random House was in upheaval, its golden reputation tarnished. Like some exotic culture explored by Jan Myrdal himself, the isle of Manhattan and its literary tribes were abuzz with whispers of fear and retribution. Once again, the scent of blood was in the air in the house of Newhouse.

Some 350 authors, literary agents, and even some of its own editors marched and picketed outside Random House headquarters. Writers like E. L. Doctorow added their own active verbs to the conflagration. In accepting the National Book Critics Circle Award in March 1990 for his best-selling *Billy Bathgate,* Doctorow worried aloud that Random House had "disfigured itself" with the Pantheon fiasco. "Even if no censorship was intended by its application of its own bottom-line criteria to its Pantheon division, the effect is indeed to still a voice, to close a door against part of the American family," Doctorow declared.

Ten years earlier, Doctorow had warned the U.S. Senate antitrust subcommittee in March 1980 about the emerging dominance of publishing houses owned by large comunications giants and its possible stifling effect on the diversity of opinion in American life.

With an artist's prophetic flair, Doctorow seemed to anticipate the cultural impact of publishers like Newhouse. As he warned: "Discovering the idealistic and mental impediments to an efficient, profitmaking machinery, the conglomerate management will eliminate them—change taste, simplify what is complex, find the personnel who will give them what they want, and gradually change the nature of books themselves, and create something else, almost-books, nonbooks, book pods, just as foods today are packaged for quick sale and mass distribution with artificial flavors that make pies and cakes, we are told, just like the ones mother used to make." Now, it seemed his concerns were coming true.

To smooth the feathers of James Michener, one of Random House's most popular writers, Si Newhouse traveled to Washington, D.C., where he and Vitale met in a hotel with Michener. As the author of thirty-three books with Random House since 1950, Michener was deeply offended by the abrupt dismissal of Bernstein and chaotic handling of the Pantheon resignations. "I said we were three men in deep trouble and I hope we realized it," Michener later recalled. In an earlier statement, he had called Vitale "an able number-cruncher," hardly a stirring endorsement. After a two-hour meeting where he listened to the company's defense, Michener was mollified and even sympathetic to Newhouse. "I think Si Newhouse has been badly hurt by all this, but he doesn't want to come out and defend himself in public," Michener said.

Only one other time would Si Newhouse personally get involved in the Pantheon mess. And again, his intervention was part of an effort to keep another well-known revenue-producing name in the fold—the cartoon character Bart Simpson.

The departure of Bart Simpson wasn't readily apparent when Vitale met in his office with a group of top Pantheon editors shortly after Schiffrin's dismissal. Each had tendered a resignation by letter. Vitale, a short man with a bulldog face, Bunsen burner blue eyes and a slight continental Italian accent, was already reassessing his position. The rumblings of the literary village, printed in the newspaper and talked about incessantly over lunch, pushed Vitale to seek a cease-fire. He had clearly miscalculated the angry response to Schiffrin's departure.

As he looked around the chairman's conference room, where glossy-covered books are displayed on the walls like trophies, Vitale stood and spoke first.

"I'm not going to accept your resignations—*not right away,*" he announced. His cool European demeanor provided the imperial suggestion that he might reconsider. Assuring them that nothing had changed at Random House, Vitale suggested they go home, take a bath, and also reconsider. The editors would have none of it.

"If everything is so wonderful and nothing is going to change, then why was André fired?" one of the editors shot back.

Vitale seemed flustered by the impertinence of Schiffrin's confreres, mostly young editors in their thirties still with a trace of long hair and the radical politics of their generation. From this modest attempt at détente, the meeting degenerated into a flurry of angry exchanges and heated words. Five of the Pantheon editors quit, taking many of their authors with them. None of this seemed to bother Vitale and Newhouse very much until they realized that one of the Pantheon editors most determined to leave was Wendy Wolf.

Just as André Schiffrin had helped to nurture Studs Terkel's writing, Wolf had recognized the remarkable cartooning talent of Matt Groening, whose work appeared in *The Village Voice,* New York City's well-known weekly. With Wolf as editor, Pantheon published a collection of Groening's work entitled *Life in Hell,* the same name given Groening's animated feature in the *Voice.* Groening later developed another set of cartoon characters called The Simpsons. These characters peopled a hit TV show and a book based on them was to be published by Pantheon for the 1990 holiday season. With his longtime editor Wendy Wolf bolting, Matt Groening and his multimillion-dollar cartoon creature—brazen Bart Simpson— were sure to follow. To keep this projected cash flow in his stable, Si Newhouse made a special effort to try to convince Wolf to stay.

Shortly after the disastrous meeting in Vitale's office, Wolf says she received a telephone call from her former boss.

"Hi, it's Si—would you like to come over for a chat?" Newhouse asked.

More than a bit dubious, Wolf nevertheless agreed to Newhouse's invitation to go over and chat at his office in the Condé Nast building. During their forty-five-minute discussion, Newhouse offhandedly confided his thoughts about how poorly he thought Random House had been operated during Robert Bernstein's tenure. Wolf was appalled and unmoved.

"He said he wanted to intervene with Random House and should have done something years before," she recalled. "It was to me a chilling statement about Bob Bernstein, one of the most respected people in the publishing business. I realized then it was not about money, but power and control."

Hopes of Newhouse reconsidering were very short-lived at Pantheon.The literary tradition of a publishing house that had once printed the works of Jean-Paul Sartre, Carl Jung, Simone de Beauvoir, Günter Grass, R. D. Laing, Ralph Nader, and countless other provocative writers and thinkers seemed to count for very little. As Wolf realized, there was just one thing Si Newhouse was after. "The only editor that they wanted to keep," as Wolf recalled, "was the one with the Simpsons."

Inside his office, Newhouse seemed remarkably distant. "You know, he's a relatively inarticulate man, very socially ill at ease," Wolf later told *Voice* writer Doug Ireland. "He was sort of *not there*—he didn't seem to have a clue as to who I was. Politics didn't come up. Money came up." Despite her private session with Newhouse in his inner sanctum, Wolf left unconvinced.

To the press, Newhouse and his staff painted a bleak picture of Pantheon's finances. After many money-losing seasons, they made it known Pantheon had lost $3 million on sales of under $20 million in 1989—the year before Vitale's arrival. "Why should Pantheon be allowed to lose a ton of money?" Vitale later asked rhetorically in an interview. "Apart from anything, this was creating a morale problem within the company." In a thinly veiled reference to his predecessor, Vitale commented, "If you're selling fifteen hundred copies of a book and printing seventy-five hundred, you don't need to have been to Harvard to know you're in trouble."

Schiffrin's supporters, including the Harvard-trained Bernstein, said the losses estimated by Vitale were overblown and that Pantheon earned $3 million alone on its backlist. Moreover, they argued that Pantheon, at the time of Schiffrin's ouster, was poised to profit from the sudden celebrity of Matt Groening's Simpsons characters as well as from those of another cartoonist, Art Spiegelman, whose sequel to his controversial comic book about the Holocaust, *Maus,* eventually became a best-seller. No one really knew for sure about Pantheon's finances except Si Newhouse. Because Random House, like the rest of Newhouse's holdings, was privately held, outsiders found it impossible to get a firm account of Pantheon's finances. "The books that S. I. Newhouse really cares about, which are the accounting books, are the only books being produced at this empire that are not open," complained Tom Engelhardt, one of Schiffrin's senior editors.

Much more than an issue of money, the uproar over Pantheon—like most primal attacks among New York's literati—was also a contest of ideology, both real and imagined. To Schiffrin's supporters, Si Newhouse's attack on Pantheon's top editorial staff was viewed not so much as a triumph of efficiency as a brutal affront on the culture. "The barbarians have taken over at Pantheon, and they might as well be producing a detergent," said Terkel, who decried Newhouse's "bottom-line" mentality as he marched with more than three hundred other writers, agents, and editors outside Random House's doors. In the inflamed rhetoric of the moment, Terkel likened the incendiary events at Pantheon to book burnings in Nazi Germany during the 1930s. This once-great publishing house had been, as one sign put it, NEWHOUSED. After more than two decades and a Pulitzer, Terkel left Pantheon to be published at a nonprofit publishing house Schiffrin later created, The New Press.

To the vociferous protesters outside Random House's doors, Alberto Vitale was nothing more than Si's straw man. The new chairman was portrayed as a numbers man who referred to books as "units" at publishing meetings, like simple widgets in some factory. Vitale compounded his image problem by telling one interviewer that at the time he was reading "very few" books for pleasure "because I don't have the time." To another inquirer, Vitale conceded his favorite author was Judith Krantz—whose books he occasionally managed to look at over the weekend—hardly the nectar imbibed by the literary gods. In keeping with the overblown metaphors of the dispute, Vitale defended his boss's view by pointing to the crumbling Communist nations of Eastern Europe: "Just look at what happened to the countries that considered 'bottom line' the most obscene expression in their vocabulary."

As the Pantheon conflagration raged for a few days in the press, the rest of the publishing industry seemed to fall into one camp or the other. Some in the media suggested the protesting writers were nothing more than spoiled children, unaware of the financial pressures of book publishing. Other publishers expressed sympathy with Newhouse's position, or suggested that Pantheon under André Schiffrin certainly didn't have a lock on quality within the company. Nevertheless, Newhouse, already infamous for his brutish sytle in human relations, became a lightning rod for a much broader criticism as he now appeared intent on seriously dismantling at least part of what was once Random House and its prestigious imprints. "Quality does not seem to be the preoccupation of Si Newhouse," commented *Le Monde,* observing the cultural clash from afar.

Around Pantheon's collapse, a sort of literary domino theory was constructed. If Si Newhouse's aggression was not stopped, many writers worried aloud, perhaps a similar fate would befall Alfred A. Knopf or other serious-minded divisions at Random House. *This meant war!* The literary armies donned their battle gear and readied the weapons used in such intellectual conflicts. A petition signed by such authors as John Hersey, Orville Schell, William Styron, Mary Gordon, Arno J. Mayer, Joyce Carol Oates, Robert Stone, Jessica Mitford, Maxine Hong Kingston, and Arthur Miller was published in *The New York Review of Books.* It called upon Newhouse "to take seriously his responsibility as a custodian of one of America's cultural treasures and to reverse his decision."

In an unusual signed editorial, *Publishers Weekly* called Schiffrin's departure a "sad day" for publishing and wondered aloud about Newhouse's true motivations for sweeping out Pantheon's top editors. "We hear that one of the complaints directed by current Random management against Pantheon . . . was that it published too many left-wing books, and why could these not be better balanced by some right-wing ones?" wrote editor John F. Baker. "In America today, the general consensus, as reflected in the media, is one of complacent, often jingoistic, enjoyment of power; the valuable task of the critic, and of publisher to that critic, is always to question that complacency and power."

Vitale and other editors said the dispute was simply a matter of finances. But some who know Si Newhouse and his private conservative outlook say he was undoubtedly ill at ease with some of Pantheon's offerings. "I think that what I've seen and heard—about the whole thing with Pantheon—is that the guy [Schiffrin] was some radical liberal guy and he simply got nuts, and he got everyone to think he was nuts," said Si's son Wynn in an interview months afterward. "There was no justification for running the company into the ground. Personally, I think he was in left field. They were writing and publishing a lot of erudite books and no one was buying them."

When he was pressed for an answer by the press, Si Newhouse—as he had when he ousted William Shawn from *The New Yorker* three years earlier—dismissed the Pantheon conflict as nothing more than a petulant reaction. "Change appears threatening and it takes a while to see what it means," Newhouse told the *Times*. "But it is surprising how much more there is to an institution like *The New Yorker* or an imprint like Pantheon than an individual. I can see why people are upset, but they do not realize that Pantheon will continue as a strong intellectual imprint."

Perhaps the most curious response, above all, was the reaction inside Random House itself. Several senior editors felt insulted, embarrassed, or personally challenged by what they perceived was the self-righteousness of Schiffrin and the Pantheon editors in leaving. One of the most outraged was Jason Epstein, one of New York's great literary lions, a founder of *The New York Review of Books* and a highly regarded book editor for such luminaries as Mailer and Doctorow. Those who watched Epstein and Schiffrin at company meetings over the years say these two talented editors seemed to resent each other deeply and jockeyed for the intellectual high ground. "He never liked André," said one person who is friendly with both men. "Jason thought he was the house intellectual and there was a tension between them."

Epstein didn't mince words about Schiffrin and his approach at Pantheon. "He didn't know what he was doing; he was very unprofessional," said Epstein. "He always lost money and Bob Bernstein always carried him."

In turn, Schiffrin said Epstein curried favor with the new management so he could tend to his outside interests. With just one entrepreneurial venture, Epstein had reportedly collected up to $1 million when *The New York Review of Books* was sold to another owner. "People no longer think of him as the one you go to with a serious intellectual book," Schiffrin replied.

A week before the ax fell at Pantheon, Epstein's essay in the *Review* detailed the new financial pressures facing book publishers. To some, it seemed like an apologia for Newhouse and his company's budget-cutting moves. Indeed, Vitale, the new chairman, photocopied Epstein's essay when it appeared and distributed it to the staff as "one of the best things

I've ever read about publishing." When Newhouse was roundly criticized for the Pantheon moves, Epstein moved to circle the wagons. He helped to draft a letter and to convince some forty top Random House editors and officials to sign this public statement supporting Newhouse's management. The letter was a clear, firm rebuke to their former colleagues. "Like Pantheon, we all strive to publish books of enduring quality," the letter stated. "But, unlike Pantheon, we have preserved our independence and the independence of our authors by supporting the integrity of our publishing program with fiscal responsibility."

Epstein wrote the letter in the editorial conference room along with Peter Gethers, then the publisher of Villard Books. "It was really weird being on the management side on a case like this, but everyone felt it was an attack on my imprint if they are saying André shouldn't have to make money," recalled Gethers. "On top of that, their stuff wasn't all that good unless you think Studs Terkel is a genius. So everyone went into a room and said we've got to respond to it. In retrospect, the smartest thing would have been to ignore it and it would have blown over. It was a total hellhole with all these people for twelve hours trying to put this letter together."

Some Random House editors felt uncomfortable with the statement— an anti-intellectual act that, they said, had no place in a great publishing house. While some like Epstein and Joni Evans were eager to sign the statement, others felt compelled by pressures from colleagues to do so. "When something ugly happens, you don't make it uglier by making a stink yourself," said one lower-level editor who was there. "I think a very few inside the building took it personally and were very petty. Times were rough, though, and people wanted to keep their jobs. I saw it as like a loyalty oath."

Among some of the company's senior staff, the letter—"that manifesto," as Epstein called it—was a necessary defense against a public slur. Epstein says he and other longtime editors like Robert Loomis and Joe Fox, who had worked with some of Random House's greatest authors, were deeply offended. "This was a great publishing institution and I hated to see it abused by someone who had failed as a publisher," Epstein explained. The controversy was aggravated, he said, because Vitale underestimated emotions and bruised egos when he arrived at Random House. "Much of it was a delayed reaction to what happened to Bob Bernstein," Epstein said.

Yet Bernstein said he was at a loss to explain the actions of Epstein and others who signed the letter during the Pantheon dispute. "I don't know why they had to do it," Bernstein said. "The idea that we could publish only 'financially responsible' books is a disingenuous statement. It's hard enough for an editor to find good books, and books that will sell. But you have to give them a feeling that they can take a chance."

Once brimming with enthusiasm about Random House, Epstein became emblematic of the changes, saying he was now content to work quietly editing books of big-name writers without worrying about the future or any philosophical differences between Bernstein and Vitale. "He doesn't have to read books," Epstein insisted, when asked about Vitale's literary credentials. "He has to please one stockholder—Si Newhouse. And he has to make it possible for the editors and authors to publish their books in an efficient and profitable way."

This message was conveyed to some of his top writers, such as E. L. Doctorow, who seemed to tone down his caustic views about Newhouse's company after talking with Epstein and others inside Random House. "There was a lot of internal stuff, which was reflected in the statement," Doctorow said in an interview months after the Pantheon furor. By then, Doctorow denied published reports saying he considered leaving Random House and he complained that his comments at the National Book Critics Circle ceremony were taken out of context by the press. "Authors and their books are important, and not their corporate nature and the difficulties that firms have," the famous novelist said. "Corporations always fight it out. That's their nature."

Undeniably, though, Si Newhouse, less than a decade after his purchase of Random House, had forever transformed its hierarchy—and, increasingly, its fundamental mission. Those who once thought Newhouse would leave Random House alone under Bernstein were struck by the widespread changes. Part of the dire reason for management changes at Random House, Newhouse acknowledged, was that "the company got so big, it needed a more hands-on style of management." Entering into the 1990s, this new publishing company was testament to Si Newhouse's belief that Random House should no longer be a mountain range, as Bernstein had once put it, but one very big mountain. With Si Newhouse at its pinnacle.

For whatever was gained, however, the idea of Random House as something special, as the "Lotusland" of Jason Epstein's youth, had been lost. "Everybody said that Random House, even after Si Newhouse bought it, wasn't one of those big conglomerates that homogenize the culture," commented Victor Navasky, editor of *The Nation*. "Well, it turns out Random House is like everyone else."

———

The dancers strutted their G-strings and fondled their naked breasts on stage as author D. Keith Mano, his tuxedo tie and jowly grin still firmly in place, walked around the room with a wad of dollar bills.

"Tip money," Mano explained to the uninitiated, money to stuff inside the garter belts of the topless dancers to show your appreciation.

Welcome to the Star Club! The upper management of Random House smiled nervously in return.

On a steamy night in August 1991, this cabaret of flesh and unrequited yearnings became home to another form of entertainment ritual—the book party.

Random House's chairman Alberto Vitale and his staff of editors celebrated the publication of Mano's new novel, appropriately entitled *Topless*, by renting out a Manhattan strip joint for the night. Mano, by day a contributing editor for *Playboy*, was overjoyed by the reception. He had already sold an option on the film rights to the novel for $500,000 and was helping to pick up the tab for this party.

Although Si Newhouse didn't show up, most of Random House's top publishers and editors made an appearance. Vitale even came with his wife. After ten years of research for his work of fiction, Mano personally selected the eight dancers for this party. They shimmied and shook their body parts until their flimsy apparel disappeared.

Usually, a book party is held in a restaurant or a well-known Manhattan bar. As an occasional gimmick, the publishing industry will locate the party at an unusual site to help publicize a new offering. But no one had ever seen anything like this. "It was the strangest night of my career," said one female writer, who felt compelled to attend for business reasons. "There were all these naked women and yet no one seemed to look at them. No one acknowledged how disconcerting it all was."

Their evasions, however, spoke volumes. Harold Evans, by then the publisher of the company's namesake imprint, came to the festivities late and without his wife, Tina Brown. He quickly departed. Another company official, Carol Schneider, kept her hands over her eyes most of the night. Jason Epstein also appeared none too pleased, but he managed to force a weak smile for a photographer from *Publishers Weekly*, the industry bible, which later managed to insert a picture of Epstein's smiling face between an even larger photograph of two dancers displaying their lower anatomy.

Suddenly, Random House, the earnest brown shoe of publishing, was developing a racy and somewhat tacky reputation. Before this strip-joint celebration, Random House also hosted a party for the American Booksellers Association convention in Las Vegas at a figure-skating show called "Nudes on Ice." Clearly, the editors at Random House were learning the dirty little secret that those at Newhouse's Condé Nast had known for more than a generation: Sex sells. The company's newfound willingness to go after the big book on sex and violence—in a way that Random House never would have before—was underlined when Sonny Mehta, publisher of the prestigious Alfred A. Knopf, agreed to publish *American Psycho* under the Vintage imprint.

The novel about a Wall Street psychopath was written by Bret Easton Ellis, then a twenty-six-year-old writer whose earlier book *Less Than Zero* told of the Yuppie noir generation living and snorting in Los Angeles. Ellis's manuscript for *American Psycho* had been accepted and then rejected by Simon & Schuster, a rival publisher once viewed as a lesser counterpart to Random House's place of editorial integrity. Despite their $300,000 advance for the novel, Simon & Schuster's management was reportedly offended by the narrative's graphic violence.

Actually, graphic violence was somehow inadequate to describe this ode to butchery. In it, Ellis's hip young protagonist—Patrick Bateman, a character whose fondness for clothing and upscale accoutrements could easily make him a typical *GQ* reader—uses Mace to subdue a female date or ties her up, bites off her breasts, and puts a starving rat up her vagina. For fun, Bateman may proceed to cut off her head and arms and go at the rest of her body with a chain saw.

When Simon & Schuster rejected the book, Ellis and his agent became inflamed. The rejection took on the mantle of pseudo-censorship and Sonny Mehta came to the rescue as a First Amendment champion. Rather than sully Knopf's good name, the home of nineteen Nobel Prize winners in literature, this work appeared under the Vintage label, another imprint overseen by Mehta. "It seems to me appropriate, given the immense coverage and curiosity about Mr. Ellis' new book, that we bring out *American Psycho* now in an original trade paperback edition, to swiftly reach the widest possible readership," Mehta said in his announcement. His quick response enabled him to sell 250,000 copies of *American Psycho*. Others saw nothing but sheer opportunism. "Enter Mr. Mehta and Vintage Books, clearly as hungry for a killing as Patrick Bateman," wrote essayist Roger Rosenblatt. "The folks at Vintage seem to me to be the special scoundrels of our tale, whether they are being cynical and avaricious or merely tasteless and avaricious. Either way, they must have a mighty low opinion of the public's ability to distinguish between art that is meaningfully sensationalistic and junk."

Whether psychopathic violence or genteel publishing, Sonny Mehta appeared fascinated by both endeavors. During a 1992 American Booksellers Association convention, Mehta stood and watched two agents engage in a bloody fistfight. Unlike other horrified onlookers, Mehta reportedly stood transfixed at the sight, smoking his cigarette as one man pummeled the other. "Fantastic, fantastic," Mehta said. "This is the first interesting thing to happen this weekend." Sudden beheadings and other dislocations within the Newhouse-owned publishing house didn't seem to affect Mehta. During Bernstein's tenure, Mehta was rumored to be on the verge of losing his job. Nevertheless, he managed to survive by displaying the political survival skills and marketing savvy needed to thrive in Si Newhouse's company.

Ajai Singh Mehta, who prefers being called Sonny, is a very stylish man who likes to wear casual black clothes and occasionally walks around the office in his stocking feet. He is often cryptic in words and actions and usually keeps his own counsel. "He's like a lizard," said one of his authors, Spaulding Gray. "Very self-contained, cool and contemplative. He listens and says nothing." At night, Mehta could be seen in some of Manhattan's nightspots with fellow editor Gary Fisketjon and other New York literary Brat Pack figures of the 1980s like writer Jay McInerney. In a profile of Mehta, *Esquire* magazine described him as a late-night partygoer who "reportedly ate little, could drink all night without becoming drunk, and seemed to revel in his companions' loss of control."

Soon after he arrived in New York, Mehta became the object of intense criticism and derision. Some press accounts described him, with his sharply-pointed Vandyke beard and intense dark eyes, almost in demonic terms, right down to his "furry little feet," as one writer put it. He had endured similar indignities in London. "English publishing was in the last throes of pretending to be a profession for gentlemen and there weren't too many people who weren't Brit in the business," Mehta recalled. "There certainly weren't too many dusky-hued people, and so I spent a lot of interviews being spoken to slowly and distinctly."

Mehta's stewardship of Knopf, one of America's great literary institutions, began uneasily. Rather than appoint his own choice, then chairman Robert Bernstein had followed the suggestion of Robert Gottlieb, who had recommended Mehta as a replacement in 1987. What appealed to Gottlieb, who had met Mehta at various international book fairs, was his flexible, insightful mind. Mehta, the son of an Indian diplomat, had traveled widely as a youth and was educated at Cambridge. For several years, he ran the London-based Pan publishing house, specializing in both mass-market and high-quality paperbacks. Some American authors—like Michael Herr, whose *Dispatches* was published in England by Mehta— praised him without reserve. He seemed an inspired, albeit unorthodox, selection for Gottlieb, who was revered as a talented book editor with an unerring eye for talent.

"Sonny is a passionate reader who really loves books," Gottlieb explained. "Second, he enjoys the business of selling books; third, he has a very strong temperament. He's a personage in his own right. Alfred certainly was that, I was considered that, and I couldn't bring into Knopf someone who didn't have an individual style."

Some criticisms of Mehta had a bit more substance. He proved himself guilty of what many top New York literary agents and authors considered the greatest sin of all: not returning phone calls. This repeated omission infuriated authors and agents alike and prompted the inevitable comparisons between Mehta and his predecessor, Gottlieb, who was considered one of America's finest book editors. Mehta's approach was more detached and aloof than the paternalistic manner of Gottlieb, who nurtured many of the writers and editors Mehta now inherited. Gottlieb's own relationship with Mehta became more complex. Although he had selected Mehta as his successor, Gottlieb never left Knopf in a sense. He continued to edit such important Knopf authors as John Le Carré and Doris Lessing, which caused some unease. "A big man leaves here and yet is still around," said Jeff Stone, then a vice president and associate publisher at Knopf and Villard. "I guess it creates a certain tension."

For a time, Mehta was despondent about the criticism aimed his way. "You walk around this place and a newcomer is someone who has been here for about five years," he complained. "So I'm really just off the boat in more senses than one." The rancor surrounding Sonny Mehta peaked when Knopf authors Robert K. Massie and J. Anthony Lukas left in a huff. *The New York Times,* sensing the confusion and funereal mood at Knopf, called Mehta an "abysmal" manager. The deathwatch was on. The phone call from Si, requesting an impromptu good-bye, appeared imminent. "There were dark forces at work," recalled Howard Kaminsky years later. "People who did not want to see Sonny succeed and who were stirring the pot, throwing in tongue of newt and toe of snail and not doing him any good."

Sometimes in private, Mehta let his own displeasure with Bernstein be known. Quietly, Bernstein was rumored to be shopping around for a replacement at Knopf, but instead, he got the ax in November 1989. A friend sent Mehta a postcard with a photograph of a mobster rubbed out in some gangland-type murder. The message was clear: Mehta had dodged the bullets for now. "It would have been a good way to go down in history if I'd lost my job for not returning phone calls," Mehta said, bemused and bemoaning his reputation.

When Vitale was appointed as new chairman, Mehta flourished and became a vocal proponent of Random House's new bottom-line ethos demanded by Newhouse. "Knopf is solidly profitable and that is how I intend to keep it," he told the *Times* in a glowing 1990 profile only two years after its critical article on his managerial ability. "Profit is one way that you can take pride in the way you publish things and insure that you can go on doing it. . . . We try to sell our writers as aggressively as those houses regarded as commercial with a capital C." In turn, Vitale found an ally in the Knopf publisher; they were both European-trained executives running one of America's best-known publishing houses. After the Pantheon fiasco, with the departure of Schiffrin and his band of editors, Vitale turned to Mehta to oversee that troubled imprint, as well as Knopf. The new company chairman praised Mehta as "without question the most brilliant publisher in the country: he is phenomenal, he has everything."

What Mehta possessed mostly was the ability to mix Knopf's highbrow fare with the keen sensibilities he had developed as a paperback publisher in Britain. His sense of story and of the American public's taste were remarkable, especially for a man who had spent nearly all his life outside of the United States. Growing up in India, Mehta had read American writers like James Baldwin, Truman Capote, William Styron, and Norman Mailer and found their voices refreshing. "They just appeared to be speaking more directly to me than anything else," Mehta said. "It was a brand-new world, less recorded, more accessible." Mehta's business acumen and his sense of marketing were just as keen. His decision to raise the suggested price from forty to fifty dollars for *The Civil War*—a Knopf book that was tied directly to the highly praised public-television documentary of the same name—would raise millions more in revenues for the company.

At heart, Mehta was unabashedly a mass-market publisher, one who brought the trappings of the cutthroat paperback business to the world of hardcovers. He was among the first trade publishers to feature hardcover books in the large cardboard display boxes (often called "dumps" in the industry) that had been used for years to display paperbacks. He published some books in a smaller, more compact format, which, by requiring more pages, ironically allowed a small text to appear as a fairly large-sized book. More importantly, Mehta had style. His magic formula required better art and graphic design, careful attention to the quality of paper, with an equal concern for the dust jacket as for the contents of a book. This often resulted in books that looked great, having a sleek, elegant appearance that increased sales considerably. "If we don't want to rely solely on best-sellers, we have to find other ways of engaging readers," Mehta said in a 1991 interview, during which he defended his aggressive marketing approach. "Everyone moves on the myth that there is a hungry readership for everything we do. And we have to adjust to the realism."

One of Mehta's most remarkable triumphs of salesmanship occurred with Josephine Hart's erotic novel *Damage,* which was published in 1991 and served for the next few years as a textbook example of graphic innovation for rival publishers. "*Damage* is certainly the granddaddy of these books," said Laurence J. Kirschbaum, president of Warner Books, after the smaller format proved to be a hit in the marketplace. "You have to give Sonny a lot of credit for realizing that size is a very important element in a book's design, equally as important as the cover art." *Damage*'s success was a grand symphony of superb marketing strokes by Mehta, with the book appearing on *The New York Times* best-seller list two weeks before most of the reviews appeared. Booksellers were alerted to *Damage*—written by first-time novelist Hart, who is the wife of Maurice Saatchi of Saatchi & Saatchi, the giant British advertising firm—by a personal letter from Mehta himself. He called it "the most shocking, haunting and erotic novel" his Knopf editors had ever read. Others compared the novel to the schlocky potboilers that might be published by houses with a less regal reputation than Knopf. Whether this claim was true or not was essentially beside the point. The personal appeal to booksellers, as well as a striking double-page ad in the *Times Book Review,* made *Damage* a winner, even though critics were lukewarm when they reviewed it. "The letter staking his reputation, the beautiful package, the spectacular ad—it was a brilliant performance on a rather dull book," another Random House editor observed.

The book party for Hart's novel, which was held at Mehta's apartment, became another triumph when Si showed up. Newhouse was obviously pleased by the changes at his book company. He exchanged pleasantries and even posed with a wide happy grin with the honored guest, Josephine Hart. Signed up with a sixty-thousand-dollar advance, *Damage* was transformed by Mehta into best-seller gold, a genuine feat of marketing genius.

Knopf was now known as much for its skills at promotion and penetrating new markets as for the quality of its literary offerings. Despite early doubts, Sonny Mehta proved himself ideally suited for Newhouse's tastes: a British-educated editor who understood mass marketing in America. He also appreciated the importance of design—the *look* of a publication— just as Alex Liberman had taught Si decades earlier at Condé Nast. (After Susan Petersen was dismissed as the head of his Ballantine division, Si told another editor that he had always been embarrassed by "the look of her covers.") Sonny Mehta's tastes were much closer to Si's. He was a bottom-line publisher with class, one with image but no illusions. Unlike Schiffrin or Bernstein, Mehta held no pretensions about his purpose. "Too many people have bitten the dust," he said, "because they've delivered an ideological statement and then not delivered the goods."

The barracuda-like atmosphere at Newhouse's Random House deepened once Harry Evans was selected in November 1990 to replace Joni Evans as the head of Little Random. Vitale pushed for this change and was relieved when Joni Evans accepted his offer to run her own small imprint, without the administrative duties of Little Random. "And there will be plenty of other changes," Vitale said in an interview a month after the switch was made at Random House. "The name of the game is change." But the arrival of a replacement with the same last name— Harry Evans, no relation to Joni but the husband of *Vanity Fair* editor Tina Brown—seemed to surprise Vitale, who had been chairman for less than a year and was now watching Si pick one of his top lieutenants. "Si made Harry take the job," one insider told *New York* magazine several months afterward. "He wanted his own boy there. Alberto's mouth dropped to the floor when he heard the news." The selection of Tina Brown's husband to run the company's flagship imprint was one more step in what some old hands decried as the "Condé Nasticizing" of Random House under Newhouse. Several editors wondered if Evans was up to the job.

Harry Evans, at the time a sixty-two-year-old journalist with an enviable track record, had a history of being sold short. In the 1970s, he was a highly regarded editor of the *Sunday Times* of London. He quit in 1982 because of a disagreement with his new boss, Rupert Murdoch. His book, *Good Times, Bad Times,* bitterly recalled his confrontations with the Australian-born press baron. (Ironically, Murdoch had agreed to write his memoirs for Random House before Evans's selection was announced. "The wheel of fortune makes me your publisher as you used to be mine," Harry Evans wrote to his former boss. Murdoch later dropped the book project). After leaving *The Times* in London, Evans, a worldly, handsome man much too proud to fade away, came to the United States and became the editor of Atlantic Monthly Press, then editor of *U.S. News and World Report,* and by 1987—after his wife had turned *Vanity Fair* into a success— he entered the Newhouse kingdom as editor in chief of *Condé Nast Trav-*

eler, a brand-new magazine promising to bring truth to the puffy world of travel writing. Evans enjoyed one of the largest editorial budgets among the Condé Nast magazines, which he lavished on writers such as William Styron and on expensive photographs by Helmut Newton. Despite a slumping economy in the late 1980s and early 1990s, Evans and his publisher at *Traveler,* Ronald Galotti, managed to carve a sizeable niche in the market against *Traveler*'s main rival, *Travel & Leisure,* the nation's top travel magazine. Once *Traveler* was hailed as a success, Harry Evans made no secret of his desire for another challenge.

Becoming the head of Little Random was a quantum leap for Harry Evans, who had a world-class Rolodex of names and contacts but only a perfunctory understanding of the book business in New York. "The grammar of the deal has changed somewhat, and of course the scale of the advances has changed," Evans told one interviewer, with more than a little understatement.

Evans's detractors attributed his hiring to his marriage to Tina Brown, a particular favorite of Si Newhouse. "He had Si's ear," recalled one Random House executive. "Harry and Tina were to the right hand of the king." And in this kingdom, Evans knew how to guard his own fiefdom. From the outset, he made it clear that he didn't want Alberto Vitale looking over his shoulder. For the first several months, Evans instructed his editors not to discuss finances with Vitale when he ventured into their offices. As this Random House editor recalled, "Harry said, 'Don't talk to Alberto.' He didn't want *anyone* to talk."

No matter how influenced by his wife, Harry Evans was even more devoted to Newhouse's big book theory. He quickly showed he could throw the big bucks around, just as he had at *Condé Nast Traveler.* Willing to pay top dollar for a big-name author or a potential blockbuster project, Evans quickly announced a number of large deals, including a reported $5 million agreement for Marlon Brando's autobiography. In 1993, Newhouse joined Evans and Vitale in a successful personal lobbying effort to get Chief of Staff Gen. Colin Powell, a hero of the Persian Gulf War, to sign for his memoir, for which he received a $6 million advance. Book publishing, Evans said, was like the oil business, because "if you strike oil, you have paid for 10 to 20 dry holes." Evans's transition from journalist to publisher was largely regarded as a success, with a 16 percent reported rise in gross sales for Little Random in his first two and half years. Several new writers were signed and nineteen books landed on the *Times*'s bestseller list in 1992, including *Vanity Fair* writer Gail Sheehy's book on menopause, *The Silent Passage,* which lasted nearly an entire year on the list. These statistics pleased Newhouse and prompted him to offer Evans another long-term contract by 1993. Evans had proved himself a worthy warrior in the war of the book deals.

As Si Newhouse increasingly exerted his will, the atmosphere at Random House was far from the genteel one of the literary house run by Cerf and Bernstein; instead it reflected the tension-filled arena of a boss who seemed to enjoy pitting one division against another. The most obvious outside competition was from Simon & Schuster—the publishing arm of the Paramount Communications empire. Although it was second to Random House in publishing trade books, Simon & Schuster was a larger publishing company overall, offering a number of educational titles besides best-sellers and traditional books.

Inside the building on East Fiftieth Street, the in-house maneuvering was even more intense. Both Newhouse and Alberto Vitale, his personally selected chairman, seemed content to foster an internal competition among Evans's three divisions—Little Random, Villard, and Times Books—and those divisions controlled by Mehta. For some proposals, authors and their agents were delighted to discover more than one of Newhouse's publishers making competing bids. "We are often in a position where several imprints within Random House are bidding on the same book," explained Peter Osnos, publisher of Times Books, "but we never bid against each other if there are only two people in the auction." Still, this practice inevitably drove up the cost of big books sold at auction.

There was a calculated madness to the buying spree. By showing his willingness to pay the most money, Newhouse often secured the biggest names in publishing, outflanking his smaller competitors and ensuring a reliable infusion of revenues in a business where little is guaranteed. There was a perverse pleasure found throughout the building in recalling tales of how one publisher attempted to outmaneuver or outperform another in-house rival. This competitiveness, for example, was exhibited in the company's updated efforts to publish the classics. For decades, Random House's Modern Library series of classics was a backlist treasure, a steady source of income for Cerf in the early days. In the early 1990s, Mehta decided to start his own Everyman's Library, an updated version of the same approach to the classics with full cloth covers, special introductions, and elegant designs. Not to be outdone, Harry Evans decided to brush off the Modern Library series, just in time for its seventy-fifth anniversary. No matter how limited the market or how much it might cost the company, neither publisher was going to be denied. Sonny Mehta particularly was a master at this game, never letting his competitiveness show. "I don't know what they're doing," he said when asked whether his offerings might undercut the Modern Library. "We've been too busy getting our own act together."

Some editors were not as adept at this game of intrigue, causing an almost constant state of unrest. In Si Newhouse's publishing world, fidelity to the boss today might be greeted with unemployment tomorrow. Although he might pass a favorable comment or drop a pleasant note about a good book, there was little sense of shared purpose. And there was every indication he liked it just this way. Indeed, many of those who signed the letter against those ingrate Pantheon editors in 1990—showing their loyalty to Newhouse's publishing company when it was under attack—found themselves not immune from sharp criticism or even dismissal.

Elisabeth Sifton was one of those who spoke against Schiffrin during the Pantheon fracas but soon fell victim in the new order of things. Sifton had enjoyed a very successful career at Viking Penguin, where she had her own imprint, until she was recruited by Mehta to join him as executive vice president at Knopf in 1987. "The opportunity to work with a house of such distinction and with Sonny Mehta, whom I admire, was irresistible," Sifton said. For a time, she served as a good soldier in Si's literary army, boasting in one 1989 interview that "the people at Knopf are highly intelligent and ferociously talented at what they do." She was sharply critical of Schiffrin's management of Pantheon and she heartily signed the letter in support of Newhouse.

Whatever hopes Sifton had of becoming Mehta's successor, though, didn't materialize. A self-described perfectionist, Sifton alienated some of her colleagues almost from the start by sending a memo at Mehta's suggestion to then chairman Bernstein about the inefficient ways that manuscripts passed through Knopf. By the early 1990s, with Alberto Vitale's arrival and Newhouse's emerging hands-on approach, Knopf's approach to publishing changed measurably. Sifton's disagreements with Mehta and with Knopf's direction became well known by others, until she finally decided to quit in April 1992. To Sifton, Knopf no longer seemed quite the same distinguished imprint she had thought she was joining five years earlier. "I chose to do this for my own good reasons," Sifton said. "But what I will say is that all of book publishing should re-examine itself, and every publishing house should be asking itself very fundamental questions about the industry."

Although she had clashed with André Schiffrin, much of the rhetoric surrounding Elisabeth Sifton's departure had the same familiar ring. In writing about her abrupt good-bye, the *Times,* like some Greek chorus to the drama unfolding at Newhouse's publishing house, quoted another publisher, who requested anonymity to express an opinion. "I think that many of us have gotten caught up in chasing best sellers and big names and are missing a lot of important works," said the faceless publisher. "And we try not to think about the compromises we make until someone like Elisabeth says, 'I've had enough' and it hits you like a splash of ice water in the face." After her departure, Sifton outdid any of the Pantheon editors. Without mentioning names, she wrote elaborate op-ed essays decrying publishing houses that followed the Newhouse big book theory. She no longer hid her sense of disappointment in Mehta, whom she considered just another sellout in Si's high-stakes world.

"When Sonny came to Knopf, he was a writer's editor," Sifton said. "Now he's a Newhouse executive."

A more spectacular failure was the loss of Joni Evans. She was one of the more innovative and creative editors to pass through Random House, yet her career seemed forever caught in the swirl of Si Newhouse's revolving-door management style. Six weeks after she arrived to start her own imprint, Bernstein asked her to take over Little Random, a move forced by his sudden dismissal of Howard Kaminsky. Although she had headed the trade book division at Simon & Schuster, Joni Evans was admittedly a reluctant administrator who preferred the enjoyment of finding new authors and exciting projects. In running Random House for the next three years, she signed a number of new authors, published thirty best-sellers and such controversial books as Julia Phillips's Hollywood memoir, *You'll Never Eat Lunch in This Town Again,* which attacked such potentates as David Geffen and Michael Ovitz.

When Bernstein was forced out of the company, Joni Evans suddenly became quite vulnerable. She was blamed for the disappointing sales of books like *Surviving at the Top,* Donald Trump's sequel to his first best-seller. There were rumors she had bumped heads too often with Sonny Mehta and that Vitale didn't trust her judgment. After the two high-profile departures of Bernstein and Schiffrin, Newhouse and his new chairman were reluctant to add Joni Evans's head to the chopping block. Instead, when she was unceremoniously replaced by Harry Evans in November 1990, she was offered something like her original deal: an imprint of her own. Characteristically, she seized the opportunity and tried to make the best of it.

Her new imprint, Turtle Bay Books, was situated in a four-story town house around the block from Random House's main headquarters. Several months before any books would appear, Evans's division was celebrated in the press like a new off-campus dormitory. The Sunday *Times* gushed ecstatically about the new imprint, with a 2,800-word feature and a remarkable picture of Evans posing with several of her top editors, all of whom happened to be young women. It became known derisively as "the hair photo." While the shot looked impressive—like a *Vogue* or *Glamour* vision of how a publishing house should appear—it made the whole venture seem less than serious. "They looked like Charlie's Angels," one editor later commented. "Suddenly the whole thing seemed like a joke, and I don't know if they ever overcame it."

As she had done successfully before, Joni Evans spent freely in search of the next blockbuster book. She paid a reported $750,000 for actor Michael Caine's autobiography, *What's It All About?* It made some regional best-seller lists but not *the* list—the Sunday *New York Times* best-seller lineup. Other books, like the highly touted *The Erotic Silence of the American Wife* or former NBC boss Brandon Tartikoff's memoirs, were disappointments. Suddenly, Evans's long-admired ability to spot a winner seemed to fade, just like her power within the company.

There was more than a touch of irony to Evans's travail. During earlier crises, she had dutifully defended Si Newhouse's moves at Random House. After Bernstein was ousted, for instance, she praised her former patron but admitted the place needed a change. Like Elisabeth Sifton and Jason Epstein, she also signed the letter rebuking the actions of the Pantheon editors. And when the switch was made to Harry Evans, easing her out of Little Random with the promise of her own imprint, with five years to prove herself, she never hinted at any resentment. "It's easier to see Alberto Vitale or Si as a monster" than as responsible publishers, she once cautioned an interviewer.

But Joni Evans's expensive digs and her failure to come up with a hit hastened the imprint's make-or-break timetable. Vitale wanted a winner at Turtle Bay, and by early 1993, he could wait no longer. The company's rumor mill let it be known that Evans's imprint was a lost cause. When she confronted Vitale about the rumors, he insisted that Turtle Bay be scaled back and that Evans fire some of her editors. She refused. This time, she didn't mince words. "I'm very disappointed in what I think is an abrupt and premature decision," she said. She was personally offered the chance to run a much smaller personal imprint from inside the main building. Instead, she left the company and her remaining books were divided among Mehta, Harry Evans, and other editors within the company. "I was finally getting to do what I really wanted to do," Evans told one interviewer. "I feel my dream was walked out on, and I know it was doable."

The fickle fortunes of Si Newhouse's publishing executives were exemplified by Erroll McDonald, another Random House editor who had mastered the art of self-promotion.

During the Pantheon contretemps, McDonald wrote a much-discussed essay in the *Times*'s op-ed page complaining about the "welfare mentality" at Pantheon. "Even though no one can dispute Pantheon's continual insolvency, a sense of entitlement to the Newhouse family's 'bottomless' fortune informed the protesters' argument," complained McDonald, then a vice president and executive editor of Vintage Books. A month later, McDonald himself was named to succeed Schiffrin as the new head of Pantheon Books—a promotion McDonald insisted had nothing to do with his essay.

McDonald had been a wunderkind in the making at Random House ever since he had been recruited off the Yale campus by novelist Toni Morrison, who was then working at Random House as an editor. Often in the overwhelming white upper-middle-class world of publishing, McDonald felt reminded of his color. As the son of a Costa Rican seamstress who had migrated to the Bedford-Stuyvesant section of Brooklyn with her family, McDonald was one of the few blacks in Random House's hierarchy. He used his flair for the dramatic to project an aura of being very hip. "There's not a club in New York that the maverick editor hasn't crashed, including the most exclusive one of all—publishing," touted an *Esquire* magazine profile about him. In it, McDonald posed in a black suit and white cotton shirt buttoned to the collar, the picture of urban sophistication, with traces of smoke from his English cigarette underlining his gestures.

For all of his fidelity to the boss, however, McDonald hardly seemed a candidate for Si Newhouse's fast track. His first brush with notoriety was as the editor for imprisoned convict Jack Henry Abbott, helping to transform Abbott's prison letters to novelist Norman Mailer into a book. In 1981, McDonald was partying with the recently released Abbott on the night before a rave newspaper review appeared about his book, *In the Belly of the Beast.* That same night, Abbott killed a man in a fight outside a bar, setting off a howl of indignation by those who felt a homicidal maniac had somehow been freed as a sort of literary cause célèbre. Inside the company, McDonald also earned a fair degree of criticism when he bumped into actor Klaus Kinski at a party and offered him $250,000 to write his autobiography. The actor's manuscript, entitled *All I Need Is Love: A Memoir* contained a reported 162 sexual encounters, complete with the names of participants and body parts. McDonald's decision to bypass the company's lawyers on the potentially libelous manuscript set off a chain reaction of recriminations with his then boss, Joni Evans, including the discovery that a rough version of the same book had already appeared in Germany. When the German publisher threatened to sue, the entire project was dropped.

Ironically, McDonald's greatest achievement at Vintage Books was in starting a line of international paperback reprints and new titles, including *Aké: The Years of Childhood* by Wole Soyinka, who won the Nobel Prize in 1986. This line, called Adventura, wound up being killed by Sonny Mehta becaue he found it too esoteric and too costly. Schiffrin's somewhat-similar fare at Pantheon—and his seemingly charmed life within Random House's management hierarchy—undoubtedly upset McDonald. McDonald viewed Schiffrin as condescending and contemptuous. "I came to see this man in his office one day," he recalled, "and he condescended to me in a manner that I will neither forgive nor forget. Ever." Few believed McDonald when he said this resentment wasn't behind his criticisms of Schiffrin. Soon afterward, though, McDonald received his own lessons on the perils of bottom-line publishing when he sought the life story of television talk-show star Oprah Winfrey.

For years, McDonald had pushed Oprah to write her autobiography, until she finally made some sort of a commitment in 1992. The exact language of the deal was never made clear publicly. (Winfrey reportedly signed a letter of agreement but not a formal book contract.) Nevertheless, with visions of a big book for the 1993 holiday season dancing in their heads, a ghostwriter for the memoir was secured and McDonald, as the editor for the project, kept in constant contact with Winfrey. He even convinced her to make an appearance at the annual American Booksellers Association convention in Miami in the spring of 1993, only a few months before her book was expected to hit the stores. At this shindig, McDonald and Mehta turned the company's publicity machine into high gear. Oprah would be a huge bonanza, the bookstore owners were told, with a first printing expected at about 750,000 copies in hardcover—not just a big book but a *humongous* one. Winfrey was welcomed with hosannas by the conventioneers and feted at a grand party hosted by Newhouse's publishing company. Oprah's as-told-to would surely bring in at least $15 to $20 million, the company's bean counters predicted.

These great expectations were perhaps too daunting, for shortly after the convention, Oprah experienced a change of heart. She didn't want to do the book, she announced, even though much of the manuscript was already completed. If anything, the overwhelming bash for her at the ABA convention convinced Oprah *not* to do it—at least for the time being. "I am in the heart of the learning curve," Winfrey said in her statement, released to the press by McDonald's boss, Sonny Mehta. "I feel there are important discoveries yet to be made." When, or if, Oprah would ever be ready to finish her autobiography was never mentioned. "A lot of things are going on in her life, including that she's lost some weight, that she wants to include," her spokeswoman said in explaining the reasons why the book was halted. Given Winfrey's well-publicized weight fluctuations, her readers could wait a lifetime for her story.

The TV star's last-minute pullout was a gross embarrassment to Newhouse's company, especially for McDonald, who instantly became the object of rampant second-guessing by his colleagues. After all, they wondered, how could Knopf make such a big fuss over someone who still hadn't signed a contract? The reverbations from the lost Oprah book would be felt at the end of the year, when Knopf's income statements would try to account for the black hole in their ledger sheet, and perhaps in the stunted advancement of McDonald's charmed career at Random House. Somehow, Sonny Mehta escaped much criticism, despite his pivotal role in the Oprah deal. He seemed impervious to embarrassment. He proved that once again when that spring the once-esteemed Alfred A. Knopf included a free pair of tasseled sequined pasties in its promotional kit for novelist Carl Hiassen's latest Florida satire, *Strip Tease*. "What's next?" *New York* magazine asked. "Marital aids with the Updike galleys?"

The reputation of the old Random House was now fading. No longer was Bennett Cerf's company perceived as the noble defender of artistic freedom in the face of repressive obscenity laws, as in the fight over James Joyce's *Ulysses*. Under Si Newhouse's ownership and the influence of such publishers as Sonny Mehta, the house of once-proud imprints was associated with extravagant promotions and cheap thrills, a house where sexual titillation and graphic violence toward women were recognized and exploited for their mass-market value. To be sure, the company's quality imprints like Knopf still published many books of recognized excellence, with a physical appearance that was second to none. But Knopf was no longer quite the same place of distinction; it was now too much like all the others. "I think he's done an excellent job," said Roger Straus about Mehta's tenure. "But it's not the Alfred Knopf it used to be."

Inside Random House, seasoned editors, trained in what was now quaintly called the old school of American book publishing, expressed bewilderment with the new chain of being in Si Newhouse's universe. The guiding principles of Bennett Cerf and later Robert Bernstein, ingrained throughout the fabric of their company, had been transformed by Si Newhouse into something very different. "When I arrived, I was told not to worry about competing with Doubleday and Simon & Schuster. We were to find good books and hope they sold well," recalled Ashbel Green, who arrived in 1964 and became one of Knopf's most respected editors. "Now we do compete for the big books."

In this regard, Sonny Mehta—professionally bold yet personally reserved, sophisticatedly "upper caste," though occasionally tacky enough to sell to the masses—was as close to a perfect Newhouse editor as could be found. He had deftly survived the various beheadings at the publishing house and had demonstrated his own taste for blood, both on the written page and in office politics. He would suggest his certain toughness was innate. "We never give up, not really, Sikhs are a war-like people," he said. Mehta harbored no sentimental illusions about himself or the readers to whom he was selling books. He said of *American Psycho:* "I think it's an ugly book, but it does have some relevance to the society it attempts to depict."

What is unique about Sonny Mehta, though, is his skill as a survivor, his ability to adapt to changing public tastes or sudden shifts in the company's in-house politics. If the big book on Oprah was a bust, there was always the spin-off possibilities from a big book on another popular favorite—dinosaurs. One of Mehta's great abilities was to increase the market for already-popular writers like Michael Crichton, whose 1990 Knopf novel, *Jurassic Park,* inspired the summer of 1993's top-grossing adventure movie of the same name. By the time the movie appeared, Newhouse's Ballantine division was ready with 7 million paperback books of the novel in print. Like some turf-minded *T rex,* the novel remained fiercely atop the *New York Times* paperback best-seller list for forty-eight straight weeks by midyear, when the movie appeared in theaters across the country. There were another 300,000 copies of a Ballantine book entitled *The Making of Jurassic Park,* which moviegoers could see displayed at one point in the film. And before his new novel for Knopf was finished, Crichton's agent, Lynn Nesbit, had made a $4 million deal for the movie rights. It was truly marketing on a monster scale.

In this cross-pollinated media world, the success of Crichton's paperback was intrinsically linked to the success of the movie by Steven Spielberg. In this new realm, certain author-screenwriters like Crichton were considered as bankable as movie superstars, with unfinished material bought sight unseen. And media conglomerates, such as the lean-and-mean Random House reconstituted by Si Newhouse, seemed like the giant carnivores envisioned on the film screen, devouring everything in sight.

Sonny Mehta represented a part of Newhouse's plan for Random House in the late 1980s and early 1990s. He seemed to understand the Condé Nast–trained sensibilities of Newhouse, who valued the elitist panache of a well-produced upscale publication but at all times stressed the bottom line. Nothing at Random House would be called "little" anymore. This was no longer a cottage industry, but a multinational business, as Mehta understood from his own experience. Throughout the late 1980s and into the 1990s, book publishing was merging into the larger scheme of mass media—the cross-pollinization of novels and best-selling biographies with movies and television, the nexus where Hollywood and publishers' row meet in cross-ownership. Si Newhouse was one of the few who controlled this unprecedented development in America's cultural life.

Those who remembered the old Random House said this new incarnation bore little resemblance to the publishing house Newhouse had purchased in 1980, shortly after his father's death. Si's first major acquisition as the head of his family's business would prove to be one of the most profitable investments ever made in publishing, rivaling any newspaper purchase by Sam Newhouse in terms of sheer cash-generating power. Despite his promise as a hands-off owner, Si carefully studied Random House's operations and then never left them alone, especially after he acquired Crown in 1988. From that point on, Random House was a different animal—too large, too corporate, and too unwieldly to be handled by anyone other than a business executive. With this purchase, Newhouse also established his own secretive, idiosyncratic methods of doing business. No longer would this shy billionaire's son remain an anonymous man. From this experience, he emerged as a dominant figure in the world's media, both feared and admired.

In transforming someone else's company into his own image, he forever changed the fundamental dynamics of American book publishing. Yet his greatest fame and personal satisfaction would not occur until he decided to prove he could start something new.

CHAPTER TEN

"Blonde Ambition"

The White House door swung open and Ronald Reagan strode confidently, almost regally, into the Map Room, like some raja in a tuxedo.

After an initial buzz of talk and movement, the room fell silent as the President and Mrs. Reagan entered, commanding a certain awe and unspoken respect. The President was already late for a state dinner with Argentina's head of state and seemed anxious to greet his foreign guests as promptly as possible. Nancy Reagan stood by her husband's side, dressed in an elegant gown and wearing pearls around her neck. They were met by a small entourage who were scheduled to watch as the Reagans had their photograph taken for a glossy, new, but financially ailing magazine—*Vanity Fair*.

In the spring of 1985, at the apex of Ronald Reagan's power, this delay for a little-known magazine was exactly the kind of interruption he could have dismissed with a wave of his hand. Tina Brown was well aware of that possibility and its fateful consequences for her magazine. Brown, a blonde thirty-one-year-old woman who could easily have been mistaken for a college intern, stood off to the side with an assistant from her magazine and a group of White House staffers who were already displeased by what was happening.

Only a few minutes earlier, the White House handlers had given strict instructions to *Vanity Fair*'s photographer Harry Benson. "This is the room where you can take the picture," a White House aide announced. "The President will come in and we will give you a few moments. And then they will have to be on their way. *Don't be long*." And then the aides and press handlers promptly left the room. When they returned with the President and Mrs. Reagan, the aides noticed that in their absence Benson had rolled up the carpet, carefully arranged the wires along the floor leading to his camera lights, and hung up a large background sheet of no-seam white paper, as if he was transforming the White House into his own personal studio. The flaks were aghast. Benson could see their unmistakable glares of stifled anger. But they remained hesitant to say anything in front of the President and his wife, lest they give the impression that something might be unplanned.

The stakes for Tina Brown, however, were much more than a matter of a successful photo op. Back in New York, she had worried for months that Si Newhouse would finally pull the plug on *Vanity Fair* as a prudent act of financial triage to his expensive gesture of reviving a once-great magazine. For months, Newhouse had been losing millions with the new *Vanity Fair*—as much as $25 million by that point. The magazine had already gone through two editors since its debut in March 1983 and still hadn't seen any signs of a turnaround after nearly a year under Brown's leadership. All but the most loyal advertisers had fled, and its largely unfocused editorial content was ridiculed by critics. Si's impatience with this mounting folly was growing, despite the urgent pleadings of his new star editor imported from Britain.

Brown determined the White House shoot with the Reagans was vitally important to the survival of *Vanity Fair*. She decided to be there personally as the President and First Lady walked in. Brown wanted to make sure everything with the photo session went according to plan—something virtually unheard of for a top American magazine editor to do. She had hired perhaps the best freelance photographer in the business for this sort of thing, the fabled Harry Benson, a wily Scotsman with an unerring eye. Benson had trained on Fleet Street, then journeyed to the United States with the Beatles twenty years earlier and never left. He knew how to outfox the President's handlers to get the kind of photo he wanted.

Gently, Benson motioned the first couple to the location where he wanted to snap their picture. And then, at just the right moment, with a cue from Benson, the *Vanity Fair* assistant next to Tina Brown flicked on a tape recorder and the music began to play.

"She takes the moonlight . . ."

The voice was distinctively Frank Sinatra, a Reagan favorite and friend, especially of the First Lady. The song was called "Nancy with a Smiling Face," a tune originally dedicated to Old Blue Eyes's daughter, but that the crooner, a converted Republican, was not ashamed to sing for Mrs. Reagan at the White House. Benson guessed correctly with the music, for it immediately drew a chuckle from both the President and First Lady. He asked them to start dancing, and they quickly obliged with a fox-trot.

Benson's camera flashed away, capturing various shots of the Reagans laughing and dipping as he urged them on. At one point, the President looked at his watch, remembering the visiting South American leader in a nearby room. "I should be there now," he said not too convincingly. "I have to be going." Mrs. Reagan, though, seemed enchanted by the moment and would have none of it. She kept dancing along with her husband.

"It's heaven when I embrace my Nancy with the laughing face . . ."

"This is a wonderful song, isn't it?" Benson said approvingly to the First Lady, trying to keep the attention diverted to the music while he kept snapping.

"Yes it is," said Mrs. Reagan, simply delighted.

Spontaneously, without any mention by Benson, Nancy Reagan kicked up her leg slightly behind her, creating an elegant pose as her husband beamed with pleasure. That shot—the Reagans dancing in each other's arms—would later become the cover for *Vanity Fair*.

Benson waited until the music stopped for what would become another two-page spread inside. He knew, at that very point, he would get another excellent opportunity from the Reagans, an old Hollywood couple. "I wanted a real close-up," Benson recalled. "Being actors of that era, those movies always finished up with a big kiss. All of those B movies finished up like that." As the music died, Benson was right there to capture every smile and wrinkle as the Reagans embraced. He flashed away as that special moment arrived: the big smooch.

Tina Brown, who stayed out of Benson's way during the entire shoot, was very pleased and thanked him as they left the White House to go their separate ways. The following morning, Benson delivered the developed photographs and Brown knew that she had a winner, if only Newhouse could be convinced to stick with the magazine a little longer.

A few weeks later in May 1985, Brown was in California, invited to appear on the Merv Griffin television show to talk about the new cover story on the Reagans. When she called back to New York, she learned Si wanted to see her as soon as possible. Unnerved by this unexpected request, Brown soon found out from her sources at the magazine that Si Newhouse had had enough: He was going to kill *Vanity Fair* after Memorial Day. By telephone, Brown contacted another key supporter on the business side and urged him to convince Newhouse to forestall any final decision at least until she returned to New York. "I didn't realize it, but everyone on the staff had sort of tentative reassignments to other magazines," Brown said years later. One rumor with the ring of truth to it had Tina Brown returning to London as the new editor of British *Vogue*.

When she arrived in New York after a red-eye flight from LA, Brown met with Newhouse inside his office and he told her of his decision. "I'm going to send you back to England and you'll be the editor of *Vogue*, because this hasn't worked." Newhouse explained. "I think we have to stop throwing money at it."

His admission was a remarkable admission of failure. For more than two years, the company had heralded the return of *Vanity Fair* in the press, and both Si and Alexander Liberman had staked much of Condé Nast's reputation on its success. *Vanity Fair* was Si's most notable start-up venture, one in which he had invested much personal pride. But *Vanity Fair*'s woes just deepened. At one point, before Tina Brown's arrival, Si was prompted to exclaim, "This is a disaster!"

Brown wasn't willing to give up without a fight. She knew there was more advertising in the pipeline and a number of upcoming stories—including the Reagan cover story—which she was confident would draw some attention. If only she could convince Newhouse to hang on a little longer.

"Please just give us a few more issues," Brown pleaded, reeling off a number of reasons why it was still premature to kill *Vanity Fair*. "We can do it. We can turn this around."

Brown's hunch proved correct. That month's *Vanity Fair*—the June 1985 issue with the cover of the first couple fox-trotting and the headline THE REAGAN STOMP— drew a great deal of media attention, with both the usual pantlike praise in the gossip columns and the indignant scorn of Reagan's detractors. Before the photos were printed, Nancy Reagan had socialite Jerry Zipkin, whom Tina once described as Mrs. Reagan's "walker," inquire within *Vanity Fair* about whether the White House portraits would be flattering. The First Lady's office was assured not to worry, with good reason—the whole issue of *Vanity Fair* seemed devoted to the Reagans and their friends.

Like a time capsule just waiting to be plucked off the newsstand and buried for some later species to dissect, study, and deconstruct, the June 1985 edition proved to be a veritable encyclopedia of the eighties, that decade of unmatchable greed, avarice, and unabashed social climbing. "The Women You Want to Sit Next To" was one picture essay, which listed some sixty-five of the most socially desirable women and offered an essay devoted to their wealth and pedigree. In her own way, Brown was like some latter-day de Tocqueville, consorting with the natives and memorializing their social customs. Every name in this issue seemed made of bold print, those celebrity and society names found sprinkled throughout the gossip columns. Indeed, Liz Smith, who was courted assiduously by Brown, was pictured in this issue tap-dancing and wearing a tux. Everyone was there: Brooke Astor, Norman Mailer, Cornelia Guest, Roy Cohn, Diane Sawyer, Rupert Murdoch, the crowd at Mortimer's, Bill Paley, Joan Juliet Buck, Betsy Bloomingdale, Bill Blass, Nan Kempner, Taki Theodoracopulos, and, of course, Jerry Zipkin.

To wrap it all together, the Reagan photo spread was accompanied by an adoring essay about the first couple's enduring romance, written by that sonneteer of the far right, William F. Buckley, Jr. "People curious to know how it is between the man and wife dancing together on the cover of *Vanity Fair* this month are going to have to put to one side their political feelings and recognize that that is the way they are," Buckley gushed.

The party-pooper Left, as usual, was appalled. The entire issue "was one of the most repulsive objects I have ever seen—all the more distasteful because it represents the cynical calculation of *Vanity Fair*'s young British editor, Tina Brown," wrote Alexander Cockburn, who declared the new magazine "is what *The New Yorker* would look like if it was edited in Los Angeles."

But Tina Brown was pleased and so was her boss, Si Newhouse. The Reagan cover was a big hit and was eventually recalled as one of the crucial moments when *Vanity Fair* turned away from the financial abyss. "They put us on the map," Brown said later of the presidential coup. "They gave Mr. Newhouse cause to think there was a light at the end of the tunnel."

The Reagans, true to the decade whose style they personified, had helped to save the magazine that would chronicle all of its excess and splendor. To Harry Benson, it seemed only fitting. "I think the Reagan years were, in some ways, the dancing years," said the photographer. "We danced ourselves into a recession—you know what I mean?"

From his earliest days at Condé Nast, Si Newhouse had heard of the glory of *Vanity Fair*. It had ceased to exist in the mid-1930s, a victim of the Depression and America's more somber times. But the memories remained vivid with Alexander Liberman, whose original mentors in the company—particularly Frank Crowninshield—were crucial to *Vanity Fair*'s success. "Since 1936, people at Condé Nast have wanted to revive *Vanity Fair*," Newhouse explained at the rebirth. And for no one was that wish more true than for Alex Liberman.

When Liberman arrived at the company in 1941, *Vanity Fair* had been dead for little more than five years. Crowninshield had been the editor of the magazine since it was renamed from the original *Dress & Vanity Fair* after five uncertain issues, starting in 1913. The rights to the name *Vanity Fair*—a defunct publication once described as a sort of *Police Gazette* of the 1880s and 1890s—had been purchased for three thousand dollars. The old *VF* was, as Crowninshield recalled, "a Broadway property never seen in a club or a lady's house." This new incarnation, however, was very much designed to be seated in the lap of luxury.

An erudite bon vivant who dressed and acted every bit the role, Crowninshield hit his stride during the 1920s, when each month the magazine celebrated the men and women who "were making life less dull and more enchanting." Walter Lippmann wrote of politics, George Jean Nathan followed the theater, and Dorothy Parker and Robert C. Benchley amused its readers. D. H. Lawrence wrote regularly for the magazine, and its contributors included Thomas Wolfe, T. S. Eliot, James Joyce, P. G. Wodehouse, Noël Coward, John O'Hara, e. e. cummings, and André Gide. The magazine reproduced in color the work of European masters like Gauguin, van Gogh, Matisse, and featured the superb photography of Edward Steichen and Cecil Beaton. Nearly every famous name in the twenties and early thirties seemed to have a connection to *Vanity Fair*, whether Gertrude Stein, who wrote about Picasso, Clare Boothe Luce, who briefly served as managing editor, or its publisher, Condé Nast, who entertained the likes of George Gershwin, Harry Houdini, and Lunt and Fontanne.

Mostly, the magazine was a reflection of Crowninshield's restless curiosity. He was born to an American painter who spent much of his career abroad, with young Francis attending schools in Paris and elsewhere until he was expelled for some act of mischief. He inherited his father's interest in art, collecting the French Impressionists and becoming one of the founders of the Museum of Modern Art (an institute where Si Newhouse would later become a favored patron). As Crowninshield once observed, "My interest in society—at times so pronounced that the word 'snob' comes a little to mind—derives from the fact that I like an immense number of things which society, money, and position bring in their train: painting, tapestries, rare books, smart dresses, dances, gardens, country houses, correct cuisine and pretty women." Both Crowninshield and his magazine were very much America's favorite dandy.

This fragile, short-lived burst of talent began to fade after the crash of 1929, when *Vanity Fair's* advertising dried up and its circulation of ninety thousand readers declined. As the nation's money woes worsened, the frivolity found in *Vanity Fair* during the previous decade was toned down. More serious articles about politics and economics were stressed up front. By 1936, the magazine was swallowed up by *Vogue,* which continued to incorporate the name inside its logo for many years afterward.

Aside from this hazy memory of greatness lost, however, the driving force behind Si Newhouse's decision to revive *Vanity Fair* was characteristically practical. His marketing surveys showed an entire generation of affluent baby boomers waiting to claim a magazine for their own. Perhaps Newhouse, who coveted the upscale demographics and ad pages of *The New Yorker,* could steal away a similar but younger audience for his new magazine. In the early 1980s, when the decision was made to go ahead, Si Newhouse placed great faith in Liberman's ability to work editorial magic. The successful creation of *Self* magazine in 1979, followed by the purchase of the revamped *Gentleman's Quarterly,* convinced Newhouse that this bold gambit—in effect, creating a whole new magazine—was worth trying. The resurrection of *Vanity Fair* was an effort truly worthy of Liberman's talents: a serious magazine of art and culture rather than simply some fashion magazine. No expense would be spared in its preparation.

Over the next year and a half, Newhouse spent as much as $15 million in start-up costs before the first issue appeared. He began by ordering a detailed marketing survey. Readers in the nation's poshest neighborhoods were asked what kind of stories they wanted to read. Teams of sales representatives from Condé Nast met with top advertisers to convince them to appear in a much-touted premiere issue in March 1983. A record-setting 168 pages of advertising were secured, many from firms that had once appeared in the old *Vanity Fair*. "I'm panting with joy," enthused Joseph Corr, listed on the masthead as *VF*'s new publisher. A direct-mail firm sent out more than 10 million pieces to potential subscribers, offering to send the initial issue of *Vanity Fair* to their home for free—the same ploy that *Self* had used in its debut. "Condé Nast is large enough so we're not intimidated by the losses we're bound to have at first," Newhouse declared confidently. "If it earns less, it'll earn less. But it'll do well."

While the marketing and advertising seemed certain, the question of what the new *Vanity Fair* would look like remained very much a mystery. For all of the vaunted rhetoric surrounding its debut, it was a magazine born of the business side rather than from a clear and compelling editorial voice. Finding the right editorial voice to go along with the desired financial result, however, would be quite a different matter. Mark Clements, whose research showed Newhouse and Liberman that there was a big potential audience for a magazine devoted to art and literature, pop culture and politics, recalled his firm's role in the start-up. "We started to track it, as is Si's desire, to see what the direction was from the beginning," Clements said. "Each editor casts a magazine, in a sense, into his or her own mold, his or her own vision as to where to go. But the role of research is to make sure you're not going down the wrong road."

The first steps in the wrong direction began when Liberman took the advice of his wife's daughter, Francine du Plessix Gray, who was a well-known author and journalist. Although Liberman was fond of calling himself a journalist, his stepdaughter was a genuinely accomplished writer. For the selection of the new *Vanity Fair* editor, she suggested someone she admired at *The New York Times*. His name was Richard Locke. An intensely serious, bespectacled man with a slightly boyish-looking face, Locke was known as a wunderkind who had been unfairly passed over to replace his friend John Leonard as editor of the *Times Book Review*. He had been a book editor at Simon & Schuster and was president of the National Book Critics Circle at the time of his selection. Si Newhouse had also heard favorable comments about Locke from Robert Gottlieb, then the editor-in-chief of Knopf. Locke had worked for Gottlieb as an assistant when they were together at Simon & Schuster. When Si talked to Locke, he was impressed by his "quickness of temperament which I think is important for being an editor." But Locke's self-assured brusqueness was off-putting to those who simply called him arrogant. Some even speculated Locke wouldn't make it to the first issue's debut.

Nevertheless, Richard Locke became the first editor of *Vanity Fair* in five decades, the chosen heir to Frank Crowninshield. He began by putting together a 172-page prototype and a staff comparable with the magazine's fabled legacy. "The old *Vanity Fair* was an exciting combination of high culture and low, entertainment and seriousness, that seemed to capture the spirit of the times. But that was the twenties," Locke said in one of several stories that appeared before its debut. "We can't bring them back and have no interest in doing so. But we hope to be able to put together a magazine that is as much a product of this time as the original was of its." For all the talk about the old *Vanity Fair,* however, the main target was *The New Yorker,* as Locke acknowledged in some private moments with his staff.

Over lunch at the grill of The Four Seasons, for example, Walter Clemons, then a book reviewer at *Newsweek,* remembers Locke's description of his dream magazine. "He had in mind a writer's magazine and I believe he felt *The New Yorker* was moribund in those days," said Clemons. "And he felt there was a need for another magazine." Many writers like Clemons were given much larger salaries then they had been earning, with the promise of a virtual free hand journalistically. For the next several months, Locke and his emerging staff shared the same floor in the Condé Nast building with *House & Garden* as they prepared *Vanity Fair*'s return.

Old friends who joined the staff, like John Leonard, were convinced that Locke was up to the task. "I think Richard had a very strong editorial concept," Leonard said in retrospect. "I'm just not sure—because I can't read his mind—how much he went ahead with his concept against their will, or how much they allowed him to go ahead with his concept and then decided it wasn't working. I just don't know." But most who were recruited for the new *Vanity Fair* grew more dubious about Locke, particularly as the deadline for the magazine's new premiere approached. When James Wolcott came aboard, he met his new editor inside his office. Locke motioned to a prototype of the magazine.

"This is not going to be a coffee table book," Locke declared, as Wolcott later remembered. "This is going to be an ongoing, cultural enterprise."

Wolcott listened to his new boss as if enduring an out-of-body experience. "Uh, oh," Wolcott thought to himself at the time. "I almost said, 'Beam me up, Scotty!' "

Although the staff had been recruited by Locke, they slowly realized that it was Alexander Liberman, and not their new editor, who was really in charge. "The basic difficulty—I was told later that I was naïve not to have known this—was that Richard didn't have the power," said Clemons. "The power was Alex Liberman. And we thought Alex Liberman was just an art director who dropped by. Little did we know that he had veto power over everything that went into the magazine." Clemons said he was startled when he saw the *Vanity Fair* prototype, which featured a Richard Avedon photo of ballet star Mikhail Baryshnikov. "My first thought was, If I had seen this, I would have never come to work for this magazine," he said. "It was all splashy layout and I saw that it wasn't the reading magazine that Richard had proposed to me." When Clemons showed a copy of the expensively produced prototype to an old colleague, the art director at *Newsweek,* he got an immediate assessment of who was in charge at *Vanity Fair.*

"Oh, I see what they're doing—it's a fast book," the art director told him. It was the start of a painful lesson for Clemons. "That was a term I didn't know," he recalled. "But that's an art director's term for a magazine you can flip through very fast and read it from the back or front or sideways. He said it was a typical Liberman production, because you can't tell the ads from the text of the magazine. And that's why advertisers love it."

The long-awaited buildup for *Vanity Fair*'s reemergence from the dead added to the overall anxiety. The company took out full-page ads in several upscale magazines trumpeting its arrival. In one ad, novelist John Irving appeared in a wrestling suit above the caption "No Contest." In another, Twyla Tharp leapt in the air above "Breakthrough." Condé Nast officials confidently predicted, "You will not find a more handsome, readable magazine in America."

The overall style was pure Liberman, the artist who was now prepared to stake his claim in the literary world. When critics pointed out that the magazine seemed unfocused, Liberman responded that "to make a guide to the reader is a bit degrading for a magazine of this level." When others questioned Locke's credentials as new editor, Liberman again responded mystically: "We take risks." Though the press was assured Richard Locke was in charge, everyone within the Condé Nast realm prepared to praise Alex Liberman for his presumed triumph. "He is obscenely proud of the marriage he has made between art and commerce," one Liberman friend told a reporter. Unflappable to the end, Liberman adopted his familiar Olympian manner and Socratic reply when challenged on the purpose of his *Vanity Fair*. "They ask what is the necessity of this magazine?" Liberman asked. "Well, what is the necessity in the world of art and creativity? That's what this magazine is about."

Things never got much clearer than that.

When the first issue finally appeared, Si Newhouse threw a party for the thirty *Vanity Fair* staff members at his East Side town house. It was a big party, with many of Manhattan's best-known literati milling around. Most staff writers had never met Newhouse, the man who paid their handsome salaries, and few engaged in conversation with him. Instead, they stared at the expensive original paintings on Newhouse's walls and wondered aloud about the true artistic taste of the man for whom they worked. Most of the chitchat in Si's circle that night was done by Liberman and Victoria Newhouse, who is much more sociable than her husband. "Victoria's warm, smart, funny, gets the joke," recalled one *Vanity Fair* staffer who was later invited to a Newhouse dinner party. "Dinner at Si's is immensely fun. It's eclectic; it's vocal; it's outspoken."

When the critical onslaught to the first issue arrived, however, the frivolity and bons mots quickly dissipated. As *Newsweek* later observed, in almost obituary style, "No magazine has ever received a ruder welcome." The reviews for the new *Vanity Fair* were simply crushing.

The *Christian Science Monitor,* somewhat uncharitably, called it "slick and superficial." *The Wall Street Journal* said the new issue was "amazingly bloated and self-indulgent." The *Washington Post* called it "incoherent gumbo." A bit less caustic, *Time* announced that *VF* "has not found its personality," while attaching a kicker that said the "liveliest bit of journalism in the new magazine" was a reprised feature about Malibu beach by James M. Cain—first published in *Vanity Fair* in 1933. *The New Republic*'s critic, Henry Fairlie, called the first issue "a mess at heart" and deeply cynical in its soul. "This new *Vanity Fair* is from Madison Avenue, literally and figuratively; it is a Madison Avenue product, a packaged brain(?)child of a publishing corporation, its accountants, and the advertisers." In perhaps the cruelest cut of all, Fairlie added, "One can have only an increased admiration for *The New Yorker* which, with much the same kind of advertising, nevertheless manages to subdue it and keep its text plainly distinct."

Even the advertisers were disgusted by the premiere issue. "The first one was too shocking, it was incredibly bad," said advertising agency chief George Lois. "I go to people around town and ask them if they understand what it is about. They don't. It's an affected magazine." The amount of advertising pages scheduled for *Vanity Fair*'s upcoming issues dropped dramatically from the record-setting debut. It seemed the huge investment was going to take much longer to recoup, if ever.

For Si Newhouse and Alexander Liberman—who were accustomed to financial success and scant critical reviews of their fashion magazines—the tidal wave of disapproval was jarring. Liberman later blamed the criticism on the prepublication hype. "And then the press pounced on the first issue with a vengeance that was perhaps more anti-Newhouse than anything else," Liberman said. If he shared the same feelings, Newhouse never showed it. To the press, Si maintained a cool demeanor, declaring that the first issue was "gutsy. It covered the waterfront." Newhouse indicated he was willing to ride out whatever bumps there were along the way. He said he wouldn't worry if *Vanity Fair* was still in the red five years later. "We never believed we were producing a perfect magazine when we relaunched *Vanity Fair*," Newhouse said, only slightly backtracking from his magazine's confident claims before its debut. "Obviously, we've got a way to go before we get the wonderful, seamless quality a mature magazine has."

Within the walls of Condé Nast, the critical bombast reverberated for weeks. Staffers who were vexed by Locke's indecisiveness now found him, as one described it, "in the bunker, paralyzed and uncommunicative." In print, the publisher, Joseph Corr, called his editor "petulant." Some blamed Newhouse for allowing the incredible ballyhoo surrounding the magazine's debut, inadvertently setting it up for disappointment against people's expectations. Despite the sharp criticisms, some staffers like John Leonard thought Locke would at least be given a chance to succeed. "A serious magazine with aspirations to be another *New Yorker* or whatever is going to have to shake down, regardless of what your concept is for it,"

Leonard said. "You don't expect to get your head lopped off after only three issues."

More than a month after the disastrous first issue, and with no sign of rebound after the second, Richard Locke was summoned to Si Newhouse's office in early May, while the rest of the staff went about its business. Whatever self-confident assurances he may have given the press, Newhouse was clearly unnerved by *Vanity Fair*'s plunging fortunes. Si had too much invested in this project to allow it to fail. Locke was told he was being replaced and to clean out his desk in two days. Later that afternoon, Locke gathered staff as they returned from lunch and informed them of his ouster. In his place was named Leo Lerman, the sixty-eight-year-old features editor of *Vogue*. Lerman was an old friend of Liberman and had joined the company in 1941, as well. Lerman was virtually the polar opposite of Locke: a genial, well-regarded editor who liked entertainment stories as well as literary treatises. He also knew his place in dealing with Alex Liberman. Staff writers later noticed that manuscripts marked in Lerman's purple felt-tipped pen, presumably after being given a final edit, were instead placed in an interoffice box for Liberman's final approval. "I want to make it into a great magazine, not what it was, but what it should be today," Lerman said for the record, playing a familiar refrain. A Condé Nast business official was trotted out to tell the *Times* that Lerman's selection was "as permanent as anything can be."

The tea-leaf readers within the company knew that good old Leo Lerman was in a holding pattern until Si and Alex could figure a way out of their predicament. Undoubtedly, there would soon be a new editor for *Vanity Fair*. The only question was who it would be.

Hardly anyone watched when Tina Brown, wearing a sequined G-string she had borrowed from another dancer, stepped onto the makeshift stage. Slowly, she started to grind to the Rolling Stones music coming from a jukebox inside a New Jersey go-go bar.

"I can't get no . . . sa-tis-fac-tion," the rock song blared.

Introduced as "Union Jackie," the all-but-nude foreign correspondent from *Punch* magazine kept her wits about her as she shook and grooved and looked out at the lunchtime crowd, a rather motley crew. As she later recounted, three construction workers took one look at the new dancer and turned their backs to play pool.

Tina Brown was barely twenty-two years old—a smart and ambitious young journalist who had already made a name for herself back in Great Britain—when she made her show-business debut in New Jersey. She was determined to take on this undercover assignment as an observer of America's mid-1970s social mores. "I wanted to come to America and I said to *Punch*, 'I'll do you five columns,'" she recalled years later. "Being the diarrhea correspondent, they have to be basically awful things. So I answered an ad in *The Village Voice* for a go-go girl in Hackensack."

In her essay, which could have been entitled "A Letter from Hackensack," Brown recounted her experiences in getting hired for the job.

"You've got a great ass," her boss, a stumpy little man known as Big Ed, reassured her before her debut. "No, really—we like our Show Go girls a little full."

Big Ed's associate, another colorful local native named Angelo, was more discriminating. "Frankly, we could book you topless," he advised. "But your crotch swivel needs a lot of practice." It was Angelo who, in a moment of inspiration, came up with Brown's nom de flesh—Union Jackie. Despite her own reservations and the concern of those who knew of her plans, Brown returned unharmed to her room at the Royalton Hotel and quickly filed her account of being an exotic dancer in the wild outback of New Jersey.

To Tina Brown, America was this wondrously bizarre country, filled with apocryphal situations like noontime voyeurs at the go-go bar in Hackensack, lovesick cops in LA, Manhattan socialites on parade at the Metropolian Museum. Like her view of England, Tina Brown's America was engaged in desperate class conflicts—a constant struggle among the A-list people, the B-list people, and those pathetic souls below. "All unaware," as she wrote of those outside the inner circle at one night's Manhattan gala, "that the evening's social apartheid meant their designer glad rags would only be for the benefit of each other."

In the late 1970s, her tales of the rich and depraved filled several columns for *Punch* and the *Sunday Times of London* and were later included in two books of her collected work. Brown's humorous and often biting writing style and her uncanny sense of the zeitgeist caught the attention of *The Tatler* magazine, which named her editor in June 1979. At the time, *The Tatler,* with a history reaching back nearly three hundred years, was a barely read relic for about ten thousand subscribers. Tina Brown, by then twenty-five, recognized *The Tatler*'s potential, spruced it up, and offered her magazine as the definitive social chronicle of an England dominated by Margaret Thatcher and the Prince of Wales's new bride. "I think the Twenties thing is going to happen all over again," she told a British interviewer in 1979 in her blunt but witty manner. "There is going to be a huge new social boom. There is going to be a reversion to sophistication and formality. After all, we've got the Tories back now. It isn't shameful to spend money anymore."

The miraculous conversion of *The Tatler*—from a dour, stuffy review of aristocracy to a vibrant, provocative magazine relying on celebrities and irreverent social commentary—earned Tina Brown a place in that honored pantheon of editors who have breathed new life into a dying publication. "As seen through the old *Tatler,* most English parties seemed to be thrown at Madame Tussaud's," Brown wrote later. Her tantalizing remedy of high- and lowbrow culture was served up with hard work, considerable skill, and sheer gall. To get an interview with Princess Caroline of Monaco, for instance, a groveling letter of introduction was placed in a box of shoes the princess had bought. Brown's style was part Fleet Street, part *Town & Country,* and always winningly irreverent and entertaining. A poke here, a poke there: no one was immune. In those years, she relied on a small staff of friends like Miles Chapman, Sarah Giles, Chris Garrett—all of whom later found jobs at *Vanity Fair*—to produce *The Tatler* with her. "When it was such a small operation, there was no one to write the pieces really, so between us, we'd write the magazine, sometimes under pseudonyms," she recalled years later. "That's what you do when you don't have a budget."

The emergence of Diana Spencer as the new Princess of Wales would help catapult *The Tatler* into the vanguard of London's social discourse. The new princess was a favorite target for Brown, who privately performed a wickedly funny imitation of Lady Di, to whom she bears a slight resemblance. "Watching the transformation of Lady Diana from a hesitant mouse into a glittering femme fatale was a source of fun and wonderment," Brown would later write in her second book, *Life as a Party.* "She was an upper-class Cinderella starving herself, streaking her hair Hollywood blonde, taking her face to the best make-up artiste in town, flaunting bare shoulders at the opera, putting to rout the time-honoured traditions of royal dowdiness and, at the same time, all her tired old gossip-column rivals. . . . I liked to think Lady Diana's transformation was the keynote to the revamped *Tatler.*"

Over the next three years, Brown learned how to edit on the fly, as she later said, and realized the importance of using attention-grabbing graphics. She pumped *The Tatler*'s tired veins with enough juicy stories to make its circulation numbers jump up to forty thousand readers. Brown's stewardship was hailed by admirers in the press and sometimes by herself as a great coup. As she later explained, "When I took her on, *Tatler* was a rather dull, stodgy deb: I put her on a diet, got her into some good designer clothes, sent her to Barbara Daly to have her face done, introduced her to bad company—she went on drugs briefly (she's off them now)—and she made a very good marriage to Condé Nast." A very good marriage indeed.

Si Newhouse and Alex Liberman were impressed by the young editor and her remarkable turnaround of *The Tatler*'s fortunes. In April 1982, Newhouse bought *The Tatler* from its owner, Gary Bogard, an Australian, who walked away with a tidy sum. By then, however, Tina Brown seemed to be wearying from the pace of running a magazine. She stayed for only a few more months, until March 1983, when she left *The Tatler* to write and travel. She remained in Newhouse's employ, though, as a consultant to *Vanity Fair.* Occasionally, during the shaky stewardships of Locke and then Lerman, Tina Brown could be found at the New York offices of *Vanity Fair,* where she was seen as a friendly, talented young woman with a telltale British accent. According to staff members, few had any idea that she might be groomed for the top spot at the magazine. Carefully, Tina Brown surveyed the wreckage. "Artistically, *Vanity Fair* was a typographical zoo, and editorially, it was aimed at readers of *The New York Review of Books* or people who wanted a short cut to culture," Brown would later comment. "The sales side was selling a crackling, witty urbane after-dinner magazine that had nothing to do with what the editors were publishing." Brown formulated her own ideas of how the magazine could still be made into a success.

Putting on a good show was always important to her. Brown had learned her flair for the dramatic from her gregarious father, George Hambley Brown, a British film producer whose first wife had been the Hollywood actress Maureen O'Hara. At Pinewood Film Studio in England, Brown's father met her mother, Bettina Kohr, who was working then as Laurence Olivier's press agent. Their daughter, Christina Hambley Brown, who later preferred the shortened version of her first name, was treated to a house full of movie stars and celebrities from both sides of the ocean. She listened to visitors like Peter Ustinov and was enraptured. "You would always find her sitting on the lap of the most important man in the room," one friend would later recall. Her father was a gentle, indulgent sort, recognizing his daughter's quick wit, keen intellect, and free spirit. Young Tina was tossed out of three different upper-crust boarding schools and infuriated her headmistresses with such regularity that father Brown developed a favorite reproach: "How depressing for you to know you failed with this talented child."

From observing her father's world, she became "a keen student of facade," as she later said, attuned to the sharp differences between image and reality. "As far as I could see, castles were always plaster, money was always funny, and the nuns came off the set for a fag."

Brown eventually enrolled in Oxford's St. Anne's College, where she developed her skills as a writer and editor. "She was so pretty, so funny, young, and feminine that the men she got to talk to never dreamed that she would remember what they said, let alone use it against them in print," one colleague on the university magazine later remembered. Through a series of breaks and raw talent, *The Times* named her Most Promising Female Journalist and she was sent to the United States in 1974 to do a story about the women's movement. At *The Times,* she met Harold Evans, then its dashing editor, a man twice her age. "My God, I was in love immediately," she recalled. "He was the sexy editor of all time, amazing in action, the Nijinsky of newsprint." They moved in together and were married in 1981 in a ceremony at the Hamptons summer home of then *Washington Post* editor Ben Bradlee and his wife, writer Sally Quinn. Evans was equally smitten but bemused enough once to list among his wife's best attributes "curiosity and ratlike cunning." After their wedding,

Brown left immediately for London and *The Tatler,* while Evans stayed at the Algonquin Hotel in Manhattan and shared old memories with a pal from the *London Sunday Times.*

Knowing how to handle older men would prove invaluable for Tina Brown in the world of Condé Nast. Her chance to edit *Vanity Fair* came in December 1983 as she was getting ready to go on vacation to Barbados. Si Newhouse called and asked her to come to lunch with Liberman and himself. Shortly afterward, Brown arrived in New York during a terrible winter storm with a limited wardrobe, which included a cheesecloth dress and a bikini. During their discussions, Si decided to offer the job to Brown. Under this arrangement, Newhouse said Leo Lerman would move out of the editor's seat and assume the title of editorial adviser. But from her observations, she knew Liberman was really running the show. If she was to take the editorship, Tina Brown indicated to Newhouse that he must promise to give her a free hand. The message was unspoken but clear that *Vanity Fair* would no longer be Alexander Liberman's to control.

"She was feisty enough to say, 'You want my thinking? You've got to let me do it without interference,' " recalled Ruth Ansel, who was brought into the company by Liberman, appointed *Vanity Fair*'s art director under Lerman, and stayed for Brown's early years. "The amazing thing about Tina is that she took a gamble. Maybe Si said okay and knew if things didn't go well, Alex would come in and interfere in a big way. But no— it was hands off for Liberman. Alex, who was there every day during Leo's time, stopped coming down. The magazine was formed by Tina and her staff and we flogged it out and created a magazine in three weeks and developed it into the *Vanity Fair* you know."

No editor at Condé Nast, at least not for forty years, had been able to drive such a hard-nosed Machiavellian bargain for control of a magazine without Alex Liberman watching overhead. A few editors like Ruth Whitney at *Glamour* or Art Cooper at *GQ,* who were highly skilled and very successful, were not dominated by Liberman as were other lesser figures in the Condé Nast hierarchy. For many years, Si had favored Liberman's system of weak editors who would tend to the details and everyday matters while Alex kept abreast of the general direction of each magazine.

This arrangement was something different, however. Newhouse's decision to give Tina Brown full control over *Vanity Fair* was surely a tribute to her skills and her ability to reverse the course of a failing magazine. It also marked her as the first major editor, with a fresh, young, strongly independent view, whom Si hired for the future, for that time when Liberman would be too old to swoop down from on high and dramatically save the day. "He's such a good poker player that when he saw it succeeding, rather than become embittered—he's a smart politician—he applauded it all and became her champion," said Ansel. "He turned a potential enemy into an ally, and the same with her. She realized he is extraordinarily helpful when you can control him. The trouble with Alex is, you can't control him. He's a mighty giant." When asked about her relations with Liberman, who had dominated the previous two *Vanity Fair* editors, Brown replied, "He's given me a clear mandate to do what I want" without providing any behind-the-scenes detail.

Tina Brown's selection as *Vanity Fair*'s new editor was met with little fanfare and few expectations of success. After all, Leo Lerman, a seasoned magazine editor, was leaving after just nine months. Most of the press portrayed *Vanity Fair* as a lost cause. "Do you know anyone who reads it anymore?" one former editor asked *Newsweek*. This perception was deadly for David O'Brasky, the magazine's new publisher, who had replaced Corr only a month before Brown was selected. Most advertising budgets were already determined for 1984, and *Vanity Fair* was looking like a sure loser. After its record-setting debut with 168 pages of advertising, Madison Avenue fled. At its worst point in July 1984, *Vanity Fair* would carry only fourteen pages of advertising. Tina Brown realized the problem and set out to change the public perception of the magazine's future. "It had become fashionable to put the boot in," Brown later said. "I felt I had to win the opinion of my peers. I had to seduce the media."

It was love at first sight. Almost from the very day of her arrival, the self-promotion never ended. Brash, funny, articulate, and charming, Brown began a series of media interviews to promote herself and the magazine, a combination that would soon become indistinguishable. "If you don't like my identity, you won't like the magazine," she told the *Washington Post*. "You're stuck with it. I have a remorsefully long shadow."

Some of her comments seemed deliberately designed to provoke or at least ruffle some feathers. "There are a lot of homosexual men in New York because the men are so frightened of the females that they turn to each other," she told one interviewer. Besides sexual conventions, Brown also stuck her finger into the side of the pompously rich. "Americans are much less ironic about their social standing," she said, after observing local titans of industry like Donald Trump and Revlon chief Ron Perlman. "Once people have made $20 million, they don't feel they should be laughed at. You get your kneecaps shot off."

Money, whether old or new, was the magic elixir of the 1980s and her reinvigorated *Vanity Fair* would bask in its allure. "*Vanity Fair* will be me responding to America," she predicted. "And let's hope I get it right." Brown, the class-conscious Oxford grad, sensed the need for social cachet among nouveaux riches—even for her boss, a second-generation billionaire. She realized *Vanity Fair* was always about more than just making money for Newhouse. "It's why faceless millionaires buy publications, so they can ring up Norman Mailer and ask him to dinner," she once explained.

To turn around *Vanity Fair*'s fortunes, it would have to become the hottest, slickest, most informed page-turner on America's newsstands.

"You've got to make it an almost illicit pleasure to get this magazine and just rip it open. Every single detail of the magazine is about screaming, *Read me! Read me! Read me! Read me!*" Brown later explained in a profile for the television show "60 Minutes." "You know—'You will die if you do not read me.' My job the whole time is one of seduction, as an editor. I am about entrapping that reader."

Upon taking the magazine's reins, Brown put together one of the most eclectic staffs in American magazine history. She announced her "first order of the day was to build up her own stable of writers to give the magazine a style of its own." True to her word, she quickly put on her spats and Condé Nast tommy gun, eliminating those unneeded staffers from early regimes ("a little blood on the floor, like Scarface," as she later described the multiple firings). Her magazine would be a "strong masculine read," she said, featuring "good, clean reporting done in a ballsy way." The cover of her first issue in May 1984 seemed to sum up Brown's expectations: a luxuriant photograph of actress Daryl Hannah blindfolded and holding two Oscars, with a headline that flashed, BLONDE AMBITION.

With Si Newhouse's largesse still available, Brown began offering un-precedented contracts for top magazine writers in New York, several of whom were given six-figure contracts—roughly twice the pay rate for most magazine writers at the time. Even kill fees for rejected articles were generous. Brown was convinced that to get the kind of stories she wanted about the rich and famous, she must pay top dollar for writers who would have the means to travel in these rarefied circles. In this regard, Si was much different from his father. He was willing to pay for editorial talent, at least for those publications read by his friends and social crowd. Writers like Gail Sheehy and Marie Brenner, two of the top feature writers at *New York* magazine, were lured away with large contracts and promises of great assignments. Brenner, one of Brown's closest confidantes, was often touted in the press as one of *Vanity Fair*'s important additions. Sheehy called attention to Brown's ever-adaptful mind. "Tina has the courage of her ignorance," said Sheehy. "If she doesn't know what some-thing means or how it works, she wants to find out. That's what makes a good editor." Perhaps the biggest coup, however, was convincing photog-rapher Annie Leibovitz to jump from *Rolling Stone* magazine. With vir-tually every issue, Leibovitz provided the distinctively stylish portraits and photos that gave *Vanity Fair* its memorable look.

Other staffers, not quite as heralded, were brought aboard for their personal connections or intimate knowledge of New York's social scene. In Los Angeles, Brown hired Angela Janklow, the daughter of literary superagent Morton Janklow. Even if young Janklow's writing "was not memorable," as one newspaper later commented, her father's network of literary and showbiz connections certainly was. Another notable example was the magazine's special projects editor Reinaldo Herrera—the dapper

S.I. Newhouse Sr. and Sons. In 1976, after the purchase of the Booth newspaper chain in Michigan—touted as the biggest newspaper deal of its time—Si Newhouse (*left*) posed with his father (*center*) and his younger brother, Donald (*right*). AP/WIDE WORLD PHOTOS.

Allard & Si & Roy. At the Horace Mann School, Allard Lowenstein was a close friend to whom Si Newhouse confided his thoughts of suicide. Although his friendship with Lowenstein would eventually fade, schoolmate Roy Cohn remained a lifelong friend.

Behind the Scenes. In the fall of 1944, Si was a comanaging editor at the school newspaper, which was edited by Lowenstein. Although Newhouse would someday become America's richest media baron, this high-school newspaper carried some of the rare stories ever to appear with his byline.

Uncertain Si. Within the Newhouse newspapers during the 1950s, young Si Newhouse was viewed as something of a buffoon, a Jerry Lewis look-alike who didn't seem to fit into his father's plans. Si is posed here with Joseph Sansone of the Newhouse's Harrisburg newspaper. UPI/BETTMAN.

The Family at Greenlands. Si's divorce from Jane Franke greatly upset his parents, Mitzi and Sam, who are seen here at the family's country estate in Greenlands, New Jersey, along with Si's brother, Donald, and his wife, Susan. This photo appeared in a 1962 *Time* magazine cover story about Sam Newhouse and his newspaper empire. BEN MARTIN/TIME MAGAZINE.

Alexander Liberman. Much of what young Si Newhouse learned about magazines, as well as modern art and New York's social circles, came from Alex Liberman (*left*). Liberman is pictured here at a social function with Chessy Patcévitch (*right*), the wife of Condé Nast president Iva Patcévitch, who oversaw the sale of the company to the Newhouses in 1959. COURTESY OF WHITCOM PARTNERS/NEW YORK HERALD TRIBUNE.

Diana Vreeland. Considered America's greatest fashion editor, Vreeland was lured from rival *Harper's Bazaar* by Liberman with Newhouse's money. Her tenure during the 1960s marked the most remarkable period in *Vogue*'s hundred-year history. In one memo, she instructed: "Today, let's think pig white." COURTESY OF WHITCOM PARTNERS/NEW YORK HERALD TRIBUNE.

Mitzi in *Vogue*. Sam Newhouse repeatedly said he bought
Condé Nast in 1959 to please his wife, Mitzi (*right*). During
the early 1960s, Mitzi traveled to Paris for the fashion shows
and listened intently to the opinions of *Vogue*'s editor, Diana
Vreeland (*left*), who made sure the new owner's wife was
mentioned in its pages. Courtesy of Whitcom Partners/New
York Herald Tribune.

***Vogue*'s Mercurial Editor and Shy Owner.** Diana Vreeland glorious reign at *Vogue* ended
with her abrupt demotion in 1971. Pictured here together shortly after Si was named *Vogue*'s
publisher in 1964, Newhouse later admitted he had a "wild nightmare" after firing the legendary Vreeland. Courtesy of Whitcom Partners/New York Herald Tribune.

Grace Mirabella. During the 1970s, Grace Mirabella, Vreeland's successor at *Vogue* focused the magazine more towards working women's concerns and revived the magazine's sagging fortunes. In 1988, her abrupt firing was announced on TV before she learned from Newhouse that Anna Wintour was her replacement. Ozier Muhammad/©1988 New York Newsday.

Master Photographer. Richard Avedon's stunning work for *Vogue* under Diana Vreeland set new standards for fashion photography. Avedon, pictured here in 1974 with some of his work, was later named by Tina Brown as the first staff photographer in the history of *The New Yorker.* Dick Yarwood /©1974 Newsday.

The Silver Fox. For a half century at Condé Nast, Alex Liberman remained the ultimate survivor in a company known for lightning-fast management turnovers. Despite his closeness with Si, Liberman was keenly aware of how "the Newhouse concept" had changed Condé Nast magazines and his own vision. Viorel Florescu/©1988 New York Newsday.

The Rat Pack. (*above left*) During the late 1950s and early 1960s, the recently divorced Si Newhouse often socialized with Roy Cohn (*left*) and their group of ambitious young friends, like entrepreneur William Fugazy, Jr. (*right*). COURTESY OF WHITCOM PARTNERS/NEW YORK HERALD TRIBUNE.

Henry Garfinkle. (*above right*) With a loan from Si Newhouse, Henry Garfinkle started what would eventually become one of the largest magazine and newspaper distribution companies in the nation. COURTESY OF WHITCOM PARTNERS/NEW YORK HERALD TRIBUNE.

Roy and Fat Tony. (*below*) In the 1980s, Roy Cohn (*right*) was "Special Counsel to Newhouse Publications" — at the same time that he was lawyer for New York Mafia leader, "Fat Tony" Salerno (*center*). At the request of mob leaders, Cohn intervened with Newhouse's Cleveland newspaper to print a misleading story that helped get Jackie Presser elected as teamsters union president. COPY OF FBI SURVEILLANCE PHOTO, COURTESY OF JAMES NEFF.

Loyal Friends. Si Newhouse's devotion to his long-time friend Roy Cohn continued until his final days, when Roy was facing disbarment and was dying from the AIDS virus. In 1986, when federal authorities filed a civil lawsuit against him for back taxes, Cohn joked with reporters in his New York City law office. ©NEW YORK NEWSDAY.

The Family Patriarch Dies. After his father's death in 1979, Si Newhouse took control of the family's media empire. Together, the brothers escorted their mother, Mitzi, at the funeral service for the family's patriarch, whose estate later became the subject of a $1 billion tax battle with the IRS. AP/WIDE WORLD PHOTOS.

America's Richest Media Tycoon. By the late 1980s, Si Newhouse (*above left*) was the self-assured chairman of America's largest private media company. Around the office, Si, with his casual clothing and short, cropped hair, could be seen working with his trademark yellow pads and marking pens. NEAL BOENZI/NYT PICTURES.

Big Names, Big Books. Soon after he and his brother bought Random House in 1980, Si Newhouse attempted to sign up Norman Mailer (*above right*) as a writer for his publishing company. Si's reliance on well-known authors, large advances and "big books" transformed Random House. OZIER MUHAMMAD/©1983 NEWSDAY.

Joni Evans. As one of the most talented editors at Random House, the career of Joni Evans seemed caught in Newhouse's revolving-door management changes. After stepping down as publisher of the company's flagship imprint, Evans (*seen here in center foreground with her staff*) started a smaller imprint called Turtle Bay Books, which was forced to close down in 1993. FRED CONRAD/NYT PICTURES.

Erroll McDonald. In a much talked-about essay in the *Times*, Erroll McDonald (*left*) complained about a "welfare mentality" at Pantheon during André Schiffrin's tenure and eventually wound up being appointed in 1990 as Schiffrin's successor. McDonald worked on convincing TV star Oprah Winfrey to finish her highly touted autobiography. BRUCE GILBERT/©NEW YORK NEWSDAY.

E. Graydon Carter. During the 1980s, Carter's *Spy* magazine upset many at Condé Nast, especially Tina Brown, with its biting humor. Carter's editorial ability was noticed by Newhouse and earned him the chance to edit *Vanity Fair*. JOHN PARASKEVAS/©1992 NEW YORK NEWSDAY.

Tina Brown. After two editors failed, Si entrusted *Vanity Fair* to a thirty-one-year-old, British-born editor whose mix of celebrity profiles with serious reporting revived *Vanity Fair* at a time when Si wanted to kill it. Her husband, Harry Evans, publisher of Random House's flagship imprint, also became a powerful figure in Newhouse's empire in the 1990s. PHOTOGRAPHY BY JEAN PAGLIUSO.

Anna Wintour. (*above left*) Supremely stylish and a Newhouse favorite, Anna Wintour replaced Grace Mirabella as editor of *Vogue* in 1988 and successfully overhauled the fashion industry's top magazine. Wintour was influential in Newhouse's decision to pick Graydon Carter as *Vanity Fair*'s new editor in 1992. NYT PICTURES.

Managed Competition. (*above right*) In 1992, Si Newhouse's switch of editors at *Vanity Fair* and *The New Yorker* seemed to catch many off guard. Tina Brown *(center)* wanted to bring *Vanity Fair*'s publisher Ronald Galotti (*left*) along with her, but Si insisted Galotti stay with the new editor, E. Graydon Carter (*right*). The internal squabbles resulted in Galotti's firing less than a year later. FRED CONRAD/NYT PICTURES.

Monopoly Money. The huge profits of the Newhouse media empire depended heavily on gaining monopoly-like newspaper franchises in places such as New Orleans and Portland. Other newspapers like the *Long Island Press* (*seen above on its last day in 1977*), which faced considerable competition, were "funerals" that were killed when the Newhouses decided they could no longer afford them. DICK KRAUS/©1977 NEW YORK NEWSDAY.

Richard Shortway. Shortway was credited by many with teaching Si about the business side of magazines. Shortway played a pivotal role as *Vogue*'s publisher. After admitting he was "burned out" and needed a change in assignment, Shortway says Newhouse dropped him as both a friend and a trusted adviser. NYT

Andy Warhol.
Si Newhouse's $100-million art collection has included several works by the famed Pop artist. After Sam Newhouse's death in 1979, Si and his mother asked Warhol to paint a portrait of the family patriarch in Warhol's distinctive style.
PAUL BERESWILL/©1979 NEWSDAY.

James Truman. One of several British-trained editors at Condé Nast, James Truman (*left*) proved he could turn around a magazine by making *Details* a success with "Generation X" young men. In 1994, Newhouse stunned the publishing industry by naming the then thirty-five-year-old Truman as Condé Nast's editorial director. ARI MINTZ/©1990 NEW YORK NEWSDAY.

William Shawn and Robert Gottlieb. Si Newhouse abruptly dismissed the legendary *New Yorker* editor, William Shawn in 1977. His replacement, Robert Gottlieb, was greeted by an angered staff and a petition demanding that he not take the job. After the announcement, Shawn met with Gottlieb to talk about the magazine's future. ©ELAINE SEIBERT.

Robert Bernstein and Bennett Cerf. Bernstein's tenure as chairman of Random House lasted for a quarter century. He is pictured here seated between Cerf and Random House cofounder Donald Klopfer (*with sales manager Lewis Miller standing*). After several differences with Newhouse, Bernstein was forced to leave in 1989. NYT PICTURES.

Barry Diller and Si. At *Vanity Fair*'s tenth anniversary party in September 1993, Si spoke with Barry Diller and contributing editor Diane Von Furstenberg. Newhouse's $500-million stake in the bid of Diller's QVC Network to buy Paramount Communications highlighted Newhouse's dominant position in controlling America's media.

Venezualan-born husband of fashion designer Carolina Herrera—who was once described in the magazine's pages as a "socialite and landowner" who frequented Mortimer's. Years earlier, as a writer for *The Tatler,* Brown had asked Reinaldo Herrera what he did with his time and all he could say was, "Busy, busy." Yet, Brown also realized that Reinaldo's ingratiating personal charm and his plentiful social contacts could be invaluable to her magazine—even if he didn't write. "Reinaldo is one of the most useful people," said one writer in 1992, explaining how Herrera served as a sort of a dressed-up assignment editor for him. "My God, you'd kill this man on the street for his Rolodex. . . . For instance in this piece I'm doing now—it's an immensely consequential series of people and Reinaldo knows them all. It's just as simple as that."

In Tina Brown's emerging menagerie of talent, another prized cockatoo was Bob Colacello, who joined *Vanity Fair* only a few weeks after he'd quit working for Andy Warhol in early 1984. A moonfaced thirty-five-year-old with thick black horn-rimmed glasses and charming personal style, Colacello grew up in suburban Long Island and, after college, introduced himself into Andy Warhol's world, becoming one of Warhol's most trusted insiders. Hired as a freelance film reviewer, Colacello eventually wound up running *Interview* magazine as its editor. While working with Warhol, Colacello adopted an accommodating editorial approach that greatly resembled Condé Nast's 'shut up and sell the merchandise' style. He once hired the same market research company used by Newhouse, Mark Clements Research, Inc., to survey *Interview*'s artsy downtown readers—the same kind of market research Si himself once mentioned to Warhol. But the mumbo jumbo of demographic statistics bored Warhol terribly, despite Colacello's hopes of enticing potential advertisers with it.

As a student of the Andy Warhol school of journalism ethics, Colacello learned to expand his role as a promoter and a marketer, hoping to convince a celebrity designer who appeared in the magazine to buy a few ads inside, as well. Colacello was clearly selling his own concept rather than someone else's brand of journalism. "Selling advertising helped me become a better editor," Colacello later wrote about his time at Warhol's magazine. "It forced me to focus on what kind of readers we wanted and how to get them, to see the magazine as a complete process, with editorial feeding circulation, circulation feeding advertising, advertising feeding editorial, rather than separate parts working against each other. That didn't mean doing everything the advertisers wanted, though we did a lot, and Andy would have had me do more."

In early 1984, Colacello quit *Interview* in a huff. Before Warhol could make amends, Colacello signed a contract with *Vanity Fair*, writing celebrity profiles and features and serving as a social tour guide for its new editor, Tina Brown. Once again, he was helping to sell a magazine's ambience and fashionableness. From running in the same circles with

Warhol, Colacello knew intimately most of the top names in New York's art market, fashion runways, media and society parties—an invaluable treasure trove of gossip and insider knowledge.

"What a party!" Tina Brown exclaimed, sitting at a table as a guest at Colacello's birthday bash shortly after his arrival at *Vanity Fair*. "This is what I want the magazine to be like—Bill Buckley on my right and Steve Rubell on my left."

Brown's class-conscious theories about why journalists had to be all dressed up were couched in the most precocious terms. "I think parties are absolutely riveting," she said. "Jane Austen said that everything happens at parties and she was right." She quickly became a budding social butterfly, throwing elaborate dinner parties for forty people and cultivating favor with well-connected New York women, like Brooke Astor, Nan Kempner, and Pat Buckley, who could help turn around the bad word on her magazine. "I realized one day that New York is a matriarchial society and the way to crack it is to win over a crucial circle of power women," she later said. She was given a salary that by the early 1990s would be estimated at $300,000, along with a $25,000 clothing allowance, car and driver, and several other perks. "To edit the magazine, you must be part of its world," she explained. "I have to be out and see the people I'm writing about to get stories. It's much fresher if you can see that world and partake of it than looking at it from outside with your nose pressed up against the window."

Despite her hype, *Vanity Fair*'s numbers didn't budge at first. Nor was her word-of-mouth very good. Brown found herself explaining things to both skeptical advertisers and celebrities who were angered by Leo Lerman's ouster. Liberman's stepdaughter, Francine du Plessix Gray, was among the set of intellectuals still upset from Richard Locke's dismissal. For a time, Brown seemed a social leper, the editor of a failing magazine in a town that does not suffer losers very well. *Vanity Fair* was doomed, it was determined, an overhyped failure of zeppelin proportions, just waiting to crash and burn—and for some, deservedly so. As with Broadway shows considered flops, New York's media had rendered a clear-cut verdict with no hope of rehabilitation. "The perceived wisdom was that a great intellectual endeavor had failed and that Condé Nast, in a Philistine spirit, had brought in Little Miss Celebrity, the wonder girl from London, to trash it up," Brown later recounted. When she attended parties soon after her arrival, she was met with disapproving stares and some who were brazen enough to tell her to her face, "I hear you're *right* down the toilet."

Working intensely to turn the magazine around and often apart from her husband, Brown sometimes regretted leaving England, where she was celebrated and well known. New York City could be a lonely and cruel place. "I dreaded going out and I dreaded going home to the tacky apartment I had rented, with disgusting leopard-skin sofas," she later recalled. "I developed some strange fantasy virus like an emotional collapse."

But Si Newhouse's opinion, as she knew, was the only one that counted. "I have no problems sticking with the magazine," Newhouse told one interviewer in mid-1985. "I'm interested in momentum." Si was hesitant to pull the plug prematurely. He had invested much money and personal capital into the revival of *Vanity Fair*. "Si's not an easy quitter, which is the great thing about him," Brown recalled years later. "He felt his instinct was correct that there was a magazine out there he wanted to do called *Vanity Fair* that would be commercially successful and capture a lost glory of the past in magazine terms that would be exciting to work on. And he was right. He's got extraordinary instincts."

Behind the scenes, however, Si's purchase of *The New Yorker* had a deeply unsettling effect upon Tina Brown—a secret she kept largely from her staff and public view until years later. She worried that she was losing favor with her patron. After all, *Vanity Fair* had been revived on the premise that it would appeal to readers who were demographically similar to those picking up *The New Yorker,* a magazine believed to be out of Newhouse's grasp. The comparisons between the two magazines could rile Brown into uncontrollable bouts of hyperbole. "My whole gimmick for this magazine is to find a *New Yorker* kind of market but update it," Brown claimed. "Much of the material that appears in *Vanity Fair* could easily appear in *The New Yorker,* and if it did, with tiny print and a little signoff, it would be hailed as first-class intellectual material."

But the bottom line was abundantly clear: If Si now owned the world-famous magazine his father and family had sought for years, why would he continue to bear *Vanity Fair*'s mounting losses? Why would he need any gimmicks when he had the sureness of a proven winner with *The New Yorker*? Although circulation improved, the losses for *Vanity Fair* by early 1985 were about $30 million and counting.

Tina Brown was almost obsessed with the fear that Newhouse's commitment wouldn't last. Repeatedly, she inquired about the fate of the magazine and about the rumors that she might be fired if the magazine didn't rebound fast enough. Newhouse was so badgered by Brown's anxiety, he eventually learned to answer her doubts in his own shorthand reply. "No, I'm not, and no, you're not," Newhouse declared after Brown once followed her boss to his gym.

Tina Brown's fears were well grounded, however. In fact, the termination of *Vanity Fair* nearly came true in May 1985, only two months after Si Newhouse had bought *The New Yorker*. For the press, of course, there were the firm denials about *Vanity Fair*'s possible demise. To *Newsweek*'s media critic Jonathan Alter, for instance, Brown repeated assurances from Newhouse that the sale of *The New Yorker* was "an entirely separate matter" from *Vanity Fair*'s fate. But, of course, the matters were intertwined.

"*The New Yorker* was the model, absolutely," Brown recalled about Newhouse's original concept for *Vanity Fair*. "People forget it now, but for many years, *The New Yorker* was a hugely commercial successful thing. Everybody wanted that cash cow. Si always loved *The New Yorker* and he saw it as a huge commercial success. So *Vanity Fair* was expected to jump into that niche and take *The New Yorker*'s advertising."

The Newhouse family's history was full of examples of the family buying out the competition and then killing the weaker of the two. In this case, Newhouse's instincts told him that he couldn't carry two magazines appealing to essentially the same demographically similar readers. It was nothing personal, just a matter of marketing and simple dollar and cents.

"It was losing too much money that Si felt it was never going to turn around," Brown recalled. "And I understand his feelings. I felt that he had been with me for only nine months. But the fact is that he had also long innings with Richard Locke and with Leo Lerman. So he was at the end of his tether and he began to think that he was throwing good money after bad. I began to get the sense that he was losing faith."

Tina Brown's dramatic plea for a few more issues would allow only a little more breathing room. She had to turn things around quickly or she would be forced to return to London as a failure.

For the Reagans dancing on *Vanity Fair*'s cover in June 1985, Brown drew upon her own social contacts with William F. Buckley, Jr., who had coedited part of Henry Kissinger's memoirs with Harry Evans. "She probably called me because she knew I was personally very close—and had been for a long time—with the Reagans," recalled Buckley, who first had dinner with Brown and Evans in the 1970s on a trip to London. "I knew her socially and I've known Harry for a long time."

Another highly publicized story, which Tina Brown extended into a two-part series starting with a lavish presentation in the August 1985 issue, profiled socialite Claus von Bülow, who had been accused of attempting to kill his wife, Sunny, with a lethal injection that left her in a coma. The story had money, sex, murder—a real-life whodunit. Dominick Dunne, the stylish former Holywood scriptwriter and novelist, turned in a chilling dissection of von Bülow's character in a way that would become a signature style for *Vanity Fair* itself. Written by Dunne in a chatty first-person manner, von Bülow's life was traced in scenes from his daughter's eighteenth birthday party at Mortimer's (with *VF*'s special projects editor, Reinaldo Herrera, among the invitees) to recollections of his father's trial as a Nazi collaborator ("He gave a good name to a bad cause . . . he dined with the wrong people") to an examination of his marriage with Sunny and why his stepchildren call him a murderer without remorse. Dunne's approach was to visit with, rather than judge, von Bülow and observe him in his natural habitat. After quizzing him Dunne observed, "Whatever one felt personally about the guilt or innocence of the man, one could not deny his charm, which was enormous, in a European, upper-class, courtly sort of way."

The photographs by Helmut Newton were, in a sense, even more provocative. Garbed in glistening black leather, von Bülow, fit and tan, stood smiling next to his new rich girlfriend, Andrea Reynolds, while Sunny von Bülow, the wife he had been convicted of attempting to kill (a verdict to be thrown out later on appeal) lay somewhere in a hospital bed, deep in deathlike sleep. The most extraordinary shot of all was the portrait of Claus, that old Teutonic cutup, demonstrating his Queen Victoria imitation, with his cheeks blown out and a white handkerchief adorning his head. It was a bizarre and compelling set of photographs and, with Dunne's novellike prose, made the entire package sensationally readable. Dunne was so excited by his encounter with von Bülow, he called Tina Brown at her summer place on Long Island's East End.

"My God!" Dunne exclaimed. "You won't believe what happened! Claus had on his black leather jacket—and then *she* had one."

Brown squeezed every bit of shock value out of the von Bülow piece, adding to the magazine's growing awareness among upscale readers and Madison Avenue types. Her unconventional formula for the magazine, and its overall voice, slowly emerged. For all of the slick and slightly overripe photos and profiles of celebrities, there remained a certain freshness and unpredictability, the expectation of finding something new and raw in every issue. It adopted the pose of a winner. "People have come to expect that they're going to find in *Vanity Fair* something to make them annoyed," she explained. "In a way, they look for it. It's important for a magazine to have lapses in taste. If you don't, you're going to be completely bland."

In her lobbying with Si Newhouse, the von Bülow profile was immensely important. As soon as she received Helmut Newton's photographs of Claus von Bülow in black leather, Tina Brown realized their value in keeping her magazine alive. She ordered her assistant to make copies late that afternoon and to send them up to Newhouse's office, "sticking it underneath his door, so at five o'clock in the morning, he'd see it and be irresistibly persuaded that we were going to make it," Brown recalled. "And much to his credit, he decided to give us another chance."

In an interview, Brown recalled that attached to the von Bülow photos, she had written a personal note: "Dear Si, are we hot or are we hot?"

Shortly after the von Bülow portfolio, Brown underlined this maxim once again in a profile of Princess Diana. In this issue, Brown devoted much of the contents to an old Condé Nast favorite—Anglomania. After returning from a trip to London, she wrote the cover story, entitled "The Mouse That Roared" and in her text repeated a rather tasteless, if prescient, observation about Diana's eclipsed husband. "The debonair Prince of Wales, His Royal Highness, Duke of Cornwall, heir to the throne, is, it seems, pussywhipped from here to eternity," she wrote. That issue, with Diana wearing a diamond tiara on the cover, sold an extra 100,000 copies on the newsstands and prompted the royal couple to respond in a television interview. The American fascination with British royalty, along with the TV-script dimensions of Charles and Diana's life together, was never lost on *Vanity Fair*'s editor and became an important part of the magazine's mix of stories. "We will do a Royals story once a year for ten years," Brown quipped. "They are a valid soap opera for readers."

Si's lingering doubts about *Vanity Fair*'s future were not put to rest until September 1985, when the second installment of the von Bülow profile appeared. Only a few months earlier, Brown had orchestrated a desperate attempt to stop Newhouse from closing the magazine. Alerted by Brown, *Vanity Fair*'s then ad director, G. Douglas Johnston, convinced Newhouse that more advertising was in the pipeline, escorting him through the advertising layout room to show him the proofs. "Doug Johnston knew it was the most important sales call of his life," Brown recalled. "He had just gotten the job and he had to sell Si on the notion that we were going to make it."

Brown also beseeched Dick Shortway to intervene. More than a year earlier, Newhouse had asked his trusted friend and *Vogue*'s publisher to act as a "rabbi" and oversee *Vanity Fair*'s business operations and offer advice. Shortway was listed as a vice president on *Vanity Fair*'s masthead. "Dick Shortway was very much an influence in those days at Condé Nast," Brown said years later. "He was very close to Si. And he was appointed very much as the unofficial uncle of *Vanity Fair*." When Tina Brown called him at home with her news, though, Shortway was surprised.

"I'm very sensitive to this magazine, and I think Si may be thinking about closing it," Brown said.

"Oh, Tina, I wouldn't believe that," Shortway assured her.

"Well, he's sending people like Doug Johnston to be interviewed over at *The New Yorker*—what does that tell you?" Brown retorted, citing names of a few others who were being interviewed for new jobs. She also mentioned her conversation with Pamela van Zandt, a Condé Nast corporate vice president. "She told me I'm frozen, that I can't hire anybody," Brown said.

"Okay, Tina," Shortway finally said, convinced that she was right. "I'll be in Si's office at seven in the morning."

The next morning, Shortway was never so blunt with his friend. "If you're going to close, just do it," Shortway told Newhouse. "Don't hang everybody by their thumbs." Shortway told him that Tina Brown was the right choice as *Vanity Fair*'s editor but that the magazine needed a better publisher.

Newhouse was genuinely disconsolate. He had gone through as many publishers as editors and was convinced the current one, David O'Brasky, who had replaced Joseph Corr, was not working out.

"Okay, what would you do?" Newhouse demanded.

Shortway said he'd get rid of O'Brasky and give the job of publisher to Johnston. And, he added, "Give Tina a vote of confidence. Tell her she's got the magazine."

Newhouse nodded and Shortway returned to his office, where he tipped off Johnston about the possible changes. An hour later, Newhouse called Shortway's office, sounding considerably chipper.

"Okay, it's done," Si announced.

"What's done?" Shortway replied.

"I fired O'Brasky and gave the job to Doug," Newhouse told him. "And I called Tina and said, 'Okay, go.'"

Tina Brown's own nervous appeal in Newhouse's office resulted in Si's agreement to extend his deadline on the magazine's fate. "I remember sitting there telling him all the things I had, the Dominick Dunne pieces, a piece by Gail Sheehy, that I had a piece I was working on myself about the Princess of Wales that I thought would make news, and it did," she said, recalling her pitch to the owner. "And I bought what he said—two years, which I knew was six months, because I'm always realistic. I believe in being realistic. I don't always believe what I'm told. He said we had two years, but I thought, six months. Realistically, we did have six months, because the losses were enormous and if we were going to continue, we had to show an upswing. And, of course, what happened was after the Reagan issue, we had Claus von Bülow in August and in October we had the Princess of Wales. Those three things—the Reagans, Claus von Bülow, and the Princess of Wales—that triple whammy of very big newsbreaks."

But what mostly impressed Brown was Newhouse's editorial instincts, his response to her list of upcoming stories and what it would mean for the magazine's fortunes. In a world of corporate media types looking anxiously at quarterly reports, Si Newhouse's personal involvement was unique in publishing and proved to be a crucial factor in *Vanity Fair*'s survival. "Where Si is remarkable is that he does understand that editorial ideas, in the end, can turn a product around," said Brown. "If the ideas are good enough, and hot enough, and interesting enough, and news-worthy enough, they can indeed make that difference. And they did indeed turn around the fortunes of *Vanity Fair*. They made us go right up there, and put us up there as something to look at. And from that moment, people took us seriously as a magazine that they couldn't afford not to look at every month."

Vanity Fair's future seemed secure enough for Tina Brown to write her first editor's letter in the front section of the magazine—a year and a half after she had assumed its editorship. "In view of this magazine's stormy launch, it seemed a good idea to wait to see if I was still around," Brown admitted in print, although not revealing how close Si Newhouse had come to killing *Vanity Fair*. "I didn't particularly want to appear in front of the curtain until we'd successfully drowned the bump and crash of noises off."

Much to the amazement of skeptics inside Condé Nast and the legion of critics outside its door, Tina Brown had pulled off a coup of remarkable proportions. She had managed to elude Alex Liberman's efforts at control and had convinced Si Newhouse to keep the cash flow coming, even when he thought he was tossing away good money after bad. *Vanity Fair* not only looked as though it would live but that it would actually thrive. The magazine's history was now delineated in terms of her arrival: before Tina and after Tina. "Before, editors here were being held captive by the marketing department, by people trying to fit the magazine into a marketing niche," Pamela Maffei McCarthy, the magazine's managing editor, later said. "Then all of a sudden comes a person with a nose for a great story and a strong visual sense."

As *Vanity Fair*'s success became more apparent in the ensuing months, Si Newhouse's comments were less tentative and somewhat revisionist. In one interview, Newhouse contended that Tina Brown's approach "is much closer to what I had in mind" from the start, even though the magazine seemed clueless for many months after its relaunch. In his own way, though, Si felt remarkably indebted to Brown for her successful rescue attempt. No longer was he facing the imminent collapse of his most ambitious project—the renaissance of a once-great magazine that he and Alex Liberman dreamed might someday rival that elusive treasure, *The New Yorker*. Now that he had both magazines, Si seemed content to keep them separate and distinct. With her unique talents and flair for publicity, Tina Brown brought an unprecedented sense of panache to an organization already known for its style and glamour, helping Si to redefine publicly the family business. No one would ever again call Newhouse's enterprise ragtag or dull.

Most importantly, Brown's ability to breathe new life into a dying publication was reminiscent of Liberman's powers, making her ever more valuable for the future. "As soon as Tina took hold, we were on the right track," Newhouse later said. "We were baffled, struggling to get the right combination of people. . . . *Vanity Fair* was waiting for the right editor, and from the time she came in, it was clear she was capable of taking the *Vanity Fair* idea and updating and restating it."

Tina Brown could see the difference in the way she was treated. Rather than sabotage or countermand her efforts, Alex Liberman praised her triumph. She responded with occasional homage in print to Liberman's artistic success or his love for Tatiana. "She's a superb co-ordinator with an extraordinary instinct for news and telling it with the vital charge a magazine should communicate," the grand master said of Brown, making sure to add that "she's growing and learning all the time." By the late summer of 1985, *The New York Times* declared Brown a success in turning around the magazine, and advertisers and the rest of the media followed its lead. Rather than being treated as an outcast, Tina Brown was now the toast of the town, one of the brightest literary stars along the Great White Way. There was more than a little irony in all this. "I think if you can survive that first year in New York, then everything can turn around," she later said. "The very same people who drummed you and gave you hell can be very nice. Nothing is sweeter than being in that second phase in New York where you have shown you can stand it."

Millions of television viewers were watching as Jodie Foster's name was called out and she glided to the podium to accept her Oscar, the very picture of a triumphant Best Actress in her moment of glory.

At home in Manhattan, Jesse Kornbluth had nodded off as the Academy Awards telecast dragged on, and he was closer to slumber than reality when he thought he heard his name being mentioned. "We fell asleep with the TV on and I came awake thinking someone was calling me," he remembered. "Then the phone started to ring."

He awoke to discover that Jodie Foster had thanked him specifically during her acceptance speech for urging her to pursue the part of the female FBI agent, Clarice Starling, in *The Silence of the Lambs*—the film that swept many of the top Oscars in 1992. The Academy Award–winning actress's decision to mention Kornbluth's name was, in a sense, one high-profile favor for another.

Back in 1988, soon after he joined *Vanity Fair*, Kornbluth wrote a cover story about Foster and her return to the limelight. Once a child star, Foster, as a young woman, suffered the worldwide ignominy of being identified as John Hinckley's fantasy girlfriend when the sordid obsessions of President Reagan's would-be assassin were made known. Foster had reentered the film industry after a hiatus of several years to attend Yale University and was now promoting a new movie. During the interview, Foster hit it off with Kornbluth, an engaging, erudite man with a quick sense of humor, and they remained friendly even after the cover story appeared.

Shortly afterward, Kornbluth, who writes screenplays in addition to his role as a journalist, received an advance copy of Thomas Harris's novel, *The Silence of the Lambs,* and he dropped Foster a note urging that she consider it. "This part is yours, and yours only," he wrote the actress. At the same time, Kornbluth also contacted the director Jonathan Demme and the producer who held the movie rights and offered to write the screenplay. The director and producer declined Kornbuth's offer. But they apparently listened to the writer's advice that they pick Jodie Foster over their favored actress at that time, Michelle Pfeiffer. The *Vanity Fair* writer fell out of touch with Foster for a couple of years afterward, until the day of the 1992 Oscars, when Kornbluth's name was mentioned prominently coast to coast.

At the elegant party for *Vogue*'s hundredth anniversary, a few nights after the Academy Awards telecast, Tina Brown was curious.

"What did you do for Jodie Foster?" she asked.

"Tina, it was weird," Kornbluth began, grinning broadly. "I did for Jodie Foster what you do for people a hundred times a day."

Kornbluth was only slightly exaggerating his admiration for Tina Brown. By the early 1990s, Brown had become the most celebrated editor in America, the talented energy behind *Vanity Fair*'s remarkable success. No longer the young upstart who struggled for attention, Brown was now a honored member of the media Establishment, capable of casting as cool and clinical an eye as any social arbiter. For writers like Kornbluth, however, Tina Brown was a generous guiding hand who seemed that rarest of treasures: an editor who values writers, or at least her star writers.

For years, Kornbluth was a staff writer at *New York* magazine, where he wrote features and became well known in social circles. After he wrote a highly detailed cover story on deadline about the death of Andy Warhol in 1987, Tina Brown's mind was made up. She gave him a contract, offering him more than double what he was making at *New York*—one of several irresistible lures she used in gathering the best pool of talent for her magazine. Once he was hired, Tina Brown asked him to lunch to discuss his first assignment. Kornbluth suggested an East Side restaurant where he seemed to know everyone.

When they sat down at a table, Tina Brown took out a large envelope, from which she pulled an eight-by-ten glossy. Unmistakably, it was a shot of Faye Dunaway in sunglasses.

"This is the cover picture that Helmut Newton took," said Brown. "How would you like to write the piece?"

"You know, Tina, I want to work for you, anyway," Kornbluth replied. "You don't have to sell me."

Her dramatic presentation was one of those endearing gestures that writers, so dependent on the kindness of strangers and deep-pocketed publishers, learned to love about Tina Brown. Along with big salaries and plush assignments, she would invite her star writers to her house for dinner parties or send them gift baskets when they were hired with cards that read, "Welcome, we're glad you're here." "Tina was the first and only editor who had paid writers, not perhaps what they're worth, but what they have to earn in order to have the life, in order to do the pieces she wants," Kornbluth said later. "I've worked for other editors who, when they see me at social events, have felt their invitations had been devalued. Tina's view is, Go out and bring something back, even if it's only a cold. Tina believes, correctly, that a lot of important activity occurs in settings that appear social."

Part of Kornbluth's appeal—like that of Reinaldo Herrera or Bob Colacello—was his intimate knowledge of New York's social scene. He was someone whom you could send to an affair all dressed up, who would never make a fool of himself and who seemed to become best friends with all the right people in attendance. He was also someone, as Brown discovered, whom you could trust to go speak with Si Newhouse and help the hapless billionaire when he faced the onerous task of public speaking.

One such event involved a Fashion Institute tribute to Condé Nast magazines. As Kornbluth remembered, "Si called Tina and said, 'I need some help doing the speech.' So she said, 'Jesse, will you go up and meet with Si?' " Kornbluth, a jack-of-all-trades, quickly agreed. As he explained, "I write speeches for people and I'm presentable, and besides, I like the corporate side of Condé Nast. It's kind of goofy and fun for me. And I don't take it seriously. So Si and I met and did some drafts." In his talk, Newhouse wanted to describe himself as a "custodian" of a great tradition, taking the focus off himself and crediting others. After several tries, Newhouse decided to write the speech himself.

"He's a shy guy who loves his work and everything about it," said Kornbluth. "And the only downside for him is having to go outside in public and represent the damn thing—it's the price he pays for owning it."

At *Vanity Fair,* cover stories on celebrities were the price of admission under Tina Brown. Punchy photos with pithy headlines and familiar faces were needed to convince impulse buyers in the supermarkets to grab the latest issue. Although the image she and others liked to promote was of a chic publication kept on chintz lounge chairs in the Hamptons, next to *Architectural Digest* and *Town & Country,* the demographics were decidedly more downscale. Once a prestigious watch manufacturer quizzed Brown about her numbers. "Tell me, what's the difference between *Vanity Fair* and *Town & Country*?" he asked. Brown's reply was fast enough to get a paper cut. "*Vanity Fair* is for the thinking rich, and *Town & Country* is for the *stinking rich,*" she said.

Inside its pages, there were no cents-off coupons, no helpful hints to buy, sell, or do. The success of each month's issue rose or fell on the heat of the cover story and its inside features. As a result, *Vanity Fair* became the most stylish practitioner of the celebrity interview, underlying the American media's increasing reliance on Hollywood for news, with the intrepid reporter usually having lunch with a star or following one around the back lot. To attract a crowd into the show tent, to gain the needed circulation to justify the maximum possible advertising rates, celebrities on the cover became necessary, preferably blonde, beautiful, and with a big new blockbuster movie. Selling celebrities, as Tina Brown seemed to envision, was just an updated sequel to the Newhouse concept at *Vogue,* where the editorial pages were often compromised by marketing needs. "We are dealing with a certain element of gossip raised to a high level," Liberman said, describing the new *Vanity Fair* in his inimitable brand of hyperbole. "Presenting personalities is the obsession of our time."

Indisputably, the cover shots of seminude sexually longing starlets were an essential component of Tina Brown's commercial success. "They are there for one reason only: they look wonderful—and they sell," she explained. In private meetings, they were the source of ridicule and delight among Brown and her laughing staff. "She is the magic bimbo who has to appear in every issue," Brown once told an interviewer as she held up the latest erotic pictures from Helmut Newton. Just another naked female body to help sell what's inside. Had any male editor in New York boasted of such an approach, he would have been sent out of town on a rail, condemned as an unreconstructed sexist. But Brown's witty sense of humor and her admitted incongruity in putting together *Vanity Fair*'s mix of stories allowed her to gloss over such things. It was certainly better than being dull. As she put it, "A sexy cover is bound to help you more than a cover of Philip Roth with his finger up his nose." This was a none-too-oblique reference to a cover photo of the novelist that had appeared during the tepid reign of Richard Locke, the magazine's first and less than lionhearted editor.

Equally unappealing, though, were some of the methods used by Tina Brown's minions to obtain cover stories. If the celebrity was important enough, it was not uncommon for *Vanity Fair* to give photo approval, quote approval, writer approval, or even ironclad assurances that certain basic questions would not be asked. Dominick Dunne, for instance, managed to tell readers in 1989 about his lunch with actress Jane Wyman but never bothered—on the instruction of Wyman's flak—to ask her about her eight-year marriage to Ronald Reagan, ostensibly the only reason for the story. (The biggest scoop for Dunne was finding out that Wyman's character was going to fall into a coma in the next season's "Falcon Crest.") Wyman even picked up the lunch tab. By the late 1980s, such deference to Hollywood celebrities and their publicity agents created a monster that even Brown complained about, though she barely acknowledged her prominent role in the media's feeding frenzy for celebrities. "We're always being beaten up in the press for doing puff pieces, yet the stars and the press agents regard us as being very tough," Brown complained. "I don't get it."

Among the *Vanity Fair* staff, there were some writers who did only celebrity profiles, others who never did celebrity profiles, and a third group who were sent on assignment if the star was big enough or if the subject matter was very sensitive. Jesse Kornbluth, like Dunne or Marie Brenner, fell into this third category, and he was suggested by Brown as the reporter for a profile on Michael Ovitz, president of the Creative Artists Agency and often described as one of Hollywood's most powerful figures. Ovitz represented many top actors and actresses—the necessary fodder for *Vanity Fair* cover stories—and was someone to be treated ever so gently. In one of the most embarrassing moments of Brown's tenure, a letter she once wrote to Ovitz somehow fell into the hands of *Spy*, the satirical magazine then edited by Graydon Carter. Her letter was remarkably fawning in tone and virtually promised Ovitz most-favored-treatment status if he cooperated. *Spy* printed the entire letter and deconstructed it with amusing asides. "While Brown doesn't entirely give away her franchise here, she does demonstrate some of the lengths to which even a powerful and relatively serious journalist will go to get a story," *Spy* said in introducing the document to its readers.

Like some journalistic Earl Scheib, Brown offered in her Ovitz letter to overhaul his old battered image and remake it with a shiny new coating. Ovitz was no mere "packager" of stars and film properties, certainly not in Brown's eyes. Instead, she wrote, "a better term for your role in the life of Hollywood would be a *catalyst:* activating creativity by a gifted sense of talent, material, timing and taste, plus, of course, extraordinary business acumen in putting it all together." The outline for a favorable article was detailed in her letter like some schematic diagram. Brown offered to fly Kornbluth to Los Angeles, if Ovitz agreed, not only because of his sophistication and writing style but because he is "knowledgeably well disposed toward CAA." In an aside, *Spy* noted that Kornbluth may be "knowledgeably well disposed" because he is also a screenwriter and "with the obvious exception of Bob Colacello, Jesse Kornbluth is perhaps the . . . *most agreeable* of all *Vanity Fair* regulars." Ovitz wound up declining Brown's offer, but *Spy* underlined how seven CAA clients appeared in *Vanity Fair* in the year after her December 1988 letter. When the letter was printed by *Spy* in August 1990, Brown was incensed.

At *Vanity Fair,* there were plenty of sacred cows besides Michael Ovitz. While the magazine took free-swinging potshots at foreign dictators, drug smugglers, or even American candidates for President, those who were truly powerful in its world were granted immunity from any real journalistic scrutiny. When Donald Trump was a high-flying entrepreneur, he learned that *Vanity Fair* was preparing a short item about how the doorknobs were falling off in Trump Tower. Shortly after this journalistic enterprise was launched, however, Brown received a call from Si Newhouse, who had gotten a call from Trump himself. Whether the offending writer knew it or not, Si had personally solicited Trump for his best-selling autobiography and Newhouse was not going to let Trump's advertising cease because of some silly little item. As a result, the story was killed. (Only after he suffered a huge financial loss in the 1990s did the magazine dare to examine Trump in any critical way.)

Top advertisers at *Vanity Fair,* in the oldest tradition of Condé Nast, were treated with kid gloves. Tina Brown made it clear that she was not encumbered by the same ethical restraints adopted by other mostly American journalists. "I don't treat advertisers as second-class citizens," Brown proclaimed, arguing that high-minded restrictions by other editors in refusing to mix with advertisers was "incredible editorial arrogance." In fact, Tina Brown's attitude helped sell ads for the magazine. As *Vanity Fair*'s then publisher, G. Douglas Johnston, boasted to *Advertising Age* in January 1988, "She works more closely with our business side than any editor at Condé Nast."

Brown's willingness to kowtow to advertisers became all too apparent in the pages of *Vanity Fair*. Within a very short period, the magazine published almost identical front covers on designer Calvin Klein and his wife in 1987 (PARTNERS IN STYLE read the headline) and an outdoors version featuring designer Ralph Lauren and his loved one in 1988 (this time with the title PARDNERS IN STYLE). Both cover pictures bore an uncanny resemblance to the look of these designers' advertising campaigns: Calvin Klein's was cool, clean, and urban; Lauren's had a rugged western style. Indeed, the cover shot of Lauren was taken by Bruce Weber, the same photographer Lauren employed for his own ads. In many journalistic quarters, this arrangement would seem too cozy. Later asked about a potential conflict in doing both sets of Lauren pictures for *Vanity Fair,* Weber replied, "You hope that magazines are going to run them the right way, but sometimes they don't. [Also], advertisers have more freedom than the magazines because the magazines are so pressured [not to offend advertisers]. That's why it's hard for the editorial pages to look as good as the ads."

These obvious valentines to *Vanity Fair* advertisers were privately ridiculed among some of its staff or rationalized as a necessary evil. Occasionally, Brown would publicly acknowledge her restrictions. "If you were producing a funny magazine, you'd have to go for people like Trump. He's up there, and you have to make fun of the gods," she said in 1986. "And then, there is also that awful commercial fact that you can't make fun of Calvin Klein, Donald Trump and Tiffany." The *Columbia Journalism Review* called attention to Brown's cozy editorial trade-offs with her advertisers, noting that gushing features in *Vanity Fair* had also been offered on other major advertisers like Gianni Versace, Bill Blass, Giorgio Armani, Karl Lagerfeld, and even Donna Karan's stepgranddaughter. Certainly, the social significance of cosmetics queen Estée Lauder's son, Ronald Lauder, then U.S. ambassador to Austria and later the erstwhile Republican candidate for New York City mayor, was hyped all out of proportion in an adoring story entitled "Our (Fabulous) Man in Vienna: Ambassador Ronald Lauder." No matter how ethically impure it might seem to outsiders, the business of trading on its front covers or feature stories to obtain lucrative advertising was an important component in Tina Brown's revival of *Vanity Fair*. As the *Columbia Journalism Review* concluded, "Tina Brown has carried this strategy to an extreme, going after some public figures like gangbusters but treating people who can bring in the ads like royalty."

The message trickled down to the troops. In talking to the *Review*, Brown's writers underlined how unimportant independent journalism was to the process of putting together a *Vanity Fair* cover story. Brooke Hayward, who wrote the Lauren feature, admitted her piece "was intended to be a rather superficial view" of the designer at his Colorado ranch. "I was not asked to do an investigative piece," said Hayward. "If Tina Brown had wanted some other kind of piece, she would have hired someone else." The author of the Calvin Klein piece was André Leon Talley, who was once part of Andy Warhol's entourage. Talley perfectly understood the intent of his story, his mission in imparting information to readers. For him, a fashion writer does not report or challenge but, rather, creates a mood to "seduce a consumer into a store." The resulting message was that some editorial pages were more serious and honest than others, a complex minefield of favors and puffery that any real journalist would tread at their own peril. "Brown sells the editorial pages of her magazine because she believes them—some of them, anyway—to be worthless," media critic Geoffrey Stokes observed. "This kind of choice is emblematic of the contempt in which Brown holds the subjects who actually sell her magazine—and, in some cases, the writers who write about them."

In all its excessive transgressions and obsessions, however, *Vanity Fair* came to reflect accurately the ethos of the 1980s, when a fascination with wealth, power, and manipulative people captured the imagination of much of the nation's big media. During the mid-eighties, the top media companies were reaping the benefits of unprecedented profit margins, buyouts, and mergers—with little thought about the excesses of corporate greed or of the widening gap between the nation's rich and poor. *Vanity Fair* celebrated the self-absorbed nouveaux riches and lionized as heroes those sultans of Wall Street junk bonds and LBO kings who leveraged the nation's future. Throughout her pages, Brown embraced and often romanticized the underlying tenets of Reaganism, despite her fashionably liberal asides in interviews. To readers of *Vanity Fair*, even those who tossed it into their grocery-store shopping carts, America was a land of people consumed with the *idea* of consuming. Its styles and social values were determined by a small, select handful—many of whom were among Tina Brown's acquaintances—and then spoon-fed and displayed to the hungry masses. "Only ordinary schleps will be famous for fifteen minutes," theorized *The Nation* about its own pages. "In *Vanity Fair*, the same people can be famous month after month." Whole sections of the magazine, like *VF*'s pictorial tributes to posh Manhattan parties and benefits, seemed calculatingly aimed at class envy, perhaps the only reason for watching frolicking millionaires at play. It was a format conducive to parody. "I'm Scared of How Desirable I Am Sometimes," was the title of one takeoff by *The New Republic,* which aped the self-absorbed celebrity interviews found in Brown's features. Nevertheless, *Vanity Fair* was also widely copied by other magazines and top newspapers. It became one of the most influential publications of its era, covering it all with a high-gloss eroticism and slightly decadent insiderish voice, like some giant traveling circus from prewar Berlin. "A hot magazine rides the Zeitgeist, defining the culture and ethos of its time," observed *Newsweek* in 1989. "Brown tapped into the preoccupations of the '80s, running with them even as she reported them. As things stand, having so exuberantly glossed the '80s, Brown now has the chance to define *fin de siècle* America the way Frank Crowninshield's *Vanity Fair* captured the '20s."

By the late 1980s, Si Newhouse was convinced that *Vanity Fair* had a great future under Brown and, after much initial consternation, the magazine might soon repay his investment. "The only thing *Vanity Fair* gave me more confidence in was Tina Brown," Newhouse admitted. At Brown's suggestion, Newhouse agreed to an expensive investment in a satellite transmission so that last-minute stories could be filed on deadline, giving *Vanity Fair* a more current, off-the-news approach than ever before. *Vanity Fair's* circulation continued to soar, from a low of 220,000 to nearly 1 million readers by the early 1990s, with each issue usually containing much more than a hundred pages of advertising. As the press became less critical and public plaudits came Brown's way, she slowly began to widen the appeal, including more serious pieces of journalism among the mix of stories. There was still the formula of Hollywood covers and stories about macabre murders and foreign despots, although now joined by more insightful, enterprising pieces on politics, business, and such social issues as famine in Africa or the spread of AIDS. One of the most notable forays into seriousness was the series of presidential candidate profiles by Gail Sheehy in 1988, which often adopted her analytic psychological approach. It paid off handsomely when the sexual adventures of the Democratic frontrunner at the time, Gary Hart, were explored in Sheehy's profile, helping to make the issue of character a key criteria among the mainstream press in examining potential Presidents.

Brown seemed to sense a change in the public's attitudes, away from the excess of the Yuppie-filled 1980s and toward an indebted nation chastened and somewhat penitent. "I am fed up with the money culture of the Reagan years, and I think the magazine reflects that," she said when named Magazine Editor of the Year in 1988 by *Advertising Age*. "We have a story on the homeless coming. We can do serious stuff. The serious stuff has had greater impact next to the fun pieces." Suddenly interrupting the cavalcade of celebrity portraits were covers featuring Jesse Jackson (one of the few African-Americans not in show business or sports to appear in *Vanity Fair* during Brown's tenure) and Soviet leader Mikhail Gorbachev. "Even if the sales of the Jesse Jackson cover are not good, it is a cover we needed to do," Brown said. Gorbachev's selection for the cover infuriated blond actress Ellen Barkin and her agent when they discovered she had been bumped inside. Barkin claimed she had been promised the cover and threatened to sue. "I felt that month Gorbachev was rather more important to world affairs than Ellen Barkin. She and I disagree on that, it seems," Brown explained later, carefully putting in the boot. "I would not have bumped Ellen Barkin off the cover in favor of Kathleen Turner. That would have been heinous, but I felt that she could live with Gorbachev or certainly be able to explain it to her friends."

By the early 1990s, Tina Brown's *Vanity Fair* still relied on her band of star writers and old friends from England, such as editors Miles Chapman and Sarah Giles, and added a few more names, like Nancy Collins and Kevin Sessums, to provide those chatty, gushing cover stories. (Sessums, the magazine's "fanfair editor," who authored some remarkably fawning portraits of such Hollywood icons as Sylvester Stallone, described Brown's idea of a good story with this simple rule: "If it makes Tina's nipples firm, then she goes with it.") Another marquee name, Norman Mailer, was added to the cast like some cameo role in the autumn of his career. Mailer made occasional appearances, with long-winded rants as the magazine's writer at large—ranting with murderous invective about Bret Easton Ellis's *American Psycho* or ranting favorably about Oliver Stone, a like-minded conspirator of the cinema. "*JFK* is bound to receive some atrocious reviews, perhaps even a preponderance of unfavorable ones, and as has been the case already, more than a small outrage is likely to be aroused in the Washington Club (that is, *The Washington Post, Newsweek, Time,* the F.B.I., the C.I.A., the Pentagon, the White House, and the TV networks on those occasions when they wish to exercise their guest privileges)," Mailer wailed in February 1992 as the new movie debuted. For faceless billionaires, part of the fun was employing Mailer to bloviate in print. "He called me and said, 'I love the magazine and I'd love to be in it,' " recalled Brown, who said *Vanity Fair*'s deal was separate from Mailer's financial arrangements with other parts of the Newhouse organization.

Despite these necessary indulgences to attract an audience, Brown launched an effort to steer the magazine slowly, like some oversized party boat, in a slightly different direction, toward a more serious tone that would reflect the times. She enlisted such fine business and cultural reporters as Peter Boyer and Leslie Bennetts, both formerly with *The New York Times*. Although Hollywood's top powers sometimes seemed to serve as an escort service for *Vanity Fair*'s front cover, inside the magazine there were now exquisitely detailed dissections by Boyer of deal making and behind-the-scenes maneuvering at such communication giants as MCA, Sony, CNN, and Walt Disney Studios. "If we said on the cover, Peter Boyer with the inside story at Sony, it wasn't some weak piece of flimflam that we put together from the clips," Brown later said. "It was a really good inside story that Hollywood would be surprised by."

Leslie Bennetts, a talented writer, would offer profiles on feminist Gloria Steinem and such entertainers as dancer Gregory Hines, but she was also a serious-enough journalist to probe into such delicate subjects as pedophilia in the Catholic Church and the failed policies of drug czar William Bennett. "I think Tina was very quick to realize that the 1980s were over—or were going to be over, before they were over—and she's been very interested in and very supportive of serious work. I don't do puff-piece movie star profiles," said Bennetts, a *Times* reporter for more than a decade. "She was very interested in going after people like me and

Peter Boyer who were very serious reporters. We don't do the glitzy stuff. I think it's a reflection of what her vision is of this era."

Both former *Times* reporters were deeply appreciative of the journalistic freedom they enjoyed under Brown. Bennetts, with young children, was allowed to work from home and kept in contact by telephone with Brown, who by then was also a working mother with two young children. "Years from now, we're going to remember this time as the best time of our lives," Boyer confided to another new staff writer, Paul Rosenfield, who was recruited from the *Los Angeles Times*. "Kind of like a dream time. And we'll know it will never happen again. We're riding a spaceship to the moon."

With her wit and style, with her producer-like flair for the dramatic, and with her family's tradition for knowing how to issue a great press release, Tina Brown turned the once bad word about *Vanity Fair* into a rave. It was the best show in town, often read cover to cover, as Brown liked to say, by the likes of Henry Kissinger as well as Warren Beatty. Si Newhouse's dream of restoring *Vanity Fair* was now complete, an unparalleled feat in publishing of transforming a dead "book" from the 1920s into the liveliest read of the 1980s. "It was a journalistic Camelot," Brown later said, recalling her era at the magazine. "We had a wonderful title. We had a proprietor who once he made his commitment backed us very vigorously and we had a wonderful staff and I was given a lot of freedom, total freedom, to do creatively what I wished to do. We were making something new and the odds were stacked at a certain point against us. And then, it began to turn and we had a wonderful sense that we were going to make it, and it was exhiliarating to be part of that feeling."

When *Vanity Fair* was nominated seven times for the prestigious National Magazine Award in 1992, including Bennetts's piece on pedophilia, Brown celebrated with a staff party. "It goes to show," she said, as confident as any editor in her prime, "when our peers are forced to sit down and actually read the magazine, they have to acknowledge the caliber of what appears in it." Everyone in the room roared with approval.

Although the magazine's reputation was still firmly rooted in glitz, Brown earnestly pointed to other meaty pieces inside her "hot book," such as T. D. Allman's various accounts from around the world, especially his piece explaining why the government of President Manuel Noriega in Panama would not fall so easily—a prescient, contrary view at the time, which defied the conventional wisdom. For most readers, Alex Shoumatoff, a *New Yorker* staff writer, was not a name that quickly came to mind when thinking of prominent *Vanity Fair* bylines. But in her own hall of fame for fine reporting, Brown often first mentioned Shoumatoff's story on Chico Mendes and his fateful effort to help preserve the Amazon rain forest ("the first eco-martyr," as Brown anointed him). There were other writers, like Ron Rosenbaum, Stephen Schiff, and James Wolcott, whose work helped to broaden the magazine's appeal. "One of the things that was very exciting to me was, when we first started *Vanity Fair* we did fluffy things because that seemed to be the feeling of the moment and we were growing and finding our way and evolving," Brown later said with slightly revisionist understatement. "But at a certain point, about three years into the magazine, we really began to add substance into the book, and it began to get very exciting to me. . . . I was very proud of the quality of our journalism. And I think we proved that you can be serious and entertaining at the same time. You can run ten-, twelve-, fifteen-thousand-word in-depth pieces of journalism that are serious and influential and sell 1.2 million copies, which is what we were doing. And the more substance we poured into the magazine, the more it sold. To me, *that* was the thrilling part."

Tina Brown's new, more serious approach was perhaps best underlined by another serious-minded investigative piece by Leslie Bennetts. Her exposé showed how Nancy Reagan, once a great benefactor of Phoenix House, the renowned drug treatment foundation, had tried to make sure its new treatment facility in California would never open. After years of preaching "Just say no"—her well-known public service message against drug abuse during her time in the White House—Mrs. Reagan caved in to pressure from her rich neighbors who worried that Phoenix House might attract all sorts of undesirables. Bennetts's story caught the former First Lady in a rank hypocrisy of the worst sort. When Tina Brown heard of the angle of the story, she seized upon it. As Bennetts recalled, "I had ten days to do the Phoenix House piece, including going to California when I was breast-feeding."

This critical treatment of Nancy Reagan was a remarkable change for a magazine that, when the Reagans were in power, pictured them not only kissing in one 1985 issue but also featured them again in 1989 waving good-bye with the headline HAPPY TRAILS—as if the two-term presidency had been just some two-reeler on a Saturday matinee. For that gala farewell edition, *Vanity Fair* gave the Reagans approval rights over their photos. It wasn't the first time, either. In a May 1986 letter to Nancy Reagan, asking for her help with another *Vanity Fair* feature about longtime devoted couples, Brown signed away any semblance of editorial independence: "I want to assure you that the feature will definitely consist of a portfolio of couples and that I would like to offer you an early opportunity to approve the photos and text."

With the Reagans out of power, though, Tina Brown's tone chilled considerably. After the Leslie Bennetts piece appeared, the ensuing controversy deeply embarrassed the former First Lady and, as if to save the day, emboldened Tina Brown to embrace Phoenix House as her own cause. In March 1990, Brown decided *Vanity Fair* would sponsor a fund-raiser in Los Angeles for Phoenix House, with an official party theme, "Just Say Yes!" It was a cruel rebuke to Mrs. Reagan's cowardly act. Undoubtedly, Tina Brown could be as scathing to those out of power as she could be ingratiating when they reigned supreme. "The evening's success had an upstated kind of 'Take that, Nancy Reagan!' theme," observed Liz Smith after attending another Brown-sponsored affair for Phoenix House in 1992. "Ever since Tina stepped in and shouldered the burden jettisoned by the former First Lady, P.H. has risen from the ashes and is the charity flavor of the decade!"

As the Los Angeles party demonstrated, Tina Brown's perceived power had grown immense, with enough influence to attract Hollywood's top producers and money-men to her event. The invitation list was a virtual roster of Tinseltown clout: former NBC chairman Grant Tinker, Twentieth Century–Fox chairman Barry Diller, Columbia's Peter Guber, Disney's Jeffrey Katzenberg, the billionaire producer and close Newhouse friend David Geffen, agents Michael Ovitz and Swifty Lazar, and many other producers, directors, and actors. In a few short years, *Vanity Fair* had become the premiere magazine to showcase an upcoming film or star, with an impact not quite seen since the mass circulation days of *Life*. But underlying Brown's glittering presence in Hollywood was the vast fortune of Si Newhouse, her benefactor back in New York, whose reach was almost without parallel.

To provide a touch of New York flair to the party, the magazine imported actor Robert Morse to present his interpretation of the late writer Truman Capote from the play *Tru,* in which he was then appearing on Broadway. Held inside a Culver City sound studio where *Gone With The Wind* was once filmed, that evening in Los Angeles seemed like a dream for those magazine staffers who were there, the culmination of Brown's long quest for social acceptance and dominance in her newfound land. She had conquered Hollywood in a way that few others had done before. "It was a pretty dazzling evening and I think it was the peak of *Vanity Fair*, at least in Hollywood," recalled Paul Rosenfield, a *Vanity Fair* contributing editor who had covered Hollywood for nearly twenty years as a reporter for the *Los Angeles Times*. "It wasn't the stars as much as it was the power—people who don't have to get dressed and go out because they're rich and powerful enough. It was interestingly seated and it showed Tina's skill. She was the daughter of a producer, and I have always seen her that way—as a great producer. She knows how to show things off, to present them. The recipe would change every month because she was producing a new show every month. That's an unusual quality for someone in magazines."

As her deliberately tart, celebrity-hyped magazine became more respectable, Brown became a ranking member of the New York literary elite. No longer the loneliest woman in town, she and her husband, Harry Evans, whom Newhouse selected as president of his Random House book imprint in 1990, hosted many parties and cocktail receptions for their friends and grateful writers. She even sponsored a back-and-forth discussion on the "character issue" in U.S. politics in the august debating chambers at Oxford University. (When she asked Gary Hart to appear on the "rogue" panel at the Oxford debate, he was reminded of those scathing Gail Sheehy profiles on him and shot back a curt reply.) With success, she became more aggressive in challenging critics. Forgetting all those "magic bimbos" and her original macho-sounding intent of formulating *Vanity Fair* into a "ballsy" magazine, she now labeled those who questioned her motives as sexist, sometimes with ample evidence. One of the most egregious examples was the way some continued to categorize *Vanity Fair* dismissively as a "woman's magazine" despite its wide appeal. At times, Brown let her annoyance show. "I honestly believe that if my name was *Tom* Brown, they wouldn't write about me in that way," she complained. "I think they're writing about me in that way because I'm a woman who beats men in the news game month after month. We crucify other news journalists with better pieces and I'm not afraid to boast about that."

By the early 1990s, Tina Brown's days on the "diarrhea" beat, dancing in Hackensack for a humorous first-person account back home, were long gone. More full in the face and of herself in general, Brown could show a matronly iciness when needed, a lightning-fast calculator of social worth. Her friends now included many powerful figures in New York, and some—like onetime *New York Daily News* publisher James Hoge or developer and media mogul Mort Zuckerman—even served as godfathers for her children. She was rhapsodized as a star on television's "60 Minutes" and was asked by the press to recommend books for the young to read. (Machiavelli's *The Prince,* she advised.) Her words, which once delighted in a certain cheeky provocation, were now more subdued and measured. "I tend to feel that you can't take on the world—it's much better to try and make alliances with the people who affect your destiny," she explained. "I have to be careful not to betray people, obviously—while not becoming bored."

Those who watched her closely, though, feared that's exactly what was happening. It was apparent in Brown's routine, with her taking longer-than-usual weekends and delegating more responsibilities to other top editors. This hint of ennui came as *Vanity Fair* was lauded as a smashing success, by virtually any measure. The magazine's circulation continued to climb astoundingly and its well of stories were surrounded by top-drawer advertising, abated little by the recession. The total amount of money Newhouse invested in *Vanity Fair*—an estimated $75 million, at least half of which was spent before Brown walked through the door as editor—still remained to be recouped fully. By 1990, the magazine was operating in the black, a remarkably quick turnaround in five years. At its most desperate moment, Brown had taken Si Newhouse's ambitious venture of reviving a long-forgotten magazine and reclaiming it for a new generation. And its voice, as she had predicted, was unmistakably hers.

For what she had achieved, Tina Brown was recognized as one of the best editors ever in America. With such acknowledged acclaim, even by some former detractors, she could venture to a convention of American newspaper publishers in 1991 and lecture them on what they were doing wrong. Tina Brown's friends and staffers began predicting that, just as she had left when *The Tatler*'s success was affirmed, her departure would be imminent. They reasoned over lunch or over the telephone that someone with her talents and boundless energy needed another challenge. Hollywood was a constant rumor. In one version, her friend Barry Diller had offered her a job. Other big names were also bandied about. Brown herself acknowledged that she had turned down two offers from Hollywood. There was a sense that Brown's ambition and drive could no longer be contained.

"Tina Brown's headed for much bigger things than *Vanity Fair*," predicted media critic Edwin Diamond in late 1991. "I guarantee you she'll dump Si Newhouse before he dumps her." Undoubtedly, Si Newhouse heard the rumblings and thought about what he would do.

That summer, Tina once again tweaked the nose of American puritanism with a cover featuring a very pregnant Demi Moore posing in the nude, her hands discreetly placed, like some Botticelli madonna with spiked hair. When Brown showed the proposed cover taken by Annie Leibovitz to Newhouse, he approved it over the qualms of some underlings. The sight of a naked pregnant woman was too much for the out-of-town magazine retailers, though, who forced *Vanity Fair* to wrap its newsstand issues in a white paper sleeve and Poly Bag. It was a delicious turn of events, for now *Vanity Fair* was being served like contraband and criticized for simply showing motherhood in all its splendor. This mini-scandal was imbibed by the gossip columnists and then swallowed whole by the mainstream media. The Demi Moore issue, which enjoyed worldwide press coverage and a huge upsurge in street sales, was positioned as a triumph for women's rights, with Tina Brown once again the social astronaut steering, in her words, "an enormously positive pushing of the envelope." It would prove to be her last big splash with the magazine she had saved.

As 1992 progressed, *Vanity Fair* was gradually becoming too predictable as it made its way out of the heyday of the eighties into the angry, resentful times of an America enraptured by a new billionaire—Ross Perot. The magazine seemed on automatic pilot, repeating its usual mix of stories in a way that was becoming too familiar. For the upcoming August 1992 issue, Demi Moore returned once again as the cover story, this time wearing a business suit painted on her naked skin, and nothing else. It was steamy and provocatively androgynous. But it was also the same idea, all too derivative and all too obvious. *Vanity Fair* was cannibalizing itself! Something had to be done! For that gravest of situations was now very apparent—the very reason cited by her editors when carving out written passages from stories that made Tina's eyes glaze or her mind begin to wander, that same queasy feeling when she held out her limp hand and then looked over your shoulder at the surrounding crowd, or when she was forced to defend herself about being starstruck, or a social climber, or—heaven knows—about those journalism ethics questions her critics were so fond of asking.

Before she was out the door, Si Newhouse realized he must make changes at the magazine that had so uniquely captured the flair of Condé Nast and given him the most notable achievement of his career. His decision would compel him to intertwine forever the futures of two magazines, *Vanity Fair* and *The New Yorker,* which he once said he would always keep separate and distinct. That promise would no longer be possible.

For at its very pinnacle of success, the worst calamity of all had struck *Vanity Fair:* Tina was bored.

CHAPTER ELEVEN

About *The New Yorker* and Si

In any Shakespearean drama, there is usually an incident or event that somehow seems to portend the future. Si Newhouse's highly dramatized takeover of *The New Yorker,* acted out on the vast tableau of the American press and infused with all the verities of an Elizabethean morality play, was no exception.

Only a few months before his purchase of *The New Yorker,* there was a minor catastrophe that somehow seemed a portent of things to come. It involved a *New Yorker* writer, Alastair Reid, who had spent most of his career sending dispatches from faraway places.

Poor Alastair Reid. After all, he was only trying to make a point.

Reid, a native Scotsman, was attempting the sort of overreaching point of view—a philosophical grandstand, if you will—that seasoned writers will occasionally foist upon the tender ears of undergraduates and grateful academics. In a newsroom of one's peers, such views might be greeted with a certain skepticism. But in the ivy-covered halls of Yale University where Reid lectured that day, they surely would understand his transcendent point: the need for a higher truth, the search for one illuminating insight greater than a mere collection of facts. "In reporting with some accuracy, at times we have to go much further than the strictly factual," Reid contended. "Facts are part of the perceived whole."

As part of this epiphany, Reid, an author of both fiction and nonfiction, admitted that he sometimes blurred the difference in the hallowed pages of *The New Yorker*—all for the cause of making things clearer and more vivid to the reader. To illustrate, Reid offered the students four examples from his work. In one *New Yorker* piece entitled "Letter from Barcelona," for example, Reid described a scene in a Spanish bar that no longer existed, a conversation in a taxicab that actually took place somewhere else, and other details and descriptions that fit nicely into his essay but did not necessarily conform to reality. These slight diversions from the literal-minded truth demanded by *The New Yorker* were, as Reid later explained it, "volunteered by me . . . as exceptional cases in which I had chosen to depart from strict factual accuracy for reasons that, while clear to me, were arguable, argument being what seminars are mean to stimulate."

On this occasion, however, Reid's prognostications about the craft—his lofty admissions of melding facts and fantasy into his work labeled nonfiction—were recorded by a skeptical student soon to become a *Wall Street Journal* reporter. If debate was what Reid was seeking, he would soon get plenty of it. In early 1984, the former Yalie exposed Reid's unorthodox views in a lengthy front-page *Journal* article that caused great controversy. In some ways, this reaction was hard to fathom, for the *Journal*'s story was not really a scoop per se. After all, Reid's admissions were certainly not a secret, having been made in a university lecture hall months before. Nor was the practice of making up conversations or details any stranger to American journalism. Nevertheless, the story about Reid's fabrications held the impact of a blockbuster piece of investigative journalism, and it was promptly picked up and trumpeted in newspapers and periodicals across the land. A WRITER FOR THE NEW YORKER SAYS HE CREATED COMPOSITES IN REPORTS, *The New York Times* front-page headline said the next day, giving the story greater currency and worldwide import.

For weeks afterward, media critics, high-minded editors, and other op-ed gadflies opined about Reid's theories, nearly all unanimous in their condemnations. For others, it was a moment of glee: the high and mighty *New Yorker* had stumbled. In beginning its account of the Reid shenanigans, *Newsweek* mimicked the style of *The New Yorker*'s "Talk of the Town" section: "A leg-pulling friend of ours who religiously reads the Talk of the Town in the *The New Yorker* writes . . . "

In the world of American journalism, other publications had returned Pulitzers or fired columnists and well-known writers for making things up. What made this transgression so shocking was that it had occurred at *The New Yorker,* which—even in the hyperkinetic, "know the price of everything" time of the mid-1980s—was still revered as something special, an institution impervious to such scandals. For nearly sixty years, the fabled writers and editors of *The New Yorker* had made it something extraordinary, from the days of Harold Ross, S. J. Perelman, James Thurber, and their witty lunchtime colleagues at the Algonquin Hotel in the 1920s and 1930s to the more somber and socially significant writing of John Updike, J. D. Salinger, Rachel Carson, John McPhee, and scores of others in the Vietnam and Watergate eras of the 1960s and 1970s. Despite its dull beige walls smudged with ink and the curmudgeonlike foibles of its staff, this place was a writers' haven, one of the few lasting citadels of excellence seemingly inured to the vagaries of corporate intrigue and financial constraints. At *The New Yorker,* the written word was king. Reid's cavalier admissions of concocting parts of his reportage shattered this illusion, like a rock through a cathedral window. It seemed to rip away the mystique of a magazine revered for its careful writing and research and its meticulous process of editing and verification by an eight-person fact-checking bureau. "The end of the world seems near now that our colleagues at *The New Yorker,* that fountainhead of unhurried fact, turn out to tolerate, even to justify fictions masquerading as facts," the *Times* wrote in an editorial, only half-jokingly.

Perhaps Reid's greatest sin was his unsteadiness about *The New Yorker's* reputation as a bedrock of editorial integrity. "Had I been writing for a tourist magazine, I could see how the readers could feel insulted. But I was writing for *The New Yorker,*" Reid later explained, still only dimly aware of the magnitude of his error.

At the outset, William Shawn, the man who had been the magazine's editor since 1952 and who personally read and approved every sentence printed in its pages, publicly defended Reid, in the same way he took care of any of his writers when they came across trouble or controversy from the outside. Yet Shawn, the very soul of *The New Yorker,* had no doubt of its mission. Before the controversy had finally subsided, Shawn wrote letters to several dozen subscribers who had been disturbed by the matter, reassuring them that *The New Yorker* was still in good hands.

And a memo from the publisher with Shawn's approval later made it clear that the magazine's standards would never again be breached:

We do not permit composites.

We do not rearrange events.

We do not create conversations.

The memo said that the widely read "Talk of the Town" section, where one of Reid's fabricated pieces had appeared, would be forever inviolate, demanding that "anything that purports to be a fact in The Talk of the Town is a fact."

But the Alastair Reid escapade, a tempest in the media's teapot that raged on for a short time during the summer of 1984, only seemed to foreshadow the much larger drama soon to envelop the entire magazine—a time when half-truths and misleading statements permeated the takeover in ownership and future direction of one of the finest magazines America had ever known.

Over the next two years, the changes at *The New Yorker* would bring about the removal of the family and major shareholders who owned it, force the "resignation" of its legendary editor Shawn, and spark a public outcry by most of the staff who demanded in a formal written petition that Robert Gottlieb, Si Newhouse's handpicked successor to Shawn, never set foot in the door. It also would set in motion a series of events in which *The New Yorker*—once the most assured of literary journals and lucrative of advertising vehicles—would become the subject of media articles wondering aloud about its decline and how it could be "fixed" for the 1990s.

In acquiring *The New Yorker* with $180 million, Si Newhouse drew upon some of the family's most time-honored traditions. Like his father, he sensed trouble in an independent family-operated publication and then pursued and gobbled it up with a price that could not be resisted. Si's father had built their newspaper empire in this piecemeal fashion, by acquiring ailing properties when death or internal rancor came to the owners and when those who survived felt they could no longer continue. Time and again, the elder Newhouse offered the opportunity for estranged but entitled family survivors to cash in. Try as he might, however, Sam Newhouse, the purveyor of lackluster newspapers in Staten Island, Cleveland, and other places, could never get his hands on a publishing jewel like *The New Yorker*. In this sense, the stunning buyout was a personal coup for Si Newhouse, who gained control of the same magazine his father had coveted but been turned down from buying many years earlier. When the hunt was over and the purchase complete in April 1985, Si Newhouse's achievement drew attention to the worldwide media empire as it had never experienced before.

A certain duplicity—a vice so roundly criticized when employed by writers like Reid but so often forgiven among wealthy media moguls—helped ease Si Newhouse's purchase of the magazine. For example, Newhouse certainly didn't seem bothered by publicly claiming in *The New York Times,* after purchasing his initial 17 percent stake, that he did not intend to seek full control of *The New Yorker*. In fact, he had previously told a broker he wished to purchase the magazine. Nor was Newhouse encumbered by his written statement that he "desires" to keep people and their jobs intact. Soon afterward, the entire business staff seemed to pass through Newhouse's equivalent of a Veg-O-Matic, which sliced and diced more than twenty ad salesmen and executives in a firing frenzy executed by *The New Yorker*'s new publisher, Steven Florio, a man who had made his mark in the Newhouse organization as publisher of *GQ*.

In dramatic fashion, the swiftly orchestrated takeover at *The New Yorker* underlined just how naïve and aloof many of its highly regarded writers and editors were about the business side of their company and just how complacent the management had become in their belief that no one would ever buy them out. "We never thought anyone would be crazy enough to actually buy it," recalled Peter Fleischmann, the man who lost the magazine his father had bequeathed him. Yet, for anyone interested, the vulnerability of *The New Yorker*—the looming threat to its long-cherished editorial integrity and independence—was right there in the magazine's annual report, lying like a time bomb amid the columns of revenues and debits for more than a decade.

Remarkably, one of the most misleading statements about the magazine's future appeared in a "Talk of the Town" essay about *The New Yorker* itself, which reassured readers during the midst of the takeover deal that all would be well under Newhouse. The essay, believed to be written in good faith by Shawn, was a recitation of the magazine's most cherished virtues and concluded that "if any single principle transcends all the others and informs all the others it is to try to tell the truth." Those lofty ideals, however, seemed weighed down by the bitter ironies involved in the Newhouse deal, which seemed to cast a pall over the magazine for years to come. Despite a pumped-up circulation drive by Newhouse—in which the magazine was being hawked on cable television and through other gimmicks—it had lost hundreds of ad pages and seemed editorially adrift. Somehow, the intangible quality of *The New Yorker*—in which it spoke to its generations of loyal readers with a certain moral authority—had seemed muted and abused in the takeover process involving Newhouse. For the first time in more than sixty years, *The New Yorker* seemed unsure of itself. Even friends of the magazine no longer were certain of its calling.

"*The New Yorker*'s most precious asset has been its authority—its ability to put an issue on the national agenda, as Rachel Carson's "Silent Spring," James Baldwin's "The Fire Next Time," and Jonathan Schell's "The Fate of the Earth" all did. The magazine's contribution to American letters and politics has been incalculable," Hendrik Hertzberg, a once and future *New Yorker* staffer, would write in the scholarly *Gannett Center Journal* five years after the sale. "Under S. I. Newhouse, its new owner (and the owner of *Vogue, Vanity Fair* and a chain of bad newspapers), who fired Shawn and replaced him with Robert Gottlieb, formerly editor-in-chief of the Alfred A. Knopf publishing house, it has continued to publish articles of high quality. But *The New Yorker* is no longer a kind of secular religion, as it once was. It is merely a magazine."

Peter Fleischmann remembered the first time he got an offer from the Newhouse family to buy *The New Yorker*. He barely had time to finish his drink before he said no.

It was sometime in the late 1960s and Fleischmann had not yet taken over the reins of the company from his father, Raoul. Perhaps sensing a change in the wind, Sam Newhouse called and invited the younger Fleischmann over to his Park Avenue town house. "It was a warm day and he suggested that I stop by for a drink," recalled Fleischmann. Without telling his father, Peter Fleischmann went to Newhouse's home after work.

As Sam accurately sensed, there was indeed change about to happen at *The New Yorker*.

Raoul Fleischmann was slowing down after years of presiding over the business side of the magazine and he was ready to retire. The heir to a yeast fortune, Raoul had escaped the obligations of running the family's bakery company by starting *The New Yorker* magazine almost on a whim, together with a card-playing buddy, Harold Ross, the magazine's founding editor. Fleischmann's investment of $700,000 and his willingness to tide over *The New Yorker*'s finances during a rough start allowed the magazine to catch on among Manhattan's smart set, finding success with its blend of humor, a wry writing touch, and an array of gentle-spirited cartoons. Ross, a hard-driving former newspaper man who at times seemed to know little about the subjects in his own magazine, proved to be a brilliant editor, a near genius at finding the magazine's voice and its audience. Like a long-shot horse that paid big at the track, *The New Yorker* was a gamble from the very start for Ross and Company and continued that way for many years.

A sense of inspired madness was the magazine's great charm, an irresistible allure for many young writers who joined its staff. Harold Ross was the maestro who made it all work. "You caught only glimpses of Ross, even if you spent a long evening with him," James Thurber, who joined the magazine in 1927, would later recall in his memoir *The Years with Ross*. "He was always in mid-flight, or on the edge of his chair, alighting or about to take off. He won't sit still in anyone's mind for a full-length portrait. After six years of thinking about it, I realized that to do justice to Harold Ross I must write about him the way he talked and lived— leaping from peak to peak." Even though Ross and Fleischmann barely spoke at times (eventually requiring that Ross's top aide, Hawley Truax, serve as a liaison between the business and editorial departments so that one side might know what the other was doing), the magazine flourished, growing plump with ads from the best New York City merchants and department stores. When Ross died in 1951, some worried about the magazine's possible demise. One of its resident wits, A. J. Liebling, predicted of *The New Yorker*'s future: "The same thing that happened to analysis after Freud died."

But during the 1950s and 1960s, the magazine enjoyed unparalleled literary and commercial success, with a tradition carried on by Fleischmann and his new editor, William Shawn. For a generation returning from World War II, *The New Yorker* was a longtime companion, having been offered in a shortened "pony" version during the war and then fattened with advertisers when the troops returned home. In 1966, *The New Yorker* enjoyed its greatest financial success, carrying 6,143 pages of advertising, rejecting another $750,000 in ads deemed unsuitable or for which there was no room, and paying a record dividend to its small group of shareholders. *The New Yorker* refused to take on any debt but also shunned using its dividends for expansion. It kept its audience select by never offering discounts except to college students. For a time, the magazine didn't publish its own telephone number. "As a business organization, it's so bad it's good," quipped John Brooks, the magazine's writer whose account of the go-go years on Wall Street in the early 1960s brilliantly captured that era.

By the late 1960s, Raoul Fleischmann, then an enfeebled man in his eighties, was already passing on much of the day-to-day responsibility for running the magazine to his only son, Peter, a forty-five-year-old World

War II veteran with a gentlemanly manner and a puckish smile. Peter Fleischmann had been preparing to take over the magazine since the 1950s, when his father beckoned him to leave his job as an investment banker at Smith Barney and join the family business. Although father and son had endured a tumultuous relationship, they were cut from the same cloth. They were both men for whom *The New Yorker* symbolized a laconic, patrician view of life. "He is a handsome, gentle, ironic man, with blue eyes, prematurely gray hair, and old-fashioned good manners," Brendan Gill wrote of Peter Fleischmann in his book *Here at the New Yorker*.

Peter Fleischmann was ready to run the magazine himself, not sell it to someone else. Still, he decided to listen to what Sam Newhouse had to offer.

As he arrived at the Newhouse home that day, Fleischmann was greeted by the newspaper tycoon and taken to the family's study, where the elder Newhouse did much of his business. On this day, Sam Newhouse, a small but dapper man nearly in his seventies, made his pitch. In his long career, he had initiated other megadeals in the newspaper industry in exactly the same way—with a friendly encounter in which he was able to judge a potential business opportunity. Often the Newhouses' best deals were made to family members willing to listen and cash in.

However, Fleischmann, who had seen rumors in the trade press about Newhouse's interest in the magazine, cut him off.

"It didn't last long enough for me to finish my drink," he recalled. "I said I wasn't interested in selling and that was it. I probably didn't tell my father about it for a week."

With what little Fleischmann knew about it, Newhouse's company struck him as an odd suitor for *The New Yorker.* The newspapers were in obscure locations like Staten Island, Syracuse, and Jamaica, New York, and were fairly pedestrian in both their appearance and their approach. The Condé Nast collection of women's fashion magazines like *Vogue, Mademoiselle,* and *Glamour* were hardly known for their writing virtuosity, either. "I didn't read any of his books," recalled Fleischmann in the jargon of the magazine industry.

Dick Shortway, Si's confidant and publisher at *Vogue,* remembered the younger Newhouse bringing up the subject during a ride in the back of a taxicab. "If you could buy *The New Yorker,* would you buy it?" Si asked him.

The answer was easy. "This was when *The New Yorker* was really in its heyday," Shortway recalled years later of that conversation in the late 1960s. "I said, I sure as hell would. Why do you ask?"

"Oh, I would, too, but my father doesn't want it," Newhouse replied, as Shortway remembered it. The subject was never brought up again.

Two decades later—the next time a Newhouse came calling on Fleischmann—the situation was much different at *The New Yorker*. In 1984, Si Newhouse was much better prepared than his father had been. And Peter

Fleischmann, whose loose control of the magazine had eroded further after his bouts with throat cancer and other illnesses, was almost totally unaware of what was to befall him. The only advance warning, Fleischmann said, came from the fluctuation in *The New Yorker*'s publicly traded stock, which caught his eye in the summer of 1984 when it wandered above $130 per share. "The stock was jiggling around and I knew that something was going on," Fleischmann said. "I thought that it might be Newhouse, but there was no way I could trace anything."

Fleischmann's suspicions were confirmed by November when he got a call one afternoon while seated in his chairman's office at the magazine. It was Si Newhouse. "I would like to make an offer to buy some stock in the magazine," Newhouse told him.

"I'd rather you didn't," Fleischmann replied with characteristic understatement.

Even though Newhouse said he was buying only a portion of available stock in the company, Fleischmann knew from that moment that Si Newhouse wanted it all.

Their brief, terse conversation was made even more difficult by Fleischmann's use of a vocal device—given to him after throat surgery—that enabled him to mouth his words. The humming device emitted a robotic sound, which made it difficult for the listener to understand, especially over the telephone. Fleischmann put the device next to his larnyx so he could be understood. It was a constant reminder of his own failing health and of his vulnerability to the right offer.

"He asked me and I said no, and then he bought it the next day," Fleischmann recalled. Immediately after Newhouse got off the telephone, Fleischmann went into action. "I called the fellow who keeps track of the stock, someone in accounting, to find out what was going on because I wanted to stop him from taking over the magazine."

The roots of Fleischmann's dilemma, however, had existed for more than a decade and he was aware of at least some of them. Following his father's death in 1969, Fleischmann was forced to rearrange his family finances so that he could pay the large sum of federal taxes on his father's estate—a fate he didn't think he could dodge. As a result, Fleischmann said his family controlled about 32 percent of the company stock and he himself held little more than 25 percent. Early in its existence, *The New Yorker* had sometimes paid its writers with stock and later awarded stock to some key officials on its business side, gradually shrinking the size of the Fleischmann share. But there was not a lot of concern, because these shareholders were as committed to *The New Yorker*'s ownership as the Fleischmanns were.

By the early 1970s, however, after he paid the estate taxes, Peter Fleischmann realized that someone with enough money and the right breaks could take the magazine away from him. He just felt that no such person existed.

On several occasions in the past, other offers had been made to buy *The New Yorker.* In the early 1960s, William Paley, chairman of the CBS broadcasting network, had made repeated overtures to the Fleischmanns, all to no avail. In the mid-1970s, Warren Buffett, the Omaha investor who then was not well known outside Wall Street circles, held a 16 percent stake in the company and was so persistent that Fleischmann arranged for him to have lunch with William Shawn, who could brief Buffett on the obstacles of taking over such an eclectic, insoluble place as their magazine. Fleischmann's hunch for fending off Buffett's friendly inquiry worked. "Peter, I see there are some very difficult problems in running this organization," Buffett later told him, after his lunch with Shawn. Without identifying Buffett by name, *The New York Times* later indicated that Shawn emphatically lectured Buffett about "the fragile equilibrium" of *The New Yorker* and how dangerously "business exploitation" would be received at this little literary flower.

By the 1980s, *The New Yorker*'s reputation was that of a national treasure, seeming to awe even corporate raiders like Ivan Boesky, who entertained the notion for a time of buying the magazine, only to demur later. Although its shares were publicly traded on the New York Stock Exchange, the magazine still acted like a private company immune to any intruder.

Many on the editorial side expressed surprise when Newhouse's purchase of 17 percent of the firm's stock was publicly announced the day after Fleischmann had received his fateful telephone call. The writers and editors—so used to the Chinese wall that existed between the editorial and business sides—seemed blissfully ignorant of the magazine's ownership problems until it was too late. Peter Fleischmann would later say that the writers had only to read *The New Yorker*'s annual report, which clearly spelled out the lack of a majority ownership at the magazine. "You don't put out a memo or a wall bulletin saying you're vulnerable to a hostile takeover," he said. "You just don't talk about it. But I never thought anyone would be fool enough to do it."

In their time-honored way, the Newhouse family assured the press that this was not the start of a hostile takeover bid. "Mr. Newhouse, chairman of Advance Publications, a holding company for the Newhouse family interests, said in a statement that the purchase was for investment purposes," the *Times* reported the next day. "He added that Advance has no plans to seek control of *The New Yorker* or to influence its management."

But Newhouse would soon move quickly to take control. In this, he was helped immeasurably by the discontent on the magazine's own board of directors, notably on the part of Philip Messinger, who had expressed displeasure for months with the way he felt *The New Yorker*'s finances were being handled. Both Messinger and another key investor, William Reik, felt that Peter Fleischmann had bungled several of the magazine's investments and alienated George Green, the magazine's president, who had left for the Hearst magazine group in May 1984. Green was well liked within the magazine and was credited with turning around its finances after a lull in advertising during the late 1970s.

After several confrontations, Fleischmann and Green had their final showdown over a multiple-page advertising supplement for computers—called an "advertorial" in the magazine world—that Green wanted to run over the objections of editor William Shawn. For years, Shawn, like his predecessor, Ross, had a traditional veto power in rejecting ads that were considered beneath the dignity of the magazine's readers or that might be confused with the actual editorial pages. But Fleischmann, adamant once his mind was determined, sided with Shawn and rejected the ads. Shortly afterward, Green resigned.

Similar confrontations had preceded the advertorial dispute, including one over Fleischmann's decision to place his son, Stephen, on the board of directors. Another sharp disagreement involved the opportunity to distribute an American version of the French fashion magazine *Elle,* a joint venture that Green had arranged with the French Hachette Publications. Shawn and J. Kenneth Bosee, the magazine's treasurer, who would soon succeed Green, felt that *Elle* was too frivolous, too inappropriate to be associated with *The New Yorker*. The debut issue of *Elle* proved to be a success and the highly stylized French magazine soon became a smash in the crowded world of American fashion magazines. But with Green's abrupt departure, Hachette's chief, Daniel Filipacchi, decided to drop the distribution arrangement with *The New Yorker,* all with the blessings of Shawn and Fleischmann.

This inner turmoil greatly upset Messinger, who had made millions from his *New Yorker* stock during Green's stewardship. In the late 1960s, Messinger had begun buying shares of *The New Yorker,* convinced that it was undervalued and that it would grow tremendously. When Warren Buffett decided to unload his shares in the mid-1970s, Messinger went on a buying spree, until he held a 13 percent stake in the company—second only to that of Peter Fleischmann. With Green's departure, Messinger increased his vociferousness at *New Yorker* board meetings. He was sometimes openly hostile to Fleischmann and his decisions. After earning a fortune from his stock, Messinger was concerned that it might begin to slip away if *The New Yorker* suddenly became a rudderless ship with Peter Fleischmann at the helm.

"Peter had been born into the job," said Messinger, who lives in Florida and tends to the fortune he made from the sale of his *New Yorker* stock. "I never thought I was dealing with a full deck there." Messinger claims that the *Elle* transaction, if it had stayed under *The New Yorker*'s purview, would have "doubled the value of the stock."

William Reik, another major investor, was also worried about *The New Yorker*. As an investment manager for Paine Webber, Reik had spent years buying up stock in the company for both himself and his clients, until he controlled approximately 14 percent in 1984. Attracted to the debt-free and family-run aspects of the company, Reik also was enamored with the prestige associated with the magazine. (He once also held similar stakes in both Tiffany's, the Fifth Avenue jeweler, and Sotheby's auction house, until they, too, were sold to an outsider at considerable profit for Reik's investments.) On occasion, Reik fancied himself someday owning the magazine, garnering enough resources to pull it off somehow. He would often share this dream with his friend, Philip Messinger.

With the departure of Green, however, both Reik and Messinger were convinced that Fleischmann—unable to make the changes necessary to keep the magazine competitive and vital—would run it into the ground. Messinger, with the more gloomy prognosis of the two investors, was determined to sell his stock. "I didn't have any choice," said Messinger, who many viewed as a traitor in the ranks. "You could either see the company get run down or have a sophisticated buyer come in. Certainly Newhouse is a sophisticated buyer." Reik remained unsure, however, and eventually did not decide to sell until his boss at Paine Webber, Donald Marron, began to show more than a passing interest in *The New Yorker*. And the guiding hand behind Marron's interest was Si Newhouse.

Newhouse had already learned about the opportunity at *The New Yorker* from a man named Abe Blinder, who had been tipped off that shares controlled in Paine Webber accounts might be in play. In the investment business, Blinder was known as a go-between in the sale of media companies, and he immediately contacted Newhouse to see whether he was interested in buying into the magazine. By all available accounts, Newhouse was quite eager. Blinder, acting as an agent for Newhouse, began contacting the magazine's shareholders—even Fleischmann—to see whether they were willing to sell. But he made little headway.

What proved to be the crucial meeting leading to the eventual sale of *The New Yorker* occurred by happenstance—when Si Newhouse bumped into Donald Marron at an art auction at Sotheby's in New York City. Marron, a politically active businessman who was a connoisseur of art as well as high finance, was Reik's boss and, at least technically, was responsible for some of the shares that Reik handled in the Paine Webber account. It was still Reik's call to make concerning the stock, but Marron from this point on would exert much greater influence on the magazine's stock.

As the trading in fine collectibles swirled about them inside the Sotheby's auction room, Newhouse inquired about Paine Webber's stake in *The New Yorker*. Newhouse's remarks seemed to suggest that Marron might help him in buying the outstanding *New Yorker* shares that were on the block. Without appearing overeager, Marron agreed to assist Newhouse, whom he knew as a fellow board member of New York's Musueum of Modern Art and as an avid collector of contemporary art. Doing business with Newhouse—even though Advance Publications was a privately held company—was an attractive notion, especially at a time in the mid-1980s when the sales of media companies were fetching large fees for those who helped arrange the deals.

The Sotheby's conversation was a source of relief for Marron, as well. After months of inquiring on his own, he was none too pleased with Reik's seeming indecision about what to do with the *New Yorker* stock, according to those involved in the sale. Deciding to take matters into his own hands, Marron invited Newhouse to discuss the stock sale further at a meeting at Marron's Park Avenue apartment the following weekend. According to writer Gigi Mahon's account of the takeover, Marron spent "several hours 'whipping up S.I.' . . . talking animatedly about what a great property *The New Yorker* was."

Newhouse needed little convincing. By the first week of November, he had decided to call and set up a meeting with Peter Fleischmann to discuss his intentions. Newhouse had already agreed to go ahead with the purchase of the Paine Webber stock and to buy Messinger's stake in the magazine. Perhaps as a courtesy, Newhouse felt it necessary to pay a visit. Or perhaps, as others later suggested, this was Si's way of assessing how much difficulty Fleischmann might pose, how vigorous the fight would be for gaining control of the magazine.

Newhouse arrived alone at Fleischmann's apartment, located in a Gothic-style landmark building on Manhattan's Upper East Side. The meeting between the two men, both the eldest sons of publishing legends, took place inside Fleischmann's wood-paneled study, where so many parties and get-togethers for the magazine had taken place. This meeting did not go well. As Fleischmann recalled, "I think he hoped that I'd be easier to get along with than I am." Newhouse told Fleischmann that he was about to buy a sizable portion of stock in the company, but he assured Fleischmann that it was for "investment purposes only," according to several accounts, including Fleischmann's own.

No matter how comforting Newhouse tried to be about his intentions, Fleischmann remained unconvinced. He correctly sensed that Newhouse was intent on owning his magazine, no matter what words he may have uttered in Fleischmann's home. "He offered to buy just a block, but I knew he wanted the whole goddamn thing," said Fleischmann. "After that, I knew he would never stop until he had the whole thing." But what the *New Yorker* chairman didn't realize was how much control Newhouse had already orchestrated.

Weeks earlier, Fleischmann had been personally told about the desire of LIN Broadcasting executives to sell their small portion of *New Yorker* stock in the account handled by Paine Webber. Donald Pels, chief of LIN Broadcasting, was alarmed about the sudden departure of *New Yorker* president George Green and, during a lunch with Fleischmann, offered to buy the magazine from him. Fleischmann politely declined the offer. He also turned down LIN's offer to sell its stock to him, allowing the shares instead to be put on the open market. But until the very end, Fleischmann remained in the dark about Si Newhouse's effort to line up both the Messinger and remaining Paine Webber blocks of stock handled by Reik. "I had no idea how he did it," Fleischmann later recalled. "I didn't find out until later."

In two decades of politely declining offers, Fleischmann viewed Si Newhouse as the least desirable suitor he had encountered for the magazine. Not only were Newhouse's publications considered inferior in Fleischmann's view but Newhouse himself didn't seem to play by the same rules that Fleischmann had tried to observe his entire life. If Newhouse was direct and bottom line–oriented, Fleischmann was gentlemanly and a bit circumspect. He was also aware at that time of the federal government's claim of chicanery involving Newhouse's income-tax payment on his father's estate. The irony was not lost on Fleischmann, who had had to reshuffle his finances following the death of his father, further diminishing his control of the magazine's stock. "I took the trouble of paying my father's estate taxes," Peter Fleischmann recalled in bitter understatement. "I am an honest man. I don't think it's something they bothered to do when their father died."

During the negotiations, Newhouse attempted to ease the transition in ownership, to smooth the all-too-apparent rough edges remaining from his hostile takeover. One afternoon, he invited Fleischmann over to his town house, which was adorned with modern art and contemporary furniture. In their own reserved ways, neither man talked much. "I gathered that he liked to do lunch," recalled Fleischmann. "But there was no way I was going to enjoy lunch with that fellow. We went straight into the dining room. He never took me upstairs to where he has a beautiful art collection."

Fleischmann, too proud and stubborn, could not bring himself to ask Newhouse why he was so insistent on buying *The New Yorker,* which had been like a family heirloom, the only occupation Peter Fleischmann had ever really known. "That's not Peter's style, it's not in his character," explained his wife, Jeanne, who first met him when she was working as a secretary to William Shawn. After they married, Peter decided that one Fleischmann was enough at *The New Yorker.* In order to be understood, Fleischmann sometimes relied on his wife to help translate his robotic sounds, the metallic hum from his voice box, for the assembly of lawyers involved in the takeover. Jeanne Fleischmann had her own view about Si Newhouse's determined quest for *The New Yorker.* "He wanted to buy it for his mother and put it on the coffee table," she said. "His father had wanted to buy it for the same reason. It was a classy thing to have, a status symbol."

As a final sale seemed near, Reik had second thoughts about selling his shares of stock. He was upset with Newhouse's roughshod handling of the transaction and still clung to a dream of becoming a last-minute white knight, saving *The New Yorker* from an unwanted interloper. "He said to me, 'Let's buy it,' but I'd say there's no way we could run the company without George Green, and he wasn't coming back," recalled Philip Messinger, who was already committed to the deal.

Despite entreaties from the staff to fight the takeover, to solicit help from other potential white knights, like multimillionaire oil heir Gordon Getty, Fleischmann gradually became resigned to the sale of the magazine he loved. "He was worth five billion, ten billion? There was no way I could fight that money," he said of Newhouse. "The only thing you can do in that situation is try to get as much money as you can for the sale."

Fleischmann's embittered feelings remained with him until he died from cancer in April 1993. "The takeover was hard to bear," Fleischmann was quoted in his obituary. "For 60 years there had been a Fleischmann on the premises and in charge, and now there was none." To be sure, some of this anguish was soothed by the fortune Newhouse paid for the magazine—a total of approximately $180 million, about $40 million of which went to the Fleischmann family. Peter and his wife owned more than 200,000 shares, along with other members of their family. Virtually overnight in the late summer of 1984, their $130-a-share stock soared, until Newhouse agreed to pay $200 a share by the following winter. If there was any pride in what had happened for Peter Fleischmann, it was in the belief he had gotten the best price he could.

"Peter did very well for his shareholders," said Jeanne Fleischmann, a very proper, cordial woman who shared her husband's assessment of Newhouse. "And he also did well by himself, but he gave a great deal of it away. He said he didn't like that dirty money."

On a winter's night in 1992—nearly seven years after the sale and a year before his death—Peter Fleischmann remembered almost every detail about Newhouse's purchase. All around his home, there were still reminders of what he had lost. As they talked that night about the sale, Peter and Jeanne sipped "flavored water" from their highball glasses with the imprint of Eustace Tilley, the magazine's famed signature caricature of a New York dandy. And on the couch, next to the fireplace and the wood-paneled walls lined with books, they relaxed on large pillows with Eustace's likeness etched into the fabric. They took care to speak with great politeness, but each wore a pained expression as they recalled the hostile takeover of *The New Yorker,* a family heirloom since 1925, by a man they now held in contempt: Si Newhouse.

"Mr. Shawn was hurt," Peter Fleischmann admitted before the night was through, "and so was I."

"I'm moved by your kind words and delighted to accept," Si Newhouse said as he stood at the Waldorf-Astoria podium, nervously following his prepared text.

The ballroom was filled with publishing executives and the clinking sound of tableware and coffee cups as Newhouse rose to accept his journalism prize. "Why I deserve it . . . or whether I deserve it . . . is another question. But, at least in one respect, I follow the precedent of past winners. I do have some fun in publishing from time to time . . . tonight being one of them."

No one needed to be reminded of Si Newhouse's recent adventures. In a few short years, he had swiftly become the premier force in American publishing, first with the successful revival of *Vanity Fair* and now with the carefully-orchestrated purchase of *The New Yorker.* On this night in January 1986, when Newhouse won the Henry Johnson Fisher Award, a prestigious magazine-industry award, he was both self-effacing and reflective. There were even signs that he was intent on keeping things as they were at *The New Yorker,* mindful of editor William Shawn's mastery and his reputation within the literary world.

"When I reminisce about my 35 years in publishing what comes to mind are the friends and associates with whom I have shared the successes and failures that are the stuff of our lives," Newhouse told the group of magazine executives. "But, especially, I think of three journalists—larger-than-life figures—each of whom has affected me in significant ways."

Naturally, the first one he mentioned was his father, S. I. Newhouse, Sr., who began the family's newspaper empire. The second influence was Alexander Liberman, Condé Nast's longtime editorial director and Si's mentor in the world of magazines. And then Si mentioned his final name.

"My third journalist is a recent acquaintance. When luck was with us last year and we were able to acquire *The New Yorker,* I became one of a few people with access to its very private and very formidable editor-in-chief, William Shawn. Around his shop, Mr. Shawn is known as Mr. Shawn. He has been described as the least-known, best-known, man in America and I believe it. One of his writers, Harold Brodkey, calls him a combination of Napoleon and St. Francis of Assisi . . . and I believe that too.

"Meeting Mr. Shawn is an event one doesn't forget. Precise, eloquent, never wasting a word or a minute, this extraordinary man is what *The New Yorker* itself is all about. These giants have made magazine publishing a memorable, meaningful activity for me."

Whatever bonhomie and high regard Newhouse felt for Shawn on this night, however, was a passing phase at best.

Almost exactly one year later, William Shawn was fired by Newhouse without—as Shawn had long hoped for—any final say in deciding his successor as editor of *The New Yorker.* The road to Shawn's abrupt departure took months to develop but seemed inevitable from the moment Newhouse bought stock in the company. The transition in leadership was neither smooth nor without rancor. In the end, it left seventy-seven-year-old Shawn, an editor of historic proportions, feeling defeated and diminished.

When Newhouse took over the magazine, Shawn was diplomatic but resolute that *The New Yorker*'s principles remain untouched. Sounding like some cautious State Department official, he told the *Times* he hoped "to establish a relationship of mutual trust" between himself and the new owner. "I would hope that as man to man we could work things out," Shawn said, refusing to consider suggestions by the staff that the magazine's sale to Newhouse include contractual provisions to safeguard its editorial independence.

"You can make a magnificent document," Shawn said. "If the people who draw up the document, or even sign the document, want to get around it, they can. And if they want to live up to it, they will. It isn't documents in the long run. It's what the people's real intentions are."

As always, Si's true intentions were indeterminable. At least from his public pronouncements, Newhouse had ultimate faith in Shawn and his ability to run *The New Yorker*. "I hope he continues to edit the magazine for a long, long time," Newhouse told the *Washington Post* for a front-cover profile in its "Style" section. "Obviously, Mr. Shawn will continue to be editor as long as he wants to be editor. He is so much *The New Yorker*. To say he is there at my sufferance would be presumptuous. He's going to be there because he's Mr. Shawn. Just as I wouldn't change the name of the magazine, I wouldn't change Mr. Shawn."

William Shawn had usually been able to figure out people's intentions ever since he became editor following Harold Ross's death in December 1951. A small, balding man with large ears and a weak smile, Shawn was the self-effacing guru for several generations of writers at the publication. No matter what the problem in a writer's life or copy, Shawn seemed to find an answer, at least one that would do for the moment. Even before Ross's death, the loyalty Shawn enjoyed among the staff was seen as remarkable and helped to catapult him into the top post. His devotion to the job was enough to convert the most devout laggard. He often would work fifteen, eighteen hours a day, six or seven days a week. His vacations were believed to be spent not along a lakeshore but by his desk at home, where there were even fewer interruptions than at the office.

His editing seemed the source of profound mystery. "Shawn's method in dealing with a writer is to convey such a high regard for a given piece of work that once it has been put in type and the moment comes for the editor to challenge certain phrases and seek certain necessary changes, the writer is pretty well convinced that the corrections will cost Shawn as much pain as they do him," wrote Brendan Gill, saying that such ordeals were necessary "only in order to bring a masterpiece from near-perfection to perfection. No author can fail to recognize the attractive logic of this proposition."

But Shawn's contributions superseded those inspirational birthing sessions with writers. His vision extended to a much broader interpretation of *The New Yorker* in the post–World War II era. He championed John

Hersey's unnerving account of the destruction wrought by the atomic bomb and personally convinced Ross to devote an entire issue in 1946 to Hersey's *Hiroshima*. This was no longer the same magazine of the 1920s, when celebrity profiles and gossipy items about Manhattan's rich were its standard fare. America had grown up. The nation had endured a torturous rite of passage during the Depression and then World War II, emerging with a different sensibility. For *The New Yorker*, there would still be cartoons or features that sometimes seemed as if they had been written by an effete Ivy League student bursting to tell his friends in a humorous offhanded way what had happened the other day. The generally light-hearted but occasionally rapier-like cartoons of such artists as Peter Arno, Saul Steinberg, Charles Addams, and Lee Lorenz peppered its pages for years. Humor could still be found with many of Woody Allen's offbeat pieces in the late 1960s, but Shawn would lament that he couldn't find other satirists good enough for the magazine's standards. Under Shawn, however, these cartoons and the magazine's humorous offhanded pieces no longer ruled the day, as they once had under Ross. The generation that came of age after World War II seemed to want more.

Shawn was determined that *The New Yorker* would continue running long in-depth pieces of journalism on important topics or issues. In 1962, Rachel Carson's *Silent Spring* served as a manifesto for environmentalists, a cause that would fully bloom among millions of Americans in the decades to come. More than eight hundred books were first excerpted in *The New Yorker*, including Truman Capote's true-crime novel *In Cold Blood*, Hannah Arendt's *Eichmann in Jerusalem*, James Baldwin's prescient warning about racism in *The Fire Next Time*, and Robert Caro's massive Pulitzer Prize–winning biography, *The Power Broker*, about Robert Moses and New York. It was Hannah Arendt who said Shawn, almost saintly in his demeanor and judgment, possessed a "moral perfect pitch."

Another writer, Thomas Whiteside, said he was encouraged by Shawn to seek out extraordinarily complex stories like his groundbreaking ex-posés on the dangers of Agent Orange and other environmental hazards. Whiteside would receive a $300,000 "genius grant" from the MacArthur Foundation in 1986 based on his *New Yorker* reporting. "He was always there to encourage," recalled Whiteside, who joined the staff in February 1950 and worked with Shawn on several articles. "His insight was such that he felt he could divine your subjective feelings. He was like an outrider and would reach out with his hand through the sheer power of his un-derstanding. He knew your state of mind to an amazing extent." To White-side and many other writers, Shawn became the essence of *The New Yorker* in the postwar generation, the key to its remarkable editorial success and its accompanying financial rewards. "Shawn is really an editor for history," Whiteside said. "I don't think what I did, for instance, would have been possible under Ross. If Ross had lived, *The New Yorker* would have died or at least have faded. Under Shawn's editorship, it became not only a good magazine but a moral force in American life."

In the same tradition, Jonathan Schell published his 1982 series of essays, *The Fate of the Earth,* about the potential holocaust from nuclear proliferation, a timely subject with particular resonancy during the early Reagan years, when the arms race was pushed to its limit. Schell's reporting drew wide attention, became a best-selling book, and was a great source of satisfaction for Shawn. In many ways, Schell was like a son to Shawn. After attending Harvard College with Shawn's own son, the actor Wallace Shawn (perhaps best known for the film *My Dinner with Andre*), Schell later joined *The New Yorker* and created a sensation in 1967 with his three-part series on Vietnam, focusing on life in the villages of Ben Suc, Quang Ngai, and Quang Tin. Schell's early reporting helped to steer intellectual opinion against the war and reflected the politically charged opinions that would come from *The New Yorker* throughout the Nixon years. Some longtime readers felt abandoned and canceled their subscriptions, but the magazine also discovered new followers among the baby boom generation of college students.

Despite these changes, *The New Yorker* was often accused of being a stultifying institution, too reverential to its traditions and mired forever in the past. The sharpest blow came from Tom Wolfe, who, in a 1965 feature in the Sunday magazine supplement of *The New York Herald Tribune,* called Shawn "the museum curator, the mummifier, the preserver-in-amber, the smiling embalmer—for Harold Ross's *New Yorker.*" Shawn's reaction to Wolfe's humorous feature indicated that things were taken a bit too seriously at *The New Yorker.* Just before Wolfe's story appeared, Shawn wrote an anxious letter to the *Herald Tribune*'s publisher, millionaire John Hay "Jock" Whitney. Characterizing Wolfe's article as "a vicious, murderous attack on me and the magazine I work for . . ." he warned that the *Herald Tribune* would be "right down in the gutter. . . . For your sake and mine, and, in the long run, even for the sake of Wolfe and his editor, Clay Felker (God help me for caring about them), I urge you to stop the distribution of that article."

In 1975, the differences between the old *New Yorker* and its postwar version were inadvertently showcased in Brendan Gill's book *Here at The New Yorker,* in which Gill assumed the bemused pose of Eustace Tilley, writing about the magazine's staff as if looking through his own monocle. Gill was one of the staff's longtime writers who seemed ill at ease with the searing, politically charged reportage of a younger generation. His book, which appeared as part of the magazine's fiftieth-anniversary celebration, was a string of vignettes straining for humor and full of self-centered observations. The magazine's vital contributions to public debates on the Vietnam War, Watergate, and other serious matters were barely mentioned. In a polite rebuke contained within Brendan Gill's book about the magazine, Shawn said that Ross was not a clumsy dolt or an "aggresively ignorant man," the subject of many amusing anecdotes (as Gill recalled at length), but, rather, a gifted and inspiring leader who knew his own limitations and augmented his staff with talented editors who allowed writers the freedom to explore the truth.

Shawn wrote in the eight-page essay contained in Gill's book:

> . . . journalistic integrity was a religious matter for him. When, once, he said that *The New Yorker* was not a magazine but a cause— Ross was a man who fled from "causes"—he was speaking, in a sense, of integrity. Ross was no moral philosopher, and his social conscience was shaky, and he knew nothing whatever about politics, but he had a profound ethical sense when it came to journalism. The truthfulness and the accuracy were part of it. The aversion to falseness was part. But there was something more. He held to some resolve—scarely ever hinted at in words—never to publish anything, never to have something written, for a hidden reason: to promote somebody or something, to pander to somebody, to build somebody up or tear somebody down, to indulge a personal friendship or animosity, or to propagandize. There were no ulterior motives, no hidden purposes, however worthy; no concealed explanations. Everything that was published in *The New Yorker* was precisely what it purported to be, was published for its own sake.

For more than half a century, Ross and then Shawn had presided over a magazine truly extraordinary in its editorial autonomy and in the success of its mission. Publishers and business types were kept at a distance. There were no reader surveys, no "focus groups," no paid advertorials appearing in the guise of staff reporting, no cents-off subscription gimmicks or gifts, hardly any other marketing tools common throughout the publishing industry. *The New Yorker*'s soul was found in the anonymous presence of Shawn, whose influence abounded but whose name never even appeared on the masthead. "If those of us now who are loosely bound together in this common enterprise manage every once in a long while to bring out an entire issue that might be called a work of art, it is because Ross, who thought he scorned works of art, prepared the way," Shawn commented.

Even admirers of Shawn's stewardship, however, began to question whether the magazine's prized features had become tired. "Under Ross, the profiles had an edge and bite that have been sadly missing—and this is Shawn's weakness as an editor—in recent years," critic Nora Ephron wrote in 1975. "In many ways, the war in Vietnam, and Shawn's decision to hammer at it, rescued the magazine from the blandness that still characterizes some of what it prints." By the early 1980s, the complaints had only lengthened. *Time*'s media writer Thomas Griffith, after praising Shawn's tenure, said the magazine's journalism had become too overwrought and too pedestrian for the casual reader. "There is a recognizable *New Yorker* kind of story," Griffith said about the magazine's fiction. "It usually involves a middle-class woman who registers a sad little recognition after some incident in which not very much happened."

The clear implication was that Shawn had overstayed his welcome. In the few interviews he granted to reporters, he shunted questions about a possible successor or retirement. He suggested those who complained about a lack of change weren't paying enough attention. "I think the magazine has changed dramatically over the years," he told an interviewer in 1975, during the magazine's fiftieth-anniversary celebration. "What is deceptive is that even though it has changed, there is considerable continuity, because from the beginning we've been striving for some kind of excellence. We wanted to write with a light touch. We wanted to be thorough in a piece of reporting, and accurate. We want to develop writers with style and individuality. . . . What we write about changes; the substance changes; what we're concerned with changes, but these other qualities could lead someone to think the magazine has not changed."

Mr. Shawn, as he was known to everyone on the staff, was not ready for the most jarring change—his own departure. For years, he had hoped that Jonathan Schell would be his heir apparent, and he tried in vain to fit him for the job. In the mid-1970s, Schell tried his hand at editing copy and there were rumors that it was part of the process of grooming him to take over someday. The staff was quick to rebel. Although Schell was an excellent journalist, many on the staff felt that he lacked the experience as an editor to succeed Shawn, who read and approved every word before it appeared in the magazine. Others worried that Schell, whose work was very political, might steer the magazine even further away from Ross's original notion that the magazine's "general tenor will be one of gaiety, wit and satire." Eventually, Shawn felt compelled to pin a two-line memo on the staff bulletin board, saying that he intended to stay for a while. Again in 1982, following the publication of Schell's *The Fate of the Earth,* there were rumors about Schell's future at the magazine, but it never came to pass. "Jonathan, as good as he was, didn't have an editor's head on his shoulders," said one writer friendly with both men. "Shawn saw Jonathan as a son, the only one capable of taking over. And Shawn tried again and again. But it just wouldn't take."

Before Newhouse took over, some board members pressed Peter Fleischmann to seek a replacement for their septuagenarian editor, but Fleischmann was hesitant to upset Shawn and had been cowed by his earlier threats to leave. In the minds of Fleischmann and several others, Shawn was crucial to the magazine's financial success. For them, the matter of finding a successor for Shawn was best pushed off for another day.

With Si Newhouse's hostile buyout in 1985, Shawn and his staff were suddenly confronted with several unpleasant realities. In his "Talk of the Town" piece, however, Shawn boldly stated his intentions never to capitulate to Newhouse, refusing to compromise the standards of his beloved magazine. "The business ownership of The New Yorker may change hands, but the idea of The New Yorker—the tradition of The New Yorker, the spirit of The New Yorker—has never been owned by anyone. It cannot be bought or sold. It exists in the minds of a group of writers, artists, editors and editorial assistants who have been drawn together by literary, journalistic, aesthetic and ethical principles they share . . . " he wrote.

Some familiar with Newhouse's methods were amazed by his restraint and rather languid response to Shawn's declaration of independence. "It was very elegantly put," Newhouse said about the "Talk of the Town" ultimatum, in one interview. "It was a great opportunity to state for the first time the basic philosophy of the magazine. I thought it was terrific. . . . It was quite refined and attractive. I couldn't have been more delighted with it."

Whether Si Newhouse's "delight" with his reception at *The New Yorker* was disingenuous or not would soon become a matter of open debate. Some close friends offered their own views about what the purchase of *The New Yorker* meant to Newhouse and his family. "I've never seen Si so excited about anything," Roy Cohn said, always offering his own spin to a story. "There's an element of class to it which he respects. It's like the crown jewel." No stranger himself to behind-the-scenes media manipulation, Cohn predicted Newhouse would put his stamp on the magazine in a matter of a year or two. "But Si is the most subtle stamper I've ever met in my life," Cohn said assuringly.

That prediction, like most Cohn observations, proved to be an amalgam of both over- and understatement. Despite his high praise for *The New Yorker*'s editor, Newhouse wanted to see the matter of Shawn's successor resolved, as well. After several months of waiting, he quietly made his move in early 1987. What transpired would profoundly affect *The New Yorker* for years to come.

Shawn had always indicated his replacement should come from within the magazine's own ranks. In a sense, *The New Yorker* under Shawn was both a dictatorship and a collegial democracy. He approved every word, with no staff meetings or any hierarchial process of editorial advice and consent. And yet, Shawn was adamant that a decision to pick his successor to run the magazine should be a mutual one, compatible with *The New Yorker*'s prickly and demanding staff of writers. In agreeing to buy the magazine, Newhouse's company agreed that "when a new editor-in-chief of *The New Yorker* is being considered, the final decision will be made by Advance, but it will consult with, and seek the advice and approval of, a group of staff members to be selected and to function in a manner then deemed appropriate by the senior editorial staff of *The New Yorker*." It was a promise Shawn felt Newhouse would honor, particularly as months passed following the tumult of the original takeover.

By late 1986, however, Si Newhouse seemed anxious for Shawn to name someone. There were rumors published in the press that Si was thinking about a number of successors, including Robert Gottlieb, editor in chief of Alfred A. Knopf, the prestigious imprint within the Newhouse-owned Random House. Shawn indicated his objections to Gottlieb, saying that the staff would never accept any outsider. Instead, Shawn told Newhouse that he favored Charles McGrath, the magazine's fiction editor, to succeed him. As part of an experiment in 1984 prior to the Newhouse sale, Shawn had selected McGrath as a co–managing editor along with fact editor John Bennet.

Chip McGrath, as he was known by just about everyone at the magazine, was a friendly, well-regarded man who had toiled diligently for years in *The New Yorker*'s vineyard. But whether he held the vision for the job was another matter. McGrath, then a thirty-nine-year-old Yale graduate who had joined the magazine as a copy editor in 1973, commuted every day from his home in the New Jersey suburbs and was viewed as a safe consensus choice. McGrath became known as the "designated experimentee," though there were doubts about his ability to lead the magazine in any other path than the one established by Shawn. "Very unlike Shawn in so many ways, he [McGrath] nevertheless shares the older man's reclusiveness and devotion to the magazine in its traditional form," commented media critic Edwin Diamond in an article that seemed to anticipate the change. "It's clear he would uphold the ways of the classic *New Yorker*. The only question is whether Shawn's man, and the magazine, are also Newhouse's."

When Shawn told Newhouse he had decided upon McGrath as a replacement, the owner seemed satisfied. Soon afterward though, Newhouse invited McGrath to dinner and began to have second thoughts. He decided that the man who should lead *The New Yorker* was Robert Gottlieb. As a longtime editor at the distinguished Knopf, Gottlieb had edited several *New Yorker* writers, including Renata Adler, Janet Malcolm, and Jonathan Schell, and was known as a man of high intellect and skill. Surely, there could not be much objection to an editor whom many knew or had worked with. Newhouse offered the job to Gottlieb and he soon accepted. Once having decided on a successor, the only obstacle that remained for Newhouse was telling Shawn.

Without consulting anyone at *The New Yorker*, Newhouse called upon Shawn at his *New Yorker* office on the afternoon of January 12, 1987, to inform him of his decision. While Newhouse was offering the editorship to Gottlieb over the holidays, Shawn had been preparing to move McGrath's office near his own so that he could increasingly assume more of Shawn's responsibilities. Shawn had no idea of what was in store when Newhouse walked into his nineteenth-floor office. For Si, the meeting was a courtesy to an editor he respected. But there was no longer any need to consult with Shawn, only to inform him of what had been decided.

Newhouse told Shawn that he wasn't happy with McGrath and that he was going to name a replacement.

"I've asked Bob Gottlieb to be the new editor," Newhouse said, according to several accounts, and then handed him a memo with Newhouse's signature saying that Shawn would "retire" on March 1.

Newhouse later said his meeting with Shawn lasted about forty-five minutes, which he spent mostly explaining his position. "Then I showed him the memo," said Newhouse. "He said he was very flattered by what I said about him, he said he was sorry I was not able to pick somebody from *The New Yorker,* and he felt it would have been better had I picked somebody from inside."

Shawn was dumbfounded but remained calm during the meeting. He attempted to dissuade Newhouse from choosing Gottlieb, or for that matter, "any outsider." But Newhouse remained adamant. Afterward, those who talked with Shawn say the seventy-nine-year-old editor was shocked and visibly dismayed. As he would later learn, Newhouse had already released the statement to the press prior to meeting with him. In this statement, Newhouse praised Shawn as "the finest editor of his time." The memo made no mention of the forced nature of his exit, however.

Before the end of the day, Shawn had written his own good-bye. It was as warm and lucid as Newhouse's missive had been cool and preemptive. With barely a moment's notice, Shawn tried to sum up his experiences at the magazine he loved.

> My feelings at this perplexed moment are too strong for farewell. . . . We have done our work with honesty and love. *The New Yorker,* . . . has been the gentlest of magazines. Perhaps it has also been the greatest, but that matters far less. What matters most is that you and I, working together . . . have tried constantly to find and say what is true.
> William Shawn

After thirty-five years as editor of *The New Yorker,* Shawn was out and his chance to determine the future leadership of the magazine gone forever.

On the day after Si Newhouse's meeting with Shawn, more than one hundred *New Yorker* staffers crammed into an editorial room, where a winding staircase connected two floors, to hear about the fate of the magazine. By *The New Yorker*'s standards, such a meeting was unprecedented.

William Shawn climbed up a few steps and leaned against the banister so that he could be seen and heard. He had been invited to address his troops, but those who prompted the gathering made it clear that the rally was not called at Shawn's instigation. During the meeting, Shawn remained in control, providing only hints at how the switch in editors had occurred. He remained polite and deferential regarding Newhouse. Nevertheless, the message got through plainly.

Many of the *New Yorker* writers expressed anger and confusion over Newhouse's sudden decision. "I'm surprised, because I thought that the succession had been worked out within the *New Yorker* staff, and that Chip McGrath was going to carry on," John Updike told the press. Rather than get upset, Updike and some *New Yorker* writers were inclined to wait and see and give Gottlieb a chance to prove himself.

But the majority of the staff, especially those close to Shawn, like longtime staff writer Lillian Ross, urged the staff to reject Newhouse's choice of Gottlieb and decided to form a committee to compose a letter requesting just such a thing. Though addressed to Gottlieb, a copy was also sent to Newhouse and made available to the media. Some staffers used the *New Yorker* telephones to call other writers and cartoonists, to win approval to add their names to the protest. In typical fashion, the three-paragraph letter was reviewed by the staff's copyreaders and fact checkers. The letter began by explaining their staff meeting, at which "there was a powerful and apparently unanimous expression of sadness and outrage over the manner in which a new editor has been imposed upon us." The letter became a declaration of independence by the outraged staffers, those with enough historical wit to call themselves the *"sans-culottes,"* a cutting reference to the French Revolution. In this revolt, they were trying to keep Shawn's head intact.

"The New Yorker has not achieved its preeminence by following orthodox paths of magazine publishing and editing," the statement read, "and it is our strange and powerfully held conviction that only an editor who has been a long-standing member of the staff will have a reasonable chance of assuring our continuity, cohesion and independence."

In its final paragraph, the protest letter made it clear that while the missive was addressed to Gottlieb, its intended audience was really Si Newhouse. "We wish to assure you . . . none of these feelings or reservations were directed against you. Many of us know you personally and professionally, and admire your splendid record at Knopf. . . . We urge that, after consultation with our owner, Mr. Newhouse, you withdraw your acceptance of the post that has been offered to you." Its valediction was signed "Sincerely and hopefully."

With that dismissive pat on the head to Gottlieb, the staff gathered once again at 5:00 P.M., more than three hours after the earlier session, to listen to a reading of "the Letter," as some were now referring to it, and to approve its submission. Eventually, 154 writers, cartoonists, and editors—including J. D. Salinger, whose prose had not appeared in *The New Yorker* for more than twenty years—placed their names on the protest document. Other names listed on the letter included Donald and Frederick Barthelme, Jamaica Kincaid, Ann Beattie, Harold Brodkey, Roger Angell, John McPhee, Ved Mehta, Howard Moss, and Calvin Trillin. Some staff members refused, including Updike, Gill, Renata Adler, and Lee Lorenz, either because they knew and liked Gottlieb or because they felt it would only exacerbate an already-wrenching situation. Whether foolish näiveté or committed idealism, a certain emotion swept throughout the staff. As Jonathan Alter observed in *Newsweek*: "The staff knows that if by some miracle it blocks Gottlieb, Newhouse's new editor will be worse. But few at the meeting seem to care. Lillian Ross might as well have been ladling Jonestown Kool-Aid."

Strangely to some, Shawn did not seem as distraught, with his forced departure all but certain, as when *The New Yorker* was bought in 1985. "He looks calmer than he did when the magazine changed ownership," longtime writer, E. J. Kahn, Jr., later observed in his published memoir. Others who were closer to Shawn say his hurt was salved by the outpouring of support from his staff. That was clear when the second meeting was called to order. Shawn, though not signing his name to any petition, certainly was not against the concept of resisting this move by Si Newhouse.

"You feel all right?" Shawn was asked by someone in the crowd at this second meeting. Shawn smiled approvingly, setting off thunderous applause in the room. For a moment, this group of iconoclasts and self-initiators was showing an uncharacteristic display of solidarity. Shawn was visibly moved by this show of emotion from his staff, according to Kahn's account and interviews with others who were there.

"We may save the magazine yet," Shawn said sotto voce.

The staff awaited Gottlieb's reply, which came the following afternoon during a strained lunchtime meeting with Shawn at his usual table at the Algonquin Hotel. With a morbid fascination, the nation's journalism community watched for a few days as *The New Yorker* seemed to convulse. The letter had made its intended splash in the press; the editorial turnover had been reduced to a soap drama. Gottlieb pointed to some of the same *New Yorker* writers whose books he had edited at Knopf, like Janet Malcolm, Renata Adler, and Jonathan Schell. "Knopf and *The New Yorker* share so many writers that it's clear my taste and judgment can't be that far from Mr. Shawn's," Gottlieb argued. "If they were very different, I don't think Mr. Newhouse would have chosen me."

In Shawn's mind, there was a great deal of difference. At a table inside the Algonquin, Shawn and Gottlieb met for the first time face-to-face, never having worked together. As a photographer flashed a camera in their faces, *The New Yorker*'s second editor conversed politely with its third, discussing whatever they could about the magazine's future. Gottlieb carried his own written reply to the staff's letter. The new editor expressed some sympathy for the feelings of the staff, but as Gottlieb firmly added, "I do intend to take up this job."

For Si Newhouse, *The New Yorker* fiasco was a source of embarrassment, once again causing a certain defensiveness about his intentions. Among the literati, Newhouse was still viewed as a philistine, the purveyor of fashion magazines with perfume scents and fly-away subscription cards stuffed in its pages. To them, Newhouse was a brute with an eye for making money, not one for cultivating writers. The staff's pent-up feelings about his ownership, the bold rebuff to his chosen successor, and Shawn's apparent unwillingness to quell the staff's uprising made Newhouse bristle. "My job was to select a man who I think can carry on in the tradition of *The New Yorker* established by Ross and Shawn, two brilliant editors," Newhouse said during the height of the controversy. "If I had found that man within the magazine, that would have been great, but I didn't feel that man existed within *The New Yorker* family and I did not compromise."

Of course, the staff could only recall Newhouse's written promises of collegiality in choosing Shawn's successor. The murky retelling of Shawn's ouster only heightened their suspicion. To the press, Newhouse would say Shawn voluntarily offered to retire by March 1, 1987. "He set the date," Newhouse told the *Times*. "He brought up the question to me about eight weeks ago." To another publication, Newhouse appeared more defensive: "Mr. Shawn is a perfectly rational man, totally committed to *The New Yorker*. He was aware of his age. If he were five or ten years younger, he'd still be editing the magazine."

But as staffers spoke with Shawn, they understood a much different story. In this version, Newhouse seized on the date of March 1 when Shawn offhandedly agreed to the idea of retiring soon. Shawn had always ducked the pressure to bow out before he got too old, yet this time he seemed sincere. For Shawn, the date was more of a target for Chip McGrath's increasing assumption of Shawn's duties rather than his formal departure.

No matter what promises were broken, Newhouse was still unaccustomed to this brand of insurrection, with an angry assemblage of editorial peasants burning their torches brightly for all to see. At Condé Nast, writers knew their place and editors were accustomed to the quick freeze (or the instant lop-off) when one fell out of favor. Shawn's refusal to go silently, or at least his unwillingness to quell the staff's objections, greatly displeased Newhouse. At the urging of several writers and editors, Shawn agreed to call Newhouse and ask for a staff meeting to hand the letter personally to Newhouse and to Gottlieb after it was written. According to several accounts, Newhouse was livid when he got the call from Shawn, and the two men agreed to meet a few hours after the tumultuous staff meeting.

When they did, Newhouse protested vehemently, asking Shawn why he would allow such a public embarrassment to occur. "Your job was to keep this from happening," Newhouse reportedly told him. The stark differences between the two men were never more distinct. Shawn replied that he was a "servant of my staff." Unaccustomed to such defiance, Newhouse insisted on his prerogatives as owner. If he was a "servant" to anyone, Si's sense of duty was to his family and future Newhouse generations, to make sure there was an orderly managerial transition at a property that had cost them nearly $200 million. There could be little, if any, future for *The New Yorker* with an old man unwilling to face the inevitable.

By about 9:00 P.M., Shawn returned to the office, "shaken" from his meeting with Newhouse, as writer E. J. Kahn later recalled. As if some form of punishment, Newhouse decided to move up Gottlieb's starting date of March 1 and install him in that position by February 15. Some say Newhouse—still seething at Shawn's actions and his tacit role in the staff's insurrection—thought seriously of throwing him out by the following Monday, January 19. Even Gottlieb, a mild-mannered person, seemed taken aback. Confrontation was not Gottlieb's style and it would only make his job more difficult in replacing such a legendary editor as Shawn. "Some people like tossing everything in the air and seeing how it all comes down," Gottlieb later told a writer, speaking in general terms. "Not me—I don't like changes or upsetting people."

Shawn left unceremoniously on Friday, February 13, 1987, after nearly six decades with *The New Yorker*. Friends and staff members took out a full-page advertisement in *Variety,* the trade publication, to thank him publicly for his contributions and achievements. He left badly hurt and still attempting to understand the real intentions of Si Newhouse—the man who, in terms of personal importance, had compared Shawn only a year before to his father, Sam, and Alexander Liberman. No longer able to affect the magazine he loved, Shawn tried to resist any bitterness. "I have never experienced or even permitted myself to contemplate a vindictive action," he later wrote to Lillian Ross. "I would rather carry around pain or disappointment or even the residue of bitterness for the balance of my life than to entertain a moment's vengeful thought."

Even years later, the unceremonious dumping of William Shawn could still anger those who were close to him. Though Si Newhouse may have seen his actions as a necessary demonstration of power, underlining who really was the boss, it was nevertheles viewed by many on the staff as a shattering of the collegial spirit, the covenant some felt with Shawn and the magazine. Jonathan Schell, whom Shawn once wanted as his successor at *The New Yorker,* was among the few staffers who quit in protest. "The hope was that Si Newhouse, despite his record, would honor his commitments and not do anything precipitous," Schell recalled. "All of this came to an end when Newhouse forced his way into the door and put Bob Gottlieb in as editor despite a written protest, in the teeth of that protest. For me, the life of *The New Yorker* I knew had been ended and was done so deceptively, through the brute force of money. I couldn't cooperate with that."

Steve Florio, the publisher of *The New Yorker,* was not formally introduced to his audience of prospective new readers. Rather, shall we say, he made his entrance with a big bang.

As part of a multimillion-dollar campaign to breathe new life into *The New Yorker,* Si Newhouse and his new publisher embarked on a widely publicized television ad campaign in late 1987. The new, upscale audience Newhouse wanted was a generation raised on TV. So the magazine's ad agency produced four commercials that would visualize actual stories from *The New Yorker.* After Newhouse's purchase of the magazine, there would be several subtle changes. But this commercial wasn't one of them.

In one of the TV ads, a nearly frozen miner was seen being rushed into a cabin by three fellow workers. The stricken man had consumed explosives and, when he was touched, a blast ignited. BOOM! When the dust settled in this rendition, one of the surviving miners was a man wearing a dark green jacket, a phony beard and a handlebar mustache. Unknown to viewers at home, that rugged survivor was Florio—*The New Yorker*'s president and publisher.

Under the old management, it was considered bad form for the magazine's publisher to appear too much in public, something that George Green was mildly rebuked for doing during his tenure as company chief. Under Newhouse, the premium was on marketing. "That's me," Florio proudly told a newspaper columnist, pointing to his television debut.

What was more remarkable was the idea that *New Yorker* stories needed to be visualized to sell the magazine. Such a concept, *New Yorker* vérité, seemed alien to the literary magazine run by William Shawn, who for years had attempted to keep the magazine's editorial integrity sacrosanct. Now, these same *New Yorker* stories were being used as copy for promotional TV ads. Things were clearly going to be different under Si Newhouse.

"Si read about Frank Perdue and said I should try it," explained Florio, referring to the king of the chicken wing, who made a fortune huckstering on the tube. Florio did his best to keep some decorum, appearing silently as a cameo player in the production. "I didn't want to appear as Steve Florio," he said. "This is my Hitchcock."

When Florio was appointed by Newhouse as the new publisher of *The New Yorker,* he was a brash thirty-six-year-old executive credited with turning around *Gentlemen's Quarterly.* As a marketing major from New York University, Florio had worked his way up the ranks at *Esquire* to become vice president and advertising director. In the spring of 1979, he came to *GQ* as publisher soon after Newhouse had purchased it. When he arrived at *The New Yorker,* Florio expressed confidence both to the business staff and to the press, saying that he could repeat the same success he had earlier enjoyed. If Newhouse was inclined to tread lightly at first on the editorial side, his newly installed publisher was determined to make his mark on an advertising staff he perceived as lazy and pampered, living in an unproductive country club atmosphere. By the end of his first year, the vast majority of business types at *The New Yorker* had been fired, retired, or left. "I just blew it out of here with a fire hose," Florio later said.

While Shawn remained editor, there was an uneasy tension, which seemed to keep Florio somewhat ill at ease. As if under instructions from Newhouse, Florio spoke deferentially of Shawn, albeit using his own terminology. "I'm a good publisher," he said, six months after taking over. "I'm not an editor. I've got a great product—and when you have an editor like William Shawn, the worst thing I could do is second-guess his moves." Florio made a transparent effort to signal Shawn's approval for the television advertising campaign. "He seems to be energized by the more aggressive selling of his words," Florio told a reporter when asked about Shawn's reaction to one ad campaign. "It's a very special property, so you don't hip-shoot."

Whatever resistance he may have received from Shawn, Florio moved ahead with his campaign to turn *The New Yorker* around just as he had at *GQ*. Those who believed in *The New Yorker*'s traditional approach were asked to suspend their beliefs. When Florio asked Hoyt Spelman, the magazine's longtime marketing director, to look into signing up more advertorials, he "prefaced his request by stating that he figured the idea of supplements would be distasteful to me, but he was going to ask me to look into them anyway," Spelman recalled. Shortly afterward, Spelman was also fired.

Both Newhouse and his publisher were convinced that they could bring the marketing hustle of Condé Nast to the inbred methods of *The New Yorker,* offering enough promotions and incentives to attract thousands more readers—"added value" gimmicks, as they are called in the parlance of the magazine business. Several of the changes were undoubtedly imperceptible to readers. For instance, some may not have noticed the magazine's profiles were now being started on the left-hand page to accommodate full-color ads that appeared on the right. And annoying insert cards and special advertising sections that looked like genuine stories on such topics as the America's Cup race could now be found in the magazine's pages.

Initially, the TV campaign seemed to pay off. Advertising, which had dropped from 3,500 pages in 1984, the year of the Newhouse takeover, to about 2,300 in 1988, climbed by about 5 percent in 1989. Circulation also grew from about 480,000 at the time Newhouse bought the magazine to more than 600,000 by 1990. When the recession of the late 1980s and early 1990s took its grip on the city's economy, however, *The New Yorker*'s fortunes turned worse. In a 1989 *New York Times* analysis entitled "How to Fix The New Yorker," the magazine was said to have plummeted from more than a $5 million annual profit at the time of its sale to a state of financial nothingness. "Many analysts now think the magazine is losing money," the *Times* said, proceeding to ask a group of media experts for their advice. "*The New Yorker* must do significant work on its editorial product," said magazine consultant Robert A. Cohen. "The advertising trade is dominated by young people who don't read magazines like *The New Yorker*. They read magazines like *Spy* and *People* that are more accessible. Young people don't understand what *The New Yorker* is all about." Another appraisal by an advertising executive was even more damaging. "There are a lot of hot, chic, contemporary magazines and if you want to show a client that you are hot, hip, and contemporary, you make advertising choices other than *The New Yorker*," said David Altshiller, head of an agency bearing his name. "In that case, the money goes to magazines that are visual pap. It's sad."

Skeptics suggested that the millions Newhouse was pouring into the magazine had not stemmed the decline in its fortunes under his stewardship. One competitor, John R. MacArthur, publisher of *Harper's Magazine,* openly questioned the circulations gains, saying they were largely the result of low-price subscriptions—an allegation that Florio vigorously denied. But another former *New Yorker* executive, well acquainted with the magazine's finances, estimated that the added costs of promotion and other gimmicks totaled $13 million, far exceeding whatever financial gains the magazine had made. "*The New Yorker* has to decide what it is," said this former executive in a 1992 interview. "In the past, it didn't go after a large circulation, but when Newhouse arrived, it seemed to view circulation as a sign of vitality. They destroyed the mystique of the publication in the eyes of the public. They made *The New Yorker* like everything else."

The New Yorker's efforts at waging a TV ad campaign and such techniques as stuffing the magazine with insert cards—whatever the short-term gains—seemed to take away its cultured, aristocratic image. In the past, the magazine had a minimal ad budget, offered virtually no discounts, and bothered readers with renewal notices only once a year. Somehow, the alchemy of its editorial quality still attracted quality advertisers, its cachet translating into cash. Under Newhouse, though, the approach was more direct, and at times *The New Yorker* looked as if it was hustling for a buck.

For the first time in decades, the unsurpassed advertising dominance of *The New Yorker* looked uncertain. "There's speculation that *The New Yorker* may be making less of a profit on circulation today because of the costs of wooing new readers," *Publishing News,* a trade magazine, would comment in February 1990. In the same article, John MacArthur was more blunt: "I think Newhouse has blown it with *The New Yorker*. The new management has lessened the perceived value of the magazine. It's not considered as elite as it once was." MacArthur accused Newhouse and Florio of "screaming to the world about how they were going to save a magazine that was, in fact, never in any real danger."

Within some circles, *The New Yorker* seemed to have adopted the same brassy self-promotional approach as other Condé Nast magazines. Some even called it "Son of *GQ*." Suddenly, *The New Yorker,* which had endured other similar lulls in advertising during its history, was being talked about as a terminal case.

When Shawn left, the pace of change increased. There was no longer quite the same dividing line between the editorial and business interests. One of the most debatable efforts—at least by the magazine's old ethical standards—was allowing staff writers to appear before the magazine's advertisers to give little talks at private lunches. On one visit, Young & Rubicam advertising executives were treated to a visit by Daniel Menaker, an editor, and Mark Singer, a writer. Brendan Gill and Pauline Kael also made outside appearances for the magazine's business side.

Others familiar with *The New Yorker*'s reputation began to notice a difference, even friendly Newhouse acquaintances like William F. Buckley, Jr. He remembers receiving an invitation to a *New Yorker* party shortly after Si purchased the magazine and being surprised by the other guests. "Since the Newhouse organization had just published one of my books, I thought I'd better accept," Buckley recalled. "It was quite obvious, the moment I got in, that it was primarily a party for the advertisers."

Although he was never a close friend, Buckley had known Si Newhouse for several years, primarily through Roy Cohn and other social acquaintances. At this party, Buckley felt familiar enough to do what many would consider the unthinkable. He walked up to Si, who was conversing with some strangers, and slung his arm around Newhouse's shoulder.

"Tell ya what, Si," Buckley said, looking around the room with his devilish smile. "I'll give you a hundred and eighty million dollars for the whole thing."

At first, Newhouse just stood there without moving, not sure whether Buckley was serious. As Buckley recalled, "His reaction was wonderful. Sort of that spastic shock that essentially shy people have, and then the sort of recognition that the time had come to smile, which he then did."

But the new coziness with advertisers was not a laughing matter to many at *The New Yorker* and it underscored a more profound worry about the magazine's integrity and future direction. "What seems to unnerve the magazine's staff most is the knowledge that the new owner might shatter their world at any time," the *Times* observed in a 1988 assessment of the post-Shawn changes at the magazine. "And there is an uncomfortable feeling that the editorial destiny of the magazine has become more closely tied to its financial performance."

Si Newhouse, aware of his reputation for abrupt firings of top editors, seemed uncharacteristically defensive about *The New Yorker.* "The New

York magazine world is a very fast track," Newhouse said. "As you know, I myself have had experience with change, and there are certain types of situations where sudden change seems better than slow change. *The New Yorker* is something else again."

Nevertheless, Si made sure that some Newhouse family traditions carried over immediately to *The New Yorker,* such as putting a Newhouse somewhere high in management. Soon after the purchase, Jonathan Newhouse, a thirty-four-year-old son of Si's Uncle Norman, was brought in to work with Florio. He later left to run the family's trendy new magazine, *Details,* aimed at young men living in the city. However, it was unclear what Jonathan Newhouse may have learned during his stay at *The New Yorker,* especially during the midst of a housecleaning.

"Jonathan was a bright kid," recalled one top *New Yorker* executive who left soon after the Newhouse takeover. "But he has a hard time making small talk. There are some very messy synapses in conversation." At a staff party, Jonathan Newhouse reportedly assured the magazine's ad director about the future, stating confidently about his family, "There's nothing wrong with *The New Yorker* that *we* can't fix."

When discussing the fate of *The New Yorker,* the talk inevitably turned to Robert Gottlieb.

In assuming the editorship from Shawn, Gottlieb, then fifty-six years old, had accepted the job of replacing a legend—a difficult task for anyone. Yet the usually unflappable Gottlieb didn't seem affected. Nearly twenty years earlier, as a much younger man, Gottlieb followed Alfred Knopf as editor of the publishing house that bears Knopf's name. In this succession, Gottlieb didn't seem overawed. And despite the staff's mass objection to his arrival at *The New Yorker,* Gottlieb didn't seem angered or intent on demanding his pound of flesh from the insurgents. He appeared to sense the need for carrying on quietly, rather than vociferously, if *The New Yorker* was to heal its wounds and survive its jarring ordeal. "I don't think he's a man who holds grudges," said Whiteside, a strong Shawn partisan. "He didn't make life difficult for people who were close to Shawn, like myself. It's something very much to his credit."

Over the first several months of his tenure, Gottlieb began the task of sorting through Shawn's backlog of finished stories and commissioned articles, honoring every financial commitment that Shawn had made to writers. He even ran a sixteen-thousand-word article by Doris Lessing (whom Gottlieb had edited at Knopf) about the Afghan warriors. The piece had been commissioned by Shawn but later rejected. Gottlieb took a greater interest in the cartoons that appeared and seemed to liven the cover art, which had grown dull and unimaginative. He made the "Talk of the Town" section a bit more "off the news," and brought in some of his own smart new writers, like reviewer Terrence Rafferty and Adam Gopnik to write about the art world. There were several nonfiction series and stories that drew considerable attention, such as the three-part excerpt from William Greider's book on the Federal Reserve and Neil Sheehan's four-part excerpt from his soon-to-be Pulitzer Prize–winning *A Bright and Shining Lie*.

What was most notable to the skittish *New Yorker* staff, however, was what Gottlieb didn't do: no wholesale firings, no severely mangled stories, no fundamental changes in assignments. Both an anxious staff and a watchful press waited for some dramatic move Newhouse-style, but Gottlieb demurred. Even the slightest change at *The New Yorker* seemed to attract attention. When the magazine gave its Table of Contents "a slightly different look," the *Times* devoted an entire story to it. "Mr. Gottlieb declined to interpret the changes to mean anything other than interest in the reader's convenience," the *Times* said, almost doubting its own account. Another *Times* story addressed the issue of color art being introduced inside the magazine. "We are not going to colorize *The New Yorker*," Gottlieb pronounced. "Cartoons and maps are not suddenly going to be in Day-Glo."

Inside his office, Gottlieb kept an array of kitsch items, such as a pint-sized Elvis doll and other plastic and porcelain novelties. Less formal than Shawn, he wore open collars and no ties, chinos and sneakers. His work schedule rarely included a power lunch like other top magazine editors. "There are four things in my life," he once told an interviewer. "Work, the ballet, reading and my family. I don't do anything else. I don't have lunches, dinners, go to plays or movies. I don't meditate, escalate, deviate or have affairs. So I have plenty of time."

Nevertheless, the burden of his office—indeed the fear of being perceived as The Man Who Ruined *The New Yorker*—seemed to have an inhibiting effect on him. Prudent to a fault and too cautious to make any real changes, Gottlieb became the new Mummifier, the unwitting keeper of Shawn's flame. "I think that by temperament I'm a conserver, not a revolutionary," Gottlieb said at the beginning of his tenure. More than five years after becoming editor, Gottlieb's *New Yorker* seemed stymied— a stunted evolution that seemed buried by the weight of a tradition impossible to live up to and with a voice that no longer applied to a new generation of readers. Once worried about wholesale changes, the staff now wondered aloud about Gottlieb's lack of direction. "I have never had a long-term vision of anything in my life," Gottlieb responded. "I started at Knopf twenty years ago with the intention of getting to the next day. Even if I were to have something as pretentious as a long-term vision, I would never articulate it. My only vision is to hope to maintain and even improve the journalistic standards we already live by."

That journalistic maintenance, with a little tinkering here and there, seemed the hallmark of Gottlieb's stewardship. He had curbed some of the excesses of Shawn's later years. For instance, Ved Mehta's anticipated three-part "Daddyji," a moving (but *barely* moving) saga of his rememberances of his father, was commissioned by Shawn but carved down to one installment by Gottlieb. Besides interesting book excerpts and notable contributions from old Shawn staffers, there was little of anything new or innovative added to *The New Yorker*'s familiar mix of stories.

With the fear of literary revilement hanging over his head, Gottlieb chose the safe route, the very approach that Newhouse had said he wanted to avoid when rejecting Chip McGrath as Shawn's successor. As Edwin Diamond would write in June 1987, several months after the Shawn departure: "Everything that Gottlieb is doing so far—from being accessible to lightening up graphics—are steps that anyone coming to Shawn's *New Yorker* would have taken. Now comes the hard part. Gottlieb has made a virtue of non-direction. He doesn't plan, he does. But without an overarching, clear and compelling vision for the magazine, Gottlieb's *New Yorker* could find its punch line turned against it: '*The New Yorker,* yes, still *The New Yorker.*'"

Some old warhorses like Brendan Gill could still be counted on to defend the fort. Less than a year after the Newhouse takeover, Gill wrote an essay for the cover of *The New York Times Book Review,* in which he reported that all was quiet on the West Side of Manhattan. "A couple of writers have left, in what amount to gestures of devotion to Shawn; other writers have learned to their dismay that lengthy, multi-part pieces may be somewhat less welcome in the magazine than they used to be," Gill wrote. "In place of turbulence, one observes a certain affirmative bustle in the editorial department." Just as Gill misunderstood Ross and Shawn, he once again failed to grasp what was transpiring.

The differences were not lost on other senior writers. Those who were not swept away with the emotion of Shawn's dismissal were willing to give Gottlieb his due. But they realized that their new leader was weak on what had been the magazine's greatest strength: journalism. Gottlieb seemed more assured on matters of fiction and other areas close to his experience as a book editor. He failed to show—certainly in comparison with Shawn at his height—a sense of anticipation for events, a curiosity about the nation, a firm sense of what to look for in reporting and writing.

The comparison with Shawn, who had basically come from running the nonfiction portion of the magazine, was striking to some of the magazine's most celebrated writers. "Although I'm sure Knopf under his management produced eight million nonfiction books and he even edited some of them, Bob's real background and interest has to do with fiction," observed Calvin Trillin. "Even nonfiction books and journalism are not the same; they are related, but they are not the same thing. So in a way, he came from a completely different background than Shawn did." Under Gottlieb, *The New Yorker*'s nonfiction pieces tended increasingly toward impressionistic essays from faraway places. All were laudable and politically correct to New York's orthodox literati, but they failed to inject any true sense of groundbreaking journalism.

For Trillin, who had signed the letter in support of Shawn but expressed some openness toward Gottlieb, there was a slow recognition of the profound differences between the two editors. "Shawn had a fantastic interest in things and he really considered journalism to be the heart of the magazine," said Trillin in an early 1992 interview. "He had a great interest in this country—that, I don't see in Bob at all. Shawn—the shy person who would ask if he was disturbing you and all that sort of thing—had a tremendous, absolute confidence in his own judgment. I'm not sure what Bob's is. Even though he's self-confident to a fault, he's not confident about what journalism is. It's all very safe, and nothing that people will get upset about, and you can't criticize it."

With such a lack of nerve and editorial clarity, The New Yorker's voice diminished and the moral authority it had once wielded began to ebb slowly. The magazine just didn't seem to matter as much anymore. As part of the vanishing act, Gottlieb was even quieter than Shawn, who had aspired only to be anonymous. "There's less in the papers these days about Gottlieb than there was about Shawn," observed another senior staff writer, who preferred not to be quoted by name about Gottlieb. "The New Yorker is not as much discussed."

That loss of editorial impact further exacerbated the wounds inflicted by Florio, who continued as Newhouse's publisher throughout the early 1990s. Florio kept a high profile, at least by The New Yorker's standards. And he continued to expound a philosophy of gimmicks and added value rather than real value. "Ultimately, a lot of companies are looking for a hook. Special ad sections are just another chip on the table," Florio told Advertising Age in March 1992. The trade publication credited Florio with introducing "advertorials to the weekly's staid pages in 1986 as a sign of its new flexibility." Indeed, the packaging together of fact and advertising claim—underlying the permeability of the magazine's once-admired Chinese wall—was a source of boasting for Florio. "In many cases," Florio concluded about The New Yorker's new brand of advertorials, "it is the deciding factor in buying one book over another."

As he did with the exploding TV commercial, Florio was merely expressing the sensibility of his boss. Like some great benefactor, Newhouse had attempted to bring along his brand of Condé Nast marketing razzamatazz to "save" The New Yorker from a slow death. Instead, he grabbed hold of the magazine against its will, failed to understand what really made it a success, and then grafted his own aesthetic onto its very being. The transplant didn't work.

More than any other publication in modern times, The New Yorker was a success driven by editorial excellence and became a must read for a generation that prized the written word. In turn, the magazine became an irresistible lure for advertisers, one of the most profitable publications ever. The New Yorker was special because it seemed distinctly apart from a world bombarded by billboards, blaring announcers, and never-ending sales hype. The magazine's quiet editorial integrity was its appeal—not an obstacle to be overcome, circumvented, or conspired against. By the 1990s, that approach had been fairly well discredited by the magazine industry and especially by the Newhouse magazines, which really knew no other world than one of marketing gimmicks, bottom-line economies, and ultimate subservience of the news side to business needs.

If the purchase of *The New Yorker* was a business venture, then Si Newhouse had truly misunderstood what he was getting into. And if he bought it, as the Fleischmanns suggested, only as a treasured ornament, like a painting or some other multimillion-dollar piece of art he might add to his collection, then Newhouse had greatly abused one of America's great literary institutions. For by the summer of 1992, it was apparent even to Si Newhouse that *The New Yorker* was dying.

CHAPTER TWELVE

"The Happiest Girl in the Whole U.S.A."

Did you make your mind up yet?"

Si Newhouse didn't like to be kept waiting. As he stood inside Tina Brown's office at *Vanity Fair* on a Thursday morning in late June 1992, he reminded her casually, almost jokingly, of the question hovering over their future together. Now that Si was resolved to make a change, he was impatient for her reply.

Only the day before, Newhouse had told Brown of his plans to replace Robert Gottlieb at *The New Yorker* and he'd offered her the editorship. For months, Si had shared his concerns about the magazine. When he asked her opinion of *The New Yorker,* Newhouse seemed genuinely pained by Brown's assessment. No one seemed to be reading it, she told him. From Newhouse's sullen reaction and his cryptic statements, it was evident Gottlieb was in trouble. And yet, for all of Newhouse's unhappiness with the magazine's direction, Brown was still surprised by the suddenness of his proposed turnover.

"Si asked me to go to *The New Yorker,* it was as simple as that," Brown later recalled of their meeting in Newhouse's office. "He asked me to go up and see him one day, and I was very, very surprised by it. We had talked about *The New Yorker,* on and off, for a year. I knew he was having a lot of thoughts about it. But I didn't expect him to make any change for at least some time. I thought Gottlieb would continue as he was. I didn't know the financial background or whatever. I didn't know it was imminent. I thought in a year, he was apt to make a change."

The magazine's bottom line couldn't wait, however. At least not by Si Newhouse's calculations.

The New Yorker's once robust advertising revenues had suffered a tremendous decline in ad pages, hastened by the public furor over Shawn's departure. Far from its mid-1960s peak of 6,000 ad pages a year, the magazine's advertising lineage had plummeted to only 2,002 for all of 1991, a drop of 18.5 percent from the year before. By June of 1992, *The New Yorker,* which was once the most profitable in the publishing industry, was rumored to be losing money, as much as $10 million a year. Rather than improve its fortunes after seven years of ownership, Si Newhouse had clearly made things worse.

In Newhouse's view, perhaps the biggest drawback to attracting advertising in the magazine was the median age of its readers, which hovered in the mid-forties. The baby boomers, who had been attracted to the magazine in the 1970s, were now nearly middle-aged. Salespeople complained about the difficulty of signing up new, expensive ads aimed at a younger, trendier market. Newhouse was alarmed at the research reports that showed *The New Yorker* was rapidly losing its audience. Ultimately, Gottlieb had to go—not so much because of his editorial stewardship of the magazine but because its demographics were all wrong.

Newhouse tried not to let on about the magazine's economic woes. His decision to change *New Yorker* editors, as he later assured *The New York Times,* "in no way arose because of business or in an attempt to solve a business problem."

But privately, the financial imperatives were clearly part of the urgency Newhouse imparted to Tina Brown. "I know the problem as it was bequeathed to me was that the readership had aged to the point that the only other magazine as old as *The New Yorker* was *Modern Maturity,*" she recalled. "Whether what Gottlieb was doing was good or not, the fact is that it was aging to the point that it could no longer be a tenable business. The fear was that it was really aging with great rapidity, that if it continued to age at that rate, there wouldn't be a readership at *The New Yorker.* It *had* to change."

Both Newhouse and Brown believed Robert Gottlieb was no longer capable of making the dramatic transformations they both felt were needed. Gottlieb appeared too much in awe of William Shawn's legacy, to the extent that he was unwilling to make any but the most minor alterations to the magazine. What he had in mind, Si told her, was something younger and bolder, to consider even some extreme measures. During their extended conversations together, Newhouse kept talking about "evolution," the need for the magazine still dominated by Shawn's presence to adapt finally to Newhouse's own lasting concept. Gottlieb failed to get the message. For that matter, even *New Yorker* publisher Steven Florio, as he later acknowledged, never quite understood what Newhouse meant by "evolving" or what was wrong with the magazine's contents. "I think I'm good at putting out the magazine the way it is," Gottlieb later told writer Michael Gross. "I didn't want, nor was I really equipped, to rethink the magazine to the extent that Si came to want. It became clear we would not agree. We couldn't be pulling in different directions. So at a given moment, we agreed to disagree."

Five years after personally selecting Gottlieb as the new editor for *The New Yorker,* Si Newhouse was, in effect, acknowledging he had been wrong. Indeed, Newhouse's intent of rejuvenating *The New Yorker,* with

Robert Gottlieb as his instrument of change, was doomed from the very beginning—mostly because of his own actions. Newhouse's awkward and eventually disastrous dismissal of Shawn made Gottlieb's job nearly impossible. Gottlieb never seemed to recover from the abject rejection of his staff, which had asked him not to come. There remained an overriding fear—long after Gottlieb showed otherwise—that he would tamper with the magazine and unalterably damage a cherished institution. "The only reason to leave the best job in publishing was to go to something else I loved," Gottlieb explained. "Why would I have gone to *The New Yorker* to undo it? I hoped to make it more of what it was—I won't use the word *better*."

Eventually, Si realized Gottlieb couldn't give him what he wanted. The time had come for a change once again. "At a certain point, Bob, who is quite conservative and quite classical, was unable or willing to see the need for further evolvement," Si explained. "In a quiet way, he decided that this wasn't a good situation and he resigned." Thankfully, Gottlieb agreed to leave without a bloody scene. His departure was certainly eased by a severance package said to be quite generous, and his own natural demeanor, which tended to avoid confrontation.

Si remained anxious about Brown's impending decision and whether there would be a smooth transition. To most observers, he was taking a considerable gamble. In effect, he was performing a head transplant—the metaphor constantly invoked by the press and staffers—by proposing to replace a failing editor with a successful one, unsure of the consequences for either magazine. Although *The New Yorker* was in trouble, *Vanity Fair* was at the top of its form, enduring the recession of the late 1980s and early 1990s with remarkable aplomb. If Brown could translate her *Vanity Fair* success (and advertising appeal) to *The New Yorker*'s weekly format, the magazine's revenues might rebound sharply and possibly return it to the ranks of the industry's biggest moneymakers.

In this proposed solution, there was little sense of irony or broken promises expressed by Newhouse. When he bought the magazine, Newhouse firmly declared, "I wouldn't make *Vanity Fair* like *The New Yorker*, and I wouldn't encourage *The New Yorker* to be like any other magazine." Now, he wanted to do just that with an editor whose own forceful, often brilliant persona always defined the magazine she edited.

While she contemplated Newhouse's offer that weekend in June 1992, Brown followed Si's suggestion of examining *The New Yorker*'s contents to figure out what was wrong and how to fix it. "They were often publishing quite superb material that wasn't being read, that was going unnoticed," Brown recalled. "That was the feeling I had when I picked up the magazine that Si asked me to look at that weekend. It was such wonderful material, so little discussed." To Brown, there didn't seem enough variety or pace, with very long pieces sometimes running together without any rest for the reader's eye. Gottlieb's *New Yorker,* she concluded, was read as "a sort of series of articles rather than as a magazine."

Gottlieb, though very talented, seemed oddly ill-equipped for the job of running *The New Yorker,* unable to translate his great skills as a book editor into a weekly magazine format. "There wasn't enough interest in the overall feeling of what that magazine did as a whole, overall object," Brown recalled. "I think that's probably because Bob Gottlieb was a books editor really. . . . He was not a journalist, and I think you need to be. Shawn was a great journalist. You have to be a great journalist to organize it."

Undoubtedly, Tina Brown was restless and needed a change. Though she denied any claims of being bored, many of her admirers on the staff, as well as the few detractors, took note of her frequent four-day workweeks and her apparent need for another, greater challenge. "This very smart Oxford girl was sort of slumming, in a way, by doing this magazine," said one editor who was hired by Brown and remained at *Vanity Fair* after she was gone. "She was always smarter than *Vanity Fair* and she knew it. At the start, she was thrilled and challenged to come here and turn things around. Once she got it working, she had essentially rejiggered the magazine to have only strong suits. It was profiles from A to Z, because most people want to read about other people. And it was glamorous, or scandalous, or about very rich people. She became, in a way, a victim of her own success formula. It became not quite as interesting for her to do."

With so much acclaim for her editorship, Tina Brown, still only thirty-eight years old, was reluctant to leave at that very moment and to increase her workload beyond the monthly pace of *Vanity Fair.* Her husband, Harold Evans, was busy overseeing Random House, a high-profile job that he had started less than two years earlier. With two small children, a boy and a girl, Brown's schedule often seemed balanced among managing one of America's best-known magazines, attending necessary social engagements at night, and finding enough time to spend with her family. From all indications, she planned to be at *Vanity Fair* to preside over the magazine's tenth birthday party in 1993. She had already instructed her staff to begin the elaborate preparations, an event that would surely underline her crowning achievements as the magazine's circulation pushed past the 1 million mark. She realized *The New Yorker,* with its weekly schedule, was a much more difficult task. At this point in her life, it seemed unlikely she could devote the same monklike attention that Shawn and Gottlieb poured into every word of every article of every issue. To bring about the kind of complete editorial overhaul Newhouse envisioned would be an enormous personal burden as well as a remarkable professional accomplishment. Nor was she eager to face the buzz saw of those Shawn loyalists and other *New Yorker* literati who would decry her arrival like some horror flick where Godzilla wrecks all the recognizable landmarks. It was the purists' worst nightmare: Tina Goes to *The New Yorker!* ("Everyone is rather jolted," a longtime staffer would later sniff. "They simply don't know where it's all headed. I guess it's headed into Tina land.")

Brown promised an answer by the following Monday morning. When the change at *The New Yorker* suddenly occurred, it seemed to catch Brown, uncharacteristicaly, off guard. "Si thinks about things and cogitates and works things out in his own mind. And then once he's made a decision, he wants to get on with it," she said, recounting the decisions leading to her arrival at *The New Yorker.* "I wanted to do it, *creatively.* But I had a lot of doubts about my family life. I felt very anxious about it. I wasn't sure it was the right decision at that moment with my children. And that's what gave me pause, really."

She spent that weekend discussing the opportunity with her husband and finally resolved to take it. Eventually, Brown's parents agreed to move to New York, where they could help with the children and ease her personal concerns. *The New Yorker* just seemed too good to pass up. If she refused, Newhouse might never offer her the chance again.

When she arrived at the Condé Nast building early Monday morning, she told Newhouse that she would accept his offer. He asked her to keep the news secret until sometime in mid-July when it would be formally announced. Even *Vanity Fair*'s publisher, Ron Galotti, later professed to being unaware of the impending change. Gottlieb was soon to depart for Japan on a previously scheduled visit to attend a translation contest. Si wanted to wait until after the July 4 holiday, when Gottlieb had returned, to make the formal announcement. Keeping a secret inside the Condé Nast building, a hothouse of rumors, proved to be impossible. Even Si couldn't be contained.

During a meeting with Florio, who for years had expressed a desire to work with Brown, Newhouse let the news slip.

"By the way, Tina accepted," Newhouse said.

Florio, far more demonstrative than his boss, was exuberant. "Oh, my God," he yelped. "It's Christmas!"

By Monday night, the word had spread around town, making its way to a softball field in Central Park. At a game involving Condé Nast *Traveler* and the staff of *Vanity Fair,* there was more talk about Tina Brown's career move than there was about who was sliding into second base. "By that point, everyone seemed to know," recalled one editor who played in the game. The rest of New York's press—with an unparalled fascination for the glamorous goings-on at Condé Nast—was quick to respond, faster than to a four-alarm fire. *The Wall Street Journal*'s reporters started making calls Monday night and other city columnists tried in vain to meet their deadlines with a verified story. With his carefully devised plans for secrecy now in tatters, Newhouse met with several of the major players at Tina Brown's East Side apartment, where it was decided press releases would be issued the next day. In his official statement, Newhouse called

Brown "the best magazine journalist in the world today." From the media's reaction to the news, it would be hard to dispute that claim.

Like General Washington's farewell to the troops, Tina Brown called her staff together for an 11:00 A.M. Tuesday meeting, where she would say good-bye. The exhilarating ordeal of transforming *Vanity Fair* into a success was already recognized as the high point of many staffers' careers. For this final adieu, emotions were overflowing from the very start of the meeting.

"I'm here to tell you some sad news," Brown said to a packed conference room filled with writers, editors, and friends. By then, everyone knew she was leaving for the *The New Yorker* and would be replaced by Graydon Carter, the former editor of *Spy* who was now running the weekly newspaper *The New York Observer*. Before she could continue, Brown began to cry. For a moment, Galotti stepped forward, talking about how difficult change was for everyone and assuring the apprehensive staff not to worry. Of course, this was impossible to do. Brown had elevated their salaries and status beyond any editor they had ever known. After regaining her composure, Brown then chimed in about the magazine's greatness and her feeling of debt to the staff. When she finished speaking, everyone in the room stood and cheered.

The next stop would not be so easy. That afternoon, Si Newhouse called a meeting of the editorial staff at *The New Yorker*. The announcement about Brown had been handed out as the staff members arrived for work. Memories of their anger over William Shawn's crudely handled firing were still relatively fresh, and this latest development seemed likely to ignite another furor. In the minds of the Shawn loyalists, Tina Brown was the quintessential Condé Nast creation and her installation would be the final blow to the seriousness of the magazine. Asked by the *Washington Post* about the staff reaction, one *New Yorker* writer said the reaction to Brown's arrival "sounded the way people sound when they hear of a sudden death—shocked, drained and numb."

Si did little to quell the uneasiness. With publisher Florio by his side, he stood in front of a lectern and announced, "The rumors are true." He then briefly explained, in the vaguest of terms, how he had decided to get rid of Gottlieb. He talked of "evolution" and the magazine's history and how Tina Brown was such a great editor. After the initial introductions and statements, Newhouse said he would entertain questions.

Calvin Trillin, known for his humorous, offhanded manner, was among the first to pose a question. He asked Newhouse to be specific about his differences with Gottlieb. Si dodged that one. Another writer inquired about the pace of change, what Newhouse felt was the appropriate "evolution" for the magazine. Si avoided that one, too.

Dressed in a light-colored summer suit, Newhouse was noticeably uncomfortable as he was then asked by a fact checker what he considered to be the essence of *The New Yorker*. Again, the response was less than satisfying. After pacing and stammering, Newhouse said there was no simple reply. Although he carefully praised Gottlieb, Newhouse responded to one question with the comment that *The New Yorker* was "too text-driven." Phrases like this, while probably appreciated by Alex Liberman, were coolly received at a magazine whose success was based on its mastery of the mother tongue. After more than seven years of grief and turmoil at a magazine that he said he had purchased in order to save, Si Newhouse still seemed unable to give the staff of *The New Yorker* a straight answer. "Everything was vague," a staff writer later commented. "It was language as a smoke screen."

When she arrived later that afternoon, Tina Brown took pains to introduce herself slowly and assure those alarmed by Newhouse's statements that her "first love" was text. She met with a group of editors privately and was later given a tour of the offices by Florio. But there was no grand meeting, no big speeches or promises made. Everything remained low-key and cordial. "I expected difficulty from the staff," she conceded, "but I had none."

The press reaction to Newhouse's changes made front-page news across the country. The fascination with Tina Brown—one of the few women ever to edit a general-interest American magazine—was the central focus of nearly every story. Some were celebratory, while others acted appalled. EDITOR OF GAUDY VANITY FAIR TO RUN STATELY JOURNAL, the *Boston Globe* declared on its front page. Si Newhouse generally refused to talk to the press except to allow himself to be interviewed by the *Times,* insisting that *The New Yorker* was not about to undergo a drastic change. "I do not know what she is going to do, but I know what she is not going to do," Newhouse said. "She is not going to go monthly. She is not going to drop the cartoons. She is not going to have some version of *Vanity Fair* at *The New Yorker.*"

At his hotel room in Japan, Robert Gottlieb watched his long-distance ouster being announced on television when his face flashed on CNN. In the middle of the night, he was awakened by reporters calling from New York City, wanting his reaction. He was the model of sanguineness, almost Gandhi-like in accepting his fate. "I don't want anyone to think that I have been treated badly," he insisted over the telephone. "Si has been extraordinarily generous to me."

Ingrid Sischy, a writer and editor who was on assignment in Japan, joined him the following morning for breakfast. She said Gottlieb wasn't bitter; he seemed almost glad the wait was over. When he returned to New York, he resumed his schedule as editor until Tina Brown took over in the fall.

Under her agreement with Newhouse, Brown worked out an arrangement where she could take off for the whole summer, leaving *Vanity Fair* immediately and planning how she would change *The New Yorker* when she arrived. "I wanted to have the whole summer to reconceive the magazine," Brown said, recalling her conversations with Newhouse. "He obviously would have preferred for me just to go in and start editing. And it was hard on us all. It was hard on Bob Gottlieb, who valiantly continued for three months through the summer, which I think was a very hard thing, and he did it with grace."

Throughout the transition, Gottlieb remained helpful and courteous, perhaps reminded of how traumatizing his own entry to the magazine had been. When she returned from a week's vacation at a Wyoming dude ranch, Brown took a temporary office on the floor below Gottlieb's office. In her own way, she returned the favor by praising Gottlieb's manners and offering her assessment of his tenure. With a slight revisionist spin, she said Gottlieb was a "transitional" editor who had cleared the way for her arrival—almost in the same way, it seemed, John the Baptist had been a "transitional" prophet. Few of the media's accounts mentioned Newhouse's decision five years earlier, when Gottlieb had been presented as the agent of change to lead *The New Yorker*. No matter how wrongheaded Newhouse's assessment may have been then, Tina Brown realized that Newhouse's verdict on Gottlieb, at least this time, was quite correct.

"I think Si's timing was impeccable," she said months later. "He gave Bob a good-enough time; he gave him five years—which is enough time to effect a good and elegant transition—and to give him a sense of whether he could also be an editor for the long run. And in the end, I think Gottlieb will be seen as a great transitional editor for *The New Yorker*. I think it would have been very, very difficult if I had followed Shawn—it would have been impossible for me and for the magazine. And I think Gottlieb's patient and curatorial approach was a very good idea and I think it helped to shore up the magazine's credibility. I think it'll enable me to then take some risks and do some creative things with the magazine and bring on new people and redesign it. Without that period in between, it would have been harder to do and achieved much less acceptance."

Eventually, some staffers noticed that gloom over his departure seeped into Gottlieb's demeanor, even dampened the mood in his kitsch-filled office with the Elvis figurine on his desk, and spilled onto the pages of the magazine. He stopped giving out long-term assignments and printed several of the stories held in the magazine's back inventory until his final issue in late September. Urged by tea-leaf-reading staffers on the magazine, a columnist for *The New York Times* performed a tongue-in-cheek deconstruction of Gottlieb's final issue, searching for several clues to his true feelings. One was the cover illustration itself, which pictured Cinderella losing her slipper at midnight. The *Times*'s translation? "The ball has ended and something is about to turn into a pumpkin," according to its sources. Other clues were found in that issue's cartoons, with more than its usual share of gallows humor. In one cartoon, a happy-looking man walks along the street singing the Broadway show tune "Oh, What a Beautiful Mornin'," with a caption that read: "In Deep Denial."

Gottlieb tried mightily to retain his slightly off-center sense of humor and firmly to deny any remorse. "Of course I'll miss it, but I am also looking forward tremendously to being free of it," the sixty-one-year-old editor told one interviewer. "The older I get, the less need I seem to feel to be a player."

When asked directly how he felt about being fired as the editor of *The New Yorker*, Gottlieb could give only a mystifying allusion to a long-forgotten country-western hit sung twenty years earlier by Donna Fargo. His answer was pure kitsch. As he insisted, "I'm The Happiest Girl in the Whole U.S.A."

The party for *Vanity Fair*'s new editor in chief, Graydon Carter, was barely in full swing when the lights dipped inside Newhouse's new apartment. Then they dipped once more, fully and deliberately.

Although Si and Victoria Newhouse had kept their East Side town house with its expensive art collection for dinner parties and social gatherings, they moved their permanent residence in the early 1990s to a grand duplex inside the UN Plaza. Many of the new staffers, sipping red wine, gawked at the exquisitely designed and spacious apartment, with its white carpets and its own expensive art collection on the walls. The flickering lights were a less-than-subtle hint. It was time to go. Si's bedtime was sometime about 9:00 P.M.; it was necessary for him to get his rest if he was to be at the Condé Nast offices before dawn the next morning.

"At precisely eight o'clock, the lights went off and on, and that was the signal we were all to leave," recalled one of the *Vanity Fair* editors who attended Newhouse's party for his new editor. "He's a little weird that way. He does show up for a surprising number of Condé Nast events. But he's very weird about his hours. They turned off the lights, and then we left."

The selection of Graydon Carter as *Vanity Fair*'s new editor was almost as mysterious.

For many *Vanity Fair* staffers, Carter was synonymous with *Spy* magazine, which Tina Brown strongly attacked after it published her adoring letter to agent Michael Ovitz—a stunt that caused Brown acute embarrassment at a time when she was trying to steer the magazine's reputation away from its Hollywood-obsessed image. She personally blamed Graydon Carter and later charged that the reprinting of the letter was sexist. "Yes, he trashed me," Brown acknowledged after the switch was made, though she claimed to hold no grudges. Yet, the notion that Carter—a man whom Brown had bad-mouthed for months after the Ovitz incident—would be picked as her successor at the magazine she had revived was very curious indeed. Even for the byzantine world of Condé Nast, this route to power was a puzzle.

Edward Graydon Carter was a college dropout who had grown up in Canada, worked at a weekly newspaper that failed, and then came to New

York City in the 1970s, landing a job as a writer for Time-Life magazines. After several jobs within that organization and feeling that he was going nowhere, Carter launched *Spy* magazine with three partners: former *Time* colleague Kurt Andersen; Tom Phillips, son of the chairman of Raytheon; and outside investor Steven Schragis. From the start, their magazine was an often-biting satirical monthly that skewered many of the 1980s icons— many of the same people who were celebrated in the pages of *Vanity Fair*. The magazine proved a remarkable hit, particularly within Manhattan and its environs. At times, *Spy*'s slick issues could be hilarious, a much-needed deflater of the high and mighty; at other times, it could be sophomoric and cruel. Graydon Carter, the somewhat heavyset editor with a sloping, flying wedge haircut, a dandy's wardrobe, and a quick wit, became a media darling to all but his targets. One of *Spy*'s most costly traits, regardless of how endearing to readers, was the ability to scare away potential advertisers with its acid tongue. "We never lost an ad, but I think we're forever closed out of a lot of advertising," Carter said in the early days of *Spy*. "We won't get Ralph Lauren ads or a Helmsley ad." Indeed, the chronic paucity of advertising was a major factor in the eventual decision to sell the magazine to a group of rich investors in 1991.

When the magazine was in its ascendancy under Carter, however, *Spy* gave voice to the angst of history's most indulged generation, the slightly adolescent howl of the pissed-off Yuppie. Its audience was the generation that embraced (yet remained deeply, *hiply* cynical about) the trappings of the Reagan years. Graydon Carter was thirty-six years old when *Spy* debuted in 1986 and was quite comfortable in his role as coeditor and social arbiter, determining who should be ridiculed next. *Spy,* modeled somewhat after *Private Eye* and the other British humor magazines, was a magazine conceived over lunch at the Harvard Club, and it never really wandered far from its elitist roots. "I think it's true that Graydon has always been a bit of a social snob. He's always been an Anglophile, that's true," said a longtime acquaintance. "He has a whole bound collection of *Punch* magazines in his apartment. You'd think when you're in his apartment that you're in a British drawing room. It's wonderful—but it's very English. He always had this sense of who was proper and who wasn't. I always felt it was more a personal code of behavior than a social code. He was very judgmental of people under this sensibility and that's part of the reason why he wanted to do *Spy*."

Such a judgmental air was, upon closer inspection, a tad ironic, for Carter was not above a little résumé puffing and social climbing himself. In attempting to raise money from investors for *Spy* in 1985, Carter claimed that he had a bachelor's degree from Carleton University in Ottawa. He also claimed to have been a speechwriter for former Canadian prime minister Pierre Trudeau and a founder of a successful monthly magazine in Canada before joining *Time*. When a *New York* magazine writer profiled Carter in 1989, however, he discovered *Spy*'s fearless leader had never graduated from Carleton, was unknown among Trudeau's top aides, and that Carter's proud Canadian magazine had actually gone bankrupt. Only when pushed did Carter tell the truth about his past. "When I came to New York, I was broke," Carter confessed, like a repentant bad little boy. "I needed a job. I was desperate. It was too late to go back to school."

Nevertheless, Carter managed to collect an estimated $2.8 million from Schragis and a broad array of investors, several of whom were the heirs to great fortunes and were intrigued by *Spy*'s intent to deflate the self-important. "There is nothing that *Spy* will not presume to understand, many things it will be amused and charmed by, and plenty of things it will mock mercilessly," Carter and his partners said in the business plan they passed around town.

Feasting on both pomp and the powerful, *Spy* enjoyed chronicling the activities of those who inhabited the Condé Nast kingdom, including Si Newhouse himself. Aside from deconstructing the Michael Ovitz "love letter," it picked apart other notable excesses found in Tina Brown's *Vanity Fair,* like the front-cover paean to advertiser Calvin Klein. When speaking of Tina Brown herself, *Spy* was particularly vicious. Her monthly editor's letters provoked hoots of laughter every month in the Condé Nast building, claimed *Spy*, which also pointed out that her new editor's photo "shows Brown looking all morning-after and tousle-haired and, curiously, serves only to highlight her nose, a proboscis that photographs much larger than it actually is." The tone and tenor of Graydon Carter's *Spy* held nothing but contempt for what he pictured as the social-climbing Brown and her craven, self-aggrandizing creation. "In *Vanity Fair,*" *Spy* observed in December 1988, "it's sometimes difficult to tell who is slurping whom."

Spy's comments about Si Newhouse were also irreverent, if a bit more obvious and tame. "His famous aversions to leisure and interaction with other human beings notwithstanding, billionaire monopolist S. I. Newhouse Jr. does, on occasion, put on hard-soled shoes and a collared shirt [to entertain] at his residence," began one *Spy* anecdote about a Newhouse dinner party. Another edition suggested Si had been separated at birth from Bianca Jagger. Sometime in 1988, Si had heard enough enthused talk about *Spy* to express interest in buying it. Still riding the crest of popularity, Carter and his partners fobbed off Newhouse's overture, reportedly before any hard numbers were discussed. By 1990, however, Carter's magazine began to appreciate Newhouse's powerful influence and its comments seemed more deferential, at least in its own way. "Is Si Newhouse a shrewd publisher or a zany one, a virtuous man or a contemptible one?" the magazine once asked. "None of us care, as long as we feel we're inside." In retrospect, the amusing comment was prescient, for Graydon Carter was soon to become an insider himself.

Anna Wintour, the editor of *Vogue* and a savvy observer of New York's social scene, recognized something about Graydon Carter that she considered necessary for her publication dedicated to fashion, design, and international celebrities. To most observers, Wintour's decision to hire him in 1988 as a contributing editor at *Vogue* seemed an odd alliance. For Carter, however, who was married with three children, the allure was obvious: an extra paycheck. Under his deal with Wintour, Carter was contracted to write several features and reviews. "I've done freelance articles for a number of publications—including *Vogue*—and it's never affected the way we report on those magazines," Carter said at the time, forswearing any possible conflict of interest or one of those tacky quid pro quos he found so offensive in *Vanity Fair*. He signed up with *Vogue*, Carter quipped, "to stave off poverty, make a car loan, and pay for my kids' school."

Once inside the Newhouse kingdom, Carter quickly adapted. This same ex-editor of *Spy*, whose magazine wondered "who was slurping whom" at *Vanity Fair*, was now remarkably capable of affecting such a tone himself in his freelance assignments for *Vogue*. Carter would prove he could slurp with the best of 'em. Even the movie stars couldn't tell the difference. When Sylvester Stallone learned that he had been interviewed for *Vogue* by the same man who had once ridiculed him in *Spy*, he was upset and cried foul. "You're kidding!" said the actor who played Rocky and Rambo in the movies. "If murder wasn't against the law, that man would no longer be with us. I try to be as candid as possible with interviewers—maybe he should have been more candid as to his background? I didn't make the connection."

In the hypersensitive atmosphere of La-La land, Graydon Carter's various minor ego-bursting transgressions at *Spy* were perceived as major felonies. The whole concept of Graydon Carter in the miscast role as *Vanity Fair*'s new editor gave shivers to some of Hollywood's most influential movers and shakers, like Warren Beatty, who made a point of publicly expressing his concern. If Hollywood really objected to Carter, it might impede *Vanity Fair*'s ability to get big stars to appear on its cover and hurt sales in shopping malls and grocery stores, where many impulse purchases of magazines are made.

But these concerns didn't matter by the summer of 1992, for inside Condé Nast, the ascension of Graydon Carter to *Vanity Fair* was recognized as a masterstoke quietly engineered by an emerging power within the company, Anna Wintour. How she pulled off such a coup was a crucial lesson in why many insiders believed she—and not the more celebrated Tina Brown—might someday wind up as the heir to Alexander Liberman, overseeing Newhouse's array of glossy magazines as the company's editorial director. Wintour's prevailing influence on the future of *Vanity Fair* went largely undetected.

Graydon Carter's selection was trumpeted by Condé Nast's formidable spin machine once Si Newhouse made his final decision. His selection was publicly seconded by Tina Brown, who, for the record, praised him as a good choice. Brown and Carter were trotted out for the smiling press photos and Si gave his usual pharaoh-like responses to friendly interviewers.

Wintour's sponsorship of Graydon Carter also underlined her eye for talent and bringing it into the company. Despite his aggressive image, Carter impressed many within the organization, including Newhouse himself, who got to meet him at various parties and Condé Nast soirees. When he dropped his editorial meat-ax, Carter could be a charming conversationalist—gregarious, cultured, and informed. He demonstrated his range with a wide variety of stories for *Vogue,* done in the Condé Nast style. After he left *Spy* in 1991, Carter showed his managerial ability by overhauling *The New York Observer* and bringing much-needed zest to that peach-colored weekly. During Carter's short tenure there, it became a knowledgeable must-read on culture and politics for Manhattan's mediaphiles, which include many inside the Condé Nast building. Carter may have charmed Si Newhouse with his Peck's Bad Boy image, but what was truly impressive was his demonstrable ability to infuse life into an editorial basket case—a skill that Newhouse treasured among his top editors.

With Tina Brown's departure, *Vanity Fair* would need a vibrant new editor who could keep the engine steaming and perhaps set a new course for the future. It seemed like a good idea to Wintour at least. So when the moment was correct, Wintour, like a good charm-school teacher helping along the progress of her star pupil, suggested Graydon Carter's name to Newhouse. Friends and close associates of Carter were convinced that Wintour got him the job at *Vanity Fair.* "Absolutely, I'm sure," said one longtime colleague. "He had a contract to work for *Vogue* and he's friendly with Wintour. I believe that's how he was brought into the organization. Si was familiar with him and so was Tina. It was not as though he was an unknown to a lot of people over there. But I presume, if he has a rabbi or mentor, it was Anna."

Just as Alex Liberman had done for decades, Anna Wintour had learned to confide her thoughts to Newhouse privately, urging a suggested name or concept that he would turn into reality. Inside Condé Nast, the trick was knowing what was best for Si Newhouse *and* oneself. Those who realized what was going on in the selection of a new *Vanity Fair* editor marveled at Wintour's adroit, discreet powers of persuasion. "If you're Machiavellian, which one tends to be in that company, maybe she wanted him because she felt he would be good but not as good as Tina and therefore not a threat to her," said one editor who knows or worked for Carter, Brown, and Wintour at various times. "I always heard the reason why he's writing for *Vogue*—and he is a good writer—but she hired him in part because it neutralized *Spy* as far as she was concerned."

There was a sudden swiftness to Newhouse's decision-making once the agonizing deliberations over *The New Yorker* ended with Gottlieb's departure. Si's demand for a yes-or-no answer within a few days caught Tina Brown without a ready replacement. As a strong hands-on editor, she didn't like to delegate too much responsibility, a luxury that her monthly magazine's schedule could afford. At *Vanity Fair,* she enjoyed the company of her top writers and was also excellent at the visual part of the magazine, especially at choosing each month's cover photo. Under Tina Brown, there was no heir apparent waiting in the wings. "Si basically pressured Tina into it," said a *Vanity Fair* staffer who later discussed it with her. "She wanted more time to think about it, and he insisted that she give an answer very quickly. Obviously, not a lot of thought had been given to who would take over at *Vanity Fair.* There was no one on staff who would have been logical, so someone else had to be brought into the picture. As I understand it, Graydon was a friend of Anna's, and he wrote for Anna and Anna recommended him to Si for the job. Things moved very quickly after that."

To Tina's loyal partisans at *Vanity Fair,* Graydon Carter was a snide usurper who used to insult them. His appointment simply appalled them. After nearly a decade of running *Vanity Fair,* Tina Brown had earned the opportunity to move to *The New Yorker.* But she had also earned the right to help name her successor at the magazine she had made into the hottest, most talked-about publication of a generation. It seemed incredible to some that Newhouse had already made up his mind on Carter before he offered Brown the job at *The New Yorker.* Tina Brown later said the former editor of *Spy* was on her short list of potential names for successor, but most believed Graydon Carter was far from her first choice.

When the question of Wintour's intervention was posed in an interview, Brown, usually brimming with informed insights, seemed defensive and unsure of herself. "I don't know," she said, after being asked whether Anna Wintour had originally suggested Graydon Carter's name to Newhouse. After a moment's pause, she then insisted Newhouse alone was the discoverer of Graydon Carter's potential. "Si wouldn't have to have Graydon suggested to him, that's what I mean about Newhouse really being an insider," Brown said. "Si was perfectly aware of what Graydon was doing at *The New York Observer* and liked it. So I'm sure the choice was Si's. Graydon needed no introduction to him. He knew him very well. He knew him socially and he knew his work."

When in doubt, Tina Brown tended to go with her favorite public portrayal of Si Newhouse—the all-knowing Wizard of Publishing. Most of the Condé Nast munchkins, tittering in the background, knew better. In effect, Brown's chief rival within the company, Anna Wintour, had been the major influence in naming the new successor at *Vanity Fair,* not Brown herself. Wintour's preeminence within Si Newhouse's inner circle, his willingness to seek and adhere to her advice, was such that he allowed this transition to occur without Brown's full support, perhaps not realizing some of the consequences. "One of the great truths you'll stumble upon about Si Newhouse is that there is less there than meets the eye," said one *Vanity Fair* editor. "Si Newhouse doesn't bring Graydon aboard because he wants Graydon to bring a new snap to *Vanity Fair;* the only reason he does is because Anna says it's a good idea or a couple of others do and he's met Graydon and Graydon's charming. He's done *The Observer,* which is elegant, and he cuts an elegant figure. If anything, Graydon told us, the only directive from Si was, 'Please just don't become *mean.*' "

In once more bringing change within his magazine empire, Si Newhouse had finally avoided the public spectacle of previous firings, those dreadful decapitations for which he had become notorious. Gottlieb was gentlemanly enough to walk the plank without a whimper. But with the solution to one problem came myriad other complications, not the least Brown's apparent resentment of Graydon Carter's selection as editor of *Vanity Fair,* the magazine to which she had all but given birth. Whether a new, kinder, and gentler Graydon Carter was preferable at *Vanity Fair* than the old hellraiser of the Reagan years would be a source of debate for months to come. While he played the amiable good sport, however, Carter fumed privately at the way he claimed Tina Brown, over at *The New Yorker,* seemed to be torpedoing him. Despite their own denials, friends and enemies acknowledged a mutual enmity between Brown and her successor. As one of Graydon Carter's closest friends observed, "They probably spend way too much time wishing the other ill."

William Shawn died quietly of a heart attack in December 1992, about two months after the much-publicized arrival of Tina Brown at his beloved magazine. Shawn's passing served as a reminder of the magazine's glorious past and of the many unnerving questions surrounding its future.

From her very first issue in early October, Tina Brown served notice that she intended on shaking up this dust-filled temple to the written word. Her debut cover featured an Edward Sorel cartoon of a bare-chested punk rocker being carried in Central Park by the mortified driver of a hansom. This sort of tension between the old and new at *The New Yorker* was a constant during Brown's transition. While she introduced photographs on a regular basis, for instance, she also revived the magazine's original Caslon typeface and returned to the use of decorative art from the days of Harold Ross as part of her new redesign. She was willing to run lengthy in-depth pieces as before, but she also increased the frequency of short items and more topical insights in the "Talk of the Town" section. And while she eased out some longtime staff writers by not renewing their contracts (Washington correspondent Elizabeth Drew among the most prominent who were let go), Brown also incorporated familiar names from *Vanity Fair* and other publications into her revised table of contents.

With Shawn's death, Tina Brown allowed a proper tribute to his memory with a twelve-page retrospective entitled "Remembering Mr. Shawn," which appeared in the final issue of 1992. The vivid recollections of his former staff, still fresh in mind more than five years after he had departed, underscored Shawn's lasting influence and the pureness of his undistracted vision. The comparisons with the present were obvious. As John Updike observed, "What was right was doubly right, somehow—aesthetics and ethics coincided—in the universe of his gentle implications. His adamancy of taste had been hardened in a buried moral fire, and his *New Yorker* was a realm from which many types of unseemliness were exluded." Robert Gottlieb, who had yet to comment meaningfully on his own tenure, remarked about the convenant of mutual trust he had discovered between Shawn and the magazine's readers. "Perhaps his most significant contribution to journalism lay in the triumph of his passionate and uncynical view of what a publication and its readers can mean to each other—a view unique in our time," Gottlieb wrote. For writers like Calvin Trillin, Shawn was a joy, a great listener with an intuitive gift for getting right to the point of a story. "The writer didn't have to worry about being second-guessed by somebody at a dinner party who had third-hand information and a confident manner," Trillin said. "Shawn wouldn't have been at the dinner party."

Afterward, Garrison Keillor, another well-known contributor, said the tribute to Shawn was a funeral dirge for the magazine "bought by a billionaire . . . who has ended the long tradition of editorial independence there." Keillor said he refused to work for Tina Brown because she simply didn't understand the essence of the magazine. *"The New Yorker* is a glorious and dear American institution, but Ms. Brown, like so many Brits, seems most fascinated by the passing carnival and celebrity show in America. Fiction, serious reporting, the personal essay, criticism, all that made *The New Yorker* great, do not engage her interest apparently. She has redesigned it into a magazine that looks and reads an awful lot like a hundred other magazines. The best writing to appear in Ms. Brown's *New Yorker,* in fact, was the section of tributes to William Shawn, which read like an obituary for *The New Yorker."*

If anything, Tina Brown was a bit perplexed by all the fuss. She believed the magazine was moving toward certain extinction unless she did something to enliven its pages and make it readable for a new audience. As was abundantly clear, she didn't envision herself becoming anonymous or encumbered in any other way by Shawn's memory. She would pay the proper lip service to his legacy of editorial independence, but not at the expense of being realistic. And part of being realistic was staying friendly with the advertisers. The same month as Shawn's death, for instance, Brown attended a party for advertiser Calvin Klein, where the new *New Yorker* editor was introduced as one of several fashion celebs paying homage to the designer. In interviews, Brown preferred to compare herself instead with another predecessor at *The New Yorker,* founding editor Harold Ross, whose jazzy sensibility she wanted to update. "Basically, my whole thrust has been to go back to Ross's magazine," she said. "It gave a writerly, newsy, interesting, intriguing feel to the contents rather than having the contents that were overpresented on a plate. . . . That's really all gone from *The New Yorker,* largely because the length of the articles really grew and grew and grew and because they really ate into the space that Ross had allocated for the really short material. I felt that was really lacking in the current *New Yorker* because there really wasn't a place to be fresh and responsive and short."

It was a brilliant public-relations move, claiming a return to the original roots of the magazine under Harold Ross, by then dead for more than forty years, and deflecting any direct comparison with Shawn's era. As she defined it, Brown was going to try something new but very much in *The New Yorker* tradition, as the spiritual heir to Harold Ross. Who could argue under this equation? Such deft positioning once again showcased her talents as a masterful manipulator of opinion, both the creator and custodian of her own literary legend. When she left *Vanity Fair,* Brown essentially wrote her own epitaph in her farewell editor's letter, enrapturing her tenure there with the grandest of spins. "*V.F.* is the quintessential postmodern magazine," Brown wrote, offering only the vaguest definition of what she meant by a *postmodern* magazine. "It is the great high-low show, able to deliver Rosanne Barr mud-wrestling side by side with Chancellor Kohl cogitating, or Demi Moore's pregnant belly side by side with Martha Graham's dance aesthetic. It is a cross-cultural synthesis that adds up to more than the sum of its parts. It is all about context, and the context of *Vanity Fair* is conducive to reading."

To assist her at *The New Yorker,* Brown brought along Maurie Perl, who once worked as Barbara Walters's press agent before she moved to *Vanity Fair.* Perl became the first formal publicity agent for *The New Yorker* in its history. Shawn never needed a press spokesperson, but Brown was convinced of the necessity. Good press clips meant good word of mouth, which was always good for business. When interviewed by a writer for the *Columbia Journalism Review,* Brown summoned an assistant to fetch an essay written about Shawn's *New Yorker* by a onetime contributor, Seymour Krim, who had complained of the magazine's intransigence two decades earlier. "The virility, adventurousness, (and) connection with the living tissue of your audience can only be restored by rebirth," wrote Krim in the copy handed out by Tina Brown. "This is not about to happen in the near future and could only occur after the present New Yorker trust fades away and twenty years hence stirs the fires of someone who buys the title and then is animated, directed, by the legend of a memorable past joined with a love for the living present." The implication was fairly clear: Si Newhouse was the savior alluded to in Krim's prophecy, and Tina Brown was the instrument of Newhouse's destiny. If there were enough comparisons to Harold Ross, perhaps she could avoid the difficulties of being compared with Shawn, the burden Gottlieb had faced when he arrived.

"We all feel that presence of Shawn in the best sense of the word," Brown said in an interview months after his death. "For me, it has not been the oppressive presence that it was for Robert Gottlieb. For Bob, it was quite intolerable many, many times, with that pressure. By the time I got here, most of that kind of emotion was gone. They found that I was willing to run a big two-part series and longer pieces and keep all the best writers, and have people like Oliver Sacks and Calvin Trillin in the magazine and nurture those people rather than firing them. As that message got out, everything's been fine. It's been a remarkably untraumatic transition. I had expected a great deal more aggravation."

If there were any lasting concerns among the editorial staff, it was that Brown would allow the magazine's business side to breach the immutable wall that Shawn had so carefully erected. More than any single characteristic, this inviolate trust—that nothing would be done except for its own literary or journalistic merit—distinguished *The New Yorker* from other publications and epitomized the very best ethic of American journalism. As one reporter wrote of the staff's mood following the arrival of Brown: "The paramount concern expressed by *New Yorker* writers is that they remain free to express their own opinions and that an absolute separation continue between their editorial domain and the magazine's business side."

This genuine editorial autonomy emerged as one of the magazine's great hallmarks, a standard that became quite influential during American journalism's high-water mark of the late 1970s and early 1980s—the post-Watergate era, when even advertising directors and other business people accepted the idea of an ethical barrier separating a major publication's financial interests from its editorial pages and sense of public service. At its peak, *The New Yorker*'s prosperity was not the result of riding the trendy waves of the zeitgeist. To the contrary, much of its financial success derived from a certain uniqueness, the clarity of its voice and good judgment in separating the timeless from the temporal, the truly important from the passing fancy. There were no obvious sellouts, no thinly veiled agendas. Pushing advertisers' products in stories, conducting endless marketing reserach, starting a magazine to fulfill a demographic niche—in short, the very hallmarks of the Condé Nast sensibility—were antithetical to Shawn's approach.

With Tina Brown, however, that tradition would no longer be observed as it once was under Shawn. In one sense, the magazine's dire financial problems forced her to be more accommodating to advertisers. The dramatic decline in advertising and the increased costs of trying to build circulation had apparently turned the magazine into a money loser. Through a series of television commercials and other promotions, the magazine's circulation rose under Gottlieb's tenure from 500,000 to 620,000 by the time he left, yet it apparently failed to enthuse advertisers. Brown wouldn't talk about exact figures, but she didn't hide the magazine's financial problems, either. Asked about her goals a few months after she arrived, Brown said, "We would like to see it in profit in five years."

Tina Brown became one of the magazine's major attractions. She was as emblematic of this era's approach to journalism as Woodward and Bernstein had been to a previous generation. With mail solicitations trumpeting the new editor, subscribers could pay only sixteen dollars for one year's worth of weekly issues—a figure way below the ninety-seven dollars paid on the newsstand and considered the lowest price before the Audit Bureau of Circulation would no longer count it as paid circulation. By trying to attract new readers with lower prices and by hawking Brown's arrival, *The New Yorker* hoped to increase its circulation base beyond 650,000 rapidly, perhaps raising circulation someday to the level of 1 million readers, as Brown had done with *Vanity Fair*. "For only 32¢ an issue, *The New Yorker* brings you the best cartoons, humor, fiction, reporting and Tina Brown . . . the best magazine editor in the country," the direct-mail cards touted.

The selling of Tina Brown's fame, at least from the tone of the magazine's promotions, seemed as important a commodity as anything else it had to offer. Coming from the worlds of Condé Nast and British journalism, Brown was accustomed to pushing her wares with advertisers, all part of working toward a magazine's success. The blurring of the lines between editorial and advertising didn't seem to alarm her as it might have an editor from within the magazine, where the concepts of editorial autonomy were much different from those found on Fleet Street or in Newhouse fashion glossies. Those steeped in Shawn's standards quickly noticed the change. As Patti Hagan, a former fact checker at the magazine and *Wall Street Journal* columnist, told the *Columbia Journalism Review:* "I'm most turned off by Marky Mark having sex in Calvin Klein's ads at the front of the book, followed a few weeks later by a signed [Susan Orlean] 'Talk of the Town' interview with Marky Mark about his underwear ads. This would never happen at the old *New Yorker*." Surely, Shawn would have objected to the florid-smelling perfume "scent strips" that Florio had installed shortly after Brown arrived—a move that readers so vehemently opposed the magazine was forced to stop using them.

Another highly touted campaign was the effort to introduce designer Gianni Versace to the pages of *The New Yorker*. Before Brown left, Versace's advertising had appeared in *Vanity Fair*. His stylish, trendy promotions were aimed at a youth-minded clientele with plenty of money, exactly the kind Brown was hoping to bring along with her to *The New Yorker*. When she arrived, the magazine acted with remarkable zeal to lure Versace's advertising for her new venue.

Much of the effort to secure Versace took place before his upcoming appearance at the awards presentation held by the Council of Fashion Designers of America. Less than two weeks after running a front-page obituary on Shawn's death, *The New York Times* printed a short little item, written matter-of-factly, briefly noting that the Italian clothes designer had "tapped" the new editor of *The New Yorker* to write a two-hundred-word biographical sketch of him for the presentation. The *Times* didn't seem to blink at this unprecedented development, certainly not in the way it had given front-page treatment to Alastair Reid's ethical transgression a decade earlier. Nor did the magazine's "business side," as Tina Brown later put it, seem to think she would be troubled about writing an ode to an advertiser.

When she read the Versace announcement in the *Times,* however, Brown says she was irritated and refused to do it, though not in a way that would offend the advertiser. Slowly, she realized how these ethical compromises could impair her reputation. After much criticism, she had developed a greater sensitivity to these sort of ethical issues in American journalism, especially after the sharp attacks on her Ralph Lauren and Calvin Klein cover stories at *Vanity Fair.* This sort of high-minded "church-state" issue was exactly the kind of journalistic mallet used by her detractors in comparing her with the venerated William Shawn. Soon after Brown arrived at *The New Yorker,* for instance, the magazine indicated that it would reduce the use of advertorials, which Florio had introduced after Newhouse purchased the magazine. (Advertorials did continue to appear through 1993, however.) "We reduced them. I don't like them," Brown said, more mindful of appearances. "I think they are sometimes confusing between advertising and editorial. You have to understand, though, that *The New Yorker* was doing not well enough to turn anything away, to be honest."

The effort to lure Gianni Versace was in full swing by the time the fashion designers show hit town in early February 1993. *The New Yorker* prepared a lavish party at Le Cirque for Versace, hosted by Brown. Inside the restaurant, on one of its walls, an elaborate tribute featured a larger-than-life photograph of model Naomi Campbell taken as part of Versace's latest advertising campaign. As much as the party celebrated his fashion award, it also marked *The New Yorker*'s success in landing the designer's ad campaign. Versace left *Vanity Fair* for what he said would be at least six months and appeared instead in the new Tina Brown–led magazine. This well-publicized departure was a blow to *Vanity Fair* at a time when many marketing analysts wondered whether up-front advertisers would stick with the magazine under Graydon Carter. "We have no reason to believe we won't be carrying Versace again in the future," said a *Vanity Fair* spokeswoman at the time. But there were no assurances Versace would return, either.

The New Yorker's success with Versace was seen as a competitive shot across the bow at Carter's shop, one of many cross-company exchanges in the difficult transition at the two magazines. Eventually, Brown learned to use the "church-state" issue in her favor, to suggest her journalistic ethics were purer than those of other editors, like her successor at *Vanity Fair.* "For instance, I've never been to the collections, the fashion collections," said Brown. "Graydon Carter—all of the editors—go to those collections to see advertisers. I never went. I didn't have to go. I got the ads anyway."

Even before Brown's arrival, things had started to change. As a top editor during Brown's tenure noticed, "the awful truth was that in the last five years, all of the church and state things had come to fall down." For all of her public assurances, though, Brown certainly had allowed her editorial staff to blur its ethical traditions, as well. The salute to Versace was part of a new tradition emerging at *The New Yorker,* a place where the business types were once forbidden to enter the editorial offices. Perhaps most noticeably, the Versace advertising campaign was shot by Richard Avedon, who only a few months earlier had been named by Brown as *The New Yorker*'s chief photographer. As part of his deal with the magazine, the extraordinarily talented lensman, by then sixty-nine years old, agreed to no other assignments for a year with any other magazine. The sense of bringing art to a magazine like *The New Yorker* appealed to him, in a way that he felt was no longer possible at *Vogue,* where the artistry of Diana Vreeland had been eroded by the desire for mass circulation. (At least this was the version Avedon offered after Anna Wintour eased him out as *Vogue*'s top photographer.) By accepting an offer from Tina Brown, Wintour's chief rival at Condé Nast, Avedon made a dramatic reemergence, swathed in the glory of being named *The New Yorker*'s first photographer, a sterling opportunity for an acknowledged master to showcase his craft. But in agreeing to work for only one magazine, Avedon continued as a commercial photographer, as well. An inherent conflict quickly developed.

The first two issues in February 1993 demonstrated Avedon's attempt to straddle the once-insurmountable ethical boundaries at *The New Yorker.* In the February first issue, a stark black-and-white photograph of Audrey Hepburn appeared in a salute to the actress who had recently died. That week, Avedon apparently was working for the editorial side. The following week, however, his work appeared again in the magazine, this time as part of a ten-page glossy advertising supplement for Gianni Versace. An even more confusing example—in which ads and editorial copy were virtually identical—could be found in Avedon's picture of a model wearing Versace's latest creations, which appeared on the August 1993 cover of *Vogue España.* A portfolio of Avedon's photos was used inside that Spanish-language edition as an editorial feature. (Of course, these Avedon shots seemed to contradict Tina Brown's claim that his work for *The New Yorker* would be exclusive.) Two months later, however, these same photos found their way into *The New Yorker,* published as an advertisement by Versace in the October eleventh issue. It was the first time in anyone's memory that the magazine had featured a centerfold layout, with a bare-breasted model wearing nothing but black leather boots, fishnet stockings, and a black see-through chemise.

When asked about a possible conflict between his two roles, Avedon mirrored the ambiguity of his longtime employer, Condé Nast, on such matters. "It's not a conflict," Avedon told the press, distilling the very essence of the Newhouse concept in his explanation. "It's a tradition. I've done ads for Revlon, Calvin Klein, Dior in the same issues of *Vogue* as my editorial pictures. An advertising assignment is one thing and editorial is another. I'm enough of a split personality to handle both sides of that little issue."

Once upon a time at *The New Yorker,* that "little issue," as Avedon put it, was a rather important principle, a source of pride for Shawn and his staff, who felt the magazine's deliberate lack of self-promotion in a world of gimmicks was part of its appeal. In another respect, though, Avedon's appraisal was correct. Under Si Newhouse's ownership, a new tradition did prevail, where commerce and journalism blend, where what was acceptable at *Vogue* was now equally acceptable at *The New Yorker.* For all of the heralded clarity of his beautiful photographs, Avedon didn't seem to grasp the fundamental conflicts in his different roles—how this might confuse the reader and how these compromises could ultimately affect the magazine's credibility. Instead, all Avedon could offer was a glib shrug of the shoulders. "Thanks to Versace, as we head for apocalypse, at least we'll be well dressed," he said.

Writers at the magazine also got into the act. Soon after she arrived, Brown objected to some staffers giving paid lectures for advertisers, including one longtime *New Yorker* writer who went with his family on a cruise financed by an advertiser. Perhaps the most complex battle on this issue occurred when Holly Brubach, the *New Yorker*'s fashion writer, agreed to pose for an advertising campaign for The Gap, a trendy retailer with stores found in many American shopping malls. (The Gap's ad campaign had long featured various celebrities and notables wearing their denim or khakis.) A full-page advertisement appeared in the May 1993 issue of *Harper's Bazaar,* with a photograph of Brubach wearing a ribbed blouse marked "$14.50." She was described in the ad simply as "fashion critic."

"She passionately wanted to do it," recalled Brown later. "I didn't like it at all; I really didn't. But she really wanted to do it and so I said, 'Okay, Holly, then you can't mention *The New Yorker.*' " When the *Times* questioned the propriety of "a reporter who covers fashion also helping to hawk one company's clothes," *The New Yorker*'s spokeswoman, Maurie Perl, explained it was permissible under Tina Brown's rules as long as she didn't use the magazine's name. After all, the magazine was now using its fabled name to hawk its own brand of sweatshirts and beach towels. Whatever moral qualms the *Times* may have had about Brubach's stint as a model apparently didn't last long. In October 1993, four months after the Gap ad, the *Times Magazine* announced its new style editor: Holly Brubach.

For her part, Brubach said the Gap ad had been approved earlier by

Gottlieb and was only part of a much larger dispute with Tina Brown. "In fact, Tina gave me her permission at the time and gave me no indication that she was against it," said Brubach, who was hired by Gottlieb in 1988. "You think of the Gap as a supermarket for fashion, and I really don't take it any more seriously than that I'm afraid, so I don't see a conflict." Brubach said her differences with Brown were over much more fundamental journalistic issues in the way fashion was written about in *The New Yorker*. In essence, Brubach said Brown wanted her to write favorable profiles about designers who advertised in the magazine. When she refused to do so, Brubach said she was on a collision course with Brown and her last two pieces for the magazine were killed.

"We had conversations about pieces that she wanted to be done, which one could impute a certain advertising motive to and that were not pieces that interested me to write," Brubach said. "Even if they couldn't afford to turn any advertising away, that doesn't mean you suddenly change your policy about how you're covering a field. *The New Yorker* had a certain respect in the fashion industry that had to do with the fact that it could not be bought."

Before Tina Brown's arrival, Brubach wrote about fashion in the same way it had been covered by her predecessor, Kennedy Fraser, and by others during Shawn's regime—with a certain detachment that angered some designers and sometimes banished Brubach to the back row at the unveiling of the following season's collections. "I think that became a real problem for Tina in terms of advertising. The fashion press is essentially a publicity organ for the industry and I refused to write about it in those terms," said Brubach. "I looked at fashion as a much broader subject—not only as what walked down the runways but as the clothes that people wore in a sort of anthropological investigation. And I think Tina was much more interested in covering the industry as a hotbed of glamour and celebrity."

Brubach said Brown's experience at *Vanity Fair* and the criticism she received from American media for her fawning treatment of advertisers had made her more aware of such ethical issues. "She doesn't come from a tradition that has these types of scruples," said Brubach. "I think she was just naïve about it." She pointed to Brown's courting of Gianni Versace and the dual role of Richard Avedon as examples where the old traditions of *The New Yorker* had given way to the new sensibilities of Tina Brown. The ethical judgments under Brown were moving close to those in magazines devoted to "fashion, which is a totally corrupt tradition to begin with," said Brubach.

These contradictory accounts about Brown and Brubach only made clear the extent to which the simple journalistic conventions of William Shawn no longer applied. At best, *The New Yorker*'s ethical standards were part of the on-the-job training for Brown. As she acknowledged, the accommodations made to advertisers and marketing at Newhouse's fashion magazines were very different from the journalistic traditions at

The New Yorker. "It *is* a different tradition," Brown replied when asked about ethical compromises. "But I will also say Si Newhouse is very smart and he would never expect me to do it. He would never want me to or expect me to. And I haven't had to. There's been nothing in the magazine that's been about pushing the advertisers. I just don't do it. It's not right. *The New Yorker* is a whole different animal to Condé Nast."

For all of the genuine concerns about Tina Brown's motives, there was an undeniable sense that *The New Yorker* had become more interesting to read, more appealing to the eye, and more talked about than any other magazine in America. Many writers found that Brown, despite her reputation as a sophisticate, could be an easy person with whom to discuss or share ideas. "She's the first nonneurotic editor in *The New Yorker's* history," quipped one old hand, more than a little seriously.

When she left *Vanity Fair,* Brown brought along some of her best writers, like James Wolcott, Marie Brenner, and Stephen Schiff, and purposely recruited other top-flight journalists, like James Stewart, the Pulitzer Prize–winning reporter and editor for *The Wall Street Journal,* and author Ken Auletta. As one of her top editors, she hired Hendrick Hertzberg, an editor at *The New Republic,* who only a few years earlier wrote that *The New Yorker*'s greatness had faded under Newhouse's ownership. Hertzberg was hired to write the new "Comment" section at the front of the magazine; this former speechwriter for President Jimmy Carter became a dauntless defender of his new boss in public. When a critical *Columbia Journalism Review* article about Tina Brown's *New Yorker* appeared, Hertzberg accused the author, Eric Utne, of being unfair, sexist, and of other journalistic high crimes.

With Bill Clinton's election as President, Brown made every effort to adapt to the new administration and to the nation's changing mood under a Democrat. After relieving Elizabeth Drew of her duties as the magazine's Washington correspondent, Brown hired Sidney Blumenthal, also a writer at *The New Republic,* as the replacement. She encouraged Blumenthal, who was considered very sympathetic to Clinton's cause during the 1992 campaign, to ingratiate her magazine with the White House's new crowd. In one fax to Blumenthal, which was purloined and passed around liberally among the Capital's press corps, Brown wrote that she and her husband wanted to attend the inauguration. "How does one do this?" she asked.

Tina Brown didn't need any lessons in how to enliven a magazine, however. From her first issues, which introduced some of the magazine's new writers, Brown tried to continually offer a new delight or provocation, not only with stories but with Avedon's often-spectacular photographs and with more biting cartoons and illustrations. Undeniably, for good or ill, people were once again talking about *The New Yorker.*

"Ms. Brown is clearly bent on shaking things up, yet holding on to some fundamentals," said *New York Times* critic Walter Goodman, who wrote a generally favorable review of Tina Brown's first issue, summarizing the mild changes. The next issue's cover was more provocative, offering a montage portrait of Malcolm X, his stern, almost-angry gaze representing a far departure from the magazine's usual idyllic, bemused sensibility of old. America was an angrier, more urbanized place, with race relations still one of its most immutable problems. Brown said her magazine would cover racial tensions rather than acting as though they didn't exist. In her distinctive fashion, she even ignited her own race controversy. When another illustration by Art Spiegelman pictured a Hasidic man kissing an African-American woman as a St. Valentine's Day fancy in February 1993, there was outrage expressed by both Jewish and black communities, compelling the media to follow the tempest. Brown replied that it was one of her best-selling covers. In its anniversary issue later that month, with the transition in full swing, *The New Yorker* offered various different artistic interpretations of Eustace Tilley—the famed dandy who represented *The New Yorker*—including an Art Spiegelman rendition in which the old boy is cut up and pasted together in jagged parts, perhaps an unintended comment on the new changes at the magazine.

Almost each week now, Brown's *New Yorker* managed to draw some comment from the press or discussion on the cocktail circuit. While she was capable of an occasional stunt or lapse in taste, there were some outstanding in-depth pieces of journalism that appeared in the magazine, like Seymour Hersh's "Nixon's Last Cover-Up," Fred Dannen's exposé on Chinese gangs, and David Remnick's reporting on Russia. Veteran journalist Paul Brodeur offered a lengthy exposé on the health dangers of radiation from high-voltage transmission lines near a California school. Almost an entire issue in December 1993 was devoted to the extraordinary account by Mark Danner of the massacre of 143 children and civilians at El Mozote and the U.S. government's successful disinformation campaign with the press in order to keep money flowing to El Salvador's regime.

At the same time, "The Talk of The Town" became more topical and less arch in style (dropping the "A friend writes . . . " construction) and there was more reliance on "casuals" and other short items to add to the magazine's overall presentation. Some of the older critics under Gottlieb were gradually replaced with a livelier crew. The regular presence of fiction began to fade from the mix under Tina Brown, until one March 1993 issue carried no short stories at all—the first time since 1946, when the magazine devoted an entire issue to John Hersey's *Hiroshima*. In June 1994, however, Brown announced a special double issue devoted to fiction, explaining that fiction "always has been, and always will be, as essential to the body and soul of *The New Yorker* as essays and reporting, reviews and cartoons."

Regardless of the great fears and trepidation about Tina Brown's stewardship, she proved all but her most ardent critics wrong with her relatively smooth transition of style and mixture of new and familiar writers. Not all of her transplants took to the unfamiliar terrain, however, notably Alexander Chancellor, an editor at London's *The Independent* newspaper who was imported to improve "The Talk of the Town" feature in the front section. Chancellor was one of several Brits hired by Brown at the magazine (such as English writer Martin Amis as tennis correspondent and *The Independent*'s Sunday film critic Anthony Lane to replace *The New Yorker*'s Michael Sragow). When she appointed him, Chancellor was given a lucrative salary and later a book deal with Brown's husband, Harry Evans, at Random House, to write a volume about his experiences in America. "I don't think he will be an annoyingly British voice," said Brown. "I think he will be a dry, droll voice, but very much connected to America in the same way as Alastair Cooke has been."

Despite these grand hopes, Chancellor had a less-than-auspicious beginning. Among some staff members who commented on his constant befuddlement, Chancellor earned the nickname "Stockdale," an allusion to the white-haired admiral who ran as Ross Perot's 1992 vice presidential candidate. There were a few embarrassing moments, such as when Chancellor tried to run an item about the arrival of a large Christmas tree at Rockefeller Center—a familiar Yuletide ritual to most New Yorkers but touted as news by the unfamiliar Brit. (Fortunately, he was persuaded otherwise and that item didn't appear.) A more embarrassing incident occurred when Chancellor printed an unsigned "Talk of the Town" piece about the trial of former East German leader Erich Honecker. As the man who had authorized the construction of the Berlin Wall, Honecker presided over one of the most repressive regimes within the old Soviet Union's bloc of nations. Yet in this piece, he was portrayed as a once-great Communist idealist, an enfeebled old man who, rather than the murderer of thirteen people who were killed trying to escape his republic, was actually a scapegoat for unified Germany's current woes. "He is not tall, but his back is straight, a symbol of incorruptibility in Germany," as the piece described Honecker, who was now "the remains of a hero, the aftermath of heroism."

After that four-page profile appeared, *Newsweek* pointed out that its author was Irene Dische, who just happened to be married to Honecker's chief defense attorney. At first, Tina Brown defended her "Talk of the Town" from any conflict-of-interest charge. "The issue is the integrity, not the identity, of the author," Brown said. After much further criticism of the Honecker item, Brown acknowledged her error. "She had written for *The New Yorker* before, so questions were not asked that should have been asked," she conceded. Shortly afterward, Chancellor left *The New Yorker*.

As a talented and very public personality, Brown was a target of more than her fair share of anonymous gossip and envious darts. But she was also capable of her own strong biases and, when sufficiently provoked, would jump out of the literary high grass to mount a vicious assault. One of the most acrimonious confrontations took place within her first month as *The New Yorker*'s editor, when the writer John Le Carré accused Brown of printing a scathing article about an upcoming biography of Rupert Murdoch. Readers were never informed that Harry Evans was portrayed unflatteringly in the book, Le Carré accused. Tina Brown's failure to reveal her conflict of interest was, Le Carré said, "one of the ugliest pieces of partisan journalism that I have witnessed in a long life of writing."

The Murdoch biography was written by William Shawcross, a friend of Le Carré, and makes only brief mention of Evans's tenure at the Sunday *Times* of London, though the book did question whether Evans had the "mental and physical stamina needed" to be the newspaper's editor. Harry Evans had written his own critical book in the mid-1980s about working for Murdoch at *The Times*. But Evans wasn't pining for a fight, at least not in public, on the Shawcross book. In his statement to the press, Evans later described himself as "simply a pass-through character in the Shawcross book anyway" and claimed he was "perfectly relaxed about it." However, Evans's wife was far from calm about it. When Le Carré made his charges, Brown quickly put on her full battlefield regalia and launched a barrage of ad hominem attacks through a transcontinental exchange of telephone faxes. In her response to Le Carré, Brown shot back: "I find that charge extraordinarily sexist. You are, of course, quite wrong in your assumption that I am banging some drum for Harry." Her letter's salutation was marked "Dear David," a reference to Le Carré's real name, David Cornwell. Brown informed him that she would be pleased to print his letter of outrage but asked him to reduce it to one paragraph. "Frankly, from yours and Willie's [Shawcross] point of view, it might pack a little more punch than sounding, as a couple of editors here thought, like a choleric colonel in Angmering-on-Sea."

Despite Brown's curt reply and attempt to be amusing in response, the Shawcross flak was taken quite seriously. TINA BROWN ACCUSED OF MISUSING NEW YORKER, the *Times* headline read, giving voice to many readers' fears about the ex-*Vanity Fair* editor. Perhaps a public feud, in the best Hollywood tradition, might stir conversation about her magazine. But in doing so, there were some disturbing questions about the character of this oh-so-new *New Yorker*. The inherent conflict of interest in the piece about the Shawcross book was clear enough and couldn't be blamed on anyone else. There seemed no good reason for Brown to print such a sharply critical piece about a book that was still three months from publication. Moreover, the dispute gave Le Carré a platform to express his overall concerns about Brown's takeover of *The New Yorker*.

"Through this little window she has given us, you can detect the entry of the degenerate British standards of journalism, and I find that deeply disturbing," Le Carré said. "Within weeks of taking over *The New Yorker*, you have sent up a signal to say that you will import English standards of malice and English standards of inaccuracy." In his response, Le Carré stressed *The New Yorker's* tradition of high standards in combining journalism and literature with a hand that was calm and deliberative. He feared a certain shrillness would come to *The New Yorker* out of the desperate need to be noticed and feared. "God protect *The New Yorker* from the English," he prayed.

Despite Le Carré's instant condemnation, what Tina Brown would do with *The New Yorker,* once America's greatest magazine, remained stubbornly undetermined by the end of 1993, with contents that could vary greatly from week to week. There were still extraordinary pieces of journalism as well as a look to the magazine that was slightly younger, faster, and breezier in style. Rather than the seamless quality Shawn had strived for, however, the magazine sometimes reflected the fractious, somewhat overcooked approach of Brown's *Vanity Fair,* where the shrill and the substantive would wind up too close to each other. Often, "the mix," as Brown described her weekly offering, seemed just too mixed up.

To judge the changes at *The New Yorker* purely on superficial alterations or graphic redesigns, however, missed the fundamental transformation made by Brown. Though some of the old *New Yorker* writers and editors were retained, the essential voice of the magazine was gone—that gentle manner that provided the perfect backdrop for powerful reporting on society's most difficult issues, a tone in which stories needed only to be well told rather than hyped. As Shawn wrote of its essence: ". . . never to publish anything, never to have something written, for a hidden reason: to promote somebody or something, to pander to somebody, to build somebody up or tear somebody down, to indulge a personal friendship or animosity, or to propagandize." This moral distinction was the single greatest loss in the takeover by Si Newhouse, who never seemed to have understood the true value of the magazine he coveted.

Under Tina Brown, the magazine's popularity with both readers and advertisers would rebound. In July 1993, a year after her selection was announced, *The New Yorker* trumpeted her success, pointing to a Simmons research survey that showed her makeover of the magazine had attracted younger, more affluent readers and prompted a 17 percent jump in advertising from the start of the year. At the same time, the magazine raised its rate base, guaranteeing to advertisers it would sell 650,000 copies of each issue, up from the previous 600,000. "Tina is certainly the head of the class," publisher Steven Florio announced. "We needed her to give us the product." To be sure, there were criticisms of Brown—for example, that she had not turned either *Vanity Fair* or *The New Yorker* into complete stand-alone successes without Si's millions. But almost always these accounts acknowledged that more than money was at stake. "Regardless of whether Vanity Fair and the new New Yorker are financially successful, Brown has fashioned them into splendid simulacra of success," observed

The New York Times in December 1993. "For a billionaire like Newhouse, this glittering appearance may well be worth more than a genuine but unsung profit."

This revamped *New Yorker,* like every other magazine Brown had edited before, adopted her engaging voice, the sensibilities and interests of an editor who was quickly excited by the contents and just as easily bored. To bring about her vision of *The New Yorker,* there were rumors that Brown would clean house indiscriminately, ushering in a totally new staff in a complete makeover. But she found herself reliant on the organizing structure put into place by Shawn, a process that allowed for an intensely complex literary publication to be produced each week. She also seemed to have developed a genuine appreciation for the talent she had already found on the premises. At first, Brown seemed swamped by the workload of a weekly magazine. In time, though, she adapted to the pace, delegating authority in a way Shawn would not have. "The momentum of a weekly is more self-generating and I've got an incredibly strong and superior team at *The New Yorker* who really are extraordinary, I must say," Brown stated. "So I'm very much reinforced in a way that is quite wonderful, in a way that I couldn't quite function without. With that weekly stress, you need a team that good."

A lasting irony of this new era was Brown's reliance on experienced staffers like Chip McGrath—the same editor who had been rejected five years earlier by Newhouse as Shawn's replacement. At that point, Newhouse wanted someone fresh, someone who would not be hesitant to spark the evolutionary changes he felt were necessary after Shawn was gone. So instead, Newhouse chose Robert Gottlieb. With that crushing rejection, no one was certain of McGrath's future at *The New Yorker.* A delicious twist of fate brought about Chip McGrath's rise as one of Brown's key editors, the deputy who oversaw the "Shouts and Murmurs" section and made sure the magazine was well edited and delivered to the printer on time. Carefully, he praised Tina Brown and dispelled the notion that she was making *The New Yorker* into just another Condé Nast publication. "The magazine has added or expanded its range," McGrath assured the loyalists. "I would say the magazine is even more unlike other magazines than it used to be."

Out of necessity, Tina Brown's *New Yorker* would likely remain an amalgam of sensibilities for some time to come. It would be up to old hands like McGrath to help Brown realize her vision of the magazine. Although Si Newhouse didn't sense a future for him as editor, McGrath was now often found helping to run the show for Tina Brown, quietly and behind the scenes—just as William Shawn had done for Harold Ross in the days when *The New Yorker* was the very best.

At the end of the workday, the pungent odor of cigarette smoke would sometimes waft through the editor's office of *Vanity Fair,* a sure sign that things had changed. When she was there, Brown strictly forbade such a practice. But now Graydon Carter could be found in his new office, puffing his favorite nonfiltered cigarettes, with both his door and perhaps a bottle of wine open. Several staffers, especially those who knew him before he was appointed, felt comfortable coming into his office to talk about a story or just to shoot the breeze.

In conversations after he arrived in 1992, Carter was often humorous, a fast draw on the one-liners. At forty-three, he seemed both relaxed and debonair. His style was certainly less intense than Brown's, but the comparisons were inevitable. "Tina ruled much more by scaring people into doing their best, while Graydon wants to charm you into doing your best," said one editor who worked with both editors and is partial to Carter. "Graydon is a wisecracking, outwardly affable guy who is inwardly harder to read. You don't really know what he's thinking or quite what he wants. He's been put in a terribly difficult situation, and when he plays it close to the vest, it makes all the sense in the world." For all of his wit and affability, however, the uncertainty with Carter sometimes showed. Carter "doesn't have the absolute conviction" of his predecessor, said this *VF* editor. "Tina could change her mind the next day, but it was just as confident."

From the very first issue under his editorship, Carter was careful to stay within the formula that Brown had established and proven a winner. He strayed and trespassed only slightly, adding a cultural column by Christopher Hitchens and a few more star writers like former *Time* essayist Roger Rosenblatt and investigative reporter Bryan Burrough, whose reporting in *The Wall Street Journal* resulted in the best-selling book, *Barbarians at the Gate*. But mostly, Graydon was playing it safe, as his first cover photograph—of actress and AIDS activist Elizabeth Taylor holding a condom—seemed to suggest. Some covers brought a strange feeling of deja vu, like the Princess Diana cover, which seemed identical to one that had appeared during Brown's reign. Because many of *Vanity Fair*'s staff writers and editors stayed on, Carter was keenly aware of Brown's methods and his occasional failures to match her standard. It took considerable time, as he admitted later, to "figure out what makes a great cover, Tina really had it down."

Many of Carter's moves seemed remarkably like an attempt to imitate Brown. He named Elise O'Shaughnessy, who had worked for Brown as *Vanity Fair*'s political editor and then at *The Observer* for Carter, as his new executive editor. He named Diane Von Furstenberg to be a contributing editor to the magazine, as if she would become *his* Reinaldo Herrera on social matters. (Her editorial contributions certainly seemed dubious. In the September 1993 issue, Von Furstenberg, who is listed on the masthead, was also featured in a two-page photo essay in which she was seen sitting in a bath, like a bejeweled Cleopatra, in the backyard of her Connecticut home. The accompanying photo caption celebrated Von Furstenberg's new Random House book, *The Bath,* which also happened to mention "her newly launched line of bath products.")

When Dominic Dunne's latest book was published, Carter hosted a private dinner party at the Morgan Library in Dunne's honor, just as Tina Brown might have in her day. Some Tina favorites like Jesse Kornbluth decided they didn't like Carter's style and departed; Annie Leibovitz now made herself available for offers other than her once-exclusive work for *Vanity Fair.* Dominic Dunne expressed a strong interest in joining his old friend and editor over at *The New Yorker,* but he was contractually stopped by Newhouse from doing so. And then there were some of Tina's people whom Carter felt he absolutely couldn't do without . . . like Hamilton South.

During Brown's tenure, Hamilton South, a handsome man in his twenties, could be found at the far end of the masthead, listed as "Director of Editorial Promotion." Brown discovered South's unique talents when he was working at Barney's, the upscale clothing store in Manhattan, which featured wonderful displays in its windows each holiday season. South's talents were in promotions and especially in putting together the gala parties fancied by Tina Brown. He acted as an appendage to Brown's astute social skills. As though he could read Tina's mind, South knew whom to seat next to one another at parties and whom Brown preferred to keep apart. When she left for *The New Yorker,* Hamilton South apparently recognized his opportunity to get ahead. "He's a real, clever operator," said one editor somewhat admiringly. "When Tina went to *The New Yorker,* he went back to Graydon and said, 'She wants me to go,' and played that game very well in getting them to bid against each other. Graydon gave him a better title." Consequently, Hamilton South, a figure virtually unknown to readers, was listed as "Editor at large" on the masthead, just above Norman Mailer, with an upgraded title and a salary said to be well into the six-figure range. No one quite seemed to know what that title meant, yet South became as integral to Graydon Carter's inner circle as he had been to Tina Brown's.

The most miraculous transformation, however, occurred within Graydon Carter himself, once the enfant terrible of New York publishing, who now acted as if he was on his best behavior. Stung by the many criticisms after Newhouse's decision to appoint him, Carter seemed to take steps to modify his actions and pattern his social behavior after his predecessor, who only a few years earlier he had mocked in print. Shortly after his announcement as editor, Carter traveled to Paris to attend the spring fashion shows, where he was spotted along the runway with his benefactor, Anna Wintour, and other Condé Nast editors. He was made the guest of honor at a dinner by Von Furstenberg at her Paris apartment. At another Vanity Fair–sponsored function in London, Carter was seated at a table with Princess Diana, where he appeared very much as the lord of the manor. "Gentlemanly discretion forbids me from commenting on our conversation," Carter told the press. "But I can assure you she is a delightful partner." Despite the smarmy bum-kissing nature (as *Spy* might have termed it) of his new public posture, Carter could also be candid about the demands of his new job. When a friend talked with him at that dinner, he asked about Carter's stewardship of the magazine. "There's much more PR than I thought there would be," Carter told his confrere.

Graydon Carter sometimes found himself trying to curry favor with those he had ridiculed only a few years before in *Spy*. If Brown's approach was trying to "build alliances" with *Vanity Fair*, Carter's style at his old magazine seemed hell-bent on burning bridges. Now as *Vanity Fair's* new editor, Carter, slightly older and perhaps wiser, was properly but somewhat disingenuously repentant. "In the 80's, it was the great thing at the right time and I loved it," he offered. "But I got a lot of that anarchistic take on the world out of my system." One of the first people he tried to cultivate was Liz Smith, the syndicated gossip columnist, who initially was unwilling to forget *Spy's* stinging comments about her. In her column, shortly after Carter's arrival, Smith noted the presence of this "controversial Anglophile" at the Paris fashion shows and repeated an old saw about him: "You can always tell a person by his aspirations."

Smith had been particularly upset with Carter ever since he and *Spy* coeditor, Kurt Andersen, showed up at a 1989 book party for author Nigel Dempster, which was attended by Smith and other *Spy* "victims," like *New York Times* columnist and former editor, A. M. Rosenthal. In her column, Smith criticized Anna Wintour and Tina Brown for inviting the bad boys from *Spy* along with them to the party, setting off a very public feud. "She's the best argument for licensing journalists, and if there was a journalism police force out there, Liz should be taken away in chains and handcuffs," Carter said with typical *Spy*-like hyperbole. "She's just an egregious bum-kisser to the famous and wealthy." He pointed out the real reason why he chose to run the Liz Smith tote board, which featured a silly photo of Smith in war paint and a list of how many times certain celebrities were mentioned by her in bold type each month. "It's always been filler, and we only keep it in because it seems to rattle her," Carter said in his best big-brat tone.

But he was right in one respect: amiable Liz Smith didn't like him very much. When Carter was selected for *Vanity Fair*, Smith's readers were treated to ruminations about her own fate with the magazine's new management. "It remains to be seen if *Vanity Fair* can maintain its thrust, popularity and vibrance under its new editor, who is not the most popular man in the world," Smith penned. "Let me put it this way. It is a lucky thing I have already been named to *Vanity Fair's* Hall of Fame, because under editor Graydon Carter, I couldn't be named dogcatcher."

For Carter, however, Liz Smith's well-read column was an important part of the word of mouth regarding his magazine. Any bad words about *Vanity Fair* might set in motion those forces that could cost him his job.

Rather than be vilified, Smith needed to be courted and fed tips, Carter learned. He could no longer afford to be mean.

Within his first few issues, Carter and his staff convinced Liz Smith to appear in a photo essay about the new look in fashion called grunge, and—poof!—there was the famous syndicated gossip columnist pictured in oversized coat, baggy pants, and looking very much like a street dude from Seattle. It was very similar to a tactic Tina Brown had employed when she arrived in the mid-1980s. At that time, Brown moved to ward off the evil spirits looming over *Vanity Fair* and assiduously charmed Liz Smith by including her prominently in a photo essay on important women. "Graydon did the same thing," said one of his top editors. "He's just learning Brown's lessons." By the spring of 1993, Liz Smith's chilliness had thawed and Graydon Carter's social rehabilitation appeared complete. Finally, Carter made his way into the realm of Most-Favored Bold Face— those who were prominently mentioned in Smith's column.

Following a White House correspondents' dinner, for instance, Carter hosted a "sizzling party," as Smith described it, inside the Washington area home of *Vanity Fair* columnist Christopher Hitchens. The guest list included Barbra Streisand and several other Hollywood friends of Bill Clinton whose names were printed as the lead item in Liz Smith's gossip column. Smith could now be counted on for an admiring word or two in her column each month about Carter's *Vanity Fair*, as she had done for Tina Brown.

Donald Trump was the source of another remarkable transformation by Carter. In the bad old days of *Spy*, Carter made no secret of his loathing for Trump, the very personification of the brash can-do hype of the 1980s. *Spy* called Trump a "short-fingered vulgarian" and satirized the New York developer and his wife, Ivana, with other assorted insults supposedly meant to be humorous. But Carter also made sure his attacks were viewed as personal. "He's a jerk," Carter told one interviewer in December 1987. "He's a little boy in a man's suit trying to . . . [pretend] that he might run for president. He should be taken seriously only in [the sense] that all alarming characters have that benign look to them. This guy's bad news."

As the new *Vanity Fair* editor, Carter was happy to make news with the former vulgarian, who attended the White House correspondents' dinner in 1993 along with Carter. Once again, Carter was making nice with former enemies—especially someone whose life story had been turned into a best-seller at the personal behest of Si Newhouse. "We buried the hatchet over lunch months ago," Carter said, playing the part of the magnanimous peacemaker. "Donald and I have a healthy, ironic relationship." Those who know Trump marvel at his ability to perceive any publicity—good, bad, or even being compared to Satan—as ultimately helping his public image. And besides, it was Graydon Carter who had started the public feud with all those nasty words and pictures. "While he skewered me in *Spy* magazine consistently, I've always respected Graydon and I have great respect for his work," said Trump. "I've called him one of the most upwardly mobile people I know, and I mean that. He's done a great job with *Vanity Fair.*"

Tina Brown was one person who didn't seem willing to forgive and forget easily. She carefully praised Carter publicly, but there was a bitter history of past grievances, hurt feelings, and perceived slights between them. The private but intense struggle over who would go and who would stay at *Vanity Fair,* like the skirmish over Hamilton South, became part of a larger battleground set up by Si Newhouse, who allowed his editors to compete among themselves as much as against rival companies. In this game of wits, Brown was a seasoned warrior who thrived and believed in the Newhouse system. "I think that most of the editors are very much aware that when Si buys something new, it could hurt their particular venture," Brown explained. "Si believes in managed competition and he thinks that's good."

In the Condé Nast version of managed competition, Graydon Carter was still a relative beginner. The pressure to compete with Brown's legacy and the constant comparisons were clearly bothersome. "Following Tina is a very tough job," he acknowledged. "I wouldn't wish it on my worst enemies." He was keenly aware of who had been a Tina favorite, and often acted accordingly. Hamilton South's worth was magnified to Carter simply because Brown wanted him, many staffers felt. "He was staying on staff to do the tenth-year birthday party as Tina's representative, but that was very divisive, because who was he really working for?" said one writer who described the situation. "Graydon's always been very paranoid about Tina. He feels that Tina is interested in destabilizing him and his operation, which I don't think is the case." Sometimes, too much was made of Brown's intentions, like her conspicuous absence at a welcoming party for Carter that was attended by Newhouse and other top Condé Nast brass. But other surviving *Vanity Fair* staffers, some of whom had worked for Brown, were sure that she was looking for ways to discreetly torpedo her successor without leaving any fingerprints.

The truly insidious maneuvers, said the insiders, were much more subtle. Take, for instance, the whereabouts of the "comp list." The comp list was the nickname for the complimentary issues of *Vanity Fair* that were rushed as soon as they arrived from the printer each month and sent by messenger to top newspapers, magazines, columnists, broadcasters, and other VIP friends and acquaintances of the magazine. It arrived like some big gift in a beautiful envelope, usually with three press releases tucked inside. Those lucky few recipients, in turn, prepared to go out and spread the news of that issue's contents to an awaiting public. Promoting *Vanity Fair* was an elaborate and financially important operation overseen by Maurie Perl and her crackerjack PR staff, who were the keepers of the comp list. When Brown left for *The New Yorker,* the list and much of the PR operation went with her. Graydon Carter was left haplessly in the lurch. "She neglected to tell Graydon that there was such a list," recalled one of Carter's editors. "And then, of course, she took Maurie Perl, too. Suddenly, all these people were beginning to bitch at their cocktail parties, saying this guy Graydon Carter clearly didn't have any respect for them because he wasn't sending them the magazine. She didn't have to do this; she could have Xeroxed the list."

There were other minor skirmishes over writers, illustrators, and story ideas. But the Condé Nast tea-leaf readers, with the political acuity of Bismarck, became convinced of Brown's intentions after reading an interview she gave to *The New York Times* in January 1993—barely a few months into Carter's tenure as *Vanity Fair*'s editor.

The entire thrust of the *Times* piece was to underscore how *Vanity Fair* was no longer quite the hot magazine now that Brown was gone. "The magazine does seem to have lost a lot of its momentum," said one advertising executive, expressing the general thesis of the piece, which, it said, was reflected by almost two dozen media directors, writers, and editors. "You don't seem to get the media hype about it." The ultimate litmus test for a magazine's hotness—the word of mouth at Manhattan cocktail parties—was once again cited as evidence. Alongside the article, Graydon Carter was pictured with a sheepish grin, standing next to a huge billboard-size replica of the latest issue, featuring Princess Diana with a tiara. Dwarfed by the billboard-size cover, Carter looked like a man too small for the job.

In the same story, Tina Brown was asked for her assessment of how Carter was doing. Through her press office, Brown sent forth the observation that "I think it's crazy to judge any editor before he puts his 10th issue to bed." Those who read Brown's comments, with the obvious suppositions in her reply, were either outraged or howled with knowing laughter.

To some, Brown's rule of thumb seemed like a hint to Si Newhouse, a public warning in advance for the boss's benefit if, after a short spell, he decided to lop off poor Graydon's head. This way, the media could say the signs of trouble were already spelled out. *Ten issues!* Graydon's friends and supporters were incensed by Brown's comments. After all, Tina Brown had at least sixteen issues before Si Newhouse thought seriously of doing something drastic in the mid-1980s, at the height of the Reagan boom years, and then gave her another extention so she could prove herself. To set up such a short test period, like some hourglass with the sands slipping quickly past, was essentially to provide the public rationale for Carter's possible ouster. "Of course it was unfair," said one close friend of Carter, who was irked by Tina Brown's remark in the *Times* piece. "She spent a lot of time on the public-relations function and it's part of her shrewdness and it's served her incredibly well. I wouldn't be surprised to find her fingerprints on the incredibly unfair story in the

Times. I wouldn't be surprised if that was part of the Tina Brown spin machine."

But *Vanity Fair*'s travail seemed more than a matter of bad press relations or some surreptitious conniving from Brown's allies, some of whom managed to tell the *Times* that the magazine had turned into "a disaster." In its first half year under Carter, *Vanity Fair* just didn't seem to have the same fresh appeal as it had once had. Some of Carter's changes at the front of the magazine, like its revised "Vanities" column, only made the magazine seem more cluttered and disjointed. Part of the magazine seemed stuck in the 1980s ("Boesky in Exile"), while other articles lacked the same attention-grabbing quality as before. Like some fading late-night television show, it seemed as if Si Newhouse had decided to present "The Best of *Vanity Fair*" and allowed Carter, like some TV fill-in host, to rerun all of Brown's favorite cover subjects: Madonna, Princess Di, and familiar crowd-pleasing blondes like Sharon Stone and Claudia Schiffer. The final issue in 1993 would feature Demi Moore, for the third time, with virtually nothing new to say.

The uncertain touch of Graydon Carter became most obvious in March 1993 when *Vanity Fair* decided to run two separate covers for the same issue: some of its readers getting a portrait of newly elected President Bill Clinton, the others being greeted by actress Andie MacDowell. Carter and his editors tried to present the two-cover idea as a novelty, a daring move that had never been attempted. At least one press report at the time, however, suggested Carter agreed to alternate the President with MacDowell's photo only after receiving a threatening complaint from MacDowell's publicist, Pat Kingsley. Given his bad-boy reputation in Hollywood, Carter could ill afford to alienate a powerful press agency that provided access to movie stars and other celebrities for *VF*'s monthly cover photos. A spokesperson for the magazine later denied the rumor of a not-so-veiled threat, but Kingsley later admitted, "If they had [called back and] said she is not on the cover then I would have had a problem."

Throughout Carter's early months, *Vanity Fair*'s circulation continued to rise, reaching 1.2 million readers. Brown's loyalists said the numbers were cresting based on the magazine's built-up reputation and they were incensed by the magazine's drift under Carter. "Graydon inherited, almost intact, the greatest magazine and editorial machine since the early days of *New York* or the legendary days of *Esquire* and all he had to do was find out how it ran and to guide it with a light hand," said one writer. "Instead, and unaccountably, he dismantled it. He couldn't learn how to run it, and it's the oddest fucking thing I've ever seen. My general take is that Graydon had been a success at everything he had ever done and had finally found a job that was too big for him."

Rather than quickly dismiss Carter as some expected, Si Newhouse stuck by his new editor. To cut off Graydon's head so soon would only exacerbate Newhouse's public image as an impatient boss with a short fuse. Si did acknowledge the drums beating in the distance, though. "I think there was a question about Graydon," Newhouse said in mid-1993. "Nobody knew what he was going to do. But the magazine is doing very well." Newhouse, like some sage media visionary, explained it all as part of his big plan. "It was in the cards that we would have some kind of fallout," Si said. "I think Graydon's doing an extraordinary job, and it shows in the circulation figures. . . . In the foreseeable future, *Vanity Fair* will regain some of the ground it's lost." For the time being, Newhouse was on record as a supporter of his new editor.

One of those who tried to keep a distance from Carter's fate was *Vanity Fair*'s publisher, Ron Galotti. A slick-haired, tough-talking businessman, Galotti brought his aggressive approach to *Vanity Fair* during the early 1990s. Within corporate Condé Nast, Galotti was widely viewed as a rising star, having worked at *Mademoiselle* and *Condé Nast Traveler* before coming to Brown's shop. His flamboyant reputation was woven of stories like that about a Rocky Mountain ski trip, when he had his red Ferrari sports car airlifted in so he could go cruising along the Colorado roadways. Galotti could be loud and sometimes caustic to fellow employees, but he nevertheless managed to keep the ad lineage growing throughout the recession.

When she left *Vanity Fair*, Tina Brown urged Si to allow her to bring Galotti over to *The New Yorker,* but Newhouse refused. Galotti suddenly became vulnerable when *Vanity Fair*'s advertising dropped by 15 percent with the switch to Graydon Carter. In a *Wall Street Journal* interview, Galotti was candid enough (some privately said too candid) to acknowledge publicly why some top advertisers pulled out of the magazine. "You don't make an editorial change at the level of Tina and not expect this," Galotti said bluntly. "There is definitely a wait-and-see attitude on the part of the advertisers. It's natural for them to sit back and be cautious about where they are placing their dollars."

However, it was unnatural for Si Newhouse to stand by and watch one of his publishers provide an excuse for advertisers not to appear in his magazine. These candid admissions seemed like a backhanded slap at Graydon Carter and gave Galotti's detractors a chance to bring out the long knives. Within the company's political circles, Galotti was viewed as a clear-cut partisan of Tina Brown and as a rival to New Yorker publisher Steve Florio, who was also interested in someday becoming the chief business executive of Condé Nast publications.

The current occupant of that job was Bernard H. Leser, the sixty-eight-year-old president and close confidant to Newhouse and editorial director Alex Liberman. For many years, Leser, who remained largely out of the limelight, had quietly managed to smooth over any hurt feelings or abrupt separations caused by Newhouse. He had played a key role in the company's European operations and had served as a wise sounding board for younger executives like Anna Wintour. "I think I am more sensitive than

Si, but Si is the greater analyst," Leser said, explaining his working relationship with Newhouse. "He is very good in a crisis, very calm, and I have never seen him lose his temper. But I probably have greater awareness of the human situation. That is what makes us a great match."

Nevertheless, Leser had little tolerance for Galotti and his volatile ways. In return, Galotti didn't hide his displeasure. "He started a rumor all over New York that he was going to replace Bernie Leser and that didn't make Bernie very happy," recalled Dick Shortway, who remained close with Leser. "For the first year or so, he did a seemingly good job, but he made a lot of enemies. He's very outspoken." Leser blamed Galotti for the advertising drop-off at *Vanity Fair* and lobbied hard with Newhouse for his ouster. Once a golden boy in the company, Galotti was now a marked man.

On the morning *The Wall Street Journal* article appeared, Galotti was intensely nervous about the reaction. "What can you do?" Galotti exclaimed to another reporter, who was writing a profile of him for a trade magazine. "I used to think that in this business perception was reality. But not anymore. We're doing great and people want to knock us."

Si Newhouse was not convinced. Two weeks after his *Wall Street Journal* interview, Galotti was summoned to Newhouse's office early on a Monday morning. The *Vanity Fair* publisher was fired and told to leave the premises within hours. A few months later, in mid-January 1994, the company announced Steven T. Florio was taking Leser's place, with his brother, Thomas Florio, publisher of *Condé Nast Traveler,* named as his successor at *The New Yorker.*

After conferring with Newhouse, Bernie Leser agreed to head the company's Pacific operations, launching a more aggressive campaign for Condé Nast magazines to appear in nations such as Japan and Korea. His move was recognized as Newhouse's attempt to prepare for a new generation of management within the company. In appointing Florio, there was little mention of the recent behind-the-scenes drama that led to Galotti's firing. "This is a very smooth running company," Newhouse maintained. "I want Steve to surprise me."

Galotti's demise was again a reminder of the limitations of Tina Brown's power within the Newhouse organization. Undoubtedly, Si was still enthralled by her gifted ability. ("There are editors and editors," he said. "I think Tina has something remarkable. I wish I knew what it was. It's undefinable. What makes a great film director a great film director?") But Brown's influence, despite her remarkable accomplishments, still seemed secondary to the status of Anna Wintour, who appeared to be quietly winning the game of "managed competition" within the organization. In public, Brown usually deflected questions about taking over for Liberman someday, expressing doubts that anyone could ever replace Liberman in Newhouse's esteem. "They have a fantastic relationship, a really, really touching relationship," Brown observed. "Si loves Alex; he really loves

Alex. I don't know what he felt about his own father, but he certainly loves Alex. He's a creative spiritual person in Si's life. He would do anything to make Alex happy. . . . He's one person who can really talk to Si about things."

For all of Brown's insights into Newhouse's character, however, Anna Wintour seemed closer to the boss, more committed to the company than the independent-minded Brown. Throughout the difficult transition, Si's support for Graydon Carter was implicitly a vote of confidence in Wintour's ability to find and develop top editorial talent. When *Vogue* was in trouble, Wintour demonstrated her ability to come in and carefully, almost effortlessly, update the image of what was still the company's most successful magazine. Even Wintour's own less-than-successful ventures didn't tarnish her image within the company—such as her short stint at *HG* (which eventually wound up being killed a few years after Wintour's departure because of Newhouse's purchase of rival *Architectural Digest* in 1993).

As she did with Graydon Carter at *Vanity Fair,* Wintour helped to place editors in top jobs throughout the company, using her direct influence with Newhouse. Wintour suggested that Newhouse put one of her top associates, Gabé Doppelt, in the post as *Mademoiselle*'s new editor in 1992—just as she had recommended James Truman, who came to the company as *Vogue*'s features editor, for *Details* in 1990. Si marveled at Truman's revamping of *Details,* which appealed to a much younger readership. "James invented the magazine from inside his head," said Newhouse, whose avid interest in *Details* underscored what appeared to be Truman's bright future within the company.

Gabé Doppelt was a friend of Tina Brown and godmother to her second child. But Anna Wintour largely fostered Doppelt's unparalled rise to editor. Doppelt was appointed to the *Mademoiselle* job even though she admitted to never really looking at the magazine until Newhouse offered her the job. Doppelt's friendship with Wintour, Truman, and so many within the Condé Nast hierarchy undoubtedly helped her ascent. After many controversial moves in less than a year—including an unbylined article about college women and lesbianism that drew criticism for its controversial nature—Newhouse stepped in and appointed a new, more mainstream editor. Doppelt's replacement, Elizabeth Crow, was described as a prototypical Newhouse editor, "a big believer" in the market-research approach of Mark Clements in deciding what to give readers.

In her discreet way, Wintour seemed to understand Si Newhouse's intensely private, multifaceted nature. She demonstrated the supreme editorial skills, like Liberman, that Newhouse felt were vital to keeping each Condé Nast magazine looking vibrant and alive. The contest between the two top women editors remained the talk of the company throughout the early 1990s and made for good copy in the press. "Everybody wants a catfight, but I didn't want to be editor of *Vogue*," Brown once said of her perceived rivalry with Wintour. "We're actually good friends. It's just that we're both high-profile editors. Gossip columns are usually written by male hacks who want to see a catfight."

The speculation over Brown and Wintour came to a surprise halt in January 1994 when Si selected James Truman, then thirty-five, as the company's new editorial director, replacing Liberman, who would remain with the company as deputy chairman–editorial. Truman's name had rarely been mentioned as a successor. But Newhouse seemed enchanted by both Truman's diffident, low-key personal style and his ability to target the young Generation X audience in their twenties. "Truman's personality is formed out of the present and a new age of technologies and readers," Newhouse told one advertising trade journal. "There won't be another Alex, but James is highly qualified to inspire."

Most agreed that James Truman would never hold the fearsome command that Alex Liberman once had. Successful editors like Ruth Whitney at *Glamour* and Art Cooper at *GQ* were too independent, with an autonomy that Newhouse had quietly allowed over the past decade as Liberman grew older. From the outset, there was an awareness of Truman's relative inexperience, particularly for what many considered one of the most powerful positions in magazine publishing. "If he starts telling me what to do, I am going to spank him and send him to bed without his dinner," warned Paige Rense, the sixtyish editor of *Architectural Digest,* in a jocular way that no Condé Nast editor would have ever dared with Liberman.

To the press, Wintour expressed her delight at Truman's appointment. With Alex's gradual departure, Wintour would remain a powerful editor in the company, with likely the most access to Newhouse's ear. Tina Brown, arguably the most talented editor in the Newhouse empire, remained uncharacteristically quiet. But several news accounts—without identifying the source—repeated the claim that both she and her husband, Harry Evans, had been offered Liberman's job earlier and turned it down. Undoubtedly, *The New Yorker* would remain Brown's fiefdom, while Truman's new job would have its certain limits. "I wouldn't say that the editors will report to James," Newhouse explained about Truman's job description. "He will be there to help editors and magazines that need help and ask for it."

During this transition period, Si's role in the company would be even more dominant, as the new appointees seemed to recognize. Shortly after their promotions were made known, Truman and Steve Florio went out for a drink to discuss the changes they foresaw for Condé Nast. "We sat there saying, "Well, I've always wanted to do this, I've always wanted to do that, do you think Si would let us do this?" Florio later recalled. "We talked about doing some outrageous things, then we'd look at each other and say, 'Naaah!' " The new management team was still very much aware of their overseers. As Florio observed, "Both James and I realize that Alex is still there and, for me, certainly, Si is still there."

Newhouse's impulsive, revolving-door style of management came full circle in March 1994 when Ron Galotti—the much-reviled *Vanity Fair* publisher whom Si had fired only a few months earlier—was re-hired as the new publisher of *Vogue*. Even by Condé Nast standards, this announcement was utterly confounding. After all, Galotti had been a chief rival against Florio for the Condé Nast president's seat which Florio had barely warmed. But recent events forced Newhouse to change his mind about Galotti. Following his ouster, Galotti returned to the Hearst organization as publisher of *Esquire* in late January 1994. Si reportedly worried that Galotti also would help Hearst in reviving the fortunes of *Harper's Bazaar* against *Vogue,* which was showing signs of slippage. *Harper's Bazaar* had revamped its format with new editor, Liz Tilberis, and gained a sizeable amount of additional advertising as the "hot book" in fashion. Suddenly, *Vogue* under Anna Wintour no longer seemed quite as indomitable as it had only a year before. As hard as it might be for many to swallow, Galotti seemed just the right tonic to revive *Vogue*'s fatigue.

Within Condé Nast, the underpinnings for this perpetual rivalry—or managed competition, as the participants preferred—were put in place by Si Newhouse, who believed that constant change was the dynamic that would preserve his family's company for another generation. Si had transformed himself from an unsure and unfocused young man into a figure described as a demanding father who seemed to enjoy pitting one sibling against another in a series of endless matchups: Tina versus Anna; Graydon versus Tina; Florio versus Galotti. After more than a decade as the company's chairman, Si Newhouse's management style—indeed his whole media organization—was renowned for eating its own. "People at the company are scared to death," one executive told the *Times* after Galotti was axed. "They feel that if it can happen to Ron and Grace Mirabella, it can happen to them." The fear of being fired abruptly, the continual overhauls and redirections—all were part of working for Newhouse. Whether his changes were beneficial for the magazines he owned or the people he employed often seemed irrelevant so long as *something* was done.

The dread of finding one's career suddenly catapulted into a black hole by displeasing Si Newhouse cast a permanent pall over his Madison Avenue headquarters. The ritual-like beheadings (beginning with a swarm of rumors and usually ending with a press release, as in Galotti's case, stating the newest victim was leaving to "pursue other interests") provided a constant source of cynical amusement for those with a taste for blood. Sometimes, the near miss could almost be as entertaining as the real thing.

That ignominious feeling of surviving the latest round of Newhouse roulette was suffered by Graydon Carter on the day Galotti was fired.

Early one morning in May 1993, Carter was summoned to Newhouse's office without any explanation. When he got there, Si told him that he was going to fire Galotti. When he arrived back downstairs in his *Vanity Fair* offices, Carter reportedly joked that he'd thought Newhouse was going to lop his head off as editor. The indignity was compounded the following morning when *The New York Post* erroneously published on its front page a headline that read: VANITY FAIR HONCHO GETS THE BOOT. And next to the *Post*'s headline was a picture of a gleeful Graydon Carter instead of what should have been Ron Galotti's face. Copies of the *Post* were quickly sold out at the newsstand in the Condé Nast building and became a sort of perverse collector's item. Carter, who might once have savored such an irony at *Spy,* was upset by the *Post*'s blunder and reports that he feared for his job. Now it was left to Liz Smith and other gossip columnists to speculate whether his job was endangered.

In his own way, Si Newhouse assured the press that he had every confidence in the future. Yes, *Vanity Fair* had lost ground, but Newhouse said he was convinced it was now back on track. No, he didn't think he was crippling one magazine to save another. And yes, Graydon Carter was doing a fine job, his numbers looked good, and his position was absolutely safe.

. . . For now.

CHAPTER THIRTEEN

Powerhouse

I *thought about what I said to you yesterday. . . ."*

The voice was familiar enough. Only the day before, this former editor of Page Six, the rock'em, sock'em gossip page of the *New York Post,* had talked expansively about her experiences with Si Newhouse and his stable of Condé Nast editors. At times, as the editor recalled, the 1980s seemed a blur of endless parties and dress-up benefits for charity, with Newhouse, tuxedoed and sphynx-like, occasionally making an appearance. The former editor had agreed to speak boldly at length and on the record about Newhouse.

There was the time this editor met Si Newhouse at a book party on the Upper West Side, a sure sign that the author's career was on the rise. And then, there was the time the Page Six editor had talked briefly with Si at some gala—just a few syllables. Maybe it was at an opening for a Larry Gagosian art show? Maybe a party for Condé Nast? What remained memorable were not Si's words, though, but the sense of power that filled the room.

"This can only hurt me if I try and look for another job and I really can't afford . . ."

Now, the editor was calling back. The expansiveness was gone and so was the offer to let her name be used for publication. The Page Six editor, who had once sniped and frolicked in the outer limits of New York tabloid journalism, was an editor at a slick magazine, sitting in a masthead perch, where a better job at Condé Nast can look awfully good—the kind of job any self-respecting Manhattan magazine editor would crave, die for . . . even shut up for. There was no telling how this might get back to Si.

"I didn't say anything to you, did I?"

Si Newhouse can hardly be held responsible for every perception, every murmur of fear or retribution—and the chronic joblessness that may ensue—by taking his name in vain.

In New York City, that cosmopolitan Olympus of American media, where the giants of communication roam and formulate the national agenda, there is but one abiding fact: Gossip rules. And what the average American learns about those who run the nation's media—the titans who control the television stations, newspapers, magazines, and book publishers—comes largely from those gossip columns and other publications devoted to chronicling the social lives of billionaires and celebrities of all sorts. In the gossip columns, the goings-on of Tina Brown, Anna Wintour, Sonny Mehta, or other Newhouse luminaries can be found among updates on Madonna, Oprah, Schwarzenegger, or Cher.

From these accounts, Si Newhouse's public image emerged as a conundrum of third-person anecdotes and brief descriptions. He remained steadfast in his refusal to supply anything but the most minimal information about his intentions or purpose. When he does speak to the press, Newhouse is far more guarded than with those who travel in his social circles—though to both he provides few details or personal insights.

In some respects, Si Newhouse can be compared to the Great Gatsby of Fitzgerald's novel, an intensely circumspect man about whom there is much public speculation. But Newhouse's name is rarely mentioned in the same rhapsodic phrases of nobility that reflected a long-ago America, the simple kind of idealized Horatio Alger–like legend that enveloped his father's reputation during the middle half of this century. As a product of the more complex and cynical times in which he lives, Si Newhouse and his assortment of family-owned media companies have become reflective of the dominant forces in today's mass media, projecting an image—with its slick self-centered ads and status-conscious editorial product—of a nation haunted by stark differences in wealth, tastes, and desires. He has become emblematic of the concentration of media into the hands of a few anonymous men, and the fact that those who hold the mirror by which America examines itself remain an unaccountable mystery to the public. "The Newhouse brothers' wealth is a staggering total for two men many Americans have never heard of," *Fortune* magazine observed in the late 1980s.

To the extent there is any lasting public impression of Si Newhouse, it remains one of power and fear. Only a few other media tycoons, like Rupert Murdoch, own companies comparable to Newhouse's, and none exceeds the size of his empire or his insistence on secrecy. As a result, virtually every aspect of Newhouse's life, even the simplest gesture, seems to be examined by his employees for its implications or hidden meanings. Anxiety pervades almost everything. When he peruses New York's midtown or SoHo art galleries on Saturday mornings, usually with multimillionaire friends like Hollywood mogul David Geffen, the impromptu visits "resemble the unexpected arrival of two four-star generals in a basic-training barracks," as the *Times* described it. Inside his headquarters,

Newhouse inspects his publications with an exacting eye but rarely takes a moment to converse with employees, creating, as one business magazine said, "a fair amount of paranoia at Condé Nast."

Ask why so many are afraid of Si Newhouse, and there are a variety of responses to be found. "Well, I'm not afraid of him," said Tina Brown, one of the few in the Newhouse organization who probably isn't. In the same response, though, she quickly added, "He's a *very* powerful man, you know. He's not at all a vindictive person. As a matter of fact, he's not petty. He forgets who's trashed him. He's bigger than that."

The fear of being cut off from Si Newhouse's company is the most common refrain when writers, editors, and other publishing types talk about him. In Manhattan, like some small literary island unto itself, Newhouse looms as a great literary god, an all-powerful benefactor with the largesse to endow writers with endless freelance assignments for his magazines or six-figure contracts with his numerous book imprints. For many top authors, Newhouse's organization may not publish their original manuscripts, but one of its subsidiaries will likely be sought for a magazine excerpt or paperback reprint. As a result, few New York writers of any reputation will consider writing about Si Newhouse's empire, though they will gossip about it incessantly.

In December 1992, for example, Suzanne Levine, editor of the *Columbia Journalism Review,* sought a seasoned journalist to examine the changes at *The New Yorker* under Tina Brown. Levine went through numerous contacts until she found an out-of-state editor willing to accept the assignment.

"Why me?" asked the editor, Eric Utne, who runs his own alternative magazine.

"You're the perfect person to do it," the *Columbia Journalism Review* told him.

When Utne pressed for the real reason, he was told flatly, "Because no one else will touch it."

In this atmosphere of fear, Si Newhouse has thrived as a silent potentate of the American communications industry, allowing his family enterprise to accumulate billions of dollars in revenues with little public scrutiny or sense of accountability to the commonweal. His quiet defiance is part of a long Newhouse family history of stonewalling or threatening retribution on those who make unwanted inquiries. For decades, whenever *Editor & Publisher*—the venerable bible of the newspaper industry—ran an item with the slightest criticism of the Newhouses, the company pulled its ads from the magazine. When a young Syracuse University graduate student in journalism during the mid-1960s tried to publish his work on the Newhouse newspaper chain, he was threatened with a lawsuit by one of Si's uncles, Ted. And in the early 1980s, author Richard H. Meeker was sued unsuccessfully by Sam Newhouse's top editorial aide after his book about Sam Newhouse and his empire was published. For that biography—which was similar in all ways but its topic to hundreds of others at Newhouse's own publishing house—Si Newhouse informed Meeker that his father was a private man and that no one from the Newhouse family would cooperate with his effort. Whether the public wanted answers or not, Si Newhouse wasn't talking.

During the laissez-faire period of the Reagan era, the Newhouse approach to journalism came into vogue. More publicly traded newspaper groups adopted the Newhouse model of cut-rate reporting, gaining one-newspaper monopolies in city after city, with a maximization of revenues on a scale that rivaled that of any other U.S. industry. In the Reagan spirit, most of the nation's media companies embraced the same closed-mouth approach as did Newhouse—with an implicit rejection of that seemingly antiquated notion that a publisher might have some obligation to the public beyond making a buck. By the 1990s, many of America's media companies finally recognized a free press for what the Newhouses always knew it to be: a powerful machine to reap an endless fortune. Eventually, many writers realized that to get paid in an increasingly con-solidated marketplace, they would have to adapt to the new rules of the game. "What we've learned is that when you're as rich and as powerful as Si Newhouse," one *New Yorker* writer told *Time* magazine, "you can do exactly what you want."

On the tiny island of Manhattan, Si Newhouse's power and influence can be acutely sensed, like that of some mighty lion roaming his natural habitat. Indeed, one must venture further into New York's literary village to understand fully its peculiar tribal customs and cryptic signposts, its rites of passage and its occasional human sacrifices.

One of the favorite watering holes for those within Newhouse's realm is the Royalton Hotel and its downstairs eatery, "44." Here, the seating arrangements are carefully prepared and studied, holding clues to who is in favor and who may soon be receiving a pink slip. More than 25 percent of this restaurant's receipts are paid from the Newhouse coffers by a phalanx of editors, writers, and business executives in his employ. Tucked behind the reservation desk, the maître d' is said to keep a book containing Condé Nast mastheads so the appropriate seating can be found. Along the back wall, there is a row of "power booths," half-moon-shaped seats in green velvet, where the Condé Nast people can be found socializing with name-brand advertisers like Calvin Klein or other fashionable celeb-rities. One newspaper, *The New York Observer,* actually printed a map of the seating plan, identifying each booth and table with the editors who sit in them and deciphering their meaning in the overall scheme of New-house's world. For Tina Brown, the Royalton holds a bit of personal history: It's the place where she stayed when on assignment for London's *Punch* in the mid-1970s and where she met writers and editors for lunch when at Vanity Fair. The Royalton is situated near both the Condé Nast building and *The New Yorker* offices and became, in an obvious comparison, what the Algonquin—located across the same street—had been for the original *New Yorker* staff.

Si Newhouse usually favored The Four Seasons and his own form of power lunches, but he had his own distant connections to the Royalton, as well. (Newhouse and Ian Schraeger, the Royalton's proprietor, once shared the same lawyer and friend—Roy Cohn, who represented the disco palace Studio 54 when it was owned by Schraeger and Steve Rubell.) Eventually, Newhouse arrived one day for lunch at the Royalton, dressed more informally than usual, wearing a sweat suit and old tennis shoes, hardly the garb worn by the rest of the Royalton crowd. Newhouse was accompanied by Gabé Doppelt, the newly selected *Mademoiselle* editor, who had called ahead and told the restaurant's manager, Brian McNally, to make sure they had one of every entrée ready so Newhouse wouldn't be kept waiting.

"Hello, Mr. Newhouse. It's a pleasure to have you here finally," said McNally when the billionaire walked through the long entrance leading to the restaurant.

Quickly, seating arrangements were changed and someone had to give up a seat to the boss. Charles Gandee, an editor at *Vogue,* sacrificed his reserved booth that day. "I was bumped [to table 21] and glad to be bumped, just to have Mr. Newhouse there," Gandee told *The Observer.*

A similar fawning attitude can be found in the newspaper columns, some of which are authored by those in Si Newhouse's employ. It is not uncommon for the hot book, controversial magazine article, or other curiosity from Newhouse's world to receive mention in the tabloid news-paper columns. Perhaps the most consistent cheerleader during the early 1990s, however, was the *New York Post*'s (and formerly *Daily News*) columnist Billy Norwich, whose society gossip column reflected his many interests, which, of course, included his fellow colleagues at Condé Nast. Norwich was editor at large at *Vogue,* and his *Post* column contained the same tone as a Condé Nast feature story—dripping in superlatives. In one column, Alex Liberman was described as a "20th-century renaissance man" who happened to be hawking his picture book on Marlene Dietrich. Charity dinners to be attended by Si Newhouse and his wife, Victoria, were given prominent mention. And he buzzed with excitement about new Condé Nast arrivals, like Gabé Doppelt, who (before her abrupt dismissal) was hailed as "one of the brightest wunderkinds working in the business today." One of Doppelt's most notable journalistic achievements while at *Vogue,* Norwich said in one dispatch, was "the Talking Fashion section, chronicling personalities through fashion, a you-are-what-you-wear history of celebrity which has been adopted by *People* magazine, the *Star,* the *Enquirer,* you name it."

A typical example of the Newhouse food chain—and Norwich's part in it—could be traced by following the vapor trail of hype for a pleasant coffee-table book entitled *Pools,* which was produced by Kelly Klein, the wife of designer Calvin Klein. This one-hundred-dollar book, as the title makes unequivocally clear, is about pools—dozens of them, sleekly arranged and photogenically lighted—and not much else. Nevertheless, first-time author Kelly Klein's book received a grand reception. Her publisher was the distinguished Alfred A. Knopf and her work was excerpted in the September 1992 issue of *Vogue*. Norwich did his part by mentioning Klein's *Pools* in two of his newspaper columns, including a rave for the party thrown by Calvin Klein and Anna Wintour, Norwich's boss at *Vogue*.

True to the mix-and-match ethics of fashion journalism, Norwich only occasionally seemed to acknowledge that this horn blowing for Newhouse's organization might be a conflict of interest. "Just because I am the so-called editor-at-large of *Vogue* in no way compromises me when I report that this do has become *the* party of the season," Norwich enthused about an upcoming celebration marking *Vogue* magazine's hundredth anniversary. Norwich perhaps thought readers would believe him. But what remains unstated in this multilayered hype is the central fact that all of these publishing ventures are traceable to one man rarely mentioned in the columns, Si Newhouse. (By late 1993, Norwich had decided to give up his daily *Post* gossip column to join Condé Nast on a more or less full-time basis and to contribute a weekly column to *The New York Observer*).

In some journalistic circles, Billy Norwich may not be viewed quite as seriously as, say, *The New York Times*. When it comes to the Newhouse organization, though, The Paper of Record seems as obsessed as any tabloid columnist around town—of course, in its own restrained, perfectly serious manner. The *Times's* rapid pulse beat for the Newhouse organization can be monitored in the small index appearing at the bottom of its business page, where a mention of Advance Publications seems to be listed almost every day. Year after year, virtually every nuance at *The New Yorker*, *Vanity Fair,* and Random House is covered faithfully by the *Times*, with the Newhouse books being reviewed far more than those of any other publishing company. Many of the *Times's* best writers and highest-level editors have published books with one of the Newhouse publishers. Others mingle on the same social circuit, like longtime art critic John Russell, who during his career managed to maintain a close friendship with Alex Liberman, write about non-art subjects for *Vogue,* and still review Liberman's latest art creations for the *Times*. "Theres always something happening at Random House, always some division or executive in the news," observed *Washington Post* critic David Streitfeld in 1991. "Partly that's because the *New York Times* is obsessed with what goes on at 201 East 50th Street, often to the exclusion of other publishers."

In the literary village of New York, the *Times* plays an enormous role as an arbiter of success and as the dispassionate chronicler of cultural trends. When it beats the drums for a book or an author, it can help make a best-seller, which is listed each Sunday in its *Book Review* and touted by small bookstores and nationwide discount chains alike as proof of a work's merit. In its own way, the *New York Times* best-seller list, which is often called simply "the list" in the trade, has become crucial to the marketing of big books by large-scale publishers like Newhouse. "No doubt the wise men (surely men) who first decided to have a *New York Times* best-seller list believed it would offer pure, neutral information," wrote Elisabeth Sifton in 1993, shortly after leaving Random House, where she had her own imprint. "They may not have envisaged a business in which author-publisher contracts, bookselling discounts and many other arrangements would relate specific percentage terms and dollar amounts to The List—so that The List itself shapes the very sales it was purporting to reflect. But the power of critical influence is alluring. And by now The List has become part of *The Times'* sense of itself, part of what it believes attracts readers and advertisers. And the publishers do nothing to dissuade it. The Faustian pact has been made."

On occasion, the *Times* coverage of Newhouse's media empire has resulted in outright controversy, such as its reportage on the sweeping changes made at Random House and at Pantheon in late 1989 and early 1990. One of those covering the story for the *Times* was Roger Cohen, a talented reporter who had been recently under contract to write a book for Newhouse's publishing company. *Times* readers were never informed about Cohen's book project—described as an "autobiography" of Gianni Agnelli, the Italian financier, publisher, and owner of Fiat Motors. Agnelli was an influential mentor of Alberto Vitale, the new Random House chairman selected by Newhouse to replace Robert Bernstein. (Vitale had managed stocks for the Agnelli family and played a role in the Agnelli company's 1974 purchase of Bantam Books, which gave Vitale his start in publishing.)

Cohen later said his book was a "dead issue" because Agnelli decided not to publish the finished manuscript, with the advance money eventually returned to Newhouse's company. But the specter of a *Times* media reporter covering the tumult at Random House while having been paid by the company to write a book about chairman Vitale's friend seemed too cozy and an obvious conflict of interest. Whether intentional or not, critics pointed out that Cohen's reporting had a decidedly pro-Newhouse spin in citing reasons for the resignation of Robert Bernstein and the upheaval at Pantheon. In his *Times* articles, Cohen managed to describe Random House as "the Cadillac of American publishing" and blamed most of the reasons for Newhouse's changes on poor money management, just as Newhouse maintained. When *Village Voice* media critic Doug Ireland mentioned Cohen's undisclosed book deal in his column, there was nary a flinch at the *Times*. In response, Joseph Lelyveld, managing editor of the *Times,* assured *The Village Voice* that Cohen "is a reporter of great integrity and if he felt he was facing a conflict of interest, he'd be the first to tell us."

Inexorably, the influence of the Newhouse concept—with its distinctive style of trendy, upscale advertising and celebrity journalism manifest in its Condé Nast magazines—seeped into the *Times*'s traditional brand of reporting. In early 1992, the *Times* introduced its own "Styles" section inside its Sunday edition, which appeared to many as a near-perfect clone of a glossy Condé Nast fashion magazine. Like some weekly version of *Vogue* or *Allure,* this newsprint section of gossip and party coverage was initially edited by Stephen Drucker, a Condé Nast alumnus, and was embraced as the wave of the future by the *Times*'s new publisher, Arthur Sulzberger, Jr. A similar transformation took place at the paper's Sunday magazine. Even the traditional wall between advertising and editorial was being debated at the *Times*.

To question Newhouse's impact on American publishing and the public weal was, especially in New York's incestuous media community, to invite hostility from the indigenes. Writing of what he called "the lost honor of American publishing" in 1991, *The New Republic*'s Jacob Weisberg demonstrated how the selection of books and emphasis on bottom-line profits had transformed Random House under Newhouse, affecting some of its most talented editors. "[Jason] Epstein is regarded by many as the Edward R. Murrow of publishing, but like all acquiring editors these days, he has far too much on his plate," Weisberg observed. "In working for a branch of a vast conglomerate owned by S. I. Newhouse, Epstein has to spend much more time thinking about how to make money than he did when the firm was owned by its founders, Bennett Cerf and Donald Klopfer." After Weisberg's article appeared, there was a thunderstorm of protest. "The general reaction was one of indignation at the mere thought of taking the argument seriously," Weisberg recalled. "As it got back to me, there were a couple of people, including some who wrote letters, who actually agreed with the piece but felt obligated to defend their editors in print."

In the literary village, with so much at stake in freelance fees and future contracts, most journalists ignored Newhouse's dominant power—something they were well aware of—even when writing about the media. Pundits may talk about the corporate greed of the 1980s and its impact on society, yet they rarely examined the nation's largest private media company or the way it affected the culture and the very notion of what journalism is today. Indeed, some of the most notable books in the early 1990s critiquing American journalism were published by Newhouse publishers— such as Susan Faludi's *Backlash* or Washington Post critic Howard Kurtz's *Media Circus*. Both discuss ethical problems at his publications but never mention Newhouse by name or hold him personally responsible for their contents. Almost always, Si Newhouse has managed to escape public scrutiny. Only the insiders seem to know the power and fear inside the Newhouse kingdom. Sometimes they can even laugh about it—nervously.

After Newhouse flexed his corporate might at *The New Yorker* and then Random House, a phony publicity release was passed along publishing circles in 1989, announcing that Random House had just purchased the Catholic Church. Printed on the company's letterhead, it mimicked the Newhouse public-relations style perfectly, with assurances by a company spokesman that the Pope would stay in place and that the Bible would be a welcome addition to its backlist.

"We don't expect to tamper with the Church's management team," the company spokesman said. "The Church will thus operate as an independent division within Random House, and the Pope will report directly to Si Newhouse."

The biggest part of the Newhouse empire lies across the Hudson River, only a few miles away from the Condé Nast headquarters in Manhattan. It is located in the building of the *Newark Star-Ledger,* where Donald Newhouse works most days. For all meaningful purposes, though, the two buildings are universes apart. Fashion magazines bring glamour and books add prestige, but the Newhouse newspapers and broadcast operations exist for one purpose only: to make money, and lots of it.

By the mid-1990s, the family's more than two dozen newspapers produced an estimated $2 billion in annual revenues and were worth close to $7 billion. The Newhouse Broadcasting cable franchises, located in several states and with more than 1 million total subscribers, were valued at close to $3 billion. As if an engineer in the steam room of a great ship, Donald Newhouse saw his essential task as that of making sure the financial engine kept humming along as it should.

Donald, like his father before him, is a creature of habit. For many years, he took the commuter train from his Park Avenue town house to Newark, until he was eventually convinced to take a private car. More so than Si, Donald resembles his late father, Sam, with a more genial-looking face, straight dark hair, and equally short stature. Donald has followed many of the same business patterns established by his father. Before his death, many of Sam's intimates thought his second son would likely lead the company when he was gone. But while his tasks remained the same as those inherited from his father, Donald never burned with an aggressive desire for conquest, not possessing the same ambition that was Sam Newhouse's lasting legacy.

A thoughtful, amiable man, Donald seemed content to manage much of the family's business and remain largely in the shadow of his father and eventually his older brother. When he died in 1979, Sam Newhouse's privately owned dailies formed the largest newspaper chain in America— topped by his final purchase of the Booth newspapers company, which was headlined in 1976 as the largest newspaper sale ever. During the 1980s and early 1990s, Si Newhouse mirrored his father's ambitiousness with a series of stunning purchases and managerial moves that made the family's name famous. Yet Si was well aware of the underlying source of the family fortune. The eldest son once called everything else "peripheral" to the cash-making prowess of the newspapers.

Donald's job has been to maintain the existing empire, not build one of his own. Unlike the world of Condé Nast, nothing about the Newhouse newspapers is very glamorous. Four of the family's newspapers are the biggest in their states of Ohio, New Jersey, Louisiana, and Oregon, yet none of them known for their journalistic excellence. In overseeing the broadcast operations, which are run on a day-to-day basis by a Newhouse cousin, Robert Miron, Donald watched the meters spin and the checks roll in from communities like Syracuse, New York, where the family owns the city's only daily newspaper and its cable-television franchise, which boasts an 80 percent penetration of the market.

Newhouse Broadcasting, despite selling its five television stations in the late 1970s, reaped a fortune from its investments in cable-television franchises in Atlanta, Syracuse, and northern New Jersey, as well as from such joint-programming ventures as the Discovery channel. The Newhouses also owned Eastern Microwave, the company that uplinks the signal of broadcast superstations, like WWOR/Channel 9 in New York, to other cable franchises across the nation. In 1990, Robert Miron, the cousin who directly supervised the cable franchises worth at least $3 billion, served as chairman of the National Cable Television Association, the industry's powerful trade organization. Donald also assumed honored positions within the newspaper industry's hierarchy, but there remained a stark contrast in business approaches between himself and his older brother.

As an empire builder, Si Newhouse ranks as one of the most dynamic media tycoons in American history, a true inheritor of his father's mantle. For instance, he has expanded his Condé Nast magazines into several foreign countries and boldly introduced new magazines to the United States, like *Vanity Fair, Self, Allure,* and *Condé Nast Traveler,* and stuck with them through the recession of the early 1990s. He's been willing to look ahead to a future generation of readers and gamble with different editorial approaches, finding success with *Details,* a magazine with a much-touted appeal to Generation X—young Americans in their teens and early twenties.

But in the same time period, the Newhouse newspaper chain seemed to tread water while other newspaper groups like Gannett, riding the crest of the 1980s go-go market, leapt forward with additional newspaper purchases. After their father's decades-long campaign of purchases, not a single newspaper was bought by the sons until they added to their collection of New Jersey newspapers by picking up the *Trenton Times.* In fact, some Newhouse newspapers, like the *St. Louis Globe Democrat* and the

Bayonne Times, were closed because they were money losers. When dailies like the *Chicago Sun-Times* became available in 1983, the Newhouses joked that there were not enough family members available to run it. By the early 1990s, the Newhouse newspaper chain was ranked fourth—still a powerful size, with a daily total circulation of some 3 million readers. But the daring, unrivaled spirit of acquisitiveness that had once characterized the Newhouse newspaper chain was gone.

Valued for the wealth that could be extracted from them, the Newhouse newspapers were, in many ways, like large antebellum plantations, where the owners held little regard for those who toiled in the fields or for the essential nature of their product. Their riches were protected by title on the properties they owned and by the accommodating way in which government allowed newspapers to secure monopoly-like dominance over entire cities and regions. The Newhouses may no longer be an industry leader, but by carefully cultivating and pruning their collection of newspapers, they could continue to acquire wealth at an undaunted pace. "It is almost impossible to wreck big monopoly newspapers," *Fortune* said in 1987, writing about the Newhouse empire. "About all they will let you do is get richer and richer."

Many of the Newhouse newspapers—and the brand of journalism they practiced—reflected the family's distant ownership, a form of local autonomy that leads to dullness, anemic reporting, and a consistent pattern of petit moral corruptness between advertisers and the editorial pages. This was more than a matter of allowing Roy Cohn to fix a story on the front page for a mobster client or a politician. Rather, it was an overall bottom-line philosophy that increasingly became the ethical standard of group newspapers in one-newspaper towns across the United States. To be sure, there were occasional exceptions at the Newhouse newspapers: here or there, a talented editor, a prize-winning series, or an inspired editorial. But excellence was usually a fleeting experience at Newhouse papers, a fond memory when talented people left for better newspapers and the usual approach returned. "Newhouse! Few people think of great journalism when the name is spoken," the *Columbia Journalism Review* commented in 1985. "Advance Publications Inc., the Newhouse holding company, has a reputation for glitzy magazines and a whole herd of bland newspapers, cash cows in a pasture, dutifully generating revenue for the new acquisition."

With this plantation-like approach, the Newhouse publications evolved by the 1990s into a very distinct two-tier system of providing information to Americans. There were the informed tony magazines and publishing houses—the Knopfs, the *Vogues,* the discriminating travel guides—read by the upper classes, those affluent people who might be encountered by Si or Donald or their socially active wives at parties in New York. For this select audience, the level of writing and quality of presentation was almost always first-rate. And then, out in the hinterlands, there were the cash cows, those old gray hulks of mediocrity that served as the only printed daily source of information for millions of Americans who would never know who the Newhouses were. Somehow, in the Newhouse equation, the quality of information seemed to depend on how demographically desirable you were. Newspapers were not a public trust but, rather, a private financial instrument to be tapped into like an annuity, with little shared return or sense of accountability to the communities they served. As a result, a newspaper like the *New Orleans Times-Picayune* could still be described by a respected journalism review—more than a decade after the Newhouses purchased it for a record-setting price—as "the bloated, sluggish, myopic giant of the Delta morn'."

For much of the 1980s, the *Times-Picayune*—with a circulation of 270,000, making it one of the largest newspapers in the South—struggled to rise above mediocrity, a Sisyphean effort resulting in only limited success. "It's a good paper, better than it's given credit for," said former editor Charles Ferguson after he abruptly left it in 1990. "We all have our bad days, of course. Our bad weeks even, but as long as you keep rolling the ball up the hill, that's what counts." Although the Newhouses owned the paper, most residents of New Orleans thought the *Times-Picayune* was owned by publisher Ashton Phelps, who was part of the private trust that sold the newspaper in 1962 but continued to oversee its operations. Phelps was overseen by Sam's brother Norman, who moved to New Orleans at the family's request but never directly managed the newspaper. Instead, the newspaper retained much of the Phelps flavor, serving New Orleans's long-established "white shoe" crowd and business interests that controlled an increasingly diverse city. "There is no community leadership on the editorial page and they ignore all kinds of important stories locally," said former columnist Ronnie Virgets, who was fired for walking away from the Democratic National Convention in Atlanta after one of his columns was killed. "It's all part of the Phelps family's tradition of not rocking the local boat."

That traditional slowness extended as well to progress on matters of race. Not until 1990, for example, did the *Times-Picayune* include African-Americans among its annual list of top-echelon society debutantes—far from an insignificant exclusion in a city with a black mayor for much of the previous decade. The most acrimonious example of the *Times-Picayune's* slowness, however, concerned the political rise of David Duke and how the Newhouse paper got scooped on probably the biggest Louisiana story of a generation. There were a number of political activists who, early in Duke's career, alerted the *Times-Picayune* to the background of this outspoken candidate for the Louisiana state legislature. Some offered a tape recording of a Duke speech before a group of Chicago neo-Nazis, as well as a wire-service photograph of Duke shaking hands with an American Nazi party official. Yet, for months afterward, there was virtually no coverage of Duke's hateful past by Louisiana's largest daily.

The *Times-Picayune* seemed satisfied with Duke's disavowal of his history as a white supremacist who had made numerous racist and anti-Semitic statements. Other newspapers, both within Louisiana and outside of the state, reported about Duke's affiliation with the Ku Klux Klan, his virulent anti-Semitism, and his authorship of a sexual-advice book for women written under a female pseudonym.

Eventually, the *Times-Picayune* began its own belated but in-depth coverage of Duke during his unsuccessful campaign for the U.S. Senate in 1990. These stories, while reiterating information from other publications, also pointed out some new details about Duke's finances and his use of plastic surgery to enhance his appearance. When Duke ran in the Louisiana gubernatorial race the following year, he galvanized the nation's attention with the threat of a neo-Nazi in the governor's chair. Embarrassed into action, the *Times-Picayune* then seemed to swing to the other extreme with news coverage that seemed deliberately designed to make sure Duke lost. (DUKE VICTORY WOULD COST LA., EXECS SAY, read one headline.) Duke's eventual loss and the *Times-Picayune*'s catch-up effort did not stop many New Orleans observers from wondering where its only city newspaper had been on this story. "Why were stories that received broad and deep attention—prominent play—in other papers treated as short, straight news stories often tucked away in the *Times-Picayune*'s Metro section?" asked press critic Jeanne W. Amend, whose accounts of the newspaper's lethargic response were later published in two prominent journalism reviews. "And why, many wondered, was there such a singular lack of analysis and synthesis in the *Times-Picayune*'s coverage of David Duke, a man with an unnerving history of racist and anti-Semitic views who suddenly disavowed the ideas he had devoutly promoted for the majority of his forty years, a story if ever there was one that warranted the press's scrutiny in Louisiana?"

Some might blame a specific reporter or editor, or maybe old Ashton Phelps, for the lapse in alerting the public to this alleged neo-Nazi in their midst, but the answer lay in the fundamental culture of Newhouse Newspapers—the plantation philosophy that dampened journalistic curiosity and gave comfort to the city's vested interests. In New York, Si Newhouse might preach about the need for change at his favored publications. Yet outside Manhattan and beyond the view of the national press, at his privately owned newspapers where his family continued to reap its fortune, the preservation of the status quo was paramount, regardless of how morally repugnant or disenfranchising to its readers.

The *Times-Picayune*'s apathetic coverage of the Duke story was not an isolated incident. Rather, it was part of a history of benign neglect by a number of the Newhouse newspapers, a trend that could be traced back more than three decades, when the *Birmingham News* was a voice for segregation in Alabama and a champion of the racist views of local demagogues like "Bull" Connor. In 1955, the Newhouse family purchased the *Birmingham News,* once again setting a benchmark for the price of a newspaper, and kept the local management in place, including Clarence Hanson as president and publisher, one of the Hanson family that sold the paper to Newhouse. "A newspaper should be a local institution—not just the expression of a personal will or whim," Newhouse editorial director Phil Hochstein said at the time of the sale. What this hands-off approach meant in Birmingham—where beatings, cross burnings, attacks on synagogues, and an atmosphere of hatred and violence prevailed—was the tacit acceptance by Newhouse of a newspaper that continued to serve as a virtual cheerleader for racial segregation in that city.

When Harrison Salisbury, one of the great reporters for *The New York Times,* went to Birmingham in 1960 to examine segregation and interracial strife in the South, he dispatched a gripping account that was published on the *Times*'s front page under the headline FEAR AND HATRED GRIP BIRMINGHAM. The Newhouse paper chose to run Salisbury's story but under a very different headline: N.Y. TIMES SLANDERS OUR CITY—CAN THIS BE BIRMINGHAM? An editorial the following day slammed Salisbury's reporting as "maliciously bigoted, noxiously false, viciously distorted," as if city commissioner Bull Connor had written it himself. When Connor sued for libel over the story, the Newhouse paper in Birmingham was very supportive of his position in their own news stories about Connor's lawsuit against the *Times*—which was eventually won by the *Times* in a landmark freedom of the press decision by the U.S. Supreme Court. Years afterward, when Connor died, his personal notes, tape recordings, and photos showed that reporters for the Newhouse paper were among the police commissioner's network of local spies. But the Newhouse family never showed any interest in curbing the clearly racist tone of its Birmingham newspaper. As its publisher, Clarence Hanson, later testified, the only discussions he ever had with the Newhouses "have been exclusively about business and financial matters."

Even after the *Birmingham News* achieved a moment of excellence, winning a Pulitzer Prize in 1991 for editorial writing, the Newhouse ethos continued to mar its reputation. While the *News* could wax poetic in its editorial pages, the newspaper assigned Dennis Washburn to write a column in its news pages designed to promote the paper's auto, restaurant, and nightclub advertisers. Washburn's column was marked as promotional in small print above, but it was printed in the same typeface as any other "objective" story in the newspaper. When the *Washington Journalism Review* published an article about the pressure auto dealers exert on newsrooms across the country, Washburn was quoted as saying, "Editorial would be extra careful about doing an exposé. . . . They probably would not jeopardize such a substantial portion of our advertisers unless it was really something major, something that affects people's lives. Their pocketbooks are something else entirely." The day after the *Washington Journalism Review* article appeared, Washburn, a twenty-three-year veteran of the newspaper, was fired for, in effect, admitting what many other journalists believed to be the dirty little secret about the *News*'s relationship with its advertisers. "The joke around town was that 'Dennis told the truth for the first time in 20 years and got fired for it,' which was the truth as I saw it," said Tim Lennox, a radio talk-show host in Birmingham.

For his part, Washburn said he regretted ever writing puff pieces about the advertisers—and only did so because the job paid more than his previous jobs as assistant city editor, travel editor, and reporter at the paper. He said the real losers were the readers who looked to the local paper for untainted news reports. "I was just telling the truth and maybe I was a fool for doing so," Washburn said in an interview a year after his firing. "It was common knowledge that auto dealers had a certain amount of influence. The type of writing in the special sections was really promotional, puff pieces that weren't really advertising or news stories, but you could barely tell the difference. The *News* does make an attempt to let readers know about it, but it's in small print. Most readers don't know the difference between these sections and the editorial copy."

This breakdown in journalistic standards was not originally part of the proud tradition at the *Portland Oregonian,* the largest newspaper in the nation's Northwest, with a daily circulation of 330,000 and 440,000 on Sundays. Unlike other previous newspapers purchased by Sam Newhouse, the *Oregonian* was already considered a financial success as well as a well-regarded newspaper capable of winning a Pulitzer Prize and serving the informational needs of Portland's citizenry. Within a few years after Newhouse bought it in 1950, the journalistic quality of the *Oregonian* began a noticeable decline, particularly after a violent strike at the newspaper. Several local leaders, like Oregon's maverick Senator Wayne Morse, expressed concern about Newhouse's dominance, especially after the owners of the city's only other competing daily, the *Oregon Journal*, sold out to Newhouse for $8 million and the paper was promptly folded into the *Oregonian's* operation.

As always, the Newhouse newspaper survived the short-lived threat of a government inquiry into its methods and prospered while the Portland economy boomed during the 1960s and 1970s. By the 1980s, the *Oregonian* was described as fat and happy, with occasional moments of excellence, like stories about the progress of school desegregation in Portland or a local medical team's efforts in Ethiopia. The *Oregonian's* bright and colorful graphics made it more appealing than some of Newhouse's other newspapers, but its local coverage remained bland. "You don't get the sense of the sweat pouring off their brow," John A. Armstrong, a former *Oregonian* editor and journalism teacher at the University of Portland, said in 1985. "It's a fatter paper now, but it's diffuse. There's a lot in the suburban sections that's just fat—ethnic restaurants, people overcoming handicaps that sort of thing—but it's more style than substance."

When the national recession of the late 1980s and early 1990s hit the Portland area, the *Oregonian,* once used to record-level profit margins, had to adapt its standards to a diminishing advertising base. By no means was the paper losing money. It is nearly impossible for a newspaper with a virtual lock on the market to lose money. But the smaller profit margins made the newspaper more sensitive to advertisers who complained about its local reporting. In 1989, for example, the newspaper's management decided to trash tens of thousands of copies of a Sunday edition simply because someone on the advertising-sales side objected to a story in the real estate section about selling a home without a broker. Rather than offend its real estate advertisers, the *Oregonian* killed the article and demoted the editor who had approved the piece. Asked about the incident, the managing editor, Peter Thompson, told *The Wall Street Journal* that the story wasn't "relevant" to its readers and was published only "through a lack of editorial monitoring, which has since been taken care of." Thompson adamantly, if not too convincingly, denied that the *Oregonian* kowtowed to its advertisers.

With a lingering national recession, the message was clear: Advertisers' concerns were to be taken more seriously than those of normal readers. In the same *Wall Street Journal* story, the *Oregonian*'s director of classified advertising, Max Taylor, acknowledged he routinely called the newsroom about complaints from advertisers. "The newsroom is always willing to listen, and always wants to improve a story if it can," the ad director said. In March 1991, when the newspaper's editors once again spiked a story sensitive to advertisers—this time, a column that criticized a big retailer for closing two neighborhood stores—the *Oregonian*'s staff became upset. Editor Thompson later called the offending column "an inadequate piece of journalism" in speaking to the *Journal,* but privately he met with small groups of reporters to assure them that the newspaper was not protecting its advertisers. Whatever hollow assurances they received from management, most reporters and editors—with their own lives and families to support—could not afford the luxury of fighting their employer over ethical standards. The subverting of traditional journalistic standards in these incidents, as the *Journal* found, resulted in a "self-editing in the newsroom," according to Ellen Heltzel, an *Oregonian* features editor at the time. "On our own, we may stay away from something sensitive."

Staying away from a story is exactly what happened shortly afterward. In the spring of 1992, the *Portland Oregonian* learned about the sexual escapades of Oregon's longtime senator Bob Packwood but chose not to print anything about several complaints from women who had worked for him. One of these women was a sixty-four-year-old reporter for the *Oregonian.* She complained that she had been kissed on the lips by the

Republican incumbent after a background interview. Yet even with Packwood running for reelection, the *Oregonian*—the only major daily in town—chose not to publish anything about what it knew, or strongly suspected, to be true. In fact, it endorsed Packwood for reelection. Immediately after the November 1992 election, the *Washington Post* ran an exposé about the women who had suffered sexual abuse and harassment at the hands of their esteemed senator. Many criticized the *Post* for waiting until after the election to print the information. Back in Oregon, people were outraged by the *Oregonian*'s failure of omission, which the newspaper later admitted in print. "I think it's inevitable that from time to time we're not going to be as aggressive as we should be," explained William A. Hillard, editor of the *Oregonian* since 1982. "And when that happens, I'm willing to take the responsibility for it."

The Packwood incident contributed further to the *Oregonian*'s image of being in bed with the power elite. A few years earlier, the paper had hired the top aide of Oregon's other U.S. senator, Mark Hatfield, to write a column for $22,000 a year, on the precondition that he wouldn't mention Hatfield. By avoiding local political scandal, the *Oregonian* seemed ripe for a national embarrassment. The disclosures about Senator Packwood further called into question the newspaper's commitment to aggressive, open-eyed journalism. Some people demanded a recall of Packwood, while readers in Portland started plastering their cars with bumper stickers that made fun of the *Oregonian*'s ad slogan: IF IT MATTERS TO OREGONIANS, IT'S IN THE OREGONIAN. Instead, the bumper sticker proclaimed: IF IT MATTERS TO OREGONIANS, IT'S IN THE *WASHINGTON POST*.

Unfortunately, the controversy seemed to overshadow the achievements of William Hillard, who was one of the few black editors at a large American newspaper and who had expanded opportunities for minorities at the *Oregonian*. At the same time Hillard was being voted in as president of the American Society of Newspaper Editors in 1993, the Newhouses brought in a new executive editor to run the newspaper, in effect, in the wake of the Packwood fiasco. But to blame Hillard or any other manager for the professional lapses of the Newhouse newspapers is to miss the broader failures allowed by the Newhouse papers on their readers. Far from a single isolated omission or momentary breach of ethics, the Newhouses have fostered a culture of apathetic reporting, cozy political relationships, and a moral ambiguity that permeates their history as stewards of a public trust.

Nowhere has that dull cash-cow mentality been more prevalent than at the Newhouses' largest newspaper, the *Newark Star-Ledger*. It is the dominant newspaper in New Jersey, with a daily circulation of 483,000, which soars on Sundays to 717,500, when the *Star-Ledger* is stuffed with local advertisements and can sometimes outweigh the bulk of *The New York Times*. While Donald Newhouse oversees the financial side of the newspaper, its editor for nearly forty years has been a crusty, no-nonsense man named Mort Pye, who married into the Newhouse family in 1942 and worked at only two daily newspapers in his career: the Newhouses' *Long Island Press* and the *Star-Ledger*. Pye was brought over by the family to Newark in 1957 to help revive the sagging *Star-Ledger,* which was a distant second to the *Newark Evening News,* a highly regarded afternoon newspaper. "I hate to speak ill of the dead, but the *Star-Ledger* was not thriving in the 1950s, even though Newark then was still a prosperous city," Pye recalled. "The paper was going downhill fast."

In its news coverage, the *Star-Ledger* favored a boosterism approach that usually ignored the corruption of local politicians and the growing strife in a city with a large minority population. During the 1960s, Mayor Hugh Addonizio proved to be a crook and city hall was influenced by organized crime, as federal authorities later contended, but readers of the *Star-Ledger* rarely got a glimpse of that reality until the mayor was indicted, convicted, and sent to jail. In 1967, the violent race riots that tore through Newark also seemed to catch the *Star-Ledger* by surprise. For the rival *Evening News,* which was already suffering the fate of many other American afternoon newspapers with the advent of television, the Newark riots brought about an economic calamity from which it never recovered. The Scudder family, which had owned the *Evening News* since 1882, decided to sell out to another company, which wound up selling its circulation list and other assets to Newhouse for $20 million. After the death of the *News* in the early 1970s, the *Star-Ledger* expanded rapidly, deliberately attempting to become the dominant newspaper in New Jersey.

"They are very bland and a gutless newspaper," says Richard Scudder, whose begrudging respect for the Newhouse financial prowess is tempered by the poor journalistic quality of the *Star-Ledger.* "They could serve the state so well, as the *News* did, but they don't care to do that. They don't use for good the considerable influence they have."

Some contend the Newhouse papers have already used too much influence behind the scenes and used their clout and pressure to improperly influence local politics. "The *Star-Ledger*'s influence is impossible to overestimate," wrote Robert Sam Anson in the *New Jersey Monthly* in 1977. "An editorial or news series in its pages can, if not make or break a candidate or issue, provide the crucial margin that will." Like a politician who wants an edifice to outlast him, Pye advocated the construction of the sprawling Meadowlands sports complex in Hackensack, New Jersey, which was first suggested in a 1967 *Star-Ledger* series and then was promoted vigorously by the newspaper until it was built. "The way he pushed the creation of the sports complex, he compromised the paper's journalistic standards," observed John Kolesar, the managing editor of a downstate paper, the *Camden Courier-Post.* "For a newspaper editor, that may not be the best memorial." Reporters at the *Star-Ledger* joked that Interstate 280, which connects Newark with the rest of the state and for which the newspaper campaigned very hard, should be called the "Pye-way." These projects, though beneficial to the *Star-Ledger,* could be perceived as being in the public interest. There were other private arrangements, however, that were clearly improper.

One of the most unethical practices by the *Star-Ledger* was pressuring campaigning politicians to place their ads in the *Star-Ledger* or else, it was suggested, the newspaper's news coverage of the candidate would suffer. In one conversation, a campaign aide for then gubernatorial candidate Thomas Kean tape-recorded his conversation with a Newhouse ad salesman who threatened poor coverage if the Kean campaign didn't spend more campaign money for *Star-Ledger* ads. The *Star-Ledger's* managing editor at the time denied that they "in any way, shape, or form trade advertising for political coverage." But its chief political reporter at that time received memos from the ad department, with a tally of which candidates were buying political ads in the paper. There were other examples, such as the political reporter who became statehouse bureau chief and wrote press releases for his "good friend" Congressman Peter Rodino; he was found giving out press releases to fellow reporters for the New Jersey Motorist Association, which listed him as secretary of the group. Several years earlier, another *Star-Ledger* political reporter covering a then-little-known prosecutor named Brendan Byrne was paid eight thousand dollars a year for public relations work by an insurance firm headed by Byrne, who eventually became New Jersey's governor. The reporter never disclosed his secret payments from Byrne to readers, and he continued to cover Byrne's activities for Newhouse's *Star-Ledger.* "The payoff is journalism's dirty little secret, the one story that almost never gets written about; seldom, in fact, even talked about," Anson commented. "It is merely there, eating away at the very foundation of journalism: the trust a reader has that a newspaper is presenting the news objectively."

The great flow of wealth from the New Jersey populace in the form of advertising and subscriptions was reflected only in the bulk of the *Star-Ledger,* with little of these revenues used by the Newhouses to make the paper better or even close to the caliber that the nation's eleventh-largest Sunday newspaper ought to be. "The Newhouse chain is community-oriented, and we do what we think is best for our area," Pye said in 1992. But in reality, the *Star-Ledger* was strip-mining the community's great advertising base without putting anything back of equal journalistic merit. Its virtual monopoly status ensured that things would never change. Among the Newhouse newspapers, the *Star-Ledger* was the biggest plantation of all, where the front page had virtually the same fifties-style ugliness and unimaginative news approach as the day Mort Pye arrived. After nearly forty years, the newspaper had yet to win a Pulitzer Prize or even the respect of its peers.

At a time when many are wondering about the future of newspapers, the Newhouse group stands as a model of the industry's persistent ills and worse habits. Although much of the Newhouse family's wealth is derived from these newspapers—found in American cities both large and small—the attention of its two proprietors is clearly elsewhere. "My brother and I have neither the inclination nor opportunity to get involved editorially in any of our publications," Si Newhouse once explained. "We learned from our father to provide sound management and build financially sound companies, and that keeps us fully occupied." In short, take the money and run. As a result, the Newhouse newspapers remain a place where every good move or earnest gesture, like the hiring of talented editors and reporters, is undermined by accounts of unprofessionalism or improper deeds.

This paradox was made apparent in 1993 when the *Columbia Journalism Review* awarded one of its laurels to the *Cleveland Plain Dealer* for an outstanding award-winning series about the dangers of shoddy radiation treatment administered by doctors and hospitals. But in the next breath, the *CJR* awarded one of its poison darts to the *New Orleans Times-Picayune* for refusing to run the same series offered by "its sister Newhouse paper," which was being distributed through the group's Newhouse News Service. The *Review* said the series never appeared in New Orleans after the wife of the *Times-Picayune* publisher, Ashton Phelps, Jr., who was a radiologist, expressed objection.

Once again, the easy fix by someone powerful enough to kill information clearly in the public interest was just further evidence of what the *Review* concluded in 1985 about Si and Donald Newhouse's approach to newspapers: "It's a system where excellence may be applauded, but it is not demanded, where no one at the top cares as deeply about the words as they do about the money," said the *Review*. "Perhaps that is the reason why the third-largest newspaper chain in the U.S. still has no great newspapers."

When the glossy magazine *HG* died in early 1993, loyal readers expressed their sorrow at losing a steady companion. "I've received such passionate, intelligent, amazing letters," said editor Nancy Novogrod after the magazine's demise was announced by Si Newhouse. "They are all really suffering grief. A void has been left in their life."

Death came to *HG* and its staff as a sudden surprise, mostly because the ninety-two-year-old magazine was reportedly still making money when Si Newhouse announced its end. *HG* had survived many different epochs and editors, including Anna Wintour's experimental tour of duty in the late 1980s, when the magazine's old name, *House & Garden,* was replaced by the trendier *HG.* Numerous readers and advertisers fled the elegant home-decorating magazine because of Wintour's precipitous changes. When Novogrod replaced Wintour in 1988, however, the hemorrhaging stopped and *HG* was again established as one of the nation's leading "shelter" magazines.

In March 1993, though, *HG* became expendable. The magazine's fate was sealed when Si Newhouse purchased *Architectural Digest,* the leader in the "shelter book" niche of the magazine industry, and another upscale magazine, *Bon Appetit,* for a reported $175 million in cash from Knapp Communications. *Bon Appetit* was expected to widen the Condé Nast company's control of the food and travel market, though most industry experts considered *Architectural Digest* to be the true gem. Although *HG* had slightly more readers (some 696,000 to 653,000), *Architectural Digest* had far more lucrative advertising pages with demographics considered elite. Most middle-class readers recognized the difference. In an issue of *HG,* you might find a usable tip or affordable layout for your own home; in *Architectural Digest,* you just looked at the lavish spreads in awe.

At the time of the sale, Bernard Leser, president of Condé Nast, gave assurances that neither one of the magazines would be closed. But two months after the sale, Newhouse and Leser announced they were going to shut down *HG*—a victim of what Newhouse called "considerable redundancy" between the two magazines. Although the readers of *Architectural Digest* and *HG* were from two very different income stratas, both publications were competing essentially for the same advertising dollar. In the time-honored Newhouse tradition of eliminating the competition or buying it out, Si made the final bottom-line decision: *HG* had to go.

For the final issue in July 1993, the editors of *HG* (some of whom were moved to other spots in the organization) considered a photograph of the entire staff waving good-bye. When Leser reportedly heard the idea, he quickly nixed it. As one staffer said, "He didn't want to put too human a face on the extinction of the magazine."

Putting a human face on extinction has not been Si Newhouse's forte. Press clippings are filled with stories about Newhouse's peculiar ways of firing people or the doublespeak phrases he uses—like "considerable redundancy"—before jettisoning an entire magazine or staff into publishing oblivion. What is often missed in the bloody saga of severed heads at Newhouse's company, however, is the broader implications of one man controlling so much of America's media. His brazen moves to buy out his rivals underline how ineffectual the government has been in preventing anti-competitive moves by huge communication conglomerates such as Advance Publications. In this respect, with much of the attention focused on the clash of personalities, Si Newhouse has skillfully obscured and screened from public inspection the overwhelming growth and dominance of his company in the 1990s. He is one of the true masters of the new Megamedia—that oligarchic group of major communications companies that control so much of what Americans consume as news and comment.

A close examination of Si Newhouse's methods immediately calls to attention those fundamentally anti-democratic forces at work in his actions and in his family's consolidation of media power. Killing the competition is one of the least-known stories.

Sam Newhouse was loath to keep "funerals," as he called newspapers without a monopoly stranglehold. In his time, he bought and killed the *Long Island Press,* the *Portland Oregon Journal,* and even the *Bayonne Times,* the same paper where Judge Lazarus had given him his start in publishing. Si and Donald Newhouse kept alive their father's tradition of killing competition by buying the subscription list of the *Cleveland Press* in a pre-arranged move and by "merging" its *New Orleans States-Item* with the more powerful *Times-Picayune* in 1980. By using these tactics—acquiring competitors' subscription lists, making secret buyout deals with rival owners, convincing friendly distributors to give better placement on the newsstands, or simply flashing enough money until the competition grabs it and leaves—S. I. Newhouse and sons have almost always prevailed.

During the 1980s, in Portland and New Orleans, this tradition continued as rivals filed lawsuits that alleged predatory pricing practices by the dominant Newhouse newspapers in those cities. These lawsuits went nowhere and made little impact on the way the Newhouses do business. At his *St. Louis Globe-Democrat,* Si Newhouse extended the family's tradition of killing newspapers, despite attempts by local, state, and federal officials to stop its closure in 1983. To some critics, the *Globe-Democrat* was hardly a model of journalistic excellence. Under Newhouse, the newspaper had become persistently mediocre and had been ranked a few years earlier by one journalism review as one of the ten worst newspapers in the nation. Still, the *Globe-Democrat* was the only other competitor in town to the *St. Louis Post-Dispatch.*

What was particularly controversial was a secret pact between Newhouse and the owners of the *St. Louis Post-Dispatch,* which only became public two decades after it was signed. Under this secret arrangement, first established in 1961, the Newhouses and their competitor agreed to combine their business operations and share the profits. In November 1983, the Newhouses decided to close the *Globe-Democrat* through this joint agreement, a move that prompted the U.S. Justice Department to intervene on antitrust grounds. As a result, the Newhouses sold the newspaper in early 1984 to Jeffrey and Debra Gluck, under whose management the *Globe-Democrat* filed for bankruptcy and later closed in November 1985.

All of this was a pretty lucrative deal. Under this arrangement, whether the Newhouses deliberately set out to kill the *Globe-Democrat* or, as happened, decided to sell to another buyer who would quickly close the paper, the company was still guaranteed a sizable cut of St. Louis's advertising revenues until the year 2034. When this twenty-two-year-old arrangement became known in 1983, some published estimates said Newhouse and the Pultizer company, which owned the *Post-Dispatch,* could share as much as $15 million each year by making St. Louis into a one-newspaper town. After the *Globe-Democrat* disappeared, the Newhouse share from the joint agreement had totaled $43.5 million by 1993. "The idea of a monopoly in St. Louis was troubling to the citizens of the area as well as to the journalism community," wrote Carolyn Tozier in the scholarly *Journalism Quarterly,* long after the *Globe* was in the industry's dustbin.

Newhouse lawyers replied that the agreement was perfectly legal. Under the Newspaper Preservation Act, the Newhouses were able to find a loophole which permitted them to kill one of the two papers. Even *The Wall Street Journal* called it a "perverse" use of the law. But since the Newhouses' actions, six other cities, including Miami and Pittsburgh, became one-newspaper towns under similar interpretations of the clearly misnomered Newspaper Preservation Act. "When you do what the Justice Department says to do, it's hard to claim you have done something wrong," said one Newhouse lawyer.

As the St. Louis experience demonstrated, most American journalists and readers, even analysts who cover the media industry, remain unaware of the details of the Newhouses' business dealings—partly because the company has always been private, but also because Si has been loath to reveal information about other parts of the family empire, even to the trusted executives of his top companies. As Steven Florio once explained about his boss, "He tries to keep the companies very separate."

By keeping companies separate, each with its own budget, revenues, and concerns, no one can be sure just how big the Newhouse media company really is. According to most industry estimates, it had become the largest privately held communications giant in America, with some nineteen thousand employees by the mid-1990s. In sheer size, the Newhouse empire was ranked at the top—or close to it—in books, newspapers, magazines, and cable-television franchises. No single individual in America's media—not Ted Turner, not Arthur Sulzberger, not Katharine Graham, not even Rupert Murdoch—owns as much as Si Newhouse or maintains so wide and influential a grip.

Surely, bigness can have its rewards. In its best form, Newhouse's bountiful supply of money and his hands-on approach allow some writers, usually at magazines like *Vanity Fair* and *The New Yorker* or at the prestigious imprints within Random House, to seek out exceptional stories and be paid well for their craft. Although Sam Newhouse seldom read his own newspapers, Si carefully examines each month's Condé Nast magazines, looking for signs of editorial fatigue. He has read or is familiar with many of the major books published by his book divisions. He knows and can appreciate good writing. In spite of his seeming lust for managerial changes, he has developed a remarkable eye for talent over the years and displays a willingness to listen to advice from his trusted aides. If a new printing plant needs to be constructed or a budding magazine needs more time to emerge, Si has proven himself an exceptional publisher who is willing to listen without immediate regard for the quarterly profit statements. In an age where publicly owned media corporations can take months to make decisions by committee, Si Newhouse's singular approach can be refreshing. In this sense, he is a quiet throwback to the days of other publishing tycoons, such as the Hearsts and Pulitzers, who were integral to the lives of their publications.

But in another respect, Newhouse has emerged as the very prototype for this new age of Megamedia—a world where information vital to people's lives is dominated by only a few huge corporations with little or no public accountability. For years, political commentators, sociologists, and media critics have warned about the growing concentration of media monopolies and the resulting threat to a democratic society. "The news media—diluted of real meaning by apolitical and sterile context, homogenized with the growth of monopoly, overwhelmingly more of a service to merchants than to the audience, and filled with frivolous material— are a threat to their own future but also to the body politic," wrote Ben H. Bagdikian in his 1983 book, *Media Monopoly.*

With advertising from big businesses being the lifeblood of most mass media, editors and publishers at groups like the Newhouse newspapers were anxious not to rock the boat with controversial stories that might offend large groups of consumers or powerful select interests. Even advertising experts like Leo Bogart, former executive vice president of the industry's Newspaper Advertising Bureau, noticed how the cultural landscape had changed in favor of this oligarchy of media powerhouses. The American media, as Bogart wrote, "is increasingly controlled by a handful of people who wield enormous power, but whose interests and energies are spread too thin to permit them to take pride in any non-commercial aspect of their endeavors. It is heavily laced with advertising, some of it so meretricious in its style of argument that it desensitizes us to the absence of integrity in human discourse—most blatantly in our political lives. Media content has been driven primarily by the need to maximize audiences for sale rather than by the desire to communicate the truth about our world or express deep thoughts and feelings."

By the early 1990s, these concerns were widespread. Newspapers with monopoly-like control existed in 98 percent of U.S. cities and were owned mostly by large companies like Advance Publications. With Newhouse's bottomless supply of revenues, Random House was purchased and became a sprawling $1 billion-a-year business. Part of this new publishing conglomerate was the Crown Publishing Group, which had been the nation's fifth-largest independent book publisher in 1980. Yet, eight years later, Crown was gobbled up by Newhouse's Random House without even the slightest hint by the Justice Department of an anti-trust problem.

This new corporate spirit with regard to publishing was felt in many corners, and within Newhouse's company it eventually led to publishers and top editors agreeing to remain silent in exchange for money. In the early 1990s, several publishers who worked for Si Newhouse agreed as part of their written contracts or severance packages not to talk publicly about their experiences or views about Newhouse's company for a period of time. In the publishing business, these were called "gag agreements."

Some like Joni Evans, the onetime publisher at Random House and Turtle Bay Books, saw nothing wrong with such arrangements. "I'm not allowed to talk about Random House," she said shortly after leaving the company in 1993. "This is my contract with the company. There is a time period on it. I can't remember how long. It [the restriction on talking] is at least a year. This isn't an exit thing. It was my employment contract with them. And it's perfectly normal."

But this enforced silence became a source of great embarrassment for some individuals who felt compelled to sign them. "People sign it because they need the money and because they want to get on with their lives," explained Martin Garbus, a lawyer who has represented Elisabeth Sifton, Pantheon's André Schiffrin, and Knopf's Sonny Mehta. In the case of André Schiffrin, for example, the gag agreement extended for a year. So while his exit from Pantheon was thoroughly discussed in the press, Schiffrin was legally bound from talking on the record, even when others at Random House freely criticized him and his reputation.

In negotiating legal contracts for his clients, Garbus, a First Amendment lawyer himself, said he was disturbed by the demands of the Newhouse organization for such a gag agreement. "It's something new, only in the last few years. It's not well known. People can sign away their First Amendment rights for money," said Garbus, who would not specify which of his clients had agreed to these provisions. "There are people who refuse to sign it. But it's happening because publishing is getting more corporate and you're getting more corporate type of things like gag agreements. It's inevitable and contradictory and you'd think the last place you'd find it is in publishing. It's hard to envision someone like Alfred Knopf ever even thinking of such a thing."

In this new media age, Newhouse publications, once viewed with disdain by their journalistic brethren, became the belle of the ball. Trendy magazines like *Vanity Fair* and *Vogue* embraced the material excesses of the Reagan years and heightened the national media craze for celebrity tidbits rather than probing analytical journalism. "The great majority of big media owners have always been happier with conservative Republicans, but in the 1980s, they had reason to be ecstatic: as they were dispensing their relentlessly positive news about Reaganism, they were being allowed by the government to create giant, monopolistic media empires," Bagdikian observed in 1992, nearly a decade after his book about media consolidation appeared. Certainly top Democrats were not immune to throwing stardust on their image, such as First Lady Hillary Rodham

Clinton, whose elegant portrait appeared in *Vogue* in late 1993. The power of Newhouse, however, extended far beyond perceived political affiliations or predilections.

The influence of Si Newhouse and his publications on American society is defined by their effect on what people think of themselves and their communities, where they spend their money, and the goals and values to which they aspire. This vision of America is of a sharply divided nation, where the quality of information—and the power that accrues from it—varies greatly by income strata and social class. Newhouse's approach celebrates those glossy magazines and elite publishing houses designed for the select audience of the rich and educated, while his chain of monopoly newspapers for the "mass" audience has traditionally emphasized financial performance over public service or journalistic distinction. There is no doubt Si Newhouse prefers the café life of Condé Nast to the K mart atmosphere of his family's newspapers. Influenced by Alexander Liberman and the opulent tradition of Condé Nast, Newhouse adopted the elitist approach of Condé Nast himself, who spoke of "class publications" aimed at what this generation of publishers would call the "demographically desirable." His magazines would serve a certain class of rich people—and people who wanted to be just like them. Newhouse updated Condé Nast's original approach with market research and such advertising devices as outserts and advertorials, which further blurred the distinction between commerce and journalism. In Newhouse publications, it is difficult to tell where the advertising stops and the news begins, and vice versa.

At the *New Orleans Times-Picayune,* for example, readers and reporters alike were confused in 1992 by a daily column that looked like a regular news story but was printed in a slightly bigger typeface and featured tales of favored advertisers and their warehouse grand openings and anniversary sales. Journalists noticed this overall trend in many American newspapers and sometimes objected to its corrupting effect on the profession. In 1992, 75 percent of business writers surveyed in an anonymous poll taken by the Society of American Business Editors and Writers said they were aware of increasing pressure by advertisers to influence the content of their pages—with 45 percent admitting it had affected the way they presented the news. But in this new era of Megamedia, in which Si Newhouse plays a major part, such journalistic concerns are usually steamrolled by a bottom-line amorality. "I'd rather it not be in the same type, and I wouldn't allow it in the business section," said Charley Blaine, the *Times-Picayune*'s business editor about his paper's special column devoted to advertisers. "It's real obvious what it is. I don't like it, but I can't stop it."

Despite their claims of editorial integrity, Newhouse's publications remain in the vanguard of co-opting newsrooms through pressure from the business side—a cynical rewriting of the ethical boundaries, in which the professional ideal of untainted and unbowed journalism is almost always lost. Nowhere was this stark difference in philosophy more apparent than at *The New Yorker*. For years through its own example, the magazine's high standards influenced much of America's journalism community. A generation of editors and reporters took this separation between the business and editorial interests as a bedrock tenet of the profession, essential to a publication's convenant with its readers. These editors could point to the financial success of Shawn's *New Yorker* and argue for the positive results of an approach which placed the reader above advertising interests. Newhouse's new ethos at *The New Yorker* was rationalized as a necessary change, that the magazine had to adapt to survive. But in compromising the magazine's ethical standards, Newhouse killed an important part of *The New Yorker*'s unique place in journalism, as if its gentle but unbending idealism was just another victim of the go-go eighties.

Likewise, the Newhouse family's plantationlike approach to its newspaper franchises present a serious challenge for those concerned with a free flow of information in a democratic society. In the Newhouse newspaper chain—with net profits estimated as much as 25 percent of its estimated total revenues—there seemed little pressure for better news gathering and more pages devoted to news. Most reporters who might agitate for improvements or reforms usually fear for their jobs, while public officials who might object to such a powerful grip on public opinion are mindful of a newspaper's editorial clout with voters. Ultimately, what can citizens expect of the only newspaper in a major city that reaps a fortune year after year and yet remains mediocre at best? Can America afford to trust publishers like Si Newhouse?

As the nation prepares for a new century, public-opinion polls show many Americans feel disenfranchised by the media, especially by lackluster daily newspapers that resemble utility companies rather than vibrant forums of diverse and insightful opinion. Certainly, the monolithic nature of Newhouse newspapers fit this description, with their maintenance of the political status quo and a fidelity to the prevailing business interests rather than those of the reader. At its worst, such as the involvement of the Mafia in compromising the Presser story at the *Cleveland Plain Dealer*, Si Newhouse has proven himself to be a suspect steward of the public trust, becoming the embodiment of what many fear about the concentration of too much American media power into too few hands. "Where once newspapers were at the very heart of the national conversation, they now seem remote, arrogant, part of the governing elite," observed *Washington Post* media critic Howard Kurtz about the newspaper industry of the 1990s. "Where once newspapers were on the front lines in exposing official corruption, they now bring up the rear, more concerned with accommodating power than challenging it."

Eventually, the specter of cities with only one daily newspaper—as well as evidence that a public trust has been repeatedly abused—may invite a kind of government regulation, perhaps of the sort that Congress imposed on the broadcasting industry in the 1930s. At that time, politicians argued that the content of radio must be regulated because of the limited number of stations on the AM dial, then the only band available. Most major cities had two or more competing newspapers. In today's America, that argument has reversed itself, with the rationale for government oversight more apt to apply to monopoly newspapers. There is now a rainbow of broadcasting options, from over-the-air VHF and UHF television stations, to sophisticated programming found on FM radio as well as AM, to cable television with multiple news and information channels. At the same time, newspapers have become more consolidated into powerful, unchallenged franchises where owners like Si Newhouse and his brother never have to account to anyone for their actions.

The Newhouses have been fortunate to live in a time when Americans make so few demands of their media owners. Rather than reinvesting money in dull newspapers in urban centers like New Orleans or Newark— where costly quality journalism is vitally needed and could have considerable impact—millions of Newhouse dollars have been diverted instead to the acquisition of upscale properties and such remakes as that of *Vanity Fair* or the expensive purchase of elitist travel or "shelter" magazines. Rather than raise the quality and ethical standards of American journalism, the brothers Newhouse have rigidly adhered to the same mediocre approach as their father, in which terms like *local autonomy* become nothing more than an excuse for doing nothing.

There is a crucial difference with Si and Donald Newhouse, however. They are not like most executives of publicly held media companies. They can be held personally responsible for the state of their publications, simply because they own them and their family's name is on them. They need not answer to a board of directors or any outside group. If they chose to, they could make the Newhouse name synonymous with journalistic excellence and a genuine voice for civic concerns and social justice. Accountability with the Newhouses, however, seems to be calibrated mostly in marketing rather than moral terms. "I think we are accountable," said Donald Newhouse, in his only comment for this book, "in that, if we are not accountable, people will not read or listen to our offerings." It is one of the lasting enigmas of American society that media barons can offer such a Hobson's choice to those living in single-newspaper towns. Nor is there much evidence that Si and his brother are troubled by such concerns.

In the past decade, Si Newhouse has been without peer, the dominant one who, as all the other major players know, casts the longest shadow in the arena of American media. He can personally devote the most money to the most ambitious project or most difficult obstacle for the longest period of time. From this realization comes the fear, the trepidation, and the begrudging admiration of those in his employ—or those who would like to be. Even his most effective advocates implicitly acknowledge his power.

"He's a very modest man, but I think he's having the time of his life now," said Tina Brown in 1993, recalling the man she had met a decade earlier when Newhouse was still quite unknown. "He's thrilled with his own successes. He can now look back on his last fifteen years and see what he's done. He created *Vanity Fair*. He launched *Self*. He launched *Traveler*. He launched *Allure*. He launched *Details*. And when you think of that, they're all success stories. That's tremendous. He's now the only show in town."

The Big Picture

Nothing matters more than the family.

Despite the vastness of the Newhouse empire, Si still diligently managed to apply his father's maxims to their company, as though he had memorized the lessons found in Sam Newhouse's book-length "memo" to his children. As the elder Newhouse prescribed: "the ties that matter are the ties to each other." Sam Newhouse's imperative to the family extended beyond nepotism to a realm where personal satisfaction and self-identity could be derived from their collective fortune.

Certainly, this was true for his eldest son. Within the Newhouse family, what made much of Si's success possible was his brother, Donald. While Si's interests increasingly drew him into the public spotlight by the mid-1990s, Donald remained content usually behind the scenes, deferring to his older brother's wishes. "I don't think they've ever had an argument," Norman Newhouse observed about the two brothers in an interview shortly after Sam's death. Some speculated that Donald was the truly powerful force within the family, the one whose sons would likely control the company in the future. Donald was a staunch supporter of the family's underlying loyalties and motivations, as much as his older brother and his father. As he testified at the 1990 tax trial over his father's estate, he was keenly aware of the downfalls of other media companies. He was determined "that we not fall into the Hearstian trap of developing big egos and rich habits, and that we continue to keep earnings in the company and build the company because we were building for ourselves, and we were building for our children and our children's children. . . ."

Si's second wife, Victoria, also realized the ideal of a self-perpetuating, ever-achieving Newhouse family was paramount to her husband; that he, the oldest son, had become the steward of his father's dream. Work—as it was for Sam Newhouse—had become Si's best way of expressing himself. "He doesn't need money and he isn't power-hungry," Victoria once said of her husband in an interview. "He is motivated by something more abstract. Perhaps it is a question of being a link in a chain—which, I suppose, is a sort of immortality."

This immortality would be hard for Si to achieve because his own three children—Samuel, Wynn, and Pamela—were sometimes reluctant participants in the Newhouse legacy. Si's divorce from Jane Franke and his demanding work schedule resulted in the almost-inevitable distance of a busy divorced parent living apart from his children. Although as a young man he had been resentful of his often-absent father, Si adopted a similar obsessive preoccupation with work, which troubled his family. On his fifty-third birthday in 1980, Si's children, by then in their mid- to late twenties, discussed why he continued the practice of arriving at work by 5:00 A.M. Even with his children, he sparingly let down his reserve.

"We talked about it endlessly, but we didn't resolve anything," Pam Newhouse later recalled. "Who knows what motivates him to get up early? When I asked him, he replied, 'Why do you get up at 7 A.M.?' The answer is prosaic rather than revealing. He works because he is disciplined and doesn't enjoy lying around. He collects paintings because he is attracted to the visual arts and he can satisfy his acquisitive side. But if you try to get to the bottom of him as a man, you'll see his reasons are profound and simple."

Pamela Newhouse's own life was far from simple. Despite her interests in becoming a writer, she never really published anyting of note, and her own private life had become just as disappointing. In November 1980, she married Verne Hendrick and two weeks afterward gave birth to Si's first grandchild, a boy, Jacob Henry Newhouse Hendrick. As an heiress to one of the world's great fortunes, Pamela asked her husband—whose annual income at the time was ten thousand dollars—to sign a prenuptial agreement the day before they married. Under the legal arrangement, Hendrick waived any future claim to the Newhouse fortune, agreeing to keep their financial affairs separate. The couple also agreed that Pamela would care for and support any children from their marriage in the event of a divorce.

The end to this marriage came swiftly. Before a court in Santo Domingo in the Dominican Republic, four months after their wedding, the young couple divorced in March 1981. The decree said their temperaments were incompatible, which "made life together unbearable." The following May, Si's company attorney, Charles Sabin, convinced a New York State judge to allow Pamela to change the name of her infant child to Jacob Henry Newhouse, with the consent of the father, who was by then living in Grand Rapids, Michigan. Family acquaintances say Pamela's life improved after this difficult marriage and that she continued to live in an apartment in Manhattan. She has never taken a prominent role in the family business, however.

Samuel Newhouse III dutifully followed his father's footsteps, becoming an executive and eventually publisher of the *Jersey Journal,* one of the papers in the family's chain. Sam III, as he often preferred to be called, also married in 1980, a month after Pamela. His vows were exchanged at a more elaborate ceremony, during which the two lighted candles given by the rabbi to Sam and his bride, Caroline, suddenly flickered and went out. Si quickly found a way to relight the extinguished candles. "That's good," the rabbi said. "A son should always get help from his family."

When not working at the *Jersey Journal,* Si's oldest son traveled with Donald and some of the other Newhouse family members to acquaint himself with the cable-television franchises owned by the Newhouses' broadcasting firm. "Sam always went along with the plans laid out for him," Pamela explained at the time. "He was the first son."

In many ways, Sam was very much like his father. He attended but never graduated from Syracuse University. He was a man who could seem relaxed and comfortable in knockabout clothes, including T-shirts and hiking boots. And he acquired the family's attentiveness to the bottom line, sometimes shouting at staff meetings about the need to curb costs. "We need the money," he instructed the family's hired hands. (In the early 1980s, he rented space at the Jersey City building to a doctor to raise an extra $850 a month.) Sam's outside interests were varied and eclectic, from scuba diving to building model airplanes, flying them off the roof of a Manhattan building that also happened to house his large-scale model trains. He gathered men's toys like his father collected art.

Whether Sam would ever be ready to assume the responsibilities of his father's job remained an open question through much of the 1980s. He seemed to lack the necessary tools and sense of gravitas. More so, Sam's chance to prove his mettle, as Si did after his father's death, still appeared years away. Si was still the boss, as his son Sam was reminded more than once. Such an occasion happened in 1987, when Sam decided to buy a seventy-two-foot yacht called the *Eagle.* He went to Fort Lauderdale to look at the boat and placed a $100,000 deposit. When Si learned of his son's intended purchase, he put his foot down. The father's power over the son was reminiscent of the time Sam Newhouse objected to young Si charging an eleven-dollar can of shaving cream to the company. Sam wrote back to the ship's owner that he would be unable to buy the *Eagle.* His father "felt very strongly that this was too large a yacht for me to purchase and maintain."

Like his father's, Sam's first marriage did not last very long. In 1988, he endured an acrimonious divorce and provided a handsome settlement to his ex-wife, who kept custody of their two sons, one of whom was named Samuel I. Newhouse IV. Young Sam stayed close to his father and continued to work diligently within the company's newspaper division. By 1994, however, he had passed forty years of age and few within the company talked about him as the Advance company's heir apparent.

No one, though, seemed to disappoint Si more in this regard than his second son, Wynn.

Wynn Newhouse was a friendly, sensitive young man who suffered a terrible freakish accident while he was working for his grandfather's flagship newspaper, the *Staten Island Advance*. Somehow, Wynn managed to catch his arm in the whirling motion of a huge printing press. His arm was nearly severed, but doctors were able to save it. "They put him over there to learn the technical end of the newspaper business and he caught it in the presses," said longtime family friend William Raidy, who recalled the shock and dismay of the whole Newhouse family over the accident. "Whatever came off, they managed to attach it again."

After the accident, Wynn became increasingly iconoclastic and removed from the family. He became someone who, as *Fortune* magazine described, "will do almost anything except what you want him to." In the 1970s, Wynn wore his hair long, which greatly displeased the elder members of his family, especially the meticulously groomed Sam Newhouse. "Wynny was always offbeat," said Raidy. "His grandfather would say, 'I won't be seen with you again unless you have a haircut!' I think Sam, though, underneath it all, admired him for it, because he defied him or whatever."

The family dispute over the length of Wynn's hair continued while he was working as a young photographer for the *Advance*. He was fired by one of his relatives when he refused to cut his hair. Rather than step into the dispute involving his son, Si kept his distance. Wynn was angered by his father's tacit acceptance. He became determined not to be a part of his family's plans, not to cede to Si's wishes. Instead, as a student at Syracuse University, where the journalism building was named after Sam Newhouse, Wynn studied computer science but never graduated. "It's a bone of contention because my father wants me to join," Wynn told an interviewer when asked whether he would become part of the family business. "One tends to build up a certain amount of resentment over being continuously pressed against."

As a Newhouse, Wynn was well acquainted with what was expected of him. "The force of my grandfather's personality is still imprinted on the entire family," Wynn said in an interview with a reporter in 1990, breaking another taboo within the clan. "It's a general drive that has come down— to succeed and to be a family. The original unity still holds up almost completely. But we're only up to the third generation. We have seen many other families that have fractured."

Wynn seemed determined to be one of the first fissures in this family-maintained monument to his grandfather's ambitions. He eventually moved to Boston, away from the family's orbit in New York, where he worked as a computer-software programmer. Wynn stayed in contact with his father, but the chill between them took years to thaw. "I don't think my father is that cold," Wynn said years later. "He does have a well-developed poker face. He doesn't always let on what he's thinking." Such ambivalent feelings also emerged during a 1991 interview with Wynn. He praised his father's intelligence yet admitted he really didn't understand

Si's emotional makeup. "I have yet to meet anyone who is his intellectual equal," said Wynn, by then thirty-six years old. "You can ask him anything and he'll have within him some knowledge of just about anything. When I was a child, I played chess with him, and I played him to a draw. But I never beat him." The Newhouse style didn't allow for weakness, for anything less than being a strong competitor in any chosen arena. There was much more to this emotional gamesmanship than chess matches, however. As friends and colleagues noted privately, Si surely wasn't pleased that as an adult Wynn had deliberately stayed away from the family business—and, in effect, from him.

Wynn had been diagnosed with multiple sclerosis, a debilitating illness that made life increasingly more difficult for him. In the early 1990s, Wynn's health was beginning to deteriorate when Si read an article about Dr. Irv Dardik, a New Jersey physician with a controversial approach to treating people with chronic types of muscular disorders. The article profiled the charismatic physician and former chairman of the U.S. Olympic Committee's Sports Medicine Council and told how he had devised a revolutionary but remarkably elemental method of using exercise (a careful regimen of rhythmic tension between athletic stress and relaxation to recoup lost energy) to improve the health of patients suffering from these ailments. Patients were usually connected to a sophisticated heart-rate monitor during exercise and reviewed daily by Dardik and his staff. The article mentioned the case studies of two patients with multiple sclerosis, including that of a thirty-year-old Philadelphia woman who made a remarkable improvement in her condition following Dardik's exercise treatments.

Si called the magazine writer who had interviewed Dardik and soon contacted the physician and asked him to meet Wynn. He was willing to arrange any treatment necessary to help his second son. Whatever the underlying reasons for Si's initiative, the physical results appeared dramatic.

"Wynn was in poor shape and he has had a rather remarkable turnaround," said one person who was involved. "For one thing, he and Si are now speaking again, which seems to be very much attributable to this whole experience. For a second thing, his physical health is much better. For a third, his mood is radically better." As evidence of his newly buoyant spirits, Wynn decided to get married. "Apparently, he's been with the same woman, but Wynn has been unable to make that decision for a long time," said this family friend. "So Si likes Irv Dardik a lot." At Wynn's wedding in 1992, Dardik was among the honored guests.

Somehow, this New Jersey doctor's soothing, rehabilitative approach eased some of the tensions between father and son. In arranging to pay someone to help heal his son, Si had once again expressed himself through deeds rather than emotions. The gesture seemed both poignant and somewhat pathetic, the late-in-life efforts of a father trying to make amends.

Dr. Dardik's intervention was an emotional salve—one more awkward, torturous schism in Si's life had been bridged through his own initiative and painful experience.

From one generation to the next, their family saga—the emotional ties that bound the Newhouses together—was built on fathers and sons, each indelibly affected by what had come before. The intensely driven Sam Newhouse and his need to achieve somehow seemed a reaction to the haplessness of his own immigrant father, Meyer. And Si's own occasional emotional desperation in his youth and his desire to find success with Condé Nast were evidence of how overpowering his father's influence had been. For Wynn, who had been caught in the family's machinery, perhaps even more tolerance was due. Nothing was more important than the family, as Si learned from his own father. But nothing could hurt so much, as well.

Art was a defining point for Si Newhouse, a measure of how his tastes had changed over the years. His deep affinity for modern art—like the mysteries of his family life or the ambivalent nature of his close friendships—were an expression of Si's enigmatic character, providing rare insight into his motivations as a human being.

This awareness of art as a personal benchmark was evident at a party at the Newhouses' town house, to which he invited some old friends and acquaintances, including Miki Denhof. Three decades earlier, Denhof was working as *Glamour*'s art director when Si joined the staff, the uncertain thirty-two-year-old son of the new owner. A cultured woman with a discernible trace of native Vienna in her voice, Denhof quickly developed friendships with both Si and his mother, Mitzi. When Si bought his first work of art in the early 1960s—a starkly painted canvas by Alex Liberman—Denhof accompanied him. "One of the Circle paintings," she recalled, referring to the geometric abstract paintings that Liberman created. From this modest investment, Si was on his way to becoming a world-renowned art collector, influenced by Liberman and the world of sculptors and painters with whom he became acquainted. By the late 1960s, Si lived in a large double town house on East Seventieth Street, which gradually evolved from a place of residence into a showcase for his art collection. When he and Victoria relocated in the early 1990s to a residence inside the United Nations Plaza, Si still kept the town house. It would be used for entertaining and as a home for his treasured art—by then estimated to be worth close to $100 million.

When Si introduced Miki Denhof to his wife for the first time, Si couldn't help but do so with an allusion to his art collection.

"This is the person with whom I bought my first painting," Si announced proudly to his wife.

Victoria, an attractive dark-haired woman who shared Si's taste for droll quips, didn't miss her cue. She turned to Denhof with a quizzical stare.

"Oh," replied Victoria, "are *you* responsible for all this madness?"

In a gallery or museum, Si seemed intrigued by the pure abstractions of beauty and truth, responding with a directness that many artists and collectors found refreshing. About art, he could maintain an uncomplicated enthusiasm and an almost childlike curiosity. "I'd go as far as to say he has a truly good eye, and that's very rare," said Fred Hughes, a longtime associate of Andy Warhol who became the executor of Warhol's estate after his death in 1987. "He does an awful lot of looking. He challenges himself and takes the trouble to look, at the primitives or at art that other people aren't aware of yet. He leaves no stone unturned. He has a true rapture for art." Newhouse remained a frequent customer of Warhol's throughout much of the 1970s and 1980s. Hughes still remembered the way Si's name would be whispered in hushed locked-jaw tones at dinner parties or as he strolled through galleries: *Mis-tah S. I. Nuuuuhauzzz Juhn-yah.*

By the early 1990s, Newhouse's primary contact with the art world and its treasures centered on a former five-dollar poster seller from California who became one of the most controversial figures in New York's art world: Larry Gagosian. This silver-haired art dealer with a spiked crew cut like Si's had a keen eye for art and an uncanny ability to secure paintings and other hard-to-get artworks that Si wanted to buy. Fast-talking and indefatigable in pursuit, Gagosian seemed like the very incarnation of Hollywood's notion of an art dealer—a Gordon Gekko among the Pollocks and de Koonings—pushing the idea of art for investment's sake to new extremes. Gagosian's nickname oozed with pure eighties adrenaline: "Go-Go." Through his patronage, Newhouse helped to finance Gagosian's meteoric escalation to the top, along with a few other deep-pocketed clients who were willing to pay millions for a desired painting. "It's no secret that we work together," Gagosian said. "His business and friendship are extremely important to me." Many other art dealers—even some friends like Fred Hughes—believed that Newhouse was privately bankrolling Gagosian's entrée into the New York art market. "It's not true that we're partners," Newhouse said in a 1989 profile of Gagosian that appeared in *Vogue.* "But I've bought so much from him that I've probably had a major role in his success. He's been the most refreshing person to come into the art world since I've been there."

The hip art dealer made no secret of his relatively modest beginnings, once working as a supermarket delivery boy, a car parker, and as an assistant manager in a record shop. In California, Gagosian turned a tiny arts-and-crafts business into a poster-selling operation, selling scenes of seascapes and cuddly kittens. He earned enough money to open his own gallery eventually and then boldly move to New York with the encouragement of his fellow art dealer Leo Castelli, who first introduced him to Newhouse. Self-invented until he could claim to be self-made, Gagosian had a direct and relentless style. Some skeptics in the art world—even Andy Warhol (who could enjoy a good payday as much as the next capitalist)—were wary of the hard-charging dealer. "Larry, I don't know, he's really weird," Warhol wrote in his diaries in November 1986. "He's weird." But Go-Go's brashness appealed to Si Newhouse; he was a man who could acquire the unobtainable. With a mansion in the Hamptons, an Upper East Side landmark carriage house with its own indoor lap pool, and always with a beautiful woman by his side, Gagosian, still in his early forties, was living an opulent lifestyle. He brought a sense of bravado and bad-boy image to the art game. "I think Mr. S. I. Newhouse has this other side that you never really figure out among his many other facets," observed Fred Hughes. "He likes that kind of person, that enjoyment of the rougher side of life in the big time."

Money helped ease Gagosian's rapid transition to respectability among his peers in New York's art market. The crowning glory took place at Sotheby's on the night of November 10, 1988, when Gagosian sat next to Si Newhouse, slowly bidding up the price of Jasper Johns's famous 1959 painting *False Starts* in increments of $250,000. In the end, Newhouse agreed to pay $17 million for the work, the highest price ever paid at that time for the work of a living artist. Initially, people in the room appeared stunned by the huge price, then burst into applause. Some even cheered as Sotheby's auctioneer smacked his gavel down to finalize the sale. The purchase was as much a public-relations triumph for Gagosian as it was a personal coup for Newhouse.

As always, Newhouse's alliance with Gagosian—like nearly all of Si's most meaningful friendships—seemed inexorably linked to the magnitude of his family's fortune and what it could buy. Indeed, a decade after he met Si Newhouse on the street corner, Larry Gagosian was recognized as one of the most influential people in the world's art market, with enough clout to hold museumlike shows in his New York galleries. In the fall of 1993, Gagosian featured a retrospective of Newhouse's great mentor and longtime friend, Alexander Liberman, whose Circle paintings were featured at his uptown gallery. At this show, Liberman's work was met once again with critical disdain, despite Newhouse's powerful influence. "As the editorial director of Condé Nast Publications, Alexander Liberman is one of the most important employees of one of Larry Gagosian's most important clients, S. I. Newhouse Jr., a fact that made it hard to approach this exhibition with anything but profound skepticism," wrote the *Times,* commenting on Liberman's "dubious career as an artist."

Alex Liberman was a rare exception in Newhouse's discreet and tightly controlled world, perhaps the only one with access to so many aspects of Si's life. For more than thirty years, their friendship had filled a void in Si's life in a way few outsiders could fully appreciate. Newhouse's admiration for him could be unbounding. Once while chatting with Si, Condé Nast executive Peter Diamandis asked him to describe Liberman. "A towering genius," Newhouse said without a moment's hesitation. Part of Liberman's "genius" was to understand Si's own complicated psyche and to instill within him a love for art. From Alex, Si learned to cast a critical, discerning eye toward contemporary art, with the same exacting gaze he usually reserved for details at work.

However, Newhouse's interests in contemporary art eventually broadened beyond his mentor's tastes and became uniquely his own. The Newhouse collection reflected the expanding circles of art dealers and contemporary artists whom Si and Gagosian favored. Liberman, who found his own public identity increasingly eclipsed by the sheer radiance of Newhouse's wealth, displayed an ambivalence about Si buying his art, until Newhouse finally stopped patronizing him. "Often I have not bought something that I thought I liked, or did like, because I got a cool response from him," Newhouse said years later. "And I think his own work has been consistently interesting. But I kind of decided not to deal with, not to collect it, because my being so close to him makes it too complicated." These deep ambivalences between them were part of the "odd, impersonal, and yet extremely close friendship that has been of great importance to both men," as Liberman's biographers, Dodie Kazanjian and Calvin Tomkins, described it.

Over time, friends like Alex Liberman and others who played a daily role in Si Newhouse's life became larger-than-life figures—cultural or political icons who were turned into dramatic characters for the theater or movies, while Si remained largely hidden from public view. There were plays and movies about Roy Cohn; a new Knopf biography, exhibitions, and a documentary about Liberman. Most notably, Diana Vreeland became an enduring legend as the epitome of fashion and taste. When she was removed by Si as *Vogue*'s editor in 1971, many expected Vreeland to retire. Instead, she gained a whole new prominence as consultant to the Costume Institute of the Metropolitan Museum of Art. Vreeland's reputation continued to grow, to the extent that *The New York Times* in 1993, four years after her death, called her simply "the greatest fashion editor who ever lived." That same year, a new play debuted about Vreeland's life, chronicling the night when she was abruptly booted from *Vogue*'s editorship. D.V.'s fate was a dramatic reminder that no matter how much employees thought they were friends with Si Newhouse or had earned his family's loyalty, the bottom line to their relationship was based strictly on business. Those who showed weakness could not be tolerated.

Dick Shortway, another longtime friend from Condé Nast, learned this hard lesson in 1986 on the day he walked into Newhouse's executive suite looking for a change.

Shortway had joined Condé Nast in 1950, nearly ten years before the Newhouses bought it. Besides Alexander Liberman, perhaps no one at

Condé Nast had worked harder with Newhouse and taught him more about the magazine business than Shortway. He was the outside guy, who, with charm and savoir faire, would meet with ad reps and salesmen for *Vogue,* allowing Si to remain inside the building at 350 Madison Avenue. In addition, Shortway was a very close friend from a time in Si's life when they were both divorced men in their thirties. He was someone who would escort Mitzi to a show or dream with Si about future plans for the magazines. He was trusted enough that he could tell Si when he was wrong without fear of being fired. When Dick Shortway took over as *Vogue's* publisher in 1975, the magazine's sagging finances had barely begun to recover. He shook things up until the fashion magazine was making plenty of money for the Newhouses. By the mid-1980s, *Vogue* was collecting more than $80 million a year in revenues, with about $20 million in pretax profit. Perhaps most importantly, Shortway had intervened at a critical point to help *Vanity Fair* survive its tumultous beginnings; it became the best-known success of Si Newhouse's career.

In 1986, when Shortway was at the peak of his powers within the company, he decided to tell his old friend Si that he needed a new challenge. It turned out to be a conversation Shortway would regret for many years afterward.

"I made a big mistake," Shortway later recalled. "At one point in my life, I walked into him and said, 'You know, I'm burned out.' And he never forgot those words."

Burned out. The words seemed forever branded across Shortway's forehead. Si knew of Shortway's desire to relocate to California, to live in a house with a pool and year-round golf and enjoy himself after nearly four decades with the company. But Si would not hear of it. "No way, there's not a job for you in California," he snapped whenever Shortway broached the issue. Shortway's admission that he was burned out seemed to deaden Si's affection for him. He was no longer a treasured friend and confidant, but an empty husk who was admitting he wasn't as valuable to the company as he once had been. A few months later, Shortway, still anxious for a new opportunity, convinced Daniel Salem to let him transfer to London to help run Condé Nast's European operations. Si reluctantly signed off on the move. Shortway never got the chance to explain to Newhouse what he meant by his admission of weakness, not until several years later.

"That's the worst statement I ever made to you," Shortway told his boss and former friend. "I didn't mean *burned out.* It was a slip of the tongue. I meant, bored. I needed a new challenge." Shortway felt that *Vogue* was running smoothly enough so that he could move to a new venue, begin a new chapter in his life. "I was getting divorced," Shortway recalled. "I wanted out of New York, to leave New York behind me forever."

In England, Shortway worked for five years with Salem and later with Si's cousin Jonathan Newhouse, trying to stem the losses in advertising as the British economy soured. In his own way, Si made sure Shortway knew of his displeasure about the move. A few months after Shortway arrived in England, Newhouse visited him on his semi-annual trip to the British company. His instant critique was pure Si.

"Well, uh, what else have you accomplished since you came over here other than lose a hundred and fifty pages in the first half of the year?" Shortway recalled Si asking.

"Si, I've been here three months—you can't blame that on me," Shortway shot back in their familiar style of banter, as though he had never left. "How's American *Vogue* doing?"

"Terrific," Newhouse said.

"Well, blame that on me."

Their friendship would never be the same after Shortway left New York. "I was three thousand miles away in a comparatively small division of his empire," he said. "Every trip to London, he'd come up to my office, sit down, stay for five, ten minutes, and chat. And that was that."

Shortway couldn't complain about his financial arrangement, however. Si's lack of personal loyalty was compensated for with a handsome check. Shortway remained a highly paid executive of the company and, with Jonathan's permission, became a vice president of Condé Nast International, based in Southern California, in 1992. Though Shortway had returned to the United States, Si no longer called for his advice or insight. As a businessman, Shortway still praises Newhouse as a publishing giant without peer. "He knows what to buy, when to buy it," Shortway said. "He's terrific as a businessman, but he likes to keep his own counsel. He doesn't want to get too close to anyone."

Shortway got close but never enough to understand Newhouse. After years of working together and being friends, Si remains very much an enigma to him. "Nobody knows him personally, old boy," Shortway said when asked for a description. "Alex probably does. I'm sure that there are some people who know him personally. But I can't say I do."

Si's world-class art collection seems only a metaphor for the changes in his life's true passion: Advance Publications. Far from its provincial origins in Staten Island, the Newhouse media empire has expanded beyond what Si ever could have imagined as a young man. The company's famous American magazines can be found in various languages in nations around the world. The name Newhouse is now truly international.

Through occasional visits and constant telephone conversations with his Paris-based cousin, Jonathan, Si kept in contact with the European operations. Condé Nast was infused with enough brand-name recognition to attract new advertisers and subscribers worldwide. "Over the years, the corporate name has become familiar to readers and has acquired an importance that it didn't used to have when we had four magazines," Si explained.

There was always an international flavor to Condé Nast. For decades in

Vogue, there was a British obsession, from secretaries with Mayfair accents to photo essays of country clubs outside London and clippings about "this season's fashionable Anglo-American marriages." The tradition continued under Newhouse with a stream of editors and writers with various forms of Her Majesty's accent. "Ground zero of the new British invasion is, of course, at Condé Nast, where proprietor S. I. Newhouse, who is not British, seems bent on collecting an editorial executive from each country of the old British Empire," remarked *Spy* magazine in February 1993, displaying some pseudo-xenophobic alarm about the tendency of American publications to give their top jobs to foreigners with English accents.

But the largest cultural exchange was going in the opposite direction, as Newhouse established strong franchises in such nations as Italy, Germany, France, Spain, and Australia. Now, the world of Si Newhouse abroad included such glossy Condé Nast titles as *The Tatler, The World of Interiors, Maison & Jardin,* and *Vogue Bambini.* New magazines like *Details* and *Allure* might be a sign of vigor in the United States, but the most remarkable potential for the family's future expansion was abroad, in becoming a global media power.

Jonathan Newhouse, as president of Condé Nast International, was the family member who supervised the company's interests in some thirty different magazines in foreign markets. He was thirty-seven years old when he was asked to give up his job as publisher of *Details* and move to Europe. Jonathan's assignment was to help and eventually take on the full-time duties of Daniel Salem, Si's close associate, who continued as chairman of the international operations on a part-time basis until he retired. A bespectacled friendly young man partial to bow ties and suspenders, Jonathan Newhouse was smart and a quick study like his father. Jonathan was one of four of Norman Newhouse's five children who went into the family business, though he was the only sibling to join Condé Nast. Among his generation, Norman was known for his great family loyalty, agreeing to move to New Orleans in the 1960s to oversee the family's regional newspapers in the South simply because his oldest brother, Sam, asked him to do so. Despite a freak accident in 1985, when he was thrown off his horse onto the concrete along a Mississippi levee, Norman remained an active part of the company until a few months before he died, in November 1988, at the age of eighty-two.

Jonathan, like his father before him, went through the family's rigorous ad hoc process of management training, with a succession of ascending jobs during the 1980s. After the purchase of *The New Yorker,* Jonathan was installed as executive vice president of that magazine, then became publisher of *Details* in February 1988. He quickly brought Newhouse marketing techniques to *Details,* which had been an independently owned operation until Si purchased it. For example, Jonathan introduced a formal media kit for *Details* to help convince potential advertisers to appear in its pages—an approach that the hip downtown magazine had never bothered with since its 1982 inception.

When Jonathan Newhouse arrived in Europe in 1989, the economic recession—soon to be felt throughout the world—was beginning to take hold in London and Paris. Nevertheless, the Newhouse family business carried on undaunted. On both sides of the Atlantic, the common wisdom was that Jonathan Newhouse would someday be the company's new chairman. "Jonathan is going to take over the company; that's what I've been told," said Tina Brown, who believes the future of the company lies with Jonathan and Steven Newhouse, Donald's son. "I get the sense that Steven is being groomed to take over the books and that Jonathan is being groomed for the magazines." Brown said Jonathan Newhouse resembles the young Si in his ability to exceed expectations. "He seems to be following in Si's footsteps in the sense that he was thrown into the deep end in Europe and proved to be very tough and very able. And quite imaginative. He's made a lot of difference."

While Jonathan remains familiar to many at Condé Nast, those with an intimate understanding of the company's financial structure say Steven is more likely to lead the whole family enterprise. He has impressed many with his quick mind and earnest demeanor; he has worked mainly in what is still the family's major source of revenues—newspapers.

Steven graduated magna cum laude from Yale University in 1979 and, after a few years as a copy editor and reporter in Springfield, Massachusetts, he became the editor of the family's *Jersey Journal,* a daily newspaper in Jersey City. He studiously attended Uncle Si's lightning-fast luncheons with his Random House executives at The Four Seasons. But he also didn't mind taking the subway to work or going to eat at the local Church's Fried Chicken with the *Journal*'s staff members. In Springfield, he volunteered to work the night shift and, according to one account, offered to chase fire engines to a warehouse blaze one night, even though he was home in bed at the time. He was once given a tour of another Newhouse newsroom, where, as he later recalled, "I felt I was being shown off as a curiosity." After all, Newhouses weren't known for their keen interest in daily journalistic matters. From these experiences, Steven later said he resolved "to put out that much more than the next guy."

To the delight of journalists, Steven didn't seem to view newspapers as mere properties. He confided to friends at the *Journal* that some in his family didn't understand why he preferred the editorial side rather than business operations of the family's publications. Randy Diamond, a former reporter at the *Journal,* told an interviewer: "He didn't come across as an heir to the Newhouse family, but as someone who wanted to know, 'How can I make this a better paper?' "

Regardless of his concern for journalism, the most important factor in Steven's favor is a stock transfer expected to take place someday. Under the terms originally set by his grandfather, Steven will inherit a major portion of the controlling stock of the parent company, Advance Publications, along with equal amounts expected to be shared by Donald's other children and Si's three children. Jonathan might become an important part of the family's future plans, but Steven's role will undoubtedly be pivotal. "From time to time, veterans of the Newhouse organization speculate that an offspring of a secondary branch of the family—say one of Norman's sons—will rise to head the business," *Fortune* magazine observed in its 1987 analysis of the company. "But nothing about Sam's will, or the history of this family, makes that seem logical. The choice instead will surely be one, or more, of the children of Si and Don."

A special arrangement with the IRS, which was made after the government dropped its appeal of the disastrous multimillion-dollar 1990 ruling in favor of the Newhouses, further confirmed this scenario. The full value of the Newhouse empire will not be taxed until Si and Donald Newhouse die, the government agreed. Only then will the byzantine fiscal structure conceived by Sam Newhouse—designed to perpetuate his family's publishing conglomerate after his death—be finally subjected to the tax burden dreaded for three generations. Whether this third group of Newhouses will rally to overcome their tax obligations (or enter into an internecine fight for control) could very well depend on Steven's abilities at filial diplomacy. What was called inconceivable by Sam Newhouse and his sons—a forced sale of the Advance conglomerate because of friction among family members—probably won't be faced as a possibility by their heirs until well into the twenty-first century.

Speculation about who would lead the Newhouses' third generation remained very premature. Si's work schedule showed no signs of letting up as he passed the traditional retirement age of sixty-five in November 1992. His business luncheons with his top executives were still as rapid-fire, though he did abandon his yellow legal pads for a computerized laptop ledger. With this gadget, Newhouse could quickly call up notations from the last luncheon with his executives or other memoranda necessary to overseeing his family's international media conglomerate. He learned to relax a little more, as well. On a summer's afternoon, he could be seen walking, relaxed and tan, along the shoreline near his new Bellport, Long Island, summer home, sporting a pair of Speedo-like swimming briefs. Early Sunday afternoons, he would return to the city, sometimes alone in the back of a rented limousine. With his dry, sardonic wit, Newhouse could even poke fun at some of his possessions. Summer residents in Bellport noticed Si had given the nickname Eustace Tiller to his modest-sized Boston Whaler, a variation on the name of *The New Yorker*'s famous dandy. For his part, Newhouse seemed unlikely ever to retire, his friends and business associates predicted. Perhaps Donald might think of retiring, they said, but Si remained too enmeshed in the running of the family's business and the collection of his art ever to give it up. "It's not what I do; it's what I am," he told one interviewer when asked about his long hours and slavish devotion to his job as chairman. As he grew older, Si's health and mortality became more important to him. Where once he had smoked fiendishly—two, three, or four packs of cigarettes a day—he now weaned himself away from the addiction, actually carrying an unlighted cigarette between his fingers for a year whenever he felt the urge to smoke.

Those who knew Si from the early days at Condé Nast marveled at how he had managed to transform himself. By the 1990s, the great and powerful S. I. Newhouse, Jr., had become a vastly different person from the shy young man they remembered thirty years before. Peter Diamandis recalled his surprise in watching Si give a speech without any of the old self-consciousness. The young man who always felt gloomy had changed, had adapted to the yoke of family responsibilities in a manner that Diamandis admired. "A lot of people would say, "Wasn't this guy lucky his father was an enormously successful guy?" Diamandis observed. "But from my vantage—having lived a while now—that wasn't a big plus, but a big minus that he overcame. And thirty-five years later, he's now a very different human. He did it by pulling himself up, psychologically, by his own boot-straps, which is more difficult than doing it financially. Now, he's a total, whole human being. He did it by the dint of his own effort."

Newhouse no longer seemed worried or concerned about what others thought of him. His father's demands were a distant memory and he had proven himself to be a worthy son, one who kept the family business alive and thriving, adding prestigious and more profitable ventures than those they already owned. The broader questions surrounding Si Newhouse's media power were for others to ponder, all of which seemed somehow irrelevant to his daily routine.

Si was busy planning for the future. In a world of increasingly sophisticated and interconnected forms of communication, Advance Publications would have to find a place beyond newsprint in order for the family's empire to survive. The investments in cable and programming were part of that strategic move for the Newhouse generations to come. Steve Newhouse was the family member on Advance Publications' multimedia team as it examined possible investments in new technologies. As usual, however, Si was pivotal in leading the family enterprise. One of the first steps in this direction was Condé Nast's decision in January 1994 to invest in a fledgling magazine named *Wired,* which is devoted to a popular presentation of the new multimedia technologies. The role of *Wired,* as one newspaper described it, was "to do for 'cyberspace' what *Rolling Stone* did for rock music," without the technical jargon.

Increasingly, Si displayed the willingness to make use of television as a form of synergy to promote and sell books and other publications. It was a remarkable turnabout. For years, Newhouse had been loath to mingle different parts of his empire in any major joint ventures. But there was a belated realization by the Newhouses that they had become a "dinosaur," as *The Wall Street Journal* said, slightly behind the curve in adapting to the interactive media. When gourmet Julia Child appeared on the QVC home-shopping network to promote her new cookbook, Random House officials were astounded that it sold ten thousand copies in thirty-five minutes. The cash-generating prowess of such new ventures was impressed upon Si Newhouse by Barry Diller, the visionary chief of the QVC Network. Diller was a social acquaintance of Si's who had attended dinners with Si at the home of Tina Brown and Harry Evans and other numerous functions. For weeks, they talked, and Si became intrigued by the possibilities.

In late 1993, after many discussions with Diller, the Newhouse brothers agreed to one of their boldest moves outside the realm of print. They decided to invest $500 million in the bid by Barry Diller's QVC Network to buy out Paramount Communications, Inc., the parent company of the well-known movie and television studio and the owner of Simon & Schuster, the giant book publisher that was Random House's main competitor. The highly publicized multibillion-dollar deal drew even greater attention when the Newhouses stepped in with their stake, joined by another giant, Cox Enterprises, which also loaned $500 million to Diller's hostile takeover bid. "It is the biggest step by far for us," Si declared in the *The New York Times*'s front-page account. In his understated way, Donald aptly predicted that giving Advance a sizable financial stake in Paramount's movies, television, and, in effect, the two largest book publishers would "give us new uses for our intellectual properties."

Indeed, the Paramount deal was a glimpse into the future—the interconnected ownerships of America's information companies in the twenty-first century. This was no simple uncontested acquisition, and bidders came from beyond the traditional news media to encompass virtually every form of mass communication. This new Megamedia was not so much about journalism as it was about entertainment options. The bidding for Paramount between Diller's QVC home-shopping network and Viacom, Inc., the owner of MTV and other cable programming, included many of the largest firms in the communications field: John Malone, the so-called king of cable, from Tele-Communications, Inc.; the video-rental giant Blockbuster Entertainment; and two regional telephone companies, Bell Atlantic and BellSouth. The winner would control Paramount's motion-picture studio, a nine-hundred-film library with such titles as *The Godfather* and *Beverly Hills Cop,* television programs like "The Arsenio Hall Show," and Simon & Schuster, along with Madison Square Garden and New York's professional basketball and hockey teams—in short, a feast of money-making opportunities for this new form of media colossus.

The prospect of Newhouse owning a share of Simon & Schuster's parent company was unsettling. During the past two decades, more than a dozen independent book publishers were lost to buyouts or mergers, while the number of companies owning America's top media outlets shrank from about fifty in 1983 to twenty a decade later. "Over the course of a generation, those who work with words have become controlled to an alarming extent by large corporate interests," warned Tom Goldstein, dean of the Graduate School of Journalism at the University of California at Berkeley, in a *New York Times* opinion essay published in December 1993, in the midst of QVC's takeover bid. "Independent newspapers, magazines and book publishers have become relics of another age." Perhaps most remarkable, as Goldstein noted, was the lack of public accountability by owners like Si Newhouse. "What would a QVC victory, extending the Newhouses' reach to their biggest book-publishing competitor, mean to the publishing world? S. I. Newhouse, a quiet investor, does not want to talk about it, and the public is left guessing."

Eventually, Diller's consortium bid of more than $10 billion for Paramount fell short and Viacom prevailed. But Si Newhouse, with his seemingly limitless personal funds and his thirst for acquisitions, once again reinforced his public image as an empire builder, a king of the new Megamedia. This dramatic and far-reaching venture was another reminder of how much Newhouse and his family's business had become one entity. Even friends and allies were reminded that much of Si's character was expressed through the actions of his company. During a break in the Paramount takeover battle, Barry Diller ran into Tina Brown at a social occasion and the two friends talked about Si. "You know you once said to me that Si is all about the work—and that phrase stuck with me," Diller told her. "All the other people I'm dealing with on this Paramount deal are about the deal. Si is the only person who is about the work. Si is excited about the creative potential of this company as opposed to the price of the deal."

There was indeed much more at stake than just another deal. To the extent he allowed any personal glimpses to interviewers over the years, Newhouse always defined himself in terms of the linear history of his family. He discouraged talk about a dynasty, yet so much of his life seemed dedicated to perpetuating just that. "We're interested in building a company," he told an interviewer. "We let the dynasty take care of itself. After all, our children are only the third generation." Each acquisition was a new addition to the family; each management change was one more step in ensuring its survival. "We will adapt to whatever the future holds that feels right for us," Si explained in early 1994 after he appointed James Truman and Steve Florio as the new leaders at Condé Nast, signaling a generational change within the company and perhaps the family itself. About this same time, Si indicated that Jonathan Newhouse would someday take his place within the magazine empire. "When I feel it is right or necessary, then Jon will take my place," he said.

The Newhouse legacy represents an extraordinary personal epic spanning the whole of twentieth-century America—from those early years when Meyer Newhouse first arrived in New York City, poor and unable to speak English, to the mid-1990s when his grandson S. I. Newhouse,

Jr., was heralded as America's richest man, a master of all forms of modern communication. Only after years of difficulty, not until his own father was gone, did Si learn to express himself fully through the family's enterprise and eventually redefine its mission. His work seemed far from over. And yet, his most remarkable achievement was already apparent: the ability to surprise, to overcome his personal fears and limitations, to exceed the expectations of those who thought they knew him best.

For so much of Si Newhouse's life, as he often professed, has been about the willingness to change.

Notes

Officially or not, a number of Newhouse executives, editors, writers, and financial executives, both past and present, were interviewed during the writing of this book. In addition, a number of longtime Newhouse family friends and former business associates agreed to be interviewed. This writer remains grateful particularly to those who are admirers of Mr. Newhouse and who, though they may not agree with all the opinions expressed herein, were gracious enough to share their thoughts and insights. Some of those listed below were interviewed briefly and answered only very limited questions about specific facts or their own direct experiences. Many others were quite generous with their time. Approximately half of the people interviewed for this book did so only after they were assured their comments would be kept as a background basis and their names not attached to their comments. Although this arrangement was hardly ideal, it allowed these people to speak candidly and, more importantly, for this author to gain a further understanding of Si Newhouse's world. This author attempted to keep anonymous quotations, especially those critical in nature, to a minimum.

Most of the other people listed below shared not only their own experiences and personal recollections of Si Newhouse on an on-the-record basis but their much broader views about publishing and the media. They also indulged this writer, who repeatedly followed up with further questioning or requests. Their gracious help is forever appreciated.

As a result of the past four years of writing, the following is a list of those who were fully or briefly interviewed or provided insights that can be acknowledged: Jeanne W. Amend, Ruth Ansel, Ben Bagdikian, John Baker, Wayne Barrett, Roldo Bartimole, Leslie Bennetts, Harry Benson, Robert Bernstein, Jason Berry, Marilyn Bobula, Leo Bogart, Thomas Bolan, Malcolm Borg, A. B. Botnick, Tina Brown, Holly Brubach, William F. Buckley, Jr., Robert Carniero, Phyllis Cerf, William H. Chafe, Noam Chomsky, John Coffee, Jr., Paul D. Colford, John Consoli, Mark Clements, Walter Clemons, Elaine Crispen, Rachel Crespin, Melvin DeFleur, Miki Denhof, Peter Diamandis, Dorothy DiCintio, E. L. Doctorow, Tom Engelhardt, Jason Epstein, Joni Evans, Jeanne Fleischmann, Peter Fleischmann, Neil Foote, Allison Frankel, Peter Fraser, William Fugazy, Cornelius Gallagher, Martin Garbus, Myron Garfinkle, Peter Gethers, George Green, Louis Oliver Gropp, Paul Haberman, John Haldenstein, Dick Haws, Mark Hellerer, Christopher Hitchens, David Hopgraph, Fred Hughes, Ray Josephs, Dodie Kazanjian, Keith Kelly, James Kornbluth, John Leonard, Lillian Levine, Larry Lowenstein, Kathleen Madden, Bea Matthews, Erroll McDonald, J. Paul McGrath, Richard H. Meeker, Sonny Mehta, John Morton, James Neff, Wynn Newhouse, David Oshinsky, Peter Osnos, Robert M. Phillips, Peter Phipps, Peter Prescott, William Raidy, Ron Rittenhauer, Paul Rosenfield, Jonathan Schell, André Schiffrin, Richard B. Scudder, Robert Shilliday, Richard Shortway, Jack Sirica, Charles Slotnik, Hoyt Spelman, Roger Stone, Studs Terkel, Dr. William Tolley, Calvin Tomkins, Calvin Trillin, Russell Twist, Véronique Vienne, Alberto Vitale, Nicholas von Hoffman, Neil Walsh, Dennis Washburn, Jacob Weisberg, Marie Winn, Tom Whiteside, Bill Woestendiek, Wendy Wolf, Jeff Yarborough, Sidney Zion.

In one fell swoop: Liz Smith, *New York Daily News,* June 2, 29, and 30, 1988. Contents of the June 29 column were also repeated during Liz Smith's reporting on the WNBC-TV program "Live at Five."

"Listen, have you heard Liz Smith?:" "Grace Mirabella and the Vagaries of Vogue," *Washington Post,* July 5, 1988.

"I'm afraid it's true": Woody Hockswender, "Changes at Vogue: A Complex Tale of Rumors and Facts," *The New York Times,* July 25, 1988; see also Dodie Kazanjian and Calvin Tomkins, *Alex: The Life of Alexander Liberman* (New York: Alfred A. Knopf, 1993).

"Change is change": Paul Richter, "Quirky Si Newhouse Becomes a Media Power," *Los Angeles Times,* November 28, 1989.

"The way it was handled": Michael Gross, "War of the Poses," *New York,* April 27, 1992.

No one was safe: William A. Henry III, "A Search for Glitz," *Time,* June 4, 1990.

"A revolving door": Henry, *Time,* June 4, 1990.

"Ahhh, the smell of freshly mowed employees": *The New Yorker,* September 28, 1992.

Margaret Case: Case's suicide is mentioned in Diana Vreeland, *D.V.* (New York: Alfred A. Knopf, 1984). See also, "Miss Case of Vogue," *Harper's Bazaar,* February 1972; Case's obituary, *The New York Times,* August 26, 1971.

The Newhouse family's estimated wealth of $13 billion: *Fortune,* September 7, 1992. Because of the privately held nature of the Newhouse empire, however, estimates of the family's wealth vary widely.

"There aren't many absolute rulers": Bonnie Angelo, "Si and Tina's Newest Act," *Time,* July 13, 1992.

their pay in separate checks: Deirdre Carmody, "At Condé Nast, Newhouse Maintains Loose Reins with a Tight Grip," *The New York Times,* July 27, 1992.

Tina Brown and Knopf's Sonny Mehta: They are listed along with Newhouse in a cover story entitled "The Cultural Elite: The Newsweek 100: Who They Really Are," *Newsweek,* October 5, 1992.

"journalistic chiffonier": A. J. Liebling, *The New Yorker,* later compiled in A. J. Liebling, *The Press* (New York: Pantheon Books, 1981).

His profit margins were estimated: interviews with John Morton and Leo Bogart, 1992.

"How he is within the family": interview with Wynn Newhouse, 1990.

"The now-bad word *advertising*": from Alexander Liberman's introduction to *Passage: A Work Record,* Irving Penn (New York: Callaway/Alfred A. Knopf, 1991); an excerpt from Liberman's introduction was reprinted in *Vogue,* October 1991.

"Last month, Ivana Trump": Carl Bernstein, "The Idiot Culture," *The New Republic,* June 8, 1992.

"My brother and I feel": Carol J. Loomis, "The Biggest Private Fortune," *Fortune,* August 17, 1987.

CHAPTER 1: MAN OF THE HOUSE

Pink roses blanketed the dark wood coffin: combined news services account of Sam Newhouse's funeral, *Newsday,* September 1, 1979; Ashton Phelps and William Tolley's comments are mentioned in this account.

That morning, newspapers across the country: Details of the Newhouse media empire at the time of Sam's death were taken from the obituary written by David J. Jacobs, *Newark Star-Ledger,* August 30, 1979.

Si Newhouse . . . didn't speak: interviews with William Tolley and William Raidy, 1992.

"I've eased up": "S. I. Newhouse and Sons: America's Most Profitable Publisher," *Business Week,* January 26, 1976.

"S.I. has to make a conscious effort": ibid.

He begged for candy: Richard Meeker, *Newspaperman: S. I. Newhouse and the Business of News* (New York: Ticknor & Fields, 1983). Further details were provided in an interview with Meeker, and through confirmation with William Tolley and Ray Josephs, the company's former longtime publicist, 1992.

Si boosted his salary: transcript of testimony and cross-examination of Si Newhouse in U.S. Tax Court, January 1989.

"You know, you're not going to find any Citizen Kane here": Jefferson Grigsby, "Newhouse, After Newhouse," *Forbes,* October 29, 1979. See also Pauline Kael, *Raising Kane* (New York: Bantam Books, 1971).

Meier Neuhaus: Details of Sam Newhouse's family life as a young boy are detailed in Meeker, *Newspaperman,* and in Sam Newhouse's own privately published memoir, *A Memo for the Children from S. I. Newhouse,* as related to and written by David Jacobs (New York: 1980), This book is available at the Library of Congress. All subsequent Sam Newhouse quotations in this chapter are from this memoir unless otherwise noted.

"Sammy, go down and take care of the paper": This was the most-repeated account of Lazarus's comment to Sam Newhouse, which was first reported in a cover story, "The Newspaper Collector," *Time,* July 27, 1962. In a 1992 interview, Calvin Trillin said he was one of the reporters for *Time* who worked on that unbylined profile. A slightly different but more emphatic version of Lazarus's quote appeared in Jacob's *Newark Star-Ledger* obituary of Newhouse. "Go downstairs and close the thing up," Lazarus ordered in that account of the exchange.

"Sammy, why do you need that?": *Newsweek,* August 17, 1964. Newhouse's recollection of it years later is contained in his memoir.

Waiting at the pier: Meeker, *Newspaperman.*

"I will not be intimidated": *A Memo for the Children.*

"If he has not debased the quality of U.S. journalism": "The Newspaper Collector," *Time.*

"Sam never pretended to be a public benefactor": ibid.

"Mr. Samuel I. Newhouse, the archetype": A. J. Liebling, *The New Yorker,* later compiled in A. J. Liebling, *The Press* (New York: Pantheon Books, 1981).

"With the *Business Week* piece": several interviews with Ray Josephs, 1992.

Samuel Isidor Newhouse: "The Newspaper Collector," *Time.*

Newhouse set up a special spy network: Meeker, *Newspaperman.*

"When [Newhouse] came to my office": Meeker, *Newspaperman.*

"The American people need to be warned": "The Newspaper Collector," *Time.*

"Going way back": testimony and cross-examination of Si Newhouse in U.S. Tax Court, January 1989.

In the mid-1930s: Meeker, *Newspaperman.*

"I'm not interested in buying funerals": "S. I. Newhouse and Sons: America's Most Profitable Publisher," *Business Week.*

"After all, if I can't sleep": This oft-repeated anecdote was included in Jacob's *Newark Star-Ledger* obituary.

"I remember years ago": interview with Wynn Newhouse, 1990.

"You know, I don't think any of us has any vanity": Grigsby, "Newhouse, After Newhouse," *Forbes.*

"I'm very hardboiled about the boys": "The Newspaper Collector," *Time.*

CHAPTER 2: IN HIS FATHER'S SHADOW

"Si was very close to my brother": Details about Allard's friendship with Si Newhouse are from an interview with Dorothy DiCintio. Lowenstein's older brother, Larry, who did not know Si well at that time, provided further information about the Lowensteins' Westchester home and about Horace Mann during the mid-1940s (interview, 1992).

Si's private pressures: Several classmates and friends who were interviewed said they directly recalled or were made aware of Si's unhappiness as a young man. Some of these details, including his thought of suicide, are mentioned in letters to Allard Lowenstein, which are found in the library archives of the University of North Carolina at Chapel Hill, as part of its Southern Historical Collection. After Lowenstein's murder in 1980, his family later donated the former congressman's voluminous personal letters and correspondence to his alma mater. All subsequent quotations from Newhouse letters to Lowenstein in this chapter are from this collection.

"I remember that Donald was more like his father": interview with William Tolley, 1992.

Young Si barely made an impression: interviews with John Halderstein and Paul Haberman, 1992.

"I did not have much time": *A Memo for the Children from S. I. Newhouse,* as related to and written by David Jacobs (New York: 1980); available at the Library of Congress. Friends and family acquaintances say the emotional distance and its impact on Si's psyche were far greater than Sam Newhouse acknowledged, however.

Si was delivered by cesarean section: ibid.

"Mrs. Newhouse prefers soft color schemes": *New York Herald Tribune,* November 26, 1957.

"It's a mess": Recollections of designer John Gerald are from Richard H. Meeker, *News-*

paperman: S. I. Newhouse and the Business of News (New York: Ticknor & Fields, 1983).

to send the boys by train to Washington, D.C.: interview with Ray Josephs, 1992.

During the summer of 1943: Details of Si's summer at the *Long Island Press* are mentioned in letters to Lowenstein and in an interview with Ray Josephs, 1992.

Goodbye, Mr. Chips: The British influence at Horace Mann was mentioned by Slotnik and other former Newhouse schoolmates, interviews 1992 and 1993.

"At the time, it was a very elitist school": interview Charles Slotnik, 1992.

"Good things come in small packages": Horace Mann yearbook, class of 1945. This book also lists the school activities in which Si Newhouse took part. Also examined were various editions of the school newspaper, including stories by Si Newhouse.

"You never heard him laugh": interview Robert Carneiro, 1993.

Newhouse's conservative views: The political discussions contained in the letters to Lowenstein underscore Si's change from the prevailing liberal Democrat view to a more conservative outlook.

For all of their plotting: The student election at Horace Mann was closely contested and still could be recalled in some detail by former classmates such as John Halderstein (interview, 1992) and Robert Carneiro (interview, 1993).

"He changed his mind about Cornell": interview with William Tolley, 1992.

But Newhouse did indeed own the newspaper: In *Newspaperman,* Meeker details how Newhouse purchased the newspaper in 1942 but gave the impression that publisher Ernest L. Owen had purchased it. According to Meeker, Sam Newhouse didn't make his secret known publicly until two years later.

Si was enchanted by the "coeds": Descriptions of the social scene at Syracuse University are contained in Newhouse's letters to Lowenstein.

Allard Lowenstein: A full discussion of Lowenstein's struggles with his own sexuality and impulses is explored in William H. Chafe, *Never Stop Running: Allard Lowenstein and the Struggle to Save American Liberalism* (New York: Basic Books, 1993).

"I think Mr. Newhouse was tough": Si's reasons for thinking of suicide were discussed by Dorothy DiCintio (interview, 1992) and in Si's letters to Lowenstein.

"Even then, there was something different": J. A. Trachtenberg, "The Newhouses: Publishing's private empire," *W,* December 19–26, 1980.

"He loved it": interview William Tolley, 1992.

"Look, I'm not going to fight it": interview with William Tolley, 1992.

"We got restless": "S. I. Newhouse and Sons: America's Most Profitable Publisher," *Business Week,* January 26, 1976.

"nice Jewish girl from the Bronx": Meeker, *Newspaperman.*

Eventually, Jane decided to change her name: This detail, along with Jane Franke's educational achievements, were cited in *The New York Times,* March 12, 1951. The *Times* published an announcement of her marriage to Si Newhouse.

Si Newhouse . . . at Sampson Air Force Base: Details of Si's military record were obtained through a Freedom of Information request processed by the National Personnel Records Center, St. Louis, Missouri.

"I think they simply grew apart": interview Ray Josephs 1992 and 1993.

"We were really too young": Trachtenberg, "The Newhouses," *W.*

"That was a bad time": Meeker, *Newspaperman.*

"He was known in the bureau as Jerry Lewis": ibid.

He dated a number of women: Details of Si's romantic life after his divorce are mentioned in Trachtenberg, "The Newhouses," *W.* They were confirmed by longtime family friends, including William Raidy and Miki Denhof, both interviewed in 1993. See also Carrie Donovan, "50 Who Mattered Most," *The New York Times Magazine,* October 24, 1993.

Rachel Crespin: A formal announcement of Si's engagement to Rachel Crespin appeared in *The New York Times,* October 29, 1962. It gave a brief history of Crespin's education and previous marriage and divorce.

"I was engaged to Si": Interview with Rachel Crespin, 1993.

"a marvelous bachelor apartment": *The New York Times*, April 6, 1966.

"The boys learned the business early and well": *A Memo for the Children from S. I. Newhouse,* as related to and written by David Jacobs (New York: 1980); available at Library of Congress.

"Nobody really knew him": Trachtenberg, "The Newhouses," *W.*

"She asked for a fashion magazine": Sam Newhouse's yarn about how he decided to buy *Vogue* was repeated in a number of places, including David Jacob's obituary in the *Newark Star-Ledger,* August 30, 1979, and in Richard Meeker, *Newspaperman: Si Newhouse and the Business of News* (New York: Ticknor & Fields, 1983). From the very beginning, however, Sam Newhouse recognized his wife would be pleased with the Condé Nast purchase.

"It seems like a good deal": Joan Kron, "Fashion's Resurgence Means Wealth, Power for Vogue Magazine," *The Wall Street Journal,* January 30, 1986.

Patcévitch told the staff: *New York Herald Tribune,* March 24, 1959. Details of the stock sale are in *Newsweek,* April 6, 1959.

"Class, not mass": Caroline Seebohm, *The Man Who Was Vogue: The Life and Times of Condé Nast* (New York: The Viking Press, 1982). A more recent rendition of the same view is contained in Gigi Mahon, "S. I. Newhouse and Condé Nast: Taking Off the White Gloves," *The New York Times Magazine,* September 10, 1989.

"taste percolates downward": Condé Nast's views were mentioned in several articles, including "A Well-Bred Magazine," *Time,* April 1, 1957.

"It becomes increasingly apparent": Gay Talese, "Vogueland," *Esquire,* July 1961.

Street & Smith: Details of Sam Newhouse's purchase of Street & Smith are in *Time,* August 31, 1959.

"I thought Mitzi": *Time,* April 1, 1959.

"It also turned out to be a present for Si": Carol J. Loomis, "The Biggest Private Fortune," *Fortune,* August 17, 1987.

"He loved it much more": interview with Ray Josephs, 1992.

"Si never went outside": interview with Peter Diamandis, 1993.

"Have you got a minute?": interview with Richard Shortway, 1993.

But by 1964, Si: *The New York Times,* September 10, 1964.

Very early one morning: In three interviews conducted in 1992 with Ray Josephs, this was probably his most vivid recollection of how Sam Newhouse's son had been transformed through his responsibilities at Condé Nast.

Alexander Liberman: Several interviews were conducted with Condé Nast employees who spoke of their experience in laying out magazines under the watchful eye of the company's editorial director. See also Marie Winn, "Liberman: Staying in Vogue," *The New York Times Magazine,* May 13, 1979.

"Un peu plus de brutalité": Véronique Vienne, "Make It Right . . . Then Toss It Away," *Columbia Journalism Review,* July/August 1991; interview with Véronique Vienne, 1992.

"Like most victims of abuse:" Véronique Vienne, "The Culture of Abuse," *Journal of Graphic Design,* American Institute of Graphic Arts, Vol. 9, No. 1, 1991. Also, interview with Vienne, 1992.

"asked me to go in and learn what made it work": This explanation was repeated by Newhouse in several articles and as part of his January 1989 testimony in U.S. Tax Court.

"is all explored": Jesse Kornbluth, "The Art of Being Alex," *New York,* October 12, 1981.

speak of Picasso's way of painting: Liberman's friendship and acquaintance with many of the twentieth century's greatest painters is reflected in his book, *The Artist in His Studio* (New York: Random House, 1959; reissued 1988). Liberman's conversance with popular culture and America's zeitgeist is mentioned in Jesse Kornbluth, "The Art of Being Alex," and in Marie Winn, "Liberman: Staying in Vogue."

"He is a Dostoevskian personality": Barbara Rose, *Alexander Liberman* (New York: Abbeville Press, 1981).

Semeon Liberman: Details about Liberman's father can be found in Rose's biography as well as in numerous profiles, including the entry on Alexander Liberman in the 1987 *Current Biography Yearbook.*

"I don't know if anyone realizes.": Rose, *Alexander Liberman.*

"Her favorite plays": "Art Lover," *The New Yorker,* November 26, 1960.

"I still remember": Rose, *Alexander Liberman.* For additional details, see also Joan Juliet Buck, "The Emigré Muse," *Vanity Fair,* March 1992.

"Those English beatings": "Art Lover."

"The eye must have rest": Lawrence Campbell, "The Great-Circle Route," *Art News,* April 1970.

"was a love that gave me everything": Buck, "The Emigré Muse."

"**Iacovleff would tell Tatiana**": Jesse Kornbluth, "The Art of Being Alex," *New York,* October 12, 1981.
"**Vogel was well aware of Liberman's talents**": Rosamond Bernier, "In the Atelier," *HG,* October 1988.
"**Great God of art directors**": Bernier, "In the Atelier."
"**A man like you must be on *Vogue!***": There are various published accounts of Liberman's testy first days under the feared Dr. Agha, including Kornbluth, "The Art of Being Alex."
"**There were great promenades**": Bernier, "In the Atelier."
"**I think most of these artists**": Liberman's view of the great artists he met while photographing for *The Artist in His Studio* was mentioned in an interview with Jed Perl for a "Revealing Moments," *Vogue,* 1988. Perl's article appeared when original 1959 book was reissued by Random House.
"**I'm grateful for my job**": "Art Lover."
"**Alex has been a surrogate father to Si**": interview with Peter Diamandis, 1993; also contained in Diamandis's comments in Sandra Salmans, "Courting the Elite at Condé Nast," *The New York Times,* Feb. 6, 1983.
"**We have never had an editorial director**": Sam Newhouse's decentralized management style, which differed markedly from the goings-on in the Condé Nast building, is mentioned in *A Memo for the Children from S. I. Newhouse,* as related to and written by David Jacobs (New York: 1980); available from the Library of Congress. For further details about Liberman's relationship with Sam Newhouse and his son, see also Dodie Kazanjian and Calvin Tomkins, *Alex: The Life of Alexander Liberman* (New York: Alfred A. Knopf, 1993).
"**She was the first editor**": After her death, "Diana Vreeland," by various contributors (including Alexander Liberman), was published in *Vogue,* December 1989.
"**Fashion must be the intoxicating release**": Lynn Darling, "The Vreeland Legend," *Newsday,* August 24, 1989.
"**Today, let's think pig white!**": Vreeland's observations are scattered in almost every story about *Vogue* during the 1960s and 1970s and was included in Mahon, "S. I. Newhouse and Condé Nast."
"**Diana seduced Mitzi Newhouse**": Amy Fine Collins, "The Cult of Diana," *Vanity Fair,* November 1993.
"**I always felt we were selling dreams**": Frank DeCaro, "The Dreams That Stuffs Are Made Of," *Newsday,* August 25, 1991.
"**She's an original**": Mary Vespa, "The Woman Who Celebrated the Beautiful People Thrives on Their Attentions," *People,* December 8, 1980.
"**Man does not live**": Stanley Kauffmann, "Through a Glass Brightly," *The New Republic,* January 11, 1964.
"**Beauty in Our Time**": Alexander Liberman, "Beauty in Our Time," *Vogue,* May 1961, along with photographic essay by Irving Penn.
"***Vogue* has always been**": "A Vogue for the New," *Newsweek,* July 31, 1971.
"**We just sat**": Kazanjian and Tomkins, *Alex.*
"**Alex, we've all known**": interview with Fred Hughes (1993), who was a longtime friend of Diana Vreeland. Variations of this anecdote have been repeated in various published accounts, as well.
"**I suppose Alex**": Winn, "Liberman: Staying in Vogue."
"**The Newhouse concept**": ibid.; interview with Marie Winn, 1993.

CHAPTER 4: THE NEWHOUSE CONCEPT

"***Vogue* decided it wanted to go middle-class**": Jesse Kornbluth, "The Art of Being Alex," *New York,* October 12, 1981.
a portrait of Sam Newhouse: Mention of Warhol's rendition of the newspaper titan is found in *The Andy Warhol Diaries,* ed. Pat Hackett (New York: Warner Books, 1989), also interview with Fred Hughes, 1993. Other Warhol quotes are from his published diaries.
"**I think they are at the forefront**": interview with Mark Clements, 1992.
"**Si was very much into research**": interview with Richard Shortway, 1993.
"**If you broaden your public**": Marie Winn, "Liberman: Staying in Vogue," *The New York Times Magazine,* May 13, 1979.
"**Under the great Diana Vreeland**": interview with Mark Clements, 1992. His comments

about the financial problems of *Vogue* were confirmed in 1993 interviews with Shortway and Diamandis and from other published accounts at that time.

"Diana Vreeland was interested in fantasy": Jennet Conant, "The Fall and Rise of a Fashion Impresarino," *Newsday,* November 30, 1988.

"It's that kind of place": "Grace Mirabella and the Vagaries of Vogue," *Washington Post,* July 5, 1988.

"Highly volatile-looking models have been cycled out": Charlotte Curtis, "Vogue, Bazaar Are Changing in Own Ways," *The New York Times,* 1971.

"I think at the midpoint of the '70s": Woody Hochswender, "Changes at Vogue: A Complex Tale of Rumors and Facts," *The New York Times,* July 25, 1988.

The "must list": Mirabella's acknowledgment of the "must list" is found in Winn, "Liberman: Staying in Vogue."

"The cold hard fact": *Advertising Age,* April 17, 1992; repeated in Ben H. Bagdikian, *The Media Monopoly* (Beacon Press, 1983); also reflected in interview with Shortway, 1993.

"Grace was so antismoking": interview Richard Shortway, 1993.

"He has to approve each cover": Winn, "Liberman: Staying in Vogue."

"Our magazines represent a certain tone": Geraldine Fabrikant, "Si Newhouse Tests His Magazine Magic," *The New York Times,* September 25, 1988.

"*GQ* was too gay": Margaret Hornblower, "Si Newhouse, the Talk of The New Yorker," *Washington Post,* May 7, 1985. Brown's comment was made in context to her observation of Newhouse at that time: "You get the sense he's really quite hip. He likes quality. *House & Garden* was making pots of money, but he didn't like it. He made it better. *GQ* was too gay. He changed it. *The New Yorker* should be so lucky as to be bought by Si Newhouse. They could have been bought by Rupert Murdoch!"

"a gay business": The comments of Anna Wintour and Art Cooper are contained in Jeff Yarbrough, "Vanity Fairies: How Gay is the Condé Nast Empire?," *The Advocate,* March 10, 1992.

"I still basically thought I was a painter": Joan Juliet Buck, "The Emigré Muse," *Vanity Fair,* March 1992.

Russian mysticism: The spiritual symbolism of Liberman's circle painting is thoroughly discussed in Barbara Rose, *Alexander Liberman* (New York: Abbeville Press, 1981). Liberman's recognition of the circle as an occult symbol, indicating higher levels of consciousness, is mentioned by Rose on page 103.

Circlism would be Liberman's challenge: ibid. Rose writes on page 167, "When Liberman began painting seriously, Picasso was clearly the influential master. 'Circlism' was his challenge to cubism." In answering a query from the Museum of Modern Art in 1960, Liberman described "Circlism" as "his answer to cubism," according to Rose.)

"If you know the collection": J. A. Trachtenberg, "The Newhouses: Publishing's private empire," December 19–26, 1980.

"This is a revival": Kornbluth, "The Art of Being Alex."

"Oh, it's so frightening": ibid.

Corcoran Gallery: *The New York Times,* April 19, 1971.

Nixon's disdain for Liberman's sculpture: Nixon's opinion of *Adam* was recounted in Michael Straight, *Twigs for an Eagle's Nest* (Devon Press, 1979) and reported in "Indifference Would Have Been Worse," *Art News,* May 1980. Liberman's reponse to Nixon ("The worst thing is indifference") is contained in the *Art News* story.

"I have always been plagued": Robert Hughes, "Sprezzatura in Steel," *Time,* April 26, 1971.

"Poverty is not conducive to good art": Kornbluth, "The Art of Being Alex."

Irving Penn: "An American Eye," *Vogue,* October 1991; *Vogue* adapted Liberman's introduction to Irving Penn, *Passage: A Work Record* (New York: Callaway/Alfred A. Knopf, 1991).

"There was once a possibility": Winn, "Liberman: Staying in Vogue."

"It was the beginning": Michael Gross, "War of the Poses," *New York,* April 27, 1992. "The period Diana was there was the last time I could express myself honestly in fashion photography," Avedon said.

"For all his cosmopolitan background": Robert Hughes, "Liberman's Eye," *Vanity Fair,* September 1988.

"kidding myself and the public": Winn, "Liberman: Staying in Vogue."

"It's a business after all": Nina Darnton, "Vogue, Self, Allure—Alex," *Newsweek,* April 8, 1991.

"Liberman found the trick": ibid.

"I'm not interested": *The New York Times,* June 9, 1981.

"The only crossover is between my brother and me": Sandra Salmans, "Courting The Elite At Condé Nast," *The New York Times,* February 6, 1983.

"Grenouille": Gigi Mahon, "S. I. Newhouse and Condé Nast: Taking Off the White Gloves," *The New York Times Magazine,* September 10, 1989; also repeated during an interview with Peter Diamandis, 1993.

"It's not that the food": *Spy,* December 1990.

"He's become daring": Daniel Machalara, "Family Newspapers: Newhouse Chain Stays with Founder's Ways and with His Heirs," *The Wall Street Journal,* February 12, 1982.

"When Si's father died": Deirdre Carmody, "At Condé Nast, Newhouse Maintains Loose Reins With a Tight Grip," *The New York Times,* July 27, 1992.

"I don't know": N. R. Kleinfield, "Heads Have a History of Rolling at Newhouse," *The New York Times,* November 2, 1989.

"I'm sure Si wished": interview with Louis Oliver Gropp, 1992; for further background, see Jennet Conant, "Keeping Up With the Joneses," *Newsweek,* September 7, 1987.

"an absolute certitude": Michael Gross, "War of the Poses."

"Alex's mind is": ibid.

"Dirt-diggers have suggested": Judith Newman, "Anna Wintour: Editor of the Year," *Adweek,* February 12, 1990.

"Perhaps I was silly": Gross, "War of the Poses."

"I think it was Bernie's persuasive power": Laurel Wentz, "Bernard Leser," *Advertising Age,* February 9, 1987. Leser explained differences in *Vogue* editors in same article.

"I'm the Condé Nast hit man": Laurence Zuckerman, "The Dynamic Duo at Condé Nast," *Time,* June 13, 1988.

"I was having a hard time personally": Gross, "War of the Poses."

"I suggested she come back": ibid.

"People either loved or hated": *Newsday,* June 7, 1990.

Elle **entered the fray:** Joan Kron, "Style Setter: Fashion's Resurgence Means Wealth, Power for Vogue Magazine," *The Wall Street Journal,* January 30, 1986; the article provided stastics showing *Vogue*'s dominance of the fashion-magazine market.

"The fact that it was": Gross, "War of the Poses."

"There are certain decisions": Kleinfield, "Heads Have a History of Rolling at Newhouse."

"These rumors and discussions": "Grace Mirabella and the Vagaries of Vogue," *The Washington Post,* July 5, 1988.

"But she just smiled": interview with Richard Shortway, 1993.

"I had a slightly different view": Conant, "The Fall and Rise of a Fashion Impresario."

She paid a reported $480,000: Craig Bromberg, "The Glitzy Brits of Condé Nast," *Washington Journalism Review,* November 1989.

"I couldn't face the replacement": Dodie Kazanjian and Calvin Tomkins, *Alex: The Life of Alexander Liberman* (New York: Alfred A. Knopf, 1993).

"I am very much in love": Melissa Sones, "Condé Nast: Corporate Makeover," *7 Days,* September 7, 1988.

"is still living": *New York Post,* August 2, 1988; Anna Wintour's comments to her staff were found in several articles.

"I'm not an advocate": Judith Newman, "Anna Wintour—Editor of the Year," *Adweek,* February 12, 1990.

"I think the magazine is superb": Kevin Haynes, "Anna's Big Year," *Women's Wear Daily,* November 10, 1989.

"Alex has a way": Winn, "Liberman: Staying in Vogue."

"Si clearly enjoys working with her": Jennet Conant, "Playing Doctor at Condé Nast," *Manhattan Inc.,* November 1988.

Amy Levin: "Condé Nast-iness?", *Newsday,* November 3, 1988. Newhouse comments included in this article.

"I'm being retired every other day": James Reginato, "The New York Newsday Interview with Alexander Liberman," *Newsday,* October 12, 1988.

"Would you mind if": Mahon, "S. I. Newhouse and Condé Nast."

BREAST OBSESSED: Randall Rothenberg, "Condé Nast Changing Style of Self," *The New York Times,* November 15, 1988.

"American journalists ramble on": Bromberg, "The Glitzy Brits of Condé Nast."

"Anthy, just go to Alex": Disney's travails at *Self* were reported in several accounts, including Bromberg's piece. Much of the detail and exchange of conversations between Newhouse and Disney were provided in a 1992 interview with an authoritative source.

"Oh, it's divine": Deirdre Carmody, "Condé Nast's Gamble: Creating Yet Another Image for Self," *The New York Times,* April 23, 1990.

"What power?": Nina Darnton, "Vogue, Self, Allure—Alex," *Newsweek,* April 8, 1991.

"He has had an enormous influence on Condé Nast": Richard David Story, "The Emperor of Taste," *New York,* December 28, 1992.

"the biggest difference": Owen Edwards, "Whose Style Is It, Anyway?" *The New York Times,* September 6, 1992; similar comments also appeared in Elizabeth Snead, "Vogue magazine celebrates a century of vision and verve," *USA Today,* March 27, 1992.

"strongly self-congratulatory air": Charles Hagen, "That Elusive Quality Called Style," April 17, 1992.

Photographers, in particular: Edwards, "Whose Style Is It, Anyway?" This article also identifies those photographers and their different client lists for advertising and magazine editorial sections.

Si kept Meisel: Helen Thorpe, "Condé Nast Bankroll Keeps Meisel in the Fold," *The New York Observer,* June 29, 1992.

"It isn't an accident": Joanne Lipman, "Big 'Outsert' Really Puts Revlon in Vogue," *The Wall Street Journal,* September 17, 1992. This article includes Hammond quote.

"There's a joke": Kazanjian and Tomkins, *Alex.*

"This is the first party of the Nineties": Paloma Picasso and Karl Lagerfeld's comments in William Norwich's column, *New York Post,* April 6, 1992.

". . . What wonderful times": Kazanjian and Tomkins, *Alex.*

"When I walk down the corridors": Kazanjian and Tomkins *Alex.*

"Youth is everyone's dream": Mahon, "S. I. Newhouse and Condé Nast."

CHAPTER 5: MY FRIEND ROY

"You know Si Newhouse": Margot Hornblower, "Si Newhouse, The Talk of *The New Yorker,*" *Washington Post,* May 7, 1985.

POWER PARTY: Bob Colacello, "Power Party," *Vanity Fair,* June 1985. Interviews with Thomas Bolan, 1992, and Peter Fraser, 1993, also provided further details about this Reagan pre-inaugural party.

One of the last telephone calls: interview with Peter Fraser (1993), who was Roy Cohn's lover and constant companion from 1981 until Cohn died of the AIDS virus at the National Institutes of Health in Bethesda, Maryland, in 1986. In interviews in 1992 and 1993, Lillian Levine, Cohn's longtime office assistant, also confirmed Newhouse's almost-daily contact with Cohn as he was dying.

"It's a phenomenon of American life": Hornblower, "Si Newhouse."

"I spent five years": Sidney Zion, *The Autobiography of Roy Cohn* (New York: Lyle Stuart, 1988). All Cohn quotes from this source unless otherwise noted.

"Roy was a crumb": interview with Dorothy DiCintio, the sister of Allard Lowenstein, 1992.

"was in many ways the most gifted demagogue": One of several extensive histories about McCarthy and the anti-Communist scare of the 1950s is Richard H. Rovere, *Senator Joe McCarthy* (New York: Harcourt, Brace and Company, 1959).

fast friendship with then FBI director J. Edgar Hoover: The extensive but heavily censored FBI file on Roy M. Cohn was obtained through a Freedom of Information request made by *Newsday* reporter Jack Sirica for his story "The FBI's Roy Cohn Files," *Newsday,* July 10, 1989. Three years later, Sirica shared these materials with this author. They show Cohn repeatedly curried favor with Hoover, sending him laudatory letters and information. The FBI files on Cohn—much of which remains heavily redacted—make no specific mention of Newhouse or any of his family's companies.

"It is very doubtful": William W. Turner, *Hoover's FBI* (New York: Dell, 1971); also cited in Arthur M. Schlesinger, Jr., *Robert Kennedy and His Times* (New York: Random House, 1978).

Clifford Case: The story of the *Newark Star-Ledger* treatment of anti-McCarthy critic Senator Clifford Case of New Jersey is found in Richard H. Meeker, *Newspaperman: S. I. Newhouse and the Business of News* (New York: Ticknor & Fields, 1983).

"The story was true": David M. Oshinsky, *A Conspiracy So Immense: The World of Joe McCarthy* (New York: The Free Press, 1982); interview with Oshinsky about Cohn and his 1979 Clifford Case interview, 1993.

"Being anti-Communist": Arthur M. Schlesinger, Jr., *Robert Kennedy and His Times.*

"I came into dinner with S. I. Newhouse": Lois Romano, "The Closing Arguments of Roy Cohn," *Washington Post,* December 21, 1985.

Henry Garfinkle: For his biography *Newspaperman,* Richard Meeker interviewed Garfinkle at length about his longtime friendship and business association with Sam Newhouse and his family's media company, including the secret three-thousand-dollar no-interest loan from Newhouse that enabled Garfinkle to buy his first newsstand. Meeker shared with this author his tape-recorded interview conducted with Garfinkle on March 30, 1981.

"Henry has two personalities": Ronald Kessler, "A Rough Dealer: Control of the Newsstands Gives Henry Garfinkle Power Over Publishers," *The Wall Street Journal,* July 3, 1969.

Cohn became the general counsel: Cohn was selected as general counsel for Garfinkle's company in August 1955, according to "Union News Names Directors," *The New York Times,* August 8, 1955.

"my best guess": interview with Myron Garfinkle, 1992.

hardball legal tactics: See "Henry Garfinkle, 80; Rose from Newsboy to Major Distributor," *The New York Times* (obituary), January 13, 1983.

a civil lawsuit against Ancorp: "Ancorp Is Sued by U.S. in Civil Action Seeking Penalties of $585,000," *The Wall Street Journal,* February 9, 1971.

there was another force: Kessler, "A Rough Dealer."

"S. I. Newhouse, Sr., was a friend": interview with Neil Walsh, a longtime friend of Roy Cohn, 1992.

"Every Saturday or Sunday": interview with William Fugazy, 1992.

"That's who his friends were": interview with Peter Diamandis, 1993.

succession of three remarkably dramatic trials: All three were extensively covered by the New York press, as well as in the remarkable profile on Cohn: Ken Auletta, "Don't Mess with Roy Cohn," *Esquire,* December 5, 1978.

underworld figures: Found in Roy Cohn's FBI file are several newspaper accounts of the trials that cite testimony about Cohn's alleged involvements with underworld figures. One *Wall Street Journal* story, March 13, 1964, concerns Cohn's alleged dealings with Dalitz, according to his FBI file documents. According to the FBI file, Cohn acknowledged meeting Miami gangster Meyer Lansky, as well, but Cohn claimed all of these meetings were social and involved no business transaction.

"I remember flying out together": interview with William Fugazy, 1992.

Dick Shortway: Shortway's recollection of the lunch with Cohn from an interview with Richard Shortway, 1993.

Roy's frantic attempts to stop Si: Nicholas von Hoffman, *Citizen Cohn: The Life and Times of Roy Cohn* (New York: Doubleday, 1988).

"Si was divorced then": interview with Neil Walsh, 1992.

"He always seemed to me": interview with Cornelius Gallagher, a Cohn friend and former New Jersey congressman, 1992.

"I remember Si": interview with Carol Horn, 1992.

Barbara Walters: Cohn and Walters's introduction and Lou Walters's Latin Quarter nightclubs are discussed in Jerry Oppenheimer, *Barbara Walters: An Unauthorized Biography* (New York: St. Martin's Press, 1990).

"Two days later": Auletta, "Don't Mess with Roy Cohn." For other details about Walters's actions on Cohn's behalf, see Bob Drogin, "Roy M. Cohn fights for His Life and Legal Career," *Los Angeles Times,* February 2, 1986.

"Barbara Walters": Romano, "The Closing Arguments of Roy Cohn."

"He's just not the marrying kind": transcript of the December 30, 1979, "60 Minutes," compiled in *60 Minutes Verbatim* (New York: Arno Press/CBS News, 1980).

"He was a great friend": von Hoffman, *Citizen Cohn: The Life and Times of Roy Cohn.*

Privately, Roy explained: ibid.

"Si is very shy": Hornblower, "Si Newhouse." In the early 1980s, Cohn was often a favored spokesman for Newhouse. "At my annual birthday party, it is my favor to him never to call upon him to make a speech," said Cohn in a 1985 *People* magazine profile of Newhouse.

"If they wanted, the Newhouses could push a few buttons": Daniel Machalara, "Family Newspapers: Newhouse Chain Stays with Founder's Ways and with His Heirs," *The Wall Street Journal,* February 12, 1982.

"I am interested in publishing successful newspapers": *A Memo for the Children from S. I. Newhouse,* as related to and written by David Jacobs (New York: 1980); available at the Library of Congress.

"Roy's power was": interview with Sidney Zion, 1992.

Hale Boggs: A version of Cohn's intervention with the Newhouses is contained in Zion, *The Autobiography of Roy Cohn;* another detailed version is contained in von Hoffman, *Citizen Cohn.*

"Go ahead and talk to him": interview with former congressman and Cohn friend Cornelius Gallagher, 1992.

"Roy used the Newhouse connection": Zion, *The Autobiography of Roy Cohn.*

a much-coveted berth: von Hoffman, *Citizen Cohn.*

Koch: A detailed examination of the political clout of Cohn and Stanley Friedman with the administration of Mayor Edward I. Koch can be found in Jack Newfield and Wayne Barrett, *City for Sale: Ed Koch and the Betrayal of New York* (New York: Harper & Row, 1988).

"The story came out": interview with Dan Janison, 1992; two other former *Advance* reporters, Terry Golway and Phil Russo, confirmed the Janison anecdote and spoke about their views about Cohn's special treatment. Richard Diamond, a Newhouse cousin and publisher of the *Staten Island Advance,* refused to be interviewed. Les Trauptman died in 1992, before he could be interviewed.

Norman Mailer: The involvement of Cohn in getting Mailer to write for Newhouse's pub-lications can be found in von Hoffman, *Citizen Cohn* and Peter Manso, *Mailer: His Life and Times* (New York: Simon & Schuster, 1985). In addition, this account was also confirmed by Peter Fraser, Cohn's companion, in an interview. Another source who was actively involved with Mailer and Cohn during this time (but didn't want to be quoted by name in this text) also confirmed the accounts provided in both the von Hoffman and Manso books. In August 1993, Norman Mailer was contacted by this author with a letter requesting an interview. Judith McNally, Mailer's assistant, said Mailer would consider questions in writing but insisted that his written response be printed in this book without editing, or not at all. In early October 1993, with the agreement of St. Martin's, this author agreed to Mailer's requirements and sent a list of five questions. After several ensuing telephone calls, McNally advised in March 1994 that Mailer was still busy writing a book and would not be able to respond in writing. However, a person authorized to speak for Mailer, who did not wish to be identified, said that Mailer met with Si Newhouse at a restaurant shortly after Random House's purchase. At that meeting, Newhouse told Mailer that "if at any time Norman would make a decision to leave Little, Brown (then Mailer's publishing house) that Newhouse would like to have him as a Random House author," said the Mailer spokesperson. "His relations with Si have been cordial ever since." When asked about Roy Cohn's involvement, which was also contained in the author's October 1993 letter, the aide said Mailer never commented about Cohn. "I do think it's interesting that Norman did not go into that," said the aide.

"I have to thank you all": Liz Smith, "Mr. Mailer's Love-Fest," *Newsday,* November 3, 1991.

"never once failed to file and pay": Roy Cohn, "You Can Beat the IRS," *Parade,* April 3, 1983. *Parade*'s editor, Walter Anderson, declined an interview, saying it has been his policy in the time since the Manso book not to speak of his experiences involving his employer, Si Newhouse.

a $7 million civil lawsuit against Cohn: Gerald McKelvey, "U.S. Sues Roy Cohn for $7M, Taking Over Tax Case from IRS," *Newsday,* April 4, 1986.

"Provocative is a euphemistic way of putting it,": interview with Thomas Bolan, 1992.

"I thought about it": This account was also confirmed by Roger Stone, a friend and political ally of Cohn, in an interview.

"With its Charles Atlas photos": Much of the laudatory media coverage of *Parade*'s cover featuring Reagan was exemplified by "So, Move Over, Jane Fonda," *Time,* December 12, 1983.

"Special Counsel" to the Newhouse Publications: Documents obtained through a Freedom of Information request to the Ronald Reagan Presidential Library provided a letter from Cohn to Reagan political aide Charles Z. Wick, head of the U.S. Information Agency, shortly after the *Parade* cover story.

"I gave him a party at Studio 54": Ken Auletta, "Don't Mess Around with Roy Cohn," *Esquire,* December 5, 1978.

"I think Si was at quite a few birthday parties": interview with Thomas Bolan, 1992.

"We went over to Studio 54": *The Andy Warhol Diaries,* ed. Pat Hackett (New York: Warner Books, 1989).

"In those days": interview with Neil Walsh, 1992.

"**I have no idea when he knew**": interview with Peter Fraser, 1993.

"**Speaking of friends**": Taki, "Regarding Roy Cohn: Not the Prince, or Queen, of Darkness," *The New York Observer,* May 3, 1993.

"**My hunch is that**": interview with Nicholas von Hoffman, who received some cooperation from the Newhouse family for his Cohn biography, 1992.

Cohn be disbarred: The appellate court agreed with a disciplinary panel's recommendation that Cohn be disbarred for refusing to pay back $100,000 he had borrowed from a client and for compelling his eighty-four-year-old millionaire friend Lew Rosenstiel, then hospitalized for a stroke and senility, to sign a document making Cohn executor of his estate. There were other allegations including that he had lied on his application for admission to the bar in Washington, D.C.

"**This was a long conversation**": interview with Fred Hughes, 1993.

"**one of the most apolitical people**": Margot Hornblower, "Si Newhouse, the Talk of The New Yorker," the *Washington Post,* May 7, 1985.

"**Si was kind of noncommittal**": interview with Thomas Bolan, 1993.

"**I don't know the piece**": *New York Post;* in a 1993 interview, Fraser also confirmed the sculpture was intended for Si.

CHAPTER 6: STOP THE PRESSES

"**I saw him once or twice**": interview with William Woestendiek, 1992.

a story of remarkable intrigue: The involvement of Si Newhouse and Roy Cohn with the *Cleveland Plain Dealer*'s coverage of Jackie Presser was examined during evidence and testimony for the federal government's trial against mob boss Anthony Salerno. In addition to several newspaper accounts of this testimony, the first extensive reporting of the Newhouse involvement was mentioined in James Neff, *Mobbed Up* (New York: Atlantic Monthly Press, 1989), and later in Kenneth C. Crowe, *Collision* (New York: Scribner's, 1993), a book about the Teamsters Union.

"**paper route**": Maggie Mahar, "All in the Family: How the Newhouses Run Their Vast Media Empire," *Barron's,* November 27, 1989.

"**extracted a deal from Si**": interview with Peter Diamandis, 1993.

Vail: In his 1983 biography of Sam Newhouse (previously cited), Meeker says the Newhouses kept Vail in place but brought in Leo Ring, an old Newhouse hand, to oversee the important decisions of the newspaper. Ring declined to be interviewed for this book.

"**the highest price ever paid**": "Newhouse Buys The Plain Dealer," *The New York Times,* March 3, 1967.

"**Complete control of The Plain Dealer**": "Why the Newhouse touch is golden," *Business Week,* March 11, 1967.

"**We are essentially a nonbureaucratic**": "S. I. Newhouse and Sons: America's Most Profitable Publisher," *Business Week,* January 26, 1976.

"**Jackie had said all these things**": Neff, *Mobbed Up.*

two-part series: Mairy Jayn Woge and Walt Bogdanich, "Charges Didn't Stop Presser as U.S. Informer," *Cleveland Plain Dealer,* August 24, 1981, and several other related *Plain Dealer* stories.

"**Good job**": Neff, *Mobbed Up.*

"**You know anybody connected with the Plain Dealer?**": The tape-recorded conversation involving Maishe Rockman and Anthony Salerno was later submitted as evidence in the federal government's Teamster-related prosecution of Salerno. This account was also confirmed in an interview (1992) with then assistant U.S. Attorney Mark Hellerer, who prosecuted the Salerno/Teamster case.

"**Tony . . . asked Roy Cohn**": direct testimony from Angelo Lonardo in *USA* vs. *Anthony Salerno et al.,* a copy of which was provided by the U.S. attorney for the Southern District of New York's public information office. Further details of Cohn's involvement are cited in FBI memos about Lonardo.

"**Here's how the play went**": This and other Hopcraft comments in Neff, *Mobbed Up.* Neff's account also mentions Si Newhouse's initial reluctance, an observation attributed to a "Teamsters insider" who attended one of the meetings. Another examination of the Cohn and Salerno influence on the Newhouse newspaper and its staff is "Mafia Influence on the Teamsters," *Cleveland Magazine,* December 1985.

"**They looked at me**": "Norman N. Newhouse dead at 82; helped build communications empire," *The Newark Star Ledger,* November 7, 1988.

Vail heard this order: What happened to Bogdanich and Vail's actions are detailed in Neff,

Mobbed Up. In December 1989, the *Washington Journalism Review* published an excerpt from Neff's book and an accompanying sidebar in which Vail responded: "At no time did we apologize. No retraction was ever printed. We just published a news story [to the effect that] the government, in a sense, had signed off on the investigation of Presser, and we had an obligation to print that." Vail declined to be interviewed for this book. According to his secretary, Carl Bankovich, Vail signed an agreement upon leaving as publisher that he would not talk about his activities at the *Plain Dealer.*

"Please be advised": "Justice closes kickback investigation of Presser," *Cleveland Plain Dealer,* October 10, 1982.

new upside-down version: "Justice closes kickback investigation of Presser," *Cleveland Plain Dealer,* October 10, 1982, which quotes Presser's lawyer, John Climaco. More than six telephone calls were made to Climaco's law office without reaching him for his account.

"He [Hopcraft] says": from transcript of Jackie Presser news conference, October 10, 1982, in Cleveland.

staff's moral disgust: "Yet Another PD Squabble," *Cleveland Magazine,* December 1982.

"It was of great concern": interview (1992) with then Assistant U.S. Attorney Mark Hellerer, who prosecuted Salerno concerning the Teamsters union, whereby the actions of Cohn and the *Plain Dealer* stories became part of the government's case.

Cole went out of his way: Norman Mlachak, "Business leadership a 'must,' Cole says," *Cleveland Press,* May 6, 1981. Cole's comments included in this article.

small part of the Cleveland Indians: Greg Stricharchuk, "Citizen Cole," *Cleveland Magazine,* December 1980.

"I'll tell you this": ibid.

"Look, I'm an amateur": sworn deposition of Si Newhouse, Jr., June 28, 1984, as part of the lawsuit *James R. Province et al* vs. *Cleveland Press Publishing Company,* U.S. District Court Northern District of Ohio, Eastern Division. In this extensive deposition, Newhouse recalled his conversation with Cole.

The secret two-page agreement: The document signed by Si Newhouse on June 10, 1982, became evidence in the *Province* case and was also cited among the findings of fact in the written opinion by U.S. District Court Judge Ann Aldrich in 1985.

When Si Newhouse's secret business deal: The first reported news about this deal was Peter Phipps and Dan Cook, "Plain Dealer Offered Cole $14.5 million to Fold Press," *Akron Beacon-Journal,* January 16, 1984; numerous follow-up stories appeared in the *Beacon-Journal.*

criminal antitrust investigation: The focus of the federal grand jury was described in Peter Phipps, "Grand jury to probe Press Closing," *Akron Beacon-Journal,* November 23, 1984; also cited in "Did Si Newhouse Conspire to Kill The Cleveland Press?", *Business Week,* July 1, 1985.

"The record is replete": comments in written opinion in the *Province* case by U.S. District Court Judge Ann Aldrich in 1985.

"Comments from the respondents": Richard Osborne, "The Fight for the Front Page," *Cleveland Magazine,* December 1980.

Alex Machaskee: Machaskee declined to be interviewed for this book. He said he disagreed with the account of events at the *Plain Dealer* described in Neff's book but would not elaborate.

"You have to remember the timing": Neff, *Mobbed Up.*

"I didn't think about it": sworn deposition of Si Newhouse, Jr., June 28, 1984.

"I just felt": Peter Phipps and Dan Cook, "Plain Dealer offered Cole $14.5 million to fold Press," *Akron Beacon Journal,* January 16, 1984.

"It occurred to us": Phipps and Cook, ibid.

"raise the specter of a possible violation": Phipps and Cook, "Plain Dealer Offered Cole $14.5 million to Fold Press." Numerous follow-up stories appeared in the *Beacon-Journal.* Widmar's directive was also included in the *Beacon-Journal* story.

"The subscription list was just a ruse": Bill Doll, "Fancy Dealing in Cleveland," *Columbia Journalism Review,* May/June 1984.

"If the Cleveland Press was going out of business": Phipps and Cook.

Ultimately, their decision to challenge: In speaking of the Newhouse-Cole matter, Twist's cover-up allegations were subsequently contained in an employee lawsuit brought by Twist (*Twist* vs. *Edwin Meese*) before the U.S. Court of Appeals in the District of Columbia Circuit. Memos from J. Paul McGrath, which mentioned that immunity had been granted to Newhouse and others in the case, were made public in that case. Twist ultimately lost his appeal concerning the Justice Department's disciplinary findings against him for being discourteous, insubordinate, and using poor judgment. Department officials said their actions against Twist had nothing to do with his cover-up allegations, which had been referred to the Justice Department's Board of Professional Responsiblity. In an interview (1992), Marilyn Bobula said she agreed with Twist's viewpoint about how the Newhouse-Cole case was mishandled. She still remained with the Justice Department, however. See also Mike Casey, "PD-Press Investigators Clashed," *Crain's Cleveland Business,* April 6, 1987. McGrath in an interview (1993) declined to talk about his actions in the case but said there was no outside pressure in the decision to grant immunity.

"Lovely day, isn't it?": "Grand Jury Grilling S. I. Newhouse," *Point of View,* June 1985.

"He was an interesting person": interview with Marilyn Bobula, 1992.

"Attention All Print Buyers": *Advertising Age,* January 30, 1984.

"The problem of the Plain Dealer's inadequacies": Roldo Bartimole, "Plain Dealer Too Comfortable," July 17, 1982; numerous issues of *Point of View* were used as references, including other *Plain Dealer* reporter comments.

"the complaints of advertisers": interview with Bill Woestendiek, 1992.

review by Howard Bray: Robert Gallagher, "Book Review Spooks Plain Dealer," *Washington Journalism Review,* December 1989. In this story, Vail's comments about it were included.

"It is for this buying public": Walter Lippmann, *Public Opinion* (New York: Free Press, 1965).

CHAPTER 7: THE ARTFUL (TAX) DODGER

"To Sam": Carol J. Loomis, "The Biggest Private Fortune," *Fortune,* August 17, 1987. Other interviews with long-time Newhouse intimates, such as William Raidy, Ray Josephs, and Dr. William Tolley, confirmed the great sense of loyalty and deference to Sam felt by his family.

Victoria de Ramel: "Samuel I. Newhouse Jr. Weds Mrs. Victoria de Ramel Here," *The New York Times,* April 15, 1973. This announcement contained some biographical information on Victoria Newhouse and additional information was obtained in interviews.

salary of $397,839: Details of the Newhouses' personal finances emerged in court papers in the case *Estate of Samuel I. Newhouse, deceased, Samuel I. Newhouse Jr. and Donald E. Newhouse* vs. *The Commissioner of Internal Revenue,* U.S. Tax Court, Washington, D.C., before Judge B. John Williams, Sr. The specific references to Donald's payments one year are contained in Richard Pollak, "The Trial of Donald and Si Newhouse," *The Nation,* March 13, 1989.

"Among the country's newspaper giants": "The Newspaper Collector," *Time,* July 27, 1962.

"The scheme's beauty": Robert J. Samuelson, *Washington Post,* March 21, 1990.

"The U.S. Tax Court": Pollak, "The Trial of Donald and Si Newhouse."

These legal papers traced: The definitive article on the Newhouse tax trial is contained in Alison Frankel, "How the Newhouses Crushed the IRS," *The American Lawyer,* May 1990, which was viewed as fair and comprehensive by both sides in the matter. Frankel was interviewed in 1992 and she shared some of the court papers from the case with this writer. The available record of this case was reviewed by the author during visits to the U.S. Tax Court. Interviews were also conducted with Robert Shilliday, Jr., the government's main attorney; Paul Scherer, the Newhouses' longtime accountant; and several of the key participants and witnesses. Previous comments of tax lawyer Richard Covey also included in this article.

Si was surprised as an adult to read: testimony of Si Newhouse in estate tax case, U.S. Tax Court, Washington, D.C.

filed tax papers with the IRS: The letter to the IRS, dated May 27, 1980 and signed by Si Newhouse, outlines the estate's summary of what it owed the government in taxes.

The Newhouses' lowball estimate: interview (1992) with newspaper expert John Morton, who was an IRS witness in this case.

the largest tax assessment: interviews with Robert Shilliday, Jr., 1992 and 1993.

"I thought the government's approach": Frankel, "How the Newhouses Crushed the IRS."

Robert Shilliday moved slowly: interviews (1992 and 1993) with Shilliday and with other courtroom observers; his opening statement was also mentioned in Frankel's story.

"The head of the family": To try to prove his point about Sam Newhouse's dominance over the company, Shilliday used this and other passages from *A Memo for the Children* *from S. I. Newhouse,* as related to and written by David Jacobs (New York: 1980), which became part of the evidence submitted by the government in the estate tax case.

"Please state your name": from the ninety-page testimony of Si Newhouse on January 5, 1989, in U.S. Tax Court in Washington, D.C. A description of Newhouse's demeanor that day and other recollections were provided by Shilliday and others.

ask the court to seal the record: John Greenwald, "Auditing the Grand Acquisitor," *Time,* October 24, 1983; see also Maggie Mahar, "All in the Family: How the Newhouses Run Their Vast Media Empire," *Barron's,* November 27, 1989. For Mahar's article, Donald Newhouse offered to be interviewed about the family's business but only if *Barron's* would wait on Mahar's story until a decision had been rendered in the tax case. Mahar quoted Donald Newhouse as saying he felt it wouldn't be "wise" or "appropriate" for a publication to comment about a matter on trial before its conclusion—a view, Mahar pointed out, that is contradicted by the Newhouse newspapers' standard everyday coverage of big-name trials. The *Barron's* piece ran without agreeing to the Newhouse request.

"He may have loved his brothers": interview with John Coffee, Jr., 1992. Coffee explained in the interview how he disagreed with the government's handling of the case.

Williams fretted aloud: Although Williams's comments were plainly stated throughout the transcript of the trial, he declined to speak for the record about the government's handling of the case.

one last big-gun expert witness: The account of Kobak's and Morton's testimonies is contained in Frankel, "How the Newhouses Crushed the IRS" and a review of available court documents. Interviews with Frankel, Shilliday, Morton, and others also provided a sense of the exchanges in the courtroom.

Rupert Murdoch: Testimony was taken on January 18, 1989.

"Baniewicz was the more zealous one": interview with John Coffee, Jr., 1992.

misidentified Richard Meeker: from trial transcripts and also cited in Frankel's account in *The American Lawyer.*

nothing short of total victory: transcripts and court documents; also Geraldine Fabrikant, "Newhouses Win Fight with IRS," *The New York Times,* March 20, 1990.

"It's hard for anyone to say": interview with Paul Scherer, 1992.

"They were consciously thinking about this": interview with John Coffee, Jr., 1992.

"members in good standing": Pollak, "The Trial of Donald and Si Newhouse."

"It is very nice": ibid.

CHAPTER 8: AT RANDOM

"I remember he was very charming that night": interview with Robert Bernstein, 1990, as well as subsequent interviews with Bernstein and his wife, Helen, 1992 and 1993. Unless otherwise noted, Bernstein quotes are from these interviews.

Edgar H. Griffiths: portrait of the RCA Corporation's then chairman from John E. Cooney, "Top Man Out: Griffith's Resignation at RCA Follows Year of Turmoil, Criticism," *The Wall Street Journal,* January 26, 1981.

"According to publishing officials": N. R. Kleinfeld, "RCA Agrees to Sell Random House to Newhouse for $65–$70 Million," *The New York Times,* February 7, 1980.

"Bennett runs Random House": "Bennett Cerf Dies; Publisher, Writer," *The New York Times,* August 29, 1971.

Ulysses: Bennett Cerf, *At Random: The Reminiscences of Bennett Cerf* (New York: Random House, 1977), which includes federal judge's comments in case.

"When Jason Epstein came over": interview with Phyllis Cerf Wagner, 1990. (After Bennett Cerf's death, she was married to former New York City mayor Robert Wagner.)

"Jason Epstein is my class editor": "Cerf to Newhouse," *The Nation,* November 27, 1989.

"We had someone ready": Cerf, *At Random.*

"I had five or six bosses": Daniel Machalara, "Family Newspapers: Newhouse Chain Stays with Founder's Ways and with His Heirs," *The Wall Street Journal,* February 12, 1982.

"I expect to see him from time to time": "Newhouse Discusses Parental Relationship to Random House," *Publishers Weekly,* February 22, 1980.

"I think it represents one of the great buys": Edwin McDowell, "The New Role of Random House," *The New York Times,* May 5, 1985.

When Si's daughter, Pamela: Bernstein's recollections in the aforementioned interviews include the encouragement that Robert Gottlieb provided to Si's daughter in her writing pursuits and reminiscences about having lunch with Newhouse and his nephew, Steve Newhouse.

"I do not like charity cases": Roger Cohen, "Changing Spirit at Random House," *The New York Times,* March 19, 1990.

"Profit was not what we were looking for": Cerf, *At Random.*

"He's in jail": Cohen, "Changing Spirit at Random House."

"It's my life—it's all I do": Edwin McDowell, "Random House Publisher a Human-Rights Activist," *The New York Times,* August 6, 1986.

"Si looks over your shoulder": McDowell, "The New Role of Random House."

"You've been fired on the front page of the Times": David Streitfeld, "Life at Random," *New York,* August 5, 1991.

"The media has decided": interview with Joni Evans, 1990.

"The press is writing stories": Fran Kiernan, "Chapter 11: The Great Publishing Crash of 1989," *7 Days,* January 24, 1990.

"We've overpaid": ibid.

"He wanted Mailer": Bernstein's lack of knowledge about the origins of the Mailer deal, and the involvement of Roy Cohn in it, only became apparent years later, he said.

"When I'm ready to do the book": Jeanie Kasindorf, "How Si Newhouse Booked Trump," *New York,* November 11, 1985. Interviews (1990) with Peter Osnos provided further details, along with an interview in 1992 with another source involved in the Trump project. This source is quoted in the text but asked not to be identified by name. In the foreword to his book *The Art of the Deal,* Trump thanked Si Newhouse, who "first came to me and convinced me to do a book despite my initial reluctance."

tried unsuccessfully to buy the Washington Post: Clark Clifford's involvement with the Newhouses in trying to buy the *Washington Post* is cited in Richard Meeker, *Newspaperman: S. I. Newhouse and the Business of News* (New York: Ticknor & Fields, 1983).

Zion said that: interview with Zion, 1990 (he told Liz Smith at that time it was approximately the same amount).

"I think Si killed it": interview with Zion, 1992.

"It's a great publishing house": McDowell, "The New Role of Random House."

"Did I know it": Joshua Hammer, "Shoot-Out on Publishers' Row," *Newsday Magazine,* January 11, 1987.

"the difference between Bendel's and Macy's": ibid.

"To a certain extent": Howard Kaminsky was originally interviewed at length in 1990. In May 1993, Kaminsky agreed again to be interviewed but shortly thereafter declined to comment about Newhouse and his company.

Si had long wanted to purchase Crown: Bill Powell, "Buying A Crown for Random House," *Newsweek,* August 29, 1988.

"resignation" . . . or retirement: Edwin McDowell, "President of Random House Out Abruptly After 23 Years," *The New York Times,* November 2, 1989, as well as other press accounts.

"the George Steinbrenner of publishing": "Surprise Ending," *The New York Times,* November 5, 1989.

"From the beginning": Jonathan Alter, "The Random House Shuffle," *Newsweek,* November 13, 1989.

"It is clear from the outpouring of affection": Calvin Reid and John F. Baker, "Bernstein Retiring from Random; Vitale is New Chairman," *Publishers Weekly,* November 17, 1989.

CHAPTER 9: CLEANING HOUSE

"You're crazy": interview with Studs Terkel, 1990.

"We selected the ideal man": Bennett Cerf, *At Random: The Reminiscences of Bennett Cerf* (New York: Random House, 1977).

"It had a special touch": interview with Noam Chomsky, 1990.

"Pantheon wanted to publish": interviews with André Schiffrin, 1990 and 1992.

"That's one hundred percent not true": interview (1990) with Alberto Vitale, during which time Vitale spoke at length about the company. During that interview, however, Vitale declined to answer any questions about Random House's owner, Si Newhouse. Vitale declined to be interviewed further in 1993 for this book.

"disfigured itself": Roger Cohen, "Top Random House Author Assails Ouster at Pantheon," *The New York Times,* March 9, 1990. In an early 1991 interview with this writer, Doctorow claimed the *Times's* quotations were out of context and not accurate.

"Discovering the idealistic and mental impediments": "Concentration in the Book-Publishing and Book-Selling Industry," Hearing Before the Subcommittee on Antitrust, Monopoly, and Business Rights of Committee on the Judiciary, United States Senate, March 13, 1980, U.S. Government Printing Office.

"I said we were three men in deep trouble": Edwin McDowell, "Michener Talks," *The New York Times,* March 28, 1990.

"I'm not going to accept": interview with Vitale and other Pantheon editors who were present during this conversation, 1990 and 1991.

"Hi, it's Si": Doug Ireland, "The Fall of the House of Pantheon," *The Village Voice,* March 13, 1990.

"He said he wanted to intervene": interview with Wendy Wolf, who recounted conversation with Newhouse, 1990.

"You know, he's a relatively inarticulate man": ibid.

"Why should Pantheon": interview with Vitale, 1990.

"The books that S. I. Newhouse really cares about": This view is repeated in various press interviews given by Thomas Engelhardt and is reflected in "At Pantheon, Closed Books," *The New York Times,* March 8, 1990.

"The barbarians have taken over": Meg Cox, "Four Editors Quit at Random House Over Aide's Firing," *The Wall Street Journal,* March 1, 1990.

NEWHOUSED: "Newhoused," *The Nation,* March 19, 1990.

Vitale: A typical description of Vitale at that time can be found in Alan Friedman, "Energetic Man of Numbers," *The Financial Times,* January 29, 1990. When asked what books he is reading for pleasure, Vitale responded: "Very few, because I don't have the time." Also, Martin Walker, "Pantheon Buried by Profit," *The Manchester Guardian.*

"Quality does not seem": *Le Monde* quotation cited by Doug Ireland, "The Fall of the House of Pantheon," *Village Voice,* March 13, 1990.

"I think that what I've seen": interview with Wynn Newhouse, 1990.

"Change appears threatening": Roger Cohen, "Changing Spirit at Random House," *The New York Times,* March 19, 1990.

"He didn't know what he was doing": interview with Jason Epstein, 1991.

"People no longer think of him": interview with André Schiffrin, 1991.

"one of the best things": interview with Vitale, 1990.

"Like Pantheon, we all strive": Thomas J. Maier, "The Ins and Outs at Random House," *Newsday Magazine,* February 24, 1991.

"It was really weird": interview with Peter Gethers, 1993. Previous interviews with Jason Epstein, Sonny Mehta, and Joni Evans in 1990 and 1991 provided further details about the composing of the letter in response to the Pantheon dispute.

"I don't know why": interview with Bernstein, 1990.

"He doesn't have to read books": interview with Jason Epstein, 1991; cited in Maier, "The Ins and Outs at Random House."

"There was a lot of internal stuff": interview with E. L. Doctorow, 1990.

"the company got so big": Cohen, "Changing Spirit at Random House."

"Everybody said that Random House": Meg Cox, "Four Editors Quit at Random House Over Aide's Firing," *The Wall Street Journal,* March 1, 1990.

"Tip money": Maureen O'Brien, "Over the Top," *Publishers Weekly,* September 6, 1993, and interviews with those who attended the Star Club party.

"It seems to me appropriate": Paul Colford, " 'Psycho' to Get Release," *Newsday,* November 17, 1990.

"Enter Mr. Mehta": Roger Rosenblatt, "Snuff This Book! Will Bret Easton Ellis Get Away with Murder?" *The New York Times Book Review,* December 16, 1990.

"Fantastic, fantastic": Richard Johnson, *New York Daily News,* May 27, 1992.

"He's like a lizard": Jennet Conant, "The Very Furry Feet of Sonny Mehta," *Esquire,* April 1993.

"furry little feet": ibid.

"English publishing was": Robert E. Sullivan, Jr., "Knopf's Uncivil War," *7 Days,* September 20, 1989.

"Sonny is a passionate reader": Conant, "The Very Furry Feet of Sonny Mehta."

"A big man leaves here": Sullivan, "Knopf's Uncivil War."

"You walk around this place": ibid.

"There were dark forces at work": Conant, "The Very Furry Feet of Sonny Mehta."

"It would have been a good way": David Streitfeld, "Life at Random," *New York,* August 5, 1991.

"Knopf is solidly profitable": Roger Cohen, "Random House Star, Sonny Mehta, Talks Profits as Well as Art," *The New York Times,* November 13, 1990.

"If we don't want to rely": interview with Sonny Mehta, 1991.

"*Damage* is certainly the granddaddy": Esther B. Fein, "Publishing," *The New York Times,* March 15, 1993.

"the most shocking, haunting and erotic": Streitfed, "Life at Random."

"The letter staking his reputation": Streitfeld, "Life at Random."

"And there will be plenty": interview with Alberto Vitale, 1990.

"Si made Harry take the job": Streitfeld, "Life at Random."

"The wheel of fortune": Edwin McDowell, "New Publisher Named in Shift at Turbulent Random House," *The New York Times,* October 31, 1990, included Evans comments.

Once *Traveler* was hailed as a success: Patrick M. Reilly, "Travel Magazine of Condé Nast Cuts Boosterism," *The Wall Street Journal,* October 1, 1990.

"if you strike oil": Geraldine Fabrikant, "Evans at Random House: Big Spender, Big Sales," *The New York Times,* March 8, 1993.

"We are often in a position": Jeannette Walls, "A Random House Divided," *New York,* January 11, 1993.

"The opportunity to work": "Elisabeth Sifton to Join Knopf as Executive Vice-President," *Publishers Weekly,* July 24, 1987.

"the people at Knopf are highly intelligent": Sullivan, "Knopf's Uncivil War."

"I chose to do this for my own good reasons": Esther B. Fein, "Book Notes," *The New York Times,* April 15, 1992.

"I think that many of us": ibid.

"When Sonny came to Knopf": Conant, "The Very Furry Feet of Sonny Mehta."

"They looked like Charlie's Angels": Phoebe Hoban, "A Random Killing at Turtle Bay," *New York,* March 1, 1993.

"It's easier to see Alberto Vitale or Si as a monster": interview with Joni Evans, 1990.

"I'm very disappointed": "A Random Killing at Turtle Bay"; Esther B. Fein, "Random House Closing a Division," *The New York Times,* February 11, 1993; Paul D. Colford, "Random House Closes Its Boutique," *Newsday,* February 11, 1993.

"welfare mentality": Erroll McDonald, "At Pantheon Books, A Welfare Mentality," *The New York Times,* March 20, 1990.

"There's not a club in New York": Vince Passaro, "The Highbrow Days and Downtown Nights of Erroll McDonald," *Esquire,* January 1991.

All I Need Is Love: *Spy,* August 1990.

"I came to see this man": Passaro, "The Highbrow . . ."

"I am in the heart of the learning curve": Sarah Lyall, "More Lessons to Learn Before Oprah Tells All," *The New York Times,* June 16, 1993; see also Charlotte Hays, "We May Never Know," *New York Daily News,* June 30, 1993.

"What's next?": *New York,* August 2, 1993.

"I think he's done an excellent job": Conant, "The Very Furry Feet of Sonny Mehta."

"When I arrived": Streitfeld, "Life at Random."

"We never give up": Conant, "The Very Furry Feet of Sonny Mehta."

Jurassic Park: *The New York Times,* June 16, 1993.

CHAPTER 10: "BLONDE AMBITION"

Ronald Reagan strode: An interview with Harry Benson (1992) and interviews with Tina Brown and William F. Buckley, Jr. (1993) provided further details to the June 1985 Reagan cover story. See also William F. Buckley, Jr., "The Way They Are" (photographs by Harry Benson), *Vanity Fair,* June 1985.

"I didn't realize it": "Flattery Will Get You Ten Pages . . . Maybe," *Spy,* August 1990.

"I'm going to send you back": interview with Tina Brown, 1993, including her recollections of the conversation with Newhouse. See also Geoffrey Stokes, "Queen Tina," *Spy,* May 1992.

"This is a disaster!": Geraldine Fabrikant, "Si Newhouse Tests His Magazine Magic," *The New York Times,* September 25, 1988.

"was one of the most repulsive objects": Alexander Cockburn, "Nausea," *The Nation,* September 7, 1985.

"Since 1936, people at Condé Nast": Sandra Salmans, "Courting the Elite at Condé Nast," *The New York Times,* February 6, 1983.

"a Broadway property": Geoffrey T. Hellman, "Last of the Species," *The New Yorker* (two parts), September 19 and 26, 1942.

"My interest in society": ibid.

"I'm panting with joy": *Fortune,* February 1983.

"Condé Nast is large enough": Salmans, "Courting the Elite at Condé Nast."

"We started to track it": interview with Mark Clements, 1992.

Francine du Plessix Gray: Jane Perlez, "Vanity Fair Sparks Sharp Reaction," *The New York Times,* March 30, 1983.

"quickness of temperament": ibid.

"The old *Vanity Fair*": Craig Unger, "Can Vanity Fair Live Again?" *New York,* April 26, 1982.

"He had in mind": interview with Walter Clemons, 1992.

"I think Richard": interview with John Leonard, 1992.

"This is not going to be a coffee table book": Tom Mathews, "High Gloss News," *Newsweek,* May 1, 1989.

"to make a guide to the reader": Perlez, "*Vanity Fair* Sparks Sharp Reaction."

"No magazine has ever received a ruder welcome": "Back to the Drawing Board at *Vanity Fair*," *Newsweek,* May 9, 1983.

"a mess at heart": Henry Fairlie, "The Vanity of *Vanity Fair*," *The New Republic,* March 21, 1983.

"The first one was too shocking": Perlez.

"And then the press pounced": Dodie Kazanjian and Calvin Tomkins, *Alex: The Life of Alexander Liberman* (New York: Alfred A. Knopf, 1993).

"gutsy": Perlez, "*Vanity Fair* Sparks Sharp Reaction."

"petulant": ibid.

Leo Lerman: Edwin McDowell, "Lerman Named Editor of Vanity Fair," *The New York Times,* April 27, 1983.

"Union Jackie": Tina Brown, "Tina Brown," *Punch,* May 5, 1976.

"I wanted to come to America": Lois Romano, "Vanity's British Import," *The Washington Post,* January 12, 1984.

"All unaware that the evening's social apartheid": Tina Brown, *Life's a Party* (North Pomfret, Vermont: David & Charles, Inc., 1984).

"I think the Twenties thing": *Sunday Telegraph Magazine,* July 29, 1979.

"As seen through the old *Tatler*": Brown, *Life's a Party.*

"When it was such a small operation": interview with Tina Brown, 1992.

"When I took her on": *Sunday Times of London,* February 20, 1983.

"Artistically, Vanity Fair was a typographical zoo": Geraldine Fabrikant, "Vanity Fair's Slick Formula," *The New York Times,* August 26, 1985.

"You would always find her sitting": Georgina Howell, "All Is Vanity Nothing Is Fair," *The Times Sunday Magazine,* 1986.

"How depressing for you": Jane McKerron, "A Brown Study," *The Times* (London), January 22, 1984.

"a keen student of facade": Brown, *Life's a Party.*

"curiosity and ratlike cunning": transcript from "Blonde Ambition," produced by Jeffrey Fager, "60 Minutes," CBS News, October 21, 1990.

"She was feisty enough": interview with Ruth Ansel, 1982.

"It had become fashionable": Elizabeth Mehren, "Road to the Fair; For Tina Brown, a Decade of Detours," *Los Angeles Times,* January 30, 1985.

"If you don't like my identity": Lois Romano, "Vanity's British Import," *Washington Post,* January 12, 1984.

"There are a lot of homosexual men": Hilary Doling, "New York as Tina Sees It," *Newsday,* November 27, 1985.

"Americans are much less ironic": Mathews, "High Gloss News."

"It's why faceless millionaires": Howell, "All Is Vanity Nothing Is Fair."

"You've got to make it": "Blonde Ambition," transcript of the "60 Minutes" program of October 21, 1990.

"first order of the day": Romano, "Vanity's British Import."

"strong masculine read": ibid.

"Tina has the courage of her ignorance": Stokes, "Queen Tina."

Angela Janklow: Bill Thomas, "Mighty Tina," *Los Angeles Times Magazine,* November 3, 1991; see also *The New York Times,* October 24, 1986.

Reinaldo Herrera: interview with Tina Brown, 1993, and a brief conversation with Herrera (1993), who talked about his job but declined to be interviewed at length. See also Brown, *Life's a Party.*

"Selling advertising helped me": Bob Colacello, *Holy Terror: Andy Warhol Close-Up* (New York: HarperCollins, 1990), including Tina Brown comment.

"The perceived wisdom": Mathews, "High Gloss News."

"I dreaded going out": Howell, "All Is Vanity Nothing Is Fair."

"I have no problems": Geraldine Fabrikant, "Vanity Fair's Slick Formula," *The New York Times,* August 26, 1985. In another interview, Newhouse said, "Vanity Fair will follow its own dynamic. There is no cause and effect as long as it is making progress," in Alex S. Jones, "An Intensely Private Family Empire," *The New York Times,* March 9, 1985.

"My whole gimmick": Janet Ungless, "Mocking the Gods Is Her Cup of Tea," *Newsday,* September 10, 1986.

"No, I'm not, and no, you're not": Fabrikant, "Vanity Fair's Slick Formula."

"an entirely separate matter": Jonathan Alter, "Trying to Buy a Legend," *Newsweek,* February 25, 1985.

"She probably called me": interview with William F. Buckley, Jr., 1993.

Claus von Bülow: Dominick Dunne, "Fatal Charm," *Vanity Fair,* August 1985 and September 1985.

"My God!": Mathews, "High Gloss News."

"The debonair Prince": Tina Brown, "The Mouse That Roared," *Vanity Fair,* October, 1985.

"We will do a Royals story": Patrick Reilly, "Fair Game for Miracle Worker," *Advertising Age,* October 24, 1988.

Brown also beseeched Dick Shortway: interviews with Shortway and Brown, 1993, including recollections of Newhouse's comments at the time.

"In view of this magazine's stormy launch": Tina Brown, "Editor's Letter—Fair's Fare," *Vanity Fair,* September 1985.

"Before, editors here were being held captive": Reilly, "Fair Game for Miracle Worker."

"is much closer to what I had in mind": Laura Landro, "For Tina Brown, Progress at Vanity Fair," *The Wall Street Journal,* March 18, 1987.

"As soon as Tina took hold": Mathews, "High Gloss News."

"We were baffled": Landro, "For Tina Brown, Progress at Vanity Fair."

"if you can survive that first year": *New York Daily News,* November 24, 1985.

"We fell asleep with the TV on": *New York Post,* April 1, 1992.

"This part is yours, and yours only": *The New York Observer,* April 6, 1992.

"What did you do for Jodie Foster?": interview with Jesse Kornbluth, 1992.

"We are dealing with a certain element": Mathews, "High Gloss News."

"They are there for one reason only": ibid.

"She is the magic bimbo": "Blonde Ambition" transcript.

"A sexy cover is bound to help": Michael Gross, "Sex Sells," *The Saturday Review,* July/August 1985.

lunch with actress Jane Wyman: Dominick Dunne, *The Mansions of Limbo* (New York: Crown, 1991).

"We're always being beaten up in the press": Bernard Weinraub, "Hollywood Still Directs Its Coverage," *The New York Times,* June 1, 1992.

promised Ovitz most-favored-treatment status: "Flattery Will Get You Ten Pages . . . Maybe," *Spy,* August 1990.

the doorknobs were falling off: Mathews, "High Gloss News."

"I don't treat advertisers": Reilly, "Vanity Fair Adds to Glitter."

PARTNERS IN STYLE: Daniel Lazare, "Vanity Fare," *The Columbia Journalism Review,* May/June 1989.

"You hope that magazines": David Hershkovits, "Bruce Weber: He's Considered Fashion's Every Angle," *Newsday,* May 25, 1989.

"If you were producing a funny magazine": Ungless, "Mocking the Gods Is Her Cup of Tea."

"Brown sells the editorial pages": Stokes, "Queen Tina."

"Only ordinary schleps": Henrietta Stackpole, "It's a Small W," *The Nation,* October 12, 1985.

"I'm Scared of How Desirable I Am Sometimes": "I'm Scared of How Desirable I Am Sometimes," *The New Republic,* November 4, 1991.

"A hot magazine rides the Zeitgeist": Tom Mathews, "High Gloss News," *Newsweek,* May 1, 1989.

"The only thing *Vanity Fair* gave me": Fabrikant, "Si Newhouse Tests His Magazine Magic."

"I am fed up": Patrick Reilly, "Fair game for miracle worker," *Advertising Age,* October 24, 1988.

"I felt that month Gorbachev was": "Blonde Ambition" transcript. Brown made a similar comment when asked why she put Cher instead of Marla Maples on her *VF* cover in November 1990, during the military buildup that led to the Persian Gulf War: "In light of the Gulf crisis, we thought a brunette was more appropriate," *Fortune,* November 19, 1990.

"If it makes Tina's nipples firm": *Newsweek,* March 9, 1992.

"I think Tina was very quick to realize": interview with Leslie Bennetts, 1992.

"Years from now": Paul Rosenfield, "The Queen and I," *LA Style,* September 1992.

"I want to assure you": A copy of the May 12, 1986, letter from Tina Brown to Nancy Reagan was obtained through a Freedom of Information request to the Ronald Reagan Presidential Library in Simi Valley, California. Brown's letter said the feature would also include such couples as Mr. and Mrs. William Buckley, Mr. and Mrs. Bob Hope, and Mr. and Mrs. Alexander Liberman.

"The evening's success": Liz Smith, *Newsday,* March 15, 1992.

"It was a pretty dazzling evening": interview with Paul Rosenfield, 1993.

"rogue" panel at the Oxford debate: Claire McHugh, "The Transom," *The New York Observer,* May 25,1992.

"I honestly believe": John Motavalli, "Tina Talks: Power and Prestige at *Vanity Fair,*" *Inside Media,* June 24, 1992.

(Machiavelli's *The Prince*): Tim Page, "Must-Reads for the '90s," *Newsday Magazine,* February 18, 1990.

"I tend to feel": Mathews, "High Gloss News."

"Tina Brown's headed": Thomas, "Mighty Tina."

CHAPTER 11: ABOUT *THE NEW YORKER* AND SI

"In reporting with some accuracy": Maureen Dowd, "A Writer for *The New Yorker* Says He Created Composites in Reports," *The New York Times,* June 19, 1984.

"volunteered by me": Reid later contested some of the implications in the *Times*'s account and the original June 18, 1984, story that appeared in *The Wall Street Journal.* His rebuttal appeared in "A Respecter of Truth in Writing," letter from Alastair Reid, *The New York Times,* July 15, 1984.

"A leg-pulling friend of ours": "There at The New Yorker," *Newsweek,* July 2, 1984.

"The end of the world": "The Fiction of Truth," *The New York Times,* July 21, 1984.

"Had I been writing for a tourist magazine": Dowd, "A Writer for The New Yorker Says He Created Composites in Reports."

"We do not permit composites": Edwin McDowell, "New Yorker Editor Calls Reporting Style Wrong," *The New York Times,* July 3, 1984.

a tempest in the media's teapot: For an example of this, see Daniel Seligman, "Compositegate Revisited," *Fortune,* August 6, 1984, and Michael Kinsley, "Dept. of Amplification: William Shawn and The Temple of Facts," *The New Republic,* July 16 and July 23, 1984.

17 percent stake: Newhouse issued a statement to this effect that was reported in Pamela G. Hollie, "Newhouse to Acquire 17% Of The New Yorker," *The New York Times,* November 14, 1984.

"We never thought anyone": interview with Peter Fleischmann, 1992.

"*The New Yorker*'s most precious asset": Hendrik Hertzberg, "Journals of Opinion," *Gannett Center Journal,* Spring 1989.

"It was a warm day": interview with Peter Fleischmann, 1992.

Fleischmann's investment of $700,000: Alden Whitman, "Raoul H. Fleischmann, Publisher of The New Yorker, Dies at 83," *The New York Times,* May 12, 1969.

"You caught only glimpses of Ross": James Thurber, *The Years with Ross* (Little, Brown & Co., 1959).

"As a business organization": Marylin Bender, *"The New Yorker:* Mannerly Maverick at 50," *The New York Times,* February 16, 1975.

"He is a handsome, gentle, ironic man": Brendan Gill, *Here At The New Yorker* (New York: Random House, 1975).

"It didn't last long enough": interview with Peter Fleischmann, 1992.

"If you could buy *The New Yorker"*: interview with Richard Shortway, 1993.

little more than 25 percent: Jonathan Alter, "Trying to Buy a Legend," *Newsweek,* February 25, 1985; also Peter Fleischmann interview, 1992.

Warren Buffett: The details of other offers were detailed by Fleischmann and are contained in Gigi Mahon, *The Last Days of The New Yorker* (New York: McGraw-Hill, 1988).

"the fragile equilibrium": Marylin Bender, *"The New Yorker:* Mannerly Maverick at 50," *The New York Times,* February 16, 1975.

Green resigned: This account is drawn from interviews (1992) with Peter Fleischmann, Philip Messinger, and another source familiar with Green's resignation.

"Peter had been born into the job": interview with Philip Messinger, 1992.

he immediately contacted Newhouse: Blinder could not be reached. But Mahon's *Last Days of The New Yorker* mentions Marron's and Blinder's involvement, and so did Messinger and Fleischmann in interviews, 1992.

"That's not Peter's style": interview with Jeanne Fleischmann, 1992.

"He said to me, 'Let's buy it' ": interview with Philip Messinger, 1992. Reik's change of heart is mentioned in Mahon's *Last Days of The New Yorker.*

"The takeover was hard to bear": Bruce Lambert, "Peter Fleischmann, 71, Who Led The New Yorker into the 1980s," *The New York Times,* April 18, 1993.

"I'm moved by your kind words": text of 1985 Newhouse speech provided by the Magazine Publishers Association; also cited in Carol J. Loomis, "The Biggest Private Fortune," *Fortune,* August 17, 1987, among others.

"to establish a relationship of mutual trust": Douglas C. McGill, "Editor of *New Yorker* Seeks 'Mutual Trust,' " *The New York Times,* March 12, 1985.

"Obviously, Mr. Shawn will continue": Margaret Hornblower, "Si Newhouse, the Talk of The New Yorker," *Washington Post,* May 7, 1985.

"Shawn's method": Gill.

a much broader interpretation of *The New Yorker:* Several interviews provided insight into Shawn's evolving vision of the magazine during the 1950s and 1960s. A sampling of different views about Shawn's tenure can be found in "Remembering Mr. Shawn," *The New Yorker,* December 28, 1992; Thomas Griffith, "Trouble in Paradise. Yes, Trouble," *Time,* January 12, 1981; Thomas Collins, "An Urbane Half Century," *Newsday,* February 21, 1975.

"He was always there to encourage": interview with Thomas Whiteside, 1992.

Jonathan Schell: Curtis Deyrup, "Jonathan Schell," *Publishers Weekly,* April 21, 1989.

"a vicious murderous attack": Louis Menand, "A Friend Writes," *The New Republic,* February 26, 1990.

"journalistic integrity": Gill, *Here At The New Yorker.* A criticism of Gill's book and Shawn's later years at *The New Yorker* is contained in Nora Ephron, *Scribble, Scribble: Notes on the Media* (New York: Alfred A. Knopf, 1978).

"If those of us now": Gill.

"Under Ross, the profiles": ibid.

"There is a recognizable": Griffith, "Trouble in Paradise. Yes, Trouble."

"I think the magazine has changed": Thomas Collins, "An Urbane Half Century," *Newsday,* February 21, 1975.

"The business ownership": "Talk Of the Town," *The New Yorker,* April 22, 1985.

"It was very elegantly put": Hornblower, "Si Newhouse, the Talk of The New Yorker."

"I've never seen Si so excited": interview, Hornblower, "Si Newhouse, the Talk of *The New Yorker.*"

"when a new editor": Mahon, *The Last Days of The New Yorker.*

a safe consensus choice: Edwin Diamond, "The Two Faces of Eustace Tilley," *New York,* November 17, 1986.

"Very unlike Shawn": ibid.

handed him a memo: the exchange between Newhouse and Shawn is recounted from interviews with several staffers who were close to Shawn and from such published accounts as Jonathan Alter, "The Squawk of the Town," *Newsweek,* January 26, 1987.

"the finest editor of his time": Edwin McDowell, "Knopf President Will Succeed Shawn as *New Yorker* Editor," *The New York Times,* January 13, 1987.

William Shawn climbed up a few steps: interviews with staff members who attended the meeting; a more detailed description can be found in Mahon, *The Last Days of The New Yorker.*

"I'm surprised": Edwin McDowell, "Staff Members, Upset, Meet at *The New Yorker*," *The New York Times,* January 14, 1987.

"there was a powerful": Edwin McDowell, "154 at *The New Yorker* Protest Choice of Editor," *The New York Times,* January 15, 1987.

listed on the letter: ibid.

"The staff knows": Alter, "The Squawk of the Town."

"He looks calmer than he did": E. J. Kahn, Jr., *Year of Change: More About The New Yorker & Me,* (New York: Viking Penguin, 1988).

"Knopf and *The New Yorker* share": McDowell, "Knopf President Will Succeed Shawn as *New Yorker* Editor."

"My job was to select a man": McDowell, "Staff Members, Upset, Meet at *The New Yorker*."

"He set the date": ibid.

"Mr. Shawn is a perfectly rational man": Edwin Diamond, "The Fate of the Earth," *New York,* January 26, 1987.

"I have never experienced": Shawn's comments were cited in the Lillian Ross essay that was part of the "Remembering Mr. Shawn" tribute in *The New Yorker,* December 28, 1992, following Shawn's death.

"The hope was that Si": interview with Jonathan Schell, 1992.

"Si read about Frank Perdue": "An Explosive Debut," *Newsday,* October 2, 1987; see also Philip H. Dougherty, "Magazine Tries New Campaigns," *The New York Times,* September 25, 1985, for more about Florio's promotional changes.

"I just blew it out of here": Mark N. Vamos, "Change at *The New Yorker* Is the Talk of the Town," *Business Week,* March 10, 1986.

"I'm a good publisher": Richard Sandomir, "I'm Strictly Business, New Yorker Boss Says," *Newsday,* December 2, 1985.

"He seems to be energized": Dougherty, "Magazine Tries New Campaigns."

TV campaign seemed to pay off: Randall Rothenberg, "*The New Yorker:* Staid No More," *The New York Times,* December 20, 1989.

$5 million annual profit: *The New Yorker* reported profits of $5.3 million in 1983 and $5.6 million in 1984, the year before Si Newhouse bought the magazine, according to Geraldine Fabrikant, "Cash vs. Cachet," *The New York Times,* June 2, 1986. See also Elizabeth Kolbert, "Soul of the Buzz Machine: Tina Brown Moves The New Yorker, at a Price," *The New York Times Magazine,* December 5, 1993.

"Many analysts now think": "How to Fix The New Yorker," *The New York Times,* November 19, 1989. Cohen's comments are included in this round table of opinions along with Altshiller.

"There's speculation": Warren Berger, "*The New Yorker:* The Image Problem Persists," *Publishing News,* February 1990.

little talks at private lunches: Menaker and Singer went to Young & Rubicam "simply to learn about the interests of young ad people," said Florio in Rothenberg, "*The New Yorker*: Staid No More." See also "Talk of the Lunch," *Newsday,* which mentions Gill and Pauline Kael.

"Since the Newhouse organization": interview with William F. Buckley, Jr., 1993.

"What seems to unnerve the magazine's staff": N. R. Kleinfield, "Rumors Outpace Changes Under *New Yorker*'s Editor," *The New York Times,* December 7, 1988.

"The New York magazine world": ibid.

"There's nothing wrong": Quotation attributed to Jonathan Newhouse is contained in Mahon, *The Last Days of The New Yorker.* Jonathan Newhouse was asked in writing for an interview for this book, but he never responded.

"I don't think he's a man": interview with Thomas Whiteside, 1992.

"a slightly different look": Herbert Mitgang, "Has Eustace Tilley Noticed? World's Not Quite the Same," *The New York Times,* April 16, 1988.

"We are not going to colorize": N. R. Kleinfield, "Inside New Yorker, a Splash of Color," *The New York Times,* February 15, 1989.

"There are four things in my life": McDowell, "Knopf President Will Succeed Shawn as *New Yorker* Editor."

"I have never had a long-term vision": Kleinfield, "Rumors Outpace Changes Under *New Yorker*'s Editor."

"Everything that Gottlieb is doing": Edwin Diamond, "After Shawn," *New York*, June 8, 1987.

"A couple of writers have left": Brendan Gill, "Still Here at *The New Yorker*," *The New York Times Book Review*, October 4, 1987.

"Although I'm sure Knopf": interview with Calvin Trillin, 1992.

"Ultimately, a lot of companies": Scott Donaton, "Advertorials Are Like a Drug," *Advertising Age*, March 9, 1992.

CHAPTER 12: "THE HAPPIEST GIRL IN THE WHOLE U.S.A."

"Did you make your mind up yet?": Michael Gross, "Tina's Turn," *New York*, July 20, 1992.

"Si asked me to go to *The New Yorker*": interview with Tina Brown, 1993.

as much as $10 million: Financial figures were reported in Patrick M. Reilly, "Tina Brown of *Vanity Fair* Will Head *The New Yorker*," *The Wall Street Journal*, July 1, 1992 and in Paul D. Colford, "Does Tina Brown Plan Big Changes? Yes and No," *Newsday*, July 7, 1992; see also Gross, "Tina's Turn." In one interview, Florio denied the magazine lost as much as $10 million, though industry analysts continued to estimate that figure for months to come.

"in no way arose because of business": Deirdre Carmody, "Tina Brown to Take Over at *The New Yorker*," *The New York Times*, July 1, 1992.

"I know the problem": interview with Tina Brown, 1993.

"I think I'm good": Gross, "Tina's Turn."

"At a certain point, Bob": Carmody, "Tina Brown to Take Over at *The New Yorker*."

"I wouldn't make *Vanity Fair*": Gross, "Tina's Turn."

"They were often publishing": interview with Tina Brown, 1993.

"Everyone is rather jolted": Reilly, "Tina Brown of *Vanity Fair* Will Head *The New Yorker*."

"By the way": Gross, "Tina's Turn."

"I'm here to tell you some sad news": ibid.

"sounded the way people sound": Charles Trueheart, "Talk of the Town," *Washington Post*, July 1, 1992. Other staffers were much more reserved in their reactions to Brown's arrival.

"The rumors are true": An account of this meeting is from interviews with Tina Brown, Calvin Trillin, and others who attended this meeting, as well as published accounts in *The New York Times*, July 1, 1992, and in Gross's definitive piece in *New York*, July 20, 1992.

"too text-driven": Trueheart, "Talk of the Town."

"I do not know what she is going to do": Carmody, "Tina Brown to Take Over at *The New Yorker*."

Gottlieb wasn't bitter: interview with Ingrid Sischy, 1993.

"I wanted to have the whole summer": interview with Tina Brown, 1993.

"I think Si's timing was impeccable": interview with Tina Brown, 1993.

He stopped giving out: "Present tense for Tina, scribes," *New York Daily News*, October 22, 1992.

"The ball has ended": Michael T. Kaufman, "Reading Between the Lines of The New Yorker," *The New York Times*, September 26, 1992.

"Of couse I'll miss it": Jim Windolf, "Tina Brown's Debut: Oct. 5 *New Yorker* Has Vanity Fair," *The New York Observer*, September 14, 1992.

She personally blamed Graydon Carter: Details of Brown's reaction to *Spy*'s publication of her letter to Mike Ovitz is from Russell Miller, "Spy Who Came into the Fold," *The Sunday Times of London*, October 11, 1992.

Edward Graydon Carter: David Blum, "Spying on Spy," *New York*, April 17, 1989. An interview (1993) with Margaret MacAngus of Carleton University's records and registration office confirmed that Carter had attended but never received a degree there.

"We never lost an ad": "This Spy Keeps an Eye on Fat Cats," *Newsday*, December 3, 1987.

"When I came to New York": Blum, "Spying on Spy." Carter refused to be interviewed for this book.

"There is nothing that *Spy*": Blum, "Spying on Spy."

"shows Brown looking all morning-after": comments about Newhouse are from *Spy*, as quoted in Gross, "Tina's Turn."

"I've done freelance articles": "Spy Man Taking Newhouse Gold," *New York*, September 19, 1988.

"You're kidding!": Liz Smith, *Newsday,* December 20, 1991.

"If you're Machiavellian": This chapter, because of its recent time frame, relied on a number of background interviews with editors, writers, and others who are friendly with Carter, Brown and Wintour, although not always contiguously.

"I don't know": interview with Tina Brown, 1993.

"What was right was doubly right": "Remembering Mr. Shawn," *The New Yorker,* December 28, 1992.

"bought by a billionaire": Eric Utne, "Tina's New Yorker," *Columbia Journalism Review,* March/April 1993. Article includes quotation from Seymour Krim.

a party for advertiser Calvin Klein: Dan Feinstein, "Style Calendar," *Newsday,* December 27, 1992.

"Basically, my whole thrust has been": Deirdre Carmody, "Her First Issue at the Ready, Tina Brown Talks About *The New Yorker,*" *The New York Times,* September 24, 1992.

"V.F. is the quintessential postmodern magazine": Tina Brown, "Editor's Letter: Signing Off," *Vanity Fair,* September 1992.

Si Newhouse was the savior: The exchange between Brown and her interviewer from the *Columbia Journalism Review* from Eric Utne, "Tina's New Yorker," *Columbia Journalism Review,* March/April 1993. Krim's quote included in this article. Sec p. 318.

"We all feel that presence of Shawn": interview with Tina Brown, 1993.

"The paramount concern": Helen Thorpe, "Off the Record," *The New York Observer,* July 13, 1992.

"We would like to see it in profit": Deirdre Carmody, "Tina Brown's Progress at *The New Yorker,*" *The New York Times,* April 12, 1993.

By trying to attract new readers: "Dirt Cheap Subscription Offer," *Newsday,* January 7, 1993.

"I'm most turned off": Utne, "Tina's *New Yorker.*"

"tapped" the new editor: Gianni Versace's purported involvement with Tina Brown was mentioned in Anne-Marie Schiro, "Art and Biographies," *The New York Times,* December 22, 1992.

"We reduced them": interview with Tina Brown, 1993.

model Naomi Campbell: *New York Daily News,* February 5, 1993.

"We have no reason to believe": *Vanity Fair* spokeswoman Beth Kseniak's comment from Jim Windolf, "Off the Record," *The New York Observer,* February 15, 1993.

"For instance, I've never been to the collections": Interview with Tina Brown, 1993.

"It's not a conflict": Degen Pener, "Through His Lens, Avedon Looks Forward and Back," *The New York Times,* February 14, 1993.

Holly Brubach: Maurie Perl's reply to Brubach's agreement to pose for Gap ads from Degen Pener, "Publishing: A Small World After All," *The New York Times,* April 25, 1993. A full-page Gap advertisement with Brubach appeared in the May 1993 issue of *Harper's Bazaar.*

"She passionately wanted": interview with Tina Brown, 1993.

"In fact, Tina gave me her permission": interview with Holly Brubach, 1993.

"It *is* a different tradition": interview with Tina Brown, 1993.

"How does one do this?": Charlotte Hays, "The Transom," *The New York Observer,* December 14, 1992.

"Ms. Brown is clearly bent on shaking things up": Walter Goodman, "Paging Through a New *New Yorker,*" *The New York Times,* September 29, 1992.

fiction began to fade: Jim Windolf, "Off the Record," *The New York Observer,* March 3, 1993.

"I don't think he": Carmody, "Her First Issue at the Ready." Earlier to the *Times* (August 20, 1992), Brown said of Chancellor: "This is the only job in the world that would have lured such a celebrated editor and writer to give up his own magazine and cross the Atlantic."

the nickname "Stockdale": Jim Windolf, "Off the Record," *The New York Observer,* December 21, 1992, which contains the Christmas tree anecdote.

"The issue is the integrity": "Let Bylines Be Bylines," *Newsweek,* January 25, 1993.

"She had written for *The New Yorker* before": Carmody, "Tina Brown's Progress at The New Yorker."

"one of the ugliest": Deirdre Carmody, "Tina Brown Accused of Misusing New Yorker," *The New York Times,* October 15, 1992, including Harry Evans comment.

"I find that charge extraordinarily sexist": ibid.

The New Yorker **trumpeted her success:** Kevin Goldman, *"New Yorker's* Makeover Attracts a Younger and Richer Audience," *The Wall Street Journal,* July 22, 1993.

"Tina is certainly the head of the class": Michael Janofsky, "Advertising," *The New York Times,* July 22, 1993.

"Regardless of whether": Elizabeth Kolbert, "Soul of the Buzz Machine: Tina Brown Moves The New Yorker, at a Price," *The New York Times Magazine,* December 5, 1993.

"The momentum of a weekly": interview with Tina Brown, 1993.

"The magazine has added": Carmody, "Tina Brown's Progress at *The New Yorker."*

"figure out what makes a great cover": Patrick M. Reilly, "Vanity Fair Looks for Comeback in Its New Life After Tina Brown," *The Wall Street Journal,* April 26, 1993.

Dominick Dunne: Degen Pener, "Reining in Tina Brown," *The New York Times,* July 19, 1992.

South's unique talents: Hamilton South's elevation on the masthead was discussed by current and former *Vanity Fair* staffers; his previous employment at Barney's was confirmed by Mallory Andrews of Barney's. South initially agreed to be interviewed for this book but then declined.

"Gentlemanly discretion": *The New York Post,* June 15, 1993.

"In the 80's, it was the great thing": Deirdre Carmody, *"Vanity Fair* is Doing Nicely, but Out of the Spotlight," *The New York Times,* January 25, 1993.

"controversial Anglophile": Liz Smith, *Newsday,* October 16, 1992.

"She's the best argument": "I Spy Feud Brewing," *Newsday,* November 27, 1989.

"It remains to be seen": Liz Smith, *Newsday,* July 2, 1992.

"sizzling party": Liz Smith, *Newsday,* May 5, 1993.

"He's a jerk": *Newsday,* December 3, 1987.

"We buried the hatchet": *The New York Observer,* May 13, 1993.

"While he skewered me": ibid.

"I think that most of the editors": interview with Tina Brown, 1993.

"Following Tina is a very tough job": Regina Joseph, "Reinventing Vanity Fair," *Inside Media,* May 12, 1993.

"The magazine does seem to have lost": Carmody, "Vanity Fair Is Doing Nicely."

"If they had [called back and] said": *New York Post,* February 9, 1993.

"I think there was a question about Graydon": Geraldine Fabrikant, "Abrupt Departure at *Vanity Fair," The New York Times,* May 11, 1993.

"It was in the cards": Reilly, "Vanity Fair Looks for a Comeback."

"You don't make an editorial change": *The Wall Street Journal,* April 26, 1993.

"I think I am more sensitive": Deirdre Carmody, "Another Pacific Passage for a Condé Nast Soldier," *The New York Times,* January 17, 1994.

"He started a rumor all over New York": interview with Richard Shortway, 1993.

"What can you do?": Regina Joseph, "Mr. Galotti Is Here to See You," *Inside Media,* May 12, 1993. After leaving Condé Nast, Galotti became publishing director of *Esquire;* see Mary Huhn, "Hearst Brings Back Galotti," *Mediaweek,* January 31, 1994.

"This is a very smooth running company": Meg Cox, "Condé Nast Names Steven T. Florio to Be Its President," *The Wall Street Journal,* January 13, 1994; see also Deirdre Carmody, "Condé Nast Switching President and Publishers," *The New York Times,* January 13, 1994, and Deirdre Carmody, "Another Pacific Passage for a Condé Nast Soldier," *The New York Times,* January 17, 1994.

"There are editors": Kolbert, "Soul of The Buzz Machine."

"They have a fantastic relationship": interview with Tina Brown, 1993.

"James invented the magazine": Candace Bushnell, "Wallflowerish Prince of Condé Nast Is Beavis and Butt-Head's Own Mencken," *The New York Observer,* September 20, 1993.

never really looking at the magazine: Clare McHugh, "A Doppelganger for Tina & Anna?" *The New York Observer,* December 12, 1992. In that same interview, Doppelt called Wintour her role model. Nevertheless, Newhouse removed Doppelt and installed a new editor at *Mademoiselle* in less than a year.

"a big believer": Jim Windolf, "Off the Record," *The New York Observer,* October 11, 1993.

"Everybody wants a catfight": Craig Bromberg, "The Glitzy Brits of Condé Nast," *Washington Journalism Review,* November 1989.

"Truman's personality": Mary Huhn, "Truman, a Dark Horse, Wins in Upset," *Mediaweek,* January 31, 1994.

"If he starts telling me": Deirdre Carmody, "Condé Nast's Visionary to Bow Out," *The New York Times,* January 26, 1994.

"I wouldn't say that the editors will report to James": Meg Cox, "James Truman Gets Star Status at Condé Nast," *The Wall Street Journal,* January 26, 1994.

"We sat there saying": Peter Stevenson, "S. I. Newhouse's Fabulous Florio Boys Leave Jones Beach for Corner Offices," *The New York Observer,* February 14, 1994.

"People at the company are scared to death": Fabrikant, "Abrupt Departure at *Vanity Fair.*"

The indignity was compounded: Carter's scare was retold by columnist Jim Windolf in *The New York Observer;* the erroneous front-page picture of Carter appeared in "Vanity Fair Honcho Gets the Boot," *New York Post,* May 11, 1993.

CHAPTER 13: POWERHOUSE

"The Newhouse brothers' wealth": Carol J. Loomis, "The Biggest Private Fortune," *Fortune,* August 17, 1987.

"resemble the unexpected arrival": Bernard Weinraub, "David Geffen—Still Hungry," *The New York Times Magazine,* May 2, 1993.

"a fair amount of paranoia at Condé Nast": Peter M. Stevenson, "New York's New Power Brokers: Power Struggle—Keith Rupert Murdoch vs. Samuel I. Newhouse Jr.," *Manhattan inc.,* September 1989.

"Well, I'm not afraid of him": interview with Tina Brown, 1993.

"Why me?": Eric Utne, "Tina's *New Yorker,*" *Columbia Journalism Review,* March/April 1993. See also Jim Windolf, "Off the Record," *The New York Observer,* December 10, 1992.

the company pulled its ads: Richard H. Meeker, *Newspaperman: S. I. Newhouse and the Business of News* (New York: Ticknor & Fields, 1983), which also includes the anecdote about the young Syracuse graduate student. Meeker's own experiences after the publication of his book are from an interview with him, 1992.

"What we've learned": Bonnie Angelo, "Si and Tina's Newest Act," *Time,* July 13, 1992.

the Royalton: Rich Cohen, "Royalton Flush," *The New York Observer,* January 11, 1993, and Georgia Dullea, "The, Uh, Royalton Round Table," *The New York Times,* December 27, 1992, including comments by McNally and Gandee.

"the Talking Fashion section": William Norwich, *New York Post,* October 2, 1992; comments on Liberman and Doppelt from other Norwich columns.

"Just because I am the so-called editor-at-large": William Norwich, *New York Post,* March 26, 1992.

John Russell: Marie Winn, "Liberman: Staying in Vogue," *The New York Times Magazine,* May 13, 1979. Russell declined to be interviewed.

"There's always something happening": David Streitfeld, "Life at Random," *New York,* August 5, 1991.

"No doubt the wise men": Elisabeth Sifton, "Book Editor Sounds a Cri de Coeur: Let's Dump the *Times* Best-Seller List," *The New York Observer,* February 22, 1993.

But the specter of a *Times* media reporter: Cohen's alleged conflicts were first reported in Doug Ireland, "Prophets of Rage," *The Village Voice,* March 27, 1990, where the response from Levyveld is mentioned. Cohen's description of Random House as the "Cadillac of American publishing" appeared in Roger Cohen, "Changing Spirit at Random House," *The New York Times,* March 19, 1990. In a February 1994 letter to this author, Cohen replied that his as-told-to account of Agnelli's life had been completed before he arrived at the *Times* in January 1990. Cohen said that Agnelli decided to stick the manuscript "in a safe in Turin rather than publish it" and later returned the advance to Random House. "As a dead issue, I doubt that it affected me one way or another," said Cohn about his *Times* coverage, "although, as your inquiries demonstrate, once things find their way into print, they take on a virtually irrepressible Nexus-fed life of their own. I would merely add that, in covering publishing in New York, I found that almost everything I wrote incurred the wrath of somebody. It's a small-town beat, awash in rumors and beset with big-city sensibilities." For the past two decades, the newspaper industry's code of ethics has been fairly uniform on reporters who have financial ties to the subject they are covering. The Associated Press Managing Editors guidelines approved in 1975, for instance, advises that: "Financial investments by staff members or other outside business interests that could conflict with the newspaper's ability to report the news or that would create the impression of a conflict should be avoided." Similar guidelines have been set forth since the 1970s by the Society of Professional Journalists, Sigma Delta Chi, and by the American Society of Newspaper Editors. In a letter, Joseph Lelyveld was asked to comment on his published quote given to Ireland concerning Cohen's book contract with Random House at that time and for any possible comments he might have about the *Times*'s coverage of the Newhouse media empire. In his response letter, Lelyveld wrote: "I can't remember talking to Doug Ireland about Roger Cohen (or, for that matter, being misquoted by him). And I can't remember anything about the context. Feel free to cite the *Voice* on what I said but I think it's a little late in the day for me to try and remember what it was all about. My mind is purged of such stuff a lot faster than the directory in my computer, I'm afraid."

its own "Styles" section: Jeannette Walls, "Styles Victims," *New York,* November 16, 1992.

the traditional wall: A discussion of the tensions between advertising and editorial is contained in Ken Auletta's profile of Arthur Sulzberger Jr., which appeared in *The New Yorker,* June 28, 1993.

"[Jason] Epstein is regarded . . . as the Edward R. Murrow": Jacob Weisberg, "Houses of Ill Repute," *The New Republic,* June 17, 1991. Weisberg's comments about his experiences after the article appeared are from an interview with him, 1992.

some of the most notable books: See Susan Faludi, *Backlash: The Undeclared War Against American Women* (New York: Crown, 1991) and Howard Kurtz, *Media Circus: The Trouble with America's Newspapers* (New York: Times Books, 1993).

"We don't expect to tamper": "The Ultimate Merger?", *Authors Guild Bulletin,* Winter 1989.

By the mid-1990s: Estimates of total annual revenues and overall worth varied widely because of the privately held nature of the Newhouse business and because of the fluctuating nature of certain methods, such as per subscriber methods of calculating a media property's worth; these figures were based on recently published estimates, such as *Hoover's Handbook of American Business 1993,* and on interviews with several media analysts.

"peripheral": Jefferson Grigsby, "Newhouse, After Newhouse," *Forbes,* October 29, 1979.

"It is almost impossible to wreck": Loomis, "The Biggest Private Fortune."

"Newhouse!": Michael Hoyt and Mary Ellen Schoonmaker, "Onward—and upward?—with the Newhouse boys," *The Columbia Journalism Review,* July/August 1985.

"the bloated, sluggish, myopic giant": from *More* magazine, as quoted in ibid.

"It's a good paper": Ron Ridenhour, "Between the Lines at The Times-Picayune," *New Orleans Magazine,* November 1990.

"There is no community leadership": ibid.

David Duke: Jeanne W. Amend, "The Picayune Catches Up with David Duke," *Columbia Journalism Review,* January/February 1992, and Jeanne Weill, "Coverage of David Duke," *St. Louis Journalism Review,* May 1991; also interviews with Amend, Jason Berry, Ron Ridenhour, Beth Rickey, and A. B. Botnick of the Anti-Defamation League in New Orleans, 1992.

"A newspaper should be a local institution": "Newhouse Buys Alabama Papers," *The New York Times,* December 2, 1955.

FEAR AND HATRED GRIP BIRMINGHAM: discussed in Harrison Salisbury, *Without Fear or Favor: An Uncompromising Look at the New York Times* (New York: Times Books, 1980) and in Meeker, *Newspaperman.*

Dennis Washburn: from "Birmingham News Fires Candid Auto Editor," *Washington Journalism Review,* November 1991; also interview with Washburn, 1992; also cited in Kurtz, *Media Circus.*

Senator Wayne Morse: Robert Shaplen, "The Newhouse Phenomenon," *The Saturday Review,* October 1960.

"You don't get the sense of the sweat": Hoyt and Schoonmaker, "Onward—and upward?—with the Newhouse boys."

Rather than offend its real estate advertisers: G. Pascal Zachary, "All The News? Many Journalists See a Growing Reluctance to Criticize Advertisers," *The Wall Street Journal,* February 6, 1992.

"The newsroom is always willing to listen": ibid.

"self-editing in the newsroom": ibid.

"I think it's inevitable": William Glaberson, "Newspaper Editors to Name a Black as President," *The New York Times,* March 29, 1993. The Packwood coverage is also cited in Kurtz, *Media Circus,* and in M. L. Stein, "Scooped," *Editor & Publisher,* December 19, 1992.

"I hate to speak ill of the dead": Jon Nordheimer, "Behind the Scenes, a Powerful Editor Lives, Breathes and Shapes His State," *The New York Times,* August 18, 1992.

Mayor Hugh Addonizio: Hoyt and Schoonmaker, "Onward—and upward?—with the Newhouse boys."

"They are very bland": interview with Richard Scudder, 1992.

"The *Star-Ledger*'s influence impossible to overestimate": Robert Sam Anson, "All The News That Money Can Buy," *New Jersey Monthly,* September 1977, which discussed ethical conflicts of the newspaper.

"The way he pushed": Nordheimer, "Behind the Scenes, a Powerful Editor Lives, Breathes and Shapes His State."

"My brother and I": Hoyt and Schoonmaker, "Onward—and upward?—with the Newhouse boys."

This paradox was made apparent: "Darts and Laurels," *Columbia Journalism Review,* March/April 1993.

"It's a system": Hoyt and Schoonmaker, "Onward—and upward?—with the Newhouse boys."

When the glossy magazine *HG* died: Craig Wilson, "Already Homesick for Doomed 'HG'," *USA Today,* May 17, 1993.

"considerable redundancy": Sheryl A. Barnett, "Lamenting the Loss of *HG,*" *Newsday,* April 22, 1993, and Deirdre Carmody, "Food and Design Magazines Are Bought by Condé Nast," *The New York Times,* March 3, 1993.

"He didn't want to put": Charlotte Hays, *New York Daily News,* May 5, 1993.

filed lawsuits that alleged: Dan Cook and Stan Crock, "Did Si Newhouse Conspire to Kill The Cleveland Press?", *Business Week,* July 1, 1985.

"The idea of a monopoly": Carolyn Tozier, "How Justice Department Viewed the St. Louis Joint Operating Agreement," *Journalism Quarterly,* Autumn 1986; "Independents Cry Foul," *Editor & Publisher,* July 18, 1987; and Stephen R. Barnett, "Anything Goes," *American Journalism Review,* October 1993; also interview with Barnett, 1992.

"When you do what the Justice Department": Staci D. Kramer, "Independents Cry Foul," *Editor & Publisher,* July 18, 1987.

"He tries to keep the companies very separate": Scott Donaton, "Condé Nast Mulls ad flexibility," *Advertising Age,* July 15, 1991.

"The news media": Ben H. Bagdikian, *The Media Monopoly,* (Beacon Press, 1983).

"is increasingly controlled": Leo Bogart, "The American Media System and Its Commercial Culture," Gannett Foundation Media Center, March 1991.

Newspapers with monopoly-like control: Ben H. Bagdikian, "Journalism of Joy," *Mother Jones,* May/June 1992.

"I'm not allowed to talk": telephone conversation with Joni Evans, 1993.

"People sign it because they need the money": interview with Martin Garbus, 1993.

Schiffrin was legally bound: interviews with André Schiffrin, 1990 and 1992.

"The great majority of big media owners": Bagdikian, "Journalism of Joy."

"I'd rather it not be in the same type": Ann Marie Kerwin, "Behind the Waltzing," *Editor & Publisher,* June 13, 1992, which included the survey by the Society of American Business Editors and Writers.

25 percent: Newspaper revenues and estimated pretax profits were found in published estimates, such as *Hoover's Handbook of American Business 1993,* and through interviews with several media analysts.

"Where once newspapers were at the very heart": Kurtz, *Media Circus.*

"I think we are accountable": Donald Newhouse comments to the author in 1993 in declining to be interviewed for this book.

"He's a very modest man": interview with Tina Brown, 1993.

EPILOGUE: THE BIG PICTURE

"the ties that matter": *A Memo for the Children from S. I. Newhouse,* as related to and written by David Jacobs (New York: privately published, 1980; available at the Library of Congress).

"I don't think they've ever had an argument": Jefferson Grigsby, "Newhouse, After Newhouse," *Forbes,* October 29, 1979.

"that we not fall into the Hearstian trap": testimony of Donald E. Newhouse in *Estate of Samuel I. Newhouse, deceased, Samuel I. Newhouse Jr. and Donald E. Newhouse* vs. *The Commissioner of Internal Revenue,* U.S. Tax Court, Washington, D.C.

"He doesn't need money": J. A. Trachtenberg, "The Newhouses: Publishing's private empire," *W,* December 19–26, 1980.

"We talked about it endlessly": ibid.

She married Verne Hendrick: details of Pamela's marriage are in court records filed in "Application of Jacob Henry Newhouse Hendrick," New York State Supreme Court, New York City, index: 11567–81, which includes the prenuptial agreement between the couple.

"Sam always went along": Trachtenberg, "The Newhouses."

He attended but never graduated from Syracuse: Samuel I. Newhouse III attended Syracuse between 1973 and 1974 but never returned, according to the registrar's office.

"We need the money": Daniel Machalara, "Family Newspapers: Newhouse Chain Stays with Founder's Ways and with His Heirs," *The Wall Street Journal,* February 12, 1982.

Sam's outside interests: Carol J. Loomis, "The Biggest Private Fortune," *Fortune,* August 17, 1987.

"felt very strongly": "No sale? Newhouse sued for $2.9M," *New York Daily News,* September 22, 1987.

His arm was nearly severed: Wynn's accident was mentioned in published accounts and in several interviews, including those with Ray Josephs and William Raidy, 1992 and 1993.

"will do almost anything": Loomis, "The Biggest Private Fortune," *Fortune,* August 17, 1987.

Si kept his distance: Si's relationship with Wynn was mentioned in William A. Henry III, "A Search for Glitz," June 4, 1990, which included an interview with Wynn.

"It's a bone of contention": "The Newhouses."

"I don't think my father is that cold": Henry "A Search for Glitz."

"I have yet to meet": interview with Wynn Newhouse, 1991.

Dr. Irv Dardik: Newhouse read Tony Schwartz, "Making Waves," *New York,* March 18, 1991. Interviews with two authoritative sources provided the account of Si's effort to help his son Wynn. Although the author conducted a 1991 telephone interview with him for a *Newsday* article, Wynn Newhouse said he didn't want to be interviewed when recontacted for this project in 1992.

"One of the Circle paintings": interview with Miki Denhof, 1993; Denhof's recollection of Si's purchase of Liberman paintings is mentioned in Dodie Kazanjian and Calvin Tomkins, *Alex: The Life of Alexander Liberman* (New York: Alfred A. Knopf, 1993).

"This is the person": This exchange was recounted by Miki Denhof, 1993.

"I'd go as far as to say": interview with Fred Hughes, 1993.

Larry Gagosian: Dana Wechsler Linden, "Must I Be A Saint?" *Forbes,* October 22, 1990.

"It's no secret": Grace Glueck, "One Art Dealer Who's Still a High Roller," *The New York Times,* June 24, 1991. As the *Times* and other published accounts indicate, there is a persistent rumor of a Newhouse bankroll behind Gagosian. "I have no backers," the art dealer replied unequivocally.

"It's not true that we're partners": Dodie Kazanjian, "Going Places," *Vogue,* November 1989.

"Larry, I don't know": *The Andy Warhol Diaries,* ed. Pat Hackett (New York: Warner Books, New York, 1989). Gagosian declined to comment for this book.

"He likes that kind of person": interview with Fred Hughes, 1993.

False Starts: Rita Reif, "Jasper Johns Painting Is Sold for $17 Million," *The New York Times,* November 11, 1988; see also Andrew Decker, "Getting the Picture," *New York,* November 9, 1992, and Alexandra Peers, "Art Prices Begin Emerging from 2-Year Slump, but Remain Far Below the Heights of '80s Boom," *The Wall Street Journal,* November 20, 1992.

"As the editorial director of Condé Nast": Roberta Smith, "Art in Review: Alexander Liberman: The Circle Paintings," *The New York Times,* September 24, 1993.

"A towering genius": interview with Peter Diamandis, 1993.

"Often I have not bought something": Kazanjian and Tomkins, *Alex: The Life of Alexander Liberman.*

That same year: "Diana Vreeland on Stage," *The New York Times,* April 27, 1993; see also "The Cult of Diana," *Vanity Fair,* December 1992.

Dick Shortway: for background on Shortway, see *The New York Times,* September 17, 1959; Isadore Barmash, "Co-Op Ads: Some Pros and Cons," *The New York Times,* August 8, 1979; further information was obtained in interviews with former colleagues, including Peter Diamandis.

"I made a big mistake": interview with Richard A. Shortway, 1993.

"Well, uh, what else have you accomplished": Newhouse exchange with Shortway is based on an interview with Shortway, 1993.

"Over the years": Mary Huhn, "The House That Si Re-Built," *Adweek,* March 1, 1993.

"Ground zero of the new British invasion": "The New British Invasion," *Spy,* February 1993.

Jonathan Newhouse: Geraldine Fabrikant, "New Head for Condé Nast International," *The New York Times,* March 14, 1989; see also Frank DeCaro, "Style, Substance and Fame," *Newsday,* October 10, 1988.

Despite a freak accident: "Norman N. Newhouse dead at 82; helped build communications empire," *Newark Star-Ledger,* November 7, 1988.

Jonathan introduced a formal media kit: Patrick Reilly, "Details-Oriented: Newhouse clout helps hip book," *Advertising Age,* March 14, 1988.

"Jonathan is going to take over the company": interview with Tina Brown, 1993.

He has impressed many: Linda Moss, "Steve Newhouse: The Family's Maverick," *Crain's New York Business,* November 20, 1989; also based on impressions of various reporters and one New Jersey publisher who asked to remain unidentified. Steven's career background was cited in *The New York Times,* September 27, 1992.

"I felt I was being shown off as a curiosity": Moss, "Steve Newhouse."

"He didn't come across as an heir": ibid.

Steven will inherit a major portion: based on Loomis, "The Biggest Private Fortune," as well as interviews with Robert Shilliday, John Morton, and others familiar with the Newhouse wills and company stock structure. After the tax court opinion on February 28, 1990, the IRS issued a press release announcing an agreement in which the "entire value of Advance [Publications]" would be taxed fully at some point in the future.

"It's not what I do": Newhouse interview with John Motavalli, cited in *The New York Observer,* April 1993.

carrying an unlighted cigarette: interview with Peter Diamandis, 1993, and confirmed by others. See also Charlotte Hays, *New York Daily News,* July 19, 1993. Si was observed in Bellport by several sources; details about his boat from *New York Post,* June 11, 1993.

Wired: See "Conde Nast Buys Interest in Multimedia Magazine," *The Wall Street Journal,* January 24, 1994.

Paramount Communications: based on numerous news accounts of QVC's bid, with Advance's $500 million investment, to buy Paramount, these articles include Meg Cox, "Newhouse Family Starts to Peer into Electronic Future," *The Wall Street Journal,* September 17, 1993, and Geraldine Fabrikant, "QVC's Hostile Bid for Paramount Wins Board Vote," *The New York Times,* December 23, 1993.

"Over the course of a generation": Tom Goldstein, "Playing Monopoly with the Media," *The New York Times,* December 10, 1993.

"You know you once said": interview with Tina Brown, 1993.

"We're interested in building a company": Trachtenberg, "The Newhouses."

"We will adapt": Scott Donaton, "Future That Feels Right for Us, Why Newhouse Is ushering in new leadership," *Advertising Age,* January 31, 1994.

Bibliography

BOOKS

Bagdikian, Ben H. *The Media Monopoly*. Boston: Beacon Press, 1983.

Barrett, Wayne. *Trump: The Deals and the Downfall*. New York: HarperCollins, 1992.

Brown, Tina. *Life's a Party*. North Pomfret, Vermont: David & Charles Inc., 1984.

Cerf, Bennett. *At Random: The Reminiscences of Bennett Cerf*. New York: Random House, 1977.

Chafe, William H. *Never Stop Running: Allard Lowenstein and the Struggle to Save American Liberalism*. New York: Basic Books, 1993.

Colacello, Bob. *Holy Terror: Andy Warhold Close-Up*. New York: HarperCollins, 1990.

Crowe, Kenneth C. *Collision: How the Rank and File Took Back the Teamsters*. New York: Scribners, 1993.

Dunne, Dominick. *The Mansions of Limbo*. New York: Crown, 1991.

Ephron, Nora. *Scribble, Scribble: Notes on the Media*. New York: Alfred A. Knopf, 1978.

Faludi, Susan. *Backlash: The Undeclared War Against American Women*. New York: Crown, 1991.

Friendly, Fred. W. *The Good Guys, the Bad Guys and the First Amendment: Free Speech vs. Fairness in Broadcasting*. New York: Random House, 1975.

Gentry, Curt. *J. Edgar Hoover: The Man and the Secrets*. New York: W. W. Norton & Co., 1991.

Gill. Brendan. *Here At The New Yorker*. New York: Random House, 1975.

Hackett, Pat, ed. *The Andy Warhol Diaries*. New York: Warner Books, 1989.

Harrison, Martin. *Appearances: Fashion Photography Since 1945*. New York: Rizzoli, 1991.

Kael, Pauline. *Raising Kane*. New York: Bantam Books, 1971.

Kahn, E. J., Jr. *Year of Change: More About The New Yorker & Me*. New York: Viking Penguin, 1988.

Kazanjian, Dodie, and Calvin Tomkins. *Alex: The Life of Alexander Liberman*. New York: Alfred A. Knopf, 1993.

Kurtz, Howard. *Media Circus: The Trouble with America's Newspapers*. New York: Times Books, 1993.

Lent, John. *Newhouse, Newspapers, Nuisances*. Exposition Press, 1967.

Liberman, Alexander. *The Artist in His Studio*. New York: Viking Press, 1960; reissued by Random House, 1988.

Liebling, A. J. *The Press*. New York: Pantheon Books, 1981.

Lippmann, Walter. *Public Opinion*. New York: Macmillan, 1922; reissued by Free Press, 1965.

Mahon, Gigi. *The Last Days of The New Yorker*. New York: McGraw-Hill, 1988.

Manso, Peter. *Mailer: His Life and Times*. New York: Simon & Schuster, 1985.

Mayer, Martin. *Making News*. New York: Doubleday, 1987.

Meeker, Richard H. *Newspaperman: S. I. Newhouse and the Business of News*. New York: Ticknor & Fields, 1983.

Neff, James. *Mobbed Up*. New York: Atlantic Monthly Press, 1989.

Newfield, Jack, and Wayne Barrett. *City for Sale: Ed Koch and The Betrayal of New York.* New York: Harper & Row, 1988.
Newhouse, S. I. *A Memo for the Children from S. I. Newhouse* (as told to David Jacobs), privately published, 1980.
Oppenheimer, Jerry. *Barbara Walters: An Unauthorized Biography.* New York: St. Martin's Press, 1990.
Oshinsky, David M. *A Conspiracy So Immense: The World of Joe McCarthy.* New York: Free Press, 1983.
Penn, Irving, with an introduction by Alexander Liberman. *Passage: A Work Record.* New York: Callaway/Alfred A. Knopf, 1991.
Reeves, Thomas C. *The Life and Times of Joe McCarthy—A Biography.* New York: Stein and Day, 1982.
Rose, Barbara. *Alexander Liberman.* New York: Abbeville Press, 1981.
Rovere, Richard H. *Senator Joe McCarthy.* New York: Harcourt, Brace and Co., 1959.
Salisbury, Harrison. *Without Fear or Favor: An Uncompromising Look at the New York Times.* New York: Times Books, 1980.
Schlesinger, Arthur M., Jr. *Robert Kennedy and His Times.* New York: Random House, 1978.
Seebohm, Caroline. *The Man Who Was Vogue: The Life and Times of Condé Nast.* New York: Viking Press, 1982.
Straight, Michael. *Twigs for an Eagle's Nest.* Devon Press, 1979.
Thurber, James. *The Years with Ross.* Little, Brown & Co., 1959.
Trump, Donald, and Tony Schwartz. *The Art of the Deal.* New York: Random House, 1988.
Turner, William W. *Hoover's FBI.* New York: Dell, 1971.
von Hoffman, Nicholas. *Citizen Cohn: The Life and Times of Roy Cohn.* New York: Doubleday, 1988.
Vreeland, Diana. *D.V.* New York: Alfred A. Knopf, 1984.
Whiteside, Thomas. *The Blockbuster Complex: Conglomerates, Show Business and Book Publishing.* Wesleyan University Press, 1981.
Wolf, Naomi. *The Beauty Myth: How Images of Beauty Are Used Against Women.* New York: William Morrow, 1991.
Zion, Sidney. *The Autobiography of Roy Cohn.* New York: Lyle Stuart, 1988.

PERIODICALS, GOVERNMENT REPORTS,
AND OTHER DOCUMENTS

Alter, Jonathan. "The Random House Shuffle." *Newsweek,* November 13, 1989.
———. "The Squawk of the Town." *Newsweek,* January 26, 1987.
———. "Trying to Buy a Legend." *Newsweek,* February 25, 1985.
Amend, Jeanne W. "The Picayune Catches Up with David Duke." *Columbia Journalism Review,* January/February 1992.
Angelo, Bonnie. "Si and Tina's Newest Act." *Time,* July 13, 1992.
Anson, Robert Sam. "All The News That Money Can Buy." *New Jersey Monthly,* September 1977.
Auletta, Ken. "Don't Mess With Roy Cohn." *Esquire,* December 5, 1978.
Bagdikian, Ben H. "Journalism of Joy." *Mother Jones,* May/June 1992.
Barmash, Isadore. "Co-Op Ads: Some Pros and Cons." *The New York Times,* August 8, 1979.
Barnett, Sheryl A. "Lamenting the Loss of HG." *Newsday,* April 22, 1993.
Barnett, Stephen R. "Anything Goes." *American Journalism Review,* October 1993.
Bartimole, Roldo. "Plain Dealer Too Comfortable." *Point of View,* July 17, 1982 (numerous issues of *Point of View* were used as references).
Bender, Marylin. "The New Yorker: Mannerly Maverick at 50." *The New York Times,* February 16, 1975.
Berger, Warren. "The New Yorker: The Image Problem Persists." *Publishing News,* February 1990.
Bernier, Rosamond. "In the Atelier." *HG,* October 1988.
Bernstein, Carl. "The Idiot Culture." *The New Republic,* June 8, 1992.
Blum, David. "Spying on Spy." *New York,* April 17, 1989.
Bogart, Leo. "The American Media System and Its Commercial Culture." Gannett Foundation Media Center, March 1991.

Bromberg, Craig. "The Glitzy Brits of Condé Nast." *Washington Journalism Review,* November 1989.

Brown, Tina. "Editor's Letter: Signing Off." *Vanity Fair,* September 1992.

Buck, Joan Juliet. "The Emigré Muse." *Vanity Fair,* March 1992.

Bushnell, Candace. "Wallflowerish Prince of Condé Nast Is Beavis and Butt-Head's Own Mencken." *The New York Observer,* September 20, 1993.

Campbell, Lawrence. "The Great-Circle Route." *Art News,* April 1970.

Carmody, Deirdre. "Another Pacific Passage for a Condé Nast Soldier." *The New York Times,* January 17, 1994.

————. "At Condé Nast, Newhouse Maintains Loose Reins with a Tight Grip." *The New York Times,* July 27, 1992.

————. "Condé Nast's Gamble: Creating Yet Another Image for Self." *The New York Times,* April 23, 1990.

————. "Condé Nast Switching President and Publishers." *The New York Times,* January 13, 1994.

————. "Condé Nast's Visionary to Bow Out." *The New York Times,* January 26, 1994.

————. "Food and Design Magazines Are Bought by Condé Nast." *The New York Times,* March 3, 1993.

————. "Her First Issue at the Ready, Tina Brown Talks About the New Yorker." *The New York Times,* September 24, 1992.

————. "Tina Brown Accused of Misusing New Yorker." *The New York Times,* October 15, 1992.

————. "Tina Brown's Progress at The New Yorker." *The New York Times,* April 12, 1993.

————. "Tina Brown to Take Over at The New Yorker." *The New York Times,* July 1, 1992.

————. "Vanity Fair Is Doing Nicely, but Out of the Spotlight." *The New York Times,* January 25, 1993.

Casey, Mike. "PD-Press Investigators Clashed." *Crain's Cleveland Business,* April 6, 1987.

Cockburn, Alexander. "Nausea." *The Nation,* September 7, 1985.

Cohen, Rich. "Royalton Flush." *The New York Observer,* January 11, 1993.

Cohen, Roger. "Changing Spirit at Random House." *The New York Times,* March 19, 1990.

————. "Random House Star, Sonny Mehta, Talks Profits as Well as Art." *The New York Times,* November 13, 1990.

————. "Top Random House Author Assails Ouster at Pantheon." *The New York Times,* March 9, 1990.

Cohn, Roy. "Could He Walk on Water?" *Esquire,* November 1972.

————. "You Can Beat the IRS." *Parade,* April 3, 1983.

Colacello, Bob. "Power Party." *Vanity Fair,* April 1985.

Colford, Paul D. "Does Tina Brown Plan Big Changes? Yes and No." *Newsday,* July 7, 1992.

————. " 'Psycho' to Get Release." *Newsday,* November 17, 1990.

————. "Random House Closes Its Boutique." *Newsday,* February 11, 1993.

Collins, Thomas. "An Urbane Half Century." *Newsday,* February 21, 1975.

Conant, Jennet. "The Fall and Rise of a Fashion Impresario: The New York Newsday Interview with Grace Mirabella." *Newsday,* November 30, 1988.

————. "Keeping Up with the Joneses." *Newsweek,* Sept. 7, 1987.

————. "Playing Doctor at Condé Nast." *Manhattan, inc.,* November 1988.

————. "The Very Furry Feet of Sonny Mehta." *Esquire,* April 1993.

Cooney, John E. "Top Man Out: Griffith's Resignation at RCA Follows Year of Turmoil, Criticism." *The Wall Street Journal,* January 26, 1981.

Cox, Meg. "Condé Nast Names Steven T. Florio to Be Its President." *The Wall Street Journal,* January 13, 1994.

————. "Four Editors Quit at Random House Over Aide's Firing." *The Wall Street Journal,* March 1, 1990.

————. "James Truman Gets Star Status at Condé Nast." *The Wall Street Journal,* January 26, 1994.

Darling, Lynn. "The Vreeland Legend." *Newsday,* August 24, 1989.

Darnton, Nina. "Vogue, Self, Allure—Alex." *Newsweek,* April 8, 1991.

DeCaro, Frank. "The Dreams That Stuffs Are Made Of." *Newsday,* August 25, 1991.

————. "Style, Substance and Fame." *Newsday,* October 10, 1988.

Decker, Andrew. "Getting the Picture." *New York,* November 9, 1992.

DeParle, Jason. "Spy Anxiety." *The Washington Monthly,* February 1989.

Deyrup, Curtis. "Jonathan Schell." *Publishers Weekly,* April 21, 1989.

Diamond, Edwin. "After Shawn." *New York,* January 8, 1987.

———. "The Fate of the Earth." *New York,* January 26, 1987.

———. "The Talk of The New Yorker." *New York,* March 25, 1985.

———. "The Two Faces of Eustace Tilley." *New York,* November 17, 1986.

Doling, Hilary. "New York as Tina Sees It." *Newsday,* November 27, 1985.

Doll, Bill. "Fancy Dealing in Cleveland." *Columbia Journalism Review,* May/June 1984.

Donaton, Scott. "Advertorials are like a drug." *Advertising Age,* March 9, 1992.

———. "Condé Nast Mulls ad flexibility." *Advertising Age,* July 15, 1991.

———. "Future That Feels Right for Us: Why Newhouse Is Ushering in New Leadership." *Advertising Age,* January 31, 1994.

Dougherty, Philip H. "Campaign for Media Planners." *The New York Times,* May 6, 1985.

———. "Magazine Tries New Campaigns." *The New York Times,* September 25, 1985.

———. "Vanity Fair's Rebirth." *The New York Times,* February 14, 1983.

Dowd, Maureen. "A Writer for The New Yorker Says He Created Composites in Reports." *The New York Times,* June 19, 1984.

Drogin, Bob. "Roy M. Cohn Fights for His Life and Legal Career." *Los Angeles Times,* February 2, 1986.

Dullea, Georgia. "The, Uh, Royalton Round Table." *The New York Times,* December 27, 1992.

Edwards, Owen. "Whose Style Is It, Anyway?" *The New York Times,* September 6, 1992.

Elliott, Stuart J. "Brown Hopes Three Times the Charm for Vanity Fair." *Advertising Age,* February 20, 1984.

Emmrich, Stuart. "Our Spy Spies on Spy's Guy." *Mediaweek,* May 20, 1991.

Fabrikant, Geraldine. "Abrupt Departure at Vanity Fair." *The New York Times,* May 11, 1993.

———. "Cash vs. Cachet at The New Yorker." *The New York Times,* June 2, 1986.

———. "Evans at Random House: Big Spender, Big Sales." *The New York Times,* March 8, 1993.

———. "New Head for Condé Nast International." *The New York Times,* March 14, 1989.

———. "Newhouses Win Fight with IRS." *The New York Times,* March 20, 1990.

———. "Si Newhouse Tests His Magazine Magic." *The New York Times,* September 25, 1988.

———. "Vanity Fair's Slick Formula." *The New York Times,* August 26, 1985.

Fairlie, Henry. "The Vanity of Vanity Fair." *The New Republic,* March 21, 1983.

Fein, Esther B. "Random House Closing a Division." *The New York Times,* February 11, 1993.

Frankel, Alison. "How the Newhouses Crushed the IRS." *The American Lawyer,* May 1990.

Gallagher, Robert. "Book Review Spooks Plain Dealer." *Washington Journalism Review,* December 1989.

Gill, Brendan. "Still Here at The New Yorker." *The New York Times Book Review,* October 4, 1987.

Glaberson, William. "Newspaper Editors to Name a Black as President." *The New York Times,* March 29, 1993.

Glueck, Grace. "One Art Dealer Who's Still a High Roller." *The New York Times,* June 24, 1991.

Goldman, Kevin. "New Yorker's Makeover Attracts a Younger and Richer Audience." *The Wall Street Journal,* July 22, 1993.

Goldstein, Tom. "Playing Monopoly with the Media." *The New York Times,* December 10, 1993.

Goodman, Walter. "Paging Through a New New Yorker." *The New York Times,* September 29, 1992.

Greenwald, John. "Auditing the Grand Acquisitor." *Time,* October 24, 1983.

Griffith, Thomas. "Trouble in Paradise. Yes, Trouble." *Time,* January 12, 1981.

Grigsby, Jefferson. "Newhouse, After Newhouse." *Forbes,* October 29, 1979.

Gross, Michael. "Madonna's Magician." *New York,* October 12, 1992.

———. "Sex Sells." *The Saturday Review,* July/August 1985.

———. "Tina's Turn." *New York,* July 20, 1992.

———. "War of the Poses." *New York,* April 27, 1992.

Hagen, Charles. "That Elusive Quality Called Style." *The New York Times,* April 17, 1992.

Hammer, Joshua. "Shoot-Out on Publishers' Row." *Newsday Magazine,* January 11, 1987.

Haynes, Kevin. "Anna's Big Year." *Women's Wear Daily,* November 10, 1989.

Hayes, Charlotte. "We May Never Know." *New York Daily News,* June 30, 1993.

Hellman, Geoffrey T. "Last of the Species." *The New Yorker,* September 19 and 26, 1942.

———. "That Was New York—Crowninshield." *The New Yorker,* February 14, 1948.

Henry, William A. III. "A Search for Glitz." *Time,* June 4, 1990.

———. "Embroidering the Facts." *Time,* July 2, 1984.

Hershkovits, David. "Bruce Weber: He's Considered Fashion's Every Angle." *Newsday,* May 25, 1989.

Hertzberg, Hendrik. "Journals of Opinion." *The Gannett Center Journal,* Spring 1989.

Hoban, Phoebe. "A Random Killing at Turtle Bay." *New York,* March 1, 1993.

Hochswender, Woody. "Changes at Vogue: A Complex Tale of Rumors and Facts." *The New York Times,* July 25, 1988.

Hollie, Pamela G. "Newhouse to Acquire 17% of The New Yorker." *The New York Times,* November 14, 1984.

Hornblower, Margaret. "Si Newhouse, the Talk of The New Yorker." *The Washington Post,* May 7, 1985.

Howell, Georgina. "All Is Vanity Nothing Is Fair." *The London Times Sunday Magazine,* 1986.

Hoyt, Michael, and Mary Ellen Schoonmaker. "Onward—and upward?—with the Newhouse Boys." *The Columbia Journalism Review,* July/August 1985.

Hughes, Robert. "Liberman's Eye." *Vanity Fair,* September 1988.

———. "Sprezzatura in Steel." *Time,* April 26, 1971.

Huhn, Mary. "Hearst Brings Back Galotti." *Mediaweek,* January 31, 1994.

———. "The House That Si Re-Built." *Adweek,* March 1, 1993.

———. "Truman. A Dark Horse, Wins in Upset." *Mediaweek,* January 31, 1994.

Ireland, Doug. "The Fall of the House of Pantheon." *The Village Voice,* March 13, 1990.

———. "Prophets of Rage." *The Village Voice,* March 27, 1990.

Jacobs, David J. "Publisher S. I. Newhouse Dies." *Newark Star-Ledger,* August 30, 1979.

Jones, Alex S. "An Intensely Private Family Empire." *The New York Times,* March 9, 1985.

Joseph, Regina. "Mr. Galotti Is Here to See You." *Inside Media,* May 12, 1993.

———. "Reinventing Vanity Fair." *Inside Media,* May 12, 1993.

Kaiser, Charles. "The Art of the Dealer." *Art News,* July 1989.

———. "Here at the New Yorker with Gottlieb, Janet Malcolm and Elvis." *Manhattan inc.,* June 1990.

———. "The Making of a Magazine." *Newsweek,* January 3, 1983.

Kauffmann, Stanley. "Through a Glass Brightly." *The New Republic,* January 11, 1964.

Kaufman, Michael T. "Reading Between the Lines of The New Yorker." *The New York Times,* September 26, 1992.

Kazanjian, Dodie. "Going Places." *Vogue,* November 1989.

Kelly, James. "Changing the Guard at 60." *Time,* March 18, 1985.

Kerwin, Ann Marie. "Behind the Waltzing." *Editor & Publisher,* June 13, 1992.

Kessler, Ronald. "A Rough Dealer: Control of the Newsstands Gives Henry Garfinkle Power Over Publishers." *The Wall Street Journal,* July 3, 1969.

Kiernan, Fran. "Chapter 11: The Great Publishing Crash of 1989." *7 Days,* January 24, 1990.

Kinsley, Michael. "Dept. of Amplification: William Shawn and the Temple of Facts." *The New Republic,* July 16 and 23, 1984.

Kleinfeld, N. R. "Heads Have a History of Rolling at Newhouse." *The New York Times,* November 2, 1989.

———. "RCA Agrees to Sell Random House to Newhouse for $65–$70 Million." *The New York Times,* February 7, 1980.

———. "Rumors Outpace Changes Under New Yorker's Editor." *The New York Times,* December 7, 1988.

Koenig, Rhoda. "The Heart of the Mehta." *New York,* March 2, 1987.

Kolbert, Elizabeth. "Soul of the Buzz Machine: Tina Brown Moves The New Yorker, at a Price." *The New York Times Magazine,* December 5, 1993.

Kornbluth, Jesse. "The Art of Being Alex." *New York,* October 12, 1981.

Krebs, Albin. "Mitzi E. Newhouse, Who Donated $1 Million for Theaters, Dies at 87." *The New York Times,* June 30, 1989.

Kron, Joan. "Style Setter: Fashion's Resurgence Means Wealth, Power for Vogue Magazine." *The Wall Street Journal,* January 30, 1986.

Lambert, Bruce. "Peter Fleischmann, 71, Who Led The New Yorker into the 1980s." *The New York Times,* April 18, 1993.

Landro, Laura. "For Tina Brown, Progress at Vanity Fair." *The Wall Street Journal,* March 18, 1987.

Lazare, Daniel. "Vanity Fare." *The Columbia Journalism Review,* May/June 1989.

Leerhsen, Charles. "A New Editor for Vanity Fair." *Newsweek,* January 16, 1984.

Liberman, Alex. "An American Eye." *Vogue,* October 1991.

——. "Beauty in Our Time." *Vogue,* May 1961, along with photographic essay by Irving Penn.

Linden, Dana Wechsler. "Must I Be a Saint?" *Forbes,* October 22, 1990.

Lipman, Joanne. "Big 'Outsert' Really Puts Revlon in Vogue." *The Wall Street Journal,* September 17, 1992.

Loomis, Carol J. "The Biggest Private Fortune." *Fortune,* August 17, 1987.

Lyall, Sarah. "More Lessons to Learn Before Oprah Tells All." *The New York Times,* June 16, 1993.

Machalara, Daniel. "Family Newspapers: Newhouse Chain Stays with Founder's Ways and with His Heirs." *The Wall Street Journal,* February 12, 1982.

Mahar, Maggie. "All in the Family: How the Newhouses Run Their Vast Media Empire." *Barron's,* November 27, 1989.

Mahon, Gigi. "S. I. Newhouse and Condé Nast: Taking Off the White Gloves." *The New York Times Magazine,* September 10, 1989.

Maier, Thomas. "The Ins and Outs at Random House." *Newsday Magazine,* February 24, 1991.

Mathews, Tom. "High Gloss News." *Newsweek,* May 1, 1989.

McDonald, Erroll. "At Pantheon Books, A Welfare Mentality." *The New York Times,* March 20, 1990.

McDowell, Edwin. "Knopf President Will Succeed Shawn as New Yorker Editor." *The New York Times,* January 13, 1987.

——. "Lerman Named Editor of Vanity Fair." *The New York Times,* April 27, 1983.

——. "Michener Talks." *The New York Times,* March 28, 1990.

——. "New Publisher Named in Shift at Turbulent Random House." *The New York Times,* October 31, 1990.

——. "The New Role of Random House." *The New York Times,* May 5, 1985.

——. "New Yorker Editor Calls Reporting Style Wrong." *The New York Times,* July 3, 1984.

——. "Nonfiction Techniques Debated Anew." *The New York Times,* June 20, 1984.

——. "154 at The New Yorker Protest Choice of Editor." *The New York Times,* January 15, 1987.

——. "President of Random House Out Abruptly After 23 Years." *The New York Times,* November 2, 1989.

——. "Random House Publisher a Human-Rights Activist." *The New York Times,* August 6, 1986.

——. "Staff Members, Upset, Meet at The New Yorker." *The New York Times,* January 14, 1987.

McGill, Douglas C. "Editor of New Yorker Seeks 'Mutual Trust'." *The New York Times,* March 12, 1985.

McHugh, Clare. "A Doppelganger for Tina & Anna?" *The New York Observer,* December 12, 1992.

McKelvey, Gerald. "U.S. Sues Roy Cohn for $7M, Taking Over Tax Case from IRS." *Newsday,* April 4, 1986.

McKerron, Jane. "A Brown Study." *The Times* (London), January 22, 1984.

Mehren, Elizabeth. "Road to The Fair; For Tina Brown, a Decade of Detours." *Los Angeles Times,* January 30, 1985.

Menand, Louis. "A Friend Writes." *The New Republic,* February 26, 1990.

Miller, Russell. "Spy Who Came into the Fold." *The Sunday Times of London,* October 11, 1992.

Moss, Linda. "Steve Newhouse: The Family's Maverick." *Crain's New York Business,* November 20, 1989.

Motavalli, John. "Tina Talks: Power and Prestige at Vanity Fair." *Inside Media*, June 24, 1992.

Newman, Judith. "Anna Wintour: Editor of the Year." *Adweek*, February 12, 1990.

Nocera, Joseph. "Spy's Demise." *The New Republic*, December 24, 1990.

Nordheimer, Jon. "Behind the Scenes, a Powerful Editor Lives, Breathes and Shapes His State." *The New York Times*, August 18, 1992.

O'Brien, Maureen. "Over the Top." *Publishers Weekly*, September 6, 1993.

Osborne, Richard. "The Fight for the Front Page." *Cleveland Magazine*, December 1980.

Passaro, Vince. "The Highbrow Days and Downtown Nights of Erroll McDonald." *Esquire*, January 1991.

Peers, Alexandra. "Art Prices Begin Emerging from 2-Year Slump, but Remain Far Below the Heights of '80s Boom." *The Wall Street Journal*, November 20, 1992.

Pener, Degen. "Publishing: A Small World After All." *The New York Times*, April 25, 1993.

———. "Reining in Tina Brown." *The New York Times*, July 19, 1992.

———. "Through His Lens, Avedon Looks Forward and Back." *The New York Times*, February 14, 1993.

Perlez, Jane. "Vanity Fair Sparks Sharp Reaction." *The New York Times*, March 30, 1983.

Phipps, Peter, and Dan Cook. "Plain Dealer Offered Cole $14.5 million to Fold Press." *Akron Beacon-Journal*, January 16, 1984.

Pollak, Richard. "The Trial of Donald and Si Newhouse." *The Nation*, March 13, 1989. 1992.

Powell, Bill. "Buying a Crown for Random House." *Newsweek*, August 29, 1988.

Reid, Alastair. "A Respecter of Truth in Writing." *The New York Times*, July 15, 1984.

Reid, Calvin, and John F. Baker. "Bernstein Retiring from Random; Vitale is New Chairman." *Publishers Weekly*, November 17, 1989.

Reif, Rita. "Jasper Johns Painting Is Sold for $17 Million." *The New York Times*, November 11, 1988.

Reilly, Patrick. "Details-Oriented: Newhouse clout helps hip book." *Advertising Age*, March 14, 1988.

———. "Fair Game for Miracle Worker." *Advertising Age*, October 24, 1988.

———. "Tina Brown of Vanity Fair Will Head The New Yorker." *The Wall Street Journal*, July 1, 1992.

———. "Travel Magazine of Condé Nast Cuts a Boosterism." *The Wall Street Journal*, October 1, 1990.

———. "Vanity Fair Adds to Glitter." *Advertising Age*, January 4, 1988.

———. "Vanity Fair Looks for a Comeback in Its New Life After Tina Brown." *The Wall Street Journal*, April 26, 1993.

Richter, Paul. "Quirky Si Newhouse Becomes a Media Power." *Los Angeles Times*, November 28, 1989.

Ridenhour, Ron. "Between The Lines at the Times-Picayune." *New Orleans Magazine*, November 1990.

Romano, Lois. "The Closing Arguments of Roy Cohn." *Washington Post*, December 21, 1985.

———. "Vanity's British Import." *Washington Post*, January 12, 1984.

Rosenblatt, Roger. "Snuff This Book! Will Bret Easton Ellis Get Away with Murder?" *The New York Times Book Review*, December 16, 1990.

Rosenfield, Paul. "The Queen and I." *LA Style*, September 1992.

Rothenberg, Randall. "Condé Nast Changing Style of Self." *The New York Times*, November 15, 1988.

———. "The New Yorker: Staid No More." *The New York Times*, December 20, 1989.

Salmans, Sandra. "Courting the Elite at Condé Nast." *The New York Times*, February 6, 1983.

Salholz, Eloise. "Mark of the Silver Fox." *Newsweek*, February 25, 1985.

Sandomir, Richard. "I'm Strictly Business, New Yorker Boss Says." *Newsday*, December 2, 1985.

Schwartz, Tony. "Making Waves." *New York*, March 18, 1991.

Seligman, Daniel. "Compositegate Revisited." *Fortune*, August 6, 1984.

Shaplen, Robert. "The Newhouse Phenomenon." *The Saturday Review*, October 8, 1960.

Sifton, Elisabeth. "Book Editor Sounds a Cri de Coeur: Let's Dump the Times Best-Seller List." *The New York Observer*, February 22, 1993.

Smith, Liz. "Mr. Mailer's Love-Fest." *Newsday*, November 3, 1991.

Smith, Roberta. "Art in Review: Alexander Liberman: The Circle Paintings." *The New York Times,* September 24, 1993.

Snead, Elizabeth. "Vogue magazine celebrates a century of vision and verve." *USA Today,* March 27, 1992.

Sones, Melissa. "Condé Nast: Corporate Makeover." *7 Days,* Sept. 7, 1988.

Stackpole, Henrietta. "It's a Small W." *The Nation,* October 12, 1985.

Stein, M. L. "Scooped." *Editor & Publisher,* December 19, 1992.

Stevenson, Peter M. "New York's New Power Brokers: Power Struggle—Keith Rupert Murdoch vs. Samuel I. Newhouse Jr." *Manhattan inc.,* September, 1989.

Stevenson, Peter. "S. I. Newhouse's Fabulous Florio Boys Leave Jones Beach for Corner Offices." *The New York Observer,* February 14, 1994.

Stokes, Geoffrey. "Queen Tina." *Spy,* May 1992.

Story, Richard David. "The Emperor of Taste." *New York,* December 28, 1992.

Streitfeld, David. "Life at Random." *New York,* August 5, 1991.

Stricharchuk, Greg. "Citizen Cole." *Cleveland Magazine,* December 1980.

Sullivan, Robert E., Jr. "Knopf's Uncivil War." *7 Days,* September 20, 1989.

Taki. "Regarding Roy Cohn: Not the Prince, or Queen, of Darkness." *The New York Observer,* May 3, 1993.

Talese, Gay. "Vogueland." *Esquire,* July 1961.

Thomas, Bill. "Mighty Tina." *Los Angeles Times Magazine,* November 3, 1991.

Thorpe, Helen. "Condé Nast Bankroll Keeps Meisel in the Fold." *The New York Observer,* June 29, 1992.

Tozier, Carolyn. "How Justice Department Viewed the St. Louis Joint Operating Agreement." *Journalism Quarterly,* Autumn, 1986.

Trachtenberg. J. A. "The Newhouses: Publishing's private empire." *W,* December 19–26, 1980.

Trueheart, Charles. "Talk of the Town." *Washington Post,* July 1, 1992.

Unger, Craig. "Can Vanity Fair Live Again?" *New York,* April 26, 1982.

Utne, Eric. "Tina's New Yorker." *Columbia Journalism Review,* March/April 1993.

Vamos, Mark N. "Change At The New Yorker Is the Talk of the Town." *Business Week,* March 10, 1986.

Vespa, Mary. "The Woman Who Celebrated the Beautiful People Thrives on Their Attentions." *People,* December 8, 1980.

Vienne, Véronique. "Make It Right . . . Then Toss It Away." *Columbia Journalism Review,* July/August 1991.

———. "The Culture of Abuse." *Journal of Graphic Design,* American Institute of Graphic Arts, Vol. 9, No. 1, 1991.

Wallach, Amei. "Art for Sale: According to Who?" *Newsday,* January 31, 1992.

Walls, Jeannette. "A Random House Divided." *New York,* January 11, 1993.

———. "Styles Victims." *New York,* November 16, 1992.

Weill, Jeanne. "Coverage of David Duke." *St. Louis Journalism Review,* May 1991.

Weinraub, Bernard. "David Geffen, Still Hungry." *The New York Times Magazine,* May 2, 1993.

———. "Hollywood Still Directs Its Coverage." *The New York Times,* June 1, 1992.

Weisberg, Jacob. "Houses of Ill Repute." *The New Republic,* June 17, 1991.

Wentz, Laurel. "Bernard Leser." *Advertising Age,* February 9, 1987.

Weyr, Thomas. "The House That Newhouse Built." *Publishers Weekly,* May 20, 1988.

Whitman, Alden. "Raoul H. Fleischmann, Publisher of The New Yorker, Dies at 83." *The New York Times,* May 12, 1969.

Wilson, Craig. "Already Homesick for Doomed 'HG'." *USA Today,* May 17, 1993.

Windolf, Jim. "Off the Record." *The New York Observer,* October 11, 1993.

———. "Tina Brown's Debut: Oct. 5 New Yorker Has Vanity Flair." *The New York Observer,* September 14, 1992.

Winn, Marie. "Liberman: Staying in Vogue." *The New York Times Magazine,* May 13, 1979.

Woge, Mairy Jayn, and Walt Bogdanich. "Charges Didn't Stop Presser as U.S. Informer." *Cleveland Plain Dealer,* August 24, 1981.

Yarbrough, Jeff. "Vanity Fairies: How Gay is the Condé Nast Empire?" *The Advocate,* March 10, 1992.

Zachary, G. Pascal. "All the News? Many Journalists See a Growing Reluctance to Criticize Advertisers." *The Wall Street Journal,* February 6, 1992.

Zuckerman, Laurence. "The Dynamic Duo at Condé Nast." *Time,* June 13, 1988.

UNBYLINED ARTICLES AND DOCUMENTS

"Alexandra Penney Parties with Pugs." *New York,* April 13, 1992.
"Ancorp Is Sued by U.S. in Civil Action Seeking Penalties of $585,000." *The Wall Street Journal,* February 9, 1971.
"An Explosive Debut." *Newsday,* October 2, 1987.
"Art Lover." *The New Yorker,* November 26, 1960.
"At Pantheon, Closed Books." *The New York Times,* March 8, 1990.
"A Well-Bred Magazine." *Time,* April 1, 1957.
"Back to the Drawing Board at Vanity Fair." *Newsweek,* May 9, 1983.
"Bennett Cerf Dies; Publisher, Writer." *The New York Times,* August 29, 1971.
"Birmingham News Fires Candid Auto Editor." *Washington Journalism Review,* November 1991.
"Blonde Ambition." Transcript of the "60 Minutes" program of October 21, 1990.
"Cerf to Newhouse." *The Nation,* November 27, 1989.
"Charlotte's Web" (column), *New York Daily News,* May 5, 1993.
"Concentration in the Book-Publishing and Book-Selling Industry." Hearing before the Subcommittee on Antitrust, Monopoly, and Business Rights of Committee on the Judiciary, United States Senate, March 13, 1980, U.S. Government Printing Office, Washington, D.C.
"The Cult of Diana." *Vanity Fair,* December 1992.
"The Cultural Elite: The Newsweek 100: Who They Really Are." *Newsweek,* October 5, 1992.
"Darts and Laurels." *Columbia Journalism Review,* March/April 1993.
"Diana Vreeland." (Various contributors, including Alexander Liberman). *Vogue,* December 1989.
"Diana Vreeland on Stage." *The New York Times,* April 27, 1993.
"Did Si Newhouse Conspire to Kill the Cleveland Press?" *Business Week,* July 1, 1985.
"Elisabeth Sifton to Join Knopf as Executive Vice-President." *Publishers Weekly,* July 24, 1987.
"The Fiction of Truth." *The New York Times,* July 21, 1984.
"50 Who Mattered Most" (compiled by Carrie Donovan). *The New York Times Magazine,* October 24, 1993.
"Flattery Will Get You Ten Pages . . . Maybe." *Spy,* August 1990.
"Grace Mirabella and the Vagaries of Vogue." *Washington Post,* July 5, 1988.
"How Si Newhouse Booked Trump." *New York,* November 11, 1985.
"I'm Scared of How Desirable I Am Sometimes." *The New Republic,* November 4, 1991.
"Independents Cry Foul." *Editor & Publisher,* July 18, 1987.
"Indifference Would Have Been Worse." *Art News,* May 1980.
"I Spy Feud Brewing." *Newsday,* November 27, 1989.
"Let Bylines Be Bylines." *Newsweek,* January 25, 1993.
"Mafia Influence on the Teamsters." *Cleveland Magazine,* December 1985.
"Miss Case of Vogue." *Harper's Bazaar,* February 1972.
"Mocking the Gods Is Her Cup of Tea." *Newsday,* September 10, 1986.
"The New British Invasion." *Spy,* February 1993.
"Newhouse Discusses Parental Relationship to Random House." *Publishers Weekly,* February 22, 1980.
"Newhoused." *The Nation,* March 19, 1990.
"The Newspaper Collector." *Time,* July 27, 1962.
"Norman N. Newhouse Dead at 82; Helped Build Communications Empire." *Newark Star-Ledger,* November 7, 1988.
"No Sale? Newhouse Sued for $2.9M." *New York Daily News,* September 22, 1987.
"Present Tense for Tina, Scribes." *New York Daily News,* October 22, 1992.
"RCA Will Sell Random House to Newhouse." *The Wall Street Journal,* February 7, 1980.
"Remembering Mr. Shawn." *The New Yorker,* December 28, 1992.
"Resurrecting a Legend." *Time,* February 21, 1983.
"Robert Miron: a coxswain's call to cable." *Broadcasting,* May 21, 1990.
"Roy Cohn vs. Bob Kennedy: The Great Rematch." *New York Daily News,* September 16, 1963.
"Samuel I. Newhouse Jr. Weds Mrs. Victoria de Ramel Here." *The New York Times,* April 15, 1973.

"S. I. Newhouse and Sons: America's Most Profitable Publisher." *Business Week,* January 26, 1976.

"So, Move Over, Jane Fonda." *Time,* December 12, 1983.

"Spy Man Taking Newhouse Gold." *New York,* September 19, 1988.

"Talk of the Town." *The New Yorker,* April 22, 1985.

"There at The New Yorker." *Newsweek,* July 2, 1984.

"This Spy Keeps an Eye on Fat Cats." *Newsday,* December 3, 1987.

"Tina Brown." *Punch,* May 5, 1976.

"The Ultimate Merger?" *Authors Guild Bulletin,* Winter 1989.

"Vanity Fair Honcho Gets the Boot." *New York Post,* May 11, 1993.

"A Vogue for the New." *Newsweek,* July 31, 1971.

"Why the Newhouse Touch Is Golden." *Business Week,* March 11, 1967.

"Yet Another PD Squabble." *Cleveland Magazine,* December 1982.

Index

About the Author

Thomas Maier has been an investigative and business reporter for *New York Newsday* since 1984, and previously worked at the *Chicago Sun-Times*. He has won several national and regional journalism honors, including the National Society of Professional Journalists' top reporting prize in 1987 for a series on police misconduct. He co-authored another *Newsday* series about the nation's waste crisis which won the national Worth Bingham award and later was published as a book, *The Rush to Burn,* Island Press, 1989. At the Columbia University Graduate School of Journalism, he won the John Patterson award for television documentary-making and his documentary, *The Mob, the Merchants and the Fulton Fish Market,* was broadcast by WNET/Channel 13. He later received a John McCloy Journalism Fellowship to Europe, which is awarded by the Columbia Journalism School and the American Council on Germany. In New York, he has won the Page One Award for Crusading Journalism, the 1990 Society of Silurians' Excellence in Journalism Award, and three first-place awards from the New York State Associated Press Association. He is a member of *Newsday*'s "Greene Team" investigative unit and was a frequent contributor to *Newsday*'s Sunday magazine, where the reporting began for this book about the Newhouse empire. Maier lives with his wife Joyce McGurrin and their three sons in Long Island, New York.